THE AGE OF
THE DEMOCRATIC REVOLUTION

THE CHALLENGE

The French Revolution had no territory of its own; in-deed, its effect was to efface, in a way, all older frontiers. It brought men together, or divided them, in spite of laws, traditions, character and language, turning enemies some-times into compatriots, and kinsmen into strangers; or rather, it formed, above all particular nationalities, an intellectual common country of which men of all nations might become citizens. . . .

When we look away from those accidental features which modified its appearance at different times and in various countries, and consider the Revolution only in itself, we see clearly that its effect was simply to abolish those political institutions which had prevailed for centuries among most European peoples . . . that it entirely destroyed, or is still destroying (for it still goes on) everything which in the old society arose from feudal and aristocratic institutions.

—ALEXIS DE TOCQUEVILLE

The Age of the Democratic Revolution

A POLITICAL HISTORY OF

EUROPE AND AMERICA, 1760 - 1800

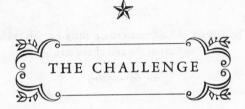

THE CHALLENGE

BY R. R. PALMER

PRINCETON, NEW JERSEY

PRINCETON UNIVERSITY PRESS

✭ PREFACE ✭

THERE have long been a great many works on the American Revolution, the French Revolution, the beginnings of the parliamentary re- form movement in Great Britain, and on Irish affairs, as also, though less known in the English-speaking world, on the several countries of continental Europe during this revolutionary era. This book attempts to bring all these national histories together. It rests heavily upon the work of others, for except in certain parts, notably Chapters I, IX, XIV, and XV, where I have been able to make use of researches of my own, it is built up from monographs, special studies, and collections of printed documents made by scholars in many countries over a long period of years. The book is therefore an example of what we have come to know as a historical synthesis, and I have accordingly thought it neces- sary to give detailed references, even at the cost of an unseemly parade of documentation, some of it in languages which I make no pretence of understanding and have been able to use only through the assistance of others. The book may be thought of also as an attempt at a compara- tive constitutional history of Western Civilization at the time of the French and American Revolutions; but "constitutional" is to be under- stood in a broad sense, without much emphasis on formal provisions, and in close connection with the political, social, and intellectual cur- rents and the actual conflicts at the time. Much of the book deals with the nature of public authority and private rights, of law, sovereignty, and political representation—or with liberty and equality, and with "fraternity" also, if fraternity be taken to mean the sense of equal membership in the community.

Naturally in the preparation of such a work I have incurred more than the usual number of obligations. Colleagues at Princeton and else- where have lent their assistance, either by calling my attention to writ- ings that I would otherwise have missed, or by reading and criticizing particular chapters. I have learned a good deal also from my students, from college seniors to authors of doctoral dissertations. Whether as stu- dents, or in some cases as research assistants, they have surveyed ma- terials for me or made studies of their own from which I have appro- priated useful items, and in more than one case they have saved me from outright errors. There are some eight persons to whom I am indebted for reading Scandinavian and East European languages. In particular I wish to thank my colleague, Professor W. F. Craven of Princeton, for his continuing help in the problems of the American

Revolution; Professors Hans Rosenberg, Jerome Blum, C. G. Sellers, and Peter Gay, and Mr. George Dangerfield, for reading and discussing various chapters with me; Professor P. Geyl of Utrecht, for his guidance in Dutch history; Professor Arne Odd Johnsen of Oslo for assistance in Norwegian and Danish; Professors D. W. Rustow and Stanley J. Stein and Mr. André Michalski of Princeton for assistance, respectively in Swedish, Portuguese, and Polish; Professor C. E. Black and Drs. R. H. McNeal and W. L. Blackwell for assistance in Russian; Dr. Peter F. Sugar for assistance in Hungarian; and my former students at Princeton, now widely dispersed, Messrs. Immo Stabreit, Demetrios Pentzopoulos, Thomas H. Kean, Elie Zilkha, and John W. Shy, and Drs. Stanley Mellon, Gordon M. Jensen, Donald Limoli, and David Gordon for various contributions whose ultimate usefulness to me they could not always foresee. I am indebted to Professor Stanley E. Howard for assistance with the proofs, and to Mr. Jeffry Kaplow for making the index. I have come to appreciate also the warm interest in the present venture shown by Mr. Herbert S. Bailey, Jr., Director of the Princeton University Press, and the careful work and exacting standards of Miss Miriam Brokaw, Managing Editor of the Press, in preparing it for publication. My debt to the Princeton University Library is very great.

To the Rockefeller Foundation, in its Division of Social Sciences, and to the Council of the Humanities of Princeton University, I wish to express thanks for financial support without which the book could not have been written, since it has been used to free me from teaching and other responsibilities for concentration on the present work. I have received smaller grants from the University Research Fund of Princeton University, mainly for the employment of occasional student assistants. I wish also to thank the editor of the *Political Science Quarterly* for permission to reprint the substance of certain articles which first appeared in its pages. No one except myself is responsible for any opinions, errors, or shortcomings in the book.

The project has grown beyond what I at first anticipated, and the present work is now seen as the first of two volumes, which together will survey the revolutionary period of the eighteenth century within the area of Western Civilization. The point of division between the two volumes is, in general, the beginning of the wars of the French Revolution. This first volume, entitled "The Challenge," will I hope be followed by a second, called "The Struggle." Further reading should make clear the full implication of these terms.

Princeton, N.J.
December 1, 1958

R. R. PALMER

★ CONTENTS ★

Preface

THE AGE OF THE DEMOCRATIC REVOLUTION

Two great parties are forming in all nations. . . . For one, there is a right of government, to be exercised by one or several persons over the mass of the people, of divine origin and to be supported by the church, which is protected by it. These principles are expressed in the formula, Church and State.

To this is opposed the new system, which admits no right of government except that arising from the free consent of those who submit to it, and which maintains that all persons who take part in government are accountable for their actions. These principles go under the formula, Sovereignty of the People, or Democracy.—G. K. VAN HOGENDORP, Rotterdam, 1791

THE AGE OF THE DEMOCRATIC REVOLUTION

A YOUNG Philadelphian of good family, Thomas Shippen, in the course of a visit to Europe, where he cultivated the acquaintance of "titled men and ladies of birth," bore a letter of introduction to Thomas Jefferson, the American Minister to France, who presented him at the court of Versailles. They arrived, one day in February 1788, "at ½ past 10 and were not done bowing until near 2." Young Shippen chatted with the Papal Nuncio and the Russian Ambassador, who "was very polite," and on meeting a woman and her two daughters who were all countesses he was introduced with all his "titles," which he thought most people believed to be hereditary. He was then paired with a German princeling for presentation to the King, who mumbled a few words while hitching on his sword. It all made the young man very conscious of his American nationality. He was "revolted" at the King's arrogance, but even more "mortified at the suppleness and base complaisance of his attendants." Such oriental splendor he thought worth seeing—once. It set him to thinking, for, as he wrote to his father, he detected ennui and uneasiness on the faces at court, and was more convinced than ever that "a *certain degree of equality* is essential to human bliss."

The underlining was Shippen's own. He added that America was peculiarly fortunate, since it provided the degree of equality that made for happiness, "without destroying the necessary subordination." No doubt his taste for equality had its limits. Descended on his mother's side from the Lees of Virginia, and on his father's from one of the founders of Pennsylvania, Thomas Shippen belonged socially to the groups that had provided many officers of government in America, and it was in fact on this ground, according to the etiquette at Versailles, that he was thought, as a mere republican, to have sufficient rank for presentation at court. On the other hand, Shippen's own father, a prominent doctor, had been a revolutionary of sorts, having acted as chief medical officer in the Continental Army. More generally, the point is that even Americans of aristocratic standing or pretensions looked on the Europe of 1788 with a certain disapproval.

This little scene at Versailles, revealed in the new edition of the *Papers of Thomas Jefferson*,[1] may serve to introduce some of the themes of the following pages, bringing together, as it does, Europe and America, monarchy and republicanism, aristocracy and an emerging democracy, and reflecting certain predilections or biases which the author at the outset confesses to sharing, without, he hastens to add, writing from any such point of view in the social scale as that of the Shippens of Philadelphia.

Let us pass from the concrete image to the broadest of historical generalizations. The present work attempts to deal with Western Civilization as a whole, at a critical moment in its history, or with what has sometimes recently been called the Atlantic Civilization, a term probably closer to reality in the eighteenth century than in the twentieth.[2] It is argued that this whole civilization was swept in the last four decades of the eighteenth century by a single revolutionary movement, which manifested itself in different ways and with varying success in different countries, yet in all of them showed similar objectives and principles. It is held that this forty-year movement was essentially "democratic," and that these years are in fact the Age of the Democratic Revolution. "Democratic" is here to be understood in a general but clear enough sense. It was not primarily the sense of a later day in which universality of the suffrage became a chief criterion of democracy, nor yet that other and uncertain sense, also of a later day, in which both Soviet and Western-type states could call themselves democratic. In one way, it signified a new feeling for a kind of equality, or at least a discomfort with older forms of social stratification and formal rank, such as Thomas Shippen felt at Versailles, and which indeed had come to affect a good many of the habitués of Versailles also. Politically, the eighteenth-century movement was against the possession of government, or any public power, by any established, privileged, closed, or self-recruiting groups of men. It denied that any

---

[1] Julian P. Boyd, ed., *The Papers of Thomas Jefferson* (Princeton, 1950-), xii, 502-04.

[2] See the paper prepared by Professor J. Godechot and myself for the international historical meeting at Rome in 1955: "Le problème de l'Atlantique du XVIIIe au XXe siècle," in *Relazioni del X Congresso Internazionale di Scienze Storiche (Roma 4-11 Settembre 1955)* (Florence, 1955), v, 175-239.

person could exercise coercive authority simply by his own right, or by right of his status, or by right of "history," either in the old-fashioned sense of custom and inheritance, or in any newer dialectical sense, unknown to the eighteenth century, in which "history" might be supposed to give some special elite or revolutionary vanguard a right to rule. The "democratic revolution" emphasized the delegation of authority and the removability of officials, precisely because, as we shall see, neither delegation nor removability were much recognized in actual institutions.

It is a corollary of these ideas that the American and the French Revolutions, the two chief actual revolutions of the period, with all due allowance for the great differences between them, nevertheless shared a good deal in common, and that what they shared was shared also at the same time by various people and movements in other countries, notably in England, Ireland, Holland, Belgium, Switzerland, and Italy, but also in Germany, Hungary, and Poland, and by scattered individuals in places like Spain and Russia.

The Revolution of Western Civilization

To obtain the right perspective on the whole era it is necessary to begin by looking at its climax at the end. This came with the Wars of the French Revolution from 1792 to 1800 or 1801. To these years I hope some day to devote a sequel, and this volume takes the story only to about 1791; but the whole period can best be understood by remembering the unprecedented struggle in which it ended. This struggle had in it something universal; as Burke said, there had been nothing like it since the Protestant Reformation had thrown all Europe into a commotion that overran all political boundaries.[3]

Burke himself, when he died in 1797, was so afraid of invasion and revolution in England that he gave orders for his remains to be secretly buried, lest triumphant democrats dig them up for desecration. Revolution broke out in Ireland in 1798. Dutch historians speak of revolution in the Netherlands in 1795, when the Batavian Republic was founded, and of a more radical movement of 1798. The Swiss feel that they were revolutionized in the Helvetic Republic of 1798. Italian writers

---

[3] The present section draws heavily on my two articles, "Reflections on the French Revolution," in *Political Science Quarterly*, LXVII (1952), 64-80, and "The World Revolution of the West, 1763-1801," *ibid.*, LXIX (1954), 1-14. See also, for bibliography, my "Recent Interpretations of the Influence of the French Revolution," in *Journal of World History*, II (1954), 173-95.

speak of revolution at Milan in 1796, at Rome in 1797, at Naples in 1798. The Cisalpine, Roman, and Parthenopean republics were the outcome. In the German Rhineland there were some who demanded annexation to France, or, that failing, the establishment of a revolutionary "Cisrhenane," or Rhineland Republic. Elsewhere in Germany the disturbance was largely ideological. The philosopher Fichte, an ardent revolutionary thinker, found it "evident" in 1799 that "only the French Republic can be considered by the just man as his true country." The city of Berlin was notably pro-French. In Poland, revolution reached a climax in 1794 with Kosciusko. In Hungary in the same year seventy-five members of a republican conspiracy were arrested. In Greece, in 1797, delegates from Athens, Crete, Macedonia, and other parts of the Greek world met at a secret conclave in Morea; they planned an uprising of all Greeks against the Ottoman Empire, if only the French would send weapons, ammunition, and a few units of the French army. A Russian found that the "charm of revolution" had penetrated "deep into Siberia."

And at the other extremity of Western Civilization, in the thinly settled American West, long after the Terror in France is supposed to have brought Americans to their senses, there was still so much lingering pro-French feeling, so much democratic and republican sentiment, so much inclination to break away from the allegedly aristocratic East, that the outgoing president, George Washington, in his Farewell Address, earnestly begged his Western countrymen to put their trust in the United States. In 1798 the popular hero, George Rogers Clark, holding a commission as brigadier-general in the army of the French Republic, attempted a secret recruiting of Kentuckians to invade and "revolutionize" Louisiana, which was then Spanish, and meant the whole territory west of the Mississippi. Blocked by an unsympathetic United States government, he fled to St. Louis, where, on the uttermost fringes of the civilized world, there was a society of French *sans-culottes* to receive him.

At Quebec in 1797 a man was hanged, drawn, and quartered as a dangerous revolutionary. At Quito, in what is now Ecuador, the first librarian of the public library was tortured and imprisoned for political agitation. A republican conspiracy was discovered at Bahia, in Brazil, in 1798. A Negro at Buenos Aires testified that Frenchmen in the city were plotting to liberate slaves in an uprising against the Spanish crown. In the High Andes, at the old silver town of Potosí, far from foreign influences on the coasts, the governor was horrified to discover men who toasted liberty and drank to France. The British government, in 1794, a year before occupying Cape Town, feared that there were too many "democrats," eager to welcome the French, among the Dutch at the Cape of Good Hope.[4]

All of these agitations, upheavals, intrigues, and conspiracies were part of one great movement. It was not simply a question of the "spread" or "impact" or "influence" of the French Revolution. Not all revolutionary agitation since 1918 has been produced by the Kremlin, and not all such agitation in the 1790's was due to the machinations of revolutionary Paris. It is true, and not without contemporary significance, that persons of revolutionary persuasion were able to install revolutionary regimes only where they could receive help from the French republican army. But revolutionary aims and sympathies existed throughout Europe and America. They arose everywhere out of local, genuine, and specific causes; or, contrariwise, they reflected conditions that were universal throughout the Western world. They were not imported from one country to another. They were not imitated from the French, or at least not imitated blindly. There was one big revolutionary agitation, not simply a French revolution due to purely French causes, and foolishly favored by irresponsible people in other countries.

This universal agitation was clear enough to contemporaries, but has not been well presented by the historians. The old classic, Sorel's *L'Europe et la Révolution française*, of which the first volume appeared in 1885, is in the older tradition of diplomatic history and international relations. It can by its very title convey a false impression, if it suggests a struggle between the French Revolution and "Europe," since the

---

[4] For the incident about Burke in the preceding paragraphs see T. W. Copeland, *Our Eminent Friend Edmund Burke: Six Essays* (New Haven, 1949), 90; for the quotation from Fichte, J. Droz, *L'Allemagne et la Révolution française* (Paris, 1949), 279; for other countries mentioned, P. F. Sugar, "The Influence of the Enlightenment and the French Revolution in Eighteenth Century Hungary," in *Journal of Central European Affairs*, XVII (1958), 348-52; A. Dascalakis, *Rhigas Velestinlis: La Révolution française et les préludes de l'indépendance hellénique* (Paris, 1937), 15; M. M. Shtrange, *Russkoye Obshchestvo i Frantsuzkaya Revolyutsiya* (Russian Society and the French Revolution, 1789-1794) (Moscow, 1956), 61 (I am indebted to Mr. W. L. Blackwell for reading this work in Russian for me); A. P. Whitaker, *The Mississippi Question 1795-1803* (New York, 1934), 155; W. Kingsford, *History of Canada* (10 vols., London 1887-1898), VII, 440-51; E. Clavéry, *Trois précurseurs de l'indépendance des démocraties sud-américaines: Miranda, Nariño, Espejo* (Paris, 1932); A. Ruy, *A primeira revoluçao social brasiliera, 1798* (Rio de Janeiro, 1942); R. Caillet-Bois, *Ensayo sobre el Rio de la Plata y la Revolucion francesa* (Buenos Aires, 1929), 76-77, 106-07; and for the Cape of Good Hope, Great Britain, Historical Manuscripts Commission, *The Manuscripts of J. B. Fortescue preserved at Dropmore* (London, 1892-1927), II, 645.

struggle was primarily between a revolutionary French government and the conservative governments and governing classes of Europe, with many Frenchmen opposed to the revolution, and many other Europeans and Americans in favor of it. At a more specialized level, there has been much research and writing in many countries. There are, for example, excellent studies of the Jacobin clubs in France, of the democratic-republican societies in the United States and of the radical societies in Great Britain, and we know that there were similar political clubs, at the same time, in Amsterdam, Mainz, Milan, and elsewhere. But only very recently has Professor Godechot undertaken to study such clubs as a whole, comparing their membership, their methods, and their stated aims. In all countries it has been the national history that has mainly occupied attention. The literature on the French Revolution is enormous, but most of it is focused on France. Italians have published abundantly on their *triennio*, the three revolutionary years in Italy from 1796 to 1799. Swiss, Belgians, Dutch, Irish, and many others have provided a wealth of materials on their respective histories at the time. The years from 1763 to 1800 have always been a staple of American historiography. But the work has been carried on in national isolation, compartmentalized by barriers of language or the particular histories of governments and states. All acknowledge a wider reality, but few know much about it. This book, in a way, is simply a putting together of hundreds of excellent studies already in existence.

Recently, probably because we live in a period of world revolution ourselves, there has been more tendency to see an analogous phenomenon at the close of the eighteenth century. Alfred Cobban and David Thomson in England have spoken of a kind of Democratic International at that time, and Louis Gottschalk of Chicago has stressed the idea of a world revolution of which the American and French Revolutions were a part. Only certain French scholars in the last decade, Lefebvre, Fugier, Godechot, have undertaken to develop the idea in detail.[5] Godechot's recently published two volumes are a remarkable work, built upon extensive and difficult researches, and analyzing the revolutionary social classes, organizations, clubs, methods, propaganda devices, ideas, objectives, and achievements with great care. They are

[5] G. Lefebvre, *La Révolution française* (Paris, 1951) in the series *Peuples et civilisations*, XIII; A. Fugier, *La Révolution française et l'Empire napoléonien* (Paris, 1954) in the series edited by P. Renouvin, *Histoire des relations internationales*, IV; and especially J. Godechot, *La Grande Nation: l'expansion révolutionnaire de la France dans le monde de 1789 à 1799* (Paris, 1956), 2 vols.

largely confined, however, to the parts of Europe actually occupied by French armies during the Revolutionary Wars, and are limited in time to the decade from 1789 to 1799; and they seem to represent a compromise, in the author's mind, between the idea of expansion of a primarily French Revolution and the idea of a more widespread upheaval in which the French Revolution was the greatest single eruption. Planned as they are, they give proportionately little attention to the English-speaking world and to Germany and Eastern Europe; and the American Revolution, its effects in Europe, and the political problems and disturbances of various European countries before the war of 1792 appear only allusively as a background.

It may be said, and it is of course true, that even if there is a world revolution in the twentieth century, its existence is of not the slightest relevancy, one way or the other, as evidence of any comparable movement at the close of the eighteenth. There is in America, and always has been, a strong body of opinion holding that the American and French revolutions were phenomena of altogether different kinds. There have always been British and European observers who have maintained that the agitation for parliamentary reform in England or Ireland, or the political overturns of the Dutch, Swiss, or Italians, were not truly revolutionary in any meaningful or modern sense. It is admittedly the purpose of this book to persuade to a contrary opinion. It is not necessary, however, to reject such ideas as simply mistaken, or to insist upon similarities where none exist. All that is necessary, or even desirable, is to set up a larger framework, or conceptual structure, in which phenomena that are admittedly different, and even different in very significant ways, may yet be seen as related products of a common impulse, or different ways of achieving, under different circumstances and against different degrees of opposition, certain recognizably common goals.

Revolution, it must be admitted, has become a distasteful word in many quarters. Americans may feel a troubled sympathy for anti-colonialist movements in Asia or Africa, and a more unanimous enthusiasm for such abortive revolutions as those attempted in Hungary or Poland in 1956; but the successful and threatening revolution of our own time, "the revolution" *par excellence*, is the one represented by communist parties, soviet republics, and, at least allegedly, the social doctrines of Karl Marx. To this revolution most readers of this book, as well as the author, feel a certain lack of cordiality. Some would dismiss all revolutions as dangerous and delusive, or even make of conservatism a kind of basic philosophy. In this case it becomes necessary—for Americans—to argue that the American Revolution was not really a revolution, but a conservative movement; I shall return to this problem. My own belief is that opposition to one revolution is no reason for rejecting all revolutions, that the value of conservatism depends on the value of what is to be conserved, that revolution must be appraised according to the ethical content and feasibility of its aims, and in terms of probable alternatives and real choices at the moment; and that the true matter for moral judgment, or for political decision, is not between the old and the new, or the conservative and the revolutionary, but the actual welfare of human beings as estimated by a reasonable calculation of possibilities in particular situations.

The parallels between the Russian and the French Revolutions, or between the twentieth-century and the eighteenth-century upheavals, are plainly apparent and cannot be honestly denied. In both there is the same story of collapse of the old system, seizure of power by new and unauthorized groups, extermination of the old institutions; confiscation, emigration, terror; attack upon the church; consolidation of the new regime in a powerful country, with the setting up of dependent states in adjacent regions; agitation threatening all established governments, frontiers, interests, classes, and views of life; cleavage of opinion, and formation of loyalties and aversions, that overrun all political borders and divide all states within. We do not like this today, and we are embarrassed to find it happening in the name of Liberty and Equality in the decade of the 1790's. We are further embarrassed by taunts from the Left, of Marxists who say that the proletarian today is only trying to do what the bourgeois once did; or that the bourgeois today, for obvious reasons, is trying to deny his own revolutionary background and suppress even the memory of it, lest it set a bad example.

It is the weakest of all replies to hold that revolution under any conditions is a sad mistake. Perhaps we should not be too squeamish; perhaps we should admit that we "bourgeois" entered upon a revolutionary era some two centuries ago. We should admit that it resembles the revolutionary era of the twentieth century. We should then add that the resemblances are largely formal, more of pattern than of substance, and involving abstractions. All wars are alike in being wars, and there is even such a thing as military science; but not all wars, or all combatants, are alike in their effects upon mankind. All revolutions resemble one another as revolutions, and there is probably even a science or technique of revolution as such; but it does not follow that all revolutions have the same effects. It is permitted to believe that a better society, more humane, more open, more flexible, more susceptible to improvement, more favorable to physical welfare and to the pursuit of higher concerns, issued from the democratic revolution of the eighteenth century than from the communist revolution of the twentieth. It is not necessary to idealize either. It is enough to say that revolution is like war, occurring when all compromise breaks down, and representing a violent clash between two or more groups over the structure of the whole society to which each belongs. We may indeed write the history of a war, or a revolution, in which we constantly deprecate the resort to violence, regret the loss of individual liberties, comment on the bad feeling between the participants, and note how all other pursuits become subordinated to one single overwhelming end. We would not thereby much elucidate the war, or the revolution; we would only be saying that we preferred peace, or that in a better world neither war nor revolution would ever be necessary.

The exact relationship of the Russian to the French Revolution has in recent decades been the subject of much careful examination. Two tendencies may be perceived: the one to associate, the other to dissociate, the two revolutions. By an "associationist" view I would not mean such an attempt as Crane Brinton's in his *Anatomy of Revolution*, in which the author looks for a pattern of revolutionary process as such, by comparative study of the English, American, French, Russian, and other revolutions. I would mean rather a view in which the French Revolution is seen as a kind of origin, partial cause, or distant prefigurement of the Russian Revolution, which insists upon "Jacobinism" as the "communism" of the eighteenth century, or sees a kind of continuing linear process in which the Russian Revolution is in some way a consequence of the French, or presents a more highly developed stage of the same process. This was of course the view of Marx, Lenin, and Trotsky, as it is of modern Soviet scholars; it is also the view of many warmly anti-Soviet and anti-communist writers, notably of Professor Talmon of the Hebrew University at Jerusalem, who traces the "origins of totalitarian democracy," or Soviet communism, back to Robespierre and Rousseau.[6] There are nowadays many others for whom Robespierre and Rousseau figure more as ancestors of totalitarianism than of democracy.

[6] J. L. Talmon, *The Rise of Totalitarian Democracy* (Boston, 1952).

It is true that Marx and his followers were close students of the French Revolution, and learned a good deal from it; this is, if anything, a good reason for the rest of us to make an independent study of the subject. It is also true that the communist movement would never have taken form as it did except for the prior occurrence of the French Revolution—as of much else in the preceding history of Russia and of Europe. It is even true that the Jacobins were in some ways something like the communists; but, not to dwell on the difference in their actual principles, the fact that the Jacobin clubs were the products of the French Revolution rather than the producers of it, never had any international organization, lasted only five years, and were closed down by revolutionaries themselves, should give pause to those wishing to pursue this parallel beyond a certain point.

"Dissociation" of the French and Russian Revolutions, at a serious level, rests upon observations of the following kind: First, the subsequent cult of the Revolution was a different thing from the French Revolution itself. This was emphasized, for example, by the late Professor Griewank of Jena. Strongly inclined to Western democratic and humane values, Griewank believed that the French of the Revolution thought in relatively practical terms of rational politics and the needs of war; and that the ballooning up of the Revolution into a vast, fearsome, perpetual, gigantic, and all-consuming force was the work in part of counterrevolutionaries who wished to discredit the real aims of the French Revolution, in part of romantic philosophers, and in part of rebellious spirits in those countries, like Germany, where real revolution had had the least effect.[7] It is apparently a fact that the modern or communist revolutions have been, so far, least successful precisely in those countries where the eighteenth-century or democratic revolution produced the most significant changes. Related to this is the thought of the American scholar T. H. von Laue, who has suggested a significant difference of kind between the Russian, Asian, and twentieth-century revolutions on the one hand, and the French, Western, and eighteenth-century revolutions on the other. Where the latter, he holds, arose as indigenous developments of their own culture, reflecting the growth of values, knowledge, and aspirations having deep native roots, the twentieth-century revolutions, whether in Russia or China, or formerly colonial areas, are alike in having been precipitated by contacts with an outside or foreign civilization, and by the stresses, mal-

[7] K. Griewank, *Der neuzeitliche Revolutionsbegriff: Entstehung and Entwicklung* (Weimar, 1955).

adjustments, feelings of backwardness, and other ambivalences ensuing thereupon.[8] The French of 1789 might feel that in respect to government or personal rights they were less favored than the British or the Americans. Like all peoples, they had been exposed to influences from outside. But the French Revolution grew directly out of earlier French history. The French were untroubled by any feeling of backwardness; they did not have to strain to keep up in a march of progress. The same is generally true of the Western world at the time. The eighteenth century saw the Revolution of the Western world; the twentieth century, the Revolution of the non-Western.

None of these ideas need command unqualified adherence. No more will be said explicitly of the twentieth century in the present book, which is a history of the eighteenth, and in which the French Revolution is associated not with modern communism but with other movements of its own time within the area of Western Civilization.

A "Democratic" Revolution: "Democrat" and "Aristocrat" in European Languages

Even if there was a general revolutionary disturbance between about 1760 and about 1800, it does not follow, without further explanation, that "democratic" is the best word to describe it. It is well known that Thomas Jefferson did not much favor the use of the word; and we often read, at least in American books, that the term in the 1790's became an epithet or smear-word, by which persons were designated against their will, and usually falsely, like persons falsely called communists at a later day. The belief that the word had no willing acceptance in the eighteenth century actually plays into the hands of the modern Left; thus a Dutch scholar has argued, partly on the mistaken ground that "democracy" was little heard in Holland before 1800, that the modern "Eastern" use of the word, implying an economic rather than a political equality, and dating from the rise of social democracy in the 1880's, is historically more legitimate than the modern "Western" use.[9] The fact seems to be that "democracy" and "democrat" enjoyed more currency before 1800 than is commonly supposed. It must be remembered that the words "liberal," "radical," and "progressive" did not exist. When moderates or conservatives wished to indicate the

---

[8] T. H. von Laue, "Die Revolution von aussen als erste Phase der russischen Revolution," in *Jahrbücher für die Geschichte Osteuropas*, IV (1956), 138-58. Mr. von Laue is an American scholar writing in German.

[9] J. van de Giessen, *De opkomst van het woord democratie als leuze in Nederland* (The Hague, 1948).

dangerous drift of the times, or when the more advanced spirits spoke of themselves, they might very well use the words "democrat" or "democracy." The reader may bear with a little evidence on this point, especially since, as the word occurs in many European languages, nothing else so vividly illustrates the international character of the movement.[10]

The word "democracy," like "aristocracy" and "monarchy," was of course as old as the Greeks or their translators, and the three terms had been in the common vocabulary of political thinkers continuously since the Middle Ages. There is some evidence that the most rural and innermost of the Swiss cantons, and some of the German free cities, thought of themselves as democratic in the eighteenth century. Except for "monarchy," however, none of the three terms seems yet to have entered the common speech. They were political scientists' words, tools of analysis, closely defined, dry in connotation, and without emotional impact. It was generally agreed that "pure democracy" could not exist, except possibly in very small states with simple habits. This was Rousseau's view as expressed in the *Social Contract*. At the most, democracy was a principle, or element, which might profitably enter into a "mixed constitution," balanced by principles of monarchy and aristocracy, as was believed to be the case in England or the Venetian Republic. It is rare, even among the *philosophes* of France before the Revolution, to find anyone using the word "democracy" in a favorable sense in any practical connection.

Some, however, can be found. There was Helvétius, who, in his private notes in refutation of Montesquieu, observed: "When the governed cannot rid themselves of the oppression of those who govern badly, it is despotism. When they can, it is democracy."[11] There was the Marquis d'Argenson, who in the 1730's allowed to circulate secretly, in manuscript, his *Considerations on the Government of France*. D'Argenson here reviews French history. He finds that the growing power of the kings has favored equality and democracy as against nobility and aristocracy. He repeatedly uses the term "democracy." He emphatically does not want it mixed with aristocracy. He speaks of "that fortunate progress of Democracy which we admire in the reigns free from civil war." He expects and hopes that this progress

---

[10] The present section reproduces parts of my article, "Notes on the Use of the Word 'Democracy,' 1789-1799," in *Political Science Quarterly*, LXVIII (1953), 203-26, to which the reader desiring documentation may refer, except for the quotations from Helvétius, Kollontay, and Wordsworth, for which references are given below.

[11] See the note by Helvétius in Montesquieu, *Oeuvres* (Paris, 1826), II, 137.

of democracy will continue. He is surprisingly like Tocqueville a century later in his view of French history—except that he is more unreservedly in favor of democracy than Tocqueville. We may note, too, in d'Argenson, the tendency to think of democracy as equality rather than as self-government, opposing it to "aristocracy," rather than to "monarchy." Both Helvétius and d'Argenson have left behind the traditional idea that only small and virtuous societies could be democratic.

The two nouns, "democrat" and "aristocrat," were coinages of the period, unknown before the 1780's. No "democrats" fought in the American Revolution; and the Age of Aristocracy, as long as it was unchallenged, heard nothing of "aristocrats." Neither word was current in English before 1789; in France, *aristocrate* crops up in the reign of Louis XVI, *démocrate* not until 1789. It may be that the words were first coined by the Dutch. It seems certain, in any case, that their first currency was in the Low Countries, in the Dutch revolution of 1784-1787 and the Belgian revolution of 1789-1791. We find *aristocraten* used by Dutch burghers as early as 1784. The Rotterdam patrician, van Hogendorp, writing in the French language in 1786, declares that his country is troubled by a cabal. "People say," he adds, "that this cabal is divided into aristocrats and democrats." "Aristocrat" entered into popular parlance among the Dutch in these years; but "democrat" remained rare, the popular party calling itself Patriot. In Belgium, however, that is, the Austrian Netherlands, in the revolt of 1789 against the emperor, the advanced party came to call itself Democrat. By January 1791 its leaders were speaking of *les braves Démocrates* and *les bons Démocrates*. One even wrote, "*Vive la Démocratie!*"

The extreme frequency of "aristocrat" in France during the Revolution is well known, and it seems to us to have been applied indiscriminately, and in fact falsely, to a great many people. To us the word means a member of an aristocratic class; it does not mean one who is an adherent of, or believer in, an aristocratic society. There is no reason, however, why it should not have had these meanings when it was coined. The word "democrat," conversely to "aristocrat," does not mean a member of a democratic class; it does mean an adherent of, or believer in, a democratic society. It is possible, therefore, that "aristocrat" was used less loosely and irrationally than is supposed, since there were undoubtedly millions of "aristocrats" in France in the extended and now obsolete sense of the word.

"Democrat" was rarely used in France, despite its currency in Belgium in 1790 and 1791. It was probably coined, in France as in Holland or Belgium, in contradistinction to "aristocrat." Ferdinand Brunot, in his tremendous history of the French language, lists two hundred and six nouns and phrases designating political alignments during the Revolution. "Democrat" is in the list, but there are many more familiar terms, such as "patriots," "Jacobins," or "sansculottes." Dubois-Crancé, the future regicide, used it in 1790 in speaking on the military policy suitable to the new France. He describes the citizen soldier—"a patriot, an honest democrat." In 1791 Brissot claimed to advocate "a popular monarchy, tending to the popular side. Such is my democracy." In 1793, when Louis XVI was executed, the drums rolled to smother the last sounds and the crowds shouted *"Vive la République!"* One young man heard, or at least reported, "Long live Democracy!" He was, however, a Greek, writing to a fellow countryman in the Greek language. It may be that "democracy" to him, not being a foreign word, could convey a feeling that it lacked for western Europeans; that he used it naturally as a translation for the Latin "republic," to express the ideals and passions that he sensed in revolutionary Paris.

With the advent of the Jacobins and the Terror, "democracy" became more frequent, though never common. It was occasionally used at the Jacobin Club, where Camille Desmoulins cried that "the English people must be exterminated from Europe, unless they democratize themselves!" Hérault-Séchelles, submitting what is called the Jacobin constitution to the Convention for adoption, praised it as "representative and democratic." The constitution itself, though in fact democratic, allowing universal male suffrage and providing measures of initiative and referendum, does not use the word.

The *locus classicus* for the word "democracy" during the French Revolution is the speech of Robespierre in the Convention on February 5, 1794. This speech is often quoted. It is the one in which he defines Virtue and Terror. What is usually quoted is Robespierre's moral exhortations rather than his remarks on democracy, although one might suppose the latter to have at least equal historical significance. Not counting sporadic occurrences, he uses the word "democracy," while specifically on the subject, eleven times in the space of seven hundred words, or in about five minutes of speaking time. "Democracy," he said, "is a state in which the people, as sovereign, guided by laws of its own making, does for itself all that it can do well, and by its delegates what it cannot. . . . Democracy is the only form of state which all the individuals composing it can truly call their country. . . . The French are the first people in the world to establish a true democracy, by calling all men to enjoy equality and the fulness of civic rights; and that, in my opinion, is the real reason why all the tyrants allied against the Republic will be defeated."

Soon after this speech the really internecine phase of the Terror began, culminating in Robespierre's own death six months later. Thereupon there was general agreement, even by revolutionaries far to the left, to regard Robespierre's ambition, or his fanaticism, as the cause of the late troubles. The association of "democracy" with Robespierre, and hence with terror, naturally tended to discredit democracy itself.

There remained in France, under the Directory, amorphous democratic groups which looked back with favor on the Constitution of the Year I (1793) and the Committee of Public Safety. They were often quite respectable people, and represented no single social class. At Toulouse, for example, they included a few of the wealthiest citizens, and many businessmen and lawyers, as well as artisans, tradesmen, and mechanics. They even won a national election in 1798, to no avail, since they were put down by a *coup d'état*. How often they employed the word "democracy" is not clear. They were called "anarchists" by the dominant republicans of the Directory, as by the royalists.

In Holland after 1795 there was an important newspaper at Amsterdam called *De Democraten*. The Amsterdam political club said it wanted the *democratisch systema*. Even the French Directory, which used the word sparingly, declared in instructions for its agent in Holland, in December 1797, that the Dutch people desired a "free and democratic constitution." About a third of the members of the Dutch constituent assembly signed a petition, in January 1798, in favor of "a democratic representative constitution." A constitutional committee, in February, affirmed to the French agent, Delacroix, that the Dutch were "capable of a greater measure of democracy than would be suitable for the French."

In parts of Germany, notably the Rhenish states, there were people whose ideas were in effect democratic, but they seem to have used the word less often than the Dutch. One clubroom, in 1792, is reported to have had a sign on its wall reading *Vive la Démocratie. Au diable les aristocrates!*—in French! The journalist Lange, in an article comparing aristocracy and democracy, boldly declared for the latter, which, he said, offered more freedom to the real inequalities of human talent. Fichte defiantly accepted the word—or, at least, refrained from explicitly repudiating it—when he got into trouble, on the charge of atheism and radicalism, at the University of Jena. In Prussia, the minister Struensee remarked to a French diplomat in 1799: "The king is a democrat in his way. . . . In a few years there will be no more privileged classes in Prussia."

In Switzerland, the constitution of the Helvetic Republic, which was proclaimed by the French in 1798, declared in its Article II that "the form of government, whatever modifications it may undergo, shall at all times be a representative democracy." Of all the written constitutions promulgated in Europe and America, in the last quarter of the eighteenth century, this is apparently the only one to call itself explicitly democratic. Its author was the Basel revolutionary, Peter Ochs, who spent a good deal of time in Paris. For the most part, in Switzerland in 1798, the favorable use of "democracy" in a modern sense appears to have been confined to the invading French. The Swiss, when they used the word favorably, generally referred to the small historic democracies of the rural cantons, which were in fact oligarchic in the eighteenth century.

It was in Italy that the word "democracy," in a favorable sense, was most commonly used in the years from 1796 to 1799. The most striking example comes from no less a person than Pius VII, two years before his elevation to the papacy. From 1785 to 1800 he was Bishop of Imola, a town in the northern part of the Papal States. Revolutionary disturbances broke out on every side when the French army, under Bonaparte, conquered Lombardy in 1796. Imola was absorbed into the Cisalpine Republic. On Christmas Eve 1797 the Bishop of Imola issued a Christmas homily to his diocese. It contains the word "democracy" eleven times within the space of a few hundred words. "The form of democratic government adopted among us, most beloved brethren," he said, "is not inconsistent with the Gospel . . ."

The Milan popular club announces: "*facciamo uno governo democratico.*" People shout: "*La Democrazia o la Morte!*" Others wish to "democratize the People," to create "a democratic base." A newspaper declares that any republic in Italy must be "a democracy, one and indivisible." Pamphlets are entitled "Resurgence of oppressed democracy" and "Democratic education for the Italian people." At Venice there is talk of creating a democracy, and Democratic Fecundity is exhibited by an engaged couple marching in a procession. At Rome a man named Martelli speaks casually of what will happen after the "democratization" of Naples and Tuscany. A proclamation reads, "Form yourselves into a democracy, People of the Roman Republic."

There is a theatrical production called "The Democratization of Heaven." There is a grand ball in honor of Bonaparte: no "ladies" and very few *seigneurs romains* were present, but this is not surprising, because "the party was democratic." And with republican Rome facing attack in 1799 by the King of Naples, the leaders try, though in vain, to make it a war for "democracy."

Use of the words in the Scandinavian and East European languages is harder to trace. Newspapers as far north as Trondheim admonished "aristocrats" in 1794. Whether republicans in Hungary used the term "democrat" I do not know. The Polish revolutionary, Kollontay, in a book written after the failure of Kosciusko's uprising, declared that the whole period since 1750 was like an "earthquake," which had given "a new aspect and a new importance to democracy."[12]

In England and Scotland the antidemocrats seem to have monopolized the word. Wordsworth did indeed say in a private letter in 1794: "I am of that odious class of men called democrats."[13] But he said it with a note of defiance which eloquently suggests the disrepute of the word. Even Thomas Paine rarely employs it, but in the third chapter of *The Rights of Man*, Part Two, he does address himself to the meaning of "republic," "aristocracy," and "democracy." "Democracy" occurs eleven times within about five hundred words. He distinguishes it from direct or "simple" democracy. "Retaining, then, Democracy as the ground, and rejecting the corrupt systems of Monarchy and Aristocracy, the representative system naturally presents itself. . . . It is on this system that the American Government is founded. It is representation ingrafted upon Democracy." There are only three texts of the period, to my knowledge, where the author uses "democracy" in a favorable sense, as often as eleven times within a few hundred words; and these three texts are those of Paine, Robespierre, and the man who became Pius VII.

In the United States, where the people were still in large measure culturally British, and in particular among those of the educated classes, there was undoubtedly some hesitation by democrats to adopt the word "democratic." The foreign origin of democracy was a favorite theme of Federalist polemics, and the justification for the Alien Act of 1798; and it seems to be true that democracy, as a word, though not

[12] Quoted by B. Lesnodorski, "Le siècle des lumières en Pologne," in Académie polonaise des sciences, *La Pologne au Xe Congrès international des sciences historiques à Rome* (Warsaw, 1955), 180.

[13] W. Knight, ed., *Letters of the Wordsworth Family from 1787 to 1855* (London, 1907), I, 66.

the reality behind it, was brought into America by the European revolution. James Monroe, after reading the Anglo-Franco-American Paine's *Rights of Man*, remarks in a letter to Jefferson, in 1791, that he agrees with the author, and that "the bulk of the [American] people are for democracy." In the following years a great many political clubs, not unlike the radical societies of Britain and Continental Europe, began to appear in various parts of the United States. Forty-two can now be identified. The first was established by Pennsylvania Germans in March 1793. It called itself the German Republican Society. The third to be organized, and the first to adopt the name "democratic," was the Democratic Society of Pennsylvania. Its members at first planned to use the name Sons of Liberty; it was the French minister, Genêt, who suggested the word "democratic" for this purpose. Sixteen others soon thereafter put "democratic" in their titles. In 1793 we find Aedanus Burke, of South Carolina, impatiently calling Jefferson a "half-way democrat" because of his stand, as Secretary of State, in favor of neutrality in the European war. The implication was that a whole-way democrat would be better. And among the countless toasts then offered at political banquets was one at Boston in 1795, which proposed for the contemplation of all lovers of liberty "one great democratic society comprehending the human race."

It is, therefore, no anachronism to apply the word "democratic" to the eighteenth-century revolution. It was the last decade of the century that brought the word out of the study and into actual politics.

A Preview of What Follows

In Western Civilization, in the middle of the eighteenth century, there was no novelty in discussions of liberty, or human equality, or law, or limited government, or constitutional rights, or the sovereignty of the people. Greek and medieval philosophy, Roman law, Christian theology, and baronial rebellions had all made contributions to one such idea or another. A marked democratic movement had expressed itself in the English revolution during the 1640's, and the history of many European towns was full of clashes between populace and patricians. Such popular movements, however, had been local, sporadic, and unsuccessful; and of general ideas, such as ultimate human equality, or government with the consent of the governed, it is well known that the more general such ideas are the more variegated and contradictory may be the actual practices with which men learn to live. Actual practice, about 1750, was such that certain old ideas, or old words and phrases, took on a new application and a wider and more urgent meaning.

If we say that a revolutionary era began about 1760, it is not because any persons or any organizations intended or worked in advance for a revolution. The modern conception of a revolutionary movement is the result, not the cause, of the revolutionary era that we are discussing. "Revolution" was a familiar word, but it usually meant no more than the revolving fortunes of governments, without great impersonal causes or any long-run direction; one might speak of Chancellor Maupeou's "revolution" in France in 1770, or the King of Sweden's "revolution" of 1772. The situation that began to develop about 1760 was revolutionary in a deeper way.

By a revolutionary situation is here meant one in which confidence in the justice or reasonableness of existing authority is undermined; where old loyalties fade, obligations are felt as impositions, law seems arbitrary, and respect for superiors is felt as a form of humiliation; where existing sources of prestige seem undeserved, hitherto accepted forms of wealth and income seem ill-gained, and government is sensed as distant, apart from the governed and not really "representing" them. In such a situation the sense of community is lost, and the bond between social classes turns to jealousy and frustration. People of a kind formerly integrated begin to feel as outsiders, or those who have never been integrated begin to feel left out. As a group of Sheffield workingmen demanded in 1794: "What is the constitution to us if we are nothing to it?"[14]

No community can flourish if such negative attitudes are widespread or long-lasting. The crisis is a crisis of community itself, political, economic, sociological, personal, psychological, and moral at the same time. Actual revolution need not follow, but it is in such situations that actual revolution does arise. Something must happen, if continuing deterioration is to be avoided; some new kind or basis of community must be formed.

What we shall see in the following chapters is a groping toward a new kind of community. With it went the struggles of opposed ideas and interests. It has often been said, on the authority of no less a person than Alexis de Tocqueville, that the French Revolution was

[14] An address to the British Nation, printed with *Proceedings of a Public Meeting at Sheffield* . . . 7 April 1794 (Sheffield, 1794), 41.

over before it began, that it was the work of men's minds before they made it the work of their hands. This idea can be misleading, for with it one may miss the whole reality of struggle. The Revolution was not merely the attempt to realize in practice ideas which had already conquered in the realm of thought. No ideas had "conquered"; there was no "climate of opinion" of any specific social or political content. The Revolution was a conflict between incompatible conceptions of what the community ought to be, and it carried out with violence a conflict that had already come into being. There is no reason to suppose (if we put aside historical metaphysics) that one side in this conflict was moribund, the other abounding with vigor; one, old and doomed in any case to extinction, the other, new and already riding upon the wave of the future. It is sufficiently enlightening to see it simply as a conflict, in which either antagonist would prevail at the expense of the other. It is hoped that readers of this book, whichever way their own sympathies may lie, may at least agree, upon finishing it, on the reality of the conflict.

In the absence of better words, and not wishing to invent more colorless sociological terms, we think of the parties to this essential conflict, so far as they may be reduced simply to two sides, as the proponents of "aristocratic" and "democratic" forms of the community, emotionally overcharged or semantically ambiguous though these words may be. It is held that both democratic and aristocratic forces were gaining strength after about 1760, that revolution came because both were rising, and that they took the form of revolution and counterrevolution at the close of the century, and of democratically and conservatively oriented philosophies thereafter. It follows that conservatism and counterrevolution were no mere "reactions" against revolution, but eighteenth-century forces against which revolution was itself a reaction. This idea is not the invention of the present author: recent works on the American Revolution emphasize the growing conservatism in British Parliamentary circles before 1775; Professor Valjavec insists that conservatism in Germany antedated the agitation of the 1790's; French historians stress the "aristocratic resurgence" preceding the eruption of 1789.[15]

The next chapter sets up one of the guiding conceptions of the book,

[15] Cf. C. R. Ritcheson, *British Politics and the American Revolution* (Norman, 1954); F. Valjavec, *Die Entstehung der politischen Strömungen in Deutschland, 1770-1815;* (Munich, 1951); and the writings of Mathiez, Lefebvre, J. Egret, and others on the French Revolution.

that of certain "constituted bodies," in Europe and America, most of them predominantly aristocratic in 1760, and including parliaments, councils, assemblies, and magistracies of various kinds. A continuing and universal theme of the period is the attempts of these constituted bodies to defend their corporate liberties and their independence, against either superior authorities on the one hand or popular pressures on the other. Resisting superior authorities, these bodies could be liberal and even revolutionary. The democratic revolutionary movement, however, came into play when persons systematically excluded from these bodies, and not content merely with the independence of these bodies as already constituted, attempted to open up their membership, change the basis of authority and representation, reconstitute the constituted bodies, or obtain a wholly new constitution of the state itself. The third chapter deals further with the philosophy and the problems which institutionalized aristocracy brought into existence. Chapter IV traces the conflicts of the aristocratic constituted bodies with kings in the 1760's and 1770's in France, Sweden, and the Hapsburg empire. Chapter V explores the clash of a similar body at the town of Geneva with its own citizens.

With Chapter VI begins the treatment of the English-speaking world, involving the structure of Parliament, the British constitution, and the American Revolution. Chapters VII and VIII consider the American Revolution, and the sense in which I believe it to have been truly revolutionary. It is shown in Chapter IX that the American Revolution, whatever its true nature, greatly added to the democratic and revolutionary spirit in Europe, to the desire, that is, for a reconstitution of government and society.

But while this spirit was rising, actual events followed the course of an aristocratic resurgence, traced in Chapters X to XIV. The parliamentary class in the 1780's in Britain and Ireland stopped the moves for democratization. Dutch, Belgian, and Swiss patricians put down the democrats in their respective countries. Whether an American upper class blocked the growth of democracy in the new United States federal constitution of 1787 is also considered. The privileged classes of the Hapsburg empire obstructed the equalizing reforms of the Hapsburg rulers. The Polish revolution failed. For a time it even seemed that the French Revolution might reinforce the privileged classes. But in the events of 1789, as explained in Chapter XV, the French revolutionaries laid down the principles of a more democratic form of state.

The book closes with further comments on the relationship of the French and American revolutions. The story is brought, for all countries, to about the year 1791, to the eve of the great war in which all these national and social developments were to be gathered together into one tremendous struggle.

ARISTOCRACY ABOUT 1760: THE
CONSTITUTED BODIES

In aristocracy, the sovereign power is in the hands of a certain number of persons. It is they who make the laws and see to their execution; and the rest of the people stand in relation to them as, in a monarchy, the subjects do to the monarch. . . . *Monarchical government, by nature, is constituted by dependent and subordinate intermediate powers. The most natural such dependent intermediate power is that of the nobility. Nobility enters in a sense into the essence of monarchy, of which the fundamental maxim is:* No monarch, no nobility; no nobility, no monarch. . . . *Abolish in a monarchy the prerogatives of lords and clergy, nobility and towns, and soon you will have either a popular or a despotic state.*—MONTESQUIEU, 1748

ARISTOCRACY ABOUT 1760: THE CONSTITUTED BODIES

EDMUND BURKE, after the American troubles began, thought that the Virginians were very much like the Poles. He would solve the American question by putting America on the same legal footing as Ireland. For Ireland he recommended the example of France, which he saw as a federal "empire," where great provinces like Brittany raised their own taxes and otherwise enjoyed extensive autonomy. Gibbon cited England, France, Venice, and Genoa to show that liberty was preserved by a gradation of social ranks. Rousseau considered the citizens of Geneva and the nobles of Venice to be much alike. The abbé Morellet, mixing in an Anglo-French reforming circle which included Turgot, Condorcet, Lord Shelburne, Bentham, Priestley, and Price, made much the same criticisms of the parlements of France and the parliament of Great Britain. Kaunitz, commenting on difficulties between the Hapsburg government and the diet of Bohemia, was reminded of similar difficulties in Hungary and Belgium.

All saw a uniformity of institutions. All had in mind those "constituted bodies" which existed everywhere in the European world, west of Russia. The term is meant to include the British and Irish parliaments, the American colonial assemblies and governors' councils, the parlements and provincial estates of France, the assemblies of estates in the Dutch and Belgian Netherlands and the princely states of the Holy Roman Empire, the diets of Sweden, Poland, Hungary, and Bohemia, and the councils of the German free cities and the city-states of Switzerland and Italy. All were different, yet all were in some ways alike.

To obtain a comparative view of these bodies has been a recognized problem of European historical research in recent years. There is a permanent committee of the International Committee of the Historical Sciences devoted specifically to the subject. It is called the International

Commission for the History of State Assemblies; scholars of many nationalities have worked under its inspiration, and many monographs have been published. Many of them have been sympathetic to corporatist political theory and correspondingly critical of the modern state and the individualist conception of legal rights. Most of this work has dealt with medieval and post-medieval times, and so is only indirectly relevant in the present context; but some of it has been directed to the European Old Regime before the French Revolution. The tendency in this case is to show the more favorable side of the Old Regime, its freedom from enforced uniformity, centralization, and all-embracing sovereign power.

According to this view, social groups with different interests or functions had rights and obligations realistically corresponding to their position. They constituted social "orders," and were represented in "estates." "In reality," says Professor Lousse, a leading exponent of the school, "there were no privileged orders in the sense that others were unprivileged, as one would be led to believe by a defective terminology created in France by the polemics of the eighteenth century. All were privileged"—but he admits that some were more privileged than others. "The domain of common law," he explains, was reduced, "but the domain of special law was much enlarged. . . . Each person's statute was adapted to his place in society, his social rank, and in a word to the function of general utility which he performed."[1] The nation was a body of cooperating groups each with appropriate obligations and rights. It was composed of "orders"—not necessarily the three "orders" made familiar by the history of the French Revolution, but orders in the sense of diverse levels in a harmonious hierarchy. "An order under the Old Regime," Professor Lousse assures us, "was not a caste but an association," not a *Geburtsstand*, or estate determined by birth, but a coming together of people with the same occupation, function, interest, or manner of life.[2] There were innumerable such orders:

[1] E. Lousse, *La société d'ancien régime: organisation et représentation corporatives* (Louvain, 1943), constituting volume VI of *Etudes présentées à la Commission internationale pour l'histoire des assemblées d'états*, 363 and 42.

[2] *Ibid.*, 255; cf. Lousse's more recent article, "Les ordres d'ancien régime n'étaient pas des castes," in *Studies Presented to the International Commission for the History of Representative and Parliamentary Institutions*, XI (Louvain, 1952). For comparative views of parliaments or estates, but not including the town councils or American assemblies treated in the following pages, see also R. H. Lord, "Parliaments of the Middle Ages and the Early Modern Period," in *Catholic Historical Review* (July 1930), 125-44; O. Hintze, "Typologie der ständischen Verfassungen des Abendlandes," in *Historische Zeitschrift* (1929), 229-48; L. Konopczynski, *Le liberum veto: étude sur le développement du principe majoritaire* (Paris, 1930).

merchants and landowners, cobblers and lawyers, peers and gentry, canons and priests, professors and civil servants. They grouped themselves at various levels, local, municipal, provincial, national. For purposes of public representation they might come together, in some countries, into estates of the realm, in France as clergy, nobility, and Third Estate.

The constituted bodies did in fact often call themselves "orders" or "estates." Most of them had in fact originated in the Middle Ages. Persons did have rights as members of groups, not abstractly as "citizens," and all persons had some legal rights, which, however, approached the vanishing point for serfs in Eastern Europe and slaves in America. But whatever may have been true in the Middle Ages, a survey of the constituted bodies of the eighteenth century forces some emendation of Lousse's picture. It is true that something like a corporate society existed, but the most noticeable similarities in the constituted bodies are to be found in two other features. First, the concept of "order," as applied in practice in the eighteenth century, frequently meant that there were some orders of men whose function was to fill positions of governance, in state or church, as distinguished from other orders whose functions were different. Secondly, there was a strong tendency, about a century old in the 1760's, toward inheritance of position in this governing elite, either by law or in fact, a tendency for influence to accumulate in a few families, or, in more abstract terms, for the institution of the family to diffuse itself through the institutions of government, not to mention those of religion. The tendency in the constituted bodies was more toward the *Geburtsstand* than toward free association.

In short, the world had become more aristocratic. Aristocracy in the eighteenth century may even be thought of as a new and recent development, if it be distinguished from the older institution of nobility. In one way it was more exclusive than mere nobility. A king could create nobles, but, as the saying went, it took four generations to make a gentleman. In another way aristocracy was broader than nobility. Countries that had no nobles, like Switzerland or British America, or countries that had few nobles of importance, like the Dutch provinces, might have aristocracies that even nobles recognized as such. There were only two hundred actual nobles in England, but all Englishmen rich enough to travel seemed *milords anglais* on the Continent. Dutch regents, scorned as mere burghers at the Peace of Westphalia, were accepted as gentlemen a hundred years later. The grandfather of Albert Gallatin was a citizen of republican Geneva who owned land across the French frontier, and who sat with the French nobility in the Estates General of 1789. Gouverneur Morris, the New York patrician, found the drawing rooms of England and the Continent open to him without condescension.

Aristocracy was nobility civilized, polished by that "refinement of manners" of which people talked, enjoying not only superiority of birth but a superior mode of life. It was a way of life as pleasing as any that mankind has ever developed, and which the middle classes were to imitate as much and as long as they could, a way of life characterized by dignified homes and by gardens and well-kept lawns, by private tutors and grand tours and sojourns at watering places, by annual migration between town and country and an abundance of respectful and unobtrusive servants. Indeed the date 1760 seems to mark a period even in the history of domestic service, at least for England. It appears that British servants were rowdy and insubordinate before this time, and terrorized house guests by their bold demand for tips; but about 1760 county meetings of the better families began to take the servant question seriously in hand, and "the transition to the more disciplined manservant of Victorian London began to take place."[3]

Aristocracy denoted also a concern for public business. The "aristocrat" (to borrow a term from eighteenth-century polemics) often had a public spirit, a desire to take part in organized government, hardly characteristic of the unruly noble of former times; or, perhaps, he only thought that governing others, being responsible for their welfare, in state or church, was the occupation most suited to a man of his standing whether or not he actually worked at this kind of occupation.

The following is a descriptive survey of the constituted bodies of the middle of the eighteenth century, with especial reference to their membership and recruitment. We move from east to west.

The Diets of Eastern Europe

The absence from Russia of bodies of the kind here described is only one of the signs that Russia, at the middle of the eighteenth century, did not belong to the region of Western Civilization. It was, however, moving in that direction. When the Empress Catherine, in

[3] D. Marshall, "The Domestic Servants of the 18th Century," in *Economica*, IX (1929), 15-40.

1767, called together a consultative assembly to sound out opinion in her domains, one of the proposals made by some noblemen was for the organization of the Russian nobility into a corporate body with corporate rights, somewhat as in Europe. Catherine, after a long delay, issued a Charter of the Nobility in 1785, as described in Chapter XII below, which by setting up provincial noble assemblies, with limited local powers, brought the Russian upper class, toward the end of our period, a little closer to the model of the European upper classes.

For most purposes Sweden (with Finland), Poland, Bohemia, and Hungary represented the eastern border of Europe.

In Sweden the years from 1719 to 1772 are known as the Age of Freedom, because at this time the Diet or Riksdag ruled without interference by the King. Indeed, these Swedish Whigs, after their revolution of 1719, had the works of John Locke translated into Swedish. The diet met in four houses, Nobles, Clergy, Burghers, and Peasants. Peasants could elect only peasants to represent them, and burghers only burghers, so that the classes or "orders" were kept apart. Nobles elected no one; every head of a noble family had the right to appear in person, but many were too poor or indifferent to do so, and added to their incomes by selling their proxies. Nobles were exempt from certain taxes, and claimed the exclusive right to high office. Government was in the hands of a council of nobles of which the King was only the chairman. During sessions of the diet executive power reverted to a secret committee of that body composed of 50 nobles, 25 churchmen, and 25 burghers (the peasants being left out as too unsuited for great affairs); the advantage to the nobility is apparent. The King was restricted in the creation of new nobles except at his coronation. It was thus assured that virtually all nobles should be born such. A law of 1762 further prescribed that no new families should be allowed to enter the chamber of nobles. The two parties, Hats and Caps, began in this decade to take on a certain class character, the Hats generally favoring the nobles, the Caps the three "unredeemed" estates, as they were called.[4]

In Poland, Bohemia, and Hungary the common feature of the diets, or assemblies of estates, was that landowners had come to monopolize them. In Poland, the towns had been excluded from the diet as long ago as 1505. In Bohemia about thirty towns had formerly been repre-

---

[4] For Sweden see Svanström and Palmstierna, *History of Sweden* (Eng. trans., Oxford, 1934), 191-92, 245-51; B. J. Hovde, *The Scandinavian Countries, 1720-1865: the Rise of the Middle Classes* (Boston, 1943), I, 177-90.

sented, but since they were largely Protestant, they were excluded during the Catholic and Hapsburg restoration in 1627; by 1755 Prague was the only town that normally sent delegates. In Hungary deputies from the towns sat in a lower house along with elected deputies of the lesser nobility or gentry, as in England; but so many townsmen were Germans that the Magyar nobility could not get along with them; all town deputies were required to vote as a body, and their vote was counted as only one vote, equal to that of a single squire, a rule reconfirmed in the turbulent Diet of 1764. Peasants in these eastern kingdoms were not represented at all; most of them were serfs. Ownership of rural land was confined to persons considered noble. In Poland and Hungary there were many small nobles, but in all three countries the great nobles or magnates were wealthy and influential. In Poland and Hungary these magnates sat by personal right, together with bishops, in an upper house of a two-chamber system, like the lords in England. In Bohemia the Hapsburgs had set up the Catholic clergy as a First Estate, but the predominance of wealthy nobles over the lesser ones was even greater than in the other two countries. In the 1780's, in Bohemia, 189 noble families owned land to the value of 600,000,000 florins; but, of these, the 15 families rated as "princely," such as the Schwarzenbergs, owned 465,000,000 florins' worth, having gained steadily throughout the century at the expense of the lesser nobles.

In Poland the diet was supreme, and the King very weak, as in Sweden until 1772. In Poland the noble landowners, great and little, prided themselves on their constitutional liberties, to the point of refusing even to be bound by majority rule, so that the diet, while supreme, could not govern, and the country in the 1760's faced partition by its monarchic neighbors. The kingdoms of Bohemia and Hungary were parts of the Hapsburg empire. The landowners in their diets had to share power with a strong dynasty. Restrained by the central government at Vienna in the eighteenth century, they were to reassert themselves vigorously in a kind of aristocratic resurgence in the 1790's.[5]

In Prussia there was no diet for the kingdom as a whole. Provincial diets or *Landtage* continued to meet, but they had lost their political powers during the century of Hohenzollern consolidation before 1740. In Prussia as elsewhere, however, the middle of the eighteenth century

[5] R. H. Lord, *Second Partition of Poland* (Cambridge, Mass., 1915); R. J. Kerner, *Bohemia in the Eighteenth Century* (N.Y., 1932); Marczali, *Hungary in the Eighteenth Century* (Cambridge, Eng., 1910).

saw a new strengthening of aristocratic institutions. The most burgher-like of Prussian kings was Frederick William I, who ruled for twenty-seven years before 1740. During his reign there was considerable upward mobility for burgher subjects. Professor Hans Rosenberg assures us that the ratio of burghers to nobles in certain high positions, which he finds to have been seven to three in 1737, was thereafter never matched in Prussia until the Weimar Republic. Frederick II was personally a man of more aristocratic tastes than his father, and his Silesian wars made it necessary for him to please the Junker nobles who commanded his army. Nobles therefore benefited substantially from the reign of the great Frederick. The King strengthened their monopoly of rural landownership, ceased to absorb their estates into the crown domain, encouraged them to set up entails, allowed their local diets to meet, and took them by preference into his army and civil service. Many Junker families, including the Bismarcks, became Prussian patriots as late as the reign of Frederick II, won over by concessions he made to their ideas.

On the other hand the Prussian civil service, one of whose functions had originally been to watch over noblemen and rustic squires, became increasingly imbued with their spirit. Burghers in the civil service obtained semi-noble status, such as exemption from certain taxes and from the jurisdiction of the lower courts. The civil service even built up its independence against the technically absolute King, gaining control of its own personnel and promotion policies, setting its own standards of training and performance, recruiting only "congenial members," becoming essentially self-selecting, a "constituted body" in the sense meant in this chapter, with a strong caste spirit, and an elitist belief in the duty of governing others for their own good. Independent in practice both of the King and of the public, possessing a strong sense of group identity and of corporate rights which outsiders did not share, the civil service in Prussia became a new estate of the realm, and was recognized as such in the Prussian Law Code of 1791.[6]

Councils and Estates of the Middle Zone

Between the eastern monarchies and France there was a broad middle zone, a world of minuscule states, princely, ecclesiastical, and repub-

[6] H. Rosenberg, *Bureaucracy, Aristocracy and Autocracy: the Prussian Experience; 1660-1816* (Cambridge, Mass., 1958), 60-74; A. Goodwin, *European Nobility in the 18th Century* (London, 1953), 83-101; W. Dorn, "The Prussian Bureaucracy in the 18th Century," in *Political Science Quarterly*, XLVII (1932), 262-66.

lican, into which Germany, Italy, Switzerland, and the Netherlands were divided. The old estates of Denmark-Norway, Bavaria, Piedmont, and Naples (like the Estates General of France and the estates of Aragon and Portugal) no longer had any meetings. Nevertheless, this middle zone had its social orders and constituted bodies, of which only a few can be noticed.

The Republic of Venice was one of the wonders of political science, famous for the ingenuity that had created an immortal frame of government, which was older than any royal house in Europe. Its citizens, that is, persons qualifying for public office, were called nobles, and nobility was strictly hereditary, determined by registration in the Golden Book. So few had been admitted, over the centuries, that where in 1367 there had been 240 noble families, there were only 111 in 1796. When the last doge was elected, in 1789, some of the older patricians complained that he was an upstart whose family had bought its way into the Golden Book as recently as 1669. In 1796, the last year of the ancient republic, with a population at that time of 130,000, only 1,218 persons attended the meeting of the Great Council, the constituted body in which all citizen-nobles met in person. It may be added, to illustrate the trend toward aristocracy, that Venetian nobles now scorned the trade on which the wealth and fame of the city were founded, and usually lived at leisure on landed estates on the dependent mainland of Venetia.[7]

Milan, like Hungary and Bohemia, belonged to the Hapsburg empire, but was governed as a separate unit. The chief public body was the Council of Decurions, 60 in number. To qualify for this council or other civic office it was necessary to be a patrician of the city. There were 297 patrician families in 1769, in a population of about 130,000. Most of these families were of merchant ancestry several generations back, but in 1652 they had introduced the rank of *cavaliere patrizio*, a kind of knightly or noble patrician, and in 1716 they had passed a rule that, to qualify as a patrician, one must prove noble status and a hundred years' residence by one's family in the city. A family lost patrician status if none of its members held office for three generations, or if a member "derogated" by going into trade. Patricians of the city and landed nobles of the surrounding duchy mixed as equals in the eighteenth century. In fact, nobles sought the more desirable status of patrician, since patricians occupied the numerous complicated magis-

---

[7] A. Bozzola, "L'ultimo doge e la caduta della Serenissima," in *Nuova Rivista Storica*, XVIII (1934), 30-58.

tracies which defended Milanese liberties against Hapsburg encroachment.[8]

In the mountains above Milan lay the cantons of Switzerland, a heterogeneous federation of small communities, some sovereign, some subject to others, but including some of the most exclusive and some of the most popular states of the day. The rural canton of Uri, for example, was one of the most democratic. Every year the villages elected a Landammann. Even here, however, the tendency to inheritance of position is apparent. That it existed in Uri suggests that it was due not merely to the ambitions of individuals but to a general willingness of most people to let others undertake public business, and the fact that only a few, under conditions of the time, had the breadth of outlook or qualities of character needed even for simple office. At any rate, the thirty-seven persons who acted as Landammann of Uri from 1700 to 1798 represented only twelve family names. For sixty-five of the ninety-eight years the Landammann was named either Bessler, Püntner, or Schmid. Son often succeeded father.[9]

Bern, on the other hand, was highly aristocratic. No one was admitted to its citizenship between 1651 and 1790, which is to say that citizenship was purely hereditary. Non-citizens might reside permanently in the town by promising to continue in the same occupation and to train one son in it. Those among the citizens who qualified to sit in the governing councils were designated as "patricians" in 1651. Eighty families held the offices in 1651, sixty-eight in 1787. The town had only about 11,000 inhabitants; its importance, and the value of its offices, lay in the fact that the town governed the country, i.e., the rural parts of the canton of Bern, as well as various "subject districts" in other parts of Switzerland. Government is said to have been honest and efficient, but it could also be profitable; a young Bern patrician could make enough to live on for life in about six years through governing one of the subject districts, such as the Vaud, the region about Lausanne.[10]

Basel was more of a middle-class or merchant aristo-democracy.

[8] F. Valsecchi, *L'Assolutismo illuminato in Austria e in Lombardia* (Bologna, 1934), II, 37-40; J. M. Roberts, "L'aristocrazia lombarda nel 18 secolo," in *Occidente*, VIII (1952), 305-25.

[9] *Dictionnaire historique et biographique de la Suisse*, "Uri."

[10] *Ibid.*, "Berne"; G. L. von Maurer, *Geschichte der Städteverfassung in Deutschland* (Erlangen, 1871), III, 760. Larger figures for the number of families qualified to hold office were given by a contemporary in 1785 (see below, p. 363); but the matter was uncertain at best, and "family" may of course mean either a household or a larger group of related persons.

Trade did not derogate, as at Milan; nor did its upper class earn a living by government, as at Bern. Half its people were citizens, half non-citizens, or *Hintersässen*, but no one received citizenship between 1763 and 1781, and in 1781 it was decided to admit no new citizens until 1790. Since the middle of the seventeenth century power had come into the hands of a few families, including the Burckhardts, to which the famous nineteenth-century historian belonged. Government was through a council which chose the magistrates and filled vacancies in its own ranks; politics within this council were dominated by the trade gilds. Of all magistrates chosen between 1529 and 1798 almost half belonged to the gild of big merchants known as the Key.[11]

Geneva, the city of Calvin and Rousseau, renowned among European intellectuals as the model republic, was an independent little place of 25,000 people, in most ways not yet really united with the Swiss confederation. The much-traveled William Coxe thought it halfway between the aristocratic and popular cantons. Five orders of persons lived under its laws; at the top, the "citizens," who had the legal right to hold office, and of whom Rousseau was one; next, the "burghers," who had the right to vote but not to hold office; next the *habitants,* who had certain rights to carry on trades in the city, but no political rights; then the *natifs,* born in the city but not of citizen or burgher parentage; and finally the *sujets,* the rural people outside the city, and governed by it. Government was by a Small Council (of twenty-five members) and a large Council of Two Hundred. The latter elected, or in fact confirmed in office from year to year, the members of the Small Council, which in turn designated the membership of the Two Hundred. By this system of mutual co-optation a few families had come to monopolize office, and so to create what was in effect a sixth order of patricians. The remaining citizens, who had the right to hold office but never did so, became indistinguishable in practice from the burghers. Burghers and citizens, some 1,500 in number, met in a kind of town-meeting along the lines of direct democracy in a General Council, and there proceeded to elect four syndics or executive officers of the city; but they elected from a slate proposed by the Small Council of twenty-five, which always put up its own members as candidates. Democracy was thus held in a tight leash at Geneva, but it never submitted entirely. As the Encyclopedia Britannica put it in 1797, "during the whole of the last century the history of Geneva affords little more

<hr/>

[11] *Dict. . . . de la Suisse,* "Bâle."

than an account of the struggles between the aristocratical and popular parties."

The most famous of all citizens of Geneva, Jean-Jacques Rousseau, was of one of the lesser families whose members never held office. Albert Gallatin, Jefferson's Secretary of the Treasury, was born a Geneva patrician in 1761. We have observed how his grandfather mixed with the French nobility. Gallatin himself tells in his memoirs, as a good Jeffersonian democrat, how he chafed at the aristocratic surroundings of his boyhood, spurned his grandmother's offer to get him a commission in a Hessian regiment bound for America, and emigrated to the New World on his own initiative instead.[12]

The free cities of Germany, some fifty in number, were in some ways like the more urban of the Swiss cantons and are of interest for the light they throw on the German middle class. Like the Swiss towns, they varied. Nuremberg, for example, was highly aristocratic—"the very El Dorado of family rule right down to our own days," as a writer in the time of Bismarck said. Its governing council and higher offices were filled by members of twenty families. These patricians permitted no one but themselves to wear swords or hats with plumes. Their sons studied and traveled at public expense. Their daughters received dowries from the city treasury. Cologne was more democratic in that, as at Basel, the gilds had in principle a good deal of influence. The Cologne gilds elected the members of the town council. But here, too, the same tendency toward self-perpetuating magistracy was apparent. Resistance of the citizens to these usurpations, sporadic since 1680, began in earnest in 1774, and lasted until the arrival of the French armies in the war of the French Revolution. Similarly at Speier the gild rule of the fourteenth century became the rule of the Thirteen in the seventeenth century and of the Five in the eighteenth—and the French in 1792 were at first regarded by many as liberators.[18]

Frankfurt was a commercial and governmental city, with a population very mixed in religion. A proverb had it that at Frankfurt the Lutherans spent their time in government, the Catholics in prayer, and the Calvinists in making money. There was also a large Jewish community. The governing council chose its own members, who served for life. Any citizen, if a Lutheran and the son of a citizen, might legally be chosen, but in fact the usual family monopolies de-

[12] *Dict. . . . de la Suisse,* "Genève"; G. Vallette, *Jean-Jacques Rousseau Genevois* (Geneva and Paris, 1911).
[18] Von Maurer, *op.cit.,* IV, 146-47, 160.

veloped in the council and the offices, of which there were no less than 500 for a town of 30,000. The citizenry had a keen sense of group identity as contrasted to the *Beisassen*, or permanent non-citizen residents. Office-holding and the ownership of real estate were privileges of the citizens, who also enjoyed more freedom in their business or occupations than the *Beisassen*. Calvinists could not belong to gilds, and Catholics only under certain restrictions. Affluent merchants yearned for nobility, and thirty-four of them in the eighteenth century obtained it by patent from the Holy Roman Empire. The uncle of Goethe, the city's most famous son, even wrote a book in the 1740's recommending creation of a merchant nobility in which a man might enjoy noble status without having to withdraw from trade. An ordinance of 1731 divided the population into five estates, or *Stände*, each to be marked by the kind of clothing it was entitled to wear. The top category was reserved for hereditary nobles who had sat in the town council for at least a hundred years—as people said.[14]

Among the German princely states there were some, like the Mecklenburgs, where assemblies of serf-owning nobles in effect ruled with little interference from the duke, and others, notably Württemberg, where the middle class was strong. The diet of Württemberg consisted of a single house, attended by fourteen Lutheran prelates and the delegates of some sixty towns. No nobles came at all; they had withdrawn from the diet as long ago as 1514, setting up as independent imperial knights and recognizing no authority in the diet. Since the Lutheran prelates had little influence, the diet represented the interests of the towns only, or rather of their several local magistracies, for it was the various burgomasters and town councillors, or persons named by them, who sat in the diet. In a population of 600,000 there were perhaps 1,500 men who chose the deputies. Yet there was at times a fairly active parliamentary life. Württemberg was often compared to England, and Charles James Fox once said that they were the only two countries in Europe to enjoy constitutional government. The philosopher Hegel made his debut, in 1797, by attacking the oligarchic character of the Württemberg estates.[15]

Of the Dutch government more will be said later. Its complexities baffle brief description. The towns were little republics, which along

[14] Voelcker, ed., *Die Stadt Goethes: Frankfurt-am-Main im achtzehnten Jahrhundert* (Frankfurt, 1932), 83-101.
[15] E. Hölzle, *Das alte Recht und die Revolution: eine politische Geschichte Württembergs in der Revolutionszeit, 1789-1805* (Munich and Berlin, 1931); J. Droz, *L'Allemagne et la Révolution française* (Paris, 1949), 112, 125.

with nobles sent deputies to estates of the seven provinces; deputies of the provinces constituted their High Mightinesses the Estates General of the United Provinces, which, together with the stadtholder, presumably ruled the country, or at least represented it in foreign affairs. Before 1748 there had been a period of almost half a century without a stadtholder, called the Age of Freedom or *ware vrijheid* (as in Sweden), during which the town oligarchies became thoroughly entrenched. "Everything tended to the domination of the few."[16] Ruling families, those holding office from generation to generation, were called regents. Each town had its regents, but those of Amsterdam were the most powerful, and had a general influence throughout the country. Their stronghold was the *vroedschap* or council of Amsterdam, a body of thirty-six men who sat for life. This council coopted its own members, chose the burgomasters of the city, and elected the deputies to the estates of Holland, which in turn preponderated in the Estates General of the union. "An alienation developed between rulers and ruled. The former became a class by itself, in which the admission of *homines novi* became very rare."[17] Government became a source of income for this upper class. The Amsterdam regents had no less than 3,600 offices at their disposal; one made 22,820 guilders by the sale of offices in seven years.

Between the fragmented republicanism of the small states just described, the magnificent monarchy of France, and the parliamentary regime of Great Britain there were obviously great differences, but the tendency to self-perpetuation in office was universal. It is illuminating to glance at the towns in England and France. They resembled those of the Netherlands and central Europe; each had its peculiar variations, but all showed their common origin in the great town-building era of the Middle Ages, from which each derived some sort of council or councils and some faint vestiges of a former popular organ of government. In both England and France, it appears, the town councils became increasingly closed organizations, and in that sense more aristocratic; but in both countries in the eighteenth century they lost out in real power, since both the Bourbon monarchy and the British Parliament, using the authority of central government

---

[16] I. H. Gosses and N. Japikse, *Handboek tot die staatkundige geschiedenis van Nederland* (The Hague, 1947), 637.

[17] *Ibid.*, 635. See also J. E. Elias, *De vroedschap van Amsterdam 1578-1795*, 2 vols. (Haarlem, 1905) and the histories of the Netherlands in English by Blok and Edmundson.

that was missing in the European middle zone, created new statutory bodies for new tasks of municipal administration.

At Lyon, for example, since the time of Henry IV, the council was made up of only five members, a mayor or *prévôt des marchands*, and four aldermen or *échevins*. The mayor was designated by the King. He alone had to be a native of the city; to become alderman it was only necessary to have lived in the city for ten years, certain property qualifications also having to be met. This rule had been forced upon the city by the royal government; it contrasts with the regulations of Swiss or German towns where a century of residence was often required, and shows how central government advanced the social and geographical mobility of the urban upper class. The council lost power over the years, but its members could console themselves with privileges; they were noble by virtue of their office, exempted from certain taxes, enjoyed special costume and escort at city expense, and could engage in wholesale trade or banking "without derogation or being reputed common." The pleasures of office were thus sufficiently attractive to encourage family ambition, and in the eighteenth century "the municipal administration recruited itself within an oligarchy of increasingly narrow scope."[18]

In England some of the towns were close corporations, others more democratic. Norwich was one of the latter, but its democracy deteriorated in the eighteenth century through public apathy and private abuse. Perhaps half the householders in 1689 were freemen, who actually voted for members of the town council. But they sold or otherwise gave their votes for other than civic reasons, and in any case the growth of new trades brought newcomers to the city who seldom took the trouble, or went to the expense, of acquiring its citizenship. The council even tried to compel people to become citizens, but there "seems to have been no great desire to become Freeman of Norwich."[19] Bristol was a close corporation. Its common council chose its own members and the public officials. It was disliked by some for its exclusiveness; on the other hand, wealthy merchants sometimes refused to accept membership in it, perhaps because they thought it too lordly, and even paid fines to avoid being included. Oligarchy might prevail *malgré lui*, so to speak, from a mere want of public spirit, or lack of confidence in the significance of public institutions.

---

[18] Kleinclausz, *Histoire de Lyon* (Paris, 1948), II, 146.

[19] S. and B. Webb, *English Local Government: Manor and Borough* (London, 1908), I, 539. See also I, 390; II, 445-70.

The Provincial Estates and Parlements of France

In France there were two kinds of bodies of a public character that played an active role in political life, as distinct from the bureaucrats and functionaries of the king. They were the Provincial Estates and the Parlements. The former resembled the assemblies of estates, diets, or parliaments found in other parts of Europe. In most of the French provinces the estates had gradually ceased to meet. In the eighteenth century they still met only in Languedoc, Brittany, Burgundy, Artois, and Bearn; and only in the first two were the Provincial Estates of any importance. In Languedoc and Brittany they exercised a power of consent to taxation by making a "free gift" to the king. This consent was sometimes forced, but they enjoyed more real freedom in dividing the tax burden among the individual taxpayers. In general, they defended the constitutional liberties of their provinces, as incorporated in the old agreements, or "contracts," by which the provinces had come under the French crown in former times.

The Estates of Languedoc met once a year. The archbishop of Narbonne always presided. The First Estate consisted of the 23 bishops of the province. The Second Estate consisted of 23 "barons," not elected by the nobles of Languedoc but appointed by the King to represent them. The Third Estate consisted of 46 "votes"—the same as the other two houses combined. These 46 votes were exercised by 68 deputies, 2 from each diocesan city, and 1 or 2 from various other towns in turn by a system of rotation. Many of these towns were what came to be called rotten boroughs in England—places once notable enough to be chosen for representation, but since decayed. Usually it was the town magistrates who attended the estates. No one was elected to the Estates of Languedoc. Voting was not by chamber, but by head. With double representation for the Third Estate, and with voting by head, the Estates of Languedoc before the Revolution enjoyed the two formal advantages demanded by the Third Estate on a national scale for the Estates General of 1789. The burghers, however, who could muster as many votes as clergy and nobles combined, by no means dominated the assembly of Languedoc. Some of the mayors who sat for towns enjoyed noble status. Two-thirds of the burgher representatives came from diocesan cities, where the influence of the bishops was strong. It was the bishops who governed in Languedoc, in cooperation with the King's agent, the intendant, because the bishops alone sat by personal right, and hence year after year, and because bishops, being often appointed for administrative talents, were willing and able to carry on public business. It was the archbishop of Narbonne who presided at the estates, and the important committees that functioned between meetings of the estates, for such matters as roads and public works, had in each case a bishop for their chairman.

The Estates of Brittany met every two years, in three houses, with vote by house, not by head. The First Estate included both bishops and other churchmen, but was less influential than in Languedoc. Forty towns sent deputies to the Third Estate, usually, as in Languedoc, the municipal mayors or councillors. To the Second or noble estate every "gentleman" of Brittany had the right to come, as in Sweden and in the subdistricts of Hungary and Poland. About 3,000 persons had the right to sit in this second chamber, and the number who actually attended never fell below 500 after 1746. Thus, though with vote by house the Third Estate possessed a veto on the two others, the estates of Brittany were dominated, or rather swamped, by nobles. Most of these were poor provincial gentry who hated taxes, viewed government and public works with suspicion, looked down on lawyers and tradespeople, and constantly disputed with the royal intendant.

The estates of Brittany and Languedoc were not declining in the eighteenth century. Both were becoming institutionally more mature. Government was becoming more complex, as taxation, conscription, road-building, postal communications, military housing, or poor relief grew more extensive. In both provinces the estates developed permanent committees and offices that remained at work between the meetings. Each province thus saw the rise of a provincial capital that was not merely the headquarters of royal officials. In Brittany after 1732 the estates almost always met at Rennes, and in Languedoc after 1736 they always met at Montpellier.[20]

The French parlements were more important than the provincial estates. A *parlement* or *conseil souverain* was at work in every part of France, each a supreme court of law for the area under its jurisdiction. All the parlements, in addition to judicial functions, exercised an executive role, supervising the keeping of order and the enforcement of their legal decisions, and also enjoyed what was in effect a

[20] For a convenient summary see E. Appolis, "Les états de Languedoc au 18e siècle: comparaison avec les états de Bretagne," in *Organisation corporative du moyen âge à la fin de l'ancien régime: études présentées a la commission internationale pour l'histoire des assemblées d'états*, ii (Louvain, 1937), 129-48.

share in legislation, claiming that they must register or "verify" every royal ordinance before it could take effect.

Seats in the parlement were for the most part owned as personal property. Members were thus neither elected nor appointed, but sat by personal right, and they could not be removed even by the King. The institution of property in office, though known almost everywhere in Europe, had been most fully developed in France and had been growing for over two hundred years. Hence, in the eighteenth century far more seats in parlement were inherited than were purchased. The King no longer sold them; they could be bought only from owners or heirs, who most often bequeathed them to sons, nephews, or sons-in-law. The *parlementaires* by 1750 thus constituted a hereditary magistracy going back three or four generations. They were now also nobles, and freely mixed and intermarried with the *noblesse de race*, descendants of the formerly feudal nobility. Their income came mainly from land ownership, and was sustained by the usual noble tax exemptions. With their legal education, their better habits of work, their living as neighbors in cities, their daily participation in public issues, their channels of regular access to the King and his ministers, and their facilities for meeting privately as recognized bodies in their several courts, the parlementary nobility by the middle of the eighteenth century had assumed a leadership over the French nobility as a whole, with which they now generally made common cause. The older landed nobility at the same time obtained a kind of trained professional leadership that it had never had before.[21]

The Parlement of Paris was the most influential, with by far the largest territorial area. It consisted of 25 "presidents" and 165 councillors, who divided up as benches of judges to hear lawsuits, and came together to discuss and act upon political questions. In addition, the 49 peers of France belonged to the Parlement of Paris; they took no part in judicial business unless the case of a very high nobleman were involved, but sat with the others, at will, if greater political matters were at stake, such as resistance to measures taken by the King or his ministers. There will be much to say of the Parlement of Paris in later chapters.

The Parlement of Dauphiny, or Grenoble, is the one of which most is known from recent historical study. It consisted of 10 "presidents"

---

[21] See F. L. Ford, *Robe and Sword: the Regrouping of the French Aristocracy after Louis XIV* (Cambridge, Mass., 1953), 188-201; J. Egret, "L'aristocratie parlementaire française à la fin de l'ancien régime," in *Revue historique*, 208 (1952), 1-14; F. Bluche, *L'origine des magistrats du Parlement de Paris au 18ᵉ siècle* (Paris, 1956).

and 54 councillors, plus 3 royal prosecuting attorneys; the bishop of Grenoble also had a right to sit, without a vote. In 1756 only 11 of the 67 were "new men," that is non-nobles or nobles of the first generation. In that year some people in the French government had the idea of a "commercial nobility," like the one dear to Goethe's uncle at Frankfurt, and such as existed in restricted form at Lyons and a few other mercantile centers—a nobility designed as an incentive to businessmen, by which they could become nobles while still remaining in business. "The very thought of a commercial nobility," announced the *parlementaires* of Grenoble, "has revolted one of the best constituted parlements of the kingdom." It was now as long ago as 1600 that most of them had had bourgeois among their progenitors. In 1762 the parlement, which like many other such councils in Europe enjoyed a free hand in determining its own membership, ruled that henceforth new members must have either parliamentary ancestry or four generations of nobility in the paternal line. Lawyers of the Grenoble bar, seeing a natural outlet for their ambitions thus blocked more than ever, protested. The parlement made a concession: it might accept a barrister on the same basis as a noble if his father, grandfather, and great-grandfather had also been barristers and if his own "merit, fortune and marriage alliances" were sufficiently worthy. The Grenoble lawyers remained dissatisfied. "It is certainly not hard to find men with four generations of nobility to make magistrates of them," one of them wrote, "but it would be impossible to find a lawyer of merit who was the fourth generation of famous lawyers."[22]

Parliaments and Assemblies in the British Isles and America

The familiar picture of the British Parliament in the eighteenth century can be profitably looked at in the context of the other constituted bodies of Europe. It consisted of King, Lords, and Commons. As Blackstone put it, the King sat in Parliament with "the three estates of the realm," the higher clergy, nobility, and commons; they and the King constituted "the great corporation or body politic of the kingdom."[23] Parliament governed; it was sovereign. "Men are con-

[22] J. Egret, *Le Parlement de Dauphiné et les affaires publiques dans la deuxième moitié du 18e siècle* (Grenoble and Paris, 1942), i, 21-24.
[23] W. Blackstone, *Commentaries on the Laws of England*, first published in 1765. Blackstone's views on Parliament are given in Chapter ii of Book i. Porritt, *Unreformed House of Commons* (Cambridge, Eng., 1903) is still standard. For most statistical data

nected with each other," said Blackstone in speaking of Parliament, "as governors and governed; or, in other words, as magistrates and people." Parliament was not supposed to follow the wishes of voters or other influences "out of doors." Representation meant that certain people assembled from various parts of the country, as in Languedoc or Württemberg, but how they were selected was hardly a matter for Parliament to concern itself with. Hence the methods by which the House of Commons was recruited seemed less peculiar to contemporaries than to modern critics who see in the House an ancestor of democratic representation.

The King in Parliament was no legal fiction, as will be seen. The House of Lords in 1760 consisted of about 230 members. Twenty-six of these were the bishops of the Church of England. Like those of Languedoc they were mostly administrators rather than religious leaders, and spent their most constructive efforts on matters of state. Each of the 200 lay lords belonged to the House by personal right; most had inherited their seats, for the frequent creation of new peers began later with the younger Pitt, but the inheritance of most of them went back no further than the preceding century, so that their noble lineage was scarcely more ancient than that of French *parlementaires*.

The House of Commons consisted of 558 members, sent up from boroughs and counties. In every county all men possessing a freehold worth forty shillings a year appeared by personal right in a county assembly, where they chose two "knights of the shire" to represent them in Parliament. Copyhold, as a form of property in land considered inferior to the freehold, did not carry with it the right of suffrage. An attempt to give the vote to copyholders in the 1750's was defeated.

Four-fifths of the members of the House of Commons sat for the boroughs, but most "burgesses" in the eighteenth century were in fact country gentlemen. It has been estimated that three-fourths of all members of the House of Commons, from 1734 to 1832, drew their main income from landed rents. In some boroughs, notably Westminster, freemen in considerable numbers actually elected their burgesses; but in most, as is well known, other and diverse methods were used

---

used here I am indebted to G. P. Judd, *Members of Parliament, 1734-1832* (New Haven, 1955). See also H. E. Witmer, *Property Qualifications of Members of Parliament* (N.Y., 1943). It will be evident to the alert reader that I do not share the revisionist admiration shown by L. B. Namier for the old House of Commons in his *Structure of Politics at the Accession of George III* (London, 1929) and other writings.

to designate the incumbents. No town had received the borough right since 1678.

Since about the year 1600 members paid their own expenses and received no remuneration, so that only men of independent income, or those patronized by the wealthy, could afford to sit in the House. An Act of 1710, by which the landed aristocracy tried to check the moneyed and business interest, held that to qualify as a knight of the shire one must own land of an annual rental value of £600, and that even to qualify as a burgess one must own land of an annual rental value of £300. It was estimated in 1740 that there were only 2,800 men in all England with £600 a year from land, and hence able legally to sit for the English counties. The Act of 1710 was often evaded (though not fully repealed until 1858); landless men did sit in the eighteenth-century House, but only through the sponsorship or connivance of landowners.

The House of Commons was elected, in a sense, and thus differed from the more purely self-perpetuating and closed constituted bodies of the Continent. But Parliament as a whole may almost be said to have recruited its own members, especially when we consider that the King, through his ministers, was part of the Parliament, and re-member that the Lords really named many members of the Commons. Many elections saw no contest at all. In seven general elections from 1760 to 1800 less than a tenth of the county seats were contested. Of the boroughs, some were purely inert in that their owners sold the seats or appointed the members without question; some seats were as much a property as seats in the French parlements. A few boroughs saw relatively democratic electoral contests; and in others small cliques and factions fought savagely, but without regard to public issues, to put their own men in the House. It may be added that Scotland sent forty-five members to the House of Commons. But the Scotch counties had fewer voters than the English, since the modern equivalent of forty fourteenth-century shillings was required in land. There were only 2,665 county voters in all Scotland, of whom 1,318 were what was frankly called "nominal and fictitious," that is, tempo-rarily provided with land by some magnate in order to deliver a vote. The Scotch boroughs were generally "closed"; 25 men, with a quorum of 13, chose the members from Edinburgh.

The eighteenth-century House of Commons has lately been sub-jected to statistical analysis. It appears that over half of all persons who sat in it for the century from 1734 to 1832 had a close blood rela-

tive in the House before them; if more were known of more distant
relationships the proportion would be higher. There were 21 Man-
nerses, 17 Townshends, and 13 Grenvilles. A Wyndham sat in every
Parliament but three from the Restoration to 1800, and indeed in half
of all Parliaments from 1439 to 1913. After 1790 the number who had
had fathers, grandfathers or greatgrandfathers in the House of Commons perceptibly increased. The trend in the eighteenth century, that
is, was toward more family rule. A quarter of all members were
baronets or sons of peers at the time they sat (i.e., noble by Continental standards); almost half were peers, sons of peers, or baronets when
they died. The trend was toward an increase in this direction. The
House elected in 1796 had 220 knights, baronets, sons of peers, and
actual peers (that is, Scotch and Irish peers not sitting in the House
of Lords). There was also a rising proportion of men who had been
to the English public schools and to Oxford and Cambridge, where
they absorbed the group spirit of a governing class. More also tended
to be career officers in the army or navy. In 1754 career officers in the
House outnumbered those trained in the law. The House elected in 1790
had 85 professional military officers, almost a sixth of its membership.
On the other hand—and the point is very significant—an increasing
proportion of the members had commercial interests, either as their
sole economic concern or in addition to their interest in the land. Here
the turning point came in the 1760's and gives weight to the old idea
of an Industrial Revolution setting in at about that time. Before 1761
only 60 or 70 of the members had any financial interest in commerce,
as had been true as far back as Elizabeth. By the 1780's the figure was
110, and it continued to rise.

The distinctive thing about the British Parliament, in contrast to
similar bodies on the Continent, was, first, its very real power, since
it governed the country, the King's ministers being part of it; and,
second, the mixing of commercial and landed interests in it, even sons
of peers sometimes having some activity in business, so that class
lines were blurred, with gentry not altogether scorning the marts of
trade, and the greater businessmen sometimes mixing with or even
related to gentry. The easy exchangeability of landed and commercial
property, and the attitude toward productivity and profit through rational management, shared by landowners and businessmen, gave a
common ground of understanding. Nevertheless, the land and the
aristocratic outlook continued to dominate.

Ireland was constitutionally a separate kingdom from Great Britain, having an autonomous though subordinate parliament of its own. "Everything was sweetly and harmoniously disposed through both islands," according to the somewhat visionary picture drawn by Edmund Burke, "for the conservation of English liberties." Hence, wishing well to the Americans, he could offer Ireland "as my model with regard to America." The Irish Parliament, like the English, had two Houses, Lords and Commons. The Lords consisted of 142 temporal peers and 22 Anglican bishops, though the population was of course mainly Catholic. The Commons consisted of 300 members from counties and boroughs, as in England; some of the boroughs were in even worse shape than those of England, that of Tulsk being described as a cluster of mud huts. In the Commons of 1775 the Duke of Leinster owned 11 seats, Mr. John Ponsonby 22. About 100 persons, 50 peers and 50 commoners, controlled two-thirds of the seats in the Irish Commons. No Catholic could be elected, and after 1727 no Catholic could vote. In any case most of a lifetime might pass without an election, since an Irish parliament lasted (until 1768) for a whole reign without renewal. In the reigns of George I and II there were no general elections except at the accession of those sovereigns.[24]

British America, and especially New England, as John Adams remarked in 1774, had "a hereditary apprehension of and aversion to lordships, temporal and spiritual."[25] There were no lords in the British colonies, except occasional Englishmen visiting or stationed there; and no bishops. But there was a good deal of hereditary standing, with an apparent trend, as in Europe, toward its increase.

Each colony had a governor's council and an elected assembly. The councils were very important: they sat as supreme courts of law, they advised the governor, and they acted as upper chambers in legislation. Individual councillors often had great influence upon elections to the assemblies. Councillors, usually twelve in each colony, were appointed by governors; and the governors, normally Englishmen appointed in England and strange to the colony, naturally chose the leading local men to help them govern. A list of all who served on the councils before the Revolution, according to the estimate of Professor Labaree, would include ninety per cent of the "first families," that is the socially prominent families, of the colonial period. By the 1760's in most colonies these families had repeatedly intermarried, until "their gene-

[24] W. Hunt, *The Irish Parliament: 1775* (London, 1907), vii-xii, 54. Burke, *Writings* (1901), ii, 171 (Conciliation with America, 1775). Lecky, *Leaders of Public Opinion in Ireland* (London, 1903), i, 78.
[25] *Works* (Boston, 1851), iv, 54, "Novanglus."

alogical trees became veritable jungles of interwoven branches, the despair of the researcher but the pride of their descendants."[26]

Visitors to the restored buildings at Colonial Williamsburg can call the scene to mind. The capitol of the royal province of Virginia stands at the end of Duke of Gloucester Street, as it stood before the American Revolution. Its floor plan is like the cross-section of a dumbbell. At one end is the room where the elected assembly, the House of Burgesses, sat on rows of benches. The other end of the building was used by the governor's council. At this end, on the second floor, is a room with twelve high-backed armchairs. Here the council sat as an upper legislative house. Directly below, on the ground floor, is a courtroom, with twelve more high-backed armchairs. Here the council sat as the supreme provincial court. The point is that the same 12 men occupied both sets of chairs. We can easily picture them gathering also, by threes and fours, in the adjoining committee rooms or at the palace half a mile away, to consult with the governor on executive business. The 12 were appointed by the governor, and while governors came and went the councillors sat, in most cases, until death or extreme old age. They were a close-knit group. Ten of them, in the year 1775, as they looked across at their assembled colleagues in the high-backed armchairs, upstairs or downstairs, saw the familiar countenances of their own relatives by blood or marriage. Ten of them knew that their own fathers or grandfathers had sat in these same seats. In the whole period from 1660 to 1774, 91 persons were appointed to the council. Nine surnames accounted for almost a third of them—Page, Byrd, Carter, Lee, and 5 others.

It was much the same in the other British American provinces. In Maryland, in 1753, 8 out of 11 sitting members had fathers or grandfathers on the council before them. In New York, 25 out of 28 councillors appointed from 1750 to 1776 bore the names of great Hudson Valley landowners. When John Wentworth, a native of the colony, became governor of New Hampshire in 1766, he had on his council his father, an uncle, two uncles by marriage, a first cousin, a first cousin once removed, a step-cousin and the husband of a cousin—8 out of 12. By 1773, after filling a number of vacancies in the interim, he had raised the number of his relatives on his council to 9. In Connecticut, the councillors were elected by the freemen. There was less of a clearly marked and intermarried governing group in this highly republican colony, but the freemen, like those of Uri in Switzer-

---

[26] L. W. Labaree, *Conservatism in Early American History* (N.Y., 1948), 3.

land, elected and reelected men of the same families year after year. "The holders of twenty-five surnames occupied two-thirds of all the places in the Connecticut magistracy. These figures coincide almost exactly with those for Virginia." A Pitkin was elected 98 times; an Allyn, 77; a Walcott, 63. Nor is it to be supposed that the whole number of persons with these names was especially large. It may be pertinent, and may satisfy those methodologists who urge the historian to divulge his own prepossessions, to remark that a few years later there were in all Connecticut only 27 families by the name of Pitkin, whereas there were 160 families by the name of Palmer, none of whose offspring seems ever to have enjoyed the slightest political importance.[27] In neighboring Rhode Island, erratic in this as in other respects, there was more turnover in governing personnel.

If the American councils, like comparable bodies in Europe, showed a strong tendency toward self-perpetuation and aristocracy, the same cannot be said with equal force for the elected assemblies. The assemblies had limited powers; each was only one part of its colonial government structure; the right to elect assemblymen was usually restricted to property owners, who, however, were often very numerous; and apathy, inconvenience, lack of time, or the badness of roads often meant that the right was not used. Representation by towns and counties, as in Britain and Europe, was very uneven. Nevertheless, in a comparative view, having in mind how the House of Commons, the Estates of Württemberg, or the Third Estate of Languedoc was recruited, remembering that in Holland or Switzerland there were few real elections at all, and recalling that the political zeal of Poles and Hungarians was possible for not more than a tenth of the population, it seems certain that the Anglo-American colonial assemblies, before the American Revolution, were the most nearly democratic bodies to be found in the world of European civilization. Practice varied from one colony to another, and more is known about some colonies than others. In New Jersey, for example, where the election of 1754 aroused enough public interest to draw out most of the voters, it is known that almost all the freeholders, or about half the adult white males, voted in Middlesex county.[28] In New England, where there were few slaves and indentured servants, and where ownership of small farms was very common, almost every adult male had the right to vote.

[27] U.S. Bureau of the Census: *Heads of Families at the First Census . . . 1790: Connecticut* (Washington, 1908).

[28] R. McCormick, *History of Voting in New Jersey* (New Brunswick, 1953), 63.

Actual voting was sporadic, but over 90 per cent of all men over twenty-one years of age actually voted at Watertown, Massachusetts, in 1757; and over 80 per cent at Weston in 1773.[29] For completeness it is worth while to mention the *cabildos* or town councils of Spanish America. The *cabildo* was the one institution in the Spanish empire allowing a measure of public representation. Some of its members were appointed by royal authority, others owned or inherited their seats by property right, so that family groups infiltrated the councils here as elsewhere. In the eighteenth century, however, with the bureaucratic development under the Spanish Bourbons, the *cabildos* of America, like the *cortes* in Spain itself, no longer enjoyed their former activity and importance. They were not to revive until the eve of the wars of independence.[30]

In summary, and here one may agree with Professor Lousse and the corporatist school already mentioned, nothing was more characteristic of the eighteenth century than constituted bodies of parliamentary or conciliar type. They existed everywhere west of Russia and Turkey. They were more universal than the institution of monarchy, more widespread than the famous middle class. All defended their liberties as they understood them; there was in many places a busy political life; discussion, protest, airing of grievances and refusal of taxes were very common. No one except a few disgruntled literary men supposed that he lived under a despotism. In defending their rights and justifying their pretensions, the constituted bodies elaborated a good deal of political theory. It was a political theory of a strongly historical kind, making much of the agreements, compacts, statutes, and charters of former times. It is not true that all eighteenth-century thought was unduly abstract or rationalistic; or, if some thinkers became belligerently rationalistic, it was because historical arguments were preempted by groups which made no secret of their exclusiveness. Nor did political thought arise merely from an emancipation of the mind, as a process of intellectual enlightenment, from the books of thinkers who defied the authorities of their time. It devel-

[29] R. E. Brown, *Middle-Class Democracy and the Revolution in Massachusetts, 1691-1780* (Ithaca, 1955), 46; F. B. Tolles, "The American Revolution Considered as a Social Movement: a Re-evaluation," in *American Historical Review* (Oct. 1954), 1-12.

[30] J. M. Ots Capdequí, "Interpretación institucional de la colonizacion española en America," in Pan American Institute of Geography and History, *Ensayos sobre la historia del nuevo mundo*, 304-07; see also the remarks of C. C. Griffin, 110-11. Ots Capdequí, *Nuevos aspectos del siglo XVIII español en America* (Bogota, 1946), 22.

oped also in close connection with actual politics, and in disputes between organized powers already well established. The next chapter sketches the political philosophy that had come to characterize the constituted bodies of Europe by the middle of the eighteenth century, and some of the problems and paradoxes presented by the growth of aristocracy up to that time.

ARISTOCRACY ABOUT 1760: THEORY
AND PRACTICE

To be bred in a place of estimation, to see nothing low and sordid from one's infancy; to be taught to respect oneself; to be habituated to the censorial inspection of the public eye . . . ; to take a large view . . . in a large society; to have leisure to read, to reflect, to converse . . . ; to be habituated in armies to command and to obey; to be taught to despise danger in the pursuit of honor and duty; to be led to a guarded and regulated conduct, from a sense that you are considered as an instructor of your fellow citizens in their highest concerns, and that you act as a reconciler between God and man; to be employed as an administrator of law and justice . . . ; to be a professor of high science . . . ; to be amongst rich traders, who from their success are presumed to have sharp and vigorous understandings . . . these are the circumstances of men that form what I should call a natural *aristocracy, without which there is no nation.*—EDMUND BURKE, 1791

The thing is perfectly harmless in itself, but it marks a certain foppery in the human character, which degrades it. . . . It talks about its fine blue ribbon *like a girl, and shows its new* garter *like a child. A certain writer, of some antiquity, says:* "When I was a child, I thought as a child; but when I became a man, I put away childish things."

The punyism of a senseless word like Duke *or* Count *or* Earl *has ceased to please. Even those who possessed them have disowned the gibberish, and as they outgrew the ricketts, have despised the rattle. . . .*

Through all the vocabulary of Adam there is not such an animal as a Duke or a Count.—THOMAS PAINE, 1791

ARISTOCRACY ABOUT 1760: THEORY
AND PRACTICE

"THERE is no more certain maxim of politics," observed Robert Walpole in 1719, "than that a monarchy must subsist either by an army or a nobility; the first makes it a despotic, the latter a free, government."[1] He was explaining his opposition to the Peerage Bill, then before Parliament, by which the earls of Stanhope and Sunderland and others of the Whig magnates intended to restrict the creation of new peers. By making the peerage more strictly hereditary, the great Whigs hoped to prevent control of the House of Lords by the King or his advisers. They wanted no repetition of what Queen Anne had done a few years before. She had simply added enough new men to the Lords to make that house agree with her on the ratification of the treaty of Utrecht. Walpole, as a commoner and country gentleman, had no desire to see the Lords put out of reach of influence by the crown, or by the crown's chief minister, as he soon became. But he did not doubt the utility of a strong body of nobles, to serve as "a balance against the democratic part of our constitution, without being formidable to the monarchy itself."

In the same year, 1719, the duke of Saint-Simon, peer of France, as haughty a nobleman as ever trod the halls of Versailles, was seriously alarmed. A plan was afoot to abolish the proprietary character of seats in the French parlements. The Regent, alarmed at the revival of the Parlement of Paris since the death of Louis XIV, was considering the creation of a new system of courts, in which property in office and hence hereditary position should have no place. The Regent wanted a parlement that would agree with him, and since it was the proprietary and hereditary nature of their seats that enabled the magistrates to resist, he proposed to buy back their

---

[1] Walpole quoted by W. S. Holdsworth, "The House of Lords 1689-1783" in *Law Quarterly Review*, XLV (1929), 449.

offices from them. This was enough to arouse Saint-Simon. Normally the first to scorn such inferior nobles as owed their nobility to government service or outright purchase by their own grandfathers, Saint-Simon now rushed to the defense of the *parlementaires*. They were, he said, a useful "check" or "barrier" against the pretensions of the papacy and the usurpations of the King.[2]

The Peerage Bill failed to pass, and the power of creating new peers remained in the British crown. The Prince Regent's ideas for abolishing property in judicial office came to nothing, and the French parlements remained predominantly hereditary. But in both countries the same response had been aroused. A commonplace of eighteenth-century political thought had been stated: that nobility was a necessary bulwark of political freedom. Whether in the interest of a more open nobility, as with Walpole, or of a more closed and impenetrable nobility, as with Saint-Simon, the view was the same. Nobility as such, nobility as an institution, was necessary to the maintenance of a free constitution.

Montesquieu, Réal de Curban, Blackstone, Warburton

Here, in the remarks of two practical observers, lay the germ of the thought of Montesquieu, a nobleman of the ancient stock who had inherited a seat in the Parlement of Bordeaux, was active in that parlement in the days of the Regency, and announced his ideas in systematic form in *The Spirit of Laws* some thirty years later. The strength of Montesquieu's book, published in 1748, lay in its firmly weaving together many diverse strands, each strand representing the position taken by actually existing institutions or groups of men. He combined the arguments of the old feudal and the new parlementary nobility in France. He put together England and France, showing that each in its way had the institutions necessary for political liberty, England through its balance of King, Lords, and Commons, France through the moderating influence of "intermediate bodies" upon the crown. He transcended a purely nobilitarian view because he included groups of all kinds among these intermediate bodies: not only the nobility, but the French parlements as associations of judges, the seigneurial and ecclesiastical courts as distinct from the royal power, the clergy and the innumerable smaller corporations within the

[2] Saint-Simon, *Mémoires*, xxxvi, 308-09.

church, the provinces and towns as corporate entities, the gilds and professional associations of all kinds. Each of these, according to Montesquieu (anticipating the views already quoted from Professor Lousse), had its own rights, legal powers, and privileges. These were no mere grants from either a sovereign people or a sovereign King. Such rights could not lawfully be curtailed; they balanced each other, and prevented the undue concentration of power. "Abolish in a monarchy," said Montesquieu, "the prerogatives of manorial lords (*seigneurs*), clergy, nobility and towns, and you will soon have either a popular or a despotic state."

But Montesquieu, in wishing to concede appropriate rights to all, thought it appropriate to allow more extended rights for the more powerful elements in society. His reading of French history, and indeed of world history as he knew it, taught him that if the "great" did not have a great share in government they would rebel against it. They were ungovernable except on their own terms; if their interests were not protected they would not be loyal. Here is what he says in his famous chapter on the British constitution:

"There are always in a state some people distinguished by birth, wealth or honors; but, if they are confounded with the rest of the people, if they have only one vote like others, the common liberty will be slavery for them, and they will have no interest in defending it. . . . Their share in legislation should therefore be proportionate to their other advantages in the state."[8]

It is hard to deny the wisdom of this observation, or the truth of the historical perceptions on which it rested: the whole interminable story of barons' wars and noble rebellions lay behind it. It may be contrasted, however, with the thought of Rousseau, when he maintained, in the *Social Contract*, that the very fact that the force of *things* tended to destroy equality was a reason why the force of *law* should be used to maintain it.

The important personages would have their proportionate share in legislation, Montesquieu went on to say, "if they form a body which has the right to check the enterprises of the people, as the people have the right to check theirs." So he recommends that the legislative power "be confided both to a body of nobles, and to a body chosen to represent the people, with the two bodies having separate assemblies and deliberations apart, and separate views and interests." And, he adds,

[8] *Esprit des lois*, Book xi, chapter vi. See also Carcassonne, *Montesquieu et le problème de la constitution française au 18ᵉ siècle* (Paris, 1926), 76-77, 84-85.

since the judiciary is in a sense "null," it is the nobles who are especially suited to balance the executive and legislative powers. This telling passage suggests a number of elucidations. First, Montesquieu was no believer in one-class rule; he really thought that the "people," i.e., persons not noble, should have a role in the state.[4] Second, he wanted to keep the classes distinct, with "separate views and interests." Third, by abstract analysis of the prerequisites of a free society, Montesquieu produces the Lords and Commons of England, with the *noblesse* and *roture* of France also present in his mind. Fourth, when he thinks of the separation or balance of powers in government, he is not thinking of the balance of executive, legislative, and judicial function, for the judicial power is in a sense "null"; he is thinking of the balance between King, nobility, and Commons, and nobility is the key element in this balance. If the French parlements serve as a balance, they are able to do so not because they are judges but because they are nobles— and hereditary nobles at that. Fifth, the later influence of Montesquieu in America should not be exaggerated. The idea of the judiciary as an equal third member in a system of government seems to have been developed by the Americans more than by Montesquieu, who saw no such staying-power in judicial office itself, unfortified by hereditary position or noble rank. Nor did all American partisans of an upper legislative chamber, during the formative years after the American Revolution, think that the role of a senate was to give proportionately greater political influence to men who already had a great share of social and economic power. Many did think so; but John Adams, at least, gave precisely the opposite reasons for creating an upper chamber, namely to prevent aristocracy by segregating the big people, "ostracizing" them to a separate chamber so that they could not infiltrate and pervert the popular house.[5] Adams, too, had read the history of Europe, and had learned from it what Montesquieu had not learned, but what is now the commonplace of our textbooks and the view more congenial

---

[4] Not that Montesquieu was without an extreme class consciousness. Cf. the note he made in 1729 on arriving in London from Holland, on a journey made in company with the Earl of Chesterfield: "A Londres, liberté et égalité. La liberté de Londres est la liberté des honnêtes gens, en quoi elle diffère de celle de Venise, qui est la liberté de vivre obscurément avec des p----- et de les épouser: l'égalité de Londres est aussi l'égalité des honnêtes gens, en quoi elle diffère de la liberté de Hollande, qui est la liberté de la canaille." *Oeuvres* (1955), III, 284-85. It is hard to see what Montesquieu could have meant by his reference to the Dutch, except that he preferred the English aristocracy (*honnêtes gens*) to the Dutch patricians, whom he seems to have regarded as *canaille*. As for the reference to the Venetians, p----- means w-----s.

[5] *Defense of the Constitutions of the United States* (1786) in *Works* (1851), IV, 290-91. See also below, pp. 271-75.

to the modern mind, namely, that a strong executive is necessary to defend the many against the few. Nothing could be more remote from the thinking of Montesquieu.

In Montesquieu's system it was "honor" that supported free monarchies, and "virtue" that supported republics, whereas despotism, the third of his three categories of states, was maintained by "fear." By "virtue" he meant civic spirit, a lack of personal ambition, a certain self-effacement when necessary for the public welfare. By "honor," on the other hand, he meant a kind of self-assertion, a consciousness of one's rank in society, a desire for recognition and public esteem, an enjoyment of external marks of high position, a sense of obligation imposed by one's standing or the known deeds of one's ancestors, a greater readiness to accept danger than to incur disgrace, a refusal to be humiliated even by a king. Because noblemen had such a sense of honor they could not succumb to the fear by which despots ruled. They would resist their own debasement, and so protect the liberties of all. There is doubtless more truth in this diagnosis than is palatable to popular equalitarians. Palatable or not, there is no disputing that for Montesquieu the preservation of political liberty presupposed a hierarchic form of society and an aristocratic code of personal honor.

The *Spirit of Laws* set forth, in an amplified and cogent form, what members of the constituted bodies of Europe had long been saying in more fragmentary ways; it was therefore immediately popular, and influential in the formulation of constitutional thought. It has often been said that Montesquieu misunderstood England; it has been alleged that the growth of cabinet government in England, and the increasing power of the House of Commons, had already put Montesquieu's emphasis on a balance between King, Lords, and Commons out of date. It seems likely, however, that Montesquieu interpreted eighteenth-century England more correctly than some later writers who sought to make England prematurely democratic. There is ground for believing that the Prime Minister was more dependent on the King than on either house of Parliament. To Holdsworth, the authority on English legal and constitutional history, it seemed that Montesquieu, and along with him Delolme, Vattel, Blackstone, and Burke, were quite right in holding the separation and balance of powers, between King, Lords, and Commons, to be the distinctive feature of the British eighteenth-century constitution, as, he says, it remained down to 1832.[6]

[6] W. S. Holdsworth, "The Conventions of the 18th Century Constitution," in *Iowa Law Review*, XVIII, 2 (Jan. 1932), 161-80. See also below, Chapter VI.

Montesquieu's book went through half a dozen French editions in three years. It was immediately translated into English, in which it reached its tenth edition by 1773. It was the best-known modern French book in America. It appeared in Dutch in 1771, in Italian in 1777, in German in 1789, in Russian in 1801, doubtless encouraged in Russia by the young patrician reformers about Alexander I. A traveler saw it in Hungary as early as 1751, translated into Latin, the official political language of the Magyars.

The extent of an influence is best seen when we find it in unexpected places, in the minds of men who are thinking of other subjects. Edmund Gibbon offers an example. Gibbon of course knew France very well. In Paris in 1763, he found that intellectuals and men of high social standing mixed more easily in that country than in England; he was a little irked to be received in France as a writer only, instead of in the quality of "a man of rank for which I have such indisputable claims."[7] Years later, as historian of the Roman Empire, he related how in A.D. 212 all subjects of the empire became Roman citizens. He found here one of the causes of subsequent despotism and degradation. He was moved to make a general observation, using some of the very language of Montesquieu. "The distinction of ranks and persons," he says, "is the firmest basis of a mixed and limited government. In France the remains of liberty are kept alive by the spirit, the honors and even the prejudices of 50,000 nobles. Two hundred families supply, in lineal descent, the second branch of the English legislature, which maintains, between the king and the commons, the balance of the constitution. . . . The perfect equality of men is the point at which the extremes of democracy and despotism are confounded."[8] So we are offered the choice, with nothing between: hereditary rank on the one hand, or "perfect equality" (and despotism) on the other.

Montesquieu was not a true conservative, because he was not satisfied with the way the Bourbon monarchy had developed and was developing in his time. Nor were the French parlements which after the mid-century drew so many arguments from Montesquieu by any means conservative, as will be seen. The Parlement of Paris in 1764 was already using the phrase, "the Sovereign, the Law and the Nation"—a forecast of "the King, the Law and the Nation" to which men took the oath of allegiance in the first years of the Revolution.[9]

[7] Quoted by Elinor G. Barber, *The Bourgeoisie in 18th Century France* (Princeton, 1955), 133.

[8] *Decline and Fall of the Roman Empire*, chap. lxiv.

[9] Flammermont, *Remontrances du parlement de Paris au 18e siècle*, II, 436.

A more purely conservative writer was Réal de Curban, an old gentleman born in 1682, who compiled six volumes on the Science of Government in his later years. They were published after his death. He anticipated the conservatism of Burke and the nineteenth century far better than Montesquieu. He takes up, for example, the much discussed institution of private ownership of public office, especially the judgeships or magistracies of the parlements. "If it is an evil," he sighs, "it is an incurable one." He poses the question: is it better to continue with it as established, or to abolish it so that the King's subjects can rise by merit alone? "Since public prejudice favors the latter opinion, which I consider false, I have thought that I ought to refute it."

Then comes the practical and conservative argument. Of course, if we were founding a new state we would not make its offices a form of property. "But when a state is established, when imperfections have become habits, and disorder itself has a usefulness to the state, prudence forbids making changes." The prudent man will conform to custom and usage. Of course we would favor the abolition of property in office if it really led to the advantages promised by the reformers, but the real consequences would be different. If magistrates did not inherit their position, says Réal, they would have to be appointed by the King, which is to say by his ministers, who, unable to know the merits of all cases in question, would in turn depend on court gossip and intrigue. Or mere intellectuals (people "with more Latin than property") would seek office, which would be undesirable; or businessmen would try to enter government service, which would also be unfortunate, since they are more useful to society in their business. In any case the present office-holders are not really so bad, since they regard their offices as investments or family occupations. Peculiar arrangements (*désordres*) "which have been introduced by public necessity and strengthened by reason of state should not and cannot be abruptly reformed. It is always dangerous for a government to pass from one extreme to another. With difficulty could one today change the means of arriving in positions of government, without undermining the loyalty of those who now occupy these positions; and it is to be feared that they would arouse the people to revolt."[10] The latter, it may be observed, is precisely what happened in France in the noble revolt of 1788 and in the counter-revolution after 1789.

Men are of course equal by nature, Réal admits; but in civil society

[10] Réal de Curban, *La Science du gouvernement* (Aix-la-Chapelle, 1751-1764), VI, 73-77.

there must be subordination. Some must give orders, others follow them. Réal cites various minor arguments, such as that variety makes the beauty of the world, that social order is willed by God, and that all is "marvelously" disposed in a great harmony; but he is willing to meet his adversaries on their own ground. "Degrees of dependence have been established only for common utility." (This is almost the language of the Declaration of the Rights of Man and Citizen of 1789.) "Why not confer this authority which must be respected upon merit rather than on external qualities?" No one would choose a ship captain for his birth; why, then, choose our governors in this way? Unfortunately, says Réal, the critics of hereditary position would be right only if men were always reasonable and just. Given men as they are, there would be no agreement on merit; each would think himself or his own leader more meritorious than others; conflict and even civil war would follow. It is better to hold to some unmistakable even if arbitrary sign, such as birth. Moreover, if a man really rose by merit, his equals and competitors would take offense, for his success would be a constant and bitter reminder of their own failures. "But in making position (*la grandeur*) depend upon birth, we soothe the pride of inferiors and make high position much less difficult to accept. There is no shame in yielding when I may say: 'I owe this to my birth.' This argument convinces the mind, without injuring it by jealousy. . . ."[11] which is to say that a society which accepts hereditary position is free from the tension, frustration, disappointment, and bitterness of a society based on rivalry for "success."

One looks up from Réal's book with a feeling that if the French had a revolution it was not because they were not forewarned, and that if modern society has developed psychological difficulties, it is not because these were not foreseen. But no attention was paid to Réal at the time, nor was there much encouragement for anyone to hold conservative opinions, outside of religion. This is because, in France, the aristocratic school was not conservative. In France the aristocracy hoped for change. It became disaffected toward the monarchy long before the middle class.

Not so in England. Here those who took part in the chief constituted bodies, the Parliament and the established church, had won out in the preceding century both against the King and against uprisings from below. Their problem was to preserve the constitution as it was. It is

[11] *Ibid.*, III, 227-30.

worth a moment to glance at two representative thinkers who wrote just before the revolutionary disturbances began.

William Blackstone went to Oxford in 1758 to occupy the newly created Vinerian professorship of law. The lectures he gave there developed into his *Commentaries on the Laws of England*. In his opening lecture he explained why English law could better be studied at Oxford than at the Inns of Court. It was because law was a proper subject of study by gentlemen who must govern the country, because at Oxford "gentlemen may associate with gentlemen of their own rank and degree," and at Oxford were assembled the future peers, future members of the House of Commons, future justices of the peace, landowners, lawyers, and clergymen. At the Inns of Court the subject was approached in too technical and vocational a way. Properly considered, the study of law was a liberal subject, a "science which distinguishes the criterions of right and wrong." Blackstone therefore proposed to impart, in addition to a certain amount of purely legal lore, a philosophical comprehension of the subject.

The philosophical arguments of the book are somewhat as follows: English constitutional liberties are "the residuum of natural liberty." They are in a sense the rights of all mankind, but by an inscrutable dispensation have been debased elsewhere while they survive in England, being "in a peculiar and emphatical manner the rights of the people of England." They are mainly the rights of personal liberty, personal security, and private property, but include also, as secondary rights calculated to preserve the primary ones, certain political rights specifying the composition and powers of Parliament. By the Rights of Persons the people are divided into certain orders, clergy and laity, nobility and commonalty; about forty status levels, from duke to laborer, are described. Rank and honors, by offering an incentive to virtuous ambition, are useful in a well-ordered state. A "body of nobility" curbs and protects both crown and people. Parliament is an autonomous body; the lords sit in their own right, and the commons serve for the kingdom as a whole, with no such dependence on their constituents as obtains in the United Provinces. Locke was mistaken in believing that, if Parliament abused its trust, the people retained a supreme power to "remove or alter" it. "So long as the English constitution lasts, we may venture to affirm that the power of Parliament is absolute and without control."[12]

[12] *Commentaries*, 1 (Philadelphia, 1860), 128, 140 ff., 144, 153, 157-60. The American

Blackstone was certainly conservative enough, even believing that no rights or wrongs existed in England except those actionable under English law. He thought that no power except Parliament itself could make changes in Parliament; certainly Parliament could not lawfully be influenced by pressures from outside. But Blackstone was not as conservative as conservatives were soon to become in the face of American and European developments. He could conceive of the possibility, in the 1750's and 1760's, of parliamentary reform. He thought it "a misfortune that deserted boroughs should continue to be summoned," and observed that "if any alteration were to be wished or suggested in the present frame of Parliament, it should be in favor of a more complete representation of the people."[13]

William Warburton, who rose to be the Bishop of Gloucester, published his *Alliance between Church and State* in 1736. He reissued it in various editions, including in the one of 1766 a lively rejoinder to Rousseau. His purpose was to justify the establishment of the Church of England, and of the Test Act designed to keep non-Anglicans out of important office. Could one sufficiently know the political writings of all languages it would doubtless be possible to find similar works from all countries in which there were religious minorities that had any recognized existence at all; for in virtually all states the holding of office was limited to persons of a preferred religion. Warburton's arguments could probably be found in Calvinist Geneva or Amsterdam, in Lutheran Württemberg or Sweden, and even in the Catholic states in the eighteenth century.

Church and state, he holds, are equals in a federal pact. It is "Hobbist" to suppose that religion was invented to facilitate government, and "papist," in his opinion, to believe that government exists to advance the cause of religion. Neither can be reduced to the other. But the church, having no power of compulsion, needs to be protected by the state. A particular religion is protected not because of its truth but because of its social utility. To argue the case for an establishment on the ground of religious truth leads to endless theological disputation. The whole "key" or "clue" to the question is to understand that a religion is established "not to provide for the true faith, but for civil utility." All religious beliefs should be tolerated, and Warburton prides himself, fairly enough, on being more indulgent than the French

---

editor, Sharswood, takes care to explain, in his notes, that in the United States the legislative body is not supreme, but exercises only powers delegated by the people.
[13] *Ibid.*, 171-80.

deists toward novel and absurd religious movements. But, he argues, it is well to single out one moderate religion for alliance with the state. The state thereby benefits because people are taught their duties, religious acrimony is minimized, and eccentric religious behavior is kept under control. The favored church benefits because its clergy are set up as an order in society, and by receiving a public endowment, in most countries in the form of tithes, become independent of voluntary contributions by the people. It is useful to have the bishops of this church sit in a parliament, where they can protect religion. It is also useful to have the bishops designated by the civil power, and to allow church assemblies only by the permission of magistrates, though of course in such matters the church should be consulted. Arguments of reason and utility, though really of universal application, show an "amazing agreement" with the existing institutions of England. Adversaries are baffled, because reason and the establishment "prove to be one and the same."[14]

Nevertheless, some will say, Warburton continues, "that every qualified subject having a right to the honors and profits in the disposal of the Magistrate, the debarring him from these advantages for matters of Opinion is a violation of the rights of the subject." Warburton grants that his other arguments may not convince such wholly unsympathetic opponents. He willingly therefore takes the argument on to higher ground. He simply denies that there is any *right* to public office at all. Or, rather, he asserts that the existing authorities may prescribe such qualifications for office as they think fit. "All places of honor and profit, in the Magistrate's disposal, are not there in the nature of a Trust, to be claimed and equally shared by the subject; but of the nature of prerogative, which he [the "magistrate"] may dispose of at pleasure, without being further accountable, than for having such places ably supplied. All right of claim then being absolutely at an end, and consequently all injustice, in excluding at pleasure, we may finish our discourse, having taken from our adversaries the great palladium of their cause."[15] No one can complain of discrimination if he happens not to have the qualifications for a job.

This statement repays careful examination. Warburton disarms his opponents not merely by denying the right to office; doubtless there is no such "right." He disarms them by explicitly declaring that government is not accountable to those it governs, that it may appoint whom

14 *Alliance of Church and State* (London, 1766), 66, 90, 115, 123, 187-205.
15 *Ibid.*, 298-300.

it pleases, and that office is not a trust but a privilege to be conferred by those who rule. Government, or "the magistrate," in this case meant the Parliament, that sublime body whose power Blackstone did not hesitate to call absolute.

Even this is not enough. The bishop has "finished his discourse," but still thinks of more to say, occupying ever higher ground of general principle—all to justify the Test Act. He enunciates the doctrine of prescription, soon to be made famous by Burke. He puts it forward as a check upon natural law. He declares that to require religious tests is not really contrary to natural law or natural right, but adds that, even if it were, religious tests would still be justified by the doctrine of prescription, which he says derives from the Roman law, and which holds that long continual possession over many years itself creates a right— often necessary to defend order and security against claims of "natural right" that may cause disturbance. Now at last, with the additional reminder that the whole question rests on the utility and not the truth of religion, he is content to close his book.[16]

Taken together, and with due regard for the differences between them, the four writers just summarized, all writing about or just before 1760, may be taken as spokesmen for the political classes of their day. The world of the constituted bodies—the parliaments, diets, assemblies of estates, councils and magistracies, each supporting and supported by the church established in its own country—would find much to agree with in Montesquieu, Réal, Blackstone, or Warburton. There would be wide agreement on the virtues of liberty, and with the idea that nobility, or at least a system of inherited ranks and distinctions, was necessary to assure it. It would be agreed that parliaments or ruling councils were autonomous, self-empowered, or empowered by history, heredity, social utility, or God; that they were in an important sense irresponsible, free to oppose the King (where there was one), and certainly owing no accounting to the "people." It would be agreed that the inequalities of position necessary to any organized society might as well be determined by inheritance, since the claims made for "merit" would be deceptive and confusing. It would certainly be agreed that there was no general right to office. It would probably be agreed, too, that what seemed unreasonable, what no one would invent if he were inventing society afresh, might still be reasonable, or at least socially useful, in a subtle or "amazing" way. And it might be agreed that prescription, long-continued practice, custom, and usage might justify or necessitate what to naïve common sense seemed very peculiar, or to sensitive consciences actually unjust.

Uses and Abuses of Social Rank

There were, however, certain problems and paradoxes created by the institution of nobility. The hierarchic character of society produced difficulties for aristocrats themselves, for those beneath them yet close enough to mix with them or aspire to join them, and for society as a whole considered as an association of human beings with practical needs to be met.

A distinction may be drawn between two kinds of rank. On the one hand there is (or was) a diffuse kind of rank, or social standing, generally derived by the individual from the family of his birth, built into his personality from childhood, conditioning his attitudes to other persons, above him, below him, or his equals; a rank or standing accompanying a person everywhere, showing in his bearing and in his clothing; in the street, in the shop, or in the drawing room; in public and in private; among his intimates and in the presence of strangers. The man of quality in the eighteenth century expected to be, and usually could be, promptly recognized as such. It was this kind of rank that Gibbon wished his French friends would see in him, when they received him merely as an accomplished man of letters. The other kind of rank may be called specific or functional. It is rank held for a particular purpose within a particular organization of limited scope, and without significance outside the organization; a rank, or position, conveying a certain authority and a certain responsibility for the achievement of certain ends, set above some ranks and below others, but only within a chain of command or a hierarchy set up for a particular purpose, and outside of which the individual is considered to be like others. A major-general in civilian clothing doing his Christmas shopping in a department store becomes merely a shopper; he takes his chances with others, and cannot expect any unusual deference. A bank president driving his car through city traffic becomes merely a driver; he takes or yields the right of way without consideration of social standing; he may grumble, but grumbling does him no good; basically he accepts, and must accept, the equality of all persons who are equally competent as drivers. Doubtless the two kinds of rank overlap, in that diffuse or social rank helps to determine occupation, and specific or functional or occupational rank carries over into personality and social standing. But the two are distinct enough. As Thomas Paine was to say later in a highly inflammatory work, if a man is called a judge or a general one may form some impression of what he is and what he does, but if he is called a duke or a count one can form no idea of what he is or does, or even whether he is a man or a baby.[17]

All societies require systems of specific rank. And a sort of diffuse rank will doubtless always exist. The peculiarity of eighteenth-century society was that specific rank was so largely determined by diffuse rank. It is probable, quite apart from the ethical merits of aristocratic and democratic institutions, that a complex and highly articulated society, moving toward what are called modernization or industrialization, will operate more efficiently, with less friction, complaint, or grievance, and with more effective discharge of its multifarious business, if specific ranks are filled with the least possible regard to diffuse rank, if generals are chosen purely for military talents and their authority is confined to strictly military affairs, if people accept each other as generals, bank presidents, motorists, or shoppers, according to circumstances of the moment, having otherwise about the same regard for all.

Europe in the eighteenth century, and Western Europe more than Eastern Europe, was already a complicated society, with elaborate mechanisms operating in the fields of government, production, trade, finance, scientific research, church affairs, and education. The allocation of personnel to these enterprises on the basis of birth and social standing could not but hamper, and even pervert (one thinks of the established churches, some of the universities, and many branches of government), the achievement of the purposes for which such institutions were designed. The old feudal days were over. It was no longer enough for a lord to look locally after the needs of his people. The persistence and even the accentuation of an aristocratic outlook derived from earlier and simpler conditions presented problems for European society itself, as well as for the individuals and classes that made it up.

Nobility in the old sense had been corrupted, so to speak, or at least turned from its early character, by two new developments which now reached their height: its association with money and wealth, and its use by governments as an instrument of rule. Wealthy men, whose grandfathers had been bourgeois, and who still owned and managed their wealth in bourgeois manner, even when it was in land, now belonged to the nobility in France and elsewhere. In England men of the same kind, while they could rarely become peers because the

[17] *Rights of Man*, Everyman edition, 60.

peerage was so small, belonged in many cases to the higher levels of aristocracy. In Holland they were regents; in Milan and elsewhere, patricians. To the advantages of money were thus added the advantages of social rank, and the inheritance of property might carry with it the inheritance of nobility or its equivalent. Wealth, thus ennobled, could give preferential access to public office, a favored position in taxation, and membership in a select body, thought to be peculiarly necessary to the freedom of the state. "Another reason operates," Turgot once said, "to render privilege most unjust and at the same time less worthy of respect. Where nobility can be acquired by a payment of money, there is no rich man that does not speedily become a noble, so that the body of the nobles includes the body of the rich, and the cause of the privileged is no longer the cause of distinguished families against a common class, but the cause of the rich against the poor."[18]

In many countries it seems that the rich were becoming richer in large measure because of their rights of special access to government—because of their favored position in an aristocratically oriented society, whether or not they enjoyed the titles of nobles. Thus even in America the families that could get on to the governors' councils, and remain there from one generation to the next, made fortunes in the eighteenth century by receiving grants of western land from the crown. In England the landowners, because of their control of Parliament, were the more able to enlarge their estates through statutory enclosures. In Bohemia the princely families added to their properties while the lesser nobles lost. The patricians of Bern made an income by governing their subject districts, and the regents of Amsterdam profited from the 3,200 offices at their disposal. In France, in the eighteenth century the King no longer commonly sold offices, which were now inherited by their owners; but he could give pensions and gratifications to whom he pleased. There was nothing specifically French in this practice. In England, too, the government did not sell offices; it gave them away as a means of maintaining its influence in Parliament or, in general, of mollifying the aristocratic class. In England by 1700 "the majority of great old families were drawing large income from various sources —colonelcies in the army, pensions, ambassadorships, etc."—which for many families equalled their incomes from landed estates.[19] The income from a mastership in chancery rose from £150 a year in 1620 to £6,000 in 1720. Shortly after 1800 the office of Chief Clerk of the

---

[18] Quoted by D. Dakin, *Turgot and the Ancient Regime* (London, 1939), 274.
[19] Habakkuk, "English Landownership 1680-1740," in *Economic History Review*, x (1939), 11.

King's Bench brought £6,200 a year to its owner, who paid £200 a year to a deputy to do the work.[20]

Thus while it is true that in some ways men governed because they were rich, it is equally true, or more so, that men were rich because they governed. Either they were able to perform public duties because they had private means, like the justices of the peace in England, or army and navy officers of certain kinds and ranks in all countries, whose salaries were too small to support the necessary manner of life. Or government itself, or various emoluments incidental to government, formed a source of income for people who were in a position to obtain them. And the people in this position were not the small politicians and grafters on the fringes of respectable society who derive a somewhat similar kind of profit from operations of government today; they were definitely of the upper class, the very guardians of liberty and of the state, peculiarly sensitive to considerations of honor; and such income from government office, or from church benefices, was thought to be especially honorable for people of this kind.

The institution of nobility, or high hereditary social rank, had also become an object to be used and manipulated by governments as a means of rule. Nobles could be turned into courtiers, as at Versailles. Or a king could make use of their great social prestige to awe the populace or impress foreign rulers, and incidentally bind the nobles more closely to himself, by making them into ambassadors or lords lieutenant or military governors with a good many ceremonial functions in addition to the practical ones. They also made good army officers, since they grew up in the habit of command; there was the additional advantage, for the king, that a nobleman turned into an army officer came under a measure of discipline. There was an increasing tendency in the eighteenth century for royal governments, which had usually established their authority in former times by drawing on the middle class, to put nobles into important civilian office. Increasingly the French intendants were nobles. In Prussia, it was in the reign of Frederick the Great that the crown for the first time favored the nobility in high office, and this remained the general practice thereafter.

Kings also could raise commoners to the nobility, or promote lower nobles to higher grades. The Hapsburgs after the reconquest of Bohemia in the 1620's had created a new Bohemian nobility to help keep the country loyal. They did the same after the reconquest of central

[20] K. W. Swart, *Sale of Offices in the 17th Century* (The Hague, 1949), 55-57.

Hungary in 1699, where such families as the Esterhazys received princely status in the eighteenth century. The Irish peerage had been created by the British crown for much the same purpose; the union of Ireland with Great Britain in 1801 was made more acceptable to Irish magnates by the creation or promotion of new batches of Irish peers. Often governments created new nobles in order to weaken or dilute the old ones. Thus the French monarchy, especially before 1700, had sold patents of nobility not only to make money but also to reward its servants, to please the ambitious middle class, and to build strength against the older feudal nobility. In England the frequent creation of new peers began in the time of George III and especially under the younger Pitt. Here, too, one purpose was to combat the aristocracy already established by creating a new one. "Pitt swamped the Whig oligarchy in the House of Lords."[21]

In general there were two possible lines of development, toward segregation or toward assimilation. A nobility or a patriciate might become more exclusive, impenetrable and purely hereditary. Or it might from time to time assimilate newcomers from the next lower classes. Exclusiveness was most rigid in the aristocratic republics, such as Venice or Bern or Nuremberg or Holland, or in monarchical states at times when the King was weak, as chronically in Poland, or during the Freedom Era in Sweden, or in England during the Whiggish generations before 1760, during which very few new peers were created. The class line was also all but impassable in the small German princely states, which had as many nobles as they needed; in the larger ones, even Prussia, and in the Austrian empire, with their more complex governments, cases of commoners rising to nobility through government service were more frequent.

It had long been easiest, in all probability, to rise to the aristocracy in England and in France. Blackstone was able to quote a sixteenth-century writer, Sir Thomas Smith: "As for gentlemen, they be made good cheap in this kingdom: for whosoever studieth the laws of the realm, who studieth in universities, who professeth the liberal sciences, and, to be short, can live idly, and without manual labor, and will bear the port, charge and countenance of a gentleman, he shall be called master, and taken for a gentleman."[22] Much the same could be said for France, where, however, the way to nobility had lain more through

---

[21] A. S. Turberville, "The Younger Pitt and the House of Lords," in *History* n. s. XXI (1937), 355.

[22] Blackstone, *Commentaries* (Philadelphia, 1860), I, 406.

government service or purchase of titles. And if in England anyone with the proper bearing could pass as a gentleman, so in France all kinds of plausible people gave themselves out to be noble.

There are signs, however, that passage from the mercantile to the aristocratic ranks was becoming less common in both countries about 1750. In England, as land ownership became more concentrated with the enclosure movement, it was the men who already owned land that were buying more land.[23] Unbreakable entails of landed estates, recognized in English law only since the Restoration, were now producing what amounted to family trusts in the third and fourth generation. There was less movement from city to country than in the Tudor period. City men who bought rural acreage often did so only to have a place of residence in the country, or meet the legal qualifications for election to Parliament; they did not become country gentry—the two classes remained distinct. "Gentlemen's sons were less commonly apprenticed in towns. By 1760 the stratification was not like a system of caste, but it roughly blocked out the division of functions between different groups of the community."[24] The justices of the peace, formerly appointed by the crown, were now appointed by the lord lieutenants of the counties, who were usually peers. "Hence by the end of the century we get a social exclusiveness amongst the justices which led them to object to anyone engaged in trade or manufacture."[25] At the highest level, that of the peerage, there was a certain opening of the gates after the Whig oligarchy lost control. The House of Lords increased in size by about fifty per cent during the two administrations of the Younger Pitt. Pitt, however, used elevation to the peerage as a reward for eminent military or diplomatic service, or to gain the support of those who controlled parliamentary boroughs. Such new peers originated in the landed class, and their elevation signified promotion within the aristocracy rather than entrance of new peers into it. The idea that elevation of businessmen to the peerage began with Pitt seems to be a groundless historical cliché, for only one of Pitt's creations was a banker and City of London man.[26] The social distance between landed and commercial classes had perhaps never been greater in England than in the days of Jane Austen and the eve of the First Reform Bill.

[23] Habakkuk, op.cit.
[24] G. N. Clark, *Wealth of England to 1760* (London, 1946), 161.
[25] W. S. Holdsworth, "The House of Lords 1689-1783," in *Law Quarterly Review,* XLV (1929), 438.
[26] Turberville, op.cit.

In France the *noblesse*, comprising tens of thousands of families, corresponded socially to what would be called gentility in England. The difference was that English gentility was a vague standing recognized by society, while French *noblesse* was a status recognized by law and defined or created by the royal power. The French noble also possessed tangible privileges such as tax advantages, which the English gentleman did not enjoy, at least not simply on any legal ground of being a gentleman. Nobility in France, however, was common enough to be the accepted symbol of prestige. Not to be noble, or nearly noble, might be almost as embarrassing in France as not to be considered of the gentlefolk in England. Many bourgeois respelled their names with a genteel or noble flourish: Robespierre as de Robespierre, Danton as d'Anton, Brissot as Brissot de Warville, Roland as Roland de la Platière. Carnot vainly tried to prove himself noble to impress the family of the girl he hoped vainly to marry.

Since the King could create nobles it was theoretically possible, in France, for the royal government to bestow the accepted prestige-symbol on successful men in all walks of life. The *élites*, as the French say, might have been assimilated to the *noblesse*, or nobility itself might have been transformed into a kind of legion of honor for men of notable achievement. Had this happened, there might have been riots and peasant uprisings, but no French Revolution.[27]

There were reformers in the French government who saw this possibility. In 1750 the government created a *noblesse militaire*. There were then about 4,000 bourgeois officers in the army, and the decree specified that all of them after thirty years' service should receive quasi-noble tax-exemptions, or nobility itself if theirs was the third generation of military service. The tendency of the government, that is, was still assimilationist rather than segregationist. But the tendency of the nobles, the "real" nobles, was more segregationist than assimilationist. The nobles by birth were often impecunious, and for economic as well as other reasons disliked bourgeois competition for military appointments. They obtained for themselves, in 1751, a new *école militaire*, in which poor boys of four generations of inherited nobility could receive education at public expense; and in 1781, just as the thirty-year period specified in the edict of 1750 came to an end, aristocratic pressure forced the government to issue the famous ordinance of that

27 M. Reinhard, "Elite et noblesse dans la seconde moitié du 18e siècle," in *Revue d'histoire moderne et contemporaine*, III (Jan.-Mar. 1956), 5-37; L. Tuetey, *Les officiers sous l'ancien régime* (Paris, 1908); E. Barber, *The Bourgeoisie in 18th Century France*, 60-62.

year, by which army commissions were in effect limited to men with four quarterings of nobility, that is, men whose noble status was duly inherited. Even at this late date, on the eve of the Revolution there appear to have been a number of generals in the French army who were not of noble birth, but these were older men who had entered the service many years before. The trend was toward aristocratic self-segregationism in the army.

If the true nobles, with their esteem for martial virtues, would not share their status with middle-class army officers there was little chance that the *élites* of civilian life could receive any such honors. The government did, at times, favor the ennoblement of businessmen. It projected a *noblesse commerçante* to correspond to the *noblesse militaire*, hoping to get nobles and their capital into business pursuits, and to make it possible for businessmen to become noble without abandoning business. A decree of 1767 allowed nobles to go into commerce without derogation. It set up procedures by which some of the *négociants*, the most well-to-do wholesale merchants, might receive certain honorific distinctions which, however, fell just short of nobility. The result was that the *négociants* were antagonized, being told in effect that they were not quite worthy of the desired rank. Such vacillation in the assimilating of businessmen to the nobility was due to many causes, to the resistance of older nobles, to the jealousy of *marchands* for *négociants*, to the difficulties of a financially hard-pressed government in granting a status that carried tax exemption, and, more generally, to the incongruousness between forms of prestige derived ultimately from land, war, or feudalism and forms of achievement arising from trade and the handling of money. The professions fared no better than business. Quite a few doctors and a few artists were ennobled, but in general no men of science, no writers and no lawyers, and only a few professional government workers. It may be pointed out that the deputies of the Third Estate who brought about the National Assembly in 1789 were almost all of them lawyers or government career men, and that they abolished nobility fairly early in the Revolution, in 1790.

Problems of Administration, Recruitment, Taxation, and Class Consciousness

Either segregation or assimilation had its difficulties. So far as privileged and hereditary aristocracy was a problem, the use of homeopathic methods, the infusion of new doses of privileged and hereditary aristocrats to allay the obstinacy of the old ones, was obviously no permanent solution. It stored up more hereditary aristocracy for the future. It maintained the aristocratic scheme of values, the admiration for aristocratic status as the proper goal of ambition, as the animating spirit or incentive throughout all walks of life. To keep movement into the aristocracy relatively open had in a certain sense a democratizing effect upon the aristocracy and upon society at large. It had, also, and perhaps more so, an aristocratizing effect upon the middle class and upon all society, for the successful merchant or lawyer could not rest easy merely with a comfortable income or the satisfactions of occupational status and what I have called functional rank, but felt obliged also to acquire a general social recognition, which would become hereditary for his children, and enable him or his children to occupy a secure vantage point from which to look downward as well as up.

Many difficulties were thus created. One was the administrative inefficiency or embarrassment that followed, in complex civilian or military organizations, when social rank and functional rank failed to correspond. It was hard for a man of high functional rank to secure respect or obedience from a subordinate whose social rank surpassed his own. A serious study of the history of army rank, that is, of the ordering of generals, colonels, majors, captains, etc., might throw light upon this curious subject. Louis XIV had systematized such purely functional rank in the French army, and had favored promotion by seniority or merit rather than by social class. The indignant Duke of Saint-Simon (who had himself failed of promotion to general), complained that in this way all men in the service were thrown into "a complete equality," with *seigneurs* mixed "in a crowd of officers of every kind," and with a gradual "forgetting by everybody, and in everybody, of all difference of person or origin," so that everyone's career came to depend "on the minister or even on his clerks."[28] To the aristocratic political school, which held that hereditary nobility was the bulwark against despotism, it seemed that by such practices a king might turn army officers, and indeed all his subordinates, into his tools or creatures. But with the aristocratic resurgence after Louis XIV's death, it was the opposite problem that prevailed. The progressive discrimination against bourgeois officers caused discontent among the bourgeoisie, and probably also, by reducing the competition between noble and bourgeois, and narrowing the field from which commissioned ranks were recruited, led to a loss of professional competence.

[28] Quoted by E. Boutaric, *Institutions militaires de la France avant les armées permanentes* (Paris, 1863), 428.

The same problem existed in civilian branches of government. In some countries, notably in Prussia and Russia, civil servants were assigned an assimilated military rank, or put in a stated order of social precedence. Even Lenin, much later, it may be recalled, was the son of a middle-class inspector of schools, who enjoyed the assimilated rank of major-general. In Germany in the eighteenth century many middle-class people were finding careers in officialdom, and facing the problem of associating with social superiors who were only their equals, or less, in official employment. The Prussian King ruled that his administrative boards should pay no attention to differences of class origin among their own members, all of whom, as civil servants, came to enjoy certain noble privileges. But the trend in other German states was the other way. In Hanover a ruling in force from 1670 to 1832 held that noble councillors should take precedence over non-noble members of the same councils; and a similar rule existed in the archbishopric of Cologne.[29]

As to effect on professional competence of socially exclusive methods of recruitment, very little seems to be systematically known. Egret's recent work on the Parlement of Grenoble is illuminating. He makes it clear that, because the parlement insisted on recruiting itself from its own sons (or from the fourth generation of nobility), its standards inevitably and lamentably declined. A royal ordinance required a minimum age of twenty-five years for an ordinary councillor, and of forty for a president or presiding judge; but the pressure to establish young men of the right families was too strong to withstand; and in 1756 half the councillors and all the presidents had come to their positions with "dispensations" for age. Other ordinances forbade fathers, sons, and brothers to belong simultaneously to the parlement, but were automatically disregarded. Members were required to have a degree in law, but the universities gave the degree with absurd facility, even telling candidates the answers to examinations in advance. Men who had no interest in law and no vocation for it as a profession, or who led scandalous personal lives most unseemly in judges, or who rarely attended the sessions but simply lived idly on their country estates, nevertheless belonged to the Parlement of Grenoble; it was their "family occupation," an investment of capital, a badge of rank; such men could of course always turn up for a political meeting, to defend

[29] F. Valjavec, *Entstehung der politischen Strömungen in Deutschland, 1770-1815* (Munich, 1951), 79; H. Rosenberg, *Bureaucracy, Aristocracy and Autocracy: the Prussian Experience* (Cambridge, Mass., 1958), 137-74.

the privileges of their bench. It must be added in fairness that in serious cases, as when it unanimously condemned one of its own members to be executed for murder, the parlement tried to do what was right; but it is not the rectitude of individuals, but the effect of the system, that is in question.[30]

It is hard not to believe that other oligarchies did not suffer from the same internal problems and produce similar disadvantages for the public. The British House of Commons, though far more broadly based than the Parlement of Dauphiny, is at least to be examined with this thought in mind. It has been argued, with a great assemblage of detailed evidence, that the system of controlled boroughs, however strange it may seem to modern eyes, did have the advantage of bringing the commercial as well as the landed interests into the House. It appears from statistical study, however, that most commercial men in the House were not the nominees of patrons but sat for the small number of open boroughs in which they were elected by actual voters. It is also argued, in favor of the eighteenth-century House of Commons, that the system allowed able young men to enter politics at an early age. This advantage, if it was one, was by no means limited to England. It was clearly due to the influence of aristocratic family connections; and was probably as widespread as this influence. In England the average age of commercial men on entrance into the House of Commons was 40, that of country gentlemen 32; in Silesia the average age of commoners upon appointment to the governing boards was 42, that of noblemen 27. Over half the members of the Parlement of Paris immediately before the French Revolution were under 35. We have just seen that half the members of the Parlement of Grenoble took their seats before their twenty-fifth birthday. In England it was only a quarter of the Commons who first took their seats at age 25 or before; but members who had had fathers or grandfathers in the House entered at an age averaging nine years younger than for others. We often hear of the youth of the French revolutionaries; we may fail to realize that the governing aristocracies of the eighteenth century were composed to a large extent of young men also.[31]

[30] Egret, *Parlement de Dauphiné*, I, 19-27.

[31] On the House of Commons see the works of Namier and Judd cited in note 23 of Chapter II. Holdsworth and Turberville also observe that the great Whigs hesitated to put into the cabinet, though not into Parliament, anyone who was not "one of themselves," and cite the fact that Edmund Burke never attained cabinet rank; see Holdsworth, *Law Quarterly Review*, XLV, 331. For Silesia see H. Rosenberg, *op.cit.*, 106; for France, J. Egret, "L'aristocratie parlementaire française à la fin de l'ancien régime," in *Revue historique*, 208 (1952), 1-14.

Ability cannot be so readily measured. There was William Pitt, prime minister at twenty-four, and a man of great talents and understanding in certain fields. It is impossible to say how many other youthful magistrates or politicians were like him, in England or elsewhere. What one knows of eighteenth-century Oxford makes one hesitate to generalize on the side of optimism; the studies at Oxford were no more difficult, and no more enlightening, than those required of young men at Grenoble. And as for the practical wisdom not to be learned at school, even Holdsworth, while praising the old House of Commons as a working institution, allows that the way in which it lost America, and alienated Ireland, constitute grave exceptions to the story of its wisdom and its triumphs. Birth and upbringing in a governing class doubtless give advantages to young men of ability and serious habits; but governing classes also produce other young men for whom a place must be found.

Another difficulty lay in the field of taxation. Outside of England, kings had pacified their nobles by granting them tax exemptions, and the republican patricians allowed various tax advantages to themselves. It is commonplace to observe that France was a rich country with a chronically impoverished government, that the inability to tax the wealthy, who were largely noble (though not all nobles were wealthy), was the basic cause of the French budgetary crisis, the mounting debt, insolvency, and revolution. Similar problems, perhaps less acute, existed elsewhere. A Dutch writer observes that the eighteenth-century United Provinces were a rich country with a poor government, and ascribes their decline as an international power in part to that fact.[32] In fact the Dutch debt was about fifteen times as heavy per capita as the French debt in the 1780's. An Austrian writer remarks that certain moneys asked by Maria Theresa of the diet of Hungary, and which the diet refused, could easily have been paid from the incomes of a few bishops and magnates.[33] No European state except Great Britain could develop its full strength under the taxation system then in use, and even the British government until about 1780 borrowed heavily from private Dutch sources. The inflexibility of the taxation system was due mainly to institutions associated with aristocracy. It might be due also in some cases to historic regional liberties, as in Brittany, Hungary, or the American colonies of Great Britain; but in Europe,

---

[32] I. H. Gosse and N. Japikse, *Handboek tot de staatkundige Geschiedenis van Nederland* (The Hague, 1947), 639.

[33] A. Arneth, *Geschichte Maria Theresas* (10 vols., Vienna, 1863-1876), VII, 112-13, 123.

if not in America, such provincial liberties gave more fiscal protection to the upper than to the lower classes.

A heightened class consciousness, with accompanying social and psychological tensions, may be listed as the last of the evils created by an increasingly aristocratic social system. It is not that the bourgeois, or persons next below the noble or patrician classes, were conscious of resentment or hostility to the aristocracy as such, though they might on occasion have unpleasant experiences with individuals. Apathy toward public affairs was very great in 1760 and even later; so far as middle-class people had no desire to participate in high position they could not resent the measures that debarred them. The most class-conscious class, or the class most sensitive to threats from other classes, real or imagined, seems to have been the aristocracy itself, with its everlasting striving for family perpetuation, its rules and ordinances requiring four quarters of nobility or a century of patrician status, its doctrine on the value of hereditary nobility for preservation of political freedom, or, in France, its theory that the older nobles were racially different, being of Frankish and Germanic origin, from the mass of the population. The bourgeois and lower classes accepted the class structure more passively as in the nature of things. Perhaps in England, among Dissenters, a sense of difference handed down from the days of the Puritan revolution kept alive a positive middle-class feeling against the Anglican and landowning aristocracy. Perhaps there was everywhere a feeling that some were born to govern, and some were not (which would correspond to the facts of the day); as long as there was acceptance of this situation we may speak of class consciousness, but not of class conflict. Bourgeois feeling was tepid on such matters. The bourgeois Voltaire had no objection to the nobility. Bourgeois radicalism, where it existed, turned rather against the church, or "ministerial despotism," or the inefficiencies or absurdities or chicaneries of government, or the ignorance and superstition believed to be inherited from the past. Such measures as were taken to cope with the essential class problem, to reduce the financial or other privileges of the nobility, or to draw middle-class people into government service or the army, were taken on the initiative of governments themselves, in the great monarchies, without bourgeois agitation and even without much bourgeois support.

The problem of the bourgeois was felt rather as a personal one. It had to do with private and family life, and with the satisfactions of prestige or recognition. The highest and most wealthy aristocracy aside, there was often little of importance, except rank itself, to distinguish two families of bourgeois and of noble status. Or, indeed, in particular cases, a bourgeois family might have more of all the world's goods, tangible and intangible, than a noble family—except rank. Mme. d'Epinay had a well-to-do acquaintance who "could not console herself at being nothing but a financier's wife."[34] Rank came to prey upon the mind. Goethe's great-uncle, J. M. von Loen, was the rich descendant of a merchant family, who became a writer, traveler, and kind of German *philosophe*. He wrote, as already mentioned, a little tract proposing a merchant nobility. Impressed by the meaninglessness of existing social classifications (which, however, he had no desire to abolish), he observed:[35]

"I see at the fair in Frankfurt a fine-looking merchant's wife sitting in her shop; she is superbly dressed, and gives orders to her servants like a princess; she knows how to greet persons of station, ordinary people and the vulgar each according to worth and condition; she judges reasonably, and brings up her children well. Her husband sits meanwhile in his office, makes decisions, disposes of thousands, and often deals with more people in an hour than others can manage to see in a day.

"On the other hand I see honest noble folk in the country that have to subject themselves to menial tasks, where the lady of the house often goes into the stable herself, hurries from store-room to kitchen to cellar, brings the lambs, pigs, hens, geese, or crops, so that in fact she is carrying on a small business yet does not derogate from her noble rank in the least. Her lord meanwhile goes about his fields scattering seed or moving dung, in the barn or the cellar, with his thrashers and hired men.

"Who would really say that, between these two ways of life, the difference was so great that only the latter would be considered noble, the former not?"

Von Loen's solution was by no means to abolish nobility, but to admit suitable people to a share in the honors it conveyed.

It may be that the class problem, and in particular the problem of the bourgeois in an aristocratic society, had become most acute in France. If so (and it is by no means certain as of the years around

[34] E. Barber, *The Bourgeoisie in 18th Century France*, 57.
[35] *Der Kaufmannsadel, Untersucht nach der Gewohnheit der heutigen Welt* (1745), quoted in H. Voelcker, *Die Stadt Goethes*, 101.

1760) it was because contact between bourgeois and noble was very common, because the bourgeois class had grown up in close conjunction with the state and the monarchy, because for generations it had expected social ascent through the holding of office, and because the French bourgeois, perhaps more than the German burgher, looked on the noble way of life as the norm of desirable living. In France the most important of the bourgeoisie were office-holders and lawyers, but even the merchants, busy, successful, enterprising, and affluent as they often were at the time, seem to have shared in the idea that commerce was a somewhat degrading occupation—thus differing from their self-satisfied counterparts in England or Holland. The French bourgeois "identified" with the aristocracy. He, too, took pride in his ancestry. For him, too, business was something to escape from and rise above. Even in the "bourgeois drama," so popular about 1760, the speeches on the dignity of trade were usually given by characters who were noblemen in disguise. A half-convinced audience, or half-convinced authors, found it more reassuring to hear middle-class life praised by their social betters. The hearty self-congratulation of Defoe in England did not exist in France.[36]

The French bourgeois wanted nothing better than to become a noble, and there was no trace of revolutionary sentiment against the nobility in 1760, nor any feeling against the hierarchic organization of society. There was already much talk of "equality"; but coming from a bourgeois it was likely to mean that he wanted to be appreciated, or, from a noble, that he was willing to mix with, or even marry into, the more affluent or interesting strata of the bourgeoisie. There was no equalitarianism of thought or feeling. But precisely because bourgeois and nobleman did mingle there were psychological problems. Whether the magic circle seemed to close or to open, there were difficulties just the same. If it closed, as when the parlements or army became more exclusive, it recalled memories of days when access had been more easy. Consternation resulted for people who had no satisfying outlet within their own class. If the circle opened, it drew newcomers in at the cost of embarrassment and emotional insecurity. Adjustment was not easy at best; the lingering effects of certain bourgeois ideas, such as the belief in thrift, hard work, and marital fidelity, prevented the full enjoyment of the lavishness, leisure, and sexual license more characteristic of the upper class. Many bourgeois women married nobles, without coming to feel really accepted by their husbands' families or

[36] Barber, *op.cit., passim.*

friends, or even by their husbands themselves. Sons of lawyers or merchants could still in individual cases enter the army; but they were never allowed to forget their inferior origins. And the same poison filtered downward. The bourgeois law students at Besançon rioted in 1772 because the son of a wigmaker had been admitted. The professors explained in vain that the universities were open to all; the youth was still taunted "for his disorderly hair and carelessness of dress."[37] At Poitiers, about the same time, the law students got into a general brawl with the younger officers of the garrison, who were nobles. Both groups had attended the same dance, where allegedly a student had given offense to a young lady of aristocratic birth by stepping on her feet. The police had to stop the ensuing disorders.[38] There was just enough separatism, and just enough mixing, to cause trouble.

[37] F. Delbeke, *L'action politique et sociale des avocats au 18e siècle* (Paris, 1927), 112-13.

[38] A. C. Thibaudeau, *Biographie: Mémoires* (Paris, 1875), 61-62.

CLASHES WITH MONARCHY

They are an assembly of republicans! Oh, well! Things as they are will last as long as I do!—LOUIS XV *on the Parlement of Paris,* 1753

The Monarch is always more a friend to Democracy which is obedient to him than to Aristocracy which stands in his way.— THE MARQUIS D'ARGENSON, 1765

CLASHES WITH MONARCHY

THE constituted bodies faced a new situation at the close of the Seven Years' War. Fighting had gone on for a generation interrupted by a few years of truce; governments had accumulated great debts, which they had now to find means to carry or repay. The search by governments for new sources of income met with resistance from magistracies or assemblies in many countries. It therefore produced constitutional crises. "From the need for money, which put into motion the machinery of reforms, arose a great drama: the clash between autonomous entities and the central power, between local governing classes and foreign rule." These words, which might apply to the dispute between the British Parliament and the American colonies after 1763, actually refer to the conflict between the Hapsburg government and the duchy of Milan.[1] Since in Hungary and Bohemia the government at Vienna was often thought of as foreign, and even in France the more autonomous provinces often felt similarly toward that of Versailles, the same formula would hold generally for the Hapsburg and Bourbon systems.

Other events, unrelated to the late wars, contributed to a change in the political atmosphere. England received a new king in 1760, Russia a new empress in 1762. The pressure of Catherine the Great upon Turkey and Eastern Europe committed the Hapsburgs to continuing military expenditure, initiated the dissolution of Poland, and helped to end the Freedom Era in Sweden. Simultaneously, and independently, the internal struggle broke out anew at Geneva.

The present and the two following chapters trace the story to about the year 1774. There are two main themes. On the one hand, the constituted bodies got into trouble with the forces of monarchy, that is, with kings and their ministers. They complained of royal encroachment, but in general, by 1774, monarchy seemed to have prevailed. This happened in Sweden, Hungary, the Milanese, France, and even

<hr />

[1] F. Valsecchi, *L'assolutismo illuminato in Austria e in Lombardia* (Bologna, 1934), I, 194.

in a way in England. In France, indeed, in an important sense, the first French revolution, one in which the people had little part, now occurred. On the other hand, there also began to be an agitation against existing constituted bodies, on the part of private persons claiming that such bodies did not adequately represent them. These are the years in which the movement for parliamentary reform first appeared in England, where, however, it was to produce no institutional change for more than fifty years. The earliest effective manifestations of democratic revolution occurred in the Anglo-American colonies and at the town of Geneva.

In any case, the constituted bodies—parliaments, diets, estates, and councils, to a large extent hereditary in membership and avowedly aristocratic in political doctrine—began to face a war on two fronts, against the Monarch on the one hand and the Multitude on the other.

The Quasi-Revolution in France, 1763-1774

Before we launch into a narrative of what happened in France it is well to make a few observations to set the story in perspective. It must be remembered that the reader of history is in a position to understand these events much better than contemporaries could. Or rather, contemporary observers were exposed to a one-sided presentation of the issues. The French parlements after the death of Louis XIV, and increasingly as the eighteenth century went on, adopted the practice of publishing their remonstrances, or formal protests, against actions taken by the royal government. These published remonstrances were of great importance in the formation of a public opinion. For the first time, the interested person could now obtain some kind of information on matters of current practical politics. He could see something of the conflict of interests behind decisions not yet made. The government, however, insisted on the maintenance of administrative privacy, or secrecy, in its affairs. Often it tried to silence the parlements, either by prohibiting publication of their remonstrances, or by temporarily "exiling" or rusticating their members. Such measures were never successfully carried through. The parlements and their allies always managed to express their views. But no one in authority within the government ever tried to explain its policies to the public. At most, certain officials in an indirect way might tolerate the printing of unorthodox opinions, as when Malesherbes in the 1750's and 1760's let the royal censorship go almost unenforced. Or other officials might engage pamphleteers to respond to tracts made public by the parlements. But at bottom the government supplied no information.

This was generally true of all countries. In England it was only in the 1760's that the substance of parliamentary debates came to be known "out of doors," or outside the two parliamentary houses; here, however, since the dominant group in Parliament was the governing group, led · by the ministers themselves, the views and purposes of government came to be known. Thus in England a public opinion could take form around practical issues and concrete decisions, whereas in France, where public opinion was beginning to grow as it did everywhere in the Atlantic world, it took rather the form of what Tocqueville called literary politics. There was no public discussion by men in executive office or hoping to be so, or by writers associated with them and informed of their intentions. Discussion was carried on rather by intellectuals, *philosophes* and *hommes de lettres*, or by pamphleteers dependent on their sponsors. It tended either to be abstract on the one hand or to reflect mere intrigue on the other. Writers at their best under these conditions might be searching or even profound; at worst, they were merely voluble, polemical, or shallow; in either case they were uninformed.

Since the actual though unknown policies of the French government were often perfectly justifiable, and could have been made to appeal to important segments of the French population, it may be said that the main victim of the withholding of public information was the French monarchy itself, and that its failure was a failure of public relations. Or, in a more general sense, the unfortunate consequence was to favor ideology at the expense of realism in French political consciousness at an important stage in its early growth. The voice of opposition to government could be heard, but not that of government itself. The irresponsible talked, where the responsible kept silent.

Even within what must be called the government it was the most irresponsible parts that were the most public. The most visible aspects of the Bourbon monarchy were the worst. The kings had in fact devised a form of public relations aimed at impressing fellow monarchs, potent feudatories, and lesser people of an earlier day when they had been more naïve. Versailles symbolized this program. The royal court at Versailles was a monument to everything grandiose, lavish, magnificent, and openly displayed. It seethed also with the trivial and the petty. It represented, in the highest degree, the influence upon government of the non-governmental, the private, the "social." Composed of the king, his wife, brothers, sisters, and relatives, his intimates and confidants and those aspiring to such position, high churchmen and princes of the blood, together with the households, retinues, and functionaries attendant upon such personages, reinforced by great noblemen and their clienteles, along with the mistresses, business agents, dependents, and servants of all and sundry, the court created an irresponsible and frothy environment in which the functioning officers of government had to work, when, indeed, they did not emanate from it in themselves. The Marquis d'Argenson, a firm upholder of monarchy against aristocracy, though inclined to be petulant after his own removal from office, described it very well, writing in 1750, privately in his diary:[2]

"The court, the court, the court! There is the whole evil.

"The court has become the only senate of the nation. The lowest lackey at Versailles is a senator, the chambermaids have a part in government. . . .

"The court prevents every reform of finances . . .

"The court corrupts the army and navy by promotions due to favoritism . . .

"The court gives us ministers without merit, authority or permanence . . .

"The court corrupts morals by teaching intrigue and venality to young men entering upon a career, instead of emulation by character and work. . . ."

It must be noted, and probably d'Argenson would admit, that these evils were due not to the court alone, but to certain oligarchic and entrenched hereditary interests in French society, of which the parlements came to be the spokesmen. But the court at Versailles was easier to see.

With its most shameful parts thus paraded before the public, and its most creditable efforts studiously concealed, the French government was an easy target for all who had a mind to be critical. The charges against it, made with increasing openness from the middle of the century until the Revolution—that it was extravagant, wasteful, despotic, and arbitrary—were all true. The parlements enunciated many liberal principles in making these charges. It was also true that the government undertook many serious reforms, but of this part of the truth much less was heard, because it was the parlements, as much

[2] *Journal et mémoires* (Paris, 1864), VI, 321-22.

as the court, that brought these reforms down in failure. And public opinion, until late in 1788, generally supported the parlements. To the modern observer today nothing is clearer than that the Bourbon monarchy, in the generation before the Revolution, seriously attempted to solve the basic problem of French society, the existence of special privileges based on legal stratification or hierarchy; and nothing is more remarkable than that the French public, bourgeois and intellectuals, seldom saw this to be the issue, took so long to develop any sense of hostility to the nobility as a class, and so widely supported the Grand Whiggery of France, the noble-aristocratic-parliamentary opposition to despotism. The government was blamed by all classes for its faults, and received credit from none for its merits.

The Parlement of Paris, together with its sister magistracies in the provinces, had had numerous clashes with the royal government for half a century, when new royal enactments in 1763 opened the way to a quasi-revolution. It was the fate of the parlements that in launching a quasi-revolution in the 1760's they opened the way for the King, who crushed them in 1770 in order to drive through certain reforms, just as in launching a real revolution in 1787 the same parlements opened the way for persons acting in the name of the nation, and bent on a program of reforms not wholly unlike the King's in 1770. Between 1774 and 1787 a kind of parliamentary-aristocratic counterrevolution was at work, as again after 1789.

Before 1770, however, as again before 1789, the parlements contributed significantly to the political education of the French people. Their repeated resistance to the crown gave a respectable precedent for more flagrant disobedience. To force the recognition of a constitutional monarchy, they formed an unauthorized and extra-legal union— what Louis XV called an "association," a word that was to take on revolutionary implications in England and America also. They emphasized "law" as the basis of authority, and they declared that certain fundamental laws, or a certain constitution by which the royal and other powers were defined, already existed in France. They forced a definition and justification of sovereign power. They brought such key words as "citizen," "nation," "country," and "natural and imprescriptible rights" into the vocabulary of official debate. Increasingly they claimed, hereditary and closed bodies though they were, to "represent" the French people, and so raised the whole problem of the nature of political representation.

The royal enactments of 1763 were tax decrees.[3] One called for an indefinite continuation of the *vingtième*, which had been expected to expire at the end of the war. The *vingtième* was the most recent and modern tax of the French monarchy, in principle a levy of a twentieth, or of one *sou* in the *livre*, of income, theoretically paid on income from all property, in practice on income from ownership of land. It was payable by nobles and commoners alike. The decree of 1763 also announced a reassessment to ascertain real income as opposed to valuations currently on the tax rolls. In France in the eighteenth century, as in the United States today, assessments tended to become frozen or stereotyped, the difference being that the mighty Bourbon monarchy lacked the flexibility in raising the rate that the smallest American municipality enjoys. Another decree laid a one per cent tax on *immeubles fictifs,* "fictitious real property," a legal term which included property in office. The *parlementaires* held their seats by virtue of property in office; as landowners they benefited from low and obsolete assessments. The controller-general, Bertin, justified the tax on offices by observing (like George Grenville explaining the Stamp Act to the American colonies) that owing to the costs of the late war it was necessary "to make sources that had not yet participated contribute to the public burdens."

The Parlements of Paris, Grenoble, Toulouse, and Rouen remonstrated strenuously. Paris insisted that the *vingtième* be levied "on the now existing rolls, without increase of valuation," under penalty of prosecution by the courts.[4] Besides urging the King to pay his debts without new taxes, and observing that half of what the taxpayer paid never reached the treasury because of faulty administration, the Parlement of Paris added a long disquisition on the French constitution. It claimed that in France there were fundamental laws, immutable by nature. By these laws the parlement had the right to "verify" legislation, i.e., authenticate it before it could take effect. By these same laws the King himself received his throne. To deny these laws, the parlement

[3] For the parlementary crisis of the 1760's see E. Glasson, *Le Parlement de Paris: son rôle politique depuis le règne de Charles VII jusqu'à la Révolution* (Paris, 1901), II, 264-347; R. Bickart, *Les parlements et la notion de souveraineté nationale au 18ᵉ siècle* (Paris, 1932); J. Flammermont, *Remontrances du Parlement de Paris au 18ᵉ siècle,* 3 vols. (Paris, 1898); J. Egret, *Le parlement de Dauphiné et les affaires publiques* (Grenoble and Paris, 1942), I, 93-121, 252-287. There is a considerable literature on the other provinces. Paul Beik, in *A Judgment of the Old Regime* (N.Y., 1944), a study of the Parlement of Provence in the 1760's, concentrates on their economic views (that the fiscal crisis was to be solved by improvement of administration and productivity instead of new taxes) rather than their political ideas or activities.

[4] M. Marion, *Dictionnaire des institutions de la France* (Paris, 1923), 557.

ominously declared, "would be to shake the solidity of the throne itself." These "laws of the State" could not be violated without bringing in doubt the very "power and authority of the said Lord King." May it please God that no one suppose "that the king is king by force, for such are the signs of robbers and pirates." The parlement took care to publish all this against the royal will.[5]

In the provinces matters went even further. The governors having received orders to force through the tax edicts, the Parlement of Toulouse put the governor of Languedoc, the duc de Fitz-James, under arrest, and the Parlement of Grenoble ordered the arrest of the lieutenant-general of Dauphiny, Dumesnil. Dumesnil, who managed to remain at large under the protection of his troops, was ostracized socially by the combined parliamentary and territorial nobility of the province; Mme. la marquise de Virieu, who was related to him, joined in the refusal to enter his house, announcing that she was "a citizen before a kinsman."[6] Regicide scrawlings appeared on the walls of buildings.

The Parlement of Paris enflamed the general agitation, and set up a three-way dispute between itself, the King, and the Parlement of Toulouse, by asserting jurisdiction in the case of Fitz-James, on the ground that as a peer he could be tried only by the peers, and that the peers sat only in the Parlement of Paris, not in any parlement of the provinces. The Fitz-James case led the Paris bench to further sweeping constitutional affirmations: that if Fitz-James had *pensé en citoyen* he would realize that he had "contracted engagements with the Nation and the laws" (that is, was not responsible to the King alone); that the essence of government was to assure the "liberty, honor and rights" of its subjects; and that the parlement was "responsible for bringing these important truths before the sacred person of the king." The parlement drew a distinction between the royal sovereignty in external and internal affairs. (The reader may be reminded of attempts sometimes made by Americans, at this time, to distinguish between parliamentary sovereignty in the internal and external affairs of the colonies.) In foreign affairs, according to this remonstrance of January 1764, the King's authority is "without limits," and "blind obedience is a duty." "But civil government, while its fulness resides entirely in the hands of the sovereign, is regulated by entirely different principles. Its object being to maintain the citizens in the enjoyment of rights

[5] Flammermont, *Remontrances*, II, 342, June 24, 1763.
[6] Quoted by Egret, *op.cit.*, I, 102.

which the laws assure them, with respect either to the sovereign or to one another, it is the law that commands, or, more precisely, the sovereign commands by the law." The history of France was reviewed to support this proposition; and, it was added, anyone telling the King the contrary offended against "the sovereign, the law and the Nation."[7]

No King of France had ever admitted to being a despot, and before this barrage of argument, collective hostility, and outright arrest of his agents, the "despot" yielded. The controller-general, Bertin, and the three provincial administrators most offensive to the parlements, Fitz-James, Dumesnil, and Harcourt in Normandy, were all replaced. The project for a tax on offices was given up. The plan for reassessment remained, but came to nothing. The year 1764 saw a striking parliamentary victory.

Matters were soon complicated again. The Assembly of the Clergy, the quinquennial convocation of the French church, met in 1765. It denounced the rising wave of anticlerical, antireligious, and general *philosophe* literature. It also, as often in the past, took action against Jansenism. The importance of Jansenism in France and Italy at this time has perhaps never been properly understood in the English-speaking world. Jansenists, as they were called by their orthodox enemies, were Catholics who inclined to a severe theology, and criticized the opulence and worldliness of the upper clergy. They had come into conflict with Rome, and been declared heretics; hence they became critical of the centralization in Rome of power in the Catholic church. The French parlements for centuries had also opposed the growth of Roman jurisdiction in France; they were hence Jansenist in a popular or sloganizing sense. They were certainly anti-Jesuit, and in 1762 had won a great victory with the expulsion of the Jesuits from France.

The Assembly of the Clergy, in 1765, in its continuing attempt to suppress Jansenism, renewed its rule that no one might receive the sacraments unless he presented a certificate—the famous *billet de confession*—stating that he had been confessed by a priest in good standing with the church. The Parlement of Paris thereupon declared all the acts of the assembly null and void. The clergy ran to the King, and the King quashed the action of the parlement. Few incidents better illustrate the role of royal absolutism as arbiter between irreconcilables —or explain the continuing popularity of absolutism in many quarters. As Voltaire put it: "There were 50,000 madmen in Paris who did not

7 Flammermont, *op.cit.*, II, 424-38, Jan. 18, 1764.

know what country the Danube or Elbe was in, who believed the universe to be shaken at its foundations by certificates of confession." For the King, he went on, to command his subjects to stop calling each other "innovators, Jansenists and semi-Pelagians was to command fools to be wise."[8] The matter is important, for Jansenism driven underground was to have an influence during the Revolution, and because the church, by the measures it used to repress it, lost the sympathy of many people who cared nothing for Jansenism.

In any case, the provincial parlements, which had been irked by the high-handedness of the Parlement of Paris in taking the Fitz-James case away from Toulouse, now all rallied to its support. All disliked clerical influence, and all objected to the abrupt annulment of an act of the Paris Parlement by the King.

Then came the *affaire de Bretagne*. Here as elsewhere the royal governor, the duc d'Aiguillon, had run afoul of the local constituted bodies. An active administrator, he had launched a great program to develop this still wild and backward province. He projected a great system of roads to join Brest and the interior of the peninsula to the main body of France. He therefore sought to conscript the peasants, who were more dependent on their local *seigneurs* in Brittany than in other parts of France, for labor in construction of roads and bridges. He wished to introduce the *corvée royale*, by which, in other parts of France, peasants were required to spend a certain number of days a year on the building or maintenance of highways. The Estates of Brittany considered road-building to be under their own jurisdiction, and were in any case dominated, as has been seen, by a swarm of ancient gentry with little interest in internal improvements. The Estates resisted d'Aiguillon, and were strongly supported by the Parlement of Rennes. Both vigorously affirmed the historic autonomy of the province. The Parlement of Rennes, instead of arresting the governor, like the parlements of Grenoble and Toulouse, declared a suspension of the courts of justice as a means of bringing pressure on the King. The King thereupon created a special tribunal to carry on judicial business at Rennes. The leader of the troublesome Breton parlement was La Chalotais. The King, to discipline La Chalotais and enforce royal authority in the province, arraigned La Chalotais and a few others before another special tribunal, set up for the purpose at Saint-Malo. The Parlement of Paris and all the other parlements of the country

[8] Voltaire, *Oeuvres* (1826), xxix, 3, 6, *Siècle de Louis XV*, chap. 36; this chapter was first published in 1768.

rushed to the defense of La Chalotais, and of the regular court system against such special administrative tribunals.

The Brittany affair thus brought to a head a movement that had gathered strength for several years. The parlements of Paris, Rennes, Grenoble, Rouen, Dijon, Toulouse, Bordeaux, and others (there were about a dozen with varying degrees of regional importance) had formed the habit of corresponding, exchanging documents, and supporting one another in altercations with the crown. They now claimed that they were parts of a general or super-parlement, a parlement of all France, of which the several actual parlements were simply subdivisions, or what they called "classes" in the older or Latin sense of the word. This parlement-in-general, they held, represented the "nation," by which they meant the people or the governed, whether of France as a whole or of Brittany and such sub-nations in particular. No law could be valid, or tax properly authorized, they asserted, without the consent of the nation as shown by its representative, the parlement.

This position assumed by the parlements was revolutionary in its implications, not only because the King rejected it, but because the law and constitutional practice of France gave it no support. Kings in the past had acknowledged the right of the several parlements to "register" legislation or remonstrate against it; but no King had ever agreed, nor parlement until recently claimed, that parlements had an actual share in the process of legislation. Nor was there any lawful ground for parlementary unity. The several parlements had not arisen by devolution from the Parlement of Paris or from the King, as they now claimed. They were coordinate with the Parlement of Paris; that of Brittany, for example, was simply the modern form of the old high court of the duke of Brittany before the incorporation of Brittany into France. France had taken form by a gradual coming together of previously separate parts, not by delegation of authority to branch offices of an original central power. The claim of the parlements to be really one parlement was in line with historic development; it showed the growth of interests, contacts, communication, and joint action on the scale of France as a whole. But constitutionally, it was without foundation. The *union des classes* was as much the assertion of new and hitherto unknown power as the Continental Congress to which a dozen British-American provinces sent delegates in 1774.

That the parlements sought to turn themselves into a true national and representative body could be abundantly documented, but one quotation from a decree of the Parlement of Rouen may suffice: "By the fundamental laws of the Monarchy the Parlement of France, the one and only public, legal and necessary council of the Sovereign, is essentially ONE, like the Sovereign whose council and organ it is, and like the political constitution of the State, of which it is the custodian and depository. . . . The Parlement is in each of its said classes [i.e. actual parlements] the plenary, universal, capital, metropolitan, and sovereign court of France."[9] And in the name of this alleged national institution the various actual parlements persisted in telling the King that he owed his position to law, that he had taken an "oath to the Nation," that a true country, or *patrie*, was one where "Law, Sovereign and State formed an indissoluble whole," that the law existed only by consent of the Nation, that Parlement alone expressed the "cry of the Nation" to the King, and watched over, for the Nation, the maintenance of its rights, its interests, and its freedom. In short, the Nation and the Law were set up, not yet expressly in opposition to the King, but as his coequal.

After ten years of such legal harangues the indolent Louis XV was goaded by the Brittany affair into a rebuttal. Early in the morning of March 3, 1766, he rode at full speed with a few companies of soldiers from Versailles to Paris. Held up at the Pont Neuf, where he knelt in the street as the Holy Sacrament was carried by, he found himself in such a traffic congestion, it is said, that he simply walked the remaining steps to the Palais de Justice. While soldiers occupied the building, a few of the magistrates received him at the steps facing the Sainte-Chapelle. It was all too sudden to constitute a formal *lit de justice*. The King had not even brought his chancellor with him, but only a few gentlemen of his court. He sat in an ordinary armchair, in his ordinary attire; the hastily assembled members of the parlement wore their usual black robes. The royal speech was then read. The session is known in French annals as the *séance de la flagellation*.[10]

"I will not allow, [said Louis XV] an association to be formed in my kingdom that would pervert the natural ties of duty and obligation into a confederation of resistance, nor an imaginary body to be introduced into the Monarchy to disturb its harmony. The magistracy does not form a body, nor an order separate from the three orders of the kingdom. The magistrates are my officers, charged with the truly royal duty of rendering justice to my subjects . . ."

[9] Bickart, *op.cit.*, 173. Bickart assembles numerous quotations from various parlements, under the topics of consent to law, national representation, and unity.
[10] Flammermont, *op.cit.*, II, 554-60.

He flatly denied that: "all the parlements form a single body divided into classes; that this body, necessarily indivisible, is essential to the Monarchy and serves as its base; . . . that it is the protector and depository of the Nation's liberty, interests and rights. . . ; that it is responsible for the public good not only to the King, but to the Nation; that it is the judge between the King and his people; that it maintains the balance of government . . . ; that the parlements cooperate with the sovereign power in the establishment of the laws . . ."

He affirmed: "In my person only does the sovereign power rest, of which the distinctive character is the spirit of counsel, justice and reason. From me alone do my courts derive their existence and their authority, but the plenitude of this authority, which they exercise in my name, remains always in me. . . . To me alone belongs legislative power without dependence or division. . . . By my authority alone do the officers of my courts proceed, not to the formation of law, but to its registration, publication and execution. . . . Public order in its entirety emanates from me, and the rights and interests of the Nation, which some dare to set up as a body distinct from the Monarch, are necessarily joined with mine, and rest only in my hands."

Respectful remonstrance, made privately and decently, he would continue to allow; but he would not allow the parlements to proclaim to all France that submission to his will was a crime, or that "the whole Nation is groaning to see its rights, liberty and security perish under a terrible power"; for in that direction lay anarchy and confusion, and he would use all the authority he had received from God to save his people from such a fate.

Never had a French King made so strong an official statement of absolutism. One might be excused for believing, in the enlightened France of 1766, that if any sovereign power existed so enormous as the King described it, and from which all law and lawful authorities derived their existence, it was too much to be located in a single man. On the other hand, one could agree with the King that the parlements, as they really were, did not represent the French people any better then he did, and that officers of justice must draw their authority from some source outside their own hereditary positions. As events were later to have it, it was the new "body," the Nation, so passively argued over by King and parlements in 1766, to which sovereign power and the source of lawful authority were to be imputed.

The parlements were not intimidated by the King's blast against them. They continued their protests, remonstrances, and obstruction.

The Brittany affair dragged on; the parlements of Paris and Rennes, while both opposing the use of administrative or prerogative courts, and upholding "law" against "circumstance," disputed with each other for jurisdiction over the hapless La Chalotais. In 1768 the royal government, moving toward economic liberalism and freedom of the market, attempted to abolish regulations on the grain trade. The parlements of Grenoble, Aix, and Toulouse favored such free trade in grain, but those of Paris and Rouen declared against it. There was also the usual opposition to taxes. In 1768 the King reactivated the *Grand Conseil*, a kind of supreme court operating directly under the King, and empowered to decide cases arising from government, or those involving conflicts of jurisdiction between the parlements. The parlements, fearing the "evocation" or transfer of their own lawsuits to this council, naturally protested, and fortified their protests by again urging the rights of the usual judiciary against administrative and presumably unfree courts.

In 1770 Louis XV decided to make an end of parlementary opposition. He put into office a reform administration composed of Maupeou as chancellor, with his aide the young lawyer, C. F. Lebrun, and the Abbé Terray as controller-general of finance.

Maupeou simply abolished the parlements, putting their members on permanent vacation, and set up a new system of law-courts in their place. He did away with property in judicial office. Judges no longer received fees from litigants for their decisions. The new judges, drawn in part from men experienced in the Grand Conseil, received a fixed salary, with assurances of secure tenure. They had no personal or proprietary right to their position. They were appointed by the crown, which, according to the edict, could now select men according to professional qualifications, without regard to financial or family considerations. The overgrown area within which the Parlement of Paris had had jurisdiction, embracing most of the interior of France, was broken up among a number of high courts, so that less travel was necessary to obtain judicial settlements. At the same time overlapping jurisdictions among courts in the city of Paris, the source of infinite confusion, expense, and delay, were clarified and redefined. The new system answered to demands that had been made sporadically for generations, and anticipated the definitive reforms carried out a generation later.

With the old parlements and their obstructive tactics done away with, the Abbé Terray launched a systematic and carefully thought out fiscal reform, aimed at a more equitable distribution of the tax burden, without regard to social class, and levied in proportion to real income. He thus resumed the program of the tax decrees of 1763 which parlementary resistance had rendered abortive. He made progress in getting modern and realistic valuations of landed income, and increased the yield of the *vingtième* by about one-half in those parts of the country where he could get reassessments made. He met with furious opposition, and though his private instructions to the intendants were full of wise and moderate counsels, he was denounced publicly all over France as a robber, an extortionist, and a minion of despotism. So great was the outburst from parlementary pamphleteers, and later from outraged authors of memoirs (it was mostly the upper classes who wrote memoirs), that Terray has in fact enjoyed a rather poor historical press ever since, though he is a hero for M. Marion, the great authority on the financial history of France.[11]

The reforming efforts of Louis XV, coming at the end of a long and unrespected reign, failed to capture the public imagination. The new courts were derisively called Maupeou parlements, and the tax reforms were considered no better than banditry. Not only were the few hundred families that had monopolized the old parlements now relegated, and hence disgruntled. The legal profession as a whole disapproved. It was hard to find men for the new positions. Public opinion, such as it was, opposed the change. It was in vain that a few writers, like the aging Voltaire, exposed the pretensions of the old parlements and heartily endorsed the new. It was in vain that a pamphleteer, perhaps hired by the government, declared that only despots or feudal lords combined judicial and legislative powers, which enlightened monarchs separated and balanced, and that if the old parlements were to triumph France would become a "republic" under "a monstrous hereditary aristocracy."[12]

The very limits of noble loyalty were strained. One excited aristocrat declared that France must be "de-Bourbonized."[13] The self-interest of the nobility in the matter is apparent. Why the country as a whole should have agreed with the aristocracy is not so clear, yet is after all understandable. The old Louis XV had lost all prestige. He was even widely hated. The government simply was not trusted. And at best

---

[11] M. Marion, *Histoire financière de la France* (Paris, 1914), I, 266-72; *id., Dictionnaire*, 558.

[12] *Réflexions d'un citoyen sur l'édit de 1770* (n.p., 1770). 9. Voltaire wrote his *Histoire du Parlement de Paris* on this occasion. Egret, *op.cit.*, 272 ff., finds that in Dauphiny the old parlement had become so unpopular that there was much support for the Maupeou reforms.

[13] Quoted by H. Carré, *La noblesse de France* (Paris, 1920), 233.

it had nothing better than enlightened despotism to offer—reform without consultation of anyone outside the bureaucracy, reform at the cost of the suppression of liberty. When Louis XV died in 1774, Maupeou and Terray were dismissed. There had been a quasi-revolution in France, but only a quasi-revolution. The nobility, through the parlements and a lesser extent the Provincial Estates, had led an attack on the monarchy. The monarchy had replied with a counterattack on the aristocracy entrenched in these constituted bodies. The parlements had laid down a broad program of constitutional liberalism. The King and Maupeou had led an assault upon privilege. But no power had changed hands. The old parlements, restored by Louis XVI, led a kind of quasi-counterrevolution, an "aristocratic resurgence," after 1774. But the last word was not spoken. Maupeou's aide, the young Lebrun, who is said to have written Maupeou's speeches to the Parlement of Paris, became a busy man in the committees of the Revolutionary assemblies, turned up as Third Consul in 1799, and was one of the chief reorganizers of France under Napoleon.

The Monarchist Coup d'Etat of 1772 in Sweden

Events in Sweden were not unrelated to those in France.[14] The young Swedish crown prince, Gustavus, arrived on a visit to Paris in 1770, just as Louis XV and Maupeou were mounting their attack on the parlements. He had come, indeed, to seek political backing and advice. The Swedish and French crowns had long been allies, having similar interests against the German powers and Russia; and from his French mentors Gustavus heard a great deal about the advantages of asserting royal authority. He heard the same from Voltaire, whose acquaintance

[14] For this account of Sweden I have drawn on B. J. Hovde, *The Scandinavian Countries, 1720-1865: The Rise of the Middle Classes*, 2 vols. (Boston, 1943), esp. I, 177-93; R. Svanström and C. F. Palmstierna, *A Short History of Sweden*, trans. from the Swedish (Oxford, 1934); D. Aimé, "La révolution suédoise de 1772," in the periodical *La Révolution française*, 1937, 144-54; and R. Nisbet Bain, *Gustavus III and His Contemporaries*, 2 vols. (London, 1894). There is a recent work by Per Erik Brolin, *Hattar och Mössor: I Borgarståndet 1760-1766* (Upsala, 1953), with a summary in English, 418-22. Brolin finds in Sweden at this time "a local manifestation of the popular forces and political ideas which made the great American and French revolutions" (422). He emphasizes the beginning of significant party politics in these years, and, as the basis of the Cap party, the dissatisfaction of merchants and craftsmen with the ruling magistracies and with "aristocracy," and the resistance of the newly developed North to the commercial regulations favoring privileged staple towns in central and southern Sweden. I am indebted to Dr. Dankwart A. Rustow of Princeton for assistance in Swedish.

he sought out at Ferney. At the opera in Paris he received the news of the death of his father. He rushed immediately back to Sweden, with promises of support from France for restoration of the power of the Swedish throne. The count de Vergennes, who a few years later was to be the chief figure in the French government in assisting American republicans against Great Britain, was sent as ambassador to Stockholm to aid the new King Gustavus III in his monarchist designs.

For half a century affairs in Sweden had been conducted by the four-chamber diet, largely dominated by the nobility, which had made the King a nonentity. Conditions in Sweden had come to have a strong resemblance to those in Poland. In both countries parties within the diet looked to foreign aid. In both countries outside powers spent money freely to bribe members of the diet in their own interest; influential Swedes and Poles regarded such gratuities as normal income consequent upon their position. The French spent 1,648,000 livres on the Swedish diet in 1769, and 1,400,000 in 1770; the British, about £42,000 (1,000,000 livres), in 1769. The French favored the party known as Hats, which, being more aggressive and military, served the purposes of French diplomacy against the expansion of Prussia and Russia. These latter powers, along with Denmark and England, sponsored the opposite party of the Caps, conceiving it to be best for government in Sweden to be more passive in the foreign field. The King of Sweden, Gustavus' father, Adolf Fredrik, was a relative of a Russian tsarina, and had received his throne in 1742 through her influence, like the King of Poland who acceded in 1764. The Swedish Queen was the sister of the King of Prussia. Both Russia and Prussia harbored designs on the territory of Sweden, especially since this still included Finland and a small area on the Pomeranian coast. A secret treaty of 1764 between Catherine and Frederick mentioned Sweden along with Poland as likely for partition. It noted also the common interest of the two rulers in preservation of the "Swedish liberties," which gave opportunities for intervention.

If Poland was partitioned in 1773, whereas Sweden escaped this fate, the main reason was doubtless the greater accessibility of Poland to the armies of the two eastern powers. But there was another reason in the social difference between the two. In Poland only the nobility counted, and it brought the country to ruin. In Sweden, with its more varied social classes, there were people who could significantly object to the rule of nobility, and from whom Gustavus III could draw support.

In Sweden the peasantry, through their village assemblies, and through representation in their own chamber in the diet, had maintained a sort of political awareness which, however rudimentary, was wholly unknown to the mute peasantry of Poland. The Swedish peasantry had been passively royalist throughout the Freedom Era. In Sweden, too, more than in Poland, a native office-holding, professional, mercantile middle class had been growing up in the eighteenth century. For a time these people mixed satisfactorily with nobles, and felt no obstruction to their ambitions. On the other hand, the fact that year after year nobleman and burgher each went apart to sit in his own house in the diet kept alive more of a sense of difference than in Denmark-Norway, where diets no longer met, and class separation was made less conspicuous by the ascendancy of the King.

Noble-vs.-burgher tensions began to mount. In 1762, in keeping with the rise of aristocratic exclusiveness that we have noted in other parts of Europe, the Swedish nobility managed to block the access of burghers to high office through further limitations on their becoming ennobled. In Sweden, as in France, though in lesser degree, the army was becoming more of an aristocratic preserve. For the Swedish officer corps we have detailed statistics, and they show that where only a third of the officers were nobles in 1719, two-thirds were nobles in 1760. It is to be observed that the year 1719, toward the close of the Northern War, was a time of full mobilization, in which more than the usual number of burghers were drawn into military service, and that the development of Swedish society during the eighteenth century created alternative civilian occupations for men of the middle class, so that the declining proportion of burgher officers cannot be wholly ascribed to the aristocratic revolution of 1719. More revealing in this connection is the changing composition of the higher military ranks, for those burghers who did adopt military careers found the higher positions more difficult to obtain. Of the higher officers in the Swedish army 26 per cent were burghers in 1719, 16 per cent in 1735, and only 11 per cent in 1760. And it was the highest nobility, not the nobility as a whole, who increasingly occupied the highest military positions.[15]

The Hat party in the mid-century became more of a noble party, while members of the other three chambers in the diet increasingly supported the Caps. There was also great dissatisfaction with the Hat policy of involvement in the Seven Years' War, in which the Hats had been induced by France to go to war with Prussia, with humiliating results. The Caps got control of the government in 1765, and introduced various liberal reforms, including great freedom for the press, relaxa-

[15] See the tables in S. Carlsson, *Ståndssamhälle och Ståndspersoner 1700-1865* (Lund, 1949), 71, 101. As late as 1865 the proportion of nobles among army officers was higher than in 1719.

tion of restraints on trade, and reduction of military expenditure. They relentlessly pursued their Hat rivals, and showed an alarming willingness to accept dependence on Russia. Hats then drove Caps from office in 1769, aided by French money; but the British, as noted, spent £42,000 to prevent the Hats from supporting royal plans for strengthening the state. The Freedom Era had thus eventuated in blind factionalism accentuated by class conflict, with the "Swedish liberties" upheld by foreign interests, when Gustavus III arrived upon the scene.

Gustavus met the Riksdag in February 1771. "Born and bred among you," he proudly declared, though in unfilial reference to both his parents, "I hold it the greatest honor to be the first citizen of a free people!"[16] The parties continued to dispute. The Caps, now controlling the three "unredeemed" chambers, demanded admission to office on grounds of "merit only." But they showed little responsibility; they arraigned Hats for trial, and actually, in 1772, at the very moment when the Polish partition was being carried out, sought closer ties with Great Britain and Russia.

Gustavus III, pressed by France, and arranging for troops to come from Finland, which, however, proved to be needless, executed an amazingly easy *coup d'etat*. He rode into the streets with a white armband, which thousands of citizens of Stockholm enthusiastically adopted. He read a speech to the diet, deploring factionalism, and alluding to the "insufferable aristocratic despotism" from which he meant to deliver the country.[17] He proclaimed a new constitution which the diet accepted. This document, in fifty-seven paragraphs, though derived primarily from earlier Swedish sources, also showed the influences of Montesquieu. It was the first written and consciously modern constitution in an era that was to produce many such. It divided power over legislation and taxation between the King and the diet, and it forbade extraordinary courts, while abolishing judicial torture, and assuring a moderate freedom of the press. A few years were to show that the Swedish nobility were not satisfied with the new arrangements. The next decade was to see an aristocratic resurgence in Sweden as elsewhere. Meanwhile, however, all seemed to pass by general acclamation. The Freedom Era was over. The country accepted its new royal leader with relief.

[16] Quoted by Bain, *op.cit.*, I, 65.
[17] *Ibid.*, 128. A French text of the Swedish constitution of 1772 is printed in L. Léouzon Le Duc, *Gustave III roi de Suède* (Paris, 1861), 347-66.

In France, there was quite a vogue for what they called the "revolution" in Sweden, soon eclipsed by more unbounded excitement over the revolution in the American colonies.

The Hapsburg Empire

The monarchy of Vienna was a kind of vast holding company, under which a great many subsidiary corporate structures remained much alive. There were the estates of the several provinces of the Austrian Netherlands, the area of the modern Belgium-Luxembourg without Liège. They represented not only the clergy and the nobility of the provinces, but also certain gild interests and certain of the Belgian cities to the exclusion of others. There were the various overlapping magistracies of Milan monopolized by the Milanese patricians. And, to omit lesser organizations, there were the diets of Bohemia and of Hungary, where town interests had been silenced and the landowning nobility and gentry entirely prevailed. The Hapsburg government was in continual conflict with these bodies, though in the 1760's and 1770's no such acute crisis developed as in France or Sweden.

It is necessary to emphasize, since after the revolutionary era it became so different, that for half a century before 1790 the Hapsburg government was one of the most enlightened in Europe, as enlightenment was then understood. Martini and Sonnenfels, professors at the University of Vienna, had great influence in affairs of state. Theirs was the pure teaching of enlightened absolutism. "A prince is the creator of his State," wrote Sonnenfels; "he can establish and develop in it what he wants, if only he takes the right measures."[18] Ministers and administrators under Maria Theresa were zealous reformers. They had to be, if the monarchy was to survive at all. In the Succession War half the Bohemian nobles had collaborated openly with the French, when the French, occupying Prague, had attempted to set up Bohemia as an independent kingdom. In 1749, therefore, after restoring her authority, Maria Theresa had annulled the Bohemian charter and greatly cut down the powers of the Bohemian diet. The Bohemian nobles, one of whose grievances was the attempt of the Hapsburg government to build up legal protection for the peasants against them, complained repeatedly of the loss of their local rights. Maria Theresa, strongly backed by Prince Kaunitz and her other advisers, refused concessions. Kaunitz wrote to her in 1763:[19]

[18] Quoted by E. Denis, *La Bohème depuis la Montagne Blanche*, 2 vols. (Paris, 1903), I, 513.
[19] Quoted by A. von Arneth, *Geschichte Maria Theresas*, VII, 30-31.

"I am a Bohemian myself, and have lands in Moravia. If I considered only my own interests I would agree with those who wish to bring the nobility and the estates more to the forefront than they now are, or let them play a role in the central administration. . . . Other sovereigns seek increasingly to limit the nobility, because the true strength of the State lies in the greater numbers of the common man, who deserves the chief consideration and yet is oppressed more in Bohemia than elsewhere. . . . I need not recall the unpleasant memory of what happened in past years with the nobility and estates of Bohemia, but will only remind Your Majesty of the obstacles to desirable measures that we meet with from the nobility and estates of Hungary, Transylvania and the Netherlands."

He might have added the patriciate of Milan.

In Bohemia, as in eastern Europe generally, the peasants were in effect serfs owing uncompensated labor service to their lords. The dispute between the Vienna government and the Bohemian diet was a battle for jurisdiction over the mass of the Bohemian population. The Vienna government drew up *urbaria*, written documents limiting and specifying the kind, the amount, and the timing of labor due to the lords. The lords preferred for all such matters to remain under their own discretion. The peasants themselves took a hand by unorganized and violent rebellion; fifteen thousand of them besieged Prague itself in 1775. The government suppressed them, but at the same time gave up all pretense of conciliation with the nobility and the diet. The *urbaria* in 1775 were officially declared to be the law. The Bohemian aristocracy remained disgruntled but silenced, since the diet was not allowed to meet for the next fifteen years.

The Hapsburg government, like others, was in need of money after the Seven Years' War. It sought, like others, to increase its revenues, in part by reaching untapped sources of taxation, in part by raising the productivity of its territories. To stimulate production it campaigned against gilds and gild restrictions, and sought to merge small local units into larger trading areas with freer internal circulation of labor, goods and investment. The tariff of 1775, for example, brought Austria, Bohemia, the Netherlands, and the Milanese—the whole monarchy except Hungary—into a single protected tariff union.

Resistance was of course met with everywhere. In the Austrian Netherlands in these years it was sporadic, though incidents were numerous, as when the estates of Luxembourg, in 1768, refused to make any accounting for their financial activities, fearing that certain hidden tax exemptions might be exposed.

At Milan certain younger members of the patrician class were beginning to feel the need of a change. Foremost among these was the economist, Pietro Verri. With a few others, including Beccaria, he founded the club called Il Caffe in 1761, which for a time published a journal of the same name. He was well acquainted with the French philosophers of the day. Indeed, a letter from the abbé Morellet to Beccaria, whose work on crimes and punishments Morellet translated into French—a letter in which Morellet described in highly unfavorable terms the politics of the Parlement of Paris in the 1760's—suggests the affinities between Milan and Paris, and the way in which reformers felt both their own efforts and the forces opposed to them to be of more than national scope.[20] Verri was to live to see, and accept, the Cisalpine Republic of 1797. At this time he pinned his hopes on the enlightened absolutism of Vienna. He entered into relations with Kaunitz and the young Joseph II, who became coregent with his mother, Maria Theresa, in 1765. "Whenever old disorders have been eradicated speedily and with success," wrote Verri, "it will be seen that it was the work of a single enlightened person against many private interests."[21]

The private interests at Milan were many-sided and complicated, though they all reflected a small number of people, the hereditary patriciate and its allies in the nobility and the church. They were entrenched in the Council of Sixty (or Decurions) of the city, in the Senate of the Duchy, and in other closed and self-perpetuating boards and councils. These bodies, and the local liberties that they represented, had been hitherto little affected by the annexation of Milan to the Austrian empire in 1714. Trouble began in the 1750's when Pompeo Neri attempted (like Louis XV's ministers in France) to introduce a census of all landed property with assessments in some correspondence to actual value. Verri, in addition, wished to get rid of the practice of tax-farming, which he thought very unfavorable in its effects on economic enterprise in the duchy. The tax-farm was in fact abolished in 1770. Such efforts of course ran up against powerfully entrenched interests. Plans for fiscal and tax reform therefore broadened out into plans for more general administrative and even constitutional change.

[20] This letter of September 1766 is reprinted by Glasson, Parlement de Paris, II, 304-06.
[21] Quoted by Donald Limoli in "Pietro Verri, a Lombard Reformer under Enlightened Despotism and the French Revolution," Journal of Central European Affairs, XVIII (1958), 260. I am indebted in these paragraphs to Mr. Limoli and to Valsecchi, Assolutismo, II, 157-94.

The power of the entrenched councils was the more absolute because each council, within its own ill-defined and overlapping domain, enacted regulations, enforced them, and judged offenders in particular cases. The reformers, both Milanese and Viennese, therefore urged separation of judicial and executive functions. The power of magistracies was made more formidable by the use of torture. In 1774 Maria Theresa, pressed by Beccaria, Verri, Martini, and Sonnenfels, abolished torture in her hereditary domains of Austria-Bohemia. In the Milanese she could act only with the consent of the local bodies, and the Senate of the Duchy pronounced torture to be necessary to government. Not until the Senate itself was destroyed by Joseph II a few years later could torture be abolished in the city of Beccaria.

Hungarian writers say of their country—as Americans have said of the British colonies on the opposite frontier of Western civilization —that new ideas were brought into it by soldiers of the Seven Years' War.[22] In 1761 Baron Orczy founded a society for the purification of the Hungarian language. The members were well aware of the contemporary French *philosophes*, and discussed political as well as linguistic matters. Montesquieu himself had spent a month in Hungary in 1728; his *Spirit of Laws* is said to have appeared in Latin, for Hungarian use, as early as 1751; and while I know of no proof of the existence of such a book, it is entirely possible that at least parts of it may have been so translated.[23] For Montesquieu's doctrine was calculated to appeal to the Magyar nobles. The idea that "intermediate bodies" should check the power of a king, and that a nobility sensitive to its honor and installed in a diet or two-chamber parliament should assure the preservation of constitutional liberty, was exactly what the Hungarians already believed. Confirmation from a famous French political scientist was a great piece of good fortune.

The diet met in June 1764. The Queen, Maria Theresa, made two important proposals. First, to pay debts from the late war, and to maintain a regular army in peacetime, she asked for an increase of taxes of about 1,000,000 florins. The old "free gift," she declared, had never been enough. Secondly, she expressed the opinion that under modern

---

[22] For these paragraphs on Hungary I depend on Arneth, *op.cit.*, VII, 111-33, and on a seminar paper and research assistance by Mr. Peter F. Sugar, who has given me the content of S. Eckhardt, *A Francia Forradalom Eszmei Magyarorszagon* (Budapest, 1924), and other works.

[23] Eckhardt, *op.cit.*, 20-28, speaks of a letter from the Englishman Calwell, in 1751, telling Montesquieu that he has seen the book in Latin at a bookstore at Pozsony (Bratislava); but I find no such letter in Montesquieu's published correspondence, and no Latin version of the *Spirit of Laws* in any of the great printed library catalogues.

military conditions the old Hungarian "insurrection," a kind of noble upsurge or militia, was inadequate. She asked that the Hungarians maintain 30,000 regular troops at their own expense, instead of the insurrection of 80,000; and since the insurrection was an obligation of nobles only, she thought it reasonable that in getting rid of this obligation the Hungarian nobles should pay the taxes which replaced it. She thus called into question the tax exemptions enjoyed by nobles and clergy.

The diet rejected both proposals. Tax exemption and the right or duty of insurrection were the marks of noble status in Hungary, privileges to which the nobility stubbornly clung. Some of the magnates were willing to consider their modification; it was the lesser gentry in the lower house that adhered most firmly to the old order. It may be recalled, to show the class character of this lower house, that this same diet of 1764 renewed the rule that all the cities represented in the chamber should exercise only a single vote, the equal of the most obscure county member. The Queen, to bring pressure, barred entrance into her Life Guard at Vienna to Hungarians. Since service for a few years in this guard had recently become a custom for young Hungarian nobles, by which they obtained some courtly and worldly experience at the metropolis (as well as being exposed to Western ideas and bound emotionally to the dynasty in their youth), the lower house grudgingly yielded, and granted 310,000 of the million asked, of which 100,000 was to maintain the purely noble Life Guard. Maria Theresa, as usual, compromised. The diet, while granting a portion of the increase asked, refused any redistribution of the tax burden. The Queen-Empress, in her final rescript, again urged that the tax burden be divided between nobles and non-nobles—in vain. The diet also antagonized her by refusing to grant the *indigenat* to certain high officials of the empire— office in Hungary was to be limited to Hungarians, who understood the Hungarian point of view. The Queen was very dissatisfied. "This diet has taught me to know people," she said. She thought she could rule better without it; no diet met again in Hungary for twenty-five years.

In summary, in the Hapsburg countries as in France and Sweden, by about the year 1774 or 1775, the various constituted bodies were under severe pressure from monarchs. The French King had crushed his parlements, the Swedish King had forced the Riksdag to accept his authority, the Hapsburg Queen-Empress was ignoring her diets of Hungary and Bohemia, and offending the corresponding bodies in Belgium and the Milanese. The diets, estates, parlements, and councils all stoutly defended liberty, and indeed stood for many genuine liberal ideas; but at the same time they palpably insisted on the maintenance or enlargement of their own privileges. It was monarchy in these countries that pressed for modernization and the general welfare.

At the same time, however, the constituted bodies in other countries saw hostilities open on the other front. Persons who were neither members of an aristocracy nor servants of a king began to move on their own initiative. This happened, between 1763 and 1774, within the narrow but not insignificant limits of the city of Geneva, and on the broader stage of the Anglo-American world, where it led to the American Revolution.

A CLASH WITH DEMOCRACY: GENEVA AND JEAN-JACQUES ROUSSEAU

We shall probably not devote to the largest monarchies articles as long as this one; but in the eyes of the philosopher the republic [of Geneva] is no less interesting than the history of great empires. . . . If our religion prevents our thinking that the Genevese have worked effectively for their happiness in the other world, reason obliges us to believe that they are about as well off as men can be in this one.—D'ALEMBERT *on Geneva in the* Encyclopédie, 1757

During the whole of the last century the history of Geneva affords little more than an account of the struggles between the aristocratical and popular parties.—Encyclopedia Britannica, 1797

Post tenebras lux.—MOTTO OF THE CITY OF GENEVA

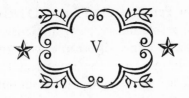

A CLASH WITH DEMOCRACY: GENEVA
AND JEAN-JACQUES ROUSSEAU

GENEVA in 1760 was a city of about 25,000 people, about the equal of Philadelphia in size, though not growing as rapidly. A man could walk across the town in fifteen minutes; the whole territory of the independent republic (which did not join the Swiss Confederation until 1814) comprised only seventy square miles. It was enclosed by the kingdoms of France and Sardinia, except for a few miles along the lake. From the Genevan point of view Sardinia was huge, and France almost infinite in extent. The city lived at the mercy of these two, or by the local balance of power between them; often enough, hostile soldiers had threatened its frontiers. A republic lying between two monarchies, a salient of Protestantism projecting into the Catholic world, its industrious people were forever on the alert, still manning their citizen guards, nervously sensitive to the outside world yet conscious of isolation from it, and filled with a self-righteous, Calvinist, or Puritan sense of superiority over their neighbors.

The city was a nursery of talents, and its chief export was its own men. It was estimated that a fifth of those who held its citizenship were habitually absent. Though it was the home of the naturalists Charles Bonnet and J. A. de Luc, men of some note in eighteenth-century science, it produced most especially men who excelled in the two fields (not unrelated, perhaps especially for Calvinists) of public finance and the philosophy of public affairs. It was the birthplace of Jacques Necker, Minister of Finance under Louis XVI of France; of Etienne Clavière, Minister of Finance in the French Republic in 1792; and of Albert Gallatin who held a similar office in the United States under President Jefferson. Burlamaqui, the esteemed writer on constitutional law, was a Genevese; as were Delolme, the expositor of the British constitution; Etienne Dumont, the discoverer and translator of Bentham; and Sismondi, the historian and economist. There were also Mallet du Pan and Sir Francis D'Ivernois, who in their youth supported the revolutionary party at Geneva, and in their mature years, in refuge in England, became well known as opponents of the revolution in France. And there was Jean-Jacques Rousseau.

Events at Geneva are of significance at various levels. Obviously nothing that happened in this tiny place could, in a crude or mechanical way, influence the world outside. But significance is not a matter of numbers only, as, indeed, had been proved by the Geneva of Calvin two centuries before. The first occasion, within the time span of this book, when a movement of modern democratic type made a positive impression on institutions of government was at Geneva in 1768. In the roles played by upper, middle, and lower classes, in the conflict between political and economic demands, and in the interplay between revolutionary and counterrevolutionary pressures, this "revolution" at Geneva even prefigured or symbolized the greater revolution that was to come in France. It was, moreover, a revolution precipitated by the presence in the neighborhood of Rousseau. It was here that the *Social Contract* produced its first explosion. Near at hand, at the same time, lived another worthy of more than local repute, namely Voltaire, on his estates at Ferney, on the French side of the Genevese frontier, but only four miles from Calvin's church. The embroilment of Rousseau and Voltaire in the politics of Geneva meant the blowing of two antithetical views of the world into a teapot tempest; or, rather, the agitations at Geneva, which in themselves were significant enough, were brought to the level of world history by the involvement of these two difficult geniuses.

Rousseau, Voltaire, and Geneva to 1762

Rousseau had been born at Geneva in 1712, but he never lived there after 1728, when, coming home one evening, he found the city gates locked, and took, at the age of sixteen, to what proved to be a wandering and unsettled life. His father was a journeyman watchmaker, in moderate circumstances, though a citizen by birth. Possibly Rousseau's Genevese boyhood helped to shape the works of his maturity; it has been persuasively shown that the republican, Protestant, and sometimes Puritan tone of his greatest writings, and even the attitude of ever watchful suspicion of the people around him, are the authentic accents of his native place.[1] What is certain, however, and necessary

[1] G. Vallette, *Jean-Jacques Rousseau Genevois* (Geneva and Paris, 1911).

to an understanding of what followed, is that Rousseau could never adjust to life in any other country as he found it. How much of his trouble was of social or psychological origin, and how much it was due to his physical malady, a urological disturbance that caused him discomfort and embarrassment throughout his life, cannot be known. He had tried to do what a young man making his way in the world was supposed to do. He had had various love affairs. He had given up his ancestral Protestantism and entered the Catholic Church. He had enjoyed the patronage of the high-born. He had used influence to be appointed secretary to the French embassy at Venice. He had written operas that were well received. He had been accepted by Diderot and other intellectual lights of Paris, where he had heard much strong talk to the effect that reason was about to dispel the fog of prejudice inherited from the ages of ignorance, that religion was a system invented by the crafty to dominate the credulous, that moral ideas were produced by social environment, and that the emancipation of the mind had caused and would cause astounding advances in the progress of civilization.

In all this Rousseau had taken part. His life, as he approached forty, was not a failure by worldly standards; yet it gave him no satisfaction. At bottom, he could accept none of it. He took nothing at face value. Even the friendly advances of his social superiors gave him a feeling of humiliation. He was afraid that acquaintances wished to patronize or exploit him. He thought the whole manner of life in France of his day artificial. Manners were too elaborate, taste too sophisticated, the conversation in the salons too clever, people of refinement too hypocritical, the theater too frivolous, religion too formal, unbelief too glib. He complained that he was never free to be himself. Even his own private life disgusted him; he lived for years with the faithful and simple (that is, uneducated) Thérèse Levasseur, secretly turning over to an orphanage the five infants that she gave him. Disturbed by his own awkwardness, social shortcomings, and moral derelictions, he felt a compulsion to publicize them to all the world, while at the same time insisting that he was not at fault, or was no worse than other men, and blaming society for his own unhappiness and that of others. Most differences of opinion about Rousseau take their departure from this point. Some, thinking him a rebel against all society and all restraint, have called him antisocial, misanthropic, anarchic, egotistical, irresponsible, and childishly evasive of all obligations. Others, holding that what he rebelled against was the specific society of his day as he knew it, have thought that this society was in fact artificial and shot through with false values, and so have found in him an authentic human protest against bad conditions. Both can be true; it is hard to imagine any society in which Jean-Jacques would have been at ease; but the only society he could rebel against was the one he knew. In any case no one denies that Rousseau was personally very uncomfortable.

He became the great revolutionary of a revolutionary age. Among contemporaries who boldly rewrote human history, arraigned kings, and exploded religion, among humane and ingenious authors who proposed this or that change in government, or the economy, or education, or the law, Rousseau alone went straight to the absolute foundation. He revolutionized the nature of authority itself. He denied the existence of authority apart from the individual over whom it was exercised. For him there were by rights no governors and governed, no rulers and no ruled. There was even no law except law willed by living men—this was his greatest heresy from many points of view, including the Christian; it was also his greatest affirmation in political theory. He was the revolutionary *par excellence* because it was a moral revolution that he called for, a revolution in the personality and in the inclination of the will. Man, according to Rousseau, should act not from custom nor rule nor command, divine or human; nor from laboriously learned principles of proper behavior; he should act freely and spontaneously according to his own better self, the divine spark within him, the virtue which might be suffocated by a bad form of society, but which a good form of society could nourish and keep alive.

It must be added that Rousseau, the great revolutionary, was revolutionary in a somewhat negative way.[2] He produced no blueprint and wrote no utopia for the future; he pointed out what was missing in existing society. He joined no movements; indeed, when approached by certain Genevese intent on a small "revolution," he would not offer to aid them. He gave no practical advice; or when he did give it, as to the Poles, was notably conservative in some of his opinions. What he did, and it was revolutionary enough, was to undermine the faith of many people in the justice of the society in which they lived. In a neurotic and exaggerated way, because he felt it more keenly, he

---

[2] See the discussion by Peter Gay, and his valuable review of the literature on Rousseau as a political thinker, particularly p. 27, in his introduction to his translation of E. Cassirer, *The Question of Jean-Jacques Rousseau* (N.Y., 1954), to which I am much indebted.

expressed the malaise that many people of the middle class came to feel in an aristocratically oriented world. But many men and women of the nobility also came to feel, in reading this eloquent and moving author, that inequalities and barriers and constrictions that they had hitherto accepted were absurd.

The great change in Rousseau's own life, his personal and internal revolution, or realization that he and humanity had been pursuing a wrong path, came in 1749 and 1750. "I began my reform," he later said, "by my articles of dress; I gave up gold lace and white stockings, took to wearing a round wig, and put aside my sword; I sold my watch, telling myself with an unbelievable joy: Thank heaven, I shall never have to know what time it is again." The simple life was made easier when one of Thérèse's brothers absconded with his twenty-two best shirts, a left-over from his days in the embassy at Venice.[3]

There were two things that he now idealized, the better to show the faults of existing society—"nature," and Geneva. In 1749 he wrote his *Discourse on the Arts and Sciences*, propounding the "paradox," as it seemed to complacent contemporaries, that technical and scientific and purely intellectual achievement, with all the wonders and complexities of modern civilization, in and of themselves made men no better. To make his point he idealized the life of the *bon sauvage*, the state of nature as it might conceivably have been prior to government and civilization; but such idealization was frankly conjectural on his part, was purely auxiliary to his real message, and was discarded in his later writings. In 1750, for much the same reasons, remembering with a warm glow the town he had left over twenty years before, he began to sign his name, Jean-Jacques Rousseau, Citizen of Geneva. In 1753, when he wrote his *Discourse on the Origins of Inequality among Men*, which included emphatic passages on the evils of property and the oppression of the poor by the rich, he actually dedicated this inflammatory work "To the Republic of Geneva."

Rousseau could not go back to nature, and did not wish to. He could go back to Geneva, and did so in 1754. He was received with mixed feelings, for the dedication was not relished; few at Geneva, and certainly not the ruling patriciate, entertained any such opinions on property and wealth as were set forth in Rousseau's discourse. But here was a native son who had become famous; and the flattered

---

[3] Cf. the chapter entitled "La 'Reforme' de Jean-Jacques" in J. Guéhenno, *Jean-Jacques Rousseau*, vol. II, *Roman et Vérité* (Paris, 1950); the quotation, from the *Confessions*, is on p. 21.

magistrates, as well as the Calvinist ministers, welcomed a prodigal who returned meekly confessing his errors. Having turned Catholic he had forfeited the citizenship which he now so proudly proclaimed. He announced his reconversion to the Reformed religion. The awful solemnities prescribed at Geneva to purge such renegades were relaxed to accommodate him. He became again a Protestant and a recognized Citizen. He stayed several months in the city, renewing or building up his acquaintance. The pure waters of the lake, the majestic and snow-capped mountains, the peace and contentment that he thought he saw in the people's faces, all symbolized for him the world as it ought to be. In the following years, particularly in his novel, the *Nouvelle Héloise*, he used Switzerland as a setting for his moral message. Thus Switzerland became a symbol for the great world that read French writers. As Mme. d'Houdetot remarked years later, after the American Revolution, there were only two countries in which she would have chosen to be born. One was America; the other, Switzerland.

Soon after Rousseau left Geneva, Voltaire arrived.[4] He craved asylum, calling himself an old man who had come there to die. He was sixty-one years old, with the most combative twenty-three years of his career yet before him. The citizens, embarrassed but flattered and charmed, as in the case of Rousseau, gave him leave to stay. The affluent and sophisticated Voltaire, who loved all civilized refinements, thereupon purchased two rural properties in nearby France, two town houses in neighboring Lausanne, and a large vacant tract (now within the city of Geneva) on which he built the chateau he called Les Délices. He began to invite prominent Genevans to his entertainments, which usually included acting in, or watching productions of, his own plays. There was a law at Geneva against theatrical representations. When the magistrates intimated to Voltaire that the law applied to him as to others, he moved from Les Délices to Ferney. But the better sort of Geneva republicans, including many of the magistrates, then repaired to Ferney to enjoy the giddy pleasures of the French neo-classic stage. A great controversy thereby began.

One of the distinguished visitors whom Voltaire's presence drew to Geneva was the philosopher d'Alembert, coeditor with Diderot of

[4] P. Chapponière, *Voltaire chez les Calvinistes*, 2nd ed. (Paris, 1936). Chapponière is a little partial to Voltaire, as Vallette is to Rousseau, in setting forth the disputes between their heroes; but both are fair-minded and well documented, and they agree in their estimate of the situation. See also B. Gagnebin, *Voltaire: Lettres inédites aux Tronchin*, 3 vols. (Geneva, 1950).

the Encyclopedia then in process of publication at Paris. Voltaire introduced him to the leading citizens and the leading ministers of the Reformed Church. D'Alembert was delighted at the rational and enlightened views that he found in these circles, and reciprocated by publishing a long article on Geneva in the Encyclopedia. It was obviously launched as a weapon against the Catholic Church. "Hell," remarked d'Alembert drily, "a principal article of belief with us, is not such today for many ministers at Geneva." He warmly praised the Protestant clergy at Geneva for their emancipation from superstition, their broad tolerance, their distaste for fanaticism, their stress on the humanity of Jesus, their attachment to natural virtue and reasonable religion. He also urged that so polished and enlightened a community should allow and even sponsor a theater.

The article caused great consternation by the shores of Lake Leman, especially among the clergy. Of course they were enlightened men of their day; of course they thought that Calvin had been too extreme, and Servetus unjustly put to death; of course they believed that Jesus had been a good man, and that reason and nature taught the same mild and uplifting truths as revealed religion. But they did not thank d'Alembert for saying so in the Encyclopedia. They did not like his editorializing their private conversation. Throughout Protestant Europe, and especially in places less intellectual than Geneva, people might form the impression that the city of Calvin had been seduced into infidelity, that the old bastion of Protestantism was no longer safe. In such circumstances they could not now change the laws of Geneva to allow a theater in their midst. The Geneva ministers, or many of them, had been led by their very real intellectual curiosity and humane sympathies into an exciting contact with Voltaire. They now saw where such philosophical associations might lead them. They drew back, and on the question of the theater became stubborn.

Rousseau rushed to their defense. He published a *Lettre à d'Alembert sur les spectacles*, which at the same time consummated his break with the *philosophes* of the Voltairean and Encyclopedist schools. The theater (for which in former days he had written himself) now signified for Rousseau the aristocratic and artificial society which he spurned. It was a false and superficial thing, a mere show, of which a sound and simple citizenry had no need. Its introduction at Geneva would be a clear sign of corruption. The question was a moral one, involving the kind of morality that underlay public life; as Rousseau's Geneva friend, Moltou, enthusiastically wrote to him, the letter to d'Alembert was "the rallying signal for all good citizens, the reproach and terror of the bad."[5]

Rousseau in answering d'Alembert was defending his idealized image of Geneva, but at the same time he had entered into a very real and practical controversy. The theater at Geneva was in fact a class amusement, and hence became a class issue. Geneva, it must be remembered, was governed by a few families who coopted themselves as members of its two main constituted bodies, the Council of Twenty-five and the Council of Two Hundred. These were the people who went to Voltaire's parties to see or act in his plays, such people as the Tronchins, one of whom was Voltaire's doctor, one his banker, and a third the procurator-general of the republic. People of wealth and leisure, drawing their income from land or old investments, they were generally pro-French in their politics, and willing to adopt the French manners and diversions which were everywhere setting the style for an international upper class. The bulk of the citizens and burghers never saw the interior of Les Délices or Ferney. They disapproved of spectacles to which they were not invited; they were politically fearful of France; and they reflected a kind of nativist reaction against the cosmopolitanism of their own aristocracy, a nativist reaction which, at Geneva, meant a renewed consciousness of their own Puritan heritage. Rousseau became their hero, as Voltaire was the favorite of the patricians. In the one camp Rousseau was the friend of virtue and the common man; in the other, a voluntary barbarian and surly enemy of the arts. That the theater was in fact a class question was abundantly shown by subsequent events; one was built at Geneva a few years later, burned down during the democratic turbulence of 1768, and rebuilt only after the aristocratic restoration of 1782, after all democratic organs in the city had been destroyed, and the democratic leaders put to flight.

Meanwhile Rousseau was going further with his meditations. In 1762 he published both *Emile* and the *Social Contract*. The Parlement of Paris condemned *Emile*. The Republic of Geneva condemned them both. It was the only government in Europe to condemn the *Social Contract* at the moment of publication. Both books, branded as "temerarious, scandalous, impious, tending to destroy the Christian religion and all governments," were solemnly lacerated and burned before the Hotel de Ville at Geneva on June 19, 1762; and Rousseau was declared liable to arrest upon entrance into the city.

It was rare at Geneva at this time to use such rigorous censorship. It is clear that the Council condemned Rousseau's two books without

[5] Vallette, *op.cit.*, p. 136.

having carefully read them; not enough time for study had intervened. It is probable that the Council wished to please the French government by this action. It is certain that they were annoyed at Rousseau for his role in the theater question, in which he had been hailed as a leader and spokesman by the discontented burghers of the city. It is probable, in view of the d'Alembert affair, that they wished to assure the world that Geneva had not fallen into unbelief. It is known that the Tronchin family spoke zealously against Rousseau in the Council; but whether Voltaire used his influence against him at this time is not clear.

At any rate the poor Jean-Jacques, who started for Switzerland after the condemnation of *Emile* in Paris, found the gates of his native city shut in his face, more purposely and more formidably than in his youth.

The Social Contract, 1762

If one were to name the one book in which the revolutionary aspirations of the period from 1760 to 1800 were most compactly embodied, it would be the *Social Contract*. Others of Rousseau's works probably had more direct and actual influence. His *Emile* presented the image, disconcerting for any professional clergy, of the reverent man who had no need for any church. His *Nouvelle Héloise* estranged readers from their over-refined mode of life. His *Discourse on Inequality* offered passages on which social revolutionaries could seize to point out the evils of private property. Rousseau's influence on education, on literature, on pure philosophy, was conveyed by these and other works.

The *Social Contract* remains the great book of the political revolution. It appeared in no fewer than thirteen editions in the French language in 1762 and 1763. There were three editions in English and one in German in 1763 and 1764; it appeared also in Russian in 1763. Thereafter, except for a solitary French edition, it was not reissued until after the Revolution began in France. Perhaps the copies in existence were enough; perhaps, as has been argued, people did not much read it after its first publication. What is certain is that the greatest vogue of the book came after the fact of revolution. The book did not so much make revolution as it was made by it. Readers did not become revolutionary from reading it; but, if they found themselves in a revolutionary situation, they might read it to gain a sense of direction, or because propagandists put it before them. The *Social Contract* appeared in thirty-two French editions between 1789 and 1799.

(There were none under Napoleon.) It was printed three times in English in 1791 and once in 1795—and thereafter not until 1905. There were two editions in Dutch in 1793-1796, four in German between 1795 and 1800, eight in Italian during the *triennio*, 1796-1799. A Latin translation circulated in manuscript copies in Hungary in the 1790's. Four editions appeared in Spanish between 1799 and 1801, and many more in Latin America after 1810. It first appeared in Hungarian in 1819, in Greek in 1828, in Polish in 1839, in Czech in 1871. There were four editions in Russian in 1906-1907, and one in Turkish in 1910. It may be observed that in most of these countries publication was preceded by revolution or attempted revolution.[6]

It is well, therefore, to analyze again this much-analyzed work. Or, at least, in the absence of strict theoretical analysis, it is useful to point out the main ideas in the *Social Contract* which appealed to men in a mood of rebellion.

The best way to understand the book is not to compare its propositions to later democratic practice, which owes little to it except on the most abstract and fundamental level; nor yet to view it as an anticipation of totalitarianism, as if free societies did not also have to issue commands; but to contrast its doctrine with the attitudes prevailing at the time it was written, of which one of the most fundamental was that some men must in the nature of things take care of others, that some had the right to govern and others the duty to obey. It was abhorrent to Rousseau to obey anything or anyone outside of and foreign to himself. Yet he was no anarchist; he accepted the need for authority and public order. "Public order in its entirety emanates from me," Louis XV declared in 1766. The constituted bodies of the day, where they were supreme, such as the Parliament in Great Britain, made somewhat the same claim to absolute sovereignty; or they argued from history and tradition, that what gave legal and compelling force to law was a legal tradition, with old charters and constitutions, inherited from the past. Rousseau, who once observed that if God wished to speak to Jean-Jacques he should not go through Moses, also thought that no free man could be expected to obey a law on the authority of another. He must comply of his free will. Even if he did what he did not wish to, paid taxes of which he did not per-

[6] Sénélier, *Bibliographie des oeuvres de Jean-Jacques Rousseau* (Paris, 1949). For the Latin manuscript see Eckhardt as cited in Chapter IV note 22 above. Parts of the *Social Contract* may have been included in selections of Rousseau's writings or in other anthologies in some languages, but hardly enough to change the tenor of the above paragraph, which refers only to publication of the work as a separate item under its own title.

sonally approve, or fought in a war which he thought to be mistaken, he must yet in a sense be following his own inclination. Otherwise he would be only yielding to force; he would act only because of necessity; he would be justified in evading as much as he could, and free to rebel at pleasure, like the nobles of Poland.

The *Social Contract* was therefore a quest for rightful authority, for a form of state in which obedience would turn into duty, while all the while an ethical philosophy stressing individual liberty was preserved. Rousseau could find no place to locate this final authority except in the community itself. Those who obey must in the last analysis command. The subject must, in the end, be the sovereign—another of the famous "paradoxes" of Rousseau.

But what was the community? Before studying the act by which a people sets up a government, says Rousseau, "it would be well to examine the act by which a people is a people; for this act, being necessarily anterior to the other, is the true foundation of society."[7] This act or agreement, "by which a people is a people," was in Rousseau's thought the one act that must be unanimous. On other and lesser questions there would be a majority and a minority. But why should a minority be bound to accept majority rule? Later generations, fearful of the domination of minorities by majorities, have often missed the force of this question, which, however, was by no means academic in the real history of Europe, where the right of minorities to ignore government, or rebel against it, had more than once led to ruin. It is right and necessary, according to Rousseau, for a minority to accept majority ruling, so long as they both agree (are "unanimous") that they constitute a people. If there is no such agreement there is no people, and no majority and minority, but only separate and hostile powers. To put it in another way, those who do not share in this agreement are not members of the people at all.

The "social contract" is this act by which a people is a people. It is an association "which protects the person and property of each associate by the common force, and in which each, uniting with all, obeys only himself and remains as free as he was before."[8] And Rousseau, amplifying this idea, conjures up some of the key words of the coming generation (the italics are his): "This public person, thus formed by the union of all, took in former times the name of *city*, and is now known as the *republic* or *body politic*, which is called by its

---

[7] *Contrat social*, Bk. I, Chap. v, ed. G. Beaulavon, 2nd ed. (Paris, 1914), 136.
[8] Bk. I, Chap. vi, *ibid.*, 138.

members the *state* when it is passive, the *sovereign* when it is active, and a *power* when compared to others of its kind. As for the associates, they take collectively the name of *people*, and individually are known as *citizens*, in that they share in the sovereign authority, and *subjects*, in that they are subject to the laws of the state."[9]

The act of association produces a General Will, the will of the community as such, which includes the willingness of minorities to abide by majority decisions, and of individuals to accept actions of government that they do not personally favor. Any member may be obliged by the community to obey this General Will: "which is to say nothing else than that he will be forced to be free."[10] Here, too, it is easy to travesty or misrepresent Rousseau's real meaning, which is perfectly consistent with a liberal and democratic practice: the existence of the community and the liberty of its members require all to respect its authority. It must be remembered that, for Rousseau, the General Will and the sovereignty of the community operate only at an abstract or distant level, as the framework or prerequisite within which more specific actions take place. Strictly speaking, he observes, the only act of sovereignty is the act of association itself. Sovereignty, though "wholly absolute, wholly sacred and wholly inviolable," is limited to general agreements (*conventions générales*). To suggest an elucidation which he does not himself give: There may be two parties in a state, which to avoid all suggestion of ideology or partisanship we may call the Greens and the Blues. If the Greens, using legal channels, and having a majority at the moment, obtain passage of a law, it is not merely a Green law but a law of the state. The Blues have voted against it, but they accept it as law, and not as a mere act of force. They obey it as such, for it gains the force of law not by will of the Greens, nor even by will of a majority only, but from the underlying general will of both Greens and Blues, a general will which is the essence of the civil community, and is the only sovereign that men need obey. If there is no such will, or such sovereign, there is no community, and no law, but only, as Rousseau says, two separate and hostile powers.

All the argument about sovereignty is set up precisely to show that the government is *not* sovereign. No one in government, not even a king, holds power by personal right of his own; none has authority independent of the authority of the governed. Their position is simply an office, a revocable trust. The people can delegate specific powers; it

---

can never delegate sovereignty. I have demonstrated, declares Rousseau, "that the depositories of the executive power are not the masters of the people, but its officers; that the people may establish or remove them as it pleases [the great democratic doctrine, and the contrary of all later totalitarianisms]; that for these officers there is no question of contracting, but only of obeying; that in undertaking the functions which the State imposes on them, they only fulfill their duty as citizens, with no right of any kind to dispute the terms."[11] Even the form or constitution of government is not absolute; it, too, is derived. A people, for example, may institute a hereditary form of government, monarchical or aristocratic. It has the ultimate right, however, to change this form of government at will. The hereditary tenure of office, by kings, lords, councillors or magistrates, gives them no untouchable inherited right. Nor is it the inheritance of a constitution that makes a constitution authoritative. The past cannot bind the present. Even the inheritance of legality is lawful because willed by the community in the eternal present—and only so long as it is so willed.

On particular forms of government Rousseau seems not to have felt very strongly. He observed that in a sense all legitimate government must be democratic: it must be willed by the sovereign people. But the people may will to have government of one kind or another. Any government of laws he would call a republic. He defines democracy as a state in which there are more citizens who are magistrates than ordinary citizens who are not magistrates; he finds this possible only in small communities, and so dismisses democracy as suited only for gods. Monarchy may be legitimate, but he has little of interest to say about it. He finds three kinds of aristocracy: natural aristocracy, or government by tribal elders; elective aristocracy, in which "wealth or power are preferred to age"; and hereditary aristocracy, in which those who inherit wealth and power also inherit governmental position. The last, says Rousseau, is the worst of all forms of government; it was also characteristic, as I have shown in preceding chapters, of almost all governments in his day. He declares that the best form of government is the second form of aristocracy, the elective. He seems to have meant a system in which the citizens elected persons to positions of government, and so to be talking about what later generations would call democracy. Nevertheless, by his own surprising definition, the persons so elected are elected for their "wealth or power."[12]

11 Bk. III, Chap. xviii, *ibid.*, 281.
12 Bk. III, Chap. v, *ibid.*, 231-32. Rousseau does also allow that election of officers will favor men of "probity, enlightenment and experience," but his whole discussion

What, then, of equality? What of the gap between wealth and destitution that he had so passionately denounced only a few years before? In the *Social Contract* inequality becomes a political problem, or a moral problem so far as it affects the maintenance of a free and lawful state. "By equality we must not understand that degrees of power and wealth should be absolutely the same." Power should never be exercised except according to law. "As for wealth, no citizen should be rich enough to be able to buy another, and none so poor as to be forced to sell himself."[13] Here, as elsewhere, it is the liberty, self-respect, and self-determination of the individual that are most important. Inequality is bad when it suppresses these. It is so bad that it must be corrected. "It is precisely because the force of things always tends to destroy equality that the force of legislation should always tend to maintain it."[14] Here was a paradox, indeed, for those who held that the rich needed special representation because they were rich; but the general idea was not especially radical or anarchic—Prince Kaunitz said the same thing to Maria Theresa in 1763, when he held that government should favor the common man against the Bohemian landlords.

It is in his discussion of representative institutions that Rousseau seems most absurd.[15] Not that he is lacking here in realistic observation. His world was full of bodies allegedly representative and elective—the third chambers in the estates of Languedoc and Brittany, the House of Commons, the Dutch estates, certain houses in the east-European diets, the ruling councils at Geneva and other towns—which almost without exception had acquired strong features of cooption and self-perpetuation, and which claimed to exercise, not a delegated power, but a power of their own. When a people is willing thus to abdicate its own powers and responsibilities, says Rousseau, it is on the brink of ruin. The English people are free only at the moment of electing members of Parliament, after which they become enslaved; had he

---

here gives less attention to the problem of merit-vs.-inheritance than that of the conservative Réal de Curban, who in defending inheritance of office concedes that the belief that office should be held for "merit" is the "popular prejudice" (see Chapter III above); or of d'Argenson, who attacks venality of office because it obstructs "the progress of Democracy" (*Considérations* [1765] p. 151). It must be recalled that Rousseau was less in contact with the real bourgeoisie of France than with intellectuals, Bohemians, and people of fashion. The *Social Contract* was a theoretical work, written by a *déraciné*, as critics hostile to Rousseau have often emphasized to their own satisfaction.

[13] Bk. II, Chap. xi, *ibid.*, 201.
[14] *Ibid.*, 202.
[15] Bk. III, Chap. xvi.

known more of elections in England he would scarcely have made even this concession. A people that turns over its military affairs to mercenaries, and its political affairs to a closed political class, the better to enjoy its own ease or pursue private business, cannot be free. In a good state men will have little private interest or private business; they will be constantly busy as citizens, attending assemblies, watching over officials, ratifying laws. They cannot delegate the law-making power, because this power is a power of sovereignty itself. He therefore denounces representative assemblies as a benighted invention of the feudal ages, and favors in effect a direct democracy of popular assemblies *en permanence.* This was to become an important idea in time of revolution. But there is no denying that the growth of an effective representative government has owed more to the aristocratic liberal than to the Rousseauist and popular democratic schools.

Much has been made of the theory of civil religion appended at the end of the *Social Contract,* and here again Rousseau can be easily misrepresented.[16] It was precisely because he proposed to grant freedom of religion, precisely because he would not associate his state with any church membership or doctrine, and because he thought that a community must nevertheless agree upon something, that he suggested in his final chapter "a purely civil profession of faith," a few simple "dogmas" of civil religion, having to do with the existence of God and the after-life, "without explanation or commentaries," and including a declaration against religious intolerance. Anyone who accepted these doctrines, or rather attitudes, and then went against them, declares our author, "should be punished with death"—a "truth" which Robespierre was to observe should best be left in the writings of Rousseau. It does not seem that these ideas of Rousseau had as much influence as has been pretended; when Robespierre tried in 1794 to institutionalize something of the sort, his own colleagues laughed behind his back; and it seems exaggerated to look here, of all possible places, for the origins of later totalitarian regimentation of the mind.

Withal, the *Social Contract* is full of conservative admonitions. Like the American Declaration of Independence, it asserts that government should not be changed for light and transient causes. "Changes are always dangerous, and established government must never be touched unless it has become incompatible with the public good; but this circumspection is a maxim of policy, not a rule of right."[17] Rousseau,

---

[16] Bk. iv, Chap. viii, *ibid.,* 240-41.
[17] Bk. iii, Chap. xviii, *ibid.,* 281.

while asserting the right, even doubts the possibility, as well as the prudence, of sweeping change. Old peoples, he says, are incorrigible; they have too many established customs and prejudices to be capable of renovation. The only possibility that he sees is in the analogy of disease. "Just as some diseases unhinge men's minds and take away their memory of the past, so there may be epochs of violence in the life of States, when revolutions have the same effects upon peoples that certain crises have upon individuals, when horror of the past acts as forgetfulness, and when the State, consumed in the fires of civil war, is born again, so to speak, from its ashes."[18] This was not a prophecy, of course, and still less a call to revolt; but it was not a bad description of what happened in France in 1793.

Rousseau's skepticism about the practicability of the ideas in the *Social Contract* was justified. It is not that these ideas were essentially visionary; most of them are better embodied in the United States today, where his influence has been slight, than in most states of Europe. They were impracticable, however, in direct proportion to the strength of those who refused to accept them. In proportion as a country lacked a real general will or sense of community, in proportion as it had a distinct ruling or privileged class insistent upon remaining so, the attempt to apply the ideas of the *Social Contract* might be self-defeating. The attempt to impose a general will where no general will existed, to create a nation in a country where influential persons preferred to remain an estate, to force people into a kind of community that they did not want, could lead only to dictatorial rule. Something of this kind happened in France during the Revolution. Revolution by its nature is a time when the general will has collapsed, the bonds of association have snapped, change by agreed upon and legal methods has become impossible. The attempt, or rather the necessity, to create a general will or solid front in France during the war with Europe after 1792 was often justified by citations of the *Social Contract,* and did in fact contribute to the quasi-totalitarianism of the Terror. But Rousseau was not, like Lenin, writing as a tactician of revolution. He did not pretend to tell how a people should go about becoming democratic. Indeed, he confused this whole issue by identifying legislative with sovereign power and by his negative attitude toward representative institutions. Primarily, he was writing a critique of the world as he knew it, of what came in due course to be called the Old Regime.

And what, in summary, was likely in his book to appeal to men

---

[18] Bk. II, Chap. viii, *ibid.*, 190.

in a mood of rebellion, and to be intolerable to those in positions of government, even at Geneva in 1762? First of all, the theory of the political community, of the people, or nation, was revolutionary in implication: it posited a community based on the will of the living, and the active sense of membership and voluntary participation, rather than on history, or kinship, or race, or past conquest, or common inheritance, or the chance of birth into an already existent political system. It denied sovereign powers to kings, to oligarchs, and to all governments. It said that any form of government could be changed. It held all public officers to be removable. It held that law could draw its force and its legality only from the community itself; as the French were to say in 1789, the will of "no body, and no individual" could be law. Not only monarchs, but also the constituted bodies of which I have said so much in preceding chapters, would be justified in believing that the *Social Contract* sapped their foundations.

The Genevese Revolution of 1768

The Geneva that anxiously watched Rousseau's approach from Paris in June 1762 was by no means the ideal city of his imagination. The confrontation that followed was to drive Rousseau to the verge of madness, and Geneva to the brink of revolution.

The old and sporadic disputes within the city had induced the governing groups, in the 1730's, to appeal to outside powers for arbitration. These powers, the kingdom of France and the cantons of Bern and Zurich, had produced the Act of Mediation of 1738, which they enforced by armed intervention. They remained the Guarantors of the Act, available for further appeal should it come into question.[19] Geneva, that is to say, like other small or weak states at the time—Sweden and Poland, or the Dutch and Venetian republics or the papal states, as will be seen—was with difficulty preserving the independent management of its own affairs.

The Act of 1738, clarifying certain older laws of the city, was in effect its constitution. It enumerated five "orders" in the state: the four Syndics; the Small Council, or Executive Council of Twenty-Five; the Council of Sixty (which was of no importance); the Council of Two Hundred; and the General Council. The General Council was a kind of town meeting. All citizens and burghers attended it. There were

---

[19] The Act was published as *Règlement de l'Illustre Médiation pour la pacification des troubles de la République de Genève* (Geneva, 1738).

about 1,500 citizens and burghers, not counting those habitually absent from the city. With their families they represented about a quarter of the population. The remaining three-quarters were either *natifs*, native born, often of several generations, but without political rights; or *habitants*, who in principle were new arrivals to whom the right of residence had been granted. Between the bulk of the citizens and the burghers there was no real difference, and they may all be referred to as Burghers. Nor was there any substantial difference between *natifs* and *habitants*, who may all be called Natives.

By the Act of 1738 the General Council met once a year, and elected the four Syndics from a list of candidates containing double the necessary number of names, submitted to it by the Small Council. The Act of 1738 specified that all candidates for the office of Syndic must be members of the Small Council, whose members in turn had to belong to the Two Hundred. The Two Hundred, conversely, were named by the Small Council. In short, the Two Hundred (on which far fewer than two hundred families sat) were the ruling aristocracy at Geneva. The Small Council and the Syndics were their executive arm; the "people" had a choice of the Syndics, but only as between candidates who belonged to the governing group. The Burghers were also confirmed by the Act of 1738 in the right of making "representations" to the Syndics and Small Council; these were protests or remonstrances to be made by groups of interested Burghers, not by the General Council as such, when they judged "proper for the good of the State."

Within this constitutional framework great economic changes were taking place. It was at this time that Switzerland became famous for watch-making. Where there had been only 680 persons employed at watch-making at Geneva in 1686, the number rose to 6,000 in 1799; it may have been even higher a decade or two before, before the loss of markets in the Revolutionary wars. The watch-makers (of whom Rousseau's father had been one) were a skilled and alert group of men. The Act of 1738 allowed Natives to enter watch-making and a few other trades; but Natives were still debarred from most occupations above the artisan level. There was no absolute occupational difference between Burghers and Natives, but in general the growth of the industry, as watch-making was called (*la fabrique*), had enriched many of the Burghers through commercial and managerial operations in connection with watches, and turned many of the Natives into a trained, self-conscious, and self-respecting body of workers. "The rapid revolution which was taking place in commerce and the arts," wrote the Genevese d'Ivernois in 1782, "made it necessary for the different classes to have contacts with each other every day."[20] But the classes were unable to get together politically.

The Burghers were a politically conscious lot, who felt that Geneva had been more democratic in former days, sensing the monopolizing of office by the patricians, legalized in 1738, as a recent usurpation. In the 1730's groups of Burghers began to meet in cafés or in each other's homes in informal *cercles*, in which as the years passed the conversation became increasingly devoted to politics. There were twelve such "circles" in the 1760's. Geneva was not misgoverned by its patricians; and the grievances of the Burghers were of the liberal kind, concerning taxes or commercial policies or individual cases of injustice or police action or arrest. The Natives did not begin to take an interest in public questions until the 1760's. Their thinking was then not so much political as economic; they were not so much concerned with who governed or how, but complained of legal exclusion from the more remunerative or prestige-conveying occupations, for which they rightly blamed the Burghers as much as the patricians.

The Burghers adopted Rousseau as their hero when he resumed his citizenship in 1754, and when in 1758 he came to their defense against Voltaire, d'Alembert and the patricians in the dispute over the theater, which involved, as has been seen, contradictory ideas of what Geneva ought to be. Their leaders were indignant when the Small Council ordered *Emile* and the *Social Contract* to be lacerated and burned, and Rousseau himself under arrest should he enter the territory of the republic. But they did nothing.

Rousseau, fleeing from Paris, was kept from Geneva by the decree of arrest, and was also refused asylum in the neighboring Vaud, a subject district of Bern. He presently settled in Neuchâtel, not far from Geneva. Neuchâtel then belonged to the King of Prussia, who extended his royal protection to the harassed republican.

With alternating moods of enthusiasm and reluctance, tossed between concern for Geneva and a desire to be rid of it forever, in an ambivalent and deeply troubled state of mind, Rousseau now entered into a series of talks with Burgher leaders who came to see him in Neuchâtel. His dream had been shattered by his condemnation; he

---

[20] F. d'Ivernois, *Tableau historique et politique des Révolutions de Genève* (Geneva, 1782), 163. The author, later knighted in England as Sir Francis D'Ivernois, was the son of the D'Ivernois who led the Burgher party and tried to work with Rousseau after 1762. This book is the main contemporary narrative.

was confused and depressed; he was hurt that no one at Geneva had yet taken any public stand in his favor; he feared that none of his fellow-citizens really cared about him or understood him. Lonely, abandoned, disappointed, and baffled, craving sympathy, and wishing to call attention to his plight, he dramatically abdicated his title of Citizen of Geneva. He thus tormented himself by surrendering what had given him so much pride. He took an irrevocable action which he may soon have secretly regretted. Three weeks later, on June 18, 1763, d'Ivernois, de Luc, and forty other citizens and burghers submitted a "representation" to the Syndics.

This document declared that there had been a breach of legality in the condemnation by the Small Council of Rousseau's two books, and that therefore the case should be referred for review to the General Council, that is, to all Burghers in town meeting assembled. The Small Council, denying any breach of legality, refused to refer the representation to the General Council. The Small Council, in its official reply, conceded the right of Burghers to make representations, but held that nothing in the Act of 1738 obliged it to transmit such representations to the General Council, if, as in this case of Rousseau, members of the Small Council were undivided and felt no uncertainty in their own minds on the legality of their decision. The Small Council pointed out, too, that the Act of 1738 forbade any of the Orders to encroach on the rights of others—that, in short, the General Council must not interfere with the conduct of government by the Small. Many representations followed the first one, and many were vetoed. Thus was launched the constitutional crisis at Geneva. For want of better names, the Burgher party called itself the Représentants, from the "representations" that they made; the party of the government were called Négatifs, because they claimed the right to negative, or veto, any Burgher representation by refusing to transmit it to the General Council.

The Small Council also deputed one of its members, J. R. Tronchin, to set forth its position more fully in a book. Tronchin did so in his *Lettres écrites de la campagne*. The friend of Voltaire, a declared enemy of Rousseau, Tronchin was a learned and accomplished man, courteous and equable in public debate, but crushing in the wealth of legal and constitutional arguments at his command. He was once called the Montesquieu of Geneva, and, like Montesquieu, put his case on a high plane. The *droit négatif* of the Small Council, he said, was like the royal veto in England, a necessary and salutary check upon the powers of the people, designed to maintain the balance in the state; it might prevent progress, but certainly prevented anarchy; it was a power that could not itself make law, but prevented capricious lawmaking by disaffected persons; hence it directly served "the great aim of a political society, to conserve itself by conserving its constitution."[21] He suggested in passing, also, that if the Burghers harked back to too many sixteenth-century precedents they might stir up the Natives. Since his more purely legal arguments seemed also to be irrefutable, the Burgher Représentants were pushed into a corner; they knew of no way to answer Tronchin, nor could they see what step they might next take. So de Luc, d'Ivernois, and other leaders went again to consult Rousseau.

Rousseau held himself apart. He was being psychologically difficult. He declared that he would never take back his citizenship even if it were offered. He was glad that some of the Burghers wished to help him, but sorry that they had acted so late. He advised them to drop the whole matter, said that he was not worthy, insisted that he would have nothing to do with it, and that he was through with Geneva. De Luc and d'Ivernois were distressed. Secretly, however, Rousseau proceeded to do the opposite. A year after the appearance of Tronchin's *Letters from the Country*, Rousseau surprised friends and enemies alike with another of his great manifestoes, the *Letters from the Mountain*. It was a rejoinder to Tronchin and the patricians. Where the *Social Contract* had been based on a reading of Hobbes and Grotius and Pufendorf and on reflections on abstract justice, the *Letters from the Mountain* were based on a close reading of the lawbooks and histories of Geneva, which Rousseau now for the first time digested in his Neuchâtel retreat. The new work included a more concrete presentation of democratic ideas than the *Social Contract*. One writer, thinking of Pascal, calls it the *Provinciales* of the democratic movement.[22] Into that we cannot go; but on the specific question now raging at Geneva Rousseau offered a clear answer. Admitting that the Small Council had the legal right of veto if a proposal for new legislation were being made, he retorted that if the charge were violation of law (as in the representation of June 1763), then the Small Council accused of such violation, however clear its own conscience, could not refuse to lay the matter before the General Council, the sovereign assembly of

---

[21] Tronchin's book is quoted at length by Vallette, *J. J. Rousseau Genevois*, 285-87. See also on these matters John S. Spink, *Jean-Jacques Rousseau et Genève* (Paris, 1934).
[22] Vallette, *op.cit.*, p. 295; "les *Provinciales* de la démocratie politique et du libéralisme religieux."

citizens of the republic. The executive could not be a permanent final judge of its own actions.

Unfortunately for Rousseau the controversy did not remain limited to this high level. Suspecting Voltaire of having been instrumental in causing his difficulties at Geneva, he took occasion in the *Letters from the Mountain* to attack Voltaire, and announced to the world that Voltaire was the true author of one of the more venomous antireligious tracts then in circulation, the *Sermon des cinquante.* Voltaire had in fact written it, but did not wish to acknowledge it, especially because, at the moment, he was trying to enlist the French government in his crusade for the rehabilitation of Jean Calas. Voltaire was irritated into a counterattack on Rousseau. He hurled another anonymous pamphlet, *Le sentiment des citoyens,* into the battle of arguments at Geneva. Siding openly with the patrician Négatifs, he raked up everything he could think of to destroy the character of Rousseau: "a man who bears upon him the dreadful marks of his debaucheries, and who, disguised as a mountebank, drags with him from village to village, and from mountain to mountain, the unfortunate woman whose mother he drove to death and whose children he exposed at the doors of an asylum."[23] The hints of venereal disease and of implication in Thérèse's mother's death were untrue. It was true, however, that Rousseau, the teacher of moral revival and family virtue, had abandoned his own five children to the nuns. This was Rousseau's great secret and hidden shame. He was later to talk about it fully enough in his *Confessions,* but in 1764 it was known only to a few. It contradicted everything he stood for and really believed; but he could not deny it, and could make no reply. To make matters worse, Voltaire had successfully mimicked the style of the Genevese pastor Vernes, whom Rousseau believed to be the author of this latest attack upon him.

Rousseau was disarmed in his dispute with the Geneva patriciate. For the Burghers he was now an embarrassing ally. It now seemed, or could be said (thanks to Voltaire), that anyone not believing literally in the Bible was really immoral. In the canton of Neuchâtel the people stoned him—a "lapidation" whose religious symbolism was not lost upon him. Believing himself misunderstood, betrayed, and crucified, he fled from Switzerland, as he had fled from Paris.

He went to England, then back to France. He now sometimes had positive hallucinations. He could not tell his enemies from his friends.

---

[23] Voltaire, *Oeuvres complètes* (52 vols., Paris, 1883-1885), xxv, 312. See also Chapponière, *Voltaire chez les Calvinistes,* 180.

He suspected them all, was convinced that a great web of conspiracy enmeshed him, that he was everywhere persecuted, that spies were watching him, that seeming friends wanted only to ridicule and undo him. Medical diagnosis of persons long since dead is absurd on the face of it, but it does seem that Rousseau was increasingly gripped by an actual neurosis. It was a neurosis which, in a personal way, foreshadowed the mass neurosis of the French Republic, when it too, proclaiming its own virtue in the face of aristocracies and churches, behaved very queerly in a world of enemies, some real, some imaginary, and some simply unknown.

At Geneva the crisis mounted. It had started with a protest against condemnation of the *Social Contract*. It may be supposed, therefore, that the leading Représentants had read the book. They were, however, sober men inclined to prefer legal and concrete historical arguments. In their official statements, designed to persuade the patricians, they never cited Rousseau, but argued from the Act of 1738 and earlier legislation at Geneva. It is important to see how some of these men were led by the actual situation into the assertion of ideas much like those of the *Social Contract*.

In January 1765 the Small Council had great difficulty in getting its candidates for Syndics elected. The slate, which included a Gallatin, obtained only about 700 votes from the 1,500 possible voters. At the end of 1765 the General Council seven times refused to elect any procurator-general and lieutenant-general at all. In this voters' strike normal government could not go forward. On January 6, 1766, the Small Council, reflecting the wishes of the governing class, therefore called in the guarantors of the Act of 1738. A few days later the General Council three times refused to elect any Syndics. That is, the Small Council repeatedly offered candidates, chosen from its own body as required by law, and the General Council refused them all. The main demand of the Représentants was no longer to have representations referred to the General Council. The main demand was now to elect only officials acceptable to the Burghers. The Act of 1738 prescribed that Syndics must come from the Small Council, but also that the General Council could "reject them, all or in part."

The issue was thus fundamental, and clearcut. Patricians and Burghers flatly disagreed on the meaning of the constitution and laws of Geneva. The Négatifs insisted on the right to veto representations, and on the necessity that *some* members from the Small Council be chosen as Syndics. The Représentants affirmed that representations could not be vetoed, and that the General Council could reject candidates any number of times, "all or in part."

It was thus necessary to define or change the law—the very essence of sovereign power. For this purpose the Genevan aristocracy appealed to outside powers—to Bern, Zurich, and France. The Burgher party declared that foreigners had nothing to do with it; that only the citizens of Geneva could be the last court of appeal on the interpretation of its law.

The Guarantor powers met. Bern and Zurich were inclined to listen to the Représentants; France was not. As Choiseul wrote to the "Magnificent Lords of Bern and Zurich," the King of France could not stand by while the Représentants at Geneva overthrew "the orders in the State" and established an "absolute Democracy" under color of the will of the people.[24] When the Représentants tried to get a memorial explaining their position transmitted to the conference of the Guarantors, the Small Council refused to transmit it. It was hardly necessary to transmit it formally, came the reply, since the Représentants had published it anyway. And they must not antagonize France. The Guarantors soon ruled in favor of the Geneva patriciate.

What were the arguments that the Représentants wished to lay before the Guarantors? That they were not innovators or rebels. That the law and history of Geneva were on their side. That the Small Council at Geneva would be "sovereign" if it could reject representations at will; but that it was really not sovereign, but only an executive. That the right to have Syndics approved by the people was the supreme guarantee of their liberties. That if the Small Council prevailed, there would be "Masters and Subjects, but there would be no more Citizens."[25]

To their own governing magistrates the Représentants addressed other arguments also. That it was unwise to appeal to outsiders in domestic affairs. That magistrates would be the stronger if they relied on their own citizens instead of relying on foreigners. "Let us pull down this wall of separation" between government and citizens; "this eternal rock on which our happiness has foundered!"[26]

[24] A letter from Choiseul to the cantons of Bern and Zurich, dated February 20 1767, has been copied in longhand into a volume of pamphlets on disputes at Geneva at this time; the volume, apparently once the property of a Genevan interested in these disputes, is now in the Princeton University Library, volume 16 of a series on Geneva.

[25] *Adresse des citoyens et bourgeois représentants de Genève au Magnifique Conseil des Vingt-Cinq de ladite Ville, avec le mémoire qui l'accompagnait, remis aux Syndics le 19 Mai 1767 par les vingt-quatre Commissaires des Représentants et trois Députés de chacun des douze Cercles.* Quotation from p. 20.

[26] *Ibid.*, 6.

In reply the Small Council naturally insisted that the Burghers should accept the decision of the Guarantors, and advanced further constitutional arguments based on the Act of 1738. It blamed the impasse of government squarely on the Représentants, observing that the Small Council was constitutionally obliged to nominate its own members for Syndics, that it had conscientiously nominated every eligible member in turn, and that the General Council, by refusing all, was nullifying the constitution. If the General Council had the right of perpetual refusal, the argument continued, then it had the power to destroy the Syndics as an Order; but the Orders of the state were constitutionally bound not to infringe upon each other. Election of Syndics had nothing to do with "sovereignty"; it was a mere executive function which the constitution assigned to the General Council.

The Small Council had the best of the constitutional argument, so that there was no recourse for the Représentants but to assert a juridical revolution—to oppose Law and Constitution with Sovereignty of the People, from which a new constitution might be derived. This was done notably in an obscurely signed pamphlet of December 1767 actually written by a young man, soon to be famous, named Delolme.[27]

"What, sir, is the Constitution? What is this unknown Being that assigns functions to the General Council, to the Sovereign of the Republic? Is it the nymph from whom Numa is said to have received his laws? . . .

"The Constitution is the totality of Laws, or Law in the collective sense. Law is the will of the Sovereign. The Sovereign in Geneva is the General Council." The General Council, as sovereign, assigns functions to others; it receives none from any higher source. It is not an Order, and cannot "infringe" on other Orders. It is the supreme lawmaker; the executive is its agent. It elects or refuses to elect whom it pleases. When it last refused election of syndics, it did so "not according to the Act of 1738, or the Edict of 1707, or of 1568, or any other edict whatsoever; it did so by the Will of the Sovereign, manifested on January 12, 1766, at four o'clock in the afternoon." Indeed, it is a more effective sovereign than any king, who is only a single man. It is both the representative and the represented. It "combines all the

---

[27] *Purification des trois points de droit souillés par un anonyme, ou Réponse à l'examen des trois points de droit traités dans les Mémoires des Représentants du 19 mai et 16 octobre, 1767.* See also E. Ruff, *Jean Louis DeLolme und sein Werk über die Verfassung Englands* (Berlin, 1934), 42-43. For Delolme's later admiration for the separation of powers in the British constitution, which was somewhat at variance with the Rousseauist views of this pamphlet, see the following chapter.

Orders; it contains all within itself; when it moves, all moves; all rights, powers and attributes of office emanate from it, and have it only for their object; and it is in all possible plenitude the Sovereign, the Nation, and the Law."[28]

This may be compared to Louis XV's resounding declaration of sovereignty, made only the year before to the Parlement of Paris. Or it may be compared to the more similar doctrine of Rousseau and the *Social Contract*. It may also be compared to the Declaratory Act of 1766 in which the British Parliament affirmed its sovereignty over America. Or to the legally less explicit Declaration of Independence, by which the American colonies took sovereign power to themselves. Or to the theory of those Frenchmen who in June 1789 repudiated the three Estates and called the National Assembly into being: "the Nation, when assembled, cannot be given orders." Matters in many quarters were reaching the point where someone had to arrogate sovereignty. In the clash of claims and counterclaims, affirmations and denials, appeals to ancient statutes and enactments made in contrary directions by contending parties, there had to be some power to decide.

At Geneva, at this time, no decision came from France, which did uphold the ruling of the Guarantors by economic sanctions, but refused to follow them with military force. A quick visit from Necker, who left his banking business in Paris, purely in his private capacity as a Genevese citizen, failed like all other such attempts to bring the parties together.

January 1768 came; it was again time for the annual election of Syndics. The General Council again three times refused to elect any. Spokesmen for the General Council and for the Two Hundred came together desperately to seek a way out. During the very night of their conference the new theater burned down; how, is not known, but it could be made to look like a Burgher outrage. The Two Hundred refused the proposals for conciliation. Burghers began carrying arms. Half the circles declared themselves *en permanence*. It was beginning to look a little like a real revolution. At this point, J. R. Tronchin, whose conservative integrity was hardly open to question, prevailed on the more moderate in the Small Council and in the Two Hundred to agree to terms. The result was the compromise Edict of 1768. It went through because many Négatifs, unconvinced, abstained from voting; they called it the Edict of Pistols.

[28] *Purification* . . . , 40-49.

The Edict of 1768 granted the General Council certain rights in election of members of the Small. It prescribed that the General Council *must* elect Syndics, who, however, might come not from the Small Council of Twenty-five but from the larger Two Hundred if necessary. It added fifty members to the Two Hundred, and provided for election of new members to it by the General Council. It also made a limited and cautious provision by which a handful of Natives could be made Burghers—for a fat fee of four thousand florins, or a little less for Natives with several generations of residence. Natives were given a few trading rights, and declared admissible to the professions of doctor, surgeon, and apothecary. The whole quarrel was patched up with no mention of the case of Rousseau that had unleashed it. Considering the height to which political argument had risen, the Edict of 1768 was a compromise indeed.

But the Genevese revolution of 1768 was a bourgeois revolution in an unquestionable sense, carried through by men legally defined as *bourgeois* and *citoyens* of Geneva. These men were scarcely conscious of the class below them as a political force. Rousseau himself, in all the study he made of Geneva politics at Neuchâtel, showed no interest in the Natives. The Natives, however, the three-quarters of the population who were not Burghers, were also beginning to agitate. They too began to hold meetings and discuss programs of action about 1765. When they submitted a petition in 1766 the Small Council called it "criminal and seditious"; the Guarantors told them they were "in the State, but not of it," since they did not constitute an Order.[29] Such language only confirmed the grievance that many Natives were beginning to feel, that they remained outsiders or second-class citizens, generation after generation. They objected, too, to the discrimination which kept them out of wholesale business and certain other trades and professions, for which they blamed the self-protectionism and economic jealousy of the Burghers. The Natives were therefore divided; some thought that they must first ally with the Burgher Représentants against the patriciate and the Small Council; others so distrusted the Burghers that they hoped to gain more by alliance with the patricians. Isaac Cornuaud, for example, a Native leader who was to favor annexation to France in 1798, and whose political career began thirty years before in these disputes of the 1760's, thought very much like a Tronchin or a Burke that Rousseau was a fanciful and dangerous thinker, that the Small Council had acted rightly in banning his books, and that the Burgher

[29] D'Ivernois, *Tableau*, 317.

Représentants were troublemakers, actuated by pride, whose new "pretensions" would if successful make the lot of the Natives worse. The Burghers, he said, wanted liberty only for themselves.[30]

Thus a pattern already appeared that was to be repeated many times later in many countries, of a lower class more interested in its economic welfare than in constitutional forms, and likely to support either Liberal or Conservative, Whig or Tory, revolution or counterrevolution as might seem best. In 1768, most of the Natives favored the Représentants, so far as they took sides at all. They received, as noted, a few concessions in the Edict of 1768, one of which, however, merely enabled a few well-to-do *natifs* to pass into the *bourgeoisie*. They continued to agitate, meet in their own "circles," publish pamphlets, and make various demands. One who refused to write *natif de Genève* after his name was banished for ten years. Some took to wearing swords, which at Geneva was a Burgher right. In 1770 a great demonstration of the Natives was put down by force, the Burghers camping in the streets to preserve order. The General Council—that is, the Sovereign People according to advanced Burgher doctrine—voted 1,182 to 99 that anyone seeking to alter the statute of the Natives might be punished even by capital punishment. The Native circles were dissolved as subversive. A number of Native leaders, including Cornuaud, fled from the city. Enough had happened to show that the Geneva middle class did not intend to share the fruits of its revolution, and that the lower class did not intend to accept it.

It is significant also, in all these events, to trace the activities of Voltaire. The departure of Rousseau left the Lord of Ferney in philosophical domination of the scene. With Rousseau gone, Voltaire ceased to be an outright partisan of the Geneva patricians. He came to conclude, as their dispute with the Représentants matured, that the two governing councils at Geneva were mere closed and privileged bodies, like the Parlement of Paris, whose obstruction to royal reforms in France at this same time he was watching with a disapproving eye. If in these years Voltaire proved his attachment to enlightened monarchy by supporting Maupeou against the French parlements, he was also converted by events at Geneva to as nearly democratic an outlook as he ever attained. The very men who had supported Rousseau— d'Ivernois, de Luc, and the others—now that Rousseau had left, and with initial embarrassments and misgivings, accepted the aid offered

---

[30] *Mémoires de Isaac Cornuaud sur Genève et la Révolution de 1770 à 1795* (Geneva, 1912), 1-9.

by Voltaire. "The more I have come to know your citizens," Voltaire wrote to d'Ivernois, "the more I have come to like them."[31] He wrote his *Idées républicaines* in praise of Geneva. The "republicanization" of Voltaire may be accounted another of the universal influences of the city by Lake Leman.

Voltaire went beyond Rousseau and the Geneva Burghers. The old mischief-maker and humanitarian actually took to befriending the Natives. He wrote a tragedy, *Les Scythes*, to exalt the virtues of a stalwart and unrefined people. He had Natives come to his house, advised them on their political tactics, and created a model village on his estates where they could pursue their watch-making and other trades when life became too difficult at Geneva. Indeed, one of the arguments of the Burghers, when they repressed the Natives in 1770, was that the whole Native question had simply been stirred up by their old enemy, Voltaire.

The Burgher revolution of 1768 at Geneva was "democratic" only in a certain sense, though an important one. It was democatic in that it was antiaristocratic, that it opposed self-perpetuation in government, that it held government officials to be only removable delegates, and countered the theory of the constituted bodies with the theory of the Sovereignty of the People. The Représentants never called their movement "democratic." But it looked like Absolute Democracy to Choiseul because it subverted the society based upon Orders. That the People need include everyone, that universal equal suffrage was the principal mark of democracy, was neither a significant theory nor an issue in practical politics at the time. Even the Geneva Natives did not clearly assert it.

The new regime was sufficiently democratic for the more vehement aristocrats not to accept it. They had not consented to it, but only abstained from voting. In 1782 there was a counterrevolution at Geneva. The Geneva aristocracy, again appealing to foreign aid, for the third time since 1738, and this time obtaining the military intervention of France, succeeded in annulling the Edict of 1768. They rebuilt their theater, and settled down to those civilized diversions of which the mad Rousseau had wanted to deprive them. Geneva, too, in the 1780's, was to have its aristocratic resurgence.

[31] Chaponnière, *op.cit.*, 214. That Voltaire's *Idées républicaines* arose not from general ideas so much as from Voltaire's involvement in and knowledge of the situation at Geneva is shown in the forthcoming work of Peter J. Gay, *Voltaire's Politics: The Poet as Realist*, to be published in 1959 by the Princeton University Press.

THE BRITISH PARLIAMENT BETWEEN
KING AND PEOPLE

The power and jurisdiction of Parliament, says Sir Edward Coke, is so transcendant and absolute, that it cannot be confined, either for causes or persons, within any bounds. . . . It hath sovereign and uncontrollable authority. . . . It can change and create afresh even the constitution of the kingdom and of parliaments themselves. . . . True it is, that what the parliament doth, no authority upon earth can undo. So that it is a matter most essential to the liberties of this kingdom that such members be delegated to this important trust as are most eminent for their probity, their fortitude, and their knowledge; for it was a known apothegm of the great lord treasurer Burleigh, "that England could never be ruined but by a parliament."—SIR WILLIAM BLACKSTONE, 1765

THE BRITISH PARLIAMENT BETWEEN
KING AND PEOPLE

OF ALL those constituted bodies of Europe, largely aristocratic in composition, which in some countries came into conflict with kings in the decade before 1775, and which at Geneva had trouble with the citizens whom they governed, the most famous and the most powerful was the Parliament of Great Britain, whose misfortune it was to be challenged from both sides at once. Or, at least, the most ardent devotees of the Houses of Parliament found Parliamentary independence being undermined by the King, in the person of George III, while at the same time a growing number of dissatisfied persons, in America, in Ireland, and in England itself, expressed increasing doubts on the independence of Parliament, invoking a higher authority which they called the People. The champions of Parliament relished neither rival. "It is our business to act constitutionally, and to maintain the independency of Parliament," said the young Charles Fox in the Commons in 1771; "whether it is attacked by the people or by the crown is a matter of little consequence."[1]

The British Constitution

There is a curious irony in the situation. The dozen years preceding the American Revolution, the years when America was profoundly alienated, and which saw the beginning of the British movement for parliamentary reform, were also the years when awestruck wonder at the glories of the British constitution reached an almost ecstatic height. The very Stamp Act Congress announced its satisfaction at living under "the most perfect form of government." "The constitution of England," declared a British book reviewer in 1775, "is without doubt the most perfect form of government that ever was devised by human

[1] *Parliamentary History*, XVII, 149.

wisdom." To John Adams it was "this stupendous fabric of human invention," even after he and other Americans no longer lived under it. The Younger Pitt, when he introduced his bill to reform the representation of the House of Commons in 1783, prefaced his speech with a prolonged apologetic, expressing his unshaken faith in the unique advantages of English liberty, as if himself incredulous that such a constitution needed any reform at all.[2] In the disputes that arose between King George's subjects in Britain and America after 1763, and in those which continued to trouble Britain itself after American independence, scarcely anyone denied that the British constitution was the most remarkable constitution in the history of the world. There was, however, some difference of opinion on the precise content of this matchless frame of state—on the concrete questions of what particular rights it guaranteed to what people, and why.

There were good reasons why all Britons, including British colonials, should have felt such self-satisfaction, and why Europeans of other nationalities should have joined in the chorus of praise. There was, for one thing, an objective ground for it. In the slums of London, or among dispossessed agricultural laborers, or pauper children, or the Irish tenantry, there were people as wretched as any in Europe. Nevertheless, there was an air of freedom in the British world, a constructive liberty which, unlike the "liberties" so common in Europe, actually added to the power of the laws and of the state; a general tolerance between classes, a forbearance toward religious minorities, a wide latitude in the expression of opinion, a relatively uncontrolled press, with much public discussion; a good deal of personal security for most of the population, together with a high degree of wealth, industry, and prosperity, of which the fruits were as evenly distributed as in other large states of Europe, for while the rich in England were probably richer than elsewhere, the English poor, in a general way, may have been a little less poor than in most parts of the Continent. Probably contemporaries were not altogether mistaken in ascribing these blessings to the form of government; at any rate, the existence of such blessings added enormously to the repute, in England and in Europe, in which the form of government was held. The spectacular victory of the Seven Years' War had the same effect. The islanders had humbled the combined powers of Austria, France, and Spain; Haps-

---

[2] For the Stamp Act Congress see L. Gipson, *Coming of the Revolution* (N.Y., 1954), 100; for the reviewer, *Critical Review*, vol. 39 (1775), p. 345; for Adams, *Defense of the Constitutions* (1786), *Works* IV (1851), 358; for Pitt, *Parliamentary History*, XXIII, 827.

burgs and Bourbons simultaneously bowed to them; they triumphed in America and in the East. Empire was on them bestowed; where Caesar's eagles never flew, as Cowper put it, none were as invincible as they. Surely the constitution of such a people must harbor the true secret by which freedom, wealth, power, and leadership might all be enjoyed at the same time.

Blackstone's *Commentaries* were published between 1765 and 1769. In the ten years from 1767 to 1777 appeared the *Rotuli parliamentorum,* the first substantial printed collection of medieval parliamentary acts. It was sponsored by the House of Lords, which was motivated both by a desire to set forth the historical evidence for its own important position in English life, and to open up, if not quite to create, the whole field of English constitutional history as a learned science. Meanwhile, the writings of Montesquieu were having their cumulative effect. Every two or three years a new edition of the *Spirit of Laws* appeared in English. Readers in England, as in the American colonies, could there find the assurance, on the authority of the great French expert on comparative government, that they lived under a constitution wholly devoted, through its ingenious separation of powers, to the preservation of liberty. Or at least they could find it if they looked for it hard enough, for Montesquieu actually gave only about a seventy-fifth part of his compendious treatise to the specific subject of the British constitution.[3]

The first book by a Continental European ever devoted wholly to that subject, and under that title, appeared at Amsterdam in French, as *La Constitution de l'Angleterre,* in 1771.[4] There was a London edition in 1775, and over twenty different London and Dublin imprints of the *Constitution of England* can be counted for the ensuing half-century. The book figured as a British political Bible until after the First Reform Bill. It did more than Montesquieu to spread an understanding of the British constitution on the Continent. It is worthy of note, and is of course a consequence of the American Revolution, that a single New York edition seems to have satisfied the American demand.

The author of the *Constitution of England* was the Genevese Delolme, one of the advanced democratic party at Geneva in 1767. He had

[3] On Blackstone and Montesquieu see Chapter III above; for the significance of the *Rotuli parliamentorum* see E. Lousse, *La société d'ancien régime: organisation et représentation corporatives* (Louvain, 1943), I, 2.

[4] G. Bonno, *La constitution britannique devant l'opinion française de Montesquieu à Bonaparte* (Paris, 1932), 118-25; E. Ruff, *Jean Louis Delolme und sein Werk über die Verfassung Englands* (Berlin, 1934).

upheld there the Sovereignty of the People against the theory of Orders within the state. So firmly did he cling to this principle that he refused to accept the compromise made at Geneva in January 1768, and a few months later went into voluntary exile. He arrived in England a stubborn democrat. Within three years he had produced his book on England, which became the classic statement of the theory of a balance among King, Lords, and Commons. It thus seems that he changed his mind, and the few who have tried to look closely at Delolme, of whose career few evidences have survived, have seen in him a significant change in a "conservative" direction, from ideas resembling those of Rousseau to ideas resembling those of Montesquieu. It is very likely that he did change his mind, because he is known to have been mixing with some of the discontented Whigs in England at the time when Lord North took charge of the government. The first edition of the collected *Letters of Junius*, published in 1772, contains in its preface a quotation from Delolme's *Constitution of England*, using the exact wording of the translation not published until three years later. Delolme clearly had made Whig acquaintances in London; someone in 1772 was engaged in translating his work. Not much more is known of Delolme, except that he stayed in England until 1800.

Yet Delolme did not become wholly a Whig, nor did he wholly give up what he had believed at Geneva. There is a unifying thought in all his political writings, one incidentally which was to appeal strongly to John Adams. It was an intense dislike of government by oligarchy, coterie, or self-perpetuating aristocracy. Hence, in the politics of Geneva he was a democrat. In the politics of Sweden his sympathies were monarchist. In 1772, immediately after the *coup d'état* of Gustavus III, he published (it was his first work published in English) *A Parallel between the English Government and the Former Government of Sweden.* He expressed here his admiration for Gustavus III, and his antipathy to the Freedom Era in Sweden, during which, he said, the nobility monopolized public life to the disadvantage of everyone else. He thought that the difference between Sweden after 1719 and England after 1689 was that in England the King remained strong, so that England had not become an aristocracy in the manner of Sweden —or of Geneva.

Delolme in fact put great emphasis on the historic role of the English crown, in a way sufficient to distinguish him from Montesquieu, of whom he is often said to be merely the popularizer, or from most of the Anglo-American Whigs and even radicals, who usually saw liberty as something won by age-long struggle against royal tyrants, and placed its beginnings in primitive Saxon times. The English constitution, says Delolme in quite modern vein, really dates from the Norman Conquest. By the conquest the monarchy imposed a strong and centralized feudalism and built a unified kingdom, unlike France; later on there was only one Parliament for the King to resort to, unlike the many assemblies with which the King of France might deal. The great power of the King fortunately overshadowed the greatest nobles, so that, as the generations passed, nobles and commoners were obliged to join forces to maintain their freedom. Delolme was impressed by the continuing authority of the British King, whom he thought to be really stronger than the King of France. As he put it, thinking of events of his own day, the King of France took care upon approaching the Parlement of Paris to overawe it with a display of "military apparatus"; the King of England at a dissolution, simply spoke a few words, telling the Parliament they were no longer a Parliament, and they were not. Such was the magic of the force of law. The King enjoyed the confidence of the people as much as Parliament did. It was "from the Nation itself," said Delolme, that the Executive in England drew its authority—from the "affection," the "consent," and the "voluntary passions of those who are subject to it."[5]

Delolme's idea of the "balance of powers" in the British constitution was thus significantly different from Montesquieu's. For Montesquieu, as for Burke, in a proper balance the role of nobility as a check upon monarchy was to be emphasized. For Delolme, as later for John Adams, the important thing was that a strong king (or executive in the case of Adams), served as a barrier against ambitions which when uncontrolled led to aristocracy. As for democracy, Delolme showed little alarm that it would turn into "anarchy." The real danger, he felt, with the experience of Geneva behind him, was that "pure democracy," or a system in which a body of citizenry supposedly governed itself, would turn into an aristocracy or oligarchy, since in popular assemblies a few ambitious individuals always got control and perpetuated their position. Against this eventuality, he thought, a strong king or executive was the best protection. England, said Delolme, was really the most nearly democratic state in Europe precisely because of its balance between King, Lords, and Commons.

According to Delolme the separation was quite distinct. The King exercised all executive power; he was the source of justice, he freely

---

[5] *Constitution of England* (London, 1775), 409.

named his ministers, he appointed to all offices, he commanded the army and navy. He was wholly independent of Parliament except in one decisive respect; he depended on it for the grant of money. Parliament made the laws; it had the initiative in legislation, and was independent of the King, except that the King might interpose his veto. Parliament was wisely divided into two houses, Lords and Commons, not so much in order to give special representation to the nobility, as Montesquieu had said, as simply to provide a countercheck against ill-advised legislation. The Commons, according to Delolme, were the duly elected representatives of the people; he defends representative government against the aspersions of his countryman, Rousseau.

In the first French editions of his book, while insisting that the British government was the best in Europe, Delolme nevertheless observed that it suffered from a few imperfections. He mentioned Old Sarum by name, and held the continued representation of decayed boroughs to be a true constitutional defect. He thought Parliament should be elected more frequently, and that something should be done to stop the arbitrary impressment of sailors. He even said that such reforms were sought by "a numerous party in the present Parliament." He declared that one of the virtues of the British government, in comparison with others, was "its greater capacity for improvement."[6]

These comments disappeared from the first English edition of 1775. The Delolme whom people read for fifty years conveyed no such reservations. Since practically nothing is known of Delolme's life, it is hard to explain the shift. He may have changed his friends, or been influenced by his translator. It is also possible that he shared in the hardening of opinion in England, the increasing tendency in some circles to idealize the constitution exactly as it was, that took place in the course of disputes with the American colonies.

Various modern authorities agree that the separation of powers was in fact the chief characteristic of the British eighteenth-century constitution, as Delolme and others maintained.[7] Parliament after 1689 was

[6] *Constitution de l'Angleterre* (Amsterdam, 1771), 263-65. This edition, the Amsterdam edition of 1774, and the first English edition of 1775 are all dedicated to the radical Earl of Abingdon, who had visited Geneva in the 1760's and been associated there with Delolme and the Genevese democrats. The later editions are dedicated to George III. On Abingdon see below, p. 180.

[7] For the workings of British government at this time I follow W. S. Holdsworth, *History of English Law* (13 vols., London, 1922-1952), x; R. Pares, *King George III and the Politicians* (Oxford, 1953); G. H. Guttridge, *English Whiggism and the American Revolution: University of California Publications in History*, xxviii (Berkeley, 1942); C. R. Ritcheson, *British Politics and the American Revolution* (Norman, 1954).

no longer subordinate to the King; but neither, until after 1832, was it subordinate to an electorate; nor was the King, or were his ministers, subordinate to the Parliament. Given a real separation of equally indispensable elements, the problem of government was to make them act together. It was the King's responsibility to keep the government going; he could lawfully appoint any combination of men that he chose to carry his government on; the only restriction on him was a practical one, that the persons so appointed must not be sufficiently distasteful to a sufficient number of persons in the Lords and Commons to make those bodies refuse money or legislation. The House of Lords was usually more amenable to the wishes of government, for various reasons: the bishops were government appointees; a few peers might still feel gratitude for a recent elevation; others hoped for promotion in the peerage, and still others for appointment as gentlemen of the Bedchamber, which gave personal access to the court and to the King. The House of Commons was socially continuous so to speak, with the Lords. In the Parliament of 1761, that is, the first Parliament to have serious trouble with America, over half the members of the House of Commons were related to baronets or peers, and three-quarters had had ancestors in the House. Lord North was the son of a peer; George Grenville and Charles Townshend were brothers of peers; others were the close associates of peers, not to say dependents, like Edmund Burke, who over a period of fifteen years received some £30,000 from the Marquis of Rockingham. As a house, however, the Commons was perhaps a bit stronger than the Lords, not because it was more representative of the country, but because it had more control over the grant of funds, and because, since its members did not often aspire to earldoms or to the Bedchamber, it had less to lose by obstinacy or opposition.

There were no parties in any definite or inclusive sense. The terms Whig and Tory had ceased to have much meaning. Groups of individuals might profess to act together in politics as "friends," but they were easily dissolved. Most members of Parliament thought of themselves as belonging to no particular following, and disapproved of the efforts of "friends" to stand or fall together in bargaining with the King for office. Cabinets did not assume or leave office as a body; ministers came and went as individuals. There was no antithesis, real or formal, between Government and Opposition. Habitual opposition was frowned upon, as in most human organizations outside the stylized limits of the modern democratic state. Most members of Parliament thought it their normal duty to lend support to the administration.

On the other hand, they expected something in return. Government was a business of the political class; and, as Professor Pares has said, there were really two political classes, a small active class within a larger passive one. The larger and more passive class included those who wanted offices, pensions, honors, status, and income, for themselves, their sons, their dependents, or their "friends," or men who had local influence in the counties, or who owned or controlled a few borough seats in return for which they expected favors. Emoluments of government, as Professor Pares puts it, played much the same part for these people as life insurance, retirement plans, or educating one's children for a profession in our own time; they were a means of securing family status. The smaller and active class, within the larger, consisted of men who had a real interest in the operation of government, who enjoyed the work, and made a career of dealing with real administrative and political problems. From this class came many ministers and most permanent public servants. For ministers, the problem was to be agreeable to the King while also satisfying a sufficient number of the passive political class. The King was the one man in the system who could not resign, or retire to his country estate. Obliged somehow always to carry on, he had to work through ministers acceptable to the two Houses, or provide them with means by which majorities in the two Houses could be obtained.

The methods by which King and ministry secured a Parliament that would work with them were summed up in the word "influence." It was this "influence" that made possible the effective functioning of government under a constitution characterized by separation of powers.[8] Influence meant primarily patronage, the award of honors, titles, promotions, pensions, and sinecures, as well as functioning offices in the church, the armed forces, the colonial administration, and the home government. By the distribution of such favors among borough owners and others in a position to determine elections, the government was usually able to get a sufficiency of cooperative knights and burgesses sent up to the House of Commons. By promise of similar favors to sitting members of both Houses, or threat of their termination, the government was usually able to get the votes without which it could not proceed. Since the matter was essential, it was very systematically handled. There are, for example, in the papers of John Robinson, the political manager for Lord North and George III, certain lists drawn

[8] W. S. Holdsworth, "The Conventions of the 18th Century Constitution," in *Iowa Law Review*, XVIII, 2 (1932), 161-80.

up in preparation for the election of 1774, showing all offices "tenable with seats in Lords and Commons."[9] It is a curious array of appointments of all kinds, honorific and remunerative, nominal and real: thirteen lords and eleven grooms of the Bedchamber, the Master of the Jewel Office, the Clerk of the Venison Warrants, Admirals and Captains of the Navy, the Master of the Hanaper, three Secretaries of State, the Secretary at War, thirty-three Governors of garrisons, the Commander-in-Chief in Great Britain, the Attorney General, the Constable of the Tower, the Lord Lieutenant of Ireland, the Clerk of the Pells, and so on in great numbers. The exchange of their political influence, or of their votes, in return for these emoluments was, of course, entirely agreeable to the political class. Indeed, it was virtually the essence of political life, except when some overwhelming crisis within the state divided men on matters of policy. There was no such crisis sufficiently momentous until the trouble with America was far advanced. Even then, under the political conditions of the day, no clear alignment was possible.

The first two Georges had let matters get somewhat out of their own hands. Certain families and "connections," rallying around the great Whig dukes—Newcastle, Bedford, Devonshire, Portland, and others— had conducted the King's government and dispensed the royal favors pretty much in their own way. When the young George III became King in 1760, he was the first native-born male sovereign of England since the Revolution. Serious, virtuous, and methodical, he was resolved to do better than his grandfather and predecessors as King—to carry in reality the responsibilities of King of Great Britain which were imposed upon him by the law.

Of George III, as of many men, it must be said that he did not intend everything that he did. It is doubtful if he had a farseeing plan of action. In effect, however, he came into collision with the Whig magnates who had long had the management of affairs. As in other countries, it was the aristocracy that set itself most firmly against the personal exercise of royal power.

George at first gave his confidence to the Scottish Earl of Bute, making him virtually his chief minister, though Bute was a member of neither Lords nor Commons. Though not illegal, this naturally antagonized the parliamentary politicians. To free himself from tutelage

---

[9] W. T. Laprade, *Parliamentary Papers of John Robinson: Camden Society, 3rd series, vol. 33* (London, 1922). See also the lists of proposed appointments in J. Fortescue, *Correspondence of King George III* (London, 1927), I, 124-55.

to his grandfather's advisers he soon brought about the resignations of the Duke of Newcastle and William Pitt. Newcastle represented the Big Whig family system; Pitt, so far as he represented anything (he had first entered Parliament via Old Sarum, the inherited family seat) was a kind of heroic personality in which much national sentiment saw itself embodied. Since Newcastle stayed in office for a time after Pitt was forced out, they could subsequently feel no solidarity with each other; the differences between Pittite Whigs and Old Whigs (soon to be called Rockingham Whigs) were in the following years to become apparent many times. Meanwhile, George III and Bute made peace with France, on terms which many Whigs and patriots thought insufficiently advantageous to Great Britain. Thus various elements were disgruntled at the beginning of the reign.

In his clash with the Whig aristocracy, and laying low of the old parliamentary leadership, the King followed in a way the pattern of enlightened monarchy on the Continent. There is a resemblance between his activities and those of Louis XV, who at the same time was opposing the French parlements and their *union des classes*, or of Maria Theresa, who was resisting and even trying to dispense with the Hungarian and Bohemian diets, or of Gustavus III, who was soon to humble the nobility of Sweden. And, indeed, many of the policies personally favored by George III were "enlightened" enough. The Octennial Act of 1768 for Ireland, the India Regulating Act of 1773, the Quebec Act of 1774, the attempts begun in 1764 to get rid of abuses in the American customs revenue, even the Stamp Act, could be abundantly justified by principles of enlightened government of the day. But in reality George III was no enlightened despot. If (to suppose the unthinkable) he had sought to loosen the control of the universities by the Church of England, or if he had sought to modernize the land tax, still levied on the land values of 1692, he would have acted as many ministers of the continental monarchs were acting at the time. He had, of course, no such intention. He would try to take control from the magnates, but trouble with the church or the landowners was far from his thoughts.

For George III was himself a Whig. He, too, gloried in the Glorious Revolution. He, too, was awed by the British constitution; he would simply restore that balance of King, Lords, and Commons which all experts declared to be its essence. He, too, would uphold Parliament against all who questioned its rights. He would, however, himself supervise the use of that influence by which Parliament was kept in step with executive programs, and which the Duke of Newcastle had so adeptly managed before him. He antagonized important groups in the parliamentary leadership, and that was enough to produce a crisis. But he did not antagonize Parliament itself; the back-benchers mostly supported him, content to be called friends of the King rather than friends of this or that private leader. In the years that followed, the King had a parliamentary majority, nor was it due solely to influence. King and Parliament stood together. The consequences were not happy, for some of their policies provoked opposition, and the bond between them, the trading in pensions and offices, was open to serious reprehension. There were men in both Britain and America who came to distrust both King and Parliament.

The First American Crisis: The Stamp Act

The expense of the Seven Years' War, and heavy indebtedness which it created for the belligerent governments, led ministers in various countries to seek untapped sources of revenue. Old tax structures, favorable to the taxpayers, existed in many places, fortified by what amounted to class privileges, as in France, or by the autonomy and regional liberty of particular provinces. In the attempt to increase revenue governments were led to call such privileges and liberties into question. Financial pressure brought pressure for constitutional change. Louis XV abolished the French parlements, in part because they stood in the way of increased taxation; his ministers then proceeded to bring assessed land values up to date, and so to raise the yield of the *vingtième*. Maria Theresa began to restrain the autonomous bodies of Lombardy. Having come "to know people" in her financial disputes with the Hungarian diet of 1764, she went on to rule without summoning the diet at all.

The problem of the British government was not dissimilar. The national debt had risen from £75,000,000 to £147,000,000 because of the war. British subjects in America paid less in taxes than in Britain. They enjoyed regional or provincial privileges in this respect, confirmed by charters or by history or by custom, somewhat like Brittany and Hungary within the Bourbon and Hapsburg empires. It seemed reasonable to King George, to Parliament, and to the Chancellor of the Exchequer, George Grenville, to distribute the tax burden by tapping sources of wealth hitherto largely exempted. There were some, like Governor Bernard of Massachusetts, who thought that a general governmental reorganization in America should precede the raising of direct taxes. Grenville decided to avoid so rash a course, and to levy a stamp tax at once; but in America as elsewhere fiscal innovation led irresistibly to constitutional innovation. The British government, to put through its fiscal and accompanying policies, had increasingly to tamper with long-recognized American customs: to suspend an assembly in New York, to strengthen courts which were not courts of common law, and in 1774 to reconstruct the whole government of Massachusetts.

Since the outburst in America began as a movement to resist taxes, it is well to attempt a comparative view of tax burdens in the Western world at the time. Writers give the most diverse impressions on this subject. Some American historians, in the effort to be impartial, allow that the British were groaning under enormous levies. Others think the Americans already paid a good share (sometimes neglecting to observe that the British treasury reimbursed Americans for their outlays during the Seven Years' War); one says, not very convincingly, that the citizens of Boston, in 1760, were paying thirteen and a half shillings in the pound. Some English writers affirm that the land tax in the eighteenth century was very heavy; others, that landowners systematically evaded paying a fair share. Contemporaries in all countries uniformly averred that they could pay no more.

It is hazardous to offer figures. High per-capita rates of taxation may reflect entirely opposite situations: either that a people is oppressively taxed, or that it is more wealthy than others. Low taxes, contrariwise, suggest either that a people is fortunate, or that it is poor. To compare the currencies of different countries is always uncertain, though perhaps less so for the eighteenth century than for the twentieth. For some countries in the eighteenth century the size of the population is so debatable as to introduce an important variable into per-capita computations. Available figures are usually for the income of central governments; one never knows what costs of local government the taxpayer paid in addition, or what other costs of government, in the form of fees or licenses, may be omitted. It may be remarked, however, that the income of central governments went mostly to pay for war and the debts due to war; and, as it dwarfed all civil expenses of central government, it probably dwarfed the expenses of local government also, much of which was carried on by unpaid officials. With due regard for all difficulties, I offer the following view of the probable tax burden per head in English shillings, in various countries about the time of the American Revolution. Figures are included for component parts of the British, French, and Hapsburg political systems, the difference of rates suggesting in part regional differences of wealth, and in part the effects of regional privilege.

APPROXIMATE ANNUAL TAX BURDEN PER HEAD
IN ENGLISH SHILLINGS[10]

	About 1765	About 1785
United Provinces		35
Great Britain	26	34
Ireland	6s 8d	10
Massachusetts	1	18
Connecticut		7d
New York		8d
Pennsylvania	1	
Maryland	1	
Virginia		5d 10
France		21
Highest Generalities		
Paris		56
Rouen		31
Lyon		25
Lowest Generalities		
Strasbourg		12
Besançon		12
Perpignan		12
Rennes		10
Austrian Monarchy		12
Austria proper		21
Bohemia-Moravia		14
Hungary proper		12
Transylvania		7
Lombardy		5
Austrian Netherlands		3s 6d
Spain		10
Sweden		9
Russia		6
Prussia		6
Poland		1

[10] The figures for 1785 are derived from E. A. W. Zimmermann, *Political Survey of the Present State of Europe in Sixteen Tables* (Dublin, 1788), except that the figures for France are from J. Necker, *De l'administration des finances*, 1784, I, 306, and that those for Massachusetts and Virginia are computed from M. Jensen, *The New Nation: a History of the United States during the Confederation, 1781-1789* (N.Y., 1950), 305 and 308. For Great Britain P. Pebrer, *Taxation, Revenue, Expenditure, Power, Statistics and Debt of the Whole British Empire* (London, 1833), 153, gives a revenue of £9,300,000 for 1765 and £14,870,000 for 1785; this has been divided by an estimated population of seven millions in 1765 and nine millions in 1785 for England, Wales, and Scotland; the resulting figure for 1785 corresponds to that given by Zimmermann. For Ireland about 1765 see G. O'Brien, *Economic History of Ireland in the 18th Century* (Dublin, 1918), 313. For the American provinces in the 1760's, see L. Gipson, *Coming of the Revolution*, 134, 136, 146; the estimates of Adam Smith

It will be seen that in the three great political systems it was the peripheral provinces, those most recently or loosely attached, and enjoying corporate liberties of their own, that paid the lowest rates. Belgians and Lombards were financially privileged within the Austrian system; Hungary and Bohemia paid less than Austria. Brittany, the Free County of Burgundy, Alsace, and Roussillon, all of which had strong provincial identity, and of which the first two possessed active Provincial Estates, were likewise favored in France. The American colonies paid no direct taxes, and not much in the way of customs duties, to the central government. The figures for America refer to money raised and spent within the several provinces. The British Americans enjoyed a lighter tax burden than any people of the Western world except the Poles—and one knows what happened to Poland.

The British Americans were already a mature people in many respects. They gave birth to men of urbanity and polish, and even of great intellectual range. The seaboard cities were not without elegance, though scarcely as sophisticated as even secondary cities in Europe, such as Dublin or Lyons. The population in 1760 was probably more than a quarter of that of Great Britain, or more than the ratio of Canada to Great Britain in population today. The economy was not primitive; it is said that British America produced more iron than Great Britain, and thirty per cent of all ships in British commerce in 1775 were built in America. There was much political life in town meetings of New England and county courthouses of the south, and in the governors' councils and the colonial assemblies. The generation that carried out the Revolution and adopted the constitution of 1787 obviously possessed great political skill. Yet it must be admitted that the Americans had much to learn. In their habit of depending on Britain they were truly provincial. They had little notion of providing for their own defense; they recognized no problems of international relations with which it was incumbent on them to deal. In the matter of taxes they were, indeed, in the state of nature;

---

given by W. G. Sumner, *The Financier and Finances of the American Revolution* (N.Y., 1892), 25, which are close to the estimates of T. Pownall, *Administration of the Colonies* (ed. 1774), 1, 162-64; see also C. J. Bullock, *Finances of the United States from 1775 to 1789* (Madison, 1895), 152. In the 1780's the federal government of the United States seems to have received somewhat less than one shilling per head of the population; see Bullock, *op.cit.*, 162-64. The British government before the Revolution, according to an estimate of R. H. Lee in 1774, received £80,000 from the American colonies in customs revenues, or about 8 d. per head of population; Sumner, *op.cit.*, 15. The increased tax burden within the American states between 1765 and 1785 was due to the war and the debt.

as late as 1778 the Continental Congress wrote to Franklin, then in Paris, that since the Americans had never been much taxed before the Revolution it would be madness to tax them now, so that the war with Britain made it urgent to obtain a loan from France. One suspects that "no taxation without representation" meant no taxation with representation, either; even Thomas Paine, in 1780, thought the Americans should pay more taxes.

As for the British, they paid, along with the Dutch, the highest taxes in proportion to population of all the peoples of Europe. The high rates signify the greater wealth of England and Holland; no comparative estimates of the proportion of public revenues to national income can be formed. The main direct tax in Britain was the land tax. Like the French *vingtième*, which it somewhat resembled, it had originated in the wars between Britain and Louis XIV, and had at first been intended as a tax on all forms of income, but had become a tax on rental from land. It was reckoned in terms of shillings per pound of income, and was levied at a rate of two or three shillings in peacetime, or four shillings in time of war. Income from land was substantially rising in this age of improving landlords, but the strength of the landed class in Parliament was strong enough to prevent any disclosure of actual income, so that landed income was assumed to be the same as in 1692. This arrangement, made soon after the Revolution, marked "the final surrender of the seventeenth-century attempt at an equitably distributed direct tax."[11] The attempt still made in the continental monarchies to bring land valuations up to date, an attempt which French parlements and other such bodies always resisted, was no longer made in England. Each shilling of land tax simply meant a flat sum of about £500,000 for the government. It was estimated in the mid-century that reassessment would have doubled the yield; that a landowner paying a four-shilling tax, and hence nominally a fifth of his income, actually paid a tenth or a twelfth. The land tax at the close of the Seven Years' War produced between a fifth and a quarter of the government's revenue. The remainder came from the customs, the excise, and the stamp tax. The stamp tax

[11] William Kennedy, *English Taxation, 1640-1799* (London, 1913), 46. See also W. R. Ward, *The English Land Tax in the 18th Century* (London, 1953), and S. Dowell, *A History of Taxation and Taxes in England from the Earliest Times* (London, 1888), III, 81-86. For the *vingtième* see the article under that heading in M. Marion, *Dictionnaire des institutions de la France aux 17ᵉ et 18ᵉ siècles* (Paris, 1923), which condenses Marion's larger writings on the subject. It is a curious fact that in 1789 the two *vingtièmes* produced 11 per cent of French government revenues; the land tax, at four shillings, about 12 per cent of British government revenues.

was relatively light, producing £281,914 in 1765, or about three per cent of government income. It was readily expansible, however; by 1790 its yield rose to £1,214,969, or almost eight per cent of government income. The trend was toward greater dependence on stamps and indirect taxes. By 1790 the four-shilling land tax was yielding only an eighth of the public revenues, though it must be noted that new taxes on windows, servants, and luxuries were aimed mainly at the well-to-do.[12]

George Grenville, sponsored by Bute and the King, becoming chief minister in April 1763, set to work to solve the problems left by the war. He devised a plan for orderly occupation of the American West, newly conquered from France, and where Pontiac's rebellion was at that very moment showing the magnitude of the Indian problem. That the colonial governments did next to nothing about this Indian uprising, which was suppressed by the British army, only emphasized the need for general and long-range planning. Grenville proposed to keep British regular troops permanently in America, to prohibit westward movement of settlers until further notice, and to acquire land titles from the Indians by peaceable and gradual negotiations. For these purposes he thought that the necessary funds might be raised in America, and so obtained enactment of the Revenue Act of 1764, and decided also to apply in America the stamp tax already familiar in England. He hoped that it would yield about £100,000, all proceeds to be spent in the colonies. It would amount to about one shilling per person per year of taxation, which seemed little enough in England, but which, the reader can see, would more than double the tax load then borne by the bucolic Americans.

Grenville spent over a year in cautious enquiries before the passage of the Stamp Act. He consulted with the colonial agents in London, and asked them to propose alternative means of raising revenue in America. He had, however, little faith that the colonial assemblies would ever provide a dependable and steady revenue for such purposes on their own initiative; he undoubtedly preferred to keep the whole matter under parliamentary control. He was assured by Chief Justice Mansfield that parliamentary taxation of British subjects in America was unquestionably legal. Enough time passed in these preparations for warnings and protests to pour across the Atlantic. Grenville decided to disregard them, considering them, not unreasonably, to be

[12] For varying amounts of the stamp tax, excise, etc., from year to year see Pebrer, op.cit., 152.

the usual complaints made by all people against new taxation. In fact, the American resistance to the Revenue Act of 1764 was already irking the British. There was already in England, even before the Stamp Act, a growing feeling that the colonists were an irresponsible people who must be brought under effectual government—that they must be made to realize the existence of central authority in the empire.[13]

The Stamp Act passed in March 1765. There was no opposition to it in Parliament. None of the later Whig friends of America spoke against it. It was assumed to be an equitable measure, which the Americans would get used to in time.

The fury of the American reaction suggests that at bottom more than money or taxation was involved. The British had entirely underestimated the strength of American feeling. They had exaggerated the degree of Anglo-American unity felt in America. From the beginning the real issue in the eyes of Americans was not the tax—granted that they disliked all taxes—but the authority by which the tax was levied. "A Parliament of Great Britain," declared John Adams in 1765, "can have no more right to tax the colonies than a Parliament of Paris."[14]

Since the Restoration, and since the Revolution of 1689, England and its colonies, particularly those in New England, had diverged more widely than they seem to have realized. Not that the colonists of English descent denied being English; they took pride in their origins. But they felt no particular sympathy for the forces that had triumphed in English life since 1660, notably the aristocratic and Anglican governing class; nor did what they knew of the realities of parliamentary politics inspire them with much confidence. On one point the truculent young John Adams and the moderate Virginia gentleman, Richard Bland, were agreed: that they enjoyed the English constitution in greater purity in America than did the English in England. And if so, asked Adams, whose fault was it?[15]

Already, in the minds of some, a sense of American distinctiveness was well developed. This was most especially true of New England,

[13] The growth of conservatism in Britain before and during the American Revolution, and in answer to the American demands, is one of the main themes of C. R. Ritcheson, *British Politics and the American Revolution* (Norman, 1954); the belief that the American and British positions of 1775-1776 were already taken in 1765 is one of the main themes of E. S. and H. M. Morgan, *The Stamp Act Crisis* (Chapel Hill, 1953).
[14] Quoted by Morgan, *op.cit.*, 140.
[15] J. Adams, *Novanglus*, 1774, in *Works* (1851), IV, 117; R. Bland, *Inquiry into the Rights of the British Colonies*, 1766, quoted by C. Rossiter, *Seedtime of the Republic* (N.Y., 1953), 273-74.

which was more acutely conscious of its own history than the other colonies, and where there was a kind of folk memory of having fled from England long ago, the better to establish a good life in a new world. This now seemed to be threatened. "Will they never let us rest in peace? . . . Is it not enough that they persecuted us out of the old world? . . . What other world remains as a sanctuary? . . ."[16] The words were written in 1763 on a different subject, but they suggest the emotions on which the Stamp Act grated. John Adams' *Dissertation on the Feudal and Canon Law,* written in 1765, just before the Stamp Act, contains a theory of the meaning of America already fully worked out: "I always consider the settlement of America with reverence and wonder, as the opening of a grand scene and design of Providence for the illumination of the ignorant, and the emancipation of the slavish part of mankind all over the earth." In Virginia the feeling was less exalted. Important Virginians did not think of their forefathers as humble or impoverished fugitives, destined to save the world; they saw them rather as gentlemen of means who had emigrated voluntarily at their own expense, but who, on setting up in America, brought all English liberties with them, including an assembly which in its own sphere was the equal of Parliament. According to a recent study of this elusive subject, during the arguments over the Stamp Act the peculiarly New England view of American origins spread to the colonies as a whole, entering deeply into the formation of American nationality. Forced to reflect upon themselves, the Americans developed a "legend of the Founding Fathers," or belief that from the very beginning America had been the refuge of political liberty. But enough such feeling already existed, in 1765, to produce an immediate, concerted, and excited resistance to the Stamp Act.

At any event, most politically conscious Americans, in all the colonies, from the moment the implications were clearly presented to them, agreed in seeing no authority in England above them except the King himself; and if Americans were still stoutly loyal in a legal sense, it may be strongly suspected (since the same was true of England in the early Hanoverian era) that they were lacking in true royalist warmth. All the arguments aimed at the British—that Parliament could levy external but not internal taxes in America, that it could levy external taxes for trade regulation, but not for revenue,

---

[16] Quoted by W. F. Craven, *The Legend of the Founding Fathers* (N.Y., 1956), 22, to which I am indebted for this whole paragraph. See also C. Rossiter, *Seedtime of the Republic* (N.Y., 1953).

etc.—were in the nature of rationalizations; the Americans really did not wish to be actually governed by the British Parliament at all, though they naturally were a little slow in saying so plainly.[17] On this there may have been more unanimity in 1765 than on any subsequent question, including independence when it came, by which time much violence had occurred, and conservatism had had a chance to form.

Resistance to the Stamp Act began in Virginia, where the house of burgesses forwarded a protest to England in May 1765, and at Boston, where in June the house of representatives, by a circular letter to the other colonial assemblies, invited them to send some of their members to a general meeting at New York, at which a common front might be presented to Parliament. During the summer staid Boston saw unedifying scenes, which were in fact revolutionary in character. A group of men of the shopkeeping and artisan class, calling themselves first the Loyal Nine and then the Sons of Liberty, and maintaining a discreet contact with prominent merchants and with a few members of the assembly (including John Adams on at least one occasion) served as intermediaries between upper and lower classes in the city. They persuaded certain rougher elements, which had staged a kind of gang warfare on the preceding Guy Fawkes day, that the Stamp Act was a threat to their liberties, and that their physical energies might find a worthier and more patriotic outlet. Someone made an effigy of Andrew Oliver, who was to be distributor of stamps under the Act, and hung it on a tree. A mob seized the effigy, paraded it about, and beheaded it. Another mob broke into the vice-admiralty court, one of the courts involved in Grenville's general reorganization, and authorized to enforce the Stamp Act. The court records were destroyed. When Thomas Hutchinson, a Bostonian of old family, who was Chief Justice and Lieutenant Governor, tried to stop these depredations, the mobs attacked his house, a new mansion in the Georgian style, systematically wrecked it, broke up the furniture, cut down the trees, and stole £900 in cash. In the face of these disturbances, and lesser ones elsewhere, the stamp distributors throughout the colonies were intimidated into resigning. The Stamp Act Congress met in New York, in more or less open defiance of the colonial governors, with these commotions ringing in their ears. Nine colonies had sent delegates, of whom the most vehement were the most influential. "It's

[17] The Morgans, *op.cit.*, 114-15, "A Note on Internal and External Taxes," argue that the Americans never made any such distinction in the admissibility of taxes levied by Parliament.

to be feared," reported General Gage, "that the Spirit of Democracy is strong amongst them."[18] By this he meant the inclination to question the governing authority of Parliament, and not merely its wisdom.

The Congress drew up a declaration. It professed "all due subordination" to Parliament. It claimed as a right of Englishmen to be taxed only by their own representatives, but observed that the colonies could not possibly be represented in the House of Commons. For the "people of Great Britain" (that is, Parliament) to vote away the property of the colonists violated the "Spirit of the British constitution." The Congress, therefore, petitioned for repeal of the Stamp Act, and for removal of the vice-admiralty courts.

Preparations were soon made to reinforce words with action. Local meetings in many places issued local manifestoes, but the first move toward concerted physical resistance took place at New London, Connecticut. There the town meeting had already furbished up the philosophy needed to undercut positive law. It asserted that a people had a right to set limits to government, and, when necessary, "to reassume their natural Rights and the Authority the Laws of Nature and of God have vested them with." On Christmas 1765 two delegates of the New York Sons of Liberty met with the Connecticut Sons of Liberty in a New London tavern. They bound themselves "to march with the utmost dispatch," if either group were endangered, and to bring about a "like association with all the colonies on the continent." The movement spread; "there can be no doubt that the colonists were getting ready to fight the British Army."[19] And the British government, having heard of the Boston riots, instructed the American governors to apply for military aid if necessary to enforce the Act.

Revolution seemed imminent in America. Force was assembling, and the doctrines had been declared. So far, to use the language of preceding chapters, it seemed a conflict between constituted bodies—between the legislative assemblies in America and the Parliament of Great Britain. Governor Bernard defined the issue as early as November 1765: "In Britain," he wrote to Lord Barrington, the Secretary for War, "the American governments are considered as Corporations empowered to make by-laws, existing only during the pleasure of Parliament. . . . In America they claim . . . to be perfect States, not otherwise dependent on Great Britain than by having the same King."[20] This remained the constitutional issue for the next eleven years.

---

[18] Morgan, *op.cit.*, 105. The Resolution of the Stamp Act Congress is printed here.
[19] *Ibid.*, 201-03.
[20] Ritcheson, *op.cit.*, 43.

The home government, with the Stamp Act nullified, its authority flouted, and its stamp distributors terrorized into resignation, now faced difficulties in England also. The Americans were reducing their commercial orders, and postponing payment of debts to British merchants, so that a trade crisis developed. The King replaced Grenville with the Marquis of Rockingham as chief minister. Rockingham led the "old" or formerly Newcastle Whigs, the most aristocratic of the Whig factions. Pitt refused to take office with Rockingham, whose government was therefore weak, depending on the "King's friends" for majorities in Parliament. The Rockingham group had seen nothing improper in the Stamp Act. They even called the Virginia resolutions "a daring attack on the constitution of this country."[21] As events unfolded, however, they were willing enough to use the American crisis to discredit the previous administration. In any case they had to take action. The choice finally coming to lie between military enforcement and repeal, the Rockingham group decided for repeal, purely on grounds of expediency, with no concession on the constitutional issue. Since the King and his friends were not yet persuaded that capitulation was wise, and since Pitt, and the friends of Pitt, already thought the Parliament should not even claim the right to levy an internal tax in America, the Rockingham group, though constituting the government, had only feeble support in the two houses. It therefore took the bold step of going "out of doors" to solicit expressions of public opinion. Rockingham's spokesmen talked with merchants all over the country. Soon petitions from merchants in Bristol, Liverpool, Glasgow, Leeds, and other towns flowed in. On the one hand Rockingham's new secretary, Edmund Burke, in his maiden speech in Parliament, upheld the supremacy of Parliament in all matters over all British subjects. On the other, the merchants, the marquis, and Burke himself held that Parliament should repeal the Stamp Act purely as a matter of practical politics. The King finally instructed those who considered themselves his friends to vote for repeal, and the Stamp Act was repealed in March 1766.

At the same time, to prevent misunderstanding in America, and to satisfy those in England who predicted dire consequences from such softness in the face of rebellion, the Rockingham Whigs and and King and his friends were in entire agreement on a further statement of law. It took the form of the Declaratory Act, modelled on

---

[21] *Ibid.*, 41.

the Declaratory Act enunciated for Ireland in 1719.[22] It may be compared also to the announcement of the King of France in the *séance de la flagellation* in Paris. The French King emphatically affirmed his sovereignty over the Parlement of Paris on March 3, 1766. The Declaratory Act, two weeks later, affirmed the sovereignty of the King-in-Parliament over the people and the assemblies of the American colonies.

The act announced that "the King's Majesty, by and with the advice and consent of the Lords Spiritual and Temporal, and of the Commons, had, hath and of Right ought to have full power and authority to make Laws and Statutes of sufficient force and validity to bind the colonies and people of America, subjects of the Crown of Great Britain, in all cases whatsoever."

Tribulations of Parliament, 1766-1774

The trouble with America turned on the question of the authority of Parliament. Anything in England, therefore, that brought the authority of Parliament under critical examination, or which cast discredit upon it, added strength to the American opposition. Contrariwise, Parliament laid itself more open to criticism in England by becoming embroiled with America.

There were beginning to be people in England who thought that Parliament did not really represent them. At the same time, George III's increasing personal influence—what was called "corruption," though the King was only doing for himself what the politicians had formerly done in his name—tended to dim the lustre of the great Areopagus. "The public does think we are a corrupt body," as Burke told the House of Commons in 1771.[23] Moreover, there were stirrings in Ireland, which also had its grievances against the British Parliament. Ireland was often cited in discussion of the American problem. Irish developments had a more than Irish significance.

When one speaks of Ireland at this time it is the Anglo-Irish who are meant.[24] They were colonists in a way, Protestant descendants of

[22] For the American Declaratory Act see the statutes 6 George III c. 12; for the Irish, 6 George I c. 65.

[23] "Speech on the Motion Made in the House of Commons, February 7, 1771, Relative to the Middlesex Election," *Writings* (Boston, 1901), VII, 62.

[24] For Ireland at this time see R. B. McDowell, *Irish Public Opinion, 1750-1800* (London, 1943), 9-51; M. Kraus, "America and the Irish Revolutionary Movement in the 18th Century," in R. B. Morris, ed., *The Era of the American Revolution* (N.Y., 1939); G. O'Brien, *Economic History of Ireland in the 18th Century* (Dublin and London, 1918); E. Curtis, *History of Ireland* (London, 1936).

the English and Scotch who had occupied Ireland in the seventeenth century, and who now constituted about a fifth of the population. Although in 1756 there was formed a Catholic Committee which later became important, the notable thing about the Catholic and native Irish in the mid-century was their silence. The Anglo-Irish in part governed and in part ignored the indigenous population. They enjoyed a certain autonomy with respect to Great Britain, so that in a formal constitutional sense Anglo-Ireland offered a model which many in England, after the repeal of the Stamp Act, thought might be suitable for America. The Irish Parliament has been briefly described in Chapter II. It was scarcely representative even of the Anglo-Irish. But it levied the Irish taxes, and it passed laws for Ireland, subject to control by the government at Westminster. It maintained 12,000 soldiers of the British army in Ireland at Irish expense; there were also certain pensions and sinecures defrayed from the Irish revenue, but available for enjoyment in England. Ireland recognized the right of the British Parliament to regulate external trade. Anglo-Irish discontent matured slowly, and flared up only when encouraged by the American Revolution. In some ways, however, it preceded that of either England or America. In Charles Lucas the Irish had "a Wilkes before Wilkes." In Molyneux they had a writer who as long ago as 1698 had contended for the equality of the Irish Parliament with the British, as Americans in the 1760's came to do for their own assemblies. They had had their Declaratory Act in 1719. By mid-century they were beginning to chafe at the trade regulations, which were, for Ireland, very severe. Designed to protect English manufacturers, the regulations permitted the export of Irish linens, but forbade any export of woolens, glass, and a number of other items from Ireland, or the levy of import taxes on English goods.

An Anglo-Irish "colonial nationalism," as Irish historians call it, thus accompanied the rise of an American colonial nationalism in the 1760's. As in America, the defeat of the French brought it to the surface. After 1763 the Anglo-Irish no longer had to fear French invasion, or the mass rising of the native Irish in collaboration with French invaders. Anglo-Irish demands for reform were increasingly heard. Anglo-Irish and Americans were conscious of common interests; the Americans read Molyneux and Lucas, and Irishmen told one another in their Parliament that the "cause of America is yours." With thousands of Presbyterian Irish emigrating to America every year, a larger proportion of the Protestant Irish than of the English had friends and relatives in America at this time.

The Lord Lieutenant sent over in 1767, Viscount Townshend (brother of the Townshend of the "Townshend Acts"), was the first viceroy permanently to reside, or to be instructed by the British government to make concessions to reformers. Townshend, aided by Lucas and the reformers, put the Octennial Act through the Irish Parliament. It was a blow at the entrenched Anglo-Irish oligarchy, since it required election of the Irish Commons every eight years instead of only at the death of the sovereign. In return, Townshend got the size of the British army maintained by Ireland raised to 15,000 men, a measure to which the Irish reformers consented reluctantly, since it was provided that 3,000 of these might be freely sent out of Ireland, presumably, in 1767, for use in America. Further reforms, for the next few years, met with obstruction. A proposal to tax the properties of absentee landlords, of whom there were about a hundred in England, came to nothing. One of the chief Irish absentees was the Marquis of Rockingham, who like others of the higher aristocracy owned land in both islands. Burke advised against the proposal; he thought it a good thing for Ireland that its magnates, who understood Ireland and its needs, should reside abroad and have seats in the Parliament at Westminster.

Many Irish were of the opinion, in 1775 and 1776, that if the British subdued and taxed America they would begin to tax Ireland also. On the other hand, the example of Ireland does not suggest that, if the Americans had not resisted, their future under a triumphant British imperial system would have been very inspiring.

In England dissatisfaction was confused, because shared in by men with different aims. There were Whigs who, in their dislike for the King's way of doing things, meant to preserve the autonomy of Lords and Commons. And there were emerging "radicals," who believed that the House of Commons should be more dependent on the voters. By "radicals," a term not used until coined by the Benthamites much later, are meant those who thought Parliament should afford a more accurate representation of the people. They were "radical" because their basic theory of representation differed from that enshrined in the constitution, or said to be enshrined in it by conservatives. It is doubtful whether men of the thirteenth century would have agreed with all that conservatives said on the subject five hundred years later. Still, there was a difference between the surviving medieval and the emerging modern ideas of who or what should be represented; the older theory went in terms of estates or communities or corporate groups; the newer, in terms of individual subjects or persons.

Discontent centered about the figure of John Wilkes. A man of unsavory private habits, author of an "Essay on Woman" generally regarded as indecent, at least until recent times, Wilkes was able, like Mirabeau, to build his public personality on the espousal of liberal principles. He was no adventurer, but a member of Parliament in touch with Pitt and other Whigs displaced from office after the accession of George III. He founded a paper in 1762, the *North Briton*, to carry on a verbal assault on the new government. The arguments were sometimes not on a high level. Wilkes made good use of the fact that the Earl of Bute's family name was Stuart. In the *North Briton* No. 45, in April 1763, he denounced "ministerial despotism," "prostitution of the crown," and vague lurking dangers of Stuart restoration.[25] George III, personally offended, spurred on his willing ministers to suppress the *North Briton*. A general warrant, that is, one not specifying anyone by name, was issued for the arrest of the publishers. The courts in 1769 declared general warrants illegal, and awarded damages to Wilkes, thus demonstrating that the law did allow more freedom of political expression in England than in most parts of Europe. Wilkes meanwhile, expelled by the House of Commons, fled to France. He was hailed there as a defender of liberty by the Parlement of Paris in its struggle against the "ministerial despotism" of Louis XV. Handkerchiefs *à la Wilkes* were for a time *à la mode* in French parlementary circles.[26]

Returning to England in 1768, he was elected to the Commons by the county of Middlesex, the environs of the city of London. The Commons expelled him again. He was again elected by Middlesex; the Commons not only declared him disqualified, but gave the seat to his opponent, who had received fewer votes. Thus in this case the Commons assumed the power to determine its own membership. A man repudiated by the county of Middlesex sat for it in the Parliament.

Wilkes' followers in 1769 founded the society of the Supporters of the Bill of Rights, the earliest in a long series of societies organized to demand parliamentary reform. They also toured the country in a

---

[25] See G. Nobbe, *The North Briton: a Study in Political Propaganda* (N.Y., 1939), 172-83, 202-24.

[26] For the handkerchiefs see F. Acomb, *Anglophobia in France, 1763-89* (Durham, 1950), 32-33. They were linen handkerchiefs imported from England with a letter from Wilkes to his Middlesex constituents printed on them.

new kind of popular political campaign. Public meetings protested against the quashing of the will of the people of Middlesex. Some 60,000 signatures were gathered for petitions. It was a large number at a time when Arthur Young judged the entire electorate of all Britain to be no more than 250,000, and when Richard Price estimated that 5,723 persons chose half the members of the House of Commons.[27] Some constituencies sent instructions on the Middlesex affair to their members of Parliament, a procedure not yet thought to be quite constitutional. "Such is the levelling principle that has gone forth," cried one member of the House, "that the people imagine they themselves should be judges over us."[28] Or as one of Wilkes' more judicious biographers puts it, the principle was now widely publicized, "perhaps for the first time, that the sovereign power was vested, not in Parliament, but in the 'great public.' "[29]

Wilkes became the hero of London, and not of the rabble only. Great merchants warmly supported him, including William Beckford, with his £100,000 a year. In 1774 Wilkes was chosen for the by no means popular office of Lord Mayor. He and his followers won the right to have debates in Parliament published in the London newspapers. It is from about this time that we can really know what was said in the two chambers. From a kind of board of directors, meeting in private to manage the affairs of the country, Parliament thus took another step toward a more modern form, in which the "great public" could keep watch on it as on a body of deputies. Elected again to the Commons, and this time admitted, Wilkes in 1776 introduced the first reform bill in that body, the Duke of Richmond introducing one also in the Lords. It had no success. Ten years before, even the conservative Blackstone had thought that some decayed boroughs might be abolished. Delolme had said so in French in 1774, but not in English in 1775. In the face of a popular movement against Parliamentary supremacy, both at home and in America, and which in America in 1775 reached the point of armed defiance, the forces of conservative opposition gathered strength.

It could be argued that the only thing the matter with Parliament was that it was too much influenced by the King. There were more who would reform its integrity than its representativeness. There were

---

[27] Young's estimate is in his *Political Essays*, 1772, 34; Price's, in his *Observations on the Nature of Civil Liberty* (London, 1776), 11.

[28] Quoted in Pares, *George III and the Politicians*, 49.

[29] H. Bleackley, *Life of John Wilkes* (London, 1917), 409. See also R. Postgate, *That Devil Wilkes* (N.Y., 1929).

more who would free it from the insidious influence of ministers, and of the King, than who wanted to bring it under the influence of a body of voters. Hence demands were frequently heard for a Place Bill, or legislation to reduce the number of offices which members of Parliament might hold. There was discussion of a Triennial Act, to make it necessary to reelect the Commons every three years instead of every seven. Radicals even talked of annual parliaments. There were proposals to increase the number of county members, who were thought to be more independent, that is, less susceptible to "influence," than those of the boroughs, by whom they were outnumbered four to one.

Critics of Parliament in England made common cause with the leaders of American discontent. And in America, while the repeal of the Stamp Act allayed the crisis, it brought no peace. The Americans in their optimism underestimated the Declaratory Act as a mere statement of legal fiction. If anything, they seemed to gloat at having forced Parliament to back down. In England the country gentlemen wished to reduce the land-tax, which had never remained at four shillings in time of peace. The King himself did not favor a reduction (in this respect showing sentiments like his contemporaries, the "enlightened despots"), nor have modern students of taxation thought the four-shilling rate oppressive, given the difference between real and nominal landed income.[30] However this may be, to the consternation of the King and his new minister, Charles Townshend, the House of Commons demonstrated its vaunted independence, and, in a surprise vote, cut the tax to three shillings, thus depriving the government of some £500,000 of revenue. Whigs joined with the King's friends in this reduction of the land-tax. Townshend, having been given to understand that the Americans would accept "external" taxes from Parliament, thereupon readily obtained enactment of his famous tariff, which levied customs duties in America on importations of paint, glass, lead, and tea. The proceeds were to be spent in America, not primarily for military protection against the Indians, as in the the plan for the Stamp Act, but rather to pay the salaries of the colonial governors, judges, and a corps of royal officials. Since the Americans had until now voted money to pay the governors in their own assemblies, the leaders of discontent feared the loss of all means of pressure upon the colonial executives, if salaries were to come from duties auto-

[30] *Correspondence of George III*, I, 454; Dowell, *History of Taxation*, III, 86.

matically collected. The use made of appointive office in England and Ireland to influence members of legislatures was also known in America.

Again, the main disturbance was in Boston. The Boston town meeting began to put pressure on the provincial assembly. It even called a "convention" of all the Massachusetts towns, which the governor disbanded as an illegal body. The Massachusetts assembly issued a circular, as in 1765, this time drafted by Samuel Adams, inviting the assemblies of the other provinces to take joint action—a move denounced in England as favoring "unwarrantable combinations." Non-importation agreements were made up and down the coast, to force British merchants, as in 1765, to demand repeal of the new taxes. Duties could not be collected on goods not imported. The Townshend duties were in effect nullified, as the Stamp Act had been.

In 1770 the King made Lord North his Prime Minister. North repealed the duties, except the one on tea. The tea duty remained as a kind of second declaratory act, asserting the rights of Parliament over all subjects of the British crown.

The new outburst in America coincided with the agitation over the Middlesex election. John Wilkes was warmly admired in America, and there was a cordial exchange of letters between him and the Boston leaders. Others of the emerging group of radicals in England, that is, men who did not believe in the structure of the Commons as it then existed, men like Major John Cartwright and Richard Price, were equally American in their sympathies. They felt, as did the Americans, that Parliament did not represent them, or indeed did not represent anyone but itself.

But the zealots of the House of Commons, as Professor Pares has remarked, being uneasily aware of the peculiarities of the electoral system, were mortally afraid of any "association" that might claim to represent anyone better than they did.[31] Any concerted manifestation of public opinion, any assembly of persons claiming the power to speak for others, contained the threat of an "anti-Parliament." According to their reading of the British constitution the House of Commons represented the people; the people neither had nor needed any other voice or representation; and meetings that claimed any representative function, or identified themselves with the "people," were to be viewed with deep suspicion. Of such unseemly pretensions were the Stamp Act Congress, the convention of Massachusetts towns, the

[31] Pares, op.cit., 52.

"unwarrantable combinations" of the colonial assemblies, and the public meetings in England that supported Wilkes in the Middlesex election. Such were soon to be the American committees of correspondence,
the Continental Congress, the Irish Volunteers, and the Yorkshire Association. And the same haunting fear of an anti-Parliament was to
be aroused, in the time of the French Revolution, by the London Corresponding Society and the Edinburgh Convention.

Of these zealots of Parliament the principal ones were Edmund
Burke and the Rockingham Whigs. A great interest attaches to their
attitude in these controversies. It is understandable that George III
and the majority in Parliament should have tried to govern America,
and in particular to have tried to distribute the tax burden between
American and British subjects. It is understandable that the Americans
should have resisted. One can see why Ireland became restless, and
why Englishmen wished to reform the House of Commons. It was
only the Whigs, however, who were in a position to offer any alternative to the policies pursued by George III. Unfortunately, they had
no alternative to offer. Parliamentary supremacy was their distinctive
doctrine, the dogma handed down from 1689, the buckler of liberty,
and the barrier against despotism. The Americans in claiming to be
under the King but not under Parliament were in fact a species of
Tories, certainly more "Tory" than George III. Only the emerging
handful of radicals in England, and the handful of followers of Pitt,
who was beginning in some ways to agree with the radicals, believed
that Parliament should not even claim the right to tax the Americans.
The formula of the Rockingham Whigs for the Americans was that
Parliament should make clear its power to tax them, but, from expediency, refrain from using it. After North repealed the Townshend
duties, this was pretty much the formula of North and the King.

Burke's famous *Thoughts on the Cause of the Present Discontents*,
written in 1770, was the classic statement of Old Whiggery at the
moment. There was, according to Burke, a profound discontent abroad
in the land, nor was it caused by a "few puny libellers." It was a
true groundswell of opposition. "When popular discontents have been
very prevalent, it may well be affirmed and supported that there has
been something found amiss in the constitution or in the conduct of
government." And he added, like Rousseau: "The people have no interest in disorder. When they do wrong, it is their error, not their
crime." The error to which the people were liable was in failing to
see that the trouble lay with the King. It was not that the King threat-

ened Parliament itself, like the Stuarts in times gone by, but that he threatened parliamentary independence. "The power of the crown, almost dead and rotten as Prerogative, has grown up anew under the name of Influence." It was a popular error, too, to favor structural changes in the Parliament. To have more voters, or more frequent elections, said Burke, would make matters worse by creating new opportunities for corruption. Our government, remarked Burke, is in any case too complicated for us to know how to reform it. Parliament should remain as it is. But it should resist the crown and its ministers.

Burke presented the issue as a clash between a kind of equalitarian despotism on the one hand and a responsible and vigorous aristocracy on the other. The court faction, he declared, wished to get rid of all "intermediate and independent importance" (one is reminded of Montesquieu), to teach "a total indifference to the persons, rank, influence, abilities, connections and character of the ministers of the crown" (one is reminded of Saint-Simon). "Points of honor and precedence were no more to be regarded . . . than in a Turkish army. It was to be avowed, as a constitutional maxim, that the King might appoint one of his footmen, or one of your footmen, for minister." This was Burke's way of saying that George III would not call the great Whig peers into the government.

The true remedy, according to Burke, must be found in Parliament itself. It lay in a good, strong legitimate sense of party—that is, of party within parliamentary circles, and in particular the party of the Rockingham Whigs. If the people would feel confidence in these natural leaders, and if the Lords and Commons would cease to give their votes passively to the ministers, whoever they might be and whatever they might do, and instead would frankly form a party to criticize the actions of government, then the dignity and independence of Parliament would be preserved. Burke's doctrine of party was to be praised by later generations. At the time, his eloquence failed to move his colleagues in Parliament, most of whom continued to see in the Rockingham Whigs only a group of malcontents out of office, and to give their votes to Lord North and the King.

The Whigs of the Burke and Rockingham persuasion, aristocratic though they were in their principles, and inclined to keep all political discussion within the bounds of Parliament itself, did greatly contribute to the awakening of extra-parliamentary or public opinion. Unheeded within the two houses, they went out of doors, and offered themselves as the leaders of an indignant people, hoping that the "people" were indignant at the same mischief as the Whigs were. At bottom, they could agree neither with the British reformers nor with the Americans. But they had invited merchants to protest against the Stamp Act. They defended Wilkes in the affair of the Middlesex elections. They fanned the discontent in America; Burke himself acted as agent for New York, and had a long correspondence with the New York assembly, in which he gave them his expert advice on how and when to resist the government in Great Britain. By their harping on the sinister designs of the King, by their hints of a kind of ministerial conspiracy to pervert Parliament, they did more than any other group in England to inculcate in America a hatred for British practices of government, and to undermine in America that respect for Parliament which it was the great Whig principle to uphold. When the Whigs said that Parliament was the proper seat of sovereignty for the whole empire, the Americans paid little attention. When they said that Parliament was corrupt, the Americans took them at their word.[32]

The Second American Crisis: The Coercive Acts and the Continental Congress

It must be admitted that the British government had many interests to consider, which the Americans significantly dismissed as foreign. The British government, in its own way, tried to do something for the West India sugar planters, the American Indians, the French Canadians, and the British taxpayers. Its policies in America were in part shaped by these needs. The Americans recognized no such needs as proper determinants of policy in America. There had ceased to be, in Rousseau's phrase, any general will for the empire as a whole, by which the Americans would accept sacrifices in the interests of others with whom they felt common ties. In 1773 the government at Westminster decided to do something for the East India Company, which had been brought to the verge of bankruptcy by its political expansion in India, and whose activities the government was now trying to subordinate to parliamentary control. The company, having an excess supply of tea, was authorized to sell 10,000,000 pounds of it in America. Since the Americans, to nullify the Townshend tea duty, had to a large extent been using smuggled tea, or none at all, they

[32] The views of Pares, Guttridge, and Ritcheson coincide in this estimate of the Old Whig attitude to America, and of Burke as a spokesman for the British aristocracy; this estimate is, indeed, a well-established one, from which only "new conservatives" and other neo-Burkeans in the United States seem to diverge.

regarded this measure as a new device to impose taxation, and hence a revival of the dispute that had lain dormant for three years.

When the Boston men dumped the company's tea in the harbor the British government lost all patience. This new outrage seemed the latest act in almost ten years of political rowdyism. For years the firebrands at Boston had raised up mobs, mocked the courts and the governor, taken the lead in convening illegal assemblages. They had now gone too far. "All men seem now to feel," wrote the King, "that the fatal compliance in 1766 has encouraged the Americans annually to increase in their pretensions."[33] Never had King George been more in agreement with his people. Even British merchants now felt little sympathy for the Americans. They resented the losses due to American non-importation agreements, but had made them good by increase of sales to Europe. There was a widespread feeling in Britain that British policy had been proved mistaken since the repeal of the Stamp Act, that the time had come to show the Americans their place.

Boston was in truth in a disturbed state, and it was in truth a real problem to set up a government there in which law would be respected. One way would have been to refashion the government so as to obtain the support of politically important or vociferous elements. This might, indeed, have led far afield; when Governor Hutchinson observed, before the Tea Party, that he saw no middle ground between parliamentary supremacy and colonial independence, the Massachusetts House of Representatives had intimated its preference for independence, as between the two. The way chosen by the British government was in part temporary coercion, and in part to reform the government of Massachusetts without further consultation of the inhabitants.

The Boston Port Act closed the harbor of Boston until the town paid damages to the East India Company. It passed the Commons without a division. The other "coercive acts," including the Massachusetts Government Act, though the Whigs objected to them in debate, went through by majorities of four to one. "The die is now cast," said the King; "the colonies must now submit or triumph." And when General Gage wrote a few months later from Boston that perhaps the Coercive Acts should be suspended, George III thought it absurd to coddle the Americans any further. "We must either master them or totally leave them to themselves and treat them as aliens."[34]

[33] *Corr. Geo. III*, III, 59.
[34] *Ibid.*, III, 131, 154.

The die was cast, indeed. It was cast when the British Parliament attempted to alter the structure of government in Massachusetts. This attempt presented the issue of parliamentary authority over the colonies in the plainest terms. The act unified Massachusetts behind the Boston insurgents, and it rallied the other colonies behind Massachusetts. It led directly to the First Continental Congress and the Revolution. There was also another and in a way larger issue raised by the Massachusetts Government Act, for the nature of the British constitution itself was brought into question. I have already said that everyone thought the British constitution to be a good thing. But the arguments following upon the Act in both Britain and America showed some significant differences of interpretation, and it is these arguments that I should like to emphasize.

The Act for Better Regulating the Government of Massachusetts Bay was in legal form an amendment to the Massachusetts charter of 1691.[35] In effect it was a new constitution, meant to be permanent. On the one hand, it reduced the powers of the various constituted bodies of Massachusetts. The governor's council, which as in other colonies acted both as an upper legislative house and as an advisory board to the governor, was in Massachusetts, by the charter of 1691, elected by the lower house. The lower house, or house of representatives, asserting itself ever more forcefully after the repeal of the Stamp Act, had refused to elect the governor's nominees to the council, so that the council, like the lower house, came to reflect the discontents at Boston. The Massachusetts Government Act of 1774 transformed the council by giving the governor the power to appoint its members; and it weakened the council by taking from it the power to ratify, and hence to veto, the governor's appointment of sheriffs. The Act weakened the lower house by taking from it the power to elect the council. It weakened the towns, whose recent habit of discussing matters of "general concern" and passing "unwarrantable resolves" it disapprovingly noted, by taking from them the right to elect panels of jurymen, and to hold meetings unless summoned by the governor, except for the one annual town meeting for the choice of local officers. On the other hand, the Act strengthened the executive power, giving the governor the right, in the King's name, to appoint his council (as in the other royal provinces), to prevent town meetings except for the annual ones, to appoint or re-move at his own discretion the sheriffs, judges, attorney general, and

---

[35] 14 Geo. III, c. 45.

marshals of the province, and to have fair juries drawn by lot from lists of eligibles assembled by the sheriffs.

The Massachusetts Government Act, though repealed in 1778 in connection with attempts at reconciliation, represented a continuing trend in British constitutional thought on colonial government. Governor Bernard of Massachusetts, since before the Stamp Act, had stressed the need of strengthening the office of governor, and of creating a more independent council on the analogy of the Lords in England. America, Bernard thought, was not yet ready for hereditary nobility (an institution which to him signified an advanced state of civilization), but meanwhile "a *Nobility* appointed by the King, for Life, and made independent, would probably give strength and stability to the American government, as effectually as an hereditary Nobility does to that of Great Britain." Years later a correspondent of Edmund Burke, in a plan of 1782 to make peace with America while keeping it in the empire, a plan intended to be liberal since it would even abolish the Navigation System, set up a "model charter" for each of the colonies—a model in which government should be in three parts: first, a governor appointed from Britain; second, an upper house of a hundred persons having real estate worth over £600 a year, sitting and voting *jure possessionum*, or elected by persons with the same qualifications, if there were more than a hundred in the province; third, a lower house elected by town freemen and county freeholders. In this plan the upper house was clearly thought of as an estate, sitting in its own right, and dependent neither on royal appointment nor on election except by its own body. The Canada Act of 1791 carried the same ideas further. For each of the provinces of Upper and Lower Canada it created a council whose members sat for life. The act empowered His Majesty to confer on these councillors the hereditary right to be summoned, and even to grant them hereditary titles; the purpose was to build up a kind of nobility among the descendants of the first councillors; and though nothing came of the idea, through lack of enthusiasm for nobility in Canada, the terms of the Canada Act yet show the preponderance of thought on the subject among the British governing class in 1791. It was the characteristic eighteenth-century idea, expressed by Walpole in 1719, that nobility was necessary to free government.[36]

[36] For Bernard's views, see Morgan, *Stamp Act Crisis*, 7-21; for Burke's correspondent, see the letter from Dr. John Gray, April 6, 1782 (to which there is no record of a reply) in the Wentworth-Woodhouse manuscripts at the Sheffield Central Library; for the Canada Act, see 31 George III c. 31 and the accompanying debates in Parliament. On Walpole see Chapter III above.

The Massachusetts Government Act of 1774 made the appointment of councillors run at the King's pleasure, that is, for indefinite terms. It said nothing of hereditary councillors, nor even of councillors for life. Its aim was to strengthen the executive, not to build the equivalent of a native nobility. Yet, John Adams was not wholly mistaken when, in his *Novanglus* of 1774, he sniffed the dangers of hereditary lordship in every breeze from Britain. For the truth is that Lord North and others who sponsored the Massachusetts Government Act seem honestly to have believed that they were about to purge the Massachusetts government of its "crudities," as North called them, and endow the province with the more highly developed advantages of the British constitution, of which the essence was agreed to be the balance between King, Lords, and Commons, or between the monarchic, aristocratic, and democratic principles in the state.

The trouble with Massachusetts, said North in the Commons, explaining the need for amending its government, was that the "democratic part" of its constitution was too strong. "There is something radically wrong in that constitution in which no magistrate for such a number of years has ever done his duty in such a manner as to enforce obedience to the laws." Hence the King's well-disposed subjects (and it was true) had been at the mercy of the turbulent and the lawless. The governor simply lacked the means to maintain law and order; he could not act without the consent of a majority of his council, which depended on election by the "democratic part"; he had no normal military force except the *posse comitatus*, the very people by whom the laws were disobeyed. The purpose of the new act, said North, was to "take the executive power from the democratic part of the government." Lord George Germain was more blunt. "I would not have men of a mercantile cast every day collecting themselves together and debating on political matters." He would frankly make the council more like the Lords, and he would have the corporate powers of towns exercised by a few individuals, as in England. "I would wish to bring the constitution of America as similar to our own as possible."[37]

Many of the Rockingham Whigs spoke against the bill. "The Americans have flourished for nearly fourscore years under that democratic charter," declared Dowdeswell, meaning the Massachusetts charter of 1691; he thought it best to leave well enough alone.[38] But the bill passed four to one.

[37] *Parliamentary History*, XVII, 1192-95.
[38] *Ibid.*, 1198.

The Whigs continued to oppose the government's program for America, their memorable spokesman at this juncture being Edmund Burke. His sympathy for the Americans even led him into statements very close to those of the radicals; he agreed that America was not even "virtually" represented in Parliament, and that to tell them they were represented as Manchester was represented, or "virtually" represented while electing no members, was to "turn to them the shameful parts of our constitution," to offer them "the slavery which we are not able to work off."[39] Burke could stomach such "slavery" for England; but since Parliament did not represent America in the same way that it was supposed to represent Great Britain, he would maintain the authority of Parliament over America at the highest and most ultimate level only, to preserve the unity of the empire, and let the Americans govern themselves in their ordinary business. The great problem, as he said in his speech on Conciliation with the Colonies in 1775, was "to admit the Americans to an interest in the constitution." He would therefore promise not to tax the Americans, while avoiding the question of right as a "Serbonian bog"; but he would keep parliamentary control over trade and navigation, since Britain drew from this control more profit than it could ever draw from taxation. As for constitutional relationships with Britain, he offered his parallel of Ireland, where the separate parliament had powers of taxation, legislation, and the maintenance of armed forces, but recognized the imperial trade controls. Burke had a vision of a great federal empire, composed of free and autonomous members presided over by a wise and superintending Parliament. Yet it is doubtful whether, in its attempt to limit the matter in dispute to the practical issue of taxation, and in its sustained refusal to dwell on the question of right, Burke's plan of 1775 offered any real basis for agreement with those who had now assumed the power to speak for America. It hardly gave them that "interest in the constitution" which Burke himself thought vital.

Burke had in fact been refuted in advance by John Adams, whose *Novanglus* appeared in 1774. Adams roundly rejected the parallel of Ireland, a conquered country, as he put it, where the Irish themselves (or Anglo-Irish) objected to their legal position. The colonies, he declared, were no part of the British Empire because there was no British Empire in any legal sense—the term was a mere journalistic expression. The colonies were not under Parliament; they recognized only the King; and George III was King of Massachusetts, or King of New

[39] "Speech on American Taxation" (April 19, 1774), *Writings* (Boston, 1901), II, 74.

York, just as he was Elector of Hanover, holding all in personal union, but with no parliamentary connection among these various domains. Of course the Americans lived under the British constitution, in the sense that each colony under the King possessed the British constitution entire within itself; but if the Americans were under the King, Lords, and Commons of Great Britain they were under a remote oligarchy with which they had no connection; or they would be like the Dutch (for Adams knew something of Europe) where the Estates of Holland had formerly been elected, but were now an oligarchy that filled its own vacancies. Parliament, he said, could not assert authority in America except by the *ultima ratio* of Louis XIV; he might have said "Louis XV" if the Boston newspapers had carried more news of France, where the claim of the French Parlements to represent the French people was in fact being currently suppressed by the French King. And if Britain persisted, said Adams prophetically, all Europe would call her a tyrant.

In England it was the radicals who were most willing to grant what the Americans really demanded, because they had no reason to be sticklers for the powers of Parliament. It was the British radicals, not the British Whigs, who corresponded to what were called Whigs in America. Thus Major John Cartwright, "father of English reform," who began a half a century of agitation for the democratizing of Parliament with his pamphlet *Take Your Choice* in 1776, published anonymously in 1774 another tract called *American Independence the Interest and Glory of Great Britain*.[40] It outlined a scheme by which the American legislatures should be really the equals of Parliament, joined in voluntary alliance under the Crown, and so anticipated better than the proposals of Burke what came later to be called dominion status. Another radical, Horne Tooke, was fined and im-

---

[40] Cartwright's views on Parliament may be judged from the full title of his well-known pamphlet, *Take Your Choice! Representation and Respect; Imposition and Contempt. Annual Parliaments and Liberty, Long Parliaments and Slavery*. Postgate remarks of Wilkes that he left no name as a Parliamentarian because he "despised" the House of Commons; *That Devil Wilkes*, 207. Another work is worthy of comment in a book devoted to the international context, since it was written by Jean-Paul Marat, then a fashionable doctor in Soho, who brought it out anonymously in an expensive format in 1774. Since the *Critical Review*, xxxvii (1774), 366-70, called it "useful," "laudable," and "intelligent," and hoped that readers would take its advice, it seems worthwhile to convey the atmosphere of the day by giving Marat's title at length: *The Chains of Slavery, a work wherein the clandestine and villainous attempts of princes to ruin liberty are pointed out and the dreadful scenes of despotism disclosed, to which is prefixed an address to the electors of Great Britain in order to draw their timely attention to the choice of proper representatives in the next Parliament* (London, 1774).

prisoned after having made himself conspicuous in the efforts of the Constitutional Society to raise £100 for the widows and children of Americans killed at Lexington and Concord. Richard Price's *Observations on Civil Liberty*, in 1776, demanded better representation of the people in the Commons, denied the omnipotence of Parliament, and defended the American rebels. John Wilkes, when he stood for Parliament in Middlesex in 1774, offered a program both of Parliamentary reform and of restoration of American rights; and when he introduced his reform bill in the Commons in 1776 he declared that the unrepresentativeness of the Parliament was a main cause of a needless American war. It was in fact a favorite idea of radicals and reformers, and long remained so (though one may question the truth of it), that if Parliament had really represented the British people America would never have been estranged.[41]

And when Burke in 1777 again pleaded for conciliation, but blamed the war with the Americans on the mere folly of ministers (and implicitly on the stupidity of the King), still refusing to recognize the conflict of principle, and insisting that Parliament must be supreme, he provoked a retort from a radical of high station, Willoughby Bertie, the fourth Earl of Abingdon. Abingdon had spent several years in the 1760's at Geneva, where he had known Delolme and taken part in the democratic movement. His reply to Burke went through five editions. A strong friend of the Americans, and thinking that government should be representative of the governed, he simply did not believe that Parliament was supreme in Britain any more than in America. "Where is the difference," he asked Burke (and it was the question that all radicals put to all Whigs), "between the despotism of the King of France and the despotism of the Parliament of England? And what is this but to erect an aristocratic tyranny in the state?"[42]

The British radicals had to live under Parliament, and had no course except to hope to reform it. The Americans did not have to live under Parliament, and refused to do so. Most Englishmen alive in 1776 were dead before Parliament gave an inch of ground. The Americans, three thousand miles away, had more freedom of action. They set up what amounted to anti-parliaments.

---

[41] Guttridge, *Whiggism*, 63, 87; Dora M. Clark, *British Opinion and the American Revolution* (New Haven, 1930), 180.

[42] Burke, "Letter to . . . the Sheriffs of the City of Bristol on the Affairs of America" (1777) in *Writings* (Boston, 1901), II, 187, 245; Abingdon, *Thoughts on Mr. Burke's Letter to the Sheriffs of Bristol on the Affairs of America* (1777), quoted by Guttridge, *op.cit.*, 94.

In Virginia, upon the news of the Boston Port Act, Thomas Jefferson drafted a resolution in support of Boston; the house of burgesses adopted it, and was thereupon dissolved by the governor. The house met illegally as an "association," denounced the Act, and summoned a "convention" of the Virginia counties. Similar conventions of counties or other self-authorized gatherings met in the other provinces. They sent delegates to an assembly that called itself the Continental Congress. The Congress issued a Declaration of Rights, and took steps to force all Americans into a concerted boycott of Great Britain.

At this First Continental Congress the delegates found that they differed on a theoretically important question. It was a question that remained alive long after American independence, and on which historians of the American Revolution have inclined to differ to this day. There were those who thought America internally unchanged by the repudiation of British authority. They justified their rebellion by appealing to their historic rights as Englishmen, or rights under the British constitution, which, they said, they wished merely to defend. As John Jay said in the Congress, they saw no need "to frame a new constitution." Others preferred to stand not on the rights of Englishmen but on the rights of man, and not on the laws in the lawbooks, but on the laws of nature. They were more willing to believe that a new era was at hand. As Patrick Henry said in the Congress: "Government is dissolved. . . . We are in a state of nature."[43]

The Congress, significantly, simply put the two together. In America, in contrast to most of Europe, nature and history were not felt to be opposites. The Americans, fundamentally, were satisfied with their own past. They thought that their rights under the British constitution were much the same as their rights as human beings under natural law. The Continental Congress, in its Declaration of Rights of 1774, appealed simultaneously to "the immutable laws of nature, the principles of the English constitution, and the several charters and compacts."[44] On this potentially ambiguous note the American Revolution began.

[43] E. C. Burnett, *The Continental Congress* (N.Y., 1941), 37.
[44] *Ibid.*, 53.

THE AMERICAN REVOLUTION:
THE FORCES IN CONFLICT

I know that for such sentiments I am called a rebel, and that such sentiments are not fashionable among the folks you see. —GOUVERNEUR MORRIS to his mother in New York, 1778

Hear thy indictment, Washington, at large;
Attend and listen to the solemn charge:
Thou hast supported an atrocious cause,
Against thy king, thy country and the laws.
—Loyalist poem, by JONATHAN ODELL, 1779

To me it will appear miraculous, if our affairs can maintain themselves much longer in their present train. If either the temper or the resources of the country will not admit of an alteration, we may expect soon to be reduced to the humiliating condition of seeing the cause of America, in America, upheld by foreign arms. . . .

It is true that our enemies as well as ourselves are struggling with embarrassments of a singular and complicated nature . . . but considering the complexion of the British nation for some time past, it is more probable these appearances will terminate in a partial reform of abuses, than in any revolution favorable to the interests of America. . . .

The general disposition of Europe is such as we could wish; but we have no security that it will remain so.—GENERAL GEORGE WASHINGTON to the President of the Congress, 1780

VII

THE AMERICAN REVOLUTION:
THE FORCES IN CONFLICT

It is a main thesis of this book that the American Revolution was a great event for the whole Eur-American world. In the Age of the Democratic Revolution the American Revolution was, after the disturbance at Geneva already recounted, the earliest successful assertion of the principle that public power must arise from those over whom it is exercised. It was the most important revolution of the eighteenth century, except for the French. Its effect on the area of Western Civilization came in part from the inspiration of its message (which in time passed beyond the area of Western Civilization), and in part from the involvement of the American Revolution in the European War of American Independence, which aggravated the financial or political difficulties of England, Ireland, Holland, and France. The climax and failure of the early movement for parliamentary reform in England, the disturbances in Ireland leading to "Grattan's Parliament" in 1782, the *Patriotentijd* and revolution of 1784-1787 among the Dutch, the reform programs of Necker and Calonne and beginnings of revolution in France, and a marked enlivening of political consciousness through the rest of Europe—all described in the following chapters—were all, in part, a consequence of the American Revolution.

The Revolution: Was There Any?

It is paradoxical, therefore, to have to begin by asking whether there was any American Revolution at all. There may have been only a war of independence against Great Britain. The British lid may have been removed from the American box, with the contents of the box remaining as before. Or there may have been a mechanical separation from England, without chemical change in America itself. Perhaps it was all a conservative and defensive movement, to secure liberties that America had long enjoyed, a revolt of America against Great Britain, carried through without fundamental conflict among Americans, by an "American consensus," in the words of Clinton Rossiter, or, as George Bancroft said a century ago, a revolution "achieved with such benign tranquillity that even conservatism hesitated to censure."[1]

A populous country, much given to historical studies, has produced an enormous literature on the circumstances of its independence. Occupied more with European than with American history, I have been able only to sample this literature. It is apparent, however, that there is no agreement on what the American Revolution was. Differences reflect a different understanding of historical fact, a difference of attitude toward the concept of revolution, or a difference of feeling on the uniqueness, if it be unique, of the United States.

The old patriotic historians, like Bancroft, who fumed against British tyranny, had no doubt that there had been a real revolution in America, even if "benignly tranquil." Writers of a liberal orientation in a twentieth-century sense, admitting that all revolutions are carried through by minorities and by violence, have said that the American Revolution was no exception. Some have seen a kind of bourgeois revolution in America, in which merchants and planters made a few concessions to the lower classes, but then, at the Philadelphia convention of 1787, rallied to the defense of property in a kind of Thermidor. Still others, of conservative temperament, sympathizing with the American loyalists, have found the ruthlessness of a true revolution in the American upheaval. It must be admitted that, for the purposes of the present book, it would be convenient to present the American part of the story in this way, on the analogy of revolutions in Europe.

But there is the contrary school that minimizes the revolutionary character of the American Revolution. Some in this school hold that there was no "democratic revolution" in America because America was already democratic in the colonial period. Thus, it has recently been shown that, contrary to a common impression, as many as ninety-five per cent of adult males had the right to vote in many parts of colonial Massachusetts. Others find the Revolution not very revolutionary because the country was still far from democratic when it became independent. They point to the maintenance of property qualifications for voting and office-holding, or the fact that estates confiscated from loyalists found their way into the hands of speculators or well-to-do people,

---

[1] C. Rossiter, *Seedtime of the Republic: the Origin of the American Tradition of Political Liberty* (New York, 1953), 352-56; G. Bancroft, *History of the United States* (Boston, 1879), III, 10-11.

not of poor farmers. Those who discount the revolutionary character of the American Revolution seem to be gaining ground. For example, thirty years ago, J. F. Jameson in his little book, *The American Revolution Considered as a Social Movement*, suggested a variety of social changes that he said took place, in landholding and land law, in the disestablishment of churches and the democratizing tendencies in an aristocratic society. The book won followers and inspired research. F. B. Tolles described the aristocratic *ancien régime* of colonial Philadelphia, dominated by Quaker grandees whose social ascendancy, he said, came to an end in the American Revolution. But in 1954 the same Professor Tolles, reviewing the Jameson thesis and summarizing the research of recent decades, concluded that, while Jameson's ideas were important and fruitful, the degree of internal or social or revolutionary change within America, during the break with Britain, should not be unduly stressed.[2]

Whether one thinks there was really a revolution in America depends on what one thinks a revolution is. It depends, that is to say, not so much on specialized knowledge or on factual discovery, or even on hard thinking about a particular time and place, as on the use made of an abstract concept. "Revolution" is a concept whose connotation and overtones change with changing events. It conveyed a different feeling in the 1790's from the 1770's, and in the 1950's from the 1930's.

No one in 1776, whether for it or against it, doubted that a revolution was being attempted in America. A little later the French Revolution gave a new dimension to the concept of revolution. It was the French Revolution that caused some to argue that the American Revolution had been no revolution at all. In 1800 Friedrich Gentz, in his *Historisches Journal* published at Berlin, wrote an essay comparing the French and American revolutions. He was an acute observer, whose account of the French Revolution did not suit all conservatives of the time, and would not suit them today; still, he made his living by writing against the French Revolution, and later became secretary to Metternich. He considered the French Revolution a bad thing, all the worse when compared to the American. He thought the American Revolution only a conservative defense of established rights against British encroachment. John Quincy Adams, then in Berlin, read Gentz's essay, liked it, translated it, and published it in Philadelphia in 1800. It served as a piece of high-toned campaign literature in the presidential election of that

<hr>

[2] F. B. Tolles, "The American Revolution Considered as a Social Movement: a Reevaluation" in *American Historical Review*, LX (October, 1954), 1-12.

year, in which the elder Adams and the Federalist party were challenged by Jefferson and the somewhat Francophile democrats. The merit of Gentz's essay, said the younger Adams in his preface, was that "it rescues that revolution [the American] from the disgraceful imputation of having proceeded from the same principles as the French." In 1955 Adams' translation of Gentz was reprinted in America as a paper-back for mass distribution, with a foreword by Russell Kirk, known as a publicist of the "new conservatism." There was something in the atmosphere of 1955, as of 1800, which made it important, for some, to dissociate the American Revolution from other revolutions by which other peoples have been afflicted.

My own view is that there was a real revolution in America, and that it was a painful conflict, in which many were injured. I would suggest two quantitative and objective measures: how many refugees were there from the American Revolution, and how much property did they lose, in comparison to the French Revolution? It is possible to obtain rough but enlightening answers to these questions. The number of émigré loyalists who went to Canada or England during the American Revolution is set as high as 100,000; let us say only 60,000. The number of émigrés from the French Revolution is quite accurately known; it was 129,000, of whom 25,000 were clergy, deportees rather than fugitives, but let us take the whole figure, 129,000. There were about 2,500,000 people in America in 1776, of whom a fifth were slaves; let us count the whole 2,500,000. There were about 25,000,000 people in France at the time of the French Revolution. There were, therefore, 24 émigrés per thousand of population in the American Revolution, and only 5 émigrés per thousand of population in the French Revolution.

In both cases the revolutionary governments confiscated the property of counterrevolutionaries who emigrated. Its value cannot be known, but the sums paid in compensation lend themselves to tentative comparison. The British government granted £3,300,000 to loyalists as indemnity for property lost in the United States. The French émigrés, or their heirs, received a "billion franc indemnity" in 1825 during the Bourbon restoration. A sum of £3,300,000 is the equivalent of 82,000,000 francs. Revolutionary France, ten times as large as revolutionary America, confiscated only twelve times as much property from its émigrés, as measured by subsequent compensations, which in each case fell short of actual losses. The difference, even allowing for margins of error, is less great than is commonly supposed. The French, to be sure, confiscated properties of the church and other public bodies in addition; but the present comparison suggests the losses of private persons.

It is my belief also, John Quincy Adams notwithstanding, that the American and the French revolutions "proceeded from the same principles." The difference is that these principles were much more deeply rooted in America, and that contrary or competing principles, monarchist or aristocratic or feudal or ecclesiastical, though not absent from America, were, in comparison to Europe, very weak. Assertion of the same principles therefore provoked less conflict in America than in France. It was, in truth, less revolutionary. The American Revolution was, indeed, a movement to conserve what already existed. It was hardly, however, a "conservative" movement, and it can give limited comfort to the theorists of conservatism, for it was the weakness of conservative forces in eighteenth-century America, not their strength, that made the American Revolution as moderate as it was. John Adams was not much like Edmund Burke, even after he became alarmed by the French Revolution; and Alexander Hamilton never hoped to perpetuate an existing state of society, or to change it by gradual, cautious, and piously respectful methods. America was different from Europe, but it was not unique. The difference lay in the fact that certain ideas of the Age of Enlightenment, found on both sides of the Atlantic—ideas of constitutionalism, individual liberty, or legal equality—were more fully incorporated and less disputed in America than in Europe. There was enough of a common civilization to make America very pointedly significant to Europeans. For a century after the American Revolution, as is well known, partisans of the revolutionary or liberal movements in Europe looked upon the United States generally with approval, and European conservatives viewed it with hostility or downright contempt.

It must always be remembered, also, that an important nucleus of conservatism was permanently lost to the United States. The French émigrés returned to France. The émigrés from the American Revolution did not return; they peopled the Canadian wilderness; only individuals, without political influence, drifted back to the United States. Anyone who knows the significance for France of the return of the émigrés will ponder the importance, for the United States, of this fact which is so easily overlooked, because negative and invisible except in a comparative view. Americans have really forgotten the loyalists. Princeton University, for example, which invokes the memory of John Witherspoon and James Madison on all possible occasions, has been chided for burying in oblivion the name of Jonathan Odell, of the class of 1759, prominent as a physician, clergyman, and loyalist satirical writer during the Revolution, who died in New Brunswick, Canada, in 1818.[3] The sense in which there was no conflict in the American Revolution is the sense in which the loyalists are forgotten. The "American consensus" rests in some degree on the elimination from the national consciousness, as well as from the country, of a once important and relatively numerous element of dissent.

Anglo-America before the Revolution

The American Revolution may be seen as a conflict of forces some of which were old, others brought into being by the event itself.

The oldest of these forces was a tradition of liberty, which went back to the first settlement of the colonies. It is true that half of all immigrants into the colonies south of New England, and two-thirds of those settling in Pennsylvania, arrived as indentured servants; but indentured servitude was not a permanent status, still less a hereditary one; the indentures expired after a few years, and all white persons soon merged into a free population.

Politically, the oldest colonies had originated in a kind of *de facto* independence from the British government. Even after the British made their colonial system more systematic, toward the close of the seventeenth century, the colonies continued to enjoy much local self-determination. Only five per cent of the laws passed by colonial assemblies were disallowed in Great Britain, and, while these often concerned the most important subjects, the infrequency of the British veto was enough to make it the exception. The elected assemblies, as already noted, were the most democratically recruited of all such constituted bodies in the Western World. In general, it was necessary to own land in order to have the right to vote for a member of the assembly, but small owner-farmers were numerous, most of all in New England; and recent studies all tend to raise the estimates of the proportion of those enjoying the franchise before the Revolution. It seems to have been above eighty per cent of adult white males in Massachusetts, half or more in New Jersey, perhaps a little under half in Virginia.[4] Many

[3] M. C. Tyler, *Literary History of the American Revolution*, 2 vols. (New York, 1897), II, p. 99, n. 3.
[4] R. E. Brown, *Middle-Class Democracy and the Revolution in Massachusetts, 1691-1780* (Ithaca, 1955), 50; R. McCormick, *History of Voting in New Jersey . . . 1664-1911* (New Brunswick, 1953), 63; C. S. Sydnor, *Gentlemen Freeholders: Political Practices in Washington's Virginia* (Williamsburg, 1952), 32, 143, appears to think that about

who had the right to vote did not often use it, and this was in part because the procedure of elections was not made convenient for the ordinary hard-working man; but non-voting also suggests an absence of grievances, or perhaps only that the common man neither expected much nor feared much from government. The elected assemblies enjoyed what in Europe would be thought a dangerously popular mandate. By 1760, decades of rivalry for power between the assemblies and the governors had been resolved, in most of the colonies, in favor of the assemblies. The idea of government by consent was for Americans a mere statement of fact, not a bold doctrine to be flung in the teeth of government, as in Europe. Contrariwise, the growing assertiveness of the assemblies made many in England, and some in America, on the eve of the Revolution, believe that the time had come to stop this drift toward democracy—or, as they would say, restore the balance of the constitution. In sum, an old sense of liberty in America was the obstacle on which the first British empire met its doom. Here the most sophisticated latest researches seem to return to the old-fashioned American patriotic historical school.

From the beginnings of British America there had also been a certain rough kind of equality. Except for slaves, the poor were less poor than in Europe, and the rich were not so wealthy. Almost a quarter of the population of England were classified as paupers in 1688; almost a tenth in 1801. There was no pauperism in America, accepted and institutionalized as such; anyone not hopelessly shiftless, or the victim of personal misfortune, could make a living. At the other extreme, on the eve of the Revolution, there were men who owned hundreds of thousands of acres, mostly vacant, the main values being speculative and in the future. It is hard to say how wealthy a wealthy colonial was. A fortune of £30,000 was thought very large in Massachusetts; Joseph Galloway of Pennsylvania was said to possess £70,000. In England in 1801 there were probably 10,000 families with an average income of £1,500 a year or more, of which the capital value would be about £30,000. There is ground for believing that in England at this time, as in the United States in 1929, five per cent of the population received over thirty-five per cent of the income. The distribution of wealth in colonial America was far more equal.[5]

---

ten per cent of the white population was qualified to vote, but this would be about half the adult males.

[5] These statements about wealth and pauperism are derived from the tables in P. Colquhoun, *A Treatise on Indigence* (London, 1806), 22, where the estimates of Gregory King for 1688 are also reproduced.

There were recognized inequalities of social rank. But rank some-how lacked the magic it enjoyed in Europe. In the migration from England and Europe, the well-situated and the high-born had been notably absent. There were Americans of aristocratic pretensions, but the most ambitious genealogy led only to some middling English gentleman's manor house; most Americans were conscious of no lineage at all, American genealogy being largely a nineteenth-century science. No American could truthfully trace his ancestry to the mists of time or the ages of chivalry—nor, indeed, could many British peers or French noblemen. It was the complaint of Lord Stirling, as the New Jersey revolutionary, William Alexander, was called, that he was *not* recognized as a lord in England. A Swedish clergyman arriving in New Jersey in 1770, to take over the old Swedish congregation on the Delaware, found that well-to-do farmers were like lesser gentry in Sweden, in their use of fine linen and fondness for good horses. The significant thing for America was that people of this style of life did not, as in Sweden, consider themselves nobles. Everyone worked, and to the Swedish newcomer it seemed that "all people are generally thought equally good."[6]

Whether religion acted as a force in the conflict of the American Revolution is disputed. Since the Worship of Reason at Notre-Dame de Paris in November 1793, there have always been those who have stressed the religious principles of the founders of the United States. It is a way of showing how different they were from Jacobins or Communists. The truth is that the age was not notably religious, and that the sentiments that burst out violently in Paris in 1793 were, as sentiments, not uncommon. We read, for example, of an Anglican rector in England who, about 1777, so admired the writings of Catherine Macaulay that "he actually placed her statue, adorned as the Goddess of Liberty, within the altar railing" of his parish church.[7] "It will never be pretended," wrote John Adams in 1786, that the men who set up the new governments in America "had interviews with the gods, or were in any degree under the inspiration of Heaven, more than those at work on ships or houses, or laboring in merchandise or agri-culture; it will forever be acknowledged that these governments were contrived by reason and the senses, as Copley painted Chatham . . . [or] as Paine exposed the mistakes of Raynal. . . ."[8] John Adams, while

---

[6] Quoted by L. Lundin, *Cockpit of the Revolution: the War for Independence in New Jersey* (Princeton, 1940), 33.

[7] E. Sitwell, *Bath* (London, 1932), 223.

[8] *Works* (1851), IV, 292-93.

differing with him in detail, had not yet broken with Thomas Paine.

Aggressive anti-Christianity did not develop in America, to the great good fortune of the future United States. It failed to develop, however, not because American revolutionary leaders were warmly religious, but because no religious body seriously stood in their way. Here again it was the weakness of conservative forces, not their strength, that made the Revolution "conservative." No church seriously opposed the political aims of the Revolution. No church figured as a first estate in colonial America, none had its dignitaries sitting in the highest councils of government, and none lost vast tracts of material property, since none possessed any.[9] The Anglican clergy generally opposed the Revolution, because of their close connection with British authority. Revolutionaries drove them out of their churches, for the same reason; worse would have happened to them had they not been so easily dislodged. In any case, even where the Anglican church was established, in New York and the South, Anglicans were not a majority of the population. At the opposite end of the religious spectrum the Quakers, because of their doctrine of non-resistance to established authority, were in effect a force to be reckoned on the British side. But they were unimportant politically outside of Pennsylvania. Over half the colonial Americans, and probably ninety per cent of New Englanders, were, vaguely or exactly, some species of Calvinists. No allegation was more common, from the British or the American loyalists, than that the whole Revolution had been stirred up by old Presbyterian disaffection. It is true that New England Congregationalists and Scotch-Irish Presbyterians did not admire some of the contemporary institutions of England, and that their ministers, when the time came, generally supported the Revolution. They probably infused, in a way hard to define, a certain religious atmosphere into the American patriot program.

A great many Americans, however, before and during the Revolution, belonged to no church at all. In conditions of constant movement, uprooting, settlement, and resettlement, probably a larger proportion

[9] The nearest thing in America to the recognition of higher clergy as lords spiritual, or as a first estate, was the fact that the commissary of the Bishop of London, at such times as such a functionary was in America, had a seat in certain governors' councils. Confiscation of church property went farthest in Virginia, where, not during the heat of revolution, but as late as 1799 and 1802, all real and movable property possessed by the Episcopal church before 1776, including church buildings themselves, was confiscated by the state. The state of Virginia persisted in this policy despite the fact that the United States Supreme Court ruled it unconstitutional in 1815. See G. M. Brydon, "The Anti-Ecclesiastical Laws in Virginia," in *Virginia Magazine of History*, LXIV (1956), 259-60.

of Americans were unchurched than in any European country. What aroused horror, when violently pursued as dechristianization in France a few years later, had gone pretty far, without violence, in America. As for the leaders of the American Revolution, it should be unnecessary to demonstrate that most of them were deists. They were strongly on the side of the best human virtues, or at least of those which were not ascetic; but they saw no connection between such virtues and religious practice. Like Jefferson in the Declaration of Independence, they appealed to the laws of Nature's God. They seem not to have felt, however, like Burke, that these laws placed serious limits upon their freedom of political action.

The simplicities in which British America had originated gave way to more complex forms of society in the eighteenth century. A liberty almost like that of the "state of nature," a liberty defined by the remoteness of government, gradually changed, especially after the British revolution of 1688, into the more organized and channelized liberty of British subjects under the British constitution. There was a bias toward equality in the foundations. The superstructure, as it was raised, exhibited palpable inequalities. As America became more civilized it began to have, like all civilized countries, a differentiation of social classes. Even the once unmanageable Quakers took on new social refinements. The Philadelphia Yearly Meeting of 1722 officially declared its "decent respect" for "ranks and dignities of men," and called for honor and obedience "from subjects to their princes, inferiors to superiors, from children to parents, and servants to masters."[10] Increasingly there was a kind of native American aristocracy. No question was of more importance for the future than the way in which this new aristocracy would develop.

The colonial aristocracy, as it took form in the eighteenth century, owed a good deal to close association with government. From New Hampshire to the far South, as has been seen in Chapter II, there were intermarried families which monopolized seats in the governors' councils, in some cases, now, to the third and fourth generation. There were Americans, close to the British authorities, who regarded themselves as the natural rulers of the country. Sometimes, like Englishmen of the class to which they would compare themselves, they expected to draw a living from public offices, to which they need devote only part of their time. This practice has been most closely

[10] F. B. Tolles, *Meeting House and Counting House: the Quaker Merchants of Colonial Philadelphia* (Williamsburg, 1948), 111-12.

studied for Maryland, where there were a number of offices in which a man could live like a gentleman, with a good deal of leisure, for £150 a year.[11]

More generally, the wealth of the growing American upper class came from early land grants, or from inheritance of land in a country where land values were always rising, or from mercantile wealth in the half-dozen seaboard cities, all of which except Charleston lay from Philadelphia to the North, or from the ownership of plantations and Negro slaves in the South. New York and the Southern provinces, because of their systems of landholding, were the most favorable to the growth of aristocratic institutions, but an upper class existed everywhere in the settled regions. In places where landed and mercantile wealth came together, as at New York and Charleston, people mixed easily with mutual regard; there was no standoffishness between "trade" and "gentry."

Without the rise of such a colonial aristocracy there could have been no successful movement against England. There had to be small groups of people who knew each other, who could trust each other in hazardous undertakings, who had some power and influence of their own, who could win attention and rally followers, and who, from an enlarged point of view, felt a concern for the welfare of the provinces as a whole. "While there are no noble or great and ancient families . . . they cannot rebel," as an observer of New England remarked in 1732.[12] A generation later such "great" families, if not noble or very ancient, could be found everywhere in the colonies.

On the other hand, the rise of such an aristocracy brought class friction and internal tension. "In many a colony in 1764," according to Professor Rossiter (whose view of an "American consensus" I do not wish to misrepresent), "civil war seemed more likely than war with Britain."[13] There was everlasting bickering over land titles, quitrents, debts, and paper money. There was complaint, in the western part of several provinces, at under-representation in the elected assemblies, or at the long distances it was necessary to go to cast a vote or to be present in a court of law. Rich and poor were not so far apart as in Europe, but they were far enough apart to cause trouble. Western Massachusetts, suspicious of Boston, was not hostile to Britain until 1774. There was a great rent riot in the Hudson valley in 1766, directed

[11] D. M. Owings, *His Lordship's Patronage: Offices of Profit in Colonial Maryland* (Baltimore, 1953).
[12] Quoted by Rossiter, *op.cit.*, 109.
[13] *Ibid.*, 115.

against the manorial system on which the Van Rensselaers and the Livingstons grew wealthy. A thousand angry western Pennsylvania farmers marched on Philadelphia in 1764, enraged that the over-represented East, and its opulent and pacifistic Quaker aristocracy, begrudged them military protection at the time of Pontiac's Indian war. The best example was afforded by the Regulators of North Carolina.

This province, though scarcely a century old, had developed a fine system of decayed boroughs on the British model. The five oldest coastal counties, thinly inhabited, enjoyed a dozen times as much representation in the assembly, per capita, as the newer uplands, so that the bulk of the people, while having the vote, could get little accomplished. Political life was most active at the county level, and in each county a few families named the judges and sheriffs, who are estimated to have embezzled over half the public funds. The governing elite, if one may so term it, unabashedly made a living off the legal business that small farmers could not avoid. A group of these farmers founded an "association" for "regulating public grievances," and these Regulators began to refuse to pay taxes. The governor finally called out the militia against them, chiefly a mounted troop of Gentlemen Volunteer Light Dragoons, in which 8 "generals" and 14 "colonels" led less than 1,300 enlisted men. The Regulators were routed in the Battle of Alamance in 1771. Seven of them were hanged. Later, when the gentry led the province into the Revolution, the British found many loyalist strongholds in the back country of Carolina.

Conflicting forces were therefore at work in America, when the Stamp Act added the conflict between America and Great Britain. Americans all but universally opposed the Stamp Act. Most of those who eventually became loyalists disapproved of British policy in the ten years before the Revolution. The doctrine of parliamentary supremacy was an innovation, accepted in England itself only since the revolution of 1689; the trend toward centralization of the empire under parliamentary authority, with attendant plans for reordering the colonial governments, was a modern development, a new force, much less old than the American liberties. On this Americans could agree. They began to disagree on the means used to uphold the American position. It was one thing to sit in meetings or submit petitions to Parliament; it was another to persist stubbornly in defiance, to insult or intimidate the King's officers, stop the proceedings of law courts, and condone the violence of mobs. Whether the British constitution really assured no taxation without representation was, after all, uncertain. It was far more certain that the British constitution secured a man against physical violence, against his having his house plundered and wrecked by political adversaries, or against being tarred and feathered for refusing to join a non-import agreement decided on by some unauthorized assembly which had no right to use force. As events unfolded, men took sides, and Americans found themselves disputing with each other on a new subject, the attitude to be taken to British law.

What happened to Plymouth Rock offers a parable. The stone on which the Pilgrims of 1620 had supposedly first set foot already enjoyed a local fame, as a symbol of what was most ancient and natively American in the New World. In 1774 a party of patriots decided to use it as the base for a liberty pole. They tried to haul it, with twenty oxen, from the shore to the town square. Under the strain, it broke in two.[14]

The Revolution: Democracy and Aristocracy

Fighting between the King's troops and the people of Massachusetts began at Lexington and Concord in April 1775. In the following December the British government put the insurgent colonists outside the protection of the British crown. The Americans were now in what they would call a state of nature, and what was in fact a condition of anarchy. Lawful authority melted away. Governors, unable to control their assemblies, undertook to disband them, only to see most of the members continue to meet as unauthorized congresses or associations; or conventions of counties, unknown to the law, chose delegates to such congresses for provinces as a whole; or local people forcibly prevented the sitting of law courts, or the enforcement of legal judgments by the sheriffs. Violence spread, militias formed, and the Continental Congress called into existence a Continental army, placing General George Washington in command.

In whose name were these armed men to act? To what civilian authority were they to be subordinated? How could the courts be kept open, or normal court decisions and police protection be carried out? If American ships, breaking the old navigation system, should enter the ports of Europe, in whose name should they appear? If diplomatic agents were sent to Versailles or the Hague, whom were they to say that they represented? If aid was to be sought from France,

[14] For this curious episode see W. F. Craven, *The Legend of the Founding Fathers* (N.Y., 1956), 32.

would the French give it for any purpose except to break up the British empire, and undo the British victory of 1763? These practical needs, together with the inflaming of feeling against England by war and bloodshed, and the extraordinary success of Thomas Paine's pamphlet, *Common Sense*, induced the Congress, more than a year after the battle of Lexington, to announce the arrival of the United States of America "among the powers of the earth," able to do "all acts and things which independent states may of right do."

With the Declaration of Independence, and the new constitutions which most of the states gave themselves in 1776 and 1777, the revolutionary colonials began to emerge from the anarchy that followed the collapse or withdrawal of British power. They sought liberty, it need hardly be said; but they also sought authority, or a new basis of order. A revolution, it has been wisely observed, is an unlawful change in the conditions of lawfulness.[15] It repudiates the old definitions of rightful authority, and drives away the men who have exercised it; but it creates new definitions of the authority which it is a duty to obey, and puts new men in a position to issue legitimate commands. The new lawfulness in America was embodied in the new constitutions, which will be considered shortly. Meanwhile, what happened in America was against the law.

The Revolution could be carried out, against British and loyal American opposition, only by the use of force. Its success "was impossible without a revolutionary government which could enforce its will."[16] Let us look simply at the case of New Jersey. Late in 1776 the danger to the patriots became very pressing, as the British pursued Washington's army across the state. One of the New Jersey signers of the Declaration of Independence was forced to recant; the man who had presided over the convention which had proclaimed independence of the state went over to the British. The state was full of open and hidden enemies of the new regime. Taxes were neither levied nor collected with any regularity; the paper money which financed the Revo-

[15] For a philosophical discussion, see P. Schrecker, *Work and History: an Essay on the Structure of Civilization* (Princeton, 1948), 206: "In the political province, a revolution may accordingly be defined as an unlawful change of the constitution, and since the constitution represents the established conditions of lawfulness, the revolutionary event appears as an unlawful change of the very conditions of lawfulness."

[16] R. C. Haskett, "Prosecuting the Revolution," in *American Historical Review*, LIX (April 1954), 578. In addition, for this paragraph, see Lundin, *op.cit.*, and the unpublished doctoral dissertation on William Paterson, by Mr. Haskett, in the Princeton University Library; also J. C. Miller, *Crisis in Freedom: the Alien and Sedition Acts* (Boston, 1951), 108, 125.

lution flooded the state, swollen by counterfeits that poured from loyalist presses in New York. Prices soared; price controls were imposed,
but were generally ineffective. The new government had no means
of enforcing its authority except the thirteen county courts carried over
from colonial times. These proved ineffectual under conditions of civil
war. Revolutionary leaders thereupon created a Council of Safety as
a temporary executive. Its twelve members were chosen by the state
legislature. They toured the state to arouse local patriots and speed
up action of the courts. They took the law into their own hands wherever they wished, hunted out suspects, ordered arrests, exacted oaths
of allegiance, punished evasion of militia service, and instituted proceedings to confiscate the property of those who openly joined the
British. One member of this Council of Safety was William Paterson,
born in Ireland, son of a storekeeper. His career had been made by
the Revolution, during which he became attorney-general to the state.
He became a heated revolutionary, detesting more than all others, as
he once said, that "pernicious class of men called moderates." His
position allowed him to buy confiscated lands on advantageous terms;
he became a well-to-do man. He lived to be a justice of the United
States Supreme Court, and a terror to democrats in the days of the
Alien and Sedition laws.

Revolutionary government as a step toward constitutional government, committees of public safety, representatives on mission to carry
revolution to the local authorities, paper money, false paper money,
price controls, oaths, detention, confiscation, aversion to "moderatism,"
and Jacobins who wind up as sober guardians of the law—how much
it all suggests what was to happen in France a few years later! With
allowance for differences of scale and intensity, there was foreshadowed
in the America of 1776 something of the *gouvernement révolutionnaire*
and even the Terror of France in 1793—except for the death sentences
and the horrors that went with them, and except for the fact that the
victims of these arbitrary proceedings never returned to political life
as an organized force, to keep alive for all time an inveterate hatred
of the Revolution.[17]

It is not easy to say why some Americans warmly embraced the
Revolution, or why others opposed it, or how many there were on each

[17] What the United States has missed by having no returned émigrés, or real
counterrevolution within its own borders, may be seen in the work of the Canadian
Arthur Johnston, dedicated to the loyalists, the "true heroes of the Revolution," and
breathing not academic revisionism but intense loathing of that event: *Myths and
Facts of the American Revolution: a Commentary on United States History as it is
Written* (Toronto, 1908).

side. Independence made it in principle necessary to choose between loyalty and rebellion. But there were many who by isolation managed to avoid commitment, or whose inclinations swayed with the course of battle, or who, torn in their beliefs, prepared passively to accept whichever authority in the end should establish itself. Numbers therefore cannot be given. It has often been repeated, as a remark of John Adams, that a third of the American people were patriot, a third loyalist, and a third neutral; but this neat summary has gone into the attic of historical fallacies; what Adams meant, when he offered it in 1815, was that a third of the Americans in the 1790's had favored the *French* Revolution, a third had opposed it, and a third had not cared.[18] The bulk of American opinion, after July 1776, seems to have been actively or potentially for independence. Positive and committed loyalists were a minority, but not therefore unimportant. They had the strength of the British empire on their side, and much also in the American tradition to support them. They believed in liberties for the colonies, and in old and historic rights under the British constitution, which, however, they felt to be less threatened by Parliament than by unruly new forces in America itself.

It is not possible to explain the division between patriot and loyalist by other or supposedly more fundamental divisions. The line coincided only locally or occasionally with the lines of conflict that had appeared before the war. Families divided, brothers often went different ways. Doubtless many a man marked himself for a lifetime by the impulsive decision of a moment. Economic and class motivations are unclear. The most firmly established merchants and lawyers tended to loyalism, but there were respected merchants and lawyers who embraced the revolution. New York and Virginia were both full of great landowners, but New York was the most loyalist province, Virginia one of the most revolutionary. Ironmasters, who had reason to object to British controls on the American iron industry, wound up in both camps. Debtors had reason to object to British attempts, over the previous half century, to limit paper money in America and stop inflation; but people do not always act from reason, and indebtedness in any case was scarcely a class phenomenon, since it was characteristic of the free-spending southern aristocracy, the businessmen in the towns, and farmers whose land was mortgaged, as well as of such actually poor people as may have been able to borrow any money. Religion

[18] J. R. Alden, *The American Revolution* (N.Y., 1954), 87, and the general discussion of loyalism in these pages.

of the Calvinist type was a force working against England, but the Presbyterians of the Carolina frontier, not eager to be governed by their own gentry, supplied many soldiers to the King. National origin had no general influence, for the Middle Colonies, the least English in origin, were stronger centers of loyalism than New England or the South. The young men, if we may judge by the infinitesimal proportion who were in the colleges, were ardently patriot. The colleges, from Harvard to William and Mary, were denounced by loyalists as hotbeds of sedition.

An obvious explanation, quite on the surface, is as good as any: that the patriots were those who saw an enlargement of opportunity in the break with Britain, and the loyalists were in large measure those who had benefited from the British connection, or who had organized their careers, and their sense of duty and usefulness, around service to the King and empire. These would include the American-born governors, Thomas Hutchinson in Massachusetts and William Franklin in New Jersey. There were also the families that customarily sat on the governors' councils or held honorific or lucrative offices under the crown. There were some in the rising American upper class who admired the way of life of the aristocracy in England, and who would imitate it as best they could.[19] Such was surely their right as British subjects, but it might alienate them from Americans generally, even many of the upper class, who were willing to have social distinctions in America develop in a new way.

It is estimated that from half to two-thirds of those who had sat on the governors' councils became loyalists.[20] For New Jersey we know exactly what happened. Of the twelve members of the provincial council in 1775, five became active and zealous loyalists, two became cautious or neutral loyalists, one went into retirement for age, and four became revolutionaries, one of whom made his peace with the British when he thought they were going to win.[21] Massachusetts had as few loyalists as any province, but when the British troops evacuated Boston in 1776 they took over 1,100 civilians with them. Of these, 102 had been councillors or officials and 18 were clergymen, mainly Anglican; but 382 were farmers, 213 were merchants "and others," and 105 came from country towns.[22] The rest were probably women and children.

[19] See, for example, C. Bridenbaugh, *Cities in Revolt: Urban Life in America, 1743-1776* (N.Y., 1955), 348-52.
[20] L. W. Labaree, *Conservatism in Early American History* (N.Y., 1948), 147.
[21] Lundin, *op.cit.*, 76-91.
[22] L. Sabine, *American Loyalists, or Biographical Sketches of Adherents to the British Crown* ... (Boston, 1847), 13.

Like the émigrés from the French Revolution, the émigrés from America came from all classes. But those connected with the English government or English church, and identifying themselves with English society and the values of the British governing class, were more numerous among loyalists than in the general population. On the other hand, lest any one thesis be carried too far, it should be pointed out that Virginia, a very English province in some ways, was so solidly patriotic that only thirteen natives of the Old Dominion ever applied to Britain for compensation for loyalist losses.[23]

The war itself polarized the issues. Each side needed strength, and the revolutionary leaders looked for it in the mass of the population, the loyalists among the ruling circles of Great Britain. In legal form, the struggle was between the sovereignty of the former colonies and the sovereignty of the British King-in-Parliament. Rebellious leaders, however, clothed themselves in the sovereignty of the "people," both in form and to a large degree in content. The social content of Parliament in the eighteenth century needs no further elaboration. The struggle, whatever men said, and whatever has been said since, was inseparable from a struggle between democratic and aristocratic forces. If the rebellion was successful, democracy in America would be favored. If it failed, if Parliament and the loyal Americans had their way, development in America would move in an aristocratic direction. In this respect the American Revolution resembled the revolutions in Europe.

That the war favored democracy in America is apparent in many ways. In some places, notably Massachusetts, the suffrage was nearly universal before the Revolution; in others, notably Virginia, the Revolution did not extend it. But in Pennsylvania the pro-British leanings of the Quaker patriciate brought them into disrepute after hostilities began; and their aversion to military solutions, at a time when any solution was bound to be military, threw power into the hands of the western farmers, who by becoming soldiers made themselves indispensable to the infant state, so that Pennsylvania developed the most democratically organized government in the new union.[24] In New Jersey the provincial congress, enjoying no legality and in rebellion against the legal authorities, sought to broaden its mandate by extending the voting franchise. In fact, petitions streamed into the Congress,

[23] Alden, op.cit., 89.
[24] E. P. Douglass, *Rebels and Democrats: The Struggle for Equal Political Rights and Majority Rule during the American Revolution* (Chapel Hill, 1955), 251-52.

urging that all householders or taxpayers should have the vote, the better to oppose enemies of the "American cause." The provincial congress in February 1776, five months before independence, granted the vote to all males at least twenty-one years old, resident in the state a year, and possessing goods worth £50 "proclamation money." With wartime depreciation of proclamation money, virtual universal manhood suffrage ensued. Voters also, after July 1776, were required to take an oath abjuring allegiance to George III, and some purists, pained by revolutionary illiberalism, have deprecated such restriction of political rights, as if the only feasible alternative would have been more democratic, and as if oaths did not exist in Britain itself, where men could still be obliged to abjure the House of Stuart.[25]

An experience of Colonel Thomas Randolph of Virginia well illustrates the same spread of democracy. Randolph, one of the many Virginia aristocrats who fought for the Revolution, was entertaining a captured British officer in his home. Three farmers came in, sat down, took off their boots, did a little spitting, and talked business with the colonel. After they left, Randolph commented to his guest on how "the spirit of independency was converted into equality, and everyone who bore arms esteemed himself on a footing with his neighbor." He added, with distaste: "No doubt, each of these men conceives himself, in every respect, my equal."[26] War, and a citizen army, had somewhat the same effects as in France after 1792. Leaders who did not fight for equality accepted it in order to win.

On the other hand, the American loyalists, who were in any case the Americans most inclined to favor hierarchic ideas, were made more so by the necessities of their position. William Eddis of Maryland, as early as 1770, thought that noblemen and bishops should be established in America as soon as possible. The commonest of all loyalist ideas was that the democratic branch, under the mixed British constitution in America, had gotten out of control. Their commonest allegation, during the war, was that the Revolution was the work of their social inferiors—"mechanics and country clowns," who had no right to dispute "what Kings, Lords, and Commons had done," as a South

---

[25] R. McCormick, *Experiment in Independence: New Jersey in the Critical Period* (New Brunswick, 1950), 35; and an unpublished doctoral dissertation in the Princeton University Library by J. R. Pole, "Reform of the Suffrage and Representation in New Jersey, 1744-1844." See also, below, 218-25. In Massachusetts the suffrage was if anything slightly restricted by the Revolution, but Massachusetts remained one of the states where the largest proportion of the population had the right to vote.

[26] Labaree, *op.cit.*, 117.

Carolina clergyman expressed it. He was driven out by his congregation.[27]

The loyalists fully expected the British army to put down the rebellion very soon. They believed that the whole disturbance had been caused by a few troublemakers, from whom the bulk of the people in America were patiently awaiting liberation. Hence, they had plans ready for the government of America after the restoration of order. These plans parallelled some of the British ideas mentioned in the last chapter. Like them, they called for the setting up in the colonies of something like a nobility. They expressed the idea that I have tried to show was so common in the eighteenth century, the idea of Blackstone and Gibbon and Montesquieu and the French parlements and many others, that some sort of nobility was a prerequisite to political liberty. There must be, in this view, an intermediate order of men having the personal right to take part in government, neither elected and hence under the influence of constituents, nor yet too amenable to influence by a king, so that they should be hereditary if possible, and at least hold office for life.

Loyal Americans congregated in New York, which was occupied by the British during most of the war. Here, as they talked over the sad state of their country, they found much on which they could agree. David Ogden of New Jersey was typical. He had served for twenty-one years on the New Jersey governor's council. After he fled to New York in January 1777, the revolutionary government in New Jersey confiscated from him twenty-three pieces of real estate, which he himself later valued at £15,231. He was one of the more prominent of the fugitives in New York, becoming a member of the Board of Refugees established there in 1779. He proposed that, after suppression of the rebellion, an American parliament be set up for all the colonies, subordinate to that of Great Britain, to consist of three branches, as in Britain: namely, a lord lieutenant, certain "barons" created for the purpose, and a house of commons chosen by the several colonial assemblies. The new parliament, incidentally, was to supervise the colleges, those "grand nurseries of the late rebellion."[28]

The case of Joseph Galloway is more fully known.[29] In 1774 he had tried to restrain the First Continental Congress by submitting a

[27] *Ibid.*, 114, 135-36.
[28] Sabine, *op.cit.*, 487.
[29] J. P. Boyd, *Anglo-American Union: Joseph Galloway's Plans to Preserve the British Empire, 1774-1788* (Philadelphia, 1941).

plan of American union, which that body had rejected as too favorable to parliamentary claims. During the war, after spending some time in New York, where he convinced himself that all Americans of any standing agreed with him, Galloway proceeded in 1778 to England, where for ten years he submitted a series of plans on colonial government to various persons in authority in London. These plans built on the plan of 1774, retaining its proposal for an autonomous inter-colonial parliament subordinate to the Parliament of Great Britain; but they added new ideas of structural reform.

The revolutionary states in America, according to Galloway, would be dissolved by the coming British victory, and the old forms of government would be forfeited by rebellion. There would therefore be a "state of nature without a civil constitution," or what he also called a Chart Blanche, "a perfect blank upon which a new policy shall be established." Opportunity would thus be afforded for certain long-needed changes. Temporarily, because of the war, there were two parties in America, the party of independence, "actuated by views of ambition and private interest," and the party favoring perpetual union with Great Britain. The former was "a mere republican party firmly attached to democratical government"; it had "vested the powers of all their new states originally and ultimately in the People." The other party, favoring union with England, preferred a "mixed form of government," to guard against abuse of power by either the sovereign or the people. Most Americans, Galloway was persuaded, were tired of being pushed about by revolutionary cliques. Most of the colonists, and certainly most men of property, would therefore welcome his plan of reorganization.

In this reorganization, the old governments of the charter provinces (Connecticut and Rhode Island) and of the proprietary provinces (Pennsylvania and Maryland) were to be abolished, and all the provinces made to conform to the same model, the balanced government of the British constitution. If Britain and America were to remain long together, it was imperative that they should have "the same customs, manners, prejudices and habits." These would then give "the same spirit to the laws." There should be an American union with a lord lieutenant or governor general representing the crown, an upper house appointed for life and with "some degree of rank or dignity above the Commons," and a lower house chosen by the various colonial assemblies. The "weight and influence" of the crown would be assured by making all offices, "civil and military, honorable and lucrative," depend on royal appointment. Thus a group of Americans would be built up, hostile to pure democracy and with an interest in mixed government and the British connection. The Americans also, declared Galloway, recurring to the almost forgotten origin of the whole controversy, would willingly pay an agreed-upon share toward military and imperial expenses, by taxing themselves through such a parliament as he outlined.

As among Americans themselves, it is clear that the Revolution involved a contest between men committed either to a more popular or a more aristocratic trend in government and society. Had the loyalists returned, received back their property, and resumed the positions of prestige and public influence which many of them had once enjoyed, it seems unlikely that the subsequent history of the United States would have been like the history that we know.

The Revolution: Britain and Europe

As between Britain and America, however, the question of internal change in America was less explicit. The British government never took official cognizance of loyalist plans. Some influence of loyalist thinking, and of British ideas resembling those of the loyalists, can be seen in the Canadian provinces, where most of the loyalists settled. But Britain had no such plans for the thirteen colonies that rebelled. Indeed, it had no plans at all, beyond the suppression of rebellion.

When hostilities began, there was a good deal of unity in England for a forcible disciplining of the Americans. Many shared the sentiments of Henry Dundas, who felt "his pride hurt, his spirit roused, his rage kindled" by the very hint that England could not "support her pretensions to empire."[30] As the war dragged on, and especially after the intervention of France, these martial enthusiasms began to subside. A war that began with wide national backing, to which only a few Whigs and a few radicals took exception, turned by 1780 into a war which everyone wanted to be rid of, with only George III persisting in his original policy, and even Lord North plaintively trying to resign.

The effects of the American Revolution in Britain and in Europe are described later. Here it need only be said, to place that Revolution more fully in its larger setting, that, just as some Americans upheld British authority and sympathized with the aristocratic order of Eu-

[30] *Parliamentary History*, xix, 1088, April 10, 1778.

rope, so there were some Europeans, and some even in the British governing class, who favored American independence, and who sympathized with the more democratic order of which the United States was already the symbol. The duke of Richmond, the first peer ever to move a parliamentary reform bill in the House of Lords, and who in fact favored universal suffrage for the House of Commons, also moved in the Lords, in April 1778, recognition of the independence of the United States.

The British government was in fact seriously handicapped, in its conflict with the colonies, by a number of embarrassments both domestic and international. France gave secret military aid to the insurgents from the beginning. Open French participation, and French attack upon Ireland, had to be considered. In December 1777, shortly before the signing of the Franco-American alliance, Lord North forwarded to George III a secret report from Paris. It affirmed that a French army was to invade Ireland, under the American flag, with promises of Irish independence. North thought the danger very considerable, since, he said, the Irish Presbyterians were pro-American "to a man," the Catholics apathetic or likely to side with the French, and the British army in Ireland too small to defend the island.[31] "America was starved for reinforcements for fear of invasion at home."[32] The need to keep troops in the home islands, at a time when military conscription was undreamed of in England, led to the employment of foreign forces. Proposals to hire as many as 50,000 Russians for use in America came to nothing. George III, as Elector of Hanover, personally disapproved of the use of German mercenaries. He even said that the German constitution forbade it. Nevertheless, the Hessians were hired; British policy and social organization required it. The use of the Hessians did more than anything else to turn American feelings toward England into hatred. It also aroused European opinion against England.

After the American victory at Saratoga, France recognized the United States, and proceeded to join it in the war against Great Britain. Lord North's government now offered a belated and untimely compromise. It repealed the Massachusetts Government Act of 1774. It repealed that old irritant, the tea duty, and put through Parliament a bill renouncing parliamentary taxation of the colonies. It despatched a peace commission to America. The commissioners were authorized to deal with the Congress "as if it were a legal body," and to yield

[31] J. Fortescue, *Correspondence of King George III* (London, 1928), III, 530.
[32] K. Feiling, *The Second Tory Party, 1714-1832* (London, 1938), 131.

everything that the Americans had officially asked before 1775. The Declaratory Act of 1766 was to stand, but Parliament would confine itself to the regulation of trade. The Americans would raise their own revenues and maintain their own army. They might even retain their Continental Congress, under the sovereignty of Parliament, if they wished to keep such an inter-colonial organization. There would be an amnesty for all involved in rebellion; on the other hand, loyalist estates would be returned, and the loyalists themselves reintegrated into American society. As for the Declaration of Independence, it would simply be superseded by a new agreement between Congress and Great Britain.[33]

It was a generous offer, though absurdly inopportune. Coming when it did, it seemed to be extorted only by force. The Americans had just won a great victory, they were securing allies in Europe, and their new states were already two years old. Leaders of the revolution in America were committed to the maintenance of the United States. Congress refused even to receive the peace commissioners, who retired in dismay to England, annoyed at the British military in America for not supporting them properly, and greatly irritated at the Americans also: William Eden wanted to harry America by fire and sword, and General Johnstone reported that two-thirds of the people in America looked longingly to England to deliver them from the tyranny of General Washington.

The government was discredited by its failures in America, and by involvement in a war with France for which it had made no adequate preparation. The reform movement in England gathered strength. Even Whigs, who saw no need of reforming Parliament, won adherents for their program of cutting down the nefarious influence of the crown. Radicalism, that is, the desire to change the composition of the Commons, grew by leaps and bounds, especially in Yorkshire and the neighborhood of London. A reforming committee at Westminster, a year before Yorktown, drew up a report that went beyond any of the new American state constitutions in its democratic theory of representation. The report, drafted by John Jebb, demanded universal manhood suffrage, the use of the ballot rather than oral voting, the annual election of Parliament, representation of voters in proportion to numbers in equal electoral districts, payment of wages to elected representatives, and removal of all property qualifications for

[33] C. R. Ritcheson, *British Politics and the American Revolution* (Norman, 1954), 258-83.

election to the Commons.[34] Here were all six points of the People's Charter to be famous in England over fifty years later.

The Whig group in Parliament, which at first hoped to make common cause with the American insurgents against George III, came to believe, after Saratoga and the Franco-American alliance, that it might after all be best for Britain if the Americans were left outside the empire. They feared that reconciliation would now bring credit upon the North ministry, or that the American Congress, if within the empire, must now be accepted as the equal of Parliament under the King. For the Whigs, it was better to recognize American independence, which would at least allow them to go on blaming the King's friends for ruining the empire. As for the radicals—not that they had any political influence—many of them believed that the British people had no quarrel with America anyway, and that the unrepresentativeness of Parliament had been a cause of the American revolt. Contrariwise, the American successes, and the perverse tendency of some people in England to applaud them, had the effect also of fortifying British conservatism. More firmness in 1765, it was argued, would have prevented the whole trouble. Concession to malcontents was a losing game; the British constitution must be upheld.

A divided Britain fought a divided America. And here a large question arises. Could the revolutionary leadership in America, divided as America was, have accomplished its purpose of independence with the resources of America alone? Was the outcome of the American War of Independence only an event in American history taking place on American soil? What would have happened if the British government had had behind it a united England and a reliable Ireland? Or if Lafayette, Kosciusko, Pulaski, de Kalb, and von Steuben had not brought their military and technical experience to the United States? Or if France had not furnished the muskets that won the battle of Saratoga, and supplied the army of Rochambeau, and fleet of de Grasse, which with Washington formed the winning combination at Yorktown?

Some writers of American history seem to feel that Britain in any case could never have suppressed the American rebellion. This may well be true. The Americans, without foreign aid, might for a long time have carried on a guerrilla resistance. They might have made the exercise of British authority impossible. The British, while long re-

[34] Printed in S. Maccoby, *The English Radical Tradition, 1763-1914* (London, 1952), 37-39.

maining in some of the seaports, might eventually have withdrawn from a country that they could not govern. To admit this much is not to answer the question. A country gaining independence in this way would not have been the country that emerged in 1783. The winners of the American war were not guerrilla chieftains. They were not obscure and hunted men out of contact with civilization. They not only made government impossible for the British; they established governments of their own. They did not represent the triumph of anarchy. America was divided, but it was not altogether, as Burke said in 1779, in a "state of dreadful confusion."[35] The Americans made a clean break with England. They came into the circle of nations as a recognized power. And they presented to the view of Europe a set of organized republican states, constituted and fashioned in a new way, of enormous interest to Europe.

The intervention of France, it may therefore appear, was one of the indispensable elements in the founding of the United States. In this sense, too, as well as in its ideological repercussions, the American Revolution was an event within an Atlantic civilization as a whole. And the Bourbon monarchy, when it helped to call the American republic into being, added another force to the forces of change in Europe.

[35] Letter of June 12, 1779 to Dr. John Erskine, in the Wentworth-Woodhouse manuscripts at the Sheffield Central Library.

THE AMERICAN REVOLUTION: THE PEOPLE

AS CONSTITUENT POWER

We hold these truths to be self-evident, that all men are created equal, that they are endowed, by their Creator, with certain unalienable rights, that among these are life, liberty, and the pursuit of happiness. That to secure these rights, governments are instituted among men, deriving their just powers from the consent of the governed, that whenever any form of government becomes destructive of these ends, it is the right of the people to alter or to abolish it. . . .—THE DECLARATION OF INDEPENDENCE OF THE UNITED STATES OF AMERICA, 1776

It is a general maxim in every government, there must exist, somewhere, a supreme, sovereign, absolute and uncontrollable power; but this power resides always in the body of the people; and it never was, or can be delegated to one man, or a few.—THE GENERAL COURT OF MASSACHU-SETTS, 1776

. . . those deluded People.—KING GEORGE III, 1775

VIII

THE AMERICAN REVOLUTION: THE PEOPLE
AS CONSTITUENT POWER

IF IT be asked what the American Revolution distinctively contributed to the world's stock of ideas, the answer might go somewhat along these lines. It did not contribute primarily a social doctrine—for although a certain skepticism toward social rank was an old American attitude, and possibly even a gift to mankind, it long antedated the Revolution, which did not so much cut down, as prevent the growth of, an aristocracy of European type. It did not especially contribute economic ideas—for the Revolution had nothing to teach on the production or distribution of goods, and the most advanced parties objected to private wealth only when it became too closely associated with government. They aimed at a separation of economic and political spheres, by which men of wealth, while free to get rich, should not have a disproportionate influence on government, and, on the other hand, government and public emoluments should not be used as a means of livelihood for an otherwise impecunious and unproductive upper class.

The American Revolution was a political movement, concerned with liberty, and with power. Most of the ideas involved were by no means distinctively American. There was nothing peculiarly American in the concepts, purely as concepts, of natural liberty and equality. They were admitted by conservatives, and were taught in the theological faculty at the Sorbonne.[1] Nor could Americans claim any exclusive

[1] See on Réal de Curban Chapter III above, and my *Catholics and Unbelievers in Eighteenth Century France* (Princeton, 1939), 126, quoting L. J. Hooke, *Religionis naturalis et moralis philosophiae principia, methodo scholastica digesta* (Paris, 1752-1754), I, 623-24: "Status is a permanent condition of man, involving various rights and a long series of obligations. It is either *natural*, constituted by nature itself, or *adventitious*, arising from some human act or institution. . . . By the *status of nature* we understand that in which men would be who were subject to no government but joined only by similarity of nature or by private pacts. . . . In the status of nature all men are equal and enjoy the same rights. For in that state they are distinguished only by the gifts of mind or body by which some excel others." Italics are the Abbé Hooke's.

understanding of the ideas of government by contract or consent, or the sovereignty of the people, or political representation, or the desirability of independence from foreign rule, or natural rights, or the difference between natural law and positive law, or between certain fundamental laws and ordinary legislation, or the separation of powers, or the federal union of separate states. All these ideas were perfectly familiar in Europe, and that is why the American Revolution was of such interest to Europeans.

The Distinctiveness of American Political Ideas

The most distinctive work of the Revolution was in finding a method, and furnishing a model, for putting these ideas into practical effect. It was in the implementation of similar ideas that Americans were more successful than Europeans. "In the last fifty years," wrote General Bonaparte to Citizen Talleyrand in 1797, "there is only one thing that I can see that we have really defined, and that is the sovereignty of the people. But we have had no more success in determining what is constitutional, than in allocating the different powers of government." And he said more peremptorily, on becoming Emperor in 1804, that the time had come "to constitute the Nation." He added: "I am the constituent power."[2]

The problem throughout much of America and Europe, for half a century, was to "constitute" new government, and in a measure new societies. The problem was to find a constituent power. Napoleon offered himself to Europe in this guise. The Americans solved the problem by the device of the constitutional convention, which, revolutionary in origin, soon became institutionalized in the public law of the United States.[3]

The constitutional convention in theory embodied the sovereignty of the people. The people chose it for a specific purpose, not to govern, but to set up institutions of government. The convention, acting as the sovereign people, proceeded to draft a constitution and a declaration of rights. Certain "natural" or "inalienable" rights of the citizen were thus laid down at the same time as the powers of government. It was the constitution that created the powers of government, defined

[2] *Correspondance de Napoleon I*, III (Paris, 1859), 314; R. M. Johnston, *The Corsican* (N.Y., 1910), 182.
[3] See, for example, J. A. Jameson, *The Constitutional Convention: Its History, Powers and Modes of Proceeding* (N.Y., 1867); H. C. Hockett, *The Constitutional History of the United States, 1776-1826* (N.Y., 1939).

their scope, gave them legality, and balanced them one against another. The constitution was written and comprised in a single document. The constitution and accompanying declaration, drafted by the convention, must, in the developed theory, be ratified by the people. The convention thereupon disbanded and disappeared, lest its members have a vested interest in the offices they created. The constituent power went into abeyance, leaving the work of government to the authorities now constituted. The people, having exercised sovereignty, now came under government. Having made law, they came under law. They put themselves voluntarily under restraint. At the same time, they put restraint upon government. All government was limited government; all public authority must keep within the bounds of the constitution and of the declared rights. There were two levels of law, a higher law or constitution that only the people could make or amend, through constitutional conventions or bodies similarly empowered; and a statutory law, to be made and unmade, within the assigned limits, by legislators to whom the constitution gave this function.

Such was the theory, and it was a distinctively American one. European thinkers, in all their discussion of a political or social contract, of government by consent and of sovereignty of the people, had not clearly imagined the people as actually contriving a constitution and creating the organs of government. They lacked the idea of the people as a constituent power. Even in the French Revolution the idea developed slowly; members of the French National Assembly, long after the Tennis Court oath, continued to feel that the constitution which they were writing, to be valid, had to be accepted by the King as a kind of equal with whom the nation had to negotiate. Nor, indeed, would the King tolerate any other view. On the other hand, we have seen how at Geneva in 1767 the democrats advanced an extreme version of citizen sovereignty, holding that the people created the constitution and the public offices by an act of will; but they failed to get beyond a simple direct democracy; they had no idea of two levels of law, or of limited government, or of a delegated and representative legislative authority, or of a sovereign people which, after acting as a god from the machine in a constituent convention, retired to the more modest status of an electorate, and let its theoretical sovereignty become inactive.

The difficulty with the theory was that the conditions under which it could work were seldom present. No people really starts *de novo;* some political institutions always already exist; there is never a *tabula rasa,* or state of nature, or Chart Blanche as Galloway posited for conservative purposes. Also, it is difficult for a convention engaged in writing a constitution not to be embroiled in daily politics and problems of government. And it is hard to live voluntarily under restraint. In complex societies, or in times of crisis, either government or people or some part of the people may feel obliged to go beyond the limits that a constitution has laid down.

In reality, the idea of the people as a constituent power, with its corollaries, developed unclearly, gradually, and sporadically during the American Revolution. It was adumbrated in the Declaration of Independence: the people may "institute new government." Jefferson, among the leaders, perhaps conceived the idea most clearly. It is of especial interest, however, to see how the "people" themselves, that is, certain lesser and unknown or poorer or unsatisfied persons, contributed to these distinctive American ideas by their opposition to the Revolutionary elite.

There were naturally many Americans who felt that no change was needed except expulsion of the British. With the disappearance of the British governors, and collapse of the old governor's councils, the kind of men who had been active in the colonial assemblies, and who now sat as provincial congresses or other *de facto* revolutionary bodies, were easily inclined to think that they should keep the management of affairs in their own hands. Some parallel can be seen with what happened in Europe. There was a revolution, or protest, of constituted bodies against authorities set above them, and a more popular form of revolution, or protest, which aimed at changing the character or membership of these constituted bodies themselves. As at Geneva the General Council rebelled against the patriciate, without wishing to admit new citizens to the General Council; as in Britain the Whigs asserted the powers of Parliament against the King, without wishing to change the composition of Parliament; as in Belgium, in 1789, the Estates party declared independence from the Emperor, while maintaining the preexisting estates; as in France, also in 1789, the nobility insisted that the King govern through the Estates-General, but objected to the transformation of the three estates into a new kind of national body; as in the Dutch provinces in 1795 the Estates-General, after expelling the Prince of Orange, tried to remain itself unchanged, and resisted the election of a "convention"; so, in America in 1776, the assemblies that drove out the officers of the King, and governed their respective states under revolutionary conditions, sought to keep control of affairs in their own hands, and to avoid reconstitution at the hands of the "people."

Ten states gave themselves new constitutions in 1776 and 1777. In nine of these states, however, it was the ordinary assembly, that is, the revolutionary government of the day, that drafted and proclaimed the constitution. In the tenth, Pennsylvania, a constituent convention met, but it soon had to take on the burden of daily government in addition. In Connecticut and Rhode Island the colonial charters remained in force, and the authorities constituted in colonial times (when governors and councils had already been elected) remained unchanged in principle for half a century. In Massachusetts the colonial charter remained in effect until 1780.

Thus in no state, when independence was declared, did a true constituent convention meet, and, as it were, calmly and rationally devise government out of a state of nature. There was already, however, some recognition of the principle that constitutions cannot be made merely by governments, that a more fundamental power is needed to produce a constitution than to pass ordinary laws or carry on ordinary executive duties. Thus, in New Hampshire, New York, Delaware, Maryland, North Carolina, and Georgia, the assemblies drew up constitutions only after soliciting authority for that purpose from the voters. In Maryland and North Carolina there was a measure of popular ratification.

Constitution-making in North Carolina, Pennsylvania, and Massachusetts

The popular pressures that helped to form American political doctrine are best illustrated from North Carolina, Pennsylvania, and Massachusetts.[4]

In North Carolina class lines had been sharply drawn by the Regulator movement and its suppression. The people of the back-country even inclined to be loyalist, not eager for an independence that might only throw them into the hands of the county gentry. In the turbulent election of October 1776 the voters knew that the assembly which they elected would draft a state constitution. There was no demand for a convention to act exclusively and temporarily as a constituent power.

[4] Here I am indebted, without sharing all his conclusions, to E. P. Douglass, *Rebels and Democrats: the Struggle for Equal Political Rights and Majority Rule during the American Revolution* (Chapel Hill, 1955).

But several counties drew up instructions for the deputies, in which the emerging doctrine was set forth clearly.

Orange and Mecklenburg counties used identical language. This is a sign, as in the case of identical phrasing in the French *cahiers* of 1789, where the matter has been carefully studied, that some person of influence and education, and not some poor farmer ruminating in his cabin, had probably written out a draft. Still, the public meetings of both counties found it to their taste. "Political power," they said, "is of two kinds, one principal and superior, the other derived and inferior. . . . The principal supreme power is possessed only by the people at large. . . . The derived and inferior power by the servants which they employ. . . . The rules by which the inferior power is exercised are to be constituted by the principal supreme power. . . ."[5] In other words, government was not a form of guardianship. Office was to be no longer a perquisite of the gentry, or "an aristocracy of power in the hands of the rich," to use their own language, but a form of employment by the people, whom they did not hesitate to call "the poor." Mecklenburg favored a unicameral legislature, Orange a bicameral one, but both called for a separation of powers. It was not that any organ of government should enjoy independence from the electorate (the essence of balance-of-power theory in the European, British, and loyalist view), but rather that the various functions of government should be defined and distributed among different men, to prevent what had happened in colonial times. The fact that before 1776 the council had possessed executive, legislative, and judicial functions, and that members of the assembly had served as justices of the peace, or had their relatives appointed judges and sheriffs, was the basis on which North Carolina had been dominated by small groups of gentry. It was popular objection to this situation, probably more than a reading of European books, that made the separation of powers a principal American doctrine.

The North Carolina constitution, as written and adopted, enlarged the electorate by granting all taxpayers the right to vote for members of the lower house. It equalized the representation by giving more deputies to the western counties. It required a freehold of 100 acres for members of the lower house, and of 300 acres for those of the upper house, who were to be elected only by voters possessing 50 acres. The governor, elected by the two houses, had to have a freehold worth

[5] *Ibid.*, 126.

£1,000. The constitution was a compromise between populace and landed gentry. It lasted until the Civil War.[6]

The situation in Pennsylvania was complex. The Quaker colony, idealized by European intellectuals as the haven of innocent equality and idyllic peace, had long been plagued by some of the most acrimonious politics in America. Quaker bigwigs had long clashed with the non-Quaker lesser orders of Philadelphia and the West. In the spring of 1776 Pennsylvania was the only colony in which the assembly was still legal under the old law. It still showed a desire for reconciliation with England, and, with it, maintenance of the old social and political system. This persistence of conservatism in high places made a great many people all the more radical. A year of open war with Britain had aroused the determination for independence, and in May 1776 a mass meeting of 4,000 people in Philadelphia demanded the calling of a constitutional convention. Various local committees got to work, and a convention was elected by irregular methods. Where the three eastern counties had formerly been heavily over-represented, the situation was now not equalized, but reversed. The West, with the same population as the three eastern counties, had 64 delegates in the convention to only 24 for the East. "The Convention in Pennsylvania was a political expedient, and not, as in Massachusetts, the cornerstone of constitutional government."[7] Its real function was to promote the Revolution, and assure independence from England, by circumventing the assembly and all other opposition. Like the more famous French Convention elected in 1792, it rested on a kind of popular mandate which did not reflect an actual majority of the population; like it, it became the government of the country during war and revolution; like it, it behaved dictatorially. The constitutions drafted in Pennsylvania in 1776, and in France in 1793, were, in their formal provisions, by far the most democratic of any produced in the eighteenth century. The Pennsylvania constitution of 1776, unlike the French constitution of the Year I, was never submitted even to the formalities of popular ratification. But the two constitutions became a symbol of what democrats meant by democracy.

The Pennsylvania constitution vested legislative power in a single house. For the executive it avoided the name and office of governor, entrusting executive power to a council and "president," a word which

---

[6] For the text of the constitutions, see F. N. Thorpe, *Federal and State Constitutions, Colonial Charters and Other Organic Laws of the . . . United States of America* (Washington, 7 vols., 1909).

[7] Douglass, *op.cit.*, 260.

then meant no more than chairman. All male taxpayers twenty-one years of age had the vote, and were eligible for any office. To sit in the assembly, however, it was necessary publicly to acknowledge the divine inspiration of the Old and New Testaments. Voters elected the legislators, the executive councillors, sheriffs, coroners, tax-assessors, and justices of the peace. Voting was by ballot. The president was chosen by the legislature and the executive council; he had no veto or appointive powers, and what powers he did have he could exercise only in agreement with his council. All officers were elected for one year, except that councillors served for three. Rotation of office was provided for; legislators, councillors, president, and sheriffs could be reelected only a certain number of times. Doors of the legislative assembly must always be open to the public. There was a kind of referendum, in that no bill passed by the assembly, short of emergency, became law until submitted for public consideration and enacted in the assembly of the following year, if there was no public objection. Officeholders received pay, but if revenues of any office became too large the assembly could reduce them. All officers and judges could be impeached by the assembly. Judges of the Supreme Court could be removed by the assembly for "misbehavior." There was an elected council of censors, or board of review, which every seven years ascertained whether the constitution had been preserved inviolate, and called a convention if amendment seemed necessary.

The Pennsylvania constitution represented the doctrine of a single party, namely the democrats, people of the kind who had formerly had little to do with government, and whose main principle was that government should never become a separate or vested interest within the state. This was indeed an understandable principle, at a time when government, in all countries in varying degree, had in fact become the entrenched interest of a largely hereditary governing class. The Pennsylvania constitution substituted almost a direct democracy, in which no one in government could carry any responsibility or pursue any sustained program of his own. Many people in Pennsylvania objected to it from the beginning. It must be remembered that the democratic constitution did not signify that Pennsylvania was really more democratic than some of the other states; it signified, rather, that Pennsylvania was more divided, and that conservatism was stronger, certain upper-class and politically experienced elements, which elsewhere took a leading part in the Revolution, being in Pennsylvania tainted with Anglophilism. Whether the constitution of 1776 was workable or not, these people soon put an end to it. It lasted only until 1790.[8]

The most interesting case is that of Massachusetts. Here the great political thinker was John Adams, who became the main author of the Massachusetts constitution of 1780, which in turn had an influence on the Constitution of the United States. In his own time Adams was denounced as an Anglomaniac and a Monocrat. In our own time some sympathizers with the eighteenth-century democrats have considered him very conservative, while on the other hand theorists of the "new conservatism" would persuade us that John Adams was in truth the American Edmund Burke. I confess that I see very little in any of these allegations.

Adams in January 1776 published some *Thoughts on Government,* for the guidance of those in the various colonies who were soon to declare independence and begin to govern themselves. This was in some ways a conservative tract. Adams thought it best, during the war, for the new states simply to keep the forms of government that they had. He obviously approved the arrangement under the Massachusetts charter of 1691, by which the popular assembly elected an upper house or council. In other ways he was not very conservative. He declared, like Jefferson, that the aim of government is welfare or happiness, that republican institutions must rest on "virtue," and that the people should support a universal system of public schools. He wanted one-year terms for governors and officials (the alternative would be "slavery"), and he favored rotation of office. He quite agreed that someday the state governors and councillors might be popularly elected, as they were in Connecticut already. He gave six reasons for having a bicameral legislature, but in none of these six reasons did he show any fear of the people, or belief that, with a unicameral legislature, the people would plunder property or degenerate into anarchy. He was afraid of the one-house legislature itself. He never committed the folly of identifying the deputies with the deputizers. He was afraid that a single house would be arbitrary or capricious, or make itself perpetual, or "make laws for their own interest, and adjudge all controversies in their own favor."[9] He himself cited the cases of Holland and the Long Parliament. The fear of a self-perpetuating political body, gathering privileges to itself, was certainly better grounded in common observation than vague alarms about anarchy or pillage.

[8] *Ibid.*, 214-86; J. P. Selsam, *The Pennsylvania Constitution of 1776: a Study in Revolutionary Democracy* (Philadelphia, 1936).
[9] *Works* (1851), IV, 196.

The *Thoughts* of 1776 were conservative in another way, if conservatism be the word. Adams had not yet conceived the idea of a constitutional convention. He lacked the notion of the people as constituent power. He had in mind that existing assemblies would draft the new constitutions, when and if any were drafted. Adams was familiar with all the high-level political theory of England and Europe. But the idea of the people as the constituent power arose locally, from the grass roots.

The revolutionary leadership in Massachusetts, including both Adamses, was quite satisfied to be rid of the British, and otherwise to keep the Bay State as it had always been. They therefore "resumed" the charter of 1691. They simply undid the Massachusetts Government Act of 1774. Some of the commonalty of Boston, and farmers of Concord and the western towns, envisaged further changes. It is hard to say what they wanted, except that they wanted a new constitution. Experts in Massachusetts history contradict each other flatly; some say that debtors, poor men, and Baptists were dissatisfied; others that all kinds of diverse people naturally owed money anyway, that practically no one was too poor to vote, and that Baptists were an infinitesimal splinter group in a solidly Congregationalist population. It may be that the trouble was basically psychological; that many people of fairly low station, even though they had long had the right to vote, had never until the Revolution participated in politics, were aroused by the Revolution, the war, and excitement of soldiering, and, feeling that affairs had always been managed by people socially above them, wanted now to act politically on their own.

Demands were heard for a new constitution. It was said that the charter of 1691 was of no force, since the royal power that had issued it was no longer valid. It was said that no one could be governed without his consent, and that no living person had really consented to this charter. Some Berkshire towns even hinted that they did not belong to Massachusetts at all until they shared in constituting the new commonwealth. They talked of "setting themselves apart," or being welcomed by a neighboring state. Echoes of the social contract floated through the western air. "The law to bind all must be assented to by all," declared the farmers of Sutton. "The Great Secret of Government is governing all by all," said those of Spencer.[10] It began to seem that a constitution was necessary not only to secure liberty but to establish authority, not only to protect the individual but to found the state.

The house of representatives proposed that it and the council, that

[10] Douglass, *op.cit.*, 178.

is, the two houses of legislation sitting together, should be authorized by the people to draw up a constitution. All adult males were to vote on the granting of this authorization, not merely those possessing the customary property qualification. In a sense, this was to recognize Rousseau's principle that there must be "unanimity at least once": that everyone must consent to the law under which he was to live, even if later, when constitutional arrangements were made, a qualification was required for ordinary voting. The council objected to a plan whereby it would lose its identity by merging with the house. A little dispute occurred, not unlike that in France in 1789 between "vote by head" and "vote by order." The plan nevertheless went through. The two houses, sitting as one, and authorized by the people, produced a constitution in 1778. It was submitted for popular ratification. The voters repudiated it. Apparently both democrats and conservatives were dissatisfied. This is precisely what happened in Holland in 1797, when the first constitution of the Dutch revolution was rejected by a coalition of opposite-minded voters.

A special election was therefore held, in which all towns chose delegates to a state convention, "for the sole purpose of forming a new Constitution." John Adams, delegate from Braintree, was put on the drafting committee. He wrote a draft, which the convention modified only in detail. The resulting document reflected many influences. It is worth while to suggest a few.

There is a modern fashion for believing that Rousseau had little influence in America, particularly on such sensible characters as John Adams. I do not think that he had very much. Adams, however, had read the *Social Contract* as early as 1765, and ultimately had four copies of it in his library. I suspect that, like others, he found much of it unintelligible or fantastic, and some of it a brilliant expression of his own beliefs. He himself said of the Massachusetts constitution: "It is Locke, Sidney, Rousseau, and de Mably reduced to practice."[11]

Adams wrote in the preamble: "The body politic is formed by a voluntary association of individuals. It is a social compact, by which the whole people covenants with each citizen, and each citizen with the whole people, that all shall be governed by certain laws for the common good."[12] The thought here, and the use of the word "cove-

[11] *Works* (1851), IV, 216. Adams also, in 1787, cited Rousseau's *Discourse on Inequality* and *Considerations on Poland* with approval, recommending the former for its picture of the evil in civilized men, the latter for its view that Poland was dominated exclusively by nobles. *Works*, IV, 409 and 367.

[12] *Ibid.*, 219; Thorpe, *op.cit.*, III, 1889.

nant," go back to the Mayflower compact. But whence comes the "social" in *social* compact? And whence comes the word "citizen"? There were no "citizens" under the British constitution, except in the sense of freemen of the few towns known as cities. In the English language the word "citizen" in its modern sense is an Americanism, dating from the American Revolution.[13] It is entirely possible that Jean-Jacques Rousseau had deposited these terms in Adams' mind. The whole passage suggests Chapter vi, Book i, of the *Social Contract*. The convention adopted this part of Adams' preamble without change.

In the enacting clause of the preamble Adams wrote: "We, therefore, the delegates of the people of Massachusetts . . . agree upon the following . . . Constitution of the Commonwealth of Massachusetts." The convention made a significant emendation: "We, therefore, the people of Massachusetts . . . agree upon, ordain and establish. . . ." The formula, *We the people ordain and establish*, expressing the developed theory of the people as constituent power, was used for the first time in the Massachusetts constitution of 1780, whence it passed into the preamble of the United States constitution of 1787 and the new Pennsylvania constitution of 1790, after which it became common in the constitutions of the new states, and in new constitutions of the old states. Adams did not invent the formula. He was content with the matter-of-fact or purely empirical statement that the "delegates" had "agreed." It was the popularly elected convention that rose to more abstract heights. Providing in advance for popular ratification, it imputed the creation of government to the people.

Adams wrote, as the first article of the Declaration of Rights: "All men are born equally free and independent, and have certain natural, essential and unalienable rights," which included defense of their lives, liberties, and property, and the seeking of "safety and happiness." The Virginia Declaration of Rights, drafted by George Mason in June 1776, was almost identical, and Adams certainly had it in mind. The Massachusetts convention made only one change in this sentence. It declared: "All men are born free and equal." The convention, obviously, was thinking of the Declaration of Independence, that is, Jefferson's more incisive rewording of Mason's Virginia declaration.

The convention had been elected by a true universal male suffrage,

---

[13] This may be readily confirmed from the Oxford Dictionary, or by comparison of definitions of "citizen" in British and American dictionaries, or by tracing the article "citizen" through successive editions of the Encyclopaedia Britannica, where the modern meaning does not appear until the eleventh edition in 1910.

but it adopted, following Adams' draft, a restriction on the franchise. To vote, under the constitution, it was necessary to own real estate worth £3 a year, or real and personal property of a value of £60. The charter of 1691 had specified only £2 and £40 respectively. The state constitution was thus in this respect more conservative than the charter. How much more conservative? Here we run into the difference between experts already mentioned.[14] A whole school of thought, pointing to a 50 per cent increase in the voting qualification, has seen a reaction of property-owners against dangers from below. Closer examination of the values of money reveals that the £3 and £60 of 1780 represent an increase of only one-eighth over the figures of 1691. Even if half the people of Boston were unfranchised, all Boston then had only a twentieth of the population of the state. In the rural areas, where farm ownership was usual, it was mainly grown sons living for a few years with their parents who lacked the vote. There seems to have been only sporadic objection to the suffrage provision.

Adams put into the constitution, and the convention retained it, that ghost of King, Lords, and Commons that now assumed the form of governor, senate, and house of representatives. Partisans of the British system, in England or America, would surely find this ghost highly attenuated. The point about King and Lords, in the British system, was precisely that they were not elected by anyone, that they were immune to popular pressure, or any pressure, through their enjoyment of life tenure and hereditary personal rights to political position. Governor and senators in Massachusetts, like representatives, both in Adams' draft and in the final document, were all elected, all by the same electorate, and all for one-year terms. To Adams (as, for example, to Delolme), it was of the utmost importance to prevent the executive from becoming the mere creature of the legislature. He even wished the governor to have an absolute veto, which the convention changed to a veto that could be overridden by a two-thirds majority of both houses. Adams continued to prefer a final veto. Jeffersonians and their numerous progeny found this highly undemocratic. In all states south of New York, at the end of the Revolution, governors were elected by the legislative houses, and none had any veto. Adams justified the veto as a means "to preserve the independence of the

---

[14] For emphasis on the conservative or reactionary character of the Massachusetts constitution, see Douglass, *op.cit.*, 189-213, and more specialized writers cited there; for the opposite view, which I follow in part, see R. E. Brown, *Middle-Class Democracy and the Revolution in Massachusetts, 1691-1780* (Ithaca, 1955), 384-400.

executive and judicial departments."[15] And since governors could no longer be appointed by the crown, an obvious way to prevent their dependence on legislatures was to have them issue, like legislators, from the new sovereign, the people. It was legislative oligarchy that Adams thought the most imminent danger. As he wrote to Jefferson in 1787: "You are afraid of the one—I, of the few."[16]

As for the phantom "lords," or senators, though they were directly elected by the ordinary voters for one-year terms, they were in a way supposed to represent property rather than numbers. They were apportioned among the counties of Massachusetts not according to population but according to taxes paid, that is, according to assessed value of taxable wealth. Suffolk County, which included Boston, thus received 6 senators out of 40, where on a purely numerical basis it would have received only four. The Maine districts, Cape Cod, and the western counties were numerically somewhat underrepresented. The three central and western counties received 11 senators, where a representation in proportion to numbers would have given them 12 or 13. Inequalities in wealth in Massachusetts, as between individuals or as between city and country, were not yet great enough to make a senate apportioned according to "property" (which included the small man's property as well as the rich man's) very different from a senate apportioned according to numbers.[17]

The Massachusetts constitution prescribed certain qualifications for eligibility. The governor was required to have a freehold worth at least £1,000, senators a freehold of £300 or £600 total estate, representatives a freehold of £100 or £200 total estate. (British law at this time required £300 or £600 *annual income* from land to qualify for the House of Commons.) These Massachusetts requirements resembled those in North Carolina, where the governor had to have a £1,000 freehold, and members of the upper and lower houses freeholds of 300 or 100 acres respectively. In the absence of comparative statistics on land values and distribution of land ownership in the two states, it is impossible to compare the real impact of these legal qualifications for office. In Massachusetts, however, whatever may have been true

---

[15] Adams, *Works* (1851), IV, 231 and 232 note.

[16] *Papers of Thomas Jefferson*, XII (Princeton, 1955), 396.

[17] Compare the apportionment of senators in the Massachusetts constitution with the population of counties in the census of 1790. The fact that the senate represented property rather than numbers is stressed by those who see the Massachusetts constitution of 1780 as a very conservative or reactionary document. I confess to sharing the impatience of Professor Brown at academic theories which dissolve under a little grade-school computation.

in North Carolina, the average 100-acre one-family farm was worth well over £300, and there were a great many such farms, so that the ordinary successful farmer could qualify for either house of the legislature, and a few well-to-do ones in almost every village might if they chose have aspired to the office of governor.[18] The requirements in Massachusetts, as set forth by John Adams, were, if anything, Jeffersonian or agrarian in their tendency, since they favored the farm population, and made it even harder for middle-class townspeople, who might own no land, to occupy public office. The aim was clearly to limit office to the substantial segment of the population, but the substantial segment was broadly defined. Still, there were people who by this definition were not "substantial," and some of them objected to these provisions, though not many would in any case have ventured to run for office or been elected if they did, in the Massachusetts of 1780.

It was Article III of the Declaration of Rights, both in Adams' draft and in the finished constitution, that caused most debate in the convention and most disagreement among the voters during ratification. This article, declaring religion to be the foundation of morality and of the state, authorized the legislature to "enjoin" people to go to church, and required the use of public funds to maintain the churches, while allowing any "subject" to have his own contribution paid to the denomination of his choice. While it received a large majority of the popular vote, 8,885 to 6,225, it was the one article which most clearly failed to obtain a two-thirds majority, and the one which may have never been legally ratified, though declared so by the convention. Those voting against it expressed a desire to separate church and state. These, in turn, included perhaps a few Baptists who favored such separation on religious principle, a great many Protestants who feared that the article might legalize Roman Catholicism, and an unknown number of people, one suspects, who were no longer very regular in attending any church at all.

The Massachusetts constitution of 1780 was adopted by a two-thirds majority in a popular referendum from which no free adult male was excluded. The vote was light, for opinion on the matter seems not to have been excited.[19] It was six years since the rebellion against King

---

[18] Brown, op.cit., 18, 394.
[19] About 23 per cent of adult males voted on ratification of the constitution of 1780, a figure which may be compared with 30 per cent of adult males voting on ratification of the French constitution of 1793, with the difference that in the France of 1793 only those voting "yes" took the trouble to vote at all (1,801,918 "ayes" to

George, and four years since the British army had left Massachusetts; doubtless many people wished to be bothered no longer. The action of the people as constituent power is, after all, a legal concept, or even a necessary legal fiction where the sovereignty of any concrete person or government is denied. It does not signify that everyone is actually engrossed in the fabrication of constitutions. On the other hand, it does not seem necessary to believe that the convention, when it declared the constitution ratified, put something over on an innocent or apathetic or reluctant people. The people of Massachusetts had rejected the constitution proposed in 1778. They could have rejected the one proposed in 1780. It was adopted, not because it was thought perfect or final by everyone, but because it offered a frame of government, or basis of agreement, within which people could still lawfully disagree. It has lasted, with many amendments, until the present day.

A Word on the Constitution of the United States

The idea that sovereignty lay with the people, and not with states or their governments, made possible in America a new kind of federal structure unknown in Europe. The Dutch and Swiss federations were unions of component parts, close permanent alliances between disparate corporate members. For them no other structure was possible, because there was as yet no Dutch or Swiss people except in a cultural sense. It was in the Dutch revolution of 1795 and the Swiss revolution of 1798 that these two bundles of provinces or cantons were first proclaimed as political nations. In America it was easier to make the transition from a league of states, set up during the Revolution, to a more integral union set up in the United States constitution of 1787. The new idea was that, instead of the central government drawing its powers from the states, both central and state governments should draw their powers from the same source; the question was the limit between these two sets of derived powers. The citizen, contrariwise, was simultaneously a citizen both of the United States and of his own

---

11,610 "no's" with some 4,300,000 abstentions). It is a question whether a vote by 23 per cent of the population should be considered "light." This percentage may have been a good measure of the politically interested population; in the annual elections of the governor the ratio of persons actually casting a vote to the total of adult white males ranged between 9 per cent and 28 per cent until it began to rise with the election of 1800. See J. R. Pole, "Suffrage and Representation in Massachusetts: A Statistical Note," in *William and Mary Quarterly*, xiv (October 1957), 590-92, and J. Godechot, *Les institutions de la France sous la Révolution et l'Empire* (Paris, 1951), 252.

state. He was the sovereign, not they. He chose to live under two constitutions, two sets of laws, two sets of courts and officials; theoretically, he had created them all, reserving to himself, under each set, certain liberties specified in declarations of rights.

It has been widely believed, since the publication in 1913 of Charles A. Beard's *Economic Interpretation of the Constitution*, that the federal constitution of 1787 marked a reaction against democratic impulses of the Revolution, and was a device by which men of property, particularly those holding securities of the state or continental governments, sought to protect themselves and their financial holdings against the dangers of popular rule. The Philadelphia convention has been represented as an almost clandestine body, which exceeded its powers, and which managed (as has also been said of the Massachusetts convention of 1780) to impose a conservative constitution on a confused or apathetic people. Recently the flimsiness of the evidence for this famous thesis has been shown by Professor Robert Brown.[20] The thesis takes its place in the history of historical writing, as a product of that Progressive and post-Progressive era in which the common man could be viewed as the dupe or plaything of private interests.

It seems likely enough that there was a conservative reaction after the American Revolution, and even a movement among the upper class (minus the old loyalists) not wholly unlike the "aristocratic resurgence" which I shall soon describe in the Europe of the 1780's. The difference is that these neo-aristocrats of America were less obstinate and less caste-conscious than in Europe. They did not agree with each other, and they knew they could not rule alone. The men at Philadelphia in 1787 were too accomplished as politicians to be motivated by anything so impractical as ideology or mere self-interest. They hoped, while solving concrete problems, to arouse as little opposition as possible. They lacked also the European sense of the permanency of class status. Thinking of an upper class as something that individuals might move into or out of, they allowed for social mobility both upward and downward. The wealthy Virginian, George Mason, at the Philadelphia convention, on urging that the upper class should take care to give adequate representation to the lower, offered it as

---

[20] R. E. Brown, *Charles Beard and the Constitution: a Critical Analysis of "An Economic Interpretation of the Constitution"* (Princeton, 1956). The critique of Beard is carried even further in a more recent work, Forrest McDonald, *We the People: The Economic Origins of the Constitution* (Chicago, 1958).

one of his reasons that, however affluent they might be now, "the course of a few years not only might, but certainly would, distribute their posterity through the lowest classes of society."[21] No one seems to have disputed this prognostication. Such acceptance of future downward mobility for one's own grandchildren, if by no means universal in America, was far more common than in Europe. Without such downward mobility there could not long remain much room for newcomers at the top, or much assurance of a fluid society. With it, there could not be a permanent aristocracy in the European sense.

It was the state legislatures that chose the delegates to the Philadelphia convention, in answer to a widely expressed demand for strengthening the federal government under the Articles of Confederation. The Philadelphia convention proceeded, not to amend the Articles, but to ignore and discard them. It repudiated the union which the thirteen states had made. Beard in 1913 found it satisfying to call this operation a revolution, a revolution from above to be sure, which he compared to a *coup d'état* of Napoleon. His critic, Professor Brown, in 1956, found it satisfying and important to deny any revolutionary action in what happened.

What did really happen? The men at Philadelphia did circumvent the state governments, and in a sense they betrayed those who sent them. They did so by adopting the revolutionary principle of the American Revolution, which had already become less purely revolutionary and more institutionalized as an accepted routine, as shown in the Massachusetts convention of 1780, which had been followed by a New Hampshire convention, and new constitution for New Hampshire in 1784. The Philadelphia convention went beyond the existing constituted bodies, that is, the state governments and the Congress under the Articles, by appealing for support directly to the people, who in each state elected, for this purpose only, conventions to discuss, ratify, or refuse to ratify the document proposed by the convention at Philadelphia. The authors of the proposed federal constitution needed a principle of authority; they conceived that "the people were the fountain of all power," and that if popularly chosen conventions ratified their work "all disputes and doubts concerning [its] legitimacy" would be removed.[22] In each state, in voting for ratifying conventions, the voters voted according to the franchise as given by their state constitutions. No use was made of the more truly revolutionary idea, still

---

[21] *Writings* of James Madison, 9 vols. (N.Y., 1902-1910), III, 47.
[22] Quoted by Brown, *op.cit.*, 140.

alive in Massachusetts in 1780, that on the acceptance of a government *every* man should have a vote. In some states the authorized voters were a great majority; in none were they a small minority. The actual vote for the ratifying conventions was light, despite protracted public discussion, because most people lost interest, or never had any, in abstract debates concerning governmental structure at the distant federal level. Eleven states ratified within a few months, and the constitution went into effect for the people of those eleven states. The remaining two states came in within three years. The whole procedure was revolutionary in a sense, but revolution had already become domesticated in America. The idea of the people as the constituent power, acting through special conventions, was so generally accepted and understood that a mere mention of the word "convention," in the final article of the proposed constitution, was thought sufficient explanation of the process of popular endorsement.

Nevertheless, men of popular principles, those who would soon be called democrats, and who preferred the arrangements of the Pennsylvania constitution, with its single-house legislature to which the executive was subordinated, found much in the new federal constitution not to their liking, at least at first sight. The new instrument reproduced the main features of the Massachusetts constitution of 1780: the strong president, the senate, the house of representatives, the partial executive veto, the independent judiciary, the separation and balance of powers. In fact, the longer tenure of offices—four years for the president, six for senators, two for representatives, in place of the annual terms for corresponding functionaries in Massachusetts—shows a reaction away from revolutionary democracy and toward the giving of more adequate authority to those entrusted with public power. The president was not popularly elected, like the governor in Massachusetts; but neither was he designated by the legislative assembly, like the president in Pennsylvania and governors in the Southern states. He was elected by an electoral college, with each state free to determine how its own share of these electors should be chosen. Although as early as 1788 almost half the states provided for popular election of presidential electors, it was not until 1828 that this became the general and permanent rule. In the federal constitution the unique feature, and key to the main compromise, was the senate. Not only did large and small states have the same number of senators, but it was the state legislatures that chose them. Since it was the state legislatures that conservative or hard-money men mainly feared in the 1780's, this provision can hardly have been introduced in the hope of assuring economic conservatism. It was introduced to mollify the states as states. In the senate the new union was a league of preexisting corporate entities. In the house of representatives it rested more directly on the people. Anyone who had the right to vote in his state could vote for a member of the lower house of Congress. In one respect the federal constitution, by its silence, was more democratic in a modern sense than any of the state constitutions. No pecuniary or religious qualification was specified for any office.

The new constitution was a compromise, but that it produced a less popular federal government, less close to the people, than that of the Articles of Confederation, seems actually contrary to the facts. It created a national arena for political controversy. There were now, for the first time, national elections in which voters could dispute over national issues. One result was the rise, on a national scale, of the Jeffersonian democratic movement in the 1790's.

Ambivalence of the American Revolution

In conclusion, the American Revolution was really a revolution, in that certain Americans subverted their legitimate government, ousted the contrary-minded and confiscated their property, and set the example of a revolutionary program, through mechanisms by which the people was deemed to act as the constituent power. This much being said, it must be admitted that the Americans, when they constituted their new states, tended to reconstitute much of what they already had. They were as fortunate and satisfied a people as any the world has known. They thus offered both the best and the worst example, the most successful and the least pertinent precedent, for less fortunate or more dissatisfied peoples who in other parts of the world might hope to realize the same principles.

Pennsylvania and Georgia gave themselves one-chamber legislatures, but both had had one-chamber legislatures before the Revolution. All states set up weak governors; they had been undermining the authority of royal governors for generations. South Carolina remained a planter oligarchy before and after independence, but even in South Carolina fifty-acre freeholders had a vote. New York set up one of the most conservative of the state constitutions, but this was the first constitution under which Jews received equality of civil rights—not a very revolutionary departure, since Jews had been prospering in New

York since 1654.[23] The Anglican Church was disestablished, but it had had few roots in the colonies anyway. In New England the sects obtained a little more recognition, but Congregationalism remained favored by law. The American revolutionaries made no change in the laws of indentured servitude. They deplored, but avoided, the matter of Negro slavery. Quitrents were generally abolished, but they had been nominal anyway, and a kind of manorial system remained long after the Revolution in New York. Laws favoring primogeniture and entail were done away with, but apparently they had been little used by landowners in any case. No general or statistical estimate is yet possible on the disposition of loyalist property. Some of the confiscated estates went to strengthen a new propertied class, some passed through the hands of speculators, and some either immediately or eventually came into the possession of small owners. There was enough change of ownership to create a material interest in the Revolution, but obviously no such upheaval in property relations as in France after 1789.

Even the apparently simple question of how many people received the right to vote because of the Revolution cannot be satisfactorily answered. There was some extension of democracy in this sense, but the more we examine colonial voting practices the smaller the change appears. The Virginia constitution of 1776 simply gave the vote to those "at present" qualified. By one estimate the number of persons voting in Virginia actually declined from 1741 to 1843, and those casting a vote in the 1780's were about a quarter of the free male population over twenty-one years of age.[24] The advance of political democracy, at the time of the Revolution, was most evident in the range of officers for whom voters could vote. In the South the voters generally voted only for members of the state legislatures; in Pennsylvania and New England they voted also for local officials, and in New England for governors as well.

In 1796, at the time of the revolution in Europe, and when the movement of Jeffersonian democracy was gathering strength in America, seven of the sixteen states then in the union had no property qualification for voters in the choice of the lower legislative house, and half of them provided for popular election of governors, only the seaboard South, and New Jersey, persisting in legislative designation of the

[23] J. R. Marcus, *Early American Jewry* (Philadelphia, 1953), II, 530.
[24] C. S. Sydnor, *Gentlemen Freeholders: Political practices in Washington's Virginia* (Williamsburg, 1952), 138-39, 143.

executive.[25] The best European historians underestimate the extent of political democracy in America at this time. They stress the restrictions on voting rights in America, as in the French constitution of 1791.[26] They do so because they have read the best American historians on the subject and have in particular followed the school of Charles Beard and others. The truth seems to be that America was a good deal more democratic than Europe in the 1790's. It had been so, within limits, long before the revolutionary era began.

Nor in broad political philosophy did the American Revolution require a violent break with customary ideas. For Englishmen it was impossible to maintain, in the eighteenth century or after, that the British constitution placed any limits on the powers of Parliament. Not so for Americans; they constantly appealed, to block the authority of Parliament or other agencies of the British government, to their rights as Englishmen under the British constitution. The idea of limited government, the habit of thinking in terms of two levels of law, of an ordinary law checked by a higher constitutional law, thus came out of the realities of colonial experience. The colonial Americans believed also, like Blackstone for that matter, that the rights of Englishmen were somehow the rights of all mankind. When the highest English authorities disagreed on what Americans claimed as English rights, and when the Americans ceased to be English by abjuring their King, they were obliged to find another and less ethnocentric or merely historical principle of justification. They now called their rights the rights of man. Apart from abstract assertions of natural liberty and equality, which were not so much new and alarming as conceptual statements as in the use to which they were applied, the rights claimed by Americans were the old rights of Englishmen—trial by jury, *habeas corpus*, freedom of the press, freedom of religion, freedom of elections, no taxation without representation. The content of rights was broadened, but the content changed less than the form, for the form now became universal.[27] Rights were demanded for human beings as such. It was not necessary to be English, or even American, to have an ethical claim

[25] W. L. Smith, *A Comparative View of the Several States with Each Other . . .* (Philadelphia, 1796). There are six tables showing comparisons.

[26] See, for example, G. Lefebvre, *La Révolution française* (Paris, 1951), 99, and *Coming of the French Revolution*, Eng. trans. (Princeton, 1947), 180-81; P. Sagnac, *La fin de l'ancien régime et la Révolution américaine 1763-1789* (Paris, 1947), 386-93, where the Beard view of issues involved in the writing and ratification of the federal constitution is clearly expounded.

[27] For a European view, see O. Vossler, "Studien zur Erklärung der Menschenrechte," *Historische Zeitschrift*, vol. 142 (1930), 536-39.

to them. The form also became more concrete, less speculative and metaphysical, more positive and merely legal. Natural rights were numbered, listed, written down, and embodied in or annexed to constitutions, in the foundations of the state itself.

So the American Revolution remains ambivalent. If it was conservative, it was also revolutionary, and vice versa. It was conservative because colonial Americans had long been radical by general standards of Western Civilization. It was, or appeared, conservative because the deepest conservatives, those most attached to King and empire, conveniently left the scene. It was conservative because the colonies had never known oppression, excepting always for slavery—because, as human institutions go, America had always been free. It was revolutionary because the colonists took the risks of rebellion, because they could not avoid a conflict among themselves, and because they checkmated those Americans who, as the country developed, most admired the aristocratic society of England and Europe. Henceforth the United States, in Louis Hartz's phrase, would be the land of the frustrated aristocrat, not of the frustrated democrat; for to be an aristocrat it is not enough to think of oneself as such, it is necessary to be thought so by others; and never again would deference for social rank be a characteristic American attitude. Elites, for better or for worse, would henceforth be on the defensive against popular values. Moreover the Americans in the 1770's, not content merely to throw off an outside authority, insisted on transmuting the theory of their political institutions. Their revolution was revolutionary because it showed how certain abstract doctrines, such as the rights of man and the sovereignty of the people, could be "reduced to practice," as Adams put it, by assemblages of fairly levelheaded gentlemen exercising constituent power in the name of the people. And, quite apart from its more distant repercussions, it was certainly revolutionary in its impact on the contemporary world across the Atlantic.

EUROPE AND THE
AMERICAN REVOLUTION

Ce vaste Continent, qu'environnent les mers,
Va tout-à-coup changer l'Europe et l'Univers.
Il s'élève pour nous, aux champs de l'Amérique
De nouveaux intérêts, une autre politique.
                                        —M. J. CHÉNIER, Charles IX, 1789
La tempesta fremente,
Che a noi salvezza e libertade apporta.
                        —VITTORIO ALFIERI, L'America libera, 1783

O Land dem Sänger teurer als Vaterland!
                                —ANON., Die Freiheit Amerikas, 1783

Mijn vrienden! ieder uwer ziet
Het heil van deezen Staat uit de Amerijksche vrijheid.
    —A. LOOSJES, De Vrij-verklaring van Noord-Amerika, 1782

K tebe dusha moia vspalena,
K tebe, slovutaia strana
Stremitsia . . .
Primer tvoi metu obnazhil.
                        —A. RADISHCHEV, Vol'nost': Oda, 1782

(For translations see Appendix II)

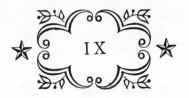

EUROPE AND THE AMERICAN REVOLUTION

The Sense of a New Era

THE FIRST and greatest effect of the American Revolution in Europe was to make Europeans believe, or rather feel, often in a highly emotional way, that they lived in a rare era of momentous change. They saw a kind of drama of the continents. This was the generation that read Raynal's *Philosophical History of European Establishments in the Two Indies*, a huge work published in Paris in 1770, which went through fifty-five editions in five or six languages within thirty years. It was a long humanitarian recital of the evils brought upon the world by European greed and colonialism. Seen against this background, the successful War of American Independence presented itself as a great act of retribution on a cosmic stage. There were many Europeans who said that America would someday, in its turn, predominate over Europe. Nor was this the view of enthusiasts only. No reports were more coldly analytical than those sent home by the Venetian ambassadors. The Venetian Ambassador in Paris observed in 1783, in a report written in secrecy and with no intention to be pompous: "If only the union of the Provinces is preserved, it is reasonable to expect that, with the favorable effects of time, and of European arts and sciences, it will become the most formidable power in the world."[1]

More than power was involved, and more than the grandiose conceptions of an embryonic geopolitics. The American Revolution coincided with the climax of the Age of Enlightenment. It was itself, in some degree, the product of this age. There were many in Europe, as there were in America, who saw in the American Revolution a lesson and an encouragement for mankind. It proved that the liberal ideas of the Enlightenment might be put into practice. It

---

[1] A. Bernardy, "La missione di Benjamino Franklin a Parigi nei dispacci degli ambasciatori Veneziani in Francia, 1776-1786," in *Archivio storico italiano* (1920), 252.

showed, or was assumed to show, that ideas of the rights of man and the social contract, of liberty and equality, of responsible citizenship and popular sovereignty, of religious freedom, freedom of thought and speech, separation of powers and deliberately contrived written constitutions, need not remain in the realm of speculation, among the writers of books, but could be made the actual fabric of public life among real people, in this world, now.

Thus was created an American myth, or mirage, or dream, "the first of those great movements of secular mysticism," to quote a recent author, "which modern man has been experimenting with for the last two hundred years." It was "essentially the belief that certain key doctrines were achieving their first realization in the United States."[2] The first realization was not to be the last. Hence came an expectancy of change, a sense of great events already begun, a consciousness of a new era, a receptivity to that attempt at world renewal soon to be made in France. And if anyone thinks that Americans had nothing to do with launching this *mystique* of world revolution, let him examine the Great Seal of the United States, conveniently printed on the back of the dollar bill, with its penetrating eye, its everlasting pyramid dated 1776, and its Latin motto: *Novus Ordo Saeclorum.*

The influence of the American Revolution in Europe has been thoroughly studied only for France. It is possible, however, by putting together sporadic pieces of evidence, some of them of uncertain significance, to present an impression of what Europe as a whole thought and felt about the events in America; and such is the purpose of this chapter. Only the immediate reaction of the years before 1789 is considered, since the French Revolution and events flowing from it had the effect of eclipsing the American Revolution in the European consciousness, and even of distorting or transfiguring it, causing some to believe in a great international or world revolution common to Europe and America both, and others to distinguish, like Gentz and J. Q. Adams, between an undesirable revolution in Europe and a revolution in America that had been no revolution at all.

There were great differences, country by country, in the way in which Europeans reacted. At one extreme, there were three countries in which admirers of the American Revolution enjoyed, or seized, the opportunity for political action in their own affairs. These three were England, Ireland, and the United Provinces. In England those who

---

[2] D. Echeverria, *Mirage in the West: A History of the French Image of American Society to 1815* (Princeton, 1956), 116, 140. This is the latest and best study of the subject for France.

most warmly sympathized with America were kept busy attending meetings, forming associations, drafting plans, and conducting propaganda for parliamentary reform. In Ireland and in the Dutch provinces they formed militia companies, wore uniforms, attended drills, and built up an actual revolutionary pressure which produced real results. As one of the Dutch leaders said, to follow the example of America meant that all should be ready, "every man with his musket."[3] Where action of such positive kind was possible there was less need to vent one's feelings in poems, orations, pamphlets and treatises on distant lands.

At the other extreme, south of the Alps and Pyrenees, the American Revolution seems in these years to have produced little commotion. Carli's *Lettere americane* of 1780 proves to be about the Lost Atlantis. It was with Latin America that these countries had their contacts, and the important works of two American-born Jesuits, in refuge in Italy after the dissolution of the Jesuit order—Molina on Chile and Clavigero on Mexico—were written in Italy during the American Revolution, on which, however, they gave no information. Knowledge of British America had long been scarce in southern Europe, and the governments there had no desire for their subjects to learn about it now. Probably beneath the political censorship there were stirrings of interest that cannot now be traced. A few pamphlets of Benjamin Franklin's appeared in Italian, but excitement in Italy over Franklin, and over the United States, was apparently greater after 1796, that is, after the Italian revolutions which accompanied the French irruption, and which freed the press and opened the way to political experimentation. I know of only one work of Italian authorship, and one of Spanish, specifically on the subject of English-speaking America, between the American and the Franco-European revolutions: Castiglioni's travels published at Milan in 1790, which showed a realistic approach to American politics, and a work published at Madrid in 1778 by Don Francisco Alvarez.

Don Francisco's is a curious production, which may give evidence of an actual curiosity about the American Revolution held down by the censorship of an apprehensive government, for although Spain joined in the American War of Independence, it naturally feared the spread of rebellion to its own American dominions. Alvarez, in his preface, declares that all eyes are on the Anglo-Americans, that the

---

[3] Quoted from J. D. van der Capellen van de Poll by H. L. Fairchild, *Francis Adrian van der Kemp* (N.Y., 1903), 56.

newspapers are full of their affairs, and that Spaniards have recently shown a commendable new interest in serious books. He proposes to give information, but he gives none. He declares that New England (probably meaning British America) is divided into eleven provinces and four counties, and that the Anglican Church is established in all of them; he says virtually nothing on the Revolution; and he drifts off into commercial topics, Indian affairs, and a miscellany of fanciful anecdotes.[4]

Between the two extremes, in the middle zone of France and Germany, there was a far more lively interest in the American Revolution than in the south, together with a more highly developed press and a wider penetration of the liberalism of the Enlightenment, while on the other hand there was no chance for private persons to do anything in the way of practical politics, as in Holland and the British Isles. The result was an incredible outburst of discussion, speculation, rhapsody, and argument, a veritable intoxication with the *rêve américain*. It is mostly with France and Germany that the following pages deal. But the theme can be set by two Swiss from Basel, Peter Ochs, the future Director of the Helvetic Republic, and his mentor, Isaac Iselin, the Swiss *philosophe* and physiocrat.

"What do you think of the success of the Americans?" wrote Ochs to Iselin in 1777. "Might it perhaps be from the side of the other continent that we shall see the realization of what you have taught about the history of mankind?"

"I am tempted to believe," replied Iselin, "that North America is the country where reason and humanity will develop more rapidly than anywhere else."[5]

Channels of Communication

Europeans were made conscious of the American Revolution in many ways, through the press, through discussions in reading clubs or Masonic lodges, through the reports of returned soldiers, and through the deliberate propaganda of Americans and others. All worked upon a basic receptivity in Europe, since the revolution in America gave the opportunity for discussion, in a colorful and dramatic context, of those general ideas about government and politics which had come to occupy the European mind.

[4] F. Alvarez, *Noticia del establecimiento y poblacion de la colonias inglesas en la America septentrionale* (Madrid, 1778).

[5] G. Steiner, ed., *Korrespondenz des Peter Ochs* (Basel, 1927), I, 102, 104.

It was in the last third of the eighteenth century that a public opinion, as such, took form, and, indeed, the very expression, "public opinion," dates in several languages from this time. It consisted in groups of people habitually interested in public events, subscribing as individuals or in clubs to newspapers and magazines, incipiently political in their outlook, not at first in the sense that they expected to take any action in politics themselves, but in the sense that they were aware of the importance of government and political institutions, and believed that there was something called the public welfare, which depended on the policies of governments and on the enlightened behavior of citizens. Such people were conscious of more than local or private problems, and of the existence of similar people, and similar problems, in distant places. This growth of communication was obviously one of the fundamental preconditions to the whole revolutionary era. It had enabled the Thirteen Colonies to stage a collective resistance to England, it now made America and Europe feel together, and it undermined, in Europe, the whole idea of government as a kind of private occupation of limited governmental circles.

The advent of public opinion was signalized by a phenomenal growth of the press, both of books and of newspapers and magazines. Books had never before been so numerous, and for the newly developing reading public America was a welcome subject, satisfying a popular taste for the exotic, or a philosophical attraction to worldwide views. The press also was less narrowly national than it later became; French was an international language for the educated, many books in French were printed in Holland and Germany, and translation soon carried many works across language frontiers. A little investigation discloses no less than twenty-six works on America that appeared in at least three languages, wholly or in large part, in the years roughly from 1760 to 1790. Fifteen of these appeared in at least four languages, most commonly in the combination of English, French, German, and Dutch, which together formed a solid zone well into eastern Europe. They are listed for reference in the accompanying table.

For the periodical press it is possible to form a quantitative impression of the growth taking place. In England it appears that 66 new magazines and newspapers were launched in the 1770's, 96 in the 1780's, and 151 in the 1790's. In Germany, because of the dispersion among many small capitals and university towns, the number of newly established periodicals (often short-lived) was astounding: 410 in the 1760's, 718 in the 1770's, 1,225 in the 1780's. Many of these were heavily

WRITINGS ON AMERICA APPEARING IN THREE OR
MORE LANGUAGES MAINLY BETWEEN 1760 AND 1790

Language or Nationality of Original: Author and Short Title	English	French	German	Dutch	Italian	Spani[sh]
AMERICAN						
Benezet, *Quakers*	1780	1783	1783			
Constitutions and Other Documents	1776ff.	1778		1787		
Crevecoeur, *American Farmer*	1782	1784	1784	1784		
Franklin, *On Emigration*, etc.	1784	1784	1786		1785	
Filson, *Kentucky*	1784	1785	1790			
Jefferson, *Notes on Virginia*	1787	1786	1789			
Paine, *Common Sense*	1776	1776	1794			
Ramsey, *Revolution in S. Carolina*	1785	1787	1794	1792		
BRITISH						
Burke, *Settlements in America*	1757	1767	1775	n.d. after 1775	1763	
Carver, *Travels in America*	1778	1784	1780	1796		
Price, *Civil Liberty*	1776	1776	1777	1776		
Price, *American Revolution*	1784	1784	1787	1785		
Robertson, *History of America*	1777	1777	1777	1778	1777	1827
FRENCH						
Brissot, *Travels in U.S.*	1792	1791	1792	n.d.		
Chastellux, *Travels in America*	1787	1785	1785			
Mably, *Government of U.S.*	1784	1784		1785		
Mirabeau, *Cincinnatus*, etc.	1785	1784	1787	1785		
Raynal, *Two Indies*	1776	1770	1774	1775	1778	1784
Raynal, *Revolution of America*	1781	1781	1782	1781		
Robin, *Travels in America*	1783	1782	1783	1782		
GERMAN						
Campe, *Discovery of America*	1799	1782	1780	1782		1803
ITALIAN						
Carli, *American Letters*		1788	1785		1780	1821
Clavigero, *Mexico*	1787		1789		1780	
Molina, *Chile*	1808	1789	1786		1782	1788
DUTCH						
De Pauw, *On the Americans*	1789	1768	1769	1771		
SWEDISH						
Kalm, *Travels in America* In Swedish, 1753	1771		1754	1772		

erudite, but many also were addressed to the public or devoted to the public welfare. For example, there were 29 newspapers and magazines in Germany before 1790 that called themselves *Der Patriot*, such as the *Hessischer Patriot*, the *Musikalischer Patriot*, etc. The number of periodicals published in France was smaller than in Germany, because of the greater centralization in Paris, and because the French depended heavily on French-language journals edited under freer conditions in Holland or at Liége. Only 40 new ones have been counted for the eight years preceding 1789, whereas 1,350 are known to have been launched in Paris alone from 1789 to 1800.[6]

With this growth of the press went the formation of reading clubs, in which friends or fellow-townsmen pooled their funds to buy books, magazines, and newspapers, and hired a room or met in a tavern to read and discuss them. It is for France that most is known about these clubs. There is even a theory, somewhat anti-revolutionary in overtones, that attributes the French Revolution, in a measure, to frequentation of these clubs by disgruntled middle-class people who naïvely supposed that they knew what was good for the country. There were, however, many such clubs in other countries; it is true that most of them turned pro-revolutionary when revolution came. Meanwhile, before 1789, the American Revolution was undoubtedly the topic of many eager discussions.

The Masonic lodges played a similar role, and their membership reached into higher social and political circles. Various branches of Masonry had spread throughout Europe and British America in the eighteenth century. The fact that Washington and other American leaders were Masons made European Masons feel akin to them, and one of the first things done by Franklin, to propagandize for America when he arrived in Paris in 1777, was to join the Lodge of the Nine Sisters. The network of Masonry, with its mysterious rituals and its select membership, which, however, was recruited without regard to social class, created an international and interclass sense of fellowship among men fired by ideas of liberty, progress, and reform. At Budapest the Masons called themselves the American Lodge. A Swiss Mason enlisted the Italo-Virginian, Philip Mazzei, in the service of Poland.

[6] The *Times*, London, *Tercentenary handlist of English and Welsh Newspapers, Magazines, and Reviews* (London, 1920); J. Kirchner, *Die Grundlagen des deutschen Zeitschriftenwesens mit einer gesamtbibliographie der deutschen Zeitschriften bis zum Jahre 1790*, 2 vols. (Leipzig, 1928); E. Hatin, *Bibliographie historique et critique de la presse périodique française* (Paris, 1866). Since Kirchner was very complete, and Hatin admitted a certain ignorance of the provincial press, the difference between Germany and France is exaggerated to an unknown extent in the above figures.

Another channel bringing an image of America to Europe was that of the returned soldiers, of whom the most memorable was the Marquis de Lafayette. The influence of America on Lafayette is well known through the researches of Professor Gottschalk. Lafayette, according to Gottschalk, was not inspired to volunteer in the American army by any idealized love of liberty already formed in France. Rather, it was his experience in America that gave him an idealized love of liberty, and made him return to France with a strong predilection toward what were called republican sentiments. He was an impressionable young man, eager for action in his military career, and the liberty that he rushed off to fight for was the "freedom of the seas," that is, a chance to strike a blow against England. He met and was closely associated with Washington, feeling toward him almost as a son; through his admiration for Washington, his wanting to think and act and speak like him, he even became a little like Washington himself.[7]

There were hundreds of other French officers who saw service with Rochambeau in 1780. For most of them the effects of their experience can only be conjectured. Some, like the Count de Ségur, were clearly inspired by what they saw of liberty and equality in America. Of Rochambeau himself, it can at least be said that he lived to accept the French Revolution; the Count de Custine, French quartermaster-general in America in 1780, commanded an army of the French Republic in 1792—and died on the guillotine. Others were unmoved in their aristocratic predilections; the Swedish Count Axel de Fersen, aide-de-camp to Rochambeau, is chiefly famous as the admirer of Marie-Antoinette and emissary of counterrevolution in 1791.

Of the Poles who fought in America, Pulaski was killed there, but Kosciusko survived to lead an attempted Polish revolution in 1794, in which national independence, and even emancipation of the serfs, were unsuccessfully asserted against the Russian and Prussian armies. British officers naturally brought home unfavorable impressions of the rebels, but it must be remembered that some pro-American British officers, like Major Cartwright, the parliamentary reformer, had refused to serve in America at all. The German auxiliaries to the British probably remained largely neutral in spirit, but General von Riedesel, the commander of the Brunswick contingent, was favorably enough impressed by the advantages of America to recommend that his sol-

---

[7] See especially the fourth volume of L. R. Gottschalk's life of Lafayette, *Lafayette between the American and the French Revolution, 1783-1789* (Chicago, 1950), 1-11

diers simply stay there at the end of the war, and a young officer named Gneisenau saw a military value in patriotically inspired militia, and tried thirty years later to introduce certain features of a democratic kind into the Prussian army.

It would be interesting to know more of the experience of enlisted men who fought in America—French, British, and German—since in this way we could trace an American influence among the lower social classes of which the enlisted ranks were then composed. An interesting attempt has recently been made in this direction.[8] It has been shown that a high proportion of the 7,000 soldiers in Rochambeau's army came from those parts of France in which agrarian insurrection and peasant revolution were most in evidence nine years later, in 1789. From this geographical coincidence it is argued that French peasants, as soldiers in America, saw how well off American farmers were, through ownership of their farms without manorial or feudal restraints; and that therefore, back in their native villages, they took a lead in stirring up revolt when the Revolution came in France. This thesis would be important if it could be more fully proved, as evidence of an actual link between common people of the two countries. It seems equally likely, however, that the geographical coincidence may be due to a third factor; that certain regions, because of bad conditions in agriculture, might both send more than an average number of men into the army, and revolt when revolt became possible. As for the 30,000 German troops who went to America, some 12,000 remained to settle there. We can only guess what was said by those who got back to Germany. Neighbors very likely heard a great deal about America from German soldiers, as well as from British and French. This may be one of the early firsthand sources of the generally favorable view of America that long characterized the working people of Europe.

A good deal of deliberate propaganda was also in the air. The British government and its sympathizers scored various successes, particularly in Holland and parts of Germany. The Dutch publicist, Isaac de Pinto, who drew part of his income from British connections, stirred up a small international controversy by two pamphlets of 1776 in which he justified the British policy toward the colonies. Since the Orange family and its adherents were as warmly partisan to England as their adversaries were to America, the American Revolution had a

---

[8] F. McDonald, "The Relation of French Peasant Veterans of the American Revolution to the Fall of Feudalism in France," in *Agricultural History*, xxv (1951), 151-61.

seriously divisive effect in the Netherlands. In Germany the British view was most fully set forth in Hanover, where the dynastic connection with England had brought about many intellectual contacts. The University of Göttingen, and especially its eminent professor, the journalist Schlözer, became the main center in Germany of anti-American feeling.[9] Echoes of the same thing in France may be heard in the words of Mallet du Pan, who remarked that in the American war "the dregs of America had fought the dregs of Europe."[10] Since Mallet du Pan and Schlözer were soon to become leading conservative writers against the French Revolution, their lack of enthusiasm for the American Revolution is worth more than passing notice. It is evidence that the two revolutions looked alike to many conservatives, and that counterrevolutionary attitudes were growing even before the French Revolution.

Many people first came to sympathize with the Americans because of dislike of England. They more readily believed that the Americans were fighting for liberty because they thought the British were tyrants. The British had become so wealthy and powerful, especially in the spectacular victories of the Seven Years' War, and they had so often taken measures to stifle the ocean-borne trade of Continental Europe, that a strong body of feeling in Europe looked on England with aversion as the modern Carthage, the ruthless monopolist of the sea, the perfidious Albion that made continental allies only to exploit them. This feeling was to be of use to Napoleon thirty years later. It was now of use to the Americans. Frederick the Great, for example, was no lover of rebellious subjects, but he was sufficiently annoyed with England to allow all sorts of pro-American sentiments to be published at Berlin.

The French government acted basically in the same way.[11] Choiseul had foreseen the American Revolution as early as 1765, and looked forward to it as a main hope for redressing the balance between France and England. The Count de Vergennes returned from Sweden in 1774, shortly after the monarchist revolution which he had helped to initiate there, to take charge of the French foreign office at the accession

[9] For information on Germany I am mainly indebted to H. P. Gallinger, *Die Haltung der deutsche Publizistik zu dem amerikanischen Unabhängigkeitskriege* (Leipzig, 1900), and to the work of my former assistant, Dr. Gordon M. Jensen.

[10] Quoted by Echeverria, *op.cit.*, 128.

[11] For what follows on France I am indebted to Echeverria, *op.cit.*, but have also used other studies, including some of my own, of my colleague Dr. H. C. Rice of the Princeton University Library, and, it need hardly be added, of Professor Gilbert Chinard.

of Louis XVI. Within a year, in 1775, Vergennes foresaw the possibility of involvement in the American crisis. He sponsored the dramatist, Beaumarchais, in rigging up a commercial company to convey French aid to the rebels. He allowed or encouraged anti-British and pro-American agitation in the press. The French government, no more addicted to republicanism than Frederick the Great, favored the appearance of a new journal called the *Affaires de l'Angleterre et de l'Amérique*. Beginning as early as 1776, two years before French official recognition of the United States, this journal published reports on the war, writings of American leaders, the Declaration of Independence, and various other documents, including several of the state constitutions.

Of all propagandists the most adroit was Benjamin Franklin. It was, in fact, a master stroke of self-advertisement for the Continental Congress to choose him as its representative at Versailles, for Franklin was the only American whose name was known in Europe at the beginning of the American Revolution. He was, however, very well known, and favorably known, for his electrical and other scientific experiments and for his defense of the colonies in England at the time of the Stamp Act. He had been a member of the French Academy of Sciences since 1772. As one who, in a famous epigram, had wrested the lightning from heaven and the scepter from tyrants, he was the perfect embodiment of what *philosophes* meant by a philosopher; self-taught, but profoundly schooled in the laws of nature; a patriot who had given years to the public service; the author, it was believed, of the constitution of Pennsylvania (he had in fact presided at the Pennsylvania convention); gallant with the ladies, yet above the foolishness of an artificial society; a plain man, the sage of Philadelphia, with an aura of Quakerism about him, who mixed with a natural equality in all social circles, and preserved his dignity, and his simple costume, when presented at Versailles to the King of France.

Franklin slipped into Paris in the last days of 1776, the unavowed agent of unrecognized revolutionaries. He left it in 1785, after nine years of adulation. A generation of Frenchmen that had worn handkerchiefs in honor of John Wilkes outdid itself to welcome Franklin, not only with handkerchiefs but with prints and engravings or anything else that might display his features: medallions and snuff-boxes, hats and canes, clocks, chinaware, watches and rings. Poetic tributes came not only from poets but from ladies and statesmen; it was Turgot who coined the line *Eripuit caelo fulmen sceptrumque tyrannis*, and the fashionable Countess d'Houdetot, in an elaborate garden party in his honor, saluted him as *Legislateur d'un monde, et bienfaiteur de deux*. At the salon of Mme. Helvétius he met Turgot, Condorcet, Volney, and Cabanis. At the Lodge of the Nine Sisters he met Voltaire, and also Brissot and Dr. Guillotin. At the Academy of Sciences, he mixed with French scientists, and was appointed to a committee, along with Lavoisier, to investigate the claims of Mesmerism. He was elected to learned societies in Lyons, Orleans, Madrid, Turin, Padua, and Rotterdam. His embrace with Voltaire at the Academy of Sciences in 1778 was the high point in all this extraordinary furor. Coming a few weeks after the signing of the Franco-American treaty, and a few months before the death of the octogenarian Voltaire, it was taken to symbolize the union of two worlds, the enlightenment of the Old joining with the liberation of the New.

Franklin in all this uproar not only performed his mission by negotiating the treaty, but publicized the United States in every way possible. He exploited his own personality, or rather the preconceptions of it that he found in France, with the serene effectiveness of a man free from personal vanity. He wrote articles for the *Affaires de l'Angleterre et de l'Amérique*. He saw to the translation of his Poor Richard and other writings. He put atrocity stories about the British and Indians into the press, and wrote a hoax on the Sale of the Hessians. He arranged with the Duke de La Rochefoucauld-Liancourt to have the American constitutions translated into French, and he instigated Mirabeau to write against the Order of the Cincinnati, of which more will shortly be said. He wrote letters of introduction for Frenchmen going to America, and he obtained the election of several to the American Philosophical Society. He listened politely to the numerous well-intentioned philosophers who came to him with plans for governing the United States. He introduced John Adams, Jefferson, Paine, and other Americans, as they one by one followed him to Europe, to the varied and important acquaintance that he had so carefully built up.

Jefferson followed Franklin as American Minister to France, and though less of a sensation than Franklin, whose triumph could never be duplicated, he carried on the same task of publicizing the United States. He was more of an intellectual than Franklin, and less Gallic in temperament; the need of strictly war propaganda was over, though French enthusiasm for America remained unbounded; so that much of Jefferson's work was in the correction of misconceptions. He published his *Notes on Virginia*, which appeared in French a year before publication in English. He worked carefully with J. N. Demeunier, who was preparing a series of articles on America for the *Encyclopédie méthodique*, carefully going over Demeunier's drafts and discussing them with him, only to conclude in the end, when they were published, that Demeunier still could not rid his mind of errors. When Jefferson's Italian friend from Virginia, Philip Mazzei, came to France, Jefferson encouraged him to write a book on America. The result was Mazzei's *Recherches historiques et politiques sur les Etats Unis*, published at Paris in 1788, in which Mazzei tried to disabuse the French public of the more farfetched ideas of Mably and Raynal. Jefferson also in these years worked closely with Lafayette, who was conducting a busy propaganda campaign of his own in favor of the United States. In 1789, at the time of the fall of the Bastille, and shortly before going home, Jefferson assisted Lafayette on the draft of a French Declaration of the Rights of Man.

During the war John Adams played a similar role in Holland, where he arrived in 1780.[12] His task was more delicate than Franklin's in France, in that the Stadtholder's government was anti-American, it being the merchants and bankers of Amsterdam who were willing, in opposition to the Prince of Orange, to lend aid to America. Adams therefore fell in with the party of incipient revolution, which included the nobleman, Van der Capellen van de Poll, the Mennonite pastor, Van der Kemp, the professor at Leiden and editor of the internationally influential Gazette de Leide, John Luzac, and the wealthy young cloth merchant, Peter Vreede, a future Director of the Batavian Republic of 1798. Adams in fact wrote rather huffily to Van der Capellen, soon after arriving, that the Dutch should reduce the power of the Stadtholder in their republic, and do something to separate the houses of Hanover and of Orange. It was more of a subversive remark than any that those discreet democrats, Franklin and Jefferson, ever allowed themselves to make in Bourbon France. Adams, whose main aim was to borrow money, found that no one would lend to America except those willing to brave British and Orange reprisals. In 1780 Capellen, Luzac, and a few others offered a few thousand guilders of their private funds. In 1782, as the anti-Orange movement mounted toward revolution, Adams' Patriot friends got a majority in the Estates Gen-

[12] For Adams' role in Holland, and the Dutch reaction, see Adams' own correspondence; H. L. Fairchild, *Francis Adrian van der Kemp* (N.Y., 1903); and W. H. de Beaufort, ed., *Brieven van en aan Joan Derck van der Capellen van de Poll* (Utrecht, 1879). Many of the letters to and from Capellen are in English or French.

eral to vote recognition of the United States, after which half a dozen Amsterdam bankers produced a loan of five millions.

Meanwhile Adams and his Dutch allies carried on a literary propaganda. Van der Kemp published a collection of American public documents, which included the Massachusetts constitution of 1780, doubtless furnished by Adams. Adams' own *History of the Dispute with America,* which he had written in 1774, also appeared in Dutch. Adriaan Loosjes wrote a poem on American independence, in which Adams figured as one of the heroes. And, like Franklin in Paris, Adams received the suggestions of well-wishers who thought that the simple Americans would appreciate the advice of enlightened Europe on how to govern the United States. An *Americansche Bybel,* containing recommendations on the management of republics, was dedicated to him in 1781.[13]

Franklin, Jefferson, and Adams, along with men like Lafayette and Kosciusko, were only the most eminent among thousands who served, in their own persons, as channels of communication between America and Europe. There was the circle that gathered about the Earl of Shelburne at Bowood, and which included Bentham, Priestley, Price, and the French abbé Morellet. There was the French literary group that lionized St. John de Crevecoeur; it included Mme. d'Houdetot and Lacretelle, and they persuaded him to turn the French translation of his famous *American Farmer* into a long sentimental idyl suited to the prevailing taste in France. There were others on the outer rim of historical visibility, such as a Dutch merchant in America named Erkalens, who as early as 1776 brought about a correspondence between Capellen van de Poll and Governors Trumbull of Connecticut and Livingston of New Jersey, so that when Adams arrived in 1780 he found Dutch-American relations already well established. There was another Erkelens who won a gold crown at Leiden in 1790 for a poem on Washington. One guesses at a connection with the merchant, despite a slight difference in spelling of the names.

We can even see dimly the beginnings of a group of international subversives, or at least of the belief in their existence. British officials suspected in 1784 that the Irish were "wrought upon by French or American emissaries." Dutch officials in 1787 were sure that certain obscure Frenchmen, who were supposed to have brought on the revolution in America, had now moved to Amsterdam to sow disaffection

---

[13] Full titles and data for works on America mentioned here and elsewhere may usually be found in J. Sabin, *A Dictionary of Books Relating to America,* 29 volumes. (N.Y., 1868-1936); or John Carter Brown Library, *Bibliotheca americana,* Part III, vol. 2 (Providence, 1871).

there. There was of course no centrally directed subversive organization of the kind with which later generations were to become familiar. There is no reason to doubt, however, that the French government might discreetly sponsor revolution in other countries, as it had done in America; or that American citizens, such as merchants, sailors, students, or other transients, if only by bragging about American liberty, might have an unsettling effect in Dublin, Amsterdam, or a hundred other cities of Europe.[14]

A few more words are due to Philip Mazzei, already mentioned. An Italian who settled in Virginia in 1773, he became active in the revolution there, and was sent to Europe in 1779 to borrow money for the state of Virginia. He returned with this mission to his native Tuscany and had many conferences with the Grand Duke, Leopold. The Grand Duke like all other informed people was very curious about the American war, but as a Hapsburg he was too skeptical of the Bourbons to assist their American protégés. Mazzei, his mission unaccomplished, then went to Paris, met Jefferson again, and wrote his *Recherches* against Mably and Raynal. He then took service with the King of Poland. In Poland, too, a kind of revolution began in 1788, and Mazzei, remaining in Paris, undertook to publicize the benefits of this revolution as he had done for the American. King Stanislas, who at first supposed political wisdom to be embodied in the British Constitution, was persuaded by his advisers to see virtue also in the new American constitutional doctrines, and to put a bust of George Washington in his study.[15]

The Depths of Feeling

America was a screen on which Europe projected its own visions. Europe was divided and restless within itself, with both aristocratic and middle-class ways of life making increasing claims to recognition. It set value both on personal merit and on inherited family status. A growing demand for equality went along with a more troubled class consciousness; and a belief that affairs should be conducted by an elite, either of bureaucratic officials or of constituted bodies that

[14] *Correspondence between William Pitt and the Duke of Rutland* (London, 1890), 24; G. W. Vreede, *Mr. Laurens Pieter van de Spiegel en zijne tijdgenooten 1737-1800* (Middelburg, 1876), III, 191; A. Cobban, *Ambassadors and Secret Agents: the Diplomacy of the First Earl of Malmesbury at the Hague* (London, 1954), 105.

[15] Mazzei's autobiography has been translated by H. R. Marraro, *Memoirs of the Life and Peregrinations of the Florentine Philip Mazzei, 1730-1816* (N.Y., 1942). On Mazzei and Grand Duke Leopold see below, p. 386. On Mazzei and King Stanislas see below, pp. 423-24.

had become largely hereditary, conflicted with a vague and widespread desire, among people hitherto outside the political scene, to take part in affairs, to do good for society, to play the patriot, to act the citizen. Views of America were of every kind, from the enthusiastic to the disgusted, from the revolutionary to the conservative, from the mystical and the moralizing to the sharply political, and from the highly unreal to the concretely realistic. I shall move in the following pages from the unpolitical to the political, and, though they are by no means the same, from the unreal to the more realistic.

The unreality of some of the writing on America must be seen to be believed, and I offer a few exhibits. Their main quality is an indifference to fact, a stylizing of the picture to suit the author's feelings. Sometimes it is *à la* Watteau, a kind of embarkation for Cythera: "They say that in Virginia the members chosen to establish the new government assembled in a peaceful wood, removed from the sight of the people, in an enclosure prepared by nature with banks of grass; and that in this sylvan spot they deliberated on who should preside over them."[16]

Sometimes it is *à la* David, teaching the theme of civic self-sacrifice, as in David's painting, *The Oath of the Horatii*, which caused a great stir at the Paris salon in 1785: "Already the cry of 'Our Country' makes itself heard, already the citizen has taken for a device this maxim, *Dulce et decorum est pro patria mori*; already his blood is ready to flow for the welfare and safety of his native land. . . . Every colonist is another Curtius, ready to leap into the gulf to save his country. . . . His blood belongs to her. . . . To shed it without reserve is the duty of a true Republican, to whom the prize of liberty makes hateful every yoke but that of the Laws and of the Deity."[17]

Sometimes it more directly echoes Plutarch and the noble Romans: "The day when Washington resigned his command in the Hall of Congress, a Crown set with jewels had been placed on the Book of the Constitutions. Suddenly Washington seized the crown, broke it, and threw it in pieces before the assembled people. How petty does the ambitious Caeasar seem before this Hero of America!"[18]

Or again the inspiration is from the classical epic, as in *L'Amérique*

[16] M. R. Hilliard d'Auberteuil, *Essais historiques et politiques sur les Anglo-Américains* (Brussels, 1782), II, 119-20.

[17] *Coup d'oeil sur la Grande Bretagne* (London, 1776), 86-87.

[18] J. B. Mailhe, *Discours qui a remporté le prix à l'Académie des Jeux Floraux en 1784, sur la grandeur et l'importance de la révolution qui vient de s'opérer dans l'Amérique Septentrionale* (Toulouse, 1784).

délivrée, which though written in French was published in Holland and dedicated to John Adams. Here in seven hundred pages of rimed hexameters, Pride, Rumor, Perfidy, and Discord bestride the stage with Minerva, Hercules, Theseus, and the Continental Congress. The author addresses the latter:

> Vénerable Congrès, d'un peuple libre et bon
> Vous avez cimenté la gloire et l'union;
> Vous avez délivré l'Amérique et ses ondes
> Des fougueux Léopards [the British],
>   du tiran des deux mondes:
> De nos vains préjugés habiles scrutateurs
> Vous êtes descendus jusqu'au fond de
>   nos coeurs:
> Vous y faites plonger un torrent de lumière,
> Qui porte la clarté dans ce triste hemisphère,
> En frappe les tirans, et de leur joug honteux
> Nous invite à briser les détestables noeuds.[19]

A footnote here declares: "This may happen sooner than we think." In other notes the author explains at length that his purpose is to combat Anglomania in Holland, and to persuade the Dutch against emigration, since they may enjoy as much liberty, equality and comfort in the Netherlands as in New York.

And indeed, beneath the literary artifice and rhetorical effusiveness that they derived from their education, we may see a kind of spiritual emigration. We can sense the psychological discomfort felt by people outside the aristocratic world, the yearning to live in a better country where solid merit would receive due recognition, the voluntary absenteeism or moral rejection of existing European society that was the ultimate cause of the coming revolution in Europe. In Europe, we are told, talent may be a sad and futile gift; it is not so in America. America is the land

> Où sans distinction de naissance et de rang,
> L'homme le plus honnête et le plus respectable,
> Le plus utile enfin, soit toujours le plus grand.[20]

The author of these verses was a *secrétaire-interprète* at the French

---

[19] Chavanne de la Giraudière, *L'Amérique délivrée* (Amsterdam, 1783), 716. For translation of metrical passages see Appendix ii.

[20] L. G. Bourdon, *Voyage d'Amérique: dialogue en vers entre l'auteur et l'abbé* (Paris, 1786), 23.

Foreign Office, and no doubt had in mind actual barriers in the way
of his own advancement. Mme. Roland, the future Girondist, had
similar feelings about her husband, one of the government inspectors
of manufactures. Meditating in 1782 on his difficulties as a public servant with men of more influence than he had, she had this to say to
him: "I abhor from the depths of my soul a State, or the social manners,
in which a virtuous man may be obliged to measure himself with a
vile creature often unworthy of his anger. What a frightful government which leaves such unequal things in balance! M. Lanthenas [a
friend of the family] is quite justified in my eyes in fleeing to Pennsylvania. I wish I were with you in the wilderness."[21]

Much the same feeling of frustration can be detected in Germany.
A professor at Giessen, in a journal which he edited at Frankfurt, observed in 1776 that the Americans were "the most fortunate people
of the whole earth . . . at least among the civilized nations. They do
not even know the names of many burdens borne by subjects in Europe."[22] And he thought it a wonder that half Europe had not already
emigrated there. Even Sprengel, one of the Göttingen circle who at first
defended England, remarked after the war that most of the American
states had become more democratic in becoming independent, that no
distinctions of class or privilege existed, and that any man by his own
talents could obtain any position. Another professor—a class of people
more in the forefront of ideas in Germany than in France or England
at this time—anonymously published a poem called "Die Freiheit
Amerikas" in the *Berliner Monatschrift* in 1783, on the occasion of
the treaty recognizing American independence. It is tempting to see
in it a symbol of Germany itself, for the author, after appealing to
Europe to rejoice and to free itself, after vaguely threatening princes
and calling nobles the plague of Europe, and after pathetically asking
America to take him to its bosom to allay his sorrows, is reminded
that he is a German, hears the clank of his chains, sees the vision fade,
and, in political helplessness, simply weeps.

> Frei bist du! (sag's im höheren Siegeston,
> Entzücktes Lied!) frei, frei nun, Amerika!

> Dein Beispiel ruft laut den Nationen:
> "Frei ist, wer's sein will, und wert zu sein ist!". . .

---

[21] *Lettres de Mme. Roland* (Paris, 1900), I, 182.
[22] H. M. G. Köster in *Neuste Staatsbegebenheiten* (Frankfurt, 1775-1779), quoted
in Gallinger, *Deutsche Publicistik*, 21-22.

O Land, dem Sänger teurer als Vaterland!
Der Sprössling deiner Freiheit steigt schnell empor
Zum Baum. . . .

The hireling soldier in America is astounded; he "turns citizen and embraces as a brother," *wird Bürger und Küsst als Bruder.* For America is the "better hemisphere,"

Wo süsse Gleichheit wohnet, und Adelbrut,
Europens Pest, die Sitte der Einfalt nicht
Befleckt, verdienstlos bessern Menschen
Trotzt . . .

And he concludes:

O, nehmt, Geliebte! nehmet den Fremdling auf,
Den müden Fremdling; lasst mich an eurer Brust
Geheimer Leiden bittre Schmerzen,
Langsam verzehrenden Kummern lindern.

Was säum' ich?—Doch die eiserne Fessel klirrt
Und mahnt mich Armen, dass ich ein Deutscher bin.
Euch seh'ich, holde Scenen, schwinden,
Sinke zurück in den Schacht, und weine.[23]

There was a similar vein in Goethe, if we may take the sentiments he ascribes to Wilhelm Meister as his own. Goethe's secret sorrows were not inflamed by any nagging sense of social inferiority; yet he, too, saw a vision of America as a land better off than old Europe, only to conclude that such ideas were a dream, and that the world of the here-and-now was the best to be hoped for—*Hier oder nirgends ist Amerika.* Goethe's other famous lines on America—*Amerika, du hast es besser Als unser Continent, das Alte*—were not written until his extreme old age, in 1827.[24]

Moral indignation passed into metaphysics, frustration into boundless hope, and the strength of feeling alone, without much need of argument, produced a kind of philosophy of history, a belief that the American Revolution marked an enormous turning point in the entire history of the human race. This was that sense of a new era already mentioned. Even conservatives, or dispassionate observers like the

[23] *Berliner Monatschrift* (1783), quoted in Gallinger, 65.
[24] See P. C. Weber, *America in Imaginative German Literature of the First Half of the Nineteenth Century* (N.Y., 1926), 32; H. Gräf, *Goethe über seine Dichtungen: Die lyrische Dichtungen* (Frankfurt-am-Main, 1914), II, 702.

Venetian ambassador to Paris, sensed that something tremendous had happened. The young Rotterdam patrician, Van Hogendorp, made a trip to America in 1782, at the age of twenty, to enlarge his knowledge of the world. He met and was chilled by George Washington; he did not believe the American union would last; he denied that the Americans, a people of farmers, should be admired or imitated in Europe. But he stated as a fact that the example of "man restored to his rights" had had wide repercussions: "In Ireland a revolution is going on without civil war and even without causing astonishment. In France, I am assured, there is much agitation. The Germans bear the yoke of an arrogant nobility with impatience. In the United Provinces power is taken from the hands to which it was entrusted. A British vessel, stopping on the way back from India at the Comoro Islands in the Mozambique Channel, finds the native inhabitants in revolt against their Arab masters; and when they ask why they have taken arms, are told: 'America is free. Could not we be?' "[25] It is curious to hear of native Africans appealing to the American Revolution a century before the European supremacy.

Learned bodies in the 1780's, in the fashion of the time, set contests for the best paper on the effects of the discovery of America upon the world. Many such papers were written in France; at least two are known at the University of Copenhagen, and one at the University of Upsala.[26] "In a little while," wrote one French enthusiast, commenting on America, "there will be nothing to which man cannot attain."[27] Another envied those who would see the close of the wonderful eighteenth century, of whose glories the American Revolution had given only an intimation. A German poem on *Das achtzehnte Jahrhundert* began by intoning,

> Und der Mensch war wieder nun Mensch, der Edlen
> Viele pflanzten emsig den Keim der Wahrheit,
> Fern an Philadelphias Ufer glühte
> Milderes Frühroth.[28]

[25] A memorandum, "Considérations sur la Révolution de l'Amérique," written at Breda, 1784, in G. K. van Hogendorp, *Brieven en Gedenkschriften* (The Hague, 1866), I, 407.

[26] N. C. Clausson, *Undersogelse om Amerikas Opdagelse har mere stadet end garnet del meunestelige Kion* (Copenhagen, 1785); J. Svedelius, *De effectu detectae Americae in Europam* (Upsala, 1802); Weber, *op.cit.*, 66.

[27] Mailhe, *op.cit.*, 29.

[28] H. S. King, *Echoes of the American Revolution in German Literature*, in *Univ. of California Publications in Modern Philology*, XIV, 2 (Berkeley, 1929), 157.

That America was the hope of the humanity, the asylum of liberty, the beacon for all ages to come, was the common talk among the more fervid in France. The Swiss Iselin apparently agreed with a letter that he published in his journal, to the effect that anyone favoring oppression of the Americans sinned against mankind. In Germany when Schlözer criticized the Americans as rebels he was answered by Jakob Mauvillon, who, defending the principle of the sovereignty of the people, found "a secret bond . . . which links the cause of the Colonies with the welfare and uplifting of the human race."[29] The Italian, Castiglioni, who was not actually much impressed by what he saw across the Atlantic, allowed nevertheless that in time the American Revolution would have momentous consequences for Europe. It would be tedious to repeat examples.

There were many who stood apart from, and even opposed, the idealization of America, nor did they include only those who, like Schlözer and the other Hanoverians, more or less deliberately publicized a British view. In Germany the warmest enthusiasts for America were generally unknown and obscure people. There was an unformulated popular sentiment in favor of America. There was in some circles a literary republicanism, but in others there was a conservatism that already used conservative language. Thus Wekhrlin, who along with Schlözer was one of the founders of modern German journalism, thought of the Americans as a rabble in arms, ridiculed those in Germany who "only learned about men in a dream world or in Masonic lodges," and held that "the great words Freedom, Constitution, Country, turn the head of some people."[30] The professional men of learning, who already heavily predominated in the expression of German opinion, tended to disapprove of rebellion, or at the most to preserve a kind of neutrality, to avoid discussion of the rights of the question, to give factual narratives of events in America, and to maintain a scholarly view by publishing the arguments and the documents from both British and American sources. Germany was full of professors of political or historical or cameralist or statistical science, and these men, along with Iselin at Basel, were mainly interested in the practical consequences of American independence, particularly the stimulus to trade now that the North Americans were free to trade directly with Europe. Yet even this view had its wider implications. Even Christian Dohm, who represented this practical view very fully (and who was to become

---

[29] *Aufsätzen über Gegenstände aus der Staatskunst* (Leipzig, 1776-1777), quoted by Gallinger, *op.cit.*, 34.

[30] Gallinger, *op.cit.*, 60.

one of the chief reorganizers of Germany under Napoleon), observed in Wieland's *Deutscher Merkur* in 1777 that an American victory would give "greater scope to the Enlightenment, new keenness to the thinking of peoples and new life to the spirit of liberty."[31]

In France the war against England, by making zeal for America coincide with French patriotism, removed the restraints both of conservatism and of mere objective study. Where many Germans saw the American war simply as an important dispute, the French saw it as a crusade. Yet even in France there were doubters. Linguet, a kind of anti-*philosophe*, attributed the American Revolution to an overdose of eighteenth-century philosophy. This was in 1777, long before Burke and others offered the same explanation of the revolution in France. Another laughed at pro-American myth-makers—those "orators, poets, panegyrists of romantic virtues and legislators of societies that will never exist."[32] Some who did in fact strongly sympathize with the Americans tried nevertheless to combat, as did Jefferson himself, the more absurd ideas that were current in France. One of these was the Marquis de Chastellux, who had been a major-general in Rochambeau's army, and who, having written a little tract *De la félicité publique*, was no enemy of the human race.

But in France, unlike Germany, the American Dream could not be kept down. There were too many who preferred dreams to reality. Brissot affords an excellent example. The French Revolution was to make him famous; he was to be the virtual head of the French government in 1792, and the man who more than anyone else took France into war with Europe. Before 1789 he was one of the not very numerous people in France who were already true revolutionaries. He was outraged at Chastellux' attempt to moderate the excitement over America. "You wish, sir, to destroy this enchantment!" he cried. "Cruel man! Even if it were an illusion would you still dissipate it? It would be dear to us, it would be useful in consoling the man of virtue. . . ."[33]

Brissot was a man with whom recent generations have been unable to feel very much sympathy, since he appeals neither to liberal constitutionalists, nor to conservatives, nor to modern revolutionaries who think him a petty bourgeois, nor to those who credit the Jacobins of the Terror with at least trying to save France from the consequences

---

[31] *Ibid.*, 19.

[32] *Discours composé en 1788 . . . sur la question: Quelle a été l'influence de la découverte de l'Amérique sur l'Europe?* (Paris, 1792), 72.

[33] J. B. Brissot de Warville, *Examen critique des Voyages de M. de Chastellux* (London, 1786), 19.

of Girondist folly. He was, if there be such a thing, a pure and natural radical. "You have a poor idea of my judgment," he wrote in 1780 to a friend who urged that change must build on existing practice, "if you think I would prefer to accept present-day practice, which I know too well. However monstrous the new theories may be, they will never equal practice in absurdity and atrocity."[34] And he thought the good fortune of America to be that drastic change could occur there: "O hundred times happy America where this reform can be executed to the foundations in every part!"

He lived in the shadowy world of political hacks and hired pamphleteers in which he had connections with the somewhat disreputable Mirabeau; but after Philip Mazzei met him, and incidentally found him living in two rooms with his children in rags, he was warned by Marmontel that Brissot "was someone to stay away from." Brissot took up all sorts of causes, not necessarily consistent. He founded the first French antislavery society. He has been called an early presocialist, and credited with the idea that property is theft; but he was also involved in speculation in Ohio River lands, and with this in mind made a trip to the United States, where he was glad to conclude that American debts would probably be paid in hard money. He still loved American virtue, but found the bosoms of ladies in New York surprisingly bare, and the custom of cigar-smoking revolting. As early as 1787 he sketched out a kind of plan of revolution, which he hoped to carry into effect through connections with the duke of Orleans. The plan was to organize a strong party—the trouble with revolutionary parties in Holland and Belgium, said Brissot, was that they did not know what they wanted—and then to exploit the dissensions between the Parlement of Paris and the King's government, to make loud demands for the Estates-General, and hold out the idea of a constitution as a rallying point. It would then be possible to "free the people and immortalize oneself."[35] The incredible triviality of the last two words was unfortunately not limited to Brissot.

Nevertheless Brissot is an exceptionally good example of the American influence. His Gallo-American Society of 1787 was a little comical. He founded it with three others, Bergasse, the Genevese Clavière, and the Americanized St. John de Crevecoeur. The first meeting, however, revealed an ideological difficulty, for Clavière found the aim of the society too narrow, since he had "devoted all his thoughts . . . to truths

[34] J. B. Brissot, *Correspondance et papiers* (Paris, 1912), 18.
[35] *Ibid.*, 150-160.

useful and beneficial for all men in general, without distinction of nation."[36] The society never had much success, influence, or membership; but we can already see the Girondist crusade of all peoples against all kings—Clavière, too, like Brissot, was a minister of state in 1792.

Soon after this attempt to found a Gallo-American Society Brissot went to the United States, and spent several months in that country during the debates over ratification of the federal constitution. He quickly grasped the essential new doctrine of the American Revolution, as I have described it in the last chapter—the idea of the people as a constituent power, creating, delimiting, and granting authority to organs of government, through the mechanism of a convention chosen for that purpose only. He returned to France in the fall of 1788, during the preparations for the Estates-General. He published, early in 1789, a "Plan of Conduct" for the deputies who were about to meet.

Here he clearly applied the American doctrine. A constitution, he declared, was "the act of apportioning the legislative, executive, and judicial powers." These grants of power could come from the people alone; for Brissot was in revolt against all constituted bodies. None of the powers thus constituted by the people had authority to change the constitution. Only a constitutional convention could do that; hence the Estates-General could not draw up a constitution for France. And whence came this device of a constituting convention? "We owe its discovery to the Free Americans, and the convention which has just formed the plan for a federal system has infinitely perfected it." Moreover, "this device or method of the Free Americans can perhaps be very easily adapted to the circumstances in which France now finds itself."[37]

The great problem (and it was a real problem) was to prevent the powers thus constituted from usurping more authority than they had been granted. According to one school, the several constituted powers of government, by watching and balancing and checking one another, were to prevent such usurpation. According to another school, which regarded the first school as undemocratic or mistrustful of the people, the people itself must maintain a constant vigilance and restraint upon the powers of government. There were partisans of both schools on

---

[36] *Ibid.*, 108. See also L. A. Vigneras, "La Société gallo-américaine de 1787," in *Bulletin de l'Institut français de Washington*, December 1952.

[37] Brissot, *Plan de conduite des députés du peuple aux Etats-Généraux de 1789* (Paris, 1789), 240-42.

both sides of the Atlantic. Brissot belonged emphatically to the second school. The Constituent Power, or People, he said, must keep a perpetual watch over government. He thought the amending process provided in the new American federal constitution to be very defective, since it left the people with no initiative to meet, to punish officials, or to effect constitutional changes. Brissot thus favored a kind of direct democracy, a continuing and detailed popular pressure upon the officers of government. This pressure, in the next few years in France, was to come from political clubs, from the press, from municipal governments or communes, and from mass demonstrations. Brissot favored it, as did Robespierre, until he was in office himself and threatened by it; both then turned against it. It was a mechanism for revolution, of no use in stabilization. Brissot saw one side of the American constitutional doctrine, that the people should ordain government. He did not see the other side, that the people having ordained government should allow themselves to be governed by it, or that having set limits they should abide by the limits, and, short of the most extreme provocation, be content with the occasional and strictly legalized power to vote unwanted officials out of office. Even the democrats in America came to accept this somewhat routinized constitutionalism. In France they did not, partly for doctrinaire and ideological reasons, partly because more than purely political forms was at stake in the French Revolution, and partly because the provocation against democratic ideas did remain very extreme. The method of the Free Americans was not, after all, altogether suited to circumstances in France.

The American Constitutions: An International Argument

It is only in France that a detailed discussion of American government seems to have taken place. Specifically political ideas about America may be traced in France, as in the case of Brissot, until they lose themselves in the conflicts of the French Revolution itself. The American state constitutions were published in France on at least five different occasions between 1776 and 1786. They were also published in Dutch, during the crisis of the Patriot movement in 1787. One cannot generalize negatively about the vast periodical literature in German, but no book containing the American constitutions seems to have appeared in Germany. It is significant that large parts of Mazzei's *Recherches historiques et politiques* appeared at Leipzig under the more feeble title of *Amerikanische Anecdoten,* and that in this work, while the new American federal constitution was included, it was translated from the French, not from the English original. Outside of France political discussion of America seldom went beyond political generalities.

The British, Irish, and Dutch were occupied by their own political activities. In Britain the parliamentary reformers were sympathetic to the Americans, and Richard Price published a short book in 1785 on how the American Revolution could become a benefit to the world. Expressing strongly the sense of a new era, he observed that the American example had already emancipated one country (by which in 1785 he must have meant Holland, or possibly Ireland) and would soon emancipate others. He gave detailed advice to the Americans on the avoidance of debt, inequalities of wealth, political corruption, and foreign trade. But he offered no critique of the American constitutions. The British reform movement antedated the American Revolution, to which it was collaterally rather than lineally related. British reformers did not have to learn from America; the Westminster group, as already noted, with a program anticipating the Chartism of the 1830's, went beyond the Americans in their theory of democratic representation. The King's party was unaware that the rebellion had any constitutional significance at all. Even Whigs, who had defended the American cause so long as it was an issue of British politics, lost interest after the Americans left the empire. In all the copious disquisitions of Edmund Burke on political questions, published and unpublished, until his death in 1796 (and I have searched them with this in mind), there is apparently not the slightest reference to the American constitutions.[38]

There was certainly an American influence in Belgium.[39] The people of these Austrian Netherlands produced few books, but they had an active periodical literature, in which lively interest and contrary opinions on America were expressed. The Abbé Feller, a founder of Belgian political journalism, and soon to be the best-known enemy of the French Revolution among Belgian writers, took an equally disapproving view of the American, and even refused to publish the Massachusetts con-

[38] Burke did specifically refer to the American constitutions in the debates in the Commons on the Canada Act in April 1791. He observed that the Americans, while lacking the materials for monarchy or aristocracy, never "set up the absurdity that the nation should govern the nation; that prince prettyman should govern prince prettyman, but formed their government, as nearly as they could, according to the model of the British constitution." It was, however, a "bare imitation"; and the English-speaking Canadians, having just fled from the American Revolution, wanted no bare imitation but the real thing. *Parliamentary History*, XXIX, 365.

[39] T. K. Gorman, *America and Belgium: a Study of the Influence of the United States upon the Belgian Revolution of 1789-1790* (London, 1925), 125-27, 157, 207-44.

stitution of 1780. The American constitutions and state papers nevertheless became widely known, and echoes of them can be found in the Belgian revolution of 1789. The declaration of independence of Flanders (each province announced its independence from the Hapsburg emperor separately) reproduced certain phrases of the American Declaration of Independence. The democratic party which briefly existed in Belgium in 1790 pointed to some of the American state constitutions for examples of what it wanted. The act of union of the United Belgian States resembled the American Articles of Confederation in its provisions and even occasionally in language. These new United States of Belgium even called their central body a Congress.

In Switzerland it is not clear whether many people had more than the general though vivid impressions of Peter Ochs and Isaac Iselin. None of the hundreds of writings published at Geneva in these years seems to have dealt with America, and the emigration of Albert Gallatin in 1780 was an act of youthful adventure without much political significance. The Genevese, like the Dutch, were preoccupied by their own continuing political crises. On the other hand, the Swiss doubtless read French and German works on America, and a modern authority on Swiss constitutional history emphasizes "the continuing importance" of the fact that, with the American Revolution, "the formal establishment of a written constitution as the basis of public law and political organization made its appearance for the first time."[40]

In Germany there was little incentive to detailed examination of American government. Some Germans, following the Anglo-Hanoverian school, thought of the American Revolution as anarchy, or set forth a historical-realistic theory of jurisprudence against the natural-rights theory or non-political "republicanism" which other Germans espoused. Nevertheless, events arising from the American war stirred up political commentary in Germany, especially in connection with the supplying of German troops to Great Britain, which many Germans disapproved. The city of Kassel, in the heart of Hesse, was in fact a main center of pro-Americanism. "For the first time in history," says a recent German writer, speaking of the sale of Hessian mercenaries, "there was a positive criticism by burghers and educated circles of the actions of the small absolutist state. We cannot doubt that these events aroused political criticism of existing conditions."[41] Reformists in Germany, however, generally hoped for improvement either through

---

[40] E. His, *Geschichte des neuern schweizerischen Staatsrechts* (Basel, 1920), I, 14.
[41] F. Valjavec, *Die Entstehung der politischen Strömungen in Deutschland, 1770-1815* (Munich, 1951), 109; Gallinger, *op.cit.*, 33.

enlightened monarchy as in the Prussia of Frederick the Great, or through the operation of diets and estates, privileged and historically constituted bodies, like the diet of Württemberg. The American constitutions had nothing to suggest along either of these lines. The idea that the "people," that is, the governed, should take part in the formation or conduct of government was unfamiliar. Only in a stray work, like Schmohl's *Nordamerika und Demokratie*, do we find a summons to the reader, and still an indefinite one, "to rise to a realization of the dignity of a free man, who feels himself to be part of the law-making power."[42] Poor Schmohl emigrated to America, but died at sea.

Probably in other countries discussion of the American governments and constitutions was even more sporadic than in Germany. We know that the gazettes of Moscow and St. Petersburg printed sympathetic reports of the American Revolution. Alexander Radishchev, in his *Voyage from Petersburg to Moscow* (for which he was exiled to Siberia) not only reprinted his *Ode to Liberty*, inspired by the American Revolution, but cited several of the American state constitutions, chiefly as an argument for liberty of the press. Radishchev, according to Catherine II, was worse than Pugachev, because he quoted Benjamin Franklin.[43]

The French, however, spurred on by certain Americans in their midst, engaged in a kind of full-dress debate on the American constitutions and American governments, examining and criticizing their features in detail.

What most impressed the French was the very act of constitution-making itself, the constituting or reconstituting of government through the principle of the people as constituent power. What they learned from America was the possibility of having a constituent assembly or a convention. The very word "convention" in this sense, which the French were to make memorable in their own way in 1792, came into the French language through translation of the American state constitutions. For the subjects of government to repudiate and dismantle their government, revert to a "state of nature," and then by

---

[42] J. C. Schmohl, *Nordamerika und Demokratie* (Copenhagen, 1782). Apparently really published at Königsberg. Quoted by Gallinger, *op.cit.*, 69; see also King, *op.cit.*, 176, and P. Merlan, "Parva Hamanniana II: Hamann and Schmohl," in *Journal of the History of Ideas* (1949), x, 567-74.

[43] Max Laserson, *The American Impact on Russia* (New York, 1950), 53-71; M. M. Shtrange, *Russkoye Obshchestvo i Frantsuzkaya Revolyutsiya* (Russian Society and the French Revolution 1789-1794) (Moscow, 1956), 43-45. I am indebted to Mr. W. L. Blackwell for reading this Russian work.

deliberate planning to constitute government anew, to invent and delimit new offices and authorities and endow them with written grants of power, was at least in a juridical sense the very essence of revolution, the practical acting out of the social contract, and the assertion of the sovereignty of the people. It is hard to believe that the French Revolution would have been very different even if the American Revolution had never happened. It is easy to show that the Americans attempted no such substantial break with their past as did the French. Nevertheless, in constitutional theory, in the belief that a people must will its own government by a kind of act of special creation, the two revolutions were much alike.

Over the specific and detailed content of the American constitutions the French discussion roamed very freely. One problem, however, preoccupied all of the French and all of the Americans in this international argument. It was the problem of how best to prevent the growth of hereditary aristocracy. French and Americans were agreed that there was one thing they did not want, though some would tolerate it as a necessary evil—"aristocracy" in the sense of legal privilege, or estates and ranks of society, or nobilities, patriciates or hereditary magistracies, or a self-selecting, exclusive, and perennial governing class, in short the "constituted bodies" as I have described them in earlier chapters. There was no agreement on how this unwanted phenomenon was to be prevented. But the disputes over the separation of powers in the American constitutions, and the furor over the Society of the Cincinnati, can best be understood against this background of aversion to the hierarchic class structure of Europe.

The argument may be said to have begun when Benjamin Franklin gave Turgot a copy of Price's *Observations on Civil Liberty*. Turgot wrote a letter of appreciation to Price, in the course of which he made some strictures on the American constitutions, which in turn prompted John Adams to write his *Defense of the Constitutions of the United States*. Adams meanwhile had been close to the Abbé Mably, who also wrote a book on the American constitutions, which seems to have annoyed Jefferson and certainly annoyed Condorcet. Jefferson's friend Mazzei, supported by Condorcet, refuted Mably. A New Jersey gentleman then demolished Adams' *Defense*, or purported to do so. His pamphlet, coming to Jefferson in Paris, was translated there with long notes by Condorcet and Dupont de Nemours, the intellectual successors to Turgot. This pamphlet was said by Morellet and Mounier, whose judgment commands respect, to have had a great influence in

France during the critical months of August and September 1789. Meanwhile, and very significantly, while the French disputed over bicameral and unicameral legislatures, and over the amount of power to be granted to the executive, John Adams and Thomas Jefferson, the future Federalist and the future Democratic Republican, do not seem really to have disagreed.

To bring this somewhat doctrinaire argument into perspective, it is necessary to point out that Turgot had been Louis XVI's principal minister from 1774 to 1776, that he had designed a great reform program to equalize the tax burden and reduce the privileges of nobility, and that he had been forced out of office by the Parlement of Paris. These events are related in a later chapter. They were a continuation of that conflict between the monarchy and the constituted bodies of which the crisis of the 1760's has already been described. In any case Turgot, from his own experience, was convinced that special bodies, orders, or classes having rights or interests peculiar to themselves were very bad, and that good government and good policy must represent the nation as a whole in an undifferentiated way. Franklin may have told him the same thing, and certainly a reading of Price would strengthen his belief that the British Parliament in no sense represented the British nation.

Turgot, therefore, in his letter to Price, written in March 1778, declared himself disappointed by the new American constitutions because they carried over too many English ideas. "Instead of bringing all the authorities into one, that of the nation," he observed, "they have established different bodies, a house of representatives, a council, a governor, because England has a house of commons, a house of lords, and a king."[44] The word "bodies," it must be understood, suggested those corporate and privileged intermediate powers lauded by Montesquieu in the preceding generation, but which Turgot and other reformers found invariably opposed to change. The word "nation," in the language of the day, signified a political community considered without regard to bodies, ranks, or classes.

Turgot vehemently disapproved of the separation of powers, or balance of "bodies," in the American governments. He was so afraid of creating a special group consciousness that he even objected to the exclusion of clergymen from American legislatures; a group of men

---

[44] John Adams, *Works*, iv, 279. Turgot's letter may also be found in his *Oeuvres* (Paris, 1912-1923), and in its place of first publication, at the end of R. Price, *Observations·on the Importance of the American Revolution and the Means of Making It a Benefit to the World* (London, 1785).

thus singled out, he feared, would develop separate interests as a "body." He believed that each American state should have a one-chamber legislature, no upper house, and a carefully restrained executive. In short, he preferred in certain respects the constitution of Pennsylvania, of which his friend Franklin was supposed to be the author. It is not that Turgot was much of a democrat; he criticized the constitutions for not sufficiently attending to the only "natural" distinction among men, the difference between those who owned and did not own land. He also thought, as a physiocrat, that the constitutions should have denied the right of government to regulate commerce, and in general should have clearly restricted the role of government to a bare minimum.

After Turgot's death Dr. Price published his letter, in 1785. John Adams immediately refuted it in three volumes. He had already made his influence felt in another way. In 1782, during the peace negotiations, he had met the Abbé Mably in Paris. He found him "polite, good-humored, and sensible," and when he was president years later he still affectionately remembered him as his old friend.[45] Mably in 1782 was an elderly philosopher who had been writing on political questions for over forty years. He now published, as his last book, some observations on the government of the United States, in the form of four letters addressed to Adams.

Mably took the opposite line from Turgot.[46] He heartily approved of the separation and balance of powers in the American constitutions, and after surveying them all, and commenting unfavorably on that of Pennsylvania, announced his preference for the constitution of Massachusetts, which of course his friend Adams had mainly written. He preferred that of Massachusetts, he said, because it placed more limits upon democracy than the others. He thus launched the notion that the one American constitution written during the war that provided for direct popular election of governor, senators, and representatives by a wide franchise was peculiarly undemocratic. Mably was denounced as an aristocrat in both France and America. He is said to have been burned in effigy in the United States. This is the same Mably who is

---

[45] For Adams' favorable opinion of Mably, which lasted throughout his life, see his *Works*, I, 350 (1782); I, 354 and 360 (1783); VIII, 554 (1797). Adams' polite request to Mably in 1782 to have his views on the American Revolution produced a rumor in France that Mably was desired by the United States to act as a kind of official expert or consultant on government; see Adams, *Works*, V, 491-96.

[46] G. B. de Mably, *Observations sûr le gouvernement et les lois des Etats-Unis d'Amérique* (Amsterdam, 1784).

also regarded as an early prophet of socialism, and who had remarked to Adams (and Adams agreed) that people who are hungry cannot be punctilious about virtue.

Mably was no "aristocrat"; he did not like aristocracy, he only feared that something of the sort was inevitable. He was painfully aware of inequalities of wealth. He thought that the rich and poor had different interests. Hence, unlike Turgot, he believed that American governments should have powers of regulation to prevent the accumulation of excessive fortunes. He felt that "germs" of aristocracy already existed in America because of the old connection with England, and that even in America, as in Europe, there were too many "prejudices" to make pure democracy feasible without civil strife. The problem, as he saw it, was on the one hand to prevent the growth of aristocracy by suitable legislation, and on the other hand to give incipient aristocracy, or men of wealth, enough of a place in the commonwealth to make them accept the government peaceably. Mably did not believe in Adams' popularly elected executive (nor did any Frenchman, or Jefferson either), but he did firmly believe in a two-chamber system with a strong senate, by which "aristocracy and democracy are held in equilibrium."

Mably wrote these comments late in 1783. At that very time, in America, the worst fears of friends of America seemed to be confirmed. The officers of the Continental Army, on disbanding, founded the Society of the Cincinnati. The Society was to be composed of former American and French officers of the War of Independence; it was to have permanent funds, periodic assemblies, and distinctive emblems and badges; and membership was to be inherited by descendants. Europeans and Americans in Europe immediately sensed the everlasting menace of hereditary social rank. Franklin in Paris, on first hearing of the Cincinnati, scoffed at them as "hereditary knights"; Adams in Holland sarcastically called the idea a "French blessing," defacing "the beauty of our temple of liberty."[47] Franklin gave a pamphlet against the Cincinnati by Aedanus Burke of South Carolina to the Count de Mirabeau to translate into French. Mirabeau, the future leader of the French Revolution, adapted and amplified it into a pamphlet of his own, *Considérations sur l'ordre de Cincinnatus*. With it he included a translation of Price's reflections on the American Revolution, and of Turgot's letter to Price, now published in French for the first time.

Mirabeau's pamphlet against the Cincinnati was a diatribe against aristocracy. Monarchies, said Mirabeau, needed special "bodies" of men;

[47] Franklin, *Works*, x, 273-81, 421; Adams, *Works*, viii, 187; ix, 524; v, 488.

in republics all men belonged to one "body" and enjoyed the same rank. The Cincinnati, he declared, echoing Franklin and Adams, violated the American constitutions and bills of rights which asserted the equality of all citizens. They would introduce into America "an eternal race of Aristocrats, who may soon usurp those insulting titles by which the European nobility crush the simple citizens, their equals and brothers."[48]

For the next two or three years, though the Society had meanwhile modified its statutes, the Cincinnati commanded a degree of attention in France that now seems out of all proportion to their true importance. Jefferson, who also disapproved of the society, tried to calm his French friends by explaining that the officers had meant no harm, and that they had had no intention of setting up an aristocratic order. But for a time no French book about America was complete without an extended and often heated treatment of this question. Perhaps the French were right; a kind of publicly honored, solemnly paraded, and rigidly hereditary Sons of the American Revolution is not nowadays to be contemplated with equanimity. In any case the French excitement reflected a profound dissatisfaction with the social order in Europe.

Meanwhile Adams, now Minister to England, was methodically compiling his *Defense of the Constitutions of the United States* against the "attack" of Turgot. It was a long survey of all republics on which Adams could find any information, ancient, medieval, and modern; democratic, aristocratic, and "regal" (England and Poland were his modern "regal republics")—an interminable setting forth of scores of examples hurriedly thrown together in a huge patchwork of long-unacknowledged quotations, connected by paragraphs of his own composition in which he gave his own thoughts on the matter. With all its defects as a piece of literary art, and with the exception of the constitutions themselves and other official American documents, the *Defense* was the most important work of American political theory before the Federalist papers. It falls neatly into place in the present book also, since it gives a comparative survey of the constituted bodies of Europe as they had come to be in the eighteenth century, finds in them a universal trend toward hereditary self-entrenchment in office, idealizes the British constitution in the manner of Delolme, expresses some basic ideas of the American Revolution, was written in Europe in an international controversy, and was designed as a polemic against

---

[48] H. G. R. de Mirabeau, *Considérations sur l'ordre de Cincinnatus, ou imitation d'un pamphlet Anglo-Américain* (London, 1784). Quotation from p. 50 of 1785 edition.

aristocratical government. Adams succeeded in making himself thoroughly misunderstood. He was even called an aristocrat; but it seems hardly possible that anyone could actually read the *Defense of the Constitutions of the United States* without seeing that aristocracy was Adams' principal bugaboo.

Adams started out with the eternal American protest against the attentions of European intellectuals: "The writer has long seen with anxiety the facility with which philosophers of greatest name have undertaken to write of American affairs, without knowing anything of them, and have echoed and re-echoed each other's visionary language."[49] He suspected that Turgot's ideas were shared by Franklin, and he feared that other Americans might be similarly misled. There were two points in Turgot's letter to Price that especially irritated him: the idea that a single elected assembly should control the whole government, and the idea that imitation of the British constitution was something for which the Americans should be blamed.

It was by obstinately insisting that his own ideas were really those of the British constitution, which he called in the *Defense* a "stupendous fabric of human invention," that Adams made himself misunderstood both by his own contemporaries and by democrats and conservatives, to denounce or to praise, in later times. This perverse New Englander, whose dislike of the England of his own day was really very intense, considered himself as English as the English, and had even boasted, in 1774, that America enjoyed the British constitution in greater purity than Britain itself. The idea of a British constitution more pure than the actual constitution of Britain was a somewhat theoretical concept, reinforced in Adams' mind by the reading of Delolme, whom he greatly admired. Delolme, it will be recalled, was by origin a Genevese democrat, an enemy of the patriciate there, whose theory of the separation of powers in England, in subtle contrast to that of Montesquieu and the English Whigs, emphasized the importance of the crown as a balance against the nobility, not the role of the nobility as a balance against the crown.

Adams' own ideas had significantly changed during the American Revolution. In his *Thoughts* of 1776 he had favored election of an upper house by the popularly elected assembly, and selection of a governor by the two houses together. In his draft of the Massachusetts constitu-

---

[49] *Defense of the constitutions of government of the United States of America, against the attack of M. Turgot . . .*, 3 vols. (London, 1787-1788). Reprinted in *Works*, IV and V. The quotation here is from *Works*, IV, 294.

tion made in 1779 he had provided for election of all three by the whole body of voters. His purpose had been to assure the independence of the three from each other, and, by emancipating the governor from the two houses, to protect the integrity of the executive and judicial powers. His emphasis on the value of a strong executive was more explicit than Delolme's, and was in fact his most distinctive political idea.

The fact that Adams' European experience was mainly in Holland, where the executive was weak and hereditary oligarchy solidly established, may have confirmed him in these ideas. At any rate, his reading of European history taught him, what it never taught most democrats, Jeffersonians or Whigs, that monarchy over the centuries had often protected the people against the nobles. "What is the whole history of the wars of the barons but one demonstration of this truth? What are the standing armies of Europe but another? These were all given to kings by the people, to defend them against aristocracies."[50] Or again, the executive "is the natural friend of the people, and the only defense which they or their representatives can have against the avarice and ambition of the rich and distinguished citizens." And it is the usual practice "of a few illustrious and wealthy citizens to excite clamors and uneasiness" against the executive, which is the essence of government.[51]

These wealthy and illustrious citizens, according to Adams, would reduce the executive to a nullity if they could. They would also nullify popular influence in the legislature if the legislature met as a single house. "The rich, the well-born and the able," he declared in a phrase often quoted out of context, "acquire an influence among the people that will soon be too much for simple honesty and plain sense, in a house of representatives. The most illustrious of them must, therefore, be separated from the mass, and placed by themselves in a senate; this is, to all honest and useful intents, an ostracism."[52] In short, the rich should be made to sit apart in a house of their own, not to protect

[50] *Works*, IV, 355.
[51] *Works*, IV, 585.
[52] *Works*, IV, 290. Adams expressed the same views in correspondence with Jefferson in later life: "Your *aristoi* are the most difficult animals to manage in the whole theory and practice of government. They will not suffer themselves to be governed." He rejected Jefferson's distinction between natural and pseudo- (or good and bad) aristocracies, regarding all forms of superiority, leadership, excellence, or talent as liable to much the same dangers of abuse. He lacked Jefferson's belief in the virtues of an elite. See his letters to Jefferson of July 9 and November 15, 1813, in P. Wilstach, *Correspondence of John Adams and Thomas Jefferson* (Indianapolis, 1925).

their own interests, and not because in a popular one-chamber system the people would despoil them, but for the opposite reason, because if the rich sat in a one-chamber house they would corrupt the popular representation, and despoil the people. It is possible to think that Adams was mistaken in believing an upper house would have the effects he expected; but it is hardly possible, since hypocrisy is one fault of which he has never been accused, to mistake the drift of his thought. It was, quite as much as Turgot's, antiaristocratic.

Adams shared with Mably a sense of the less agreeable traits of human nature. He did not expect much from the unaided virtue and enlightenment of either common or uncommon men—it was his one trait of conservatism. Americans, he repeatedly said, were no different from and no better than Europeans. "There is no special Providence for Americans, and their nature is the same as that of others."[53] Toward the end of his work, as with inexhaustible patience he analyzed the minuscule medieval republic of Montepulciano, he went into a digression on the American Cincinnati, whose fancy for hereditary honors and titles seemed to him to show the beginning of the very process which he had now traced in Europe and in antiquity dozens of times. In America, too, he thought, people easily fell into the habit of accepting the leadership of a few families; in the simplest New England town meetings, he observed, men of the same families were elected to office for four and five generations. In America, too, there were "aristocratical passions," insatiable like all passions—pride, vanity and ambition, the love of gold, the love of praise, the love of domination, the love of position. There were tendencies to lead and to follow, to dominate and to submit; there was a love of equality, but also a love of inequality, a desire to possess or to excel. Since these traits could not be eradicated, the problem was to combine, adapt, utilize, and restrain them for the public good.

The burden of Adams' *Defense* was therefore to show that if America followed Turgot's advice it would end up like most of Europe. As soon as all power was in one assembly, a few individuals would appropriate it for themselves. It was from faulty arrangement of government, from ignorance of the doctrine of separation of powers, from failure to provide an independent executive and to divide the legislature into two houses, that Geneva, Venice, Holland, Poland, and many others had fallen under self-perpetuating oligarchic rule. He particularly invited Americans to study the experience of the people of Geneva, "as

[53] *Works*, IV, 401.

enlightened as any," who, however, had supinely given up their freedom, because they had never learned that the people should combine with the syndics, and the syndics with the people, against patrician encroachments. At Geneva, he warned, a mere dual balance between an aristocratic and a democratic assembly had been proved to be futile; it was necessary to have a third power, an independent executive. Likewise to have a single chamber balanced by an independent executive would be only to have two armies drawn up in battle. There must be a third element, a senate, to provide a balance.

Adams, like Delolme, arguing that the British constitution was the best in Europe, because it balanced the crown, the aristocracy, and the people, was obliged by the necessities of his theory to believe the people were really represented in the eighteenth-century House of Commons. He was aware that the House needed reform if it was to be representative in any meaningful sense, as Delolme himself had been in 1771; but he had no such strong feelings on the matter as Turgot and Price and many others. To think that the Commons had become socially akin to the Lords, or that the lower house was influenced, infiltrated, or "corrupted" by the upper, would be to surrender his whole argument. In this one respect Adams, too, was a doctrinaire, and what he could not assimilate was a particular set of facts. His adversaries had reason to think him unreasonably Anglophile. Yet his doctrine is still clear, whether or not it corresponded to the facts of British public life. The doctrine was that an upper house and an independent executive would prevent aristocratic domination.

Adams further perplexed his readers by his careless use of the word "orders." This was a fighting word for reformers. It signified corporate bodies and legal stratification. Adams sometimes made himself clear enough. "In America," he said, "there are different orders of *offices*, but none of *men*."[54] But he liked to refer to the executive, senate, and popular assembly as "orders" of government, and to insist that good government must be a "balance of three orders," so that, though he was neither a monarchist nor an aristocrat, and thought it best for executive and senate to be popularly elected, his readers may be excused if they thought him an apologist for King, Lords, and Commons. His book was really too long even for contemporaries; his ideas were smothered by the profusion of exotic examples, most of which did deal with real aristocracies and real kings.

[54] *Works*, IV, 380.

Adams sent a copy of the *Defense* to Jefferson in Paris, who pronounced it a useful and illuminating work, and tried to get it translated.[55] In this he failed; it was not translated into French until 1792. Its length would deter a translator; it is possible also that Frenchmen of the kind interested in translation of American books, such as Morellet, Condorcet, Dupont, or Brissot, were repelled by its doctrine, or apparent doctrine, of the necessity for three "orders." Many of the French with whom Jefferson mixed were partisans of Turgot. They admired neither the British constitution, nor aristocracy, nor "orders," nor the balance of powers within government. It is possible that Jefferson's own experience with his *Notes on the State of Virginia* is of some relevancy here.

Jefferson had written these *Notes* before leaving America, and had had two hundred copies printed for private circulation. His aim in part, like that of Adams in the *Defense*, was to correct the vagaries of European savants on America, notably the views made current by de Pauw and Buffon, to the effect that America was an unfavorable habitat for living things, that the animals were more puny and the human beings less vigorous than in Europe, and that human culture in America showed a tendency to deteriorate. Jefferson also commented on the constitution of Virginia. He listed certain defects in it, in particular the domination over executive and judiciary by the legislative assembly, in which Jefferson saw the danger of "elective despotism"—a term which for Jefferson seems to have meant what Adams called "aristocracy." Jefferson also included, in the *Notes*, a draft constitution for Virginia which he had made in 1783, when it was thought that a state constitutional convention would soon assemble. In this draft he provided for a clear separation of powers. He strengthened the position of governor by proposing a five-year term. He provided for senators to be elected by the voters, though indirectly by way of electors. Though he wished to broaden the franchise, and to reduce the overrepresentation of tidewater counties, Jefferson's draft constitution of 1783 for Virginia was in important respects less democratic than Adams' draft of 1779 for Massachusetts, since neither the governor nor the senate was to be directly elected by voters. Also, it never went into effect; Virginia had no new constitution until 1830. But in wishing to strengthen the executive, separate the three powers, and widen the franchise Jefferson's thought moved in the same direction as Adams'.

[55] Jefferson, *Papers* xi (Princeton, 1955), 177.

One of the privately printed copies of *Notes on Virginia* came into the hands of the Abbé Morellet, who began to translate it, without Jefferson's approval, for publication in France. Morellet took various liberties with the text. For one thing, he did not include, in his translation, Jefferson's draft constitution of 1783. It is certain that Jefferson would want this draft to appear, for Demeunier, working under his guidance, published it in the *Encyclopédie*, and the London edition of the *Notes*, published the following year under Jefferson's supervision, also included it.[56]

Why did Morellet omit Jefferson's proposed constitution from his *Observations sur la Virginie?* We may never know the answer to this question. He may have tired of his task of translation, or thought the draft unimportant. Or he may have found it awkward for his own purposes. Morellet was associated with the followers of Turgot in France, and with parliamentary reform groups in England. For these partisans of the American Revolution, who despite criticisms yet believed that the American constitutions were an epoch-making contribution to political science, it was inconvenient to find the eminent Jefferson, the former governor, proposing a new constitution for his own state. Nor did it suit their requirements to find Jefferson demanding a more independent executive and such "British" ideas as a separation and balance of powers.

Adams' book remaining unknown in France, and the more jarring ideas of Jefferson being brushed aside, the counterattack of the Turgot school fell upon the now deceased Abbé Mably. Philip Mazzei arrived in Paris, mixed with Morellet, Condorcet, and others, and with Jefferson's blessing wrote his four-volume work to correct French misconceptions of the United States. The whole second volume was a refutation of Mably. Mazzei also included in his book two tracts by Condorcet, one on the influence of the American Revolution on Europe, the other on "the uselessness of separating the legislative power among several bodies."

Mazzei's complaint against Mably—except as he thought that Mably shared in a general wrong-headedness about America—was that Mably was a kind of crypto-aristocrat, pessimistically harping on the "prejudices" that Americans shared with Europe, and dissatisfied with everything in the American constitutions except the restraints that

[56] Jefferson, *Observations sur la Virginie* (Paris, 1786); *Notes on the State of Virginia* (London, 1787); critical edition of the same edited by William Peden (Williamsburg, 1955); *Encyclopédie Méthodique: Economie Politique*, article "Virginie."

they placed on democracy. He ridiculed Mably's idea that the constitution of Massachusetts would, in contrast to that of Pennsylvania, allow the inevitable transition to aristocracy to occur peaceably. It was one of Mably's delusions, said this friend of Jefferson, to suppose that the constitution of Massachusetts was really less democratic than that of other states.[57]

More interest attaches to the views of Condorcet, the friend and biographer of Turgot, the intellectual luminary of the revolution soon to come in France. Like Turgot, he wanted a single assembly to represent simply the nation as such. Like Turgot and many others, in all countries, including England, he was aware of the realities in British public life: "Inequality of representation may render it illusory, as in England."[58] Like Brissot, with whom he was to be closely associated in the politics of the Revolution, he would prevent the usurpation of power by making the single assembly dependent on frequent election, by providing for referendums and initiative on the part of the voters, and by detailed declarations of rights. Like the physiocrats, he would give almost unlimited economic freedom. And, like the mathematician that he was, his ideas were alarmingly self-evident, abstract, absolute, and simple.

Recognition of natural rights in America, he declared, "teaches that these rights are everywhere the same," and that all men in all countries should enjoy all of them with one exception—the right to vote, which "the virtuous citizen must know how to renounce in some constitutions."[59] In fact, though the Revolution was to make him accept a manhood suffrage, Condorcet in 1788 would give a full vote only to persons (men or women, for he was an early sponsor of women's rights, and Mme. Condorcet was an upper-class Mme. Roland) who possessed enough landed property to live on the income without working. To smaller land-owners he would give corresponding fractional votes. Precautions against the abuse of power were the less necessary, he asserted, in proportion as the declaration of rights was more specific and extended. This declaration must forbid hereditary distinctions, make all offices elective, prohibit regulation of commerce, occupation, or religion, and abolish all taxes except the tax on the product of land. Any piece of legislation affecting the people's rights must be ratified by the people itself, "because either the solution of questions is self-evident

---

[57] P. Mazzei, *Recherches historiques et politiques sur les Etats-Unis,* 4 vols. (Paris, 1788), II, 75-77.
[58] *Ibid.,* I, 287.
[59] *Ibid.,* IV, 248.

and agreed upon, or cannot be legitimately found except by the people as a whole."[60] The people, as just noted, meant the proprietors of land. And America proved all this:[61] "In observing how the Americans have founded their peace and happiness on a few maxims that seem the naïve expression of what common sense could have dictated to all men, we shall cease to vaunt those complex machines . . . where so many counter-weights are supposed to produce a balance. . . . We shall see the danger . . . of those systems in which the law, and hence truth, reason and justice, its immutable base, are forced to change according to temperature, to bend before usages consecrated by prejudice, or the absurdities adopted by each people." Or, as Brissot said at this time, "Should the thermometer determine human rights?" Or as Dupont de Nemours wrote to Jefferson, "there is a perfect government, the *beau idéal* of government," better than even the Americans yet have, but which the nations will enjoy some day because of the *perfectibilité de l'esprit humain*.[62] Nothing could be further from Mably, or from Adams, or even from Jefferson, all of whom preferred to trust in institutional arrangements rather than in human nature or mere declared rights, to prevent the usurpation of power.

A climax to the argument here narrated came with a pamphlet published in America as a rebuttal to Adams and Delolme, and translated into French under a different title, *Examen du gouvernement de l'Angleterre*, with long anonymous notes by Condorcet, Dupont de Nemours, and Philip Mazzei. It is illuminating to comment on the role of this same pamphlet in the two countries.[63]

Its author was believed to be Governor Livingston of New Jersey, but was actually John Stevens. Stevens was of what passed in America as the upper class. His father had sat for thirteen years on the New Jersey governor's council before the Revolution, but had turned patriot during the war; he himself had acquired a mile-square loyalist estate, for £18,340, overlooking the Hudson, the present site of Stevens Institute, a pleasant tract which he was then laying out in parks and

---

[60] *Ibid.*, I, 331.

[61] *Ibid.*, IV, 254.

[62] *Papers of Thomas Jefferson* XII (Princeton, 1955), 326.

[63] John Stevens, *Observations on government, including some animadversions on Mr. Adams' Defense of the Constitutions . . . and on Mr. Delolme's Constitution of England*. By a Farmer of New Jersey (N.Y., 1787). The French version was *Examen du gouvernement de l'Angleterre comparé aux constitutions des Etats-Unis* (Paris, 1789). This pamphlet, published anonymously, was long attributed to William Livingston. See A. D. Turnbull, *John Stevens: An American Record* (N.Y., 1928). For the French version see R. Ciampini, *Lettere di Filippo Mazzei alla corte di Polonia* (Bologna, 1937), 121.

driveways on the English model. Stevens was later to achieve fame, and greater wealth, as the inventor of the screw propeller and builder of steamboats and railroads.[64]

John Stevens was persuaded that John Adams was trying to foist aristocracy upon the United States. We Americans, declared Stevens, enjoy "perfect equality" as a nation of small farmers; there has never been and is not now a trace of aristocracy among us; we have no orders, ranks, or nobility. Our governments are nearly perfect democracies because our governors are our agents; it is a fallacy to suppose that all men must have the right to vote in a democratic system. A balance of orders may be necessary in Europe, but America is different, and Adams and Delolme will never convince us that we need any such "orders" here, any "independent and self-existing powers," or any "interest separate from that of the community at large." Nevertheless, says Stevens, it is of course wise to have a second chamber of legislation, and to give the executive and the judiciary a power of restraining the legislature.

The interest of this pamphlet, in America, lies in the fact that this affluent landed gentleman supposes himself to be a democrat, more so than Adams, and that, even in refuting Adams, he still favors a constitutional separation of powers. His dispute with Adams arose from a misunderstanding, whether willful or not; for Adams had never said that there should be hereditary ranks and orders of men in America. Fundamentally Adams and Stevens agreed on what was desirable. Those who disagreed had been silenced or left the country.

In France the same pamphlet had a different significance. It appeared in French in the early weeks of 1789, on the eve of the elections to the Estates General. There was a general belief that France would soon receive a new constitution, and Condorcet and Dupont, in adapting this American pamphlet, and spurred on by Mazzei and possibly

[64] At about the time when John Stevens, under the anonymity of a "farmer of New Jersey," wrote his critique of John Adams, his father, John Stevens, Sr., described by Forrest McDonald as a "wealthy capitalist" and investor "in both real and personal property," sat in the New Jersey state convention to ratify the federal constitution. The elder Stevens then owned land valued at £62,500, and had interests in small manufacturing enterprises. Since the New Jersey convention voted unanimously to ratify the federal constitution, it would appear that the elder Stevens approved of it, though it embodied pretty much the views of John Adams which the younger Stevens was simultaneously attacking. The younger Stevens in 1787 was a heavy holder of continental paper (to the extent of $28,000); he was the sort of man, and of the sort of family, which, according to Beard's form of economic interpretation, should have agreed with John Adams instead of attacking him. But this "farmer of New Jersey" talked like a pre-Jeffersonian democrat. On the two Stevenses see F. McDonald, *We the People: The Economic Origins of the Constitution* (Chicago, 1958), 127.

by Jefferson, intended to clear the ground for a French constitution by discrediting the British constitution as a model. That the American Stevens actually favored a threefold separation of powers was confusing; but then Stevens himself had been unclear, for he did roundly denounce the government of England and the society of ranks and orders. In any case the notes to the translation, furnished by Condorcet and Dupont, and longer than the translation itself, could straighten out the matter. In these notes the annotators either elaborated or contradicted their author as best suited their purpose. They gained the prestige of American precedent for their attack on England and on aristocratic society. They disagreed on the matter of constitutional powers; they declared, unlike Stevens, that an upper chamber, and an executive equipped with a veto, were useless imitations of the discredited British constitution. There need be only a single omnicompetent assembly, checked by frequent election, by direct intervention of the people, and by declaration of rights.

The *Examen du gouvernement de l'Angleterre*, thus originating as an American reply to Adams, did have an effect in France in the crucial year 1789. The Abbé Sieyès added a note on it in the third edition of his famous tract on the Third Estate. He hailed it as a useful work showing the need of a single representative body. It was referred to repeatedly in the constitutional debates in the Assembly later in the year. Mounier, the leader in these debates of the group desiring a strong executive and a bicameral legislature, thought that this refutation of Adams had done much to undermine his own views. The Abbé Morellet, more conservative in 1789 than in 1787, was of the same opinion. Both of them wrote pamphlets in reply to "Governor Livingston" and his French annotators.

The French Constituent Assembly, in the decisions made in September 1789, provided no upper chamber of legislation, and the burden of thought was against a strong and independent executive. For six years France was in effect to be ruled by a single assembly, subject to the pressures of a direct democracy and sporadic popular intervention.

Obviously no pamphlet or war of pamphlets determined the constitutional decisions made in France in 1789. The situation in France was very different from that in America. In France an upper chamber would mean a chamber composed largely of the higher nobility, and the executive was bound to mean King Louis XVI, who by June 1789 had got himself into the position of supporting the nobility against the Third Estate. There were really two meanings in the doctrine of the separation of powers, which the Americans could keep separate and which the French could not. There was the idea of separation of social classes, the old idea of Montesquieu, expressible in the formula of King, Lords, and Commons. There was the idea of separation between functions of government, expressible in the formula of executive, senate, and assembly. The French were not free to have the latter without the former. For them a "senate" must mean a body of nobles; the executive must mean the King, hereditary and unelected, or ministers who, as they in fact still were in England, would be primarily agents of the King. In America the senators were not lords, nor were the governors kings; they were temporary occupants of office, with no personal right to the exercise of public authority. In all the muddle of arguments all Americans since the defeat of the loyalists agreed upon this—John Adams, John Stevens, Jefferson, and Franklin alike. In France the essence of the revolution of 1789 was the revolt of the Third Estate against the nobility. With a hostile nobility to overcome, and a king sympathetic with the nobility to contend with, the creation of an upper house and a strong independent executive was simply not among the possible choices for men interested in furthering the French Revolution.

The effects in Europe of the War of American Independence will become apparent in the next chapters. The effects of the American Revolution, as a revolution, were imponderable but very great. It inspired the sense of a new era. It added a new content to the conception of progress. It gave a whole new dimension to ideas of liberty and equality made familiar by the Enlightenment. It got people into the habit of thinking more concretely about political questions, and made them more readily critical of their own governments and society. It dethroned England, and set up America, as a model for those seeking a better world. It brought written constitutions, declarations of rights, and constituent conventions into the realm of the possible. The apparition on the other side of the Atlantic of certain ideas already familiar in Europe made such ideas seem more truly universal, and confirmed the habit of thinking in terms of humanity at large. Whether fantastically idealized or seen in a factual way, whether as mirage or as reality, America made Europe seem unsatisfactory to many people of the middle and lower classes, and to those of the upper classes who wished them well. It made a good many Europeans feel sorry for themselves, and induced a kind of spiritual flight from the Old Regime.

TWO PARLIAMENTS ESCAPE REFORM

Parliamentary reform, I am still sure, must *sooner or later be carried in* both *countries. If it is well done, the sooner the better.* . . . . *For God's sake, do not persuade yourself, in the meantime that the measure* . . . *is inconsistent with either the dignity or the tranquillity and facility of government. On the contrary, I believe* they *ultimately depend upon it.*—WILLIAM PITT, Prime Minister of Great Britain, to the Duke of Rutland, Lord Lieutenant of Ireland, 1784

The great object of most of these reformers is to prepare the destruction of the Constitution by disgracing and discrediting the House of Commons.—EDMUND BURKE, Member of Parliament for Malton, 1784

X

TWO PARLIAMENTS ESCAPE REFORM

As WE now, after long considering the American Revolution and its influence, return to pick up the trail of events in a dozen European countries, it is well to look back upon some of the main points staked out since the beginning of this volume. The makings of a great conflict were accumulating in Europe, a conflict that was to reach its height during the last years of the century and that may be called the Great Democratic Revolution, in that it was primarily a revolt against aristocracy in its numerous manifestations. Aristocracy was entrenched in a multitude of constituted bodies—estates, diets, councils, and parliaments, and in the established churches in view of the social origins of the higher ecclesiastical personnel. The simultaneous growth of both aristocratic and middle-class ideals and ambitions produced stresses of many kinds. By 1774, or the eve of the American Revolution, the constituted bodies were yielding before contrary pressures. On the one hand, enlightened monarchy, in its own way, worked toward a greater equality as among the subjects of government: the Maupeou administration overcame the parlements in France, Gustav III ended the noble hegemony in Sweden, Maria Theresa sought to circumvent the various diets and councils of her composite realms. On the other hand, at Geneva, a kind of democratic or burgher party had asserted itself against the patricians with some success. In England the parliamentary patriciate saw its independence endangered both by King George III, who was determined to subdue the Whig magnates, and by the beginnings of a democratic agitation which held that the House of Commons should be really elected by, and reflect the wishes of, the people whom it was deemed to represent. The American Revolution broke with both Parliament and King. It put into effect many of the ideas of the Enlightenment, and offered the example, through its written constitutions and its constitutional conventions, of the people acting as a constituent power.

In the years between 1774 and 1789, or between the beginnings of the American and of the French Revolutions, the stresses and conflicts grew more acute. Events in America aroused the sense of a new era in Europe, encouraged a negative attitude in Europe toward European institutions, and induced a belief in the possibility of change in the directions desired by persons hitherto excluded from political life. The influence of America, and of much indigenous European development, operated in general in a democratic direction. But real events in Europe, as distinguished from the stirring up of ideas, seemed to be going the opposite way.

It has become commonplace among writers of French history to think of an "aristocratic resurgence" in France before the Revolution. It is illuminating to apply the same concept to a wider area. In the fifteen years before the French Revolution the British and Irish parliaments escaped even a moderate reform, the Dutch Patriots rose and were suppressed, the Genevese patriciate drove out the democrats, the Swedish nobility chafed against Gustav III (who was assassinated by a nobleman in 1792), the Maupeou program collapsed in France, the Belgian and Hungarian estates revolted against the Hapsburg monarchy, the Russian nobility received a charter from Catherine II, the Polish nobility began to build a gentry republic, and the lawyers of Prussia labored to codify the *Ständestaat* in the *Preussisches Allgemeine Landrecht*, which was promulgated in 1791, and stands as an instructive counterpart to the first French revolutionary constitution issued in that year. A philosophy of what was to be called conservatism began to appear. In the circumstances of the day, it was in effect a defense of the existing constituted bodies, hence heavily historical, and aristocratic. Edmund Burke first gave a full expression to his major ideas, not in writing against the French Revolution of 1789, but in opposing the reform of Parliament in 1784.

There was, in short, a widespread aristocratic resurgence, or perhaps only a "surgence," a rising bid for power and recognition, or successful offensive against antiaristocratic forces, whether monarchic or democratic, at the very time when other developments, one of which was the impact of the American Revolution, made a great many people less willing than ever to accept any such drift of affairs. The great disturbance of the 1790's can be understood only against the background of these conflicting trends.

We begin with what happened in the British Isles.

The Arming of Ireland: "Grattan's Parliament"

In both islands, during the later years of the American war, an organized force of public opinion developed outside of Parliament and against it, a kind of anti-Parliament, claiming to represent the people of the country better than Parliament itself and thus to bring a rightful pressure upon it. Since the constitutional doctrine of the day recognized no power above or outside of Parliament (except possibly God and his laws), the claims of any such pressure groups were thought to be, and in fact were, more or less extra-legal and more or less revolutionary in implication. In Ireland (as in Holland) this extra-legal organization took to arms. In England it remained purely civilian. But the arming of Ireland was hailed as a great advantage by many English reformers.[1]

There were two levels of conflict in Ireland: first, the desire of the Irish Parliament for emancipation from the British Parliament, and, second, the desire of many people in Ireland to reform the Irish Parliament itself. It will come as no surprise to readers of political history to learn that the Irish Parliament welcomed extra-parliamentary or popular support in its struggle against Westminster, and that, once emancipated from the Parliament of Great Britain, it tended to believe that such extra-parliamentary activity was unnecessary and improper.

Ireland in the 1770's had about 4,500,000 people, or over half as many as England. More than 3,000,000 were Catholics, who, somewhat like the "natives" of Geneva, were legally debarred from political life, even from the vote, and from most of the desirable or remunerative occupations. Somewhat under a million were Presbyterians, most heavily concentrated in Ulster and laboring under the same political disabilities as in England. They could vote, if they had the required qualifications. They were legally debarred by religion from no occupation except higher government service. Most of them were farmers on easily terminable leases. Many also worked as linen weavers in their cottages. The remaining 450,000 were Anglicans, concentrated in the east but found all over the island. Anglicans owned five-sixths of the land, but there were a few Catholic peers, and a number of Catholic gentry, for though the purchase of land by a Catholic had been forbidden, its

---

[1] For Ireland at this time see R. B. McDowell, *Irish Public Opinion 1750-1800* (London, 1943); G. O'Brien, *Economic History of Ireland in the 18th Century* (Dublin and London, 1918); B. Inglis, *The Freedom of the Press in Ireland 1784-1841* (London, 1954); E. Curtis, *History of Ireland* (London, 1936). Also, for connections between Irish and English reform movements, H. Butterfield, *George III, Lord North and the People* (London, 1949).

inheritance under certain restrictions was allowed. Few Presbyterians were upper class; like the English Dissenters, they were thought to be susceptible to "republicanism." Educated Catholics and Protestants had begun to get along with each other peaceably, but such broad-mindedness had not yet spread very far through society. Dublin was a cosmopolitan city, the administrative, commercial, legal, educational, and fashionable capital of the island, its articulate citizens mainly Anglican, graced by new parks and fine Georgian buildings, and rapidly growing, claiming, with 150,000 people, to be the fifth largest city of Europe. Belfast was still a small provincial town.

The Irish Parliament, as already explained, represented the Anglican or Anglo-Irish community, though in the peculiar fashion of the time, for where in England it was estimated that 5,723 persons controlled half the seats in the House of Commons, only about a hundred controlled two-thirds of those in the Commons of Ireland. Many of these oligarchs worked habitually with the Castle—Dublin Castle, the seat of the Lord Lieutenant and the British authorities—so that the crown was normally able, as in England, to "influence" Parliament in the desired direction. In any case, by the famous Poynings' Law, enacted as long ago as 1494 to control the Anglo-Irish magnates, no bill could be introduced in the Irish Parliament without the previous consent of the English Privy Council, through its agent the Lord Lieutenant. This law was the symbol of the subordination of the Irish Parliament, which, however, did legislate pretty freely on internal matters. Most of the legislation against Catholics was the work of the Irish Parliament, not the British. After the mid-century the British government usually showed more indulgence toward Irish Catholics than did the Irish government in Ireland.

The Anglo-Irish, like the Americans, were well satisfied with their English culture. They were aware, too, that their position as against the native Catholics depended ultimately on British protection. Nevertheless, they often defended Irish interests against the English. Though Ireland was not taxed by the British Parliament, and maintained its own army, administration, and debt, it was subject to trade controls enacted in Britain for the protection of British merchants. These controls forbade Ireland to export woolens and other goods that might compete, or to levy tariffs against England, or in general to trade with Europe or the British colonies except through intermediaries in England. Ireland lived by the export of beef, pork, butter, and linens. There was always a balance-of-trade problem, since landowners and pensioners resident in England took out almost £1,000,000 a year. Despite all disadvantages, there was a considerable business growth in Ireland after the mid-century. The Irish Parliament wished to get rid of the trade regulations enacted in England.

The impact of the troubles with America was very direct. American non-importation agreements, followed after the outbreak of hostilities by British embargoes, caused a sudden and ruinous decline in the export of linens and provisions. All classes felt the blow: landlords could not collect rents, nor farmers pay them; weavers were thrown out of work; and merchants saw their stocks pile up unsold in Dublin, Cork, and the depots of London. The proverbial poverty of the Irish poor was worse than ever.

Then, in April 1778, John Paul Jones, in the United States warship *Ranger*, sailed unopposed into Belfast harbor. Troops had been withdrawn for the American war; there were never enough, in any case, to guarantee security in wartime against a French invasion with which it was expected that the Catholic population would collaborate. The French did have plans for invasion, and soon financed John Paul Jones's small American flotilla. In Ireland people of the middling and upper ranks rushed to defend themselves, organized neighborhood companies, procured arms, assembled for drills, and adopted "neat and elegant" uniforms. These companies were at first exclusively Protestant. Such leading men as the Duke of Leinster and the Earl of Charlemont accepted positions of command. The British government, on the advice of the Lord Lieutenant, countenanced them and even supplied weapons, though with some misgiving, under the fear of invasion.

Thus originated the Irish Volunteers. They were entirely different from the White boys, Steel boys, Peep-of-Day boys, or Defenders who throughout this whole period carried on an underground violence among the depressed agricultural masses. It was the difference between Pugachev and Radishchev, as Catherine II might say; the Irish Volunteers read Benjamin Franklin. They were overwhelmingly sympathetic to the American rebellion and well informed of its progress. It was not against John Paul Jones that they meant to defend themselves, but against the French and agrarian insurrection. Nor indeed was the movement merely defensive; the Volunteers seized the opportunity of the American rebellion and the French war to bring pressure on England, to demand for Ireland the "liberty" for which others were fighting in America. There were 40,000 volunteers in arms by the end of 1779, organized, officially approved, and perfectly in the open. Their drills and musters brought them together for the exchange of ideas and adoption of programs. Delegates from the companies, meeting in regional assemblies, further spread political consciousness and communication throughout the island.

The Volunteers represented the Protestant and middle-class "nation in arms," but commanded as they were by dukes and earls, with sponsors like Henry Grattan and other reformers in the Irish Parliament, and with no hostility from the Catholics, they represented also, in 1779 and 1780, before the more cautious spirits took alarm, a degree of unity in Irish opinion such as had never existed before and was never to exist again. The awakening of the newspaper press, the outburst of political pamphlets, the formation of non-importation associations against England, the resolutions passed by normal civilian bodies, such as grand juries and county meetings, all added to the agitation. The broadest basis for agreement was the demand for a relaxing of the trade controls to relieve the economic crisis. There was a great desire for legislative autonomy for the Irish Parliament. Many wanted parliamentary reform; and a few dreamers undoubtedly, with the American example before them, were already beginning to think of total separation from England.

The government of Lord North, enmeshed in the American difficulties, trapped in a war with France for which it had optimistically made no preparation, and bedeviled by British merchants who wanted no competition from Ireland, especially after losing American markets, was unable to act speedily or decisively on the Irish demands. It is not that the British were immovable. The Irish Octennial Act of 1768, described above, has been called the first piece of parliamentary reform in the history of the two islands; and concessions to the Catholics, allowing them to take leases on land, had begun in the 1770's, probably to prevent their lending support to Protestant malcontents. But the British delayed on the trade concessions. There was meanwhile no force in the country capable of disarming the Volunteers. The Irish Parliament, sensing the quasi-military backing of the Volunteers, took the unprecedented step of refusing to vote money supplies except for a period of six months. Before pressure of this kind, and the continuing boycott of British goods, which the Volunteers made the more effective by their organization and publicity, the British yielded. The first real concessions came in 1780. The British Parliament amended the trade controls to allow export of Irish woolens and glasswares and trade with the colonies. But these concessions came so late, so grudgingly, and so obviously under pressure of armed defiance, that they inspired no confidence and won no credit for the British. And it was thought that what Parliament gave it could take away.

Agitation therefore continued. A Volunteer convention, with delegates from 143 companies, met at Dungannon in Ulster. It was presided over by the Earl of Charlemont and the two leading reformers in the Irish Parliament, Henry Flood and Henry Grattan. Flood was a reformer of more drastic type, who had even tried to tax absentee landlords. Grattan was a kind of Whig, primarily interested in Irish parliamentary liberties. The convention passed resolutions repudiating the power "of any other than the King, Lords, and Commons of Ireland to make laws to bind this kingdom." Meanwhile Cornwallis had surrendered at Yorktown. The British ministry was helpless and its policies wholly discredited. In England, too, a vociferous reform movement had arisen, of which Fox was now the chief spokesman within the parliamentary governing class. The English reformers looked on those of Ireland as allies against the same evils.

In 1782 the British gave the Irish what they seemed to want, and what the Americans had seemed to want in 1775, namely, freedom from the Parliament of Great Britain, and a coordinate status for their own Parliament under the crown. Poynings' Law and the Declaratory Act of 1719 were rescinded. The Irish Parliament was now "free," and the two kingdoms were supposedly equal. For a moment there was great joy in Ireland. It was indeed a momentous hour. Never had England so relaxed its hold on the lesser island. An applauding Parliament at Dublin, expressing the real enthusiasm of the country, voted a national award of £50,000 to the patriot hero, Henry Grattan.

England had yielded before the armed strength of the Volunteers, whose numbers rose to 80,000 by 1782. It must be noted, however, that the Volunteer companies, spirited as they were, were never put to the test. The way in which the very similar Dutch free companies melted away before a few Prussian regiments in 1787 suggests what might have happened if a few Hessian regiments had landed at Dublin. The English, who might conceivably have shifted troops after the surrender at Yorktown, must be given credit for not making the experiment. As it turned out it was the Americans who were put to the test, and by surviving it secured concessions for Ireland. Many Irish, in their American sympathies, gladly admitted as much. "It was on the plains of America," wrote one in 1782, "that Ireland obtained her freedom."[2]

"Grattan's Parliament," as the independent Irish Parliament has always been called, lasted from 1782 until the Act of Union with Great Britain in 1801. It represented the apogee of the "Protestant nation," which is to say of the Anglican nation, for Catholics still had no political rights, and although Presbyterians were relieved from the Test Act in 1780 very few of them, in the real circumstances of Anglican monopoly, had anything to do with the government. It was a time of prosperity for the manufacturing, trading, and landowning classes. The slow process of integrating the Catholics into the community went gradually on. Catholics were permitted to buy land in 1782. The strictly penal code against them was finally liquidated, though still with hesitation; for example, the movement to allow a Catholic college in Ireland was defeated, and Catholics desiring higher education for their children continued to send them to France or Belgium. Nor could any Catholic vote for a member of Parliament until England was again at war, in 1793.

The era of Grattan's Parliament was in fact one of increasing frustration. Even the Irish Whigs found parliamentary autonomy disappointing. The Lord Lieutenant, an Englishman, still reigned as viceroy at the Castle. He received his instructions from London, and his job, as before, was to get the Irish Parliament to conform to policies set in Great Britain. He had the same means of influence at his disposal. There was less of cabinet responsibility in Ireland than even in England, where it was embryonic; the doctrine of King, Lords, and Commons, of separate and equal status of executive and legislative, applied to Ireland with full force. Nor did abolition of the trade controls bring satisfaction, for Britain continued in the old habit of considering Ireland strategically joined to it but economically foreign. With really foreign countries the Irish now could trade without impediment from Britain, and they now had commercial access to the British colonies, but these included only the establishments in America and West Africa. That inescapable Mother of Parliaments, sitting at Westminster, continued to forbid Irish trade in the area of the East India Company charter, the whole region from the Cape of Good Hope eastward to the Strait of Magellan, and it also imposed high import duties on Irish goods coming into Great Britain. Irish printed

[2] McDowell, op.cit., 40; see also M. Kraus, "America and the Irish Revolutionary Movement in the 18th Century," in Era of the American Revolution (N.Y., 1939), 332-48.

linens entering Britain paid a 65 per cent duty; British printed linens entering Ireland paid only 10 per cent. The same disparities applied to many other products. Demands for an Irish protective tariff collapsed under the fear of British retaliation. Demands for an equalization of duties, which Pitt supported when he became Minister, were abandoned under the agonized outcries of British manufacturers. Manchester, just launching into its famous industrial revolution, and not yet converted to free trade, sent in a petition with 55,000 signatures against any tariff concessions to the Irish.[3]

Nor did Grattan's Parliament satisfy anyone slightly tinged with democracy. It was the same old Irish Parliament, more independent than ever. It is not necessary to take an Irish nationalist view of the matter. So moderate an observer as the diplomat Harold Nicolson, in his life of his great-great-grandfather, the United Irishman, Hamilton Rowan, observes that Grattan's Parliament was nothing but the Anglo-Irish vested interest more or less emancipated from higher control.[4] It was the ascendancy governing the natives and the dissenters.

The Volunteers refused to disband. They persisted in their armed deliberations, now urging reform of the electoral machinery of the Irish Commons. There were henceforth two discernible currents in the program of electoral reform. One proposed, while leaving all else unchanged, to grant the vote to those few property-owning and substantial Catholics who could qualify under the existing system. This plan, which simply looked to the removal of Catholicism as a disability, was favored by Grattan, and by Burke in England, himself of Irish birth by a Catholic mother. Given the tepidity of religious feeling among educated persons in the eighteenth century, and considering that the Irish Catholic bishops (without consulting the pope) had formally denied that the pope had any civil or temporal power in Ireland, the idea of granting the franchise to the substantial Catholics was not a very bold or alarming step, though in Ireland it raised many well-grounded apprehensions. The other plan, favored by the Volunteers, looked to a renovation of decayed boroughs, abolition of borough-mongering, and allowing of real freedom and actual elective powers to the electorate. It was a popular plan, and enjoyed wide support; but its sponsors were weakened by disagreement on giving the vote

---

[3] The petition was printed in the *Annual Register, 1784-1785*, 362-64. See also O'Brien, *op.cit.*

[4] H. Nicolson, *The Desire to Please: a Story of Hamilton Rowan and the United Irishmen* (London and New York), 1943, 66.

to the Catholics. There were those who predicted, and the next hundred years were to vindicate their predictions, that political power in the hands of the Catholics would subvert all Ireland as then known, undo all the effects of the seventeenth-century conquests, overturn property, dissolve the established church, and even bring English civilization into question.

The Irish reform movement reached a climax in 1783 and 1784. It was closely related to the corresponding movement in England, to which we can now turn before taking up the reform bills in the Parliaments of the two countries.

The "Association" Movement in England

In England the new political movement centered about the idea of "association," in which Professor Herbert Butterfield has seen not merely a passing disturbance but one of the grand dates of all English history. "Our French Revolution," he has written, "is in fact that of 1780—the revolution that we escaped."[5] He insists that the movement was quasi-revolutionary, because it affirmed that assemblies of private persons, forming spontaneously throughout the country, were more representative than Parliament itself, both in being truer spokesmen of the people's wishes, and in having the power to take binding action in their name. It must again be recalled that by the accepted ideas Parliament was supposed to be "absolute," according to Blackstone, or so independent that it must resist pressure from either King or people, as Fox had said in 1771.

At the same time, and somewhat inconsistently with the doctrine of parliamentary absolutism, it was held that members of the House of Commons, being sent up by constituencies in boroughs and counties, could not themselves change these constituencies, much less destroy them by outright abolition of decayed boroughs. Blackstone himself was too logical to believe this; he even held that Parliament could make and remake the constitution, and thought it regrettable that depopulated boroughs should continue to have members in Parliament. But it was an argument much favored by opponents of electoral reform; it is found even in the highly Whiggish *Letters of Junius*. It had a convincing sound—how could Parliament destroy its own

[5] H. Butterfield, *George III, Lord North and the People, 1779-1780* (London, 1949), vi. For this whole section I am mainly indebted to this important work. See also G. S. Veitch, *The Genesis of Parliamentary Reform* (London, 1913); S. Maccoby, *English Radicalism, 1762-1785* (London, 1955).

makers?—and it led to rethinking on the ultimate sources of lawful power. If it was true that Parliament could not change the constituencies of the House of Commons, then there must be some other power that could do so, some really final and technically absolute power. In England this could not be the King; what then could it be but the People? Here again we may note how the idea of the sovereignty of the people, far from being the product of abstract speculation, arose in the needs of debate against claims to inviolability made by constituted bodies.

The reform movement that reached its height in the Wilkes agitations subsided during the 1770's. It had set many precedents in its use of public meetings, its organization of opinion outside Parliament, its instruction of members, and its view of them as deputies answerable to their electors. It had won publication of parliamentary debates, and produced the first reform bill in 1776. The bill of course failed to pass, and nothing more happened. Wilkes sat in the Commons from 1774 to 1790, but he had no further role of importance.

The American war was at first popular in England, but as it proved more difficult to conduct, and broadened into a war with France, a good deal of British opinion turned against it, and blamed it on the stupidity, misgovernment, or despotism of the King. The rising taxes made necessary by the war gave offense to many of all classes, who, being dissatisfied with the government and its policies, attributed their financial troubles to "corruption," that is, the award of pensions, sinecures, or other expensive gratifications to the toadies, favorites, or political minions of the crown. Such practices were no greater or more expensive than ever, but they made a good target for discontent.

Demands for a change thus revived about 1778, among larger segments of the population than in the days of Wilkes and Liberty ten years before. There were two main centers of disaffection, which spread, merged, and fell apart. One was among the landowners of Yorkshire, led by Christopher Wyvil. The other carried on the radicalism of London, which now centered more in the adjoining city of Westminster. Two distinct programs of reform were in the air: an "economical reform" to reduce pensions, sinecures, and ornamental offices, and so save the taxpayers' money and abate the royal power to "corrupt" or influence Parliament; and a political or electoral reform to alter the composition of the Commons. The first was one that good Whigs could heartily endorse, and its high moral tone and promise of lower taxes gave it a wide appeal. The second was more radical; and though some, like Wyvil, concluding that a corrupted Parliament would not abolish the means of its own corruption, moved on to political reform as the necessary goal, others, like Burke and many Whigs, in order to avert electoral change, increasingly made a crusade of economical reform itself.

Wyvil brought about a county meeting at York, in December 1779, representing in principle all the freeholders and gentry of Yorkshire. Six hundred attended, including five dukes and earls and the Marquis of Rockingham. They claimed to represent landed wealth within the county worth £800,000 a year. They passed resolutions on the deplorable trend of public events, warned against the growing influence of the crown, and urged the need of economical reform. They declared that a degenerate government would do nothing except under organized public pressure, and to illustrate their meaning they pointed with approval to what was happening in Ireland. They set up a committee of correspondence to establish contact with similar meetings elsewhere. Wyvil, moderating his own desire for electoral reform, let them emphasize economical reform as offering a broader basis of agreement.

News of the Yorkshire meeting was hailed with enthusiasm in London, to which Wyvil repaired, and which became the main center of the whole movement. "Join as the Irish do!" cried one London newspaper. "It is not by speaking or voting in the House of Commons, Sir, that this country is to be saved," said another. "The Associations in America," declared a third, meaning the non-importation and other pre-revolutionary associations in the colonies, "have set an example. . . . This example has been followed in Ireland."[6]

Throughout England, in towns and counties, meetings on the model of the Yorkshire meeting assembled, and after a few resolutions, appointed committees, in which a few leading spirits took on the management of affairs. In February 1780, the London and Westminster committees sent a circular to all the others, inviting them to send deputies to an assembly in London, "to consider a Plan of Association." Only twelve counties and four towns responded, apparently because of shortage of time, but these in turn resolved to form a General Association, or what Sir George Savile proposed to call a National Assembly. This association was to examine the public accounts, and to work for parliamentary reform, that is, for annually elected Parliaments, for "tests" by which candidates must promise to adhere to pro-

6 Quotations from Butterfield, op.cit., 210.

grams demanded by their constituents, and for the addition of one hundred county members. It may be recalled that four-fifths of the members of the House of Commons sat for boroughs, and that though most burgesses were country gentlemen the rural population was thus underrepresented; the point, however, was that the boroughs were highly susceptible to manipulation, so that an increase of county members was a commonly proposed means to assure a freer and purer House.

Meanwhile, certain of the Parliament Whigs, including Charles James Fox, had become active in the town and county meetings. Fox had now become a reformer, and even a tribune of the people, delivering eloquent speeches in the Westminster meeting, praising the American rebels (with whom England was still at war), and loudly applauding the Irish Volunteers. The Whigs, indeed, at this time, in Butterfield's phrase, adopted a doctrine of "near revolution."[7] To their old fondness for the Revolution of 1688 they added a taste for the conveniently distant revolution in America, for the revolutionary ferment in Ireland, and for appeals to the majesty of the people of England, compounding all into a terrible medicine to be inflicted on Lord North and King George III. Fox declared that the Irish Volunteers were a good thing even if they were illegal, and he even endorsed the radical idea that members of Parliament were only "delegates" of the people. Scion of a wealthy Whig family (he and his brothers had to be bailed out of £140,000 in gambling debts in 1774), Fox was a man of warm and generous nature, who came to sponsor all manner of liberal causes and was courageously to oppose the war with Revolutionary France; but in his sympathy for parliamentary reform, he seemed sometimes to lack a steadiness of cold conviction, and be less of a reformer than either of the two Pitts or their friend, the Earl of Shelburne. In any case, Shelburne (the elder Pitt being dead, the younger not yet in Parliament) also now entered into the tumult of meetings and committees. With Fox and Shelburne, the Rockinghamite and the Pittite Whigs, joining forces with a great national upsurge of extra-parliamentary opinion, it seemed for a moment, in 1780, as if their combined forces might both put an end to George III's experiments with personal rule, and bring about some measure of democratization of the House of Commons. There were thoughts of a less baronial Magna Carta, a "second Runnymede."

Wyvil and the reformers, however, in their distrust of Parliament, regarded the appearance of Fox and other members of Parliament in

[7] *Ibid.*, 172-73.

their midst as an infiltration. To a Parliament that had claimed independence of the people, they responded by proposing an association independent of Parliament, an extra-parliamentary but representative body that should act upon Parliament and reform it. Within the various county and town meetings there thus took place a struggle for leadership, between reformers who were members of Parliament and reformers who, from the outside, did not believe that Parliament ever would or could really reform itself.

The call for a General Association, a veritable anti-Parliament, threw the reformers into disarray. The Rockingham Whigs (Shelburne showed more inclination to radicalism) now took alarm. They declared—rightly enough from a legal point of view—that the deputies at London had no real representative character, and no real representative powers. Meetings throughout the country were dubious and divided. Gentry and freeholders were annoyed at corruption, taxes, extravagance, and parliamentary subservience to the crown, but they could not bring themselves to impugn the grandeur of the British constitution, or to believe that Parliament should be dictated to by unauthorized persons like themselves. At the Wiltshire meeting, to which both Fox and Shelburne belonged, the committee cautiously decided that if any association ever met it should demand no more than economical reform, and the full meeting would agree to no association at all. Nottingham, in county meeting, feared "self-created assemblies." Sussex warned against "General Associations apparently tending to overrule the legislature," and Hertfordshire did not want the legislature "overawed" by committees of correspondence. America and Ireland, observed the *Annual Register*, had made the very words "association" and "committee" sound suspicious. And even in Yorkshire, where the movement to "overawe" Parliament had first gathered strength among men boasting £800,000 of income, there were sobering second thoughts. Yorkshire, under the nominal four-shilling land tax, really paid only one shilling in the pound of actual rents. Conservatives were quick to hint at the probable consequences of reform.[8]

Whigs everywhere disputed with radicals, as the Whigs everywhere fled from the association idea, and even refused to submit to electoral tests. Most meetings would go no further than to ask for economical reform. Parliamentary reformers divided. Wyvil and his followers concluded that parliamentary reform could come only with the support

---

[8] *Ibid.*, 246-51; W. R. Ward, *English Land Tax in the 18th Century* (London, 1953), 125.

of the landed class, and advocated only a more uniform and effective representation of property owners. The popular reformers became more self-conscious in identifying their opponents and in formulating their own aims. One of them burst out in the Essex meeting: "I have never yet heard of an aristocracy [and he meant the Rockingham Whigs and the Parliament] from ancient Rome to modern Venice that was not the universal tyrant and inquisitor of the species."[9] It was at this time, in May 1780, that the Westminster meeting, as already noted in connection with the American Revolution, drafted its far-reaching proposals for parliamentary reform, which went beyond the American constitutions in their theory of representation, and anticipated the six points of the People's Charter, including universal suffrage for all adult males.[10]

Then in June 1780 came the Gordon riots, an irrelevant episode, unconnected with projects of association or of reform, but which crippled and discredited the democratic movement by exposing the violence endemic at the bottom of society. A mild act of Catholic relief, passed by Parliament in 1778, had aroused ancestral terrors of popery, particularly among the lower classes, which, in Britain as in Ireland, did not yet share that religious magnanimity that educated persons had come to feel. Lord George Gordon, a Scotsman, and an eccentric of the kind admired by the British when harmless (he died a converted Jew), became the leader of the no-popery forces in London. The misery of the poor, and the absence of effective police, made mobs a chronic danger in all great cities. On June 2 Lord George entered the House of Commons (of which he was a member, being the son of a duke), to present a petition against legislation in favor of Catholics. Large crowds accompanied him, wearing the blue cockade originated by Wilkes, who, however, opposed the present demonstration. They "overawed" Parliament in an actual sense, pulling the wigs off two lords, and chasing a bishop across the adjoining roofs. The next day a full-grown riot took possession of London, and held it for a week. Whole Catholic neighborhoods were burned, as were the houses of judges and lawyers. The Fleet, Newgate, and King's Bench prisons went up in flames, and two thousand prisoners wandered free. On one night thirty-six separate fires were visible. Probably there was less physical destruction in Paris during the whole French Revolution, if we except the demolition of the Bastille.

[9] Butterfield, *op.cit.*, 295.
[10] See above, p. 208, and Maccoby, *op.cit.*, 320.

The mob was put down mainly by John Wilkes, who headed a body of volunteers before the arrival of military reinforcements. Several were killed, hundreds wounded. Wilkes, long known to some as an agitator, was now a traitor in the eyes of the populace. The democratic branch of the reformers was silenced. Henceforth any notion of giving a vote to all adult males had a great resistance to overcome.

No General Association ever met. There was no second Runnymede. No National Assembly ever convened in England. The difficulty of holding any such assembly that did not start from some legally accepted base, such as the colonial legislatures in America or the French Estates General of 1789, was made abundantly clear. The association idea evaporated, leaving for a while a vaguely subversive aura about the word, and slowly passing, in the long run, into the idea of the modern political party, as a private and unofficial, but at the same time public and organized, body, apart from government, yet using government and bringing pressure upon it.

Yet the meetings and murmurs throughout the country had their effect. Streams of petitions, while deferentially law-abiding, still showed a widespread dissatisfaction with royal and ministerial influence. The opposition in Parliament, the two great Whig factions, were temporarily able to capture a majority from Lord North. The result was the Dunning resolution adopted in April 1780 by the Commons: that "the influence of the crown has increased, is increasing, and ought to be diminished." The next logical step would be to reduce this influence by abolishing some of the offices and pensions through which it was exercised, but this step the Whigs were for a while unable to take—because, it is seriously alleged, at the critical moment the young blades of the Rockingham party made off for the Newmarket races. The Dunning resolution itself, however, though nothing but a resolution, gave some indication that Parliament was not inevitably controlled by the King, that it could at times respond to public opinion, that it might, after all, be capable of some measure of self-reform. It thus temporarily quieted the political agitation, as did the Gordon riots that shortly followed.

Lord North recaptured his majority, but in 1782 was finally allowed to resign by the King, who at last in desperation, with America lost, Ireland rebellious, and England much disgruntled, called his enemies the Whigs into office, and put Rockingham, Fox, and Shelburne into the cabinet. The Whigs opened negotiations with the United States, and conceded parliamentary independence to Ireland.

The Whigs also in 1782 obtained the enactment of Burke's bill for Economical Reform, or as Burke had called it in 1780, a "Plan for the better security of the independency of Parliament." The beauty of economic reform was that, by saving the taxpayer's money through the reduction of offices, it seemed simultaneously to relieve Parliament from the wrath of the public, and to reduce the means of influence brought to bear by the King. Burke's plan had many merits, and did contribute to the modernization of government. It abolished the clusters of idle but lucrative offices that clung to the Principality of Wales, the Duchy of Lancaster, the County of Chester, and other survivals of former times, "principalities," as Burke called them, which retained "the apparatus of a kingdom for the jurisdiction over a few private estates." It abolished also certain honorific appointments in the royal household, with considerable difficulty, "because the King's turnspit in the King's kitchen was a member of Parliament." It turned over the King's table, wardrobe, and kennels to appropriate contractors or employees: "It is not proper that great noblemen should be the keepers of dogs." It introduced more order into public accounting. Burke himself, as Paymaster of the Forces in the short-lived Rockingham government, an office in which his predecessors had often enriched themselves by the flexible handling of large sums of money, introduced the novel practice of depositing the funds in the Bank of England, and put himself on a salary. I cannot resist the observation that the salary fixed upon was £4,000, five times more than Alexander Hamilton received as Secretary of the Treasury in 1789. Burke explained that, while cutting out sinecures, he meant to have the really important offices of state handsomely paid, so as to attract the right kind of men, and keep up the necessary "representation."[11]

Actually, the Economical Reform of 1782 saved less than £50,000 a year.[12] In an annual budget of £12,500,000 this was imperceptible to the taxpayer. Nor, as it turned out, was it enough to emancipate Parliament from the King. The King could win any election; his problem was to find someone able and willing to head up his government. George III, buffeted and discomfited, obliged finally to part with North, and even to bring in the Whigs, was not really beaten. He survived quite well the "near revolution" of 1780, and even Rockingham's three months in office. He found the man he needed in young William Pitt.

[11] Quotations in this paragraph are from Burke's speech on economical reform.
[12] J. Sinclair, *History of the Public Revenue of the British Empire* (London, 1803), II, 85.

Entering Parliament at the age of twenty-two, enjoying high office with Shelburne the following year, and himself Prime Minister the year after that, Pitt dissolved Parliament in 1784. Older and more edifying histories declare that he sensed an aroused country in his favor, and swept into power as the nation's candidate against an embarrassed monarch. The truth is that Pitt was the King's man, and that, before his dissolution of Parliament, he had the expert advice of John Robinson, the King's manager, who, after exhaustive calculations, assured him that the crown controlled enough boroughs to give him a victory.[13]

Pitt did not basically agree with George III. Pitt had his principles, which were usually good ones, but he also respected the principles of the royal master. He held office for almost two decades by respecting the King's wishes when he could not change them. Here again, as in the days of the Stamp Act, there was a remote and ludicrous English analogy to the enlightened despotism of the Continent, which the Whiggish traditions of English history have perhaps concealed. With Pitt in office the aristocracy was kept at a distance. As Lady Holland, the great Whig hostess, was to remark in the days of the French Revolution, Pitt really had no more regard for the aristocracy than any member of the London Correseponding Society. And Pitt did accomplish a good deal of fiscal and administrative reconstruction by making himself useful to the crown. But, as with reforming ministers in other countries, there were important sacrifices that he had to make. In England as elsewhere, in the 1780's, the aristocracy was not dislodged.

The young Pitt, among his other qualities, was a serious believer in the need for parliamentary reform. He carried over, in his younger days, some of the popular ideas of Shelburne and his father. He himself introduced three reform bills. They came at the same time as the reform bill in Ireland, and the two kingdoms can be considered together.

The Reform Bills and Their Failure

The extra-parliamentary pressure, quasi-military in Ireland, civilian in England, built up to force action upon the two Parliaments, was

---

[13] W. T. Laprade, *Parliamentary Papers of John Robinson 1774-1784* (London, 1922) in *Camden Society Third Series*, vol. 33. That Pitt took and retained office as the King's man, and not by a popular, parliamentary, or liberal triumph over George III, is the thesis of D. G. Barnes, *George III and William Pitt, 1783-1806* (London, 1939). It is shared by Pares, Butterfield, Feiling, and other British writers.

"revolutionary" only in a certain sense. Only insofar as the Parliaments were constitutionally independent, and clamor out of doors, or even orderly public opinion, was a phenomenon on which Parliament was free to act, or not to act, according to its own unforced judgment of the national interests, can outside pressures be described by so strong a word. In another sense the most advanced ideas of reformers were not revolutionary in the least. None went beyond the idea of a more equal representation in the House of Commons. None attacked the Lords or the crown in any basic way, and none anticipated the actual workings of cabinet government, which was a conception, rather, promoted by the parliamentary Rockingham Whigs. Reformers dwelt on the majesty of the people. But the British and Irish reformers never really took up the theory developed in the American Revolution, the theory of the people as constituent power. None thought that any General Association, or what Sir George Savile called a "National Assembly," should actually *create* government. All venerated the British constitution, properly understood, and free from "abuses"; none thought of replacing the existing constitution by another or a newly authorized one. None demanded a written document drafted by a constituent convention. At most, reformers wanted the people to "constitute" the Commons, that is, to make it up by their free votes and turn it into a body of delegates. There was no idea that the people should explicitly "constitute" the whole apparatus of government.

These observations may be kept in mind as we survey the reform bills and the conservative arguments against them.

In Ireland, after the winning of legislative independence, the Volunteers not only refused to disband, but rapidly grew in numbers, even admitting and arming Catholics as recruits. Grattan and the Irish Whigs, who had so recently praised them as armed patriots willing to fight for their country, now regarded them as an anarchic menace to lawful authority. The Volunteers, who for some time had met in regional conventions, decided to hold a Grand National Convention at Dublin in November 1783. It was the first body calling itself a national convention in a world that was to know many such in the next fifteen years. Uniformed and armed delegates from all parts of the island marched through Dublin amid the cheers of the population. They deliberated under the chairmanship of the Earl of Charlemont, who had consented to come in the hope of moderating the proceedings. There was much disagreement on the enfranchisement of Catholics, which was finally decided against, so that the proposals automatically excluded two-thirds of the population. The reform program resolved upon has been thought moderate enough by later historians. It demanded that Parliament be elected every three years, that no life pensioners be allowed to sit unless specifically reelected, that all Protestant freeholders and holders of long leases of at least £10 a year be given the vote, if actually resident, and that decayed constituencies, having less than two hundred voters, should no longer be represented in the House of Commons.[14]

Henry Flood, an officer of the Volunteers, proceeded the short distance through the Dublin streets from the session of the convention to the Parliament building, where he forthwith introduced these proposals as a bill. He appeared in uniform, with a few other members, and so gave a welcome opening to the opponents of reform, since he did in fact raise the question of the propriety of a parliamentary body yielding to men in arms. After long speeches, the bill was voted down, 150 to 60. The year 1784 saw even more hectic agitation. Catholics were increasingly admitted to the Volunteer companies. The beginnings of the United Irishmen could already be seen. The *Volunteer Journal* and other radical newspapers grew more excited, demanding a protective tariff for starving workers, pointing enthusiastically to America, printing cartoons in which gibbets for traitors were featured, or various notables were tarred and feathered. The Dublin reformers called together a new national body, which this time they called a "congress." This American word aroused unbounded hopes and wild apprehensions. The Congress assembled through more or less legal channels, by the summons of sheriffs for election of delegates in their counties. Most sheriffs refused to comply, but several did, including the sheriff of Dublin. The Attorney General arrested him, and also suppressed the radical newspapers, so that the freedom of the press enjoyed for the past several years in Ireland was now permanently restrained. The Congress met behind closed doors, but did nothing except to pass resolutions, and faded away early in 1785.

It is clear that the Irish reform movement, though its most advanced leaders were already very radical, commanded a wide support throughout the country. All three members of the Stewart family then in the Irish Commons, including the father of the future Lord Castlereagh,

---

[14] There is a narrative account of the convention in T. Wright, *History of Ireland* (London and New York, n.d.), II, 469-74. For other details, including the resolutions of the convention and provisions of its reform bill, see *Memoirs of the Life and Times of Henry Grattan by his Son* (London, 1849), III, 143-46.

voted for the bill brought from the Convention by Henry Flood in 1783. Even the Congress of 1784 could boast of a peer and four baronets. A moderate writer estimates that the upper and middle classes of Ireland, except for those profiting or hoping to profit from the existing system (who were indeed numerous), favored a reform of Parliament at this time, though not at the cost of civil struggle, and, for many, not at the dictation of uniformed men in the House of Commons.[15]

It is the arguments of the antireformers that are most interesting, since those of the reformers are familiar enough, and those of conservatives, who were the successful party, were soon to spread throughout Europe. The grand debate in the Irish Parliament took place at the time of the National Convention and Flood's bill at the end of 1783. Some of the speeches resemble those of Edmund Burke, who was in habitual correspondence with Ireland, but whether Burke influenced Irishmen like Sir Hercules Langrishe, or was influenced by them, is impossible to say.

The first crushing oration was delivered by Yelverton, who turned the whole discussion from the merits of reform to the merits of the convention from which Flood had unwisely brought the bill. The truth seems to be that the Irish government and Parliament did not really fear the convention. Both General Burgoyne, now commanding the army in Ireland, and the Lord Lieutenant wrote to London that there was nothing to worry about. They reassured Charles Fox, who had declared in 1780 that he approved the Volunteers even though illegal, and who now, in 1783, being in responsible office, was adjuring them to suppress the convention and pay no attention whatsoever to its petitions. There was nothing to be afraid of, reported the Lord Lieutenant, because the convention was hopelessly divided on the Catholic question. He had himself, as Lord Lieutenant, through friends who belonged to it, taken steps to divide and confuse it on the religious issue.[16]

The Irish conservatives, relieved of real fears, launched the more easily into broad statements of principle. The question, said Yelverton, was "whether this house or the convention are the representatives of the people." It was whether "we are here to register the edicts of another assembly, or receive propositions at the point of the bayonet." It was whether Ireland, now a "free state," should squander its "inheritance" and its "blessings under our happy constitution." Mr. George Ponsonby warned against the secret machinations of English

---

[15] McDowell, *op.cit.*, 110.   [16] Grattan, *op.cit.*, III, 131.

radicals, and against "all the system-mongers in Europe," no two of whom, he alleged, ever agreed on any plan of reform. (His father owned twenty-two seats in the Irish House.) Sir Hercules Langrishe thought the bill "subversive of the constitution," of a constitution that was "the admiration and envy of all nations and all ages." In Ireland they were privileged to enjoy "ancient charters that had taken root in the constitution and are the growth of so many centuries." One must dread the "perplexities, the dangers, the difficulties presented by these sages of reform. Good God, is the mind of man never to be satisfied!"[17]

It must be admitted that the Anglo-Irish lost little time in appreciating their "inheritance."

In England, though the ardors of the Association movement were somewhat abated, the Whigs allowed the young Pitt, newly in Parliament, to introduce a reform bill as early as May 1782. It failed by a vote of 161 to 141 in a House of 558. Shelburne and the old Chathamite Whigs generally supported it, as did Fox, Sheridan, and the Duke of Richmond, but the bulk of the Rockingham Whigs, including Burke, satisfied that Parliament would regain its freedom through economic reform, voted against it. Pitt tried another bill in 1783, with the same lack of success. In 1784 Alderman Sawbridge, a leader of the London reformers, introduced another reform bill, against the advice of Pitt, who thought it inopportune, but who spoke in its favor. In 1785 Pitt introduced still another bill, making it one of his major proposals as head of the ministry. That is to say, parliamentary reform was no longer a mere agitation carried on a wave of public opinion. It was a serious measure offered in due parliamentary fashion by the government.

Pitt made his bill of 1785 as moderate as he thought possible in order to overcome the opposition, such as that expressed by Burke. He proposed to abolish only thirty-two of the most depopulated boroughs (in which the voters, if there were any, would henceforth vote as residents of their counties), and to transfer the seats thus made available either to the more populous counties or to the growing towns such as Manchester. Since copyhold, over the centuries, had in effect become a form of ownership of land, he would add the 40-shilling copyholders to the 40-shilling freeholders as voters in the counties. He would also enfranchise certain long leaseholders. Since in a few boroughs there

[17] Speeches are quoted at length in Wright, *op.cit.*, II, 474-81.

[306]

were propertyless persons who had the voting right, and who, paradoxically, would lose it by reform (as they did in 1832), Pitt proposed to indemnify these "potwallopers" to the extent of £1,000,000. Their vote was regarded as a property right.

Pitt was weakened, however, not only by the resistance of those who opposed any alteration of Parliament in principle, but by the failure of the new industrialists, in the unrepresented Midland towns, to lend him enough support. Pitt at this same time was working to equalize the tariff duties between England and Ireland. He was therefore unpopular in Manchester, Birmingham, Leeds, and Sheffield, which abstained from petitioning for passage of his reform bill. This was significant, at a time when Manchester got up a petition with 55,000 signatures against tariff concessions to Ireland. Pitt then gave up his tariff plans. It thus seemed that Burke was right when he said that places sending no members to Parliament were nevertheless "represented," and had their interests carefully watched over. Manchester, with no members in Parliament, could sway the tariff policy of England and profoundly influence its relations with Ireland, just as Yorkshire, which had few members, and where no election was contested between 1760 and 1800, continued to enjoy a favored position under the land tax.

Pitt's reform bill of 1785 may thus be thought of, somewhat like the Maupeou reforms in France, as the project of an enlightened government acting in the long-run interests of the country, rather than as a measure demanded by powerful forces in society at large. Like its predecessors, it failed to pass, by 248 against 174.

Pitt in 1785 was repudiated on the two measures on which he set most store, the reform of Parliament and the reform of commercial relations with Ireland. He could at this point either resign, or seek a coalition with Fox or North, or remain in office by depending on the King. There was no constitutional requirement that he resign, and he had a kind of personal feud with Fox. He remained Prime Minister by cooperating with the King. He never again brought up the subject of parliamentary reform, and remained content with such fiscal or administrative improvements as he could persuade the King to accept.

George III thus won out in the long constitutional crisis that had been going on for twenty years. If he did not rule personally, he ruled through Pitt, letting him have his high principles and ideas, and persuading him when necessary to defer or modify their application.

Constitutional change came to a standstill until 1832. King and Parliament remained "separated" and "balanced," and in effect made to work together by "influence." The aristocracy continued to hold forth in Parliament, and to accept the favors of the crown. As for the "people," some cared more for other things than the vote, like the industrialists of the Midlands, or the perfervid anti-Catholics of London. Others continued to hold meetings, form societies, and write pamphlets on reform of the representation. They were soon to be stirred up again during the French Revolution.

Here, as in Ireland, an especial interest attaches to the conservative arguments against the reform bills, because it was at this time that Edmund Burke codified his chief ideas. Burke's philosophy was ultimately to be of such importance that, like that of Rousseau's *Social Contract*, it demands attention in a section by itself.

The Conservatism of Edmund Burke

The best way to show that Burke's philosophy of conservatism was not a critique of the French Revolution, and was not directed against the more doctrinaire or purely rationalistic aspects of the Enlightenment, is to show how fully its principles were formed before the French Revolution, and that it was directed against practical proposals made in England, by Englishmen, for England.

He was Anglo-Irish, born in Dublin in 1729, the son of an Anglican attorney and a Catholic mother. He became an eloquent writer, a man of feeling, and an expatriate, in many ways surprisingly like Jean-Jacques Rousseau. He accepted the English aristocracy in a way that Rousseau never accepted the French; he was in turn accepted as an able follower and a friend by the Whig dukes and the Marquis of Rockingham, but they did not exactly regard him as one of themselves, and when they came briefly into office in 1782 they made him Paymaster of the Forces but would not give him cabinet rank. Together with his brother and cousin, at the beginning of his parliamentary career, he bought a country house in Buckinghamshire for £20,000, a price which he was wholly unable to afford, so that he was under constant strain for many years to keep up his style of living. When Rockingham died in 1782 he cancelled a debt of £30,000 owed him by Burke. Burke's career was a series of disappointments, for the Rockingham Whigs were out of office from 1766 to 1782, and in 1782 their term of office was cut short by Rockingham's death, so that Burke lost his lucrative position as paymaster almost immediately on receiving it, and did not even obtain a pension until 1795.[18]

Burke warmly identified himself with anything and anyone in which he believed. When rumors, which were in fact true, began to circulate about the dubious financial practices of the brother and cousin with whom he lived, he refused to believe them. He considered such talk as a persecution of himself. Of his own honesty there is no doubt, but he did benefit from his relatives' income, some of which helped to pay for the grand house and landed property that they occupied jointly. Somewhat similarly, he could believe no evil of the British constitution, and accept no criticism, if at all basic, of the House of Commons. Nor would he admit that he personally benefited from the political habits of the day, or see the proponents of parliamentary change as anything but wrongheaded men. It is in fact in his adulation of Parliament that we may see the unifying force behind the various political positions that he took. His carefully qualified attitude on American questions, his opposition to George III, his framing of the doctrines of party responsibility for the Rockingham Whigs, his sponsoring of economic reform, his opposition to electoral reform, and, in later years, his fear of the corruption of Parliament by East Indian nabobs, can all be explained as a warm defense of parliamentary dignity and independence. It is possible that he idealized Parliament all the more because he was not natively English, having spent his youth in the Anglo-Irish outpost of Dublin. One thinks of Herder idealizing German culture from outposts on the Baltic.

Beginning about 1780 or 1782, however, the House showed an unwillingness to listen to him. Members would bait him to make him angry, or noisily walk out when he rose to speak. For one so dedicated to the greatness of Parliament such cutting insults were a painful blow. He felt irritated, frustrated, unappreciated, surrounded by enemies, wounded in the depths—like Rousseau. The notion of Burke as a judicious observer of a turbulent revolutionary age is entirely a later concoction. His contemporaries were dismayed by his outbursts of unstable emotionalism.

"They represent him as actually mad," said Boswell to Johnson.

"Sir," answered the doctor, who was, indeed, no Whig, "if a man

[18] For Burke's personality, see the illuminating essays by T. W. Copeland, *Our Eminent Friend, Edmund Burke* (New Haven, 1949); for the finances of the Burke brothers and their cousin see D. Wecter, *Edmund Burke and His Kinsmen* (Boulder, 1939) in *University of Colorado Studies*, 1.

will appear extravagant as he does, and cry, can he wonder that he is represented as mad?"[19]

Burke was capable of a good deal of hard work, and of amassing exact knowledge on large and complex subjects, such as the history of trade with the American colonies, or the jungle of emoluments at the King's disposal, or the details of the case of Warren Hastings. He has been praised, indeed, and contrasted with French *philosophes* and British radicals, for his avoidance of metaphysical abstractions, and for his insistence on taking account of reality, facts, consequences, real choices, and possible actions. The contrary could as well be argued— that his gift lay on the plane of general statement, and his weakness in the perception and diagnosis of real events. Sir Ernest Barker has declared that Burke violated his own principles in his critique of the French Revolution, that in denouncing political "metaphysics" he became himself metaphysical, and failed altogether to see what the French Revolution was really about.[20] He could understand only that with which he could sympathize. He could understand the Irish Catholics but not the Irish reformers. He could understand the Americans as long as he thought them Whigs irritated at royal misgovernment; but in his insistence on parliamentary trade controls over the colonies, his offering them Ireland as a model, his belief in 1777 that America might return under "the paternal care and nurture" of Parliament, and his utter indifference to the new American constitutions that were exciting all Europe, he showed little comprehension of what really happened to the American people in his lifetime.

He was capable, too, of liberal and humane ideas. Many of his wisest apothegms could be quoted by reformers. In one of his earliest writings he ridiculed the lawyers' idea that the constitution was changeless.[21] Defending the Wilkesite agitation in 1770, he denied that it was stirred up by "a few puny libelers." "When popular discontents have been very prevalent," he said on this occasion, "it may well be affirmed and supported that there has been generally something found amiss in the constitution or the conduct of government."[22] He never said as much of any later discontents, however "prevalent," in England or elsewhere, in which his own sympathies or party loyalties were not

---

[19] Copeland, *op.cit.*, 70.

[20] E. Barker, "Edmund Burke et la Révolution française," in *Revue philosophique,* Sept.-Dec., 1939, 129-60.

[21] *Writings* (Boston, 1901), VII, 476. "An essay towards an abridgement of the English history," 1758.

[22] *Ibid.*, I, 439, 441. "Thoughts on the cause of the present discontents," 1770.

aroused. He could call the non-representation of Manchester one of "the shameful parts of our constitution"—when he was defending the Americans against Lord North in 1774.[23] He saw nothing disconcerting in it on other occasions. He could coin the very formula of the impatient progressive: "There is a time when men will not suffer bad things because their ancestors have suffered worse."[24] He made this remark in arguing for his Economic Reform. What we miss is the ability to perceive, in an objective way, the relevancy of such maxims to the ideas of other men.

There was one context in which he was willing to argue from an elevated position, to appeal to that "great rule of equality, which is grounded upon our common nature," that natural law or "substance of original justice" of which all human laws were only declaratory.[25] There was one context in which he could freely affirm that no one should be excluded from the commonwealth, that if excluded they might turn revolutionary or subversive, that without some degree of equality men could not be fellow citizens, that the whole empire should have "one common bottom of equality and justice."[26] Such phases might apply to the whole reforming and revolutionary movement of his day, to the whole dissatisfaction with self-enclosed governing bodies, and to the whole principle of the democratic state as it developed in later times. He applied them in the context of Irish Catholic disabilities.

Burke was never conservative abstractly or obstinately or dogmatically, from a mere principle of conservatism as a value in itself. Even in the *Reflections on the French Revolution* he allowed for a right of revolution; his objection to the French was that they needed no revolution, that they had made "an unforced choice, a fond election of evil."[27]

[23] *Ibid.*, II, 74. "Speech on American taxation," 1774.

[24] *Ibid.*, II, 279. "Speech on a plan for better security of the independence of Parliament," 1780.

[25] *Ibid.*, VII, 326. "Fragments of a tract relative to the laws against popery in Ireland," about 1765.

[26] Letter to Dermott, Aug. 17, 1779, in Burke correspondence, I, 813, in Wentworth-Woodhouse manuscripts at Sheffield; *Writings*, IV, 220, "Letter to a peer of Ireland on the penal laws against Catholics," 1782; and various utterances in the 1790's, *ibid.*, IV, 292, VII, 369, 379, 398, 423, where he now rejects natural right as a ground for granting the franchise to otherwise qualified Catholics and argues that they must be given a share in the constitution and a sense of participation and citizenship lest they turn Jacobin, i.e., revolutionary.

[27] On the right of revolution, *ibid.*, III, 410. "Reflections," 1790: "I do admit that too critical an inquiry might not be advisable into the means of freeing the world. . . . The tenderest minds, confounded with the dreadful exigence in which morality submits to the suspension of its own rules in favor of its own principles, might turn aside

This objection rested in turn on the judgment, or feeling, that French government and society before 1789 were, on balance, good. His approval of France before 1789 is apparent in many of his speeches and writings, as when he offered the federalism of the French provinces as a model for the British empire, or again, in 1780, pointed to the current reforms of Necker as an example of the economic reform that he desired in England.

Burke's conservative sentiments, like his liberal ones, arose in a concrete and human way from strong emotions. As he was powerfully held by the vision of a great British empire, or by the plight of the Irish Catholics, so he had a profound feeling for English society and for the British constitution and Parliament. And the same disproportion between far-reaching generalizations and the specific issues to which they applied, a disproportion that we have just observed in his liberal sentiments, is to be found in even greater measure in his conservative ones. He could call up the image of a great and just commonwealth of equal citizens to obtain the vote for a handful of Irish Catholic freeholders. He could invoke pictures of wholesale desolation in arguing against very limited proposals for change. It is a disproportion that suggests an emotional origin, but also, in all candor, a taste for rhetoric in the grand manner, the habits of a highly articulate man of letters in politics.

A few examples:

It is proposed (in 1769) to enlarge the electorate. But if people get the idea that "our constitution is not so perfect as it ought to be" the authority of Parliament is undermined, and ruin follows.[28] It is proposed to relieve certain Anglican clergymen of subscription to the Thirty-Nine Articles. This must not be done. Why not? Because the Anglican clergy must accept the doctrines made legal by Parliament, "because dissent, not satisfied with toleration, is not conscience, but ambition," and because "no legislature was ever so absurd as to tax its people to support men for teaching and acting as they please."[29] Infidels are bad. Why? Because they are "outlaws of the constitution of the human race."[30] Taxation of Irish absentee landowners would be bad. Why? Because it would subvert the principle of common citizen-

---

whilst fraud and violence were accomplishing the destruction of a pretended nobility. . . ." The Jacobins would not have put it otherwise.

[28] *Ibid.*, I, 371. "Observations on a late publication . . . ," 1769.

[29] *Ibid.*, VII, 11, 13. "Speech on the Acts of Uniformity," 1772.

[30] *Ibid.*, VII, 36. "Speech on a bill for the relief of Protestant Dissenters," 1773.

ship in the empire.[31] He calls up a dreadful vision of lawsuits, litigations, prosecutions, frenzy, of "society dissolved, industry interrupted, ruined—of those personal hatreds that will never be suffered to soften, those animosities and feuds which will be rendered immortal, those quarrels which are never to be appeased—morals vitiated and gangrened in the vitals."[32] What has occasioned this horrifying prognostication? Is it the Reign of Terror in France? No, it is a proposal that Parliament be elected every three years instead of every seven. Similarly, as a landowner of Buckinghamshire, he wrote to his county meeting, at the time of the Association movement, that the plan to add a hundred county members to the Commons would alter the "constitution of Parliament itself."[33]

When electoral reform became an issue of practical politics, sponsored four times in close succession by men in responsible office, Burke prepared a speech in which he assembled his arguments against it. This speech was never delivered, for the good reason that no one would listen to it. At the time of Pitt's reform bill of 1783 Burke rose to speak, but declined to do so because so many members were walking out. In the following year, at the time of Sawbridge's bill, Burke got into an altercation on the floor of the House with Pitt. Pitt declared that the American war had been due to defective representation in Parliament. Burke hotly denied this, and a general hubbub followed, with "some of the young members vociferating so loudly as to prevent Mr. Burke from being distinctly heard." Burke tried repeatedly to launch into a connected discourse, saying that he had "something to say which he conceived to be well worth their hearing," but finally gave up under the clamor that he said "oppressed" him. An undelivered speech, found at his death among his papers, is probably what he conceived to be worth the members' hearing on June 16, 1784. Had they listened, they would have heard no discussion of the terms of any particular reform bill, but a beautifully compact statement of what was to become philosophical conservatism.[34]

[31] *Ibid.*, VII, 121-34. "A letter . . . on the Irish absentee tax," 1773.
[32] *Ibid.*, VII, 80. "Speech on a bill for shortening the duration of Parliaments," 1780.
[33] *Ibid.*, VII, 293. "Letter to the chairman of the Buckinghamshire meeting," 1780.
[34] *Parliamentary History*, XXIV, 1,001. The refusal to give Burke a hearing was not due to pressure of time, since twelve speeches by others followed. Burke, *Writings*, VII, 89-104, "Speech on a motion . . . to inquire into the state of the representation of the Commons in Parliament." Some of Burke's editors, including the editor of the Boston edition of 1901, here cited, attribute this speech, or intended speech, to May 17, 1782, others to June 16, 1784. I have chosen the latter date because of the incident reported in the parliamentary history for that day, and because it seems likely that Burke

Burke, in this speech to which no one would listen, attributed the demand for electoral reform to a theory—the false theory of "the supposed rights of man." "They lay it down that every man ought to govern himself, and that where he cannot go, himself, he must send his representative; that all other government is usurpation. . . . Nine tenths of the reformers argue thus—that is, on the natural right." (He had himself justified the claims of Irish Catholics by natural right.) But, he now said, the British constitution did not derive its authority from any such source as natural right, nor did the Commons represent men as men, "as a collection of individuals." The constitution rested on prescription. (I have shown how Bishop Warburton had appealed to prescription, as a barrier to natural right, in defending the Test Act.) "Our constitution is a prescriptive constitution; it is a constitution whose sole authority is, that it has existed time out of mind." Prescription was a better source of rightful authority than election, because prescription showed the real "choice of the nation." This, he said, anticipating a famous passage in the *Reflections on the French Revolution*, where society was called a contract between the dead, the living and the yet unborn, was because "a nation is not an idea only of local extent and individual momentary aggregation. . . . [The nation's choice, as shown by prescription,] is a deliberate choice of ages and generations; it is a constitution made by what is ten thousand times better than choice; it is made by peculiar circumstances, occasions, tempers, dispositions, and moral, civil and social habitudes of the people, which disclose themselves only in a long space of time."

Here the question was how the real will of a political community could be ascertained. For Rousseau, as for Genevese democrats, or the authors of the American constitutions, this will must be felt and exercised by living persons in the present. For Burke the real will could be observed at work only over a long period of time. The two views were not necessarily contradictory, nor should either be dismissed as false, but they would coincide only in a relatively unchanging society, or in one not conscious or desirous of political change. One view was calculated to justify change and assert liberty. Burke's view was de-

would have codified his opposition to reform on the occasion of the third recently attempted reform bill rather than of that of 1782. It would be worth while to attempt an exact dating of this speech from Burke's unpublished papers. If written in 1784, this important statement of Burke's position would be influenced by events in Ireland also, and perhaps by speeches in the Irish Parliament in 1783, quoted above, since Burke was in close correspondence with Ireland.

signed to resist change, and to confine liberty within the limits of such liberties, if any, as might be inherited. Burke's view represented also a distrust of the reason of consciously reasoning, living men. "The individual is foolish, the multitude is foolish, but the species is wise."

As for the House of Commons, he went on, it too existed prescriptively. It had always been the same, composed of knights, citizens, and burgesses, representing not persons or individuals, but the corporate units of shires, cities, and boroughs without regard to population. No change was necessary in the recruitment of the House, and certainly no conversion to a radically new system of personal representation, because, on a practical ground, no change could be expected to do anyone any good. England had long been free, happy, and prosperous with its Parliament. Indeed, rightly understood, England already enjoyed equal representation. "You have an equal representation because you have men equally interested in the prosperity of the whole." If thirty-six sat for Cornwall, and only six for Lancashire, it made no difference. The truth that may be found in this particular allegation is that the thirty-six Cornish members certainly did not represent Cornwall, and that the Manchester industrialists, or Yorkshire landowners, as I have said, did not, or did not yet, feel much material disadvantage from political underrepresentation.

With that disproportion already noted, Burke proceeded to identify a few proposed changes in the electoral system with violation of the order of nature, or of God's plan for the government of the world. "There is an order that keeps things fast in their place: it is made to us, and we are made to it. Why not ask another wife, other children, another body, another mind?" (Or as Sir Hercules said in Ireland: "Good God! Is the mind of man never to be satisfied!") And he proceeded to identify electoral changes with total subversion: "The great object of most of these reformers is to prepare the destruction of the Constitution by disgracing and discrediting the House of Commons." And to declare that only what existed was possible, and that to criticize government was to invite anarchy. "For to discredit the only form of government which we either possess or can project, what is this but to destroy all government? And this is anarchy." And to conclude with an arresting image: he would never abuse the constitution of his country, he would never "cut it in pieces, and put it in the kettle of any magician, in order to boil it, with the puddle of their compounds, into youth and vigor."[35]

---

[35] All quotations in the preceding three paragraphs may be found within the fifteen

Much could be said on the philosophical implications of this speech, as, for example, that the offering of no alternative except stark chaos made him a kind of Hobbesian of the unreformed Parliament, or that the identification of the real, the right, the rational, and the possible made him a kind of predecessor to Hegel. Much has been said in these later times, at least in America, on the religion of Edmund Burke. It is true that he disliked declared infidels, sympathized with all hierarchical churches, and was much in favor of the Church of England, but his religion, so far as I can see, consisted in a kind of attribution of the social order to the will of God, and in a kind of humility which was by no means a personal humility, but a belief, or expressed belief, in the limitations of the human mind, and a distrust of reason (though "the species is wise") which really meant a distrust of the reason of those persons who did not agree with him. As for the realism of his approach to practical issues, his idealization of the England of his day seems scarcely closer to fact than the roseate optimism, with respect to the future, of a Dupont de Nemours or a Condorcet. As for the wisdom of some of his great utterances, there are many of them that I would not question for a moment in the abstract. I would only question their relevancy to the circumstances that elicited them. This is to question his common sense—as his contemporaries did.

The point to be emphasized in the present connection is that Burke's conservatism was well formed long before the French Revolution. It was not shaped, in 1784, by the spectacle of real revolution, nor by dislike of public disorder, nor by resistance to illegal leadership or to law-breaking, nor by opposition to mobs, none of which accompanied the reform bills brought up in the British Parliament between 1782 and 1785. It was directed against the Enlightenment only insofar as the Enlightenment was a habit of mind, not only of French *philosophes,* but of various Americans, British, and Europeans whose number included William Pitt. Burke's conservatism was really directed against the democratization of government even by peaceful means—not even against universal suffrage or annual Parliaments, which Pitt was far from endorsing, but against the ideas of personal representation, or of political change at the will of the living, or of the right to abolish

---

pages of the speech cited. On Burke's "order that keeps things fast in their place," compare the Parlement of Paris in 1776, appealing, to oppose Turgot's reform of the *corvée*, to an order that "takes its source in divine institutions . . . a law of the Universe which despite efforts of the human mind . . . etc." See below, p. 451.

institutions for which there was little reason except history on the one hand or narrow vested interest on the other.

In any case, Burke's conservatism had as yet little influence, because no one would pay attention long enough to find out what it was. Even men intending to vote as he wished walked out when he rose to speak—they did not need such elegant arguments. The reform of Parliament in the 1780's failed in both England and Ireland. The parliamentary oligarchies triumphed over the reformers.

The "Appellation of Citizen" vs. the Test Act

A word must be added on a related matter, the attempt of English Protestant Dissenters to obtain equality of civil rights. This reached its height between 1787 and 1790, and has been called, like the Association movement, "England's unsuccessful Revolution."[36]

The Dissenters were Protestants who would not take communion in the Church of England, or subscribe to its Thirty-Nine Articles. They were divided in the eighteenth-century among Independents, Presbyterians, and Baptists. About a sixth of all English clergymen were Dissenters, but the Dissenters were a much smaller proportion of the whole population. They were most numerous in the towns and among merchants and business people, though many of the latter were Anglican. Rare among the Anglican gentry, and with few followers among the poor, whose inclinations to Methodism were still held within the established church, the Dissenters as a group were self-consciously and self-righteously middle-class. They had been tolerated since 1689, in that their belief and worship were not interfered with. They were also free to vote for members of Parliament, and to sit in the Commons, though few did.

Dissenters, however, by the Test Act, could lawfully hold no office by appointment of the crown in the civil government or in the army and navy. They could not, by the Corporation Act, belong to any municipal corporation in the boroughs or hold even the lowest of town offices. Hence they played little part in local politics, and were unlikely to be sent to Parliament by boroughs in which the Anglican corporation named the members. No admitted Dissenter could take a degree from either of the two universities. Though predominantly

[36] A. Lincoln, *Some Political and Social Ideas of English Dissent, 1763-1800* (Cambridge, Eng., 1938), 2 and 183. The following section is drawn largely from this book.

a business group, Dissenters were forbidden, by extensions of the Test Act, to occupy positions of management in the Bank of England, or in the East India, South Sea, and Russia Companies. The rigors of the law were softened by the easygoing attitudes of the time, for in fact a certain number of Dissenters held forbidden posts, either by occasional and purely formal communion in the Anglican church, or because the authorities paid no attention. Though subject in such cases to the dangers of denunciation and punishment, they seem not to have lived in fear. Nor, as a prospering group, did they have much strictly economic grievance. It seems likely that they came to feel a sense of indignity—to object to discrimination.

The same legal disabilities applied even more effectively to the Catholics. There were both Dissenting and Catholic leaders who, by the 1780's, conceived of a civil state in which all of them, along with Jews, might enjoy the same rights without regard to religion. They could not, however, lead their followers in this direction. Most Dissenters still felt the old horror of popery, and usually thought, in urging recognition for themselves, that they strengthened their case by dissociating it clearly from the Catholics. The inability of the Dissenters to combine with Catholics, or even to stay combined with each other, together with the lack of heavy material grievance, naturally weakened the assault on entrenched Anglicanism.

There still clung to the Dissenters, in the majority view, an unpleasant odor of the old Puritanism and the king-killing of 1649. They were felt not to have the right attitude toward the national institutions, to harbor a sour-faced disaffection in church and state. Actually, like the French Protestants, who lived under even worse disabilities until the Revolution, the Dissenters were patriotic and loyal. About 1760, however, they began to exhibit a new political consciousness. In 1771 a group of Cambridge undergraduates petitioned for relief from the Thirty-Nine Articles; they were refused. Dissenters were prominent among English sympathizers with the American Revolution, and especially with Puritan New England. Few except Dissenters expressed any interest in the new American constitutions, with their separation of political rights from religious affiliation. The role of Presbyterians in the Irish disturbances was well known. In the Association movement of 1780 the Dissenters were very active; 2,000 of them signed the Yorkshire petition, and they had a majority in the county meetings of Cambridgeshire and Kent. In conservative eyes they were susceptible to all kinds of dubious causes; they seemed antimonarchical and "republican," until, as their historian puts it, "the progress of events made 'Jacobin' a more modish form of vituperation."[37]

The abatement of true religious conflict, the sense of the enlightenment of the age, the promulgation of American principles, the relief of Irish Presbyterians from the Test Act, and the growing wealth and importance of the Dissenting community, a byproduct of growth of the commercial classes throughout Western Europe, all contributed to a mood of optimism among the Dissenters, who, at a great meeting of deputies of the three denominations in January 1787, decided to attack the barriers against them directly, by petitioning Parliament for repeal of the Corporation and Test Acts. Three bills to this effect were introduced, in 1787, 1789, and 1790.

The interesting thing, in the broad view, is that the English Dissenters, who had originated for the most part as Calvinists a few generations before, had now come, by the needs of their situation as they saw them, to use the language and conceptions of the European revolution. They thought of themselves as "unprivileged." As their sponsor (an Anglican) in the House of Commons put it on May 8, 1789, they asked only "the usual privileges and general benefits of citizenship." They wished access to public office and honors, like the French Third Estate which met at Versailles in that same week. They insisted that they bore no grudge toward the Establishment, and declared that some established religion was good for society, again like the French in 1789, but what they wanted was a secular state, in which religious belief, or lack of it, should have nothing to do with one's role in the political order. The deepest human community should be political, not religious. The descendants of men who, a century and a half ago, as Calvinists, had thought that the State should be under the guidance of a true church, now held that the church or churches should be within and in a way under the state, a state which conferred equal citizenship on its people, and derived its authority from their collective sovereignty. The English Dissenters, or their leaders, had traveled the path of the Genevese Rousseau. They wished to be "children of the State" though not of the Church—to forget religious difference, and "bury every name of distinction in the common appellation of citizen."[38]

The years 1789 and 1790 saw heated controversy. Never had Dissenters of the great towns, Leicester, Nottingham, and others, been so active in support of those of London. The methods of the Associations of 1780 were revived; there was a plan for a national convention of Dissenters, which never materialized, but continued to alarm the defenders of Anglicanism. In March 1790 the bill to repeal the Test and Corporation Acts was defeated for the third time, 294 to 105.

Conservatism hardened, and it hardened in defense of the Test Act and the existing arrangements to protect the Church of England. The beauties of the British constitution were again set up to public wonder. To the Dissenters' argument that the two acts were only pieces of legislation, obsolete measures which, at most, might have been justified a century and more ago, it was replied that the acts were of the very fabric of "our excellent constitution." When the Dissenters pointed to religious freedom in America, Pitt answered, "The American constitution resembles ours neither in church nor state."[39] When the Dissenters appealed to natural rights, Burke found their position too abstract, and offered a preview in the House of Commons of his forthcoming *Reflections on the Revolution in France*. Most of all, the defenders of the existing arrangements used the arguments of Warburton, of which a survey was given earlier in this book: it was not an affair of religious belief; anyone remained free to believe as he wished and would be willingly tolerated; it was only a matter of "civil convenience," for in England an establishment of religion was found to be socially useful, and it was only reasonable for persons not well affected toward such an establishment to be kept from the public power by which it might be injured. Warburton's argument of prescription was also brought forward; the acts were over a century old, they had grown into the body of English public life. They represented the wisdom of ancestors. And likewise employed was his view of the terms of political office. "It was in the power of every government," said Lord North in the debate of May 1789, "to prescribe the persons to fill the offices of power."[40] No one could complain if Parliament, the sovereign body, made communion in the national church, or any other qualification, a prerequisite to official position.

The agitation raised by the Dissenters' petition, as by the movement for parliamentary reform, and by the American Revolution, had forced men to commit themselves to conflicting theories of public authority and of individual rights. The British Isles were to exhibit little solidarity toward the issues of the French Revolution, or in the war that followed.

[39] *Parliamentary History*, xxviii, 413.　　　　[40] *Ibid.*, xxviii, 18.

DEMOCRATS AND ARISTOCRATS—DUTCH,
BELGIAN, AND SWISS

Do we see in the Austrian Netherlands, or in the United Netherlands . . . that confidence in one another, and in the common people, which enabled the United States to go through a revolution?—JOHN ADAMS, London, 1787

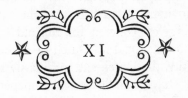

DEMOCRATS AND ARISTOCRATS—DUTCH, BELGIAN, AND SWISS

IT IS unfortunate that the affairs of the smaller European peoples do not enter more fully into our general histories, for their experience has been illuminating. The very words "democrat" and "aristocrat," as observed above in the first chapter, were coined in the Dutch and Belgian troubles of the decade from 1780 to 1790. In both countries the common pattern of the time was especially evident. Constituted bodies—in this case town councils and estate-assemblies—determining their own membership within a closed system, claimed to represent the country and to rule in their own right. Both asserted their powers and liberties against a "prince"—the Prince of Orange in the case of the Dutch, the Austrian Emperor in that of the Belgians—and both, after 1780, found a new popular party fighting at their side. The new party, which was neither exactly popular not yet a party in a more modern sense, at first felt no difference of purpose from its allies. As the controversies developed, however, the new party began to brand its allies, or erstwhile allies, as "aristocrats," and to favor an actual reconstitution of the old constituted bodies, so that these bodies would become representative in a new kind of way, either by actual choice at the hands of voters outside their own ranks, or through a broadening of membership to reflect wider segments of the population.

The United Netherlands comprised the seven Dutch provinces, Holland, Utrecht, Zeeland, Overyssel, Gelderland, Friesland, and Groningen, which together ruled over Drenthe and northern Brabant. The Austrian Netherlands, of which Brabant and Flanders were the most important, were the ten provinces which had remained under the Spanish crown in the sixteenth-century wars, and had passed to Austria in 1714. They were loosely attached to the Hapsburg system, and in firm possession of local liberties, until the reign of Joseph II. Political interest, both Dutch and Belgian, was highly particularistic, provincial, and even municipal, especially for the town magistrates and the members of provincial estates. It was the "democrats" in both countries who, having less concern for the old vested bodies, developed a somewhat more national all-Dutch or all-Belgian feeling. Both countries were wealthy, the Dutch extraordinarily so. Beyond that, the parallel ceases. The Dutch had long been independent, the Belgians long dependent on a foreign crown. The Dutch government was a republic, the Belgians belonged to an international monarchy. The Dutch Estates General, their High Mightinesses, were deemed to be sovereign, and the Prince of Orange was a semi-royal official, "stadtholder" in each of the provinces, and captain-general of the union. The Belgian Estates General, like the French, no longer really existed; it assembled under revolutionary conditions in January 1790. The chief executive in Belgium was the Governor-General, an Austrian.

The Dutch Patriot Movement

The United Provinces was a small country, much of which could be seen from the top of Utrecht cathedral, at least according to a traveling Englishman who claimed to distinguish fifty-one towns from that elevated point. With fewer than two million people it had less than half the population of Ireland. Its interests and importance, however, were universal. Dutch shipping and trade were on every sea. There were Dutch colonies in the West Indies, at the Cape of Good Hope, in Ceylon, and in Java, and Dutch merchants were the only Europeans allowed to trade in Japan. The Dutch were the great international capitalists. In 1777 they owned forty per cent of the British national debt, and by 1796 the entire foreign-held national debt of the United States was in their hands.

Dutch affairs had become closely entwined with those of England. Both the political successes and the commercial growth of Great Britain in the eighteenth-century were heavily financed by Dutch investors. In international politics the Dutch had followed the British lead since the days of William III. William V, stadtholder from 1751 to 1795, was himself married to a Prussian princess, but his mother was English, and in fact William II, William III, and William IV had all married the daughters of English kings. The House of Orange was the next thing to royalty, and the unfortunate William V, whose stadtholderate was to be terminated by revolution in 1795, bore a dismaying resemblance to Louis XVI. He was quite unable to make a decision, cope with events, or undertake any new line of policy. "I wish I were dead," he wrote in 1781, "that my father had never been stadtholder. . . . I feel I have no ability to be at the head of so many affairs." To the painter's eye of Sir Joshua Reynolds he looked "very like King George, but not so handsome; he has a heavy look . . . with somewhat a round belly."[1]

It was the American war that precipitated the abortive revolution known as the Patriot movement.[2] There had been the usual intellectual preparation. Dutch writers had played little role in the European Enlightenment; the Amsterdam regents, like those of Geneva, had suppressed Rousseau's Social Contract when it appeared; and there was no legalized freedom of the press before 1795. But in fact the Dutch press had long been active, and many books and magazines in the international language, French, had their place of publication in Holland. Nowhere was the periodical press older or better established, yet Dutch historians, like others, attribute the first appearance of specifically political journals to about the year 1770. Here as elsewhere a public opinion, or an opinion on matters of public concern outside the circles of government, was beginning to form.

An early spokesman of the new ideas was J. D. van der Capellen tot de Pol, who was also one of the first of the Dutch who openly favored the American rebels.[3] He was a nobleman of Overyssel, one of the "land provinces" which long remained apart from the financial and maritime interests of Holland. He was thus uninvolved with the influential magnates of Amsterdam.

Capellen first called attention to himself in 1775. There was in the Dutch service a certain Scotch Brigade, which the British government expressed a desire to borrow for use in America against the insurgents.

[1] P. Geyl, De Patriottenbeweging (Amsterdam, 1947), 47; letter of Sir J. Reynolds to Edmund Burke, August 14, 1781, in the Wentworth-Woodhouse collection at the Central Library, Sheffield.

[2] On the Patriot movement, see P. Geyl, op.cit., I. Vijlbrief, "De Patriottencris, 1780-1787" in Algemeene Geschiedenis der Nederlanden, VIII, 128-69 (Utrecht, 1955); I. H. Gosses and N. Japikse, Handboek tot de staatkundige Geschiedenis van Nederland (The Hague, 1947), 674-717; P. J. Blok, History of the People of the Netherlands, Eng. trans., V, 172-272 (London and New York, 1912); Helen L. Fairchild, Francis Adrian van der Kemp: an autobiography with extracts from his correspondence (N.Y., 1903); C. M. Davies, Memorials and Times of Peter Philip Jurian Quint Ondaatje (Utrecht, 1870) in Werken uitgegeven door het Historisch Genootschap gevestigd te Utrecht, new series, no. 13.

[3] On Van der Capellen see the above and W. H. de Beaufort, Brieven van en aan Joan Derk Van der Capellen van de Poll (Utrecht, 1879), which is no. 27 in the series of the Utrecht Historical Society just cited. Many of Van der Capellen's letters and papers, as of other Dutch figures of the period, are in French or English.

The stadtholder, William V, asked for favorable action on this request in the several provincial estates. In the Estates of Overyssel, van der Capellen eloquently opposed the despatch of the Scotch Brigade, and succeeded in blocking it. He also broke all precedent by violating the secrecy of discussion in the estates, and making known his opinions to the public. On another occasion he took the lead in persuading the Estates of Overyssel to abolish certain *corvées*, by which peasants had owed two days of labor service a year. He was in touch with parliamentary reformers in England, translated Richard Price's *Essay on Civil Liberty* in 1776, and corresponded with the revolutionary governors of Connecticut and New Jersey. He lent 20,000 French *livres'* worth of his own money to the Americans as early as 1778. Well informed on American, British, and Dutch affairs, he was one of the first international figures of the incipient democratic revolution.

Around Capellen there gathered a circle of men, pro-American and dissatisfied with Dutch conditions, who were later to lead the democratic wing of the Patriots. These were for the most part well-to-do burghers, many of them bankers, merchants, owners of manufacturing establishments, printers and publishers, or professors at Utrecht or Leiden. They were upper middle-class, but so were most people of any consequence in the country. Their class standing could not really be defined economically. It was more readily defined by the permanent exclusion from state affairs of persons like themselves, including their fathers and presumably their children, either because they did not belong to the families that controlled the town councils, or because they were not members of the Dutch Reformed Church. In the United Provinces, as in England, despite liberal toleration and economic prosperity for dissenters, only members of the official church could take part in government, military command, or the Bank of Amsterdam and the East India Company. More were excluded than in England on this ground, since a third of the population was Catholic, and another ten per cent either Jews or Protestant sectaries. Capellen's group included the Mennonite pastor Van der Kemp, J. Luzac, editor of the famous French-language *Gazette de Leide*; and P. Paulus, P. Vreede, R. Schimmelpenninck, and others who were to be prominent in the Patriot movement, and again in the revolutionary Batavian Republic after 1795. These, too, were the men with whom John Adams most easily associated on reaching Holland in 1780, and from whom he was first able to borrow money for the American Congress.

The American war also aroused many of the old in-group, who were called the "regents," in distinction from ordinary "burghers" or mere "inhabitants." The regent families filled the town councils, such as the council of thirty-six which governed Amsterdam; and these town oligarchies in turn, working with the stadtholder or against him, controlled the provincial estates and the Estates General. The Estates of Holland, for example, consisted of eighteen votes for eighteen towns, plus one member, with one vote, for all the nobility of the province. The Dutch regents were a hereditary aristocracy, but an unusual one in that they drew their large incomes from finance and trade.[4] For two hundred years a strong party within the regents had quarreled with the House of Orange, and had twice dispensed with it altogether, in a kind of perpetual opposition which the Dutch called Loevestein, a sort of Whiggery in which the people had no concern. The old anti-Orangism became again acute during the War of American Independence, because William V remained firmly committed to England, while many of the regents sought to break their connections with, and dependency on, the British economic and naval power.

The Orange party of William V, in the complex disputes that followed, drew its strength from the Prince's court and retainers, from men who owed their offices and position to him, from the church-minded people of the Reformed Church, and indirectly from the mass of the people, who had no political interest or organization, cared little for the problems of their social superiors, and by a kind of popular royalist predilection looked on the Prince of Orange as if he really were their King. In the showdown, the Orange party was rebuilt by Great Britain.

The Americans, on declaring their independence, threw off the British trade regulations and invited direct commerce with the Continent of Europe. Commercial men of Amsterdam, both those who were regents and those who were not, hastened to engage in this lucrative new traffic. The city of Amsterdam, which is to say its regents, even made a secret treaty in 1778 with a representative of the United States. An enthusiasm for the American Revolution swept over the great commercial metropolis. When eight United States ships docked

---

[4] J. E. Elias, *Geschiedenis van het amsterdamsche Regentenpatriciaat* (The Hague, 1923), a work written with an Orangist animus against the old regents, found (p. 238) that all 37 Amsterdam burgomasters from 1752 to 1795 had commercial connections, in contrast to only 2 out of 24 for the period 1718-1748. In the stadtholderless period before 1748 the regents seem to have lived rather from the income of office and government. Virtually all known leaders of the Patriot movement, says Elias, had traded "illicitly" with France and America after 1775.

there in 1779, they found that a Dutch lady had composed a song, in English, in ten stanzas, in their honor.[5]

That Amsterdam could thus determine its own foreign policy, to say the least, revealed the particularism, the internal division, and the unworkable confusion of uncentralized powers in the republic as set up long ago by the Union of Utrecht. Amsterdam was naturally supported in its course by the French, who wished to bring its merchant marine and its capital into the war, and denounced by the British and by the Orange party. In 1780 Great Britain declared war on the United Provinces, and began to assail the Dutch shipping and colonies.

It must be remembered that British colonial and commercial primacy was widely felt to be of recent growth, quite possibly soon to end. American and French military successes persuaded many Dutch capitalists that the British empire had already passed its zenith, and even that British securities were no longer a good investment. In 1780, on the eve of war with the Dutch, the British government was able to borrow, with difficulty, only about a million guilders in Holland. Two years later the French government borrowed 5,000,000 guilders in a single day. A sum of the same size was loaned in that year to the United States of America, and Dutch capital also flowed into private American land and canal companies. On the eve of the French Revolution, French credit remained strong in Holland, so far were practical men from supposing the French monarchy to be tottering. In 1782 Dutch investments in Britain stood at 280,000,000 guilders, as against only 25,000,000 in France. Comparable figures are not available for the following years, but, in 1786, Dutch income from French securities almost equalled that from British. In the absence of other means of satisfactory measurement, this flight of Dutch capital suggests the substantial character and the strength of the Patriot movement.[6]

In broadest terms, the Patriot party, at the outset, was an unstable compound of regent and popular elements, anti-Orange and anti-British, produced by the crisis of the Fourth English War, as the Dutch call the War of American Independence. The Dutch, outside the Orange party, saw the war as a defense of their shipping, their navy,

[5] F. Edler, *The Dutch Republic and the American Revolution* (Baltimore, 1911), is diplomatic history of the narrowest kind. The Dutch lady's song is printed in A. Loosjes, *Gedenkzuil ter gelegenheid der Vrij-verklaaring van Noord-Amerika* (Amsterdam, 1782).

[6] For these details on Dutch capital see C. H. Wilson, *Anglo-Dutch Commerce and Finance in the 18th Century* (Cambridge, Eng., 1941), 189-204; J. P. Manger, *Recherches sur les relations économiques entre la France et la Hollande pendant la Révolution française, 1785-1795* (Paris, 1923), 17; E. Baasch, *Holländische Wirtschaftsgeschichte* (Jena, 1927), 205-06.

and their colonies from the depredations of the British fleet. The Prince and his supporters, less sensitive on these matters, accused the Amsterdam merchants of stirring up a needless war with England to satisfy their own greed. The Patriots, rallying to the defense of Amsterdam, accused the Orange party of subverting Dutch national interests through a ruinous partiality for Great Britain.

Two pamphlets of 1781 drew the issues. One, *A Political Remonstrance against the True System of Amsterdam*, by the Orangist R. M. van Goens, denounced the antistadtholderian machinations of that city back to 1581, with especial emphasis on its recent disgraceful involvement with the American rebels. It was followed by *An Address to the Netherlands People*, written anonymously by Van der Capellen tot de Pol. Copies were found in the streets of the Dutch cities, scattered at night by men secretly organized by the pastor Van der Kemp. The pamphlet caused an uproar. "The press cannot be restrained," wrote the delighted Adams, who was there. The Estates of Holland condemned it as subversive, forbade people to read it, and offered a reward to anyone revealing its author's identity, which nevertheless remained unknown for many years. The historian Pieter Geyl calls *An Address to the Netherlands People* the first piece of writing in which anyone ever addressed the Dutch people as a national unit. The author of this inflammatory tract, writes another, was no Loevesteiner—*hij was democraat!*[7]

Capellen's pamphlet was a long tirade against the House of Orange, which, he said, had conspired to become a monarchy for two hundred years, had always despised the merchants of Amsterdam, ingratiated itself with England and embroiled the country with France, preferring to build up an army for its own purposes, while neglecting the navy, and surrounding itself with a fawning lot of grandees. Capellen likewise assaulted the regent oligarchs, whom he also accused of entrenching themselves since the sixteenth century. It was time for the Dutch people to recover their rights. A nation, he said, was like a commercial concern in that its magistrates were only employees; the Dutch people owned the "Society of the United Netherlands," just as shareholders owned the East India Company. He pointed also to America, which now had a good government because its officers were elected. He denounced William V for getting his own sycophantic admirers into the town councils, the Provincial Estates, the Estates General, and the ad-

[7] Geyl, 53; Vijlbrief, 136.

ministrative departments of the union. Only determination and a show of force would make them responsible to the country.

"Assemble in your towns and villages. Meet peaceably, and elect from among yourselves a moderate number of courageous, virtuous and pious men; choose good Patriots that you can trust. Send these as your deputies to the places of assembly of your several provincial estates, and order them in the name and by the authority of this nation, to make an inquiry, by and with the estates of the other provinces, into the reasons for the extraordinary inertia with which the arming of the country against a formidable and active enemy is being handled. Order them also . . . to choose a council for His Highness . . .

"Provide for the freedom of the press, the one support of your national liberty. . . .

"Arm yourselves, elect those who must command you . . . and in all things proceed like the people of America, with modesty and composure."[8]

The unknown author was indeed a *democraat*, and even a revolutionary in a way. He urged a popular arming, as in Ireland and America, and the formation of self-authorized citizen groups, which, like the Irish convention and the American committees, or like the associations in England, should claim to represent the country better than any organ of government, and to bring upon the existing constituted bodies a pressure not recognized as legitimate in the history or constitution of the country. He did not propose to abolish anything, beyond a few "abuses." Nor did he clearly envisage the creation of anything new. He was far from the American theory of a constituent power. He had in mind, rather, a public inspection or scrutiny over the multitude of councils, estates, boards, colleges, and magistracies of the historic republic. He made little appeal to the "philosophy" of the day. He did not argue from the enlightenment of the age, or nature and reason, or the social contract, or human rights, or liberty and equality in the abstract. He was aroused by the unreliability of his own government in a time of war. Pointing to common-sense analogies, like stock ownership in a business enterprise, or the American rebellion (still before Yorktown), he arrived at an affirmation of popular sovereignty. He did so for an immediate purpose, to displace a small governing group which could not otherwise be opened up or removed.

[8] Van der Capellen tot de Pol, *Aan het Volk van Nederland*, as quoted by P. Geyl, *Patriotten beweging*, 53-54. This pamphlet was translated into English as *An address to the People of the Netherlands* (London, 1782).

He looked backwards as well as forwards, as did many like him in Britain and America, and his arguments were historical in their character if not in the accuracy of their content. He hoped to return to a freer regime which he believed to have existed before hereditary oligarchy had closed in. Even three years later, when Capellen's circle produced the nearest thing to a constitutional project, they called it the *Grondwettige Herstelling,* or constitutional "restoration." They here declared, with due precaution against influence of the real lower classes or populace, that the Dutch constitution, when rightly understood, was and properly always had been, "democratic."[9] It was the failure of such arguments to accomplish anything in the 1780's that forced men into the more radical positions of the 1790's. In Holland, as in England, even the first stirrings in a democratic direction brought on a systematic conservative reply. The learned Adrian Kluit, one of the founders of historical jurisprudence in the Netherlands, was so irritated by the *Grondwettige Herstelling* that he answered it with a pamphlet, in 1785, *The sovereignty of the Estates of Holland defended against the modern doctrine of people's government (Volksregering,* the word then mainly used for "democracy"). The issue lay between the alleged sovereignty of constituted bodies and the alleged sovereignty of the people.[10]

Regent and popular Patriots were able for a time to cooperate. It had become the custom, since 1748, for the Prince to place his own appointees in the self-coopting councils, or the estate assemblies, or in offices to which these bodies had the right to elect, by the practice of

[9] The Dutch Patriots seem to have used the words "democracy" and "democrat" infrequently in application to themselves. J. van de Giessen, *De opkomst van het woord democratie als leuze in Nederland* (The Hague, 1948), finds that the use of "democracy" as a catchword began with social democracy in the 1880's, and that the "Eastern" use of the term, emphasizing equality of income and opportunity, is historically more accurate than the "Western." While this seems at best only partly true, the author's claim that self-accepted use of the term was more common among the Patriots of the 1780's than among the Batavians after 1795 is undoubtedly mistaken.

[10] A. Kluit, *De souvereiniteit der Staaten van Holland, verdedigt tegen de hededaggsche leere der volks-regering . . .* (Groningen, 1785). Kluit also in 1782 published a work in Latin significantly entitled *De potestate ordinum,* "On the power of the [socio-legal] orders," and one called *De rechten van den mensch in Frankrijk geen gewaande rechten in Nederland* (Amsterdam, 1793), "The rights of man in France no so-called rights in the Netherlands." On Kluit see E. Lousse, *La société d'ancien regime: organisation et representation corporatives* (Louvain, 1943), I, 13, and *Nieuw Nederlandsch Biografisch Woordenboek,* III, 696-98. There is little ground for agreeing with Lousse's remark that Dutch democrats like Van der Capellen were *gagnés aux idées de J. J. Rousseau.* For Rousseau on the sovereignty of the people see above p. 122. For the argument of the present book, that the idea of the sovereignty of the people, which was indeed the essential revolutionary idea of the period, arose from the needs of political debate against claims to sovereignty made by constituted bodies see above pp. 134-36 (Geneva), 197-98, 214-24, 228 (America), 295, 319 (England).

sending in the names of men who were acceptable to him, and who were thereupon elected. Van der Capellen called this practice *insluipsel*, an insidious "slipping in"; and the Orangist Van Goens, explaining Dutch affairs to the Duke of Portland, called it a prerogative not exactly legal, but one which gave the Prince "an influence in the assemblies and magistracies without which he would be a phantom." It will be seen that this *insluipsel* was somewhat like that "influence" which enabled the British crown and ministry to govern through the aristocracy in the Parliament. It is likely that without some such "influence" there could be no effective direction of government, given the extraordinary dispersion and separation of powers among independent bodies that characterized the Dutch republic. What was needed was either less, or more, than resistance to *insluipsel*. But on reduction of the Prince's authority all Patriots could agree. In 1782 and 1783 many towns declared his power of recommending for office abolished.[11]

Amsterdam became the center of regent opposition, while the discontents of those outside the regent families were seen most clearly at Utrecht. Burghers began to arm, as urged by Van der Capellen. They organized Free Corps in the various towns, adopted uniforms, drilled, listened to speeches, and sent delegates to national meetings. They armed against vaguely sensed dangers of "violence from without and within," against the menace of the small standing army and the ancient militia commanded by Orangist officers, against invasion by the British, or a little later by Austrians from the side of Belgium; against the obstinacy of the Prince; and, finally, against the "aristocrats." Among early democrats no principle was more common than that free citizens must serve as soldiers, and the Estates of Holland, in 1785, even decreed a small-scale anticipation of the famous French *levée en masse*. The Free Corps opened their ranks to Protestant sectaries and to Catholics. Van der Kemp, the Mennonite pastor, once delivered a sermon in uniform. They were mainly middle class, for the citizen soldiers usually though not always had to furnish their own weapons and uniforms; nor did they wish to stir up the multitude, which in any case showed little inclination to join. Nevertheless, it was in these Free Corps that the democratic wing of the Patriots came to have an organized existence. With the first meeting of a National As-

[11] On *insluipsel* see Vijlbrief, 144; on *une influence dans les assemblées*, etc., *Brieven aan R. M. van Goens en onuitgegeven stukken hem betreffende* (3 vols., Utrecht, 1886), III, 208; on the role of "influence" in the eighteenth-century British constitution, Holdsworth and others as cited in Chapter VI above.

sembly of Free Corps, held at Utrecht in December 1784, Dutch burghers outside the regent class met and discussed political action for the first time.[12]

The situation at Utrecht, though complicated, is worth special attention, as a concrete example of the kind of questions at stake, throughout the United Provinces and indeed throughout Europe, and to illustrate the groping and *ad hoc* way in which a democratic doctrine was formulated. The province had originated as a medieval bishopric in the Holy Roman Empire, though there had been no bishop in residence since the Reformation. Its highest body was the assembly of three orders or estates—technically the clergy, the nobility, and the Third. Certain lay appointees of the stadtholder now functioned as the "clergy." The stadtholder influenced the second estate, the nobility, by his power to increase the number of its deputies at will. The third estate consisted of deputies from the city of Utrecht and four other towns; actually, by his "influence," the stadtholder had the town councils depute the men he named. The city of Utrecht was governed by its council and burgomasters. It was the custom for the council, on filling vacancies in its own body or selecting the burgomasters, to select men, within the regent group, whose names were notified to it by the Prince.

During the disturbances of 1783 a petition of 700 burghers urged the council to fill a recent vacancy without recourse to the Prince's recommendation. The councillors agreed, and made their own appointment. William V protested. The council, to gain support against William V and his partisans, invited the burghers to make a further statement of their desires. The Free Corps of the city, led by a student at the University named Ondaatje, thereupon proposed that the Prince's power to name members of the provincial estates be done away with. This also coincided with the wishes of a majority of the council. But the Free Corps and the burghers made further proposals. They wished to elect spokesmen to sit with the council, discuss taxation and appointments along with the regents, and share in defense of the liberties of Utrecht against the Prince. By an act signed with 1,215 names, 24 *geconstitueerden*, "constituted persons," were elected, 2 from each company in the municipal Free Corps plus 8 burghers. The names of the 1,215 have been preserved. They were of the middling ranks of a small eighteenth-century city: shopkeepers, carpenters, master shoemakers,

[12] For the Free Corps see the works cited in note 2 above, and in particular Mrs. Davies, *Ondaatje*, for a concrete picture of the Free Corps of Utrecht; for the *levée en masse* in Holland, see the *Gazette de Leyde*, November 1784 to January 1785.

and the like. Since there were less than 30,000 inhabitants in the city, 1,215 adult males would in effect be about a fifth of the population. The council, with mounting reluctance, accepted the existence of these "constituted persons" at its side. More was to come, for Ondaatje and the Free Corps, recalling how burgomasters had been chosen by guilds in the Middle Ages, now demanded that the burghers take part in election of these officials. The council demurred, observing that there had been no such popular choice of burgomasters since the days of the Emperor Charles V—long before the independence of Utrecht or the formation of the federal republic.

The Patriot coalition now began to fall apart. The regents of Utrecht, secure hitherto in the town council, had not intended, in liberating themselves from the Prince of Orange, to fall into the hands of burghers of the city. Like the upholders in England of the House of Commons, they believed the public good to require their "independence." The town council, backed by the Provincial Estates, where the fear of democracy also pushed aside the fear of Orange, decided to put Ondaatje under arrest, though to do so would be an affront to the 1,215 who had signed the burgher electoral act, plus several hundred more in the Free Corps, and so constitute a declaration of war on virtually the entire politically conscious population of the city. At this time the first meeting of the National Assembly of Free Corps from all the United Provinces took place in Utrecht. The delegates were loud in Ondaatje's defense. They denounced the "aristocratic cabal." Ondaatje received honors in all parts of the country, including a doctorate at the University of Leiden. He made a bold speech to the Utrecht council. "Have we, in making you independent of the stadtholder, made you also independent of ourselves? . . . Is the council house yours, or ours?"[13]

Two years of confusion followed, in Utrecht and elsewhere. While many initially anti-Orange regents backed away, the Patriot movement nevertheless gathered strength. The educated, the professional people, the large religious minorities, wished it well. The French government promised it support, seeing it as anti-British. The fact that the spring of 1785 was the period of heaviest selling of British securities, and hence of Dutch investment in France and America, suggests that there were a good many men of means in the movement, that it was no flurry among the young, the impressionable, and the idealistic. There was

[13] For these events at Utrecht see Davies, *Ondaatje*, 1-89; Geyl, *Patriottenbeweging*, 101-12; Vijlbrief, 150. There is a longer study by Vijlbrief, with an all too short summary in English: *Van Anti-Aristocratie tot Democratie: Een bijdrage tot de politieke en sociale Geschiedenis der Stad Utrecht* (Amsterdam, 1950).

something with which William V could have allied against the regent oligarchs. He could, in principle (had he been a different man), have raised the standard of an Orange democracy, and begun to lay foundations for a more broadly based political state in the Netherlands. Perhaps this lost chance has always seemed more real to historians than it did to contemporaries.[14] Yet there were some who saw it then, including the young G. K. van Hogendorp, who years later, in 1814, was to become a national hero by his role in restoring the House of Orange as a true national monarchy, with a relatively liberal constitution. Hogendorp was no democrat. He did not believe that people could govern themselves. Just returned from America, he thought of the Americans as rustics from whom nothing in politics could be learned. He was of a Rotterdam regent family whose social position gave him the ear of William V. A young and self-confident patrician, he observed that the times were times of widespread disturbance, unlike anything since the Reformation, that people all over Europe were going to obtain representative institutions, that the role of the chief of state should everywhere be to hold the balance between *le peuple et les grands*, and that the House of Orange, in the present troubles, "should incline more to the democrats than to the aristocrats, since the former at least claim to represent the good of the people."[15]

William V could take no such advice. Like Louis XVI a few years later, he could not disown his privileged classes, though these privileged classes had long been the main source of embarrassment to his family. He could not bring himself to seem to abandon his church, or to ally with new men tossed up from what appeared to him to be the depths of society. "No democracy" became his watchword—not even any Orange democracy. He became the rallying point for all antidemocratic forces in the country, in which Orange stalwarts were increasingly joined by rebellious regents in flight from popular rule.

There were, of course, some of the regents who persisted in opposition to the Prince and his policies, some from an inveterate anti-Orangism, others with a more progressive idea that the time had come to broaden the terms of participation in public life. These formed the Assembly of Patriot Regents, and in 1786 they even gained control in three of the provinces, Holland, Groningen, and Overyssel. The Estates of Holland deposed the Prince from his offices of stadtholder and captain-general. The embattled Patriot Regents had to give ear

---

[14] On William V's "lost chance," Geyl, 115-17; Vijlbrief, 132.
[15] G. K. van Hogendorp, *Brieven en Gedenkschriften* (The Hague, 1866-1903), I, 411, 437, 443; II, 55-61.

to the Free Corps, and the demands of these excited groups of armed and uniformed burghers became ever more clearly "democratic." "Freedom is an inalienable right belonging to all citizens (*aan alle de burghers*) of the Netherlands confederation," declared the Provincial Assembly of the Armed Corps of Holland, meeting at Leiden. "This liberty would be a deceptive shadow if representatives were to be independent of those whom they represent; and their appointment by the people, by a firmly settled plan, is the most appropriate way to prevent this independence."[16] In 1786 the Utrecht burghers finally put an end to their old council and chose a new one by general election— "a true revolution," says Professor Geyl.

The National Assembly of Free Corps, again meeting in Utrecht, despatched Van der Kemp to confer with the Assembly of Patriot Regents sitting at Amsterdam. The two organizations published a joint declaration in the newspapers (though many Patriot Regents hesitated to sign), which may stand as the most advanced official statement of the abortive Dutch revolution. It declared for "the true republican form of government in our commonwealth, namely a government by representation of the people . . . with a stadtholdership subordinate thereto." And it repudiated "a government by one man, or any system of independent family rule . . . that chokes off the reasonable and respectful voice of the people."[17]

To oppose one-man government and family-rule simultaneously, remarks Professor Geyl, was hopeless. Henceforth the Prince and the oligarchs knew that they stood or fell together. Even so, they had little strength. Disarrayed, frightened, at odds with themselves, and with no program, they could not agree on which way to turn. "Our salvation can come only from foreign powers," the Orangist Van Goens had prophetically observed to the Duke of Portland in 1783.[18] In 1787 his prophecy came to pass.

From the beginning the French government had favored the Patriots, and lent them a secret assistance which was willingly accepted. A Patriot victory in Dutch internal affairs might result in a more or less permanent Franco-Dutch alliance; and the combination of French and Dutch maritime and economic strength was a contingency that British policy must at all costs seek to avoid. The British, however, had a good deal of anti-British feeling in the Netherlands to contend with. It was the Fourth English War that had touched off the Patriot explosion; and when the British not only captured 80,000,000 guilders' worth of

[16] Geyl, *Patriottenbeweging*, 124-25.   [17] *Ibid.*, 139-40.
[18] *Brieven aan R. M. van Goens . . .* , III, 220.

Dutch shipping during the war, but insisted at the peace table on keeping the Dutch post at Negapatam in India, and on obtaining certain rights in the East Indian archipelago, they did not further endear themselves in Dutch commercial circles. Frederick the Great advised his niece, the Princess of Orange, to avoid dependency on the "pirates of the channel." His advice was no more heeded than that of Leopold II to his sister, Marie Antoinette, a few years later. The Princess of Orange, and the Orange party in general, continued to believe that true Dutch interests were the same as those of Great Britain. They urged the British to use financial inducements with anti-Orange regents (£100,000 might win over the province of Friesland); and there were some in Zeeland who even proposed, rather than submit to the Patriots, to withdraw the province from the Dutch union, put it under British protection, give the British fleet a base at Flushing, and annex the Zeeland share in the Dutch East India Company to that of England. National feeling was not yet highly developed, and especially not among the cosmopolitan upper classes. The Princess of Orange, however, and her followers, aware that an open association of the Prince with the British would only damage him still further in Dutch opinion, strongly advised that the British work behind the scenes.[19]

This is precisely what began to happen when Sir James Harris arrived as British minister at the Hague in December 1784. There ensued a long series of intrigues and counterintrigues between Harris and the French agents, each backing and backed by their partisans among the Dutch, as recently recounted in detail by Professor Alfred Cobban of the University of London. In 1787 the Free Corps came to open blows with the Prince's troops, and civil war began in the Netherlands. The French government, now in serious financial and even revolutionary difficulties itself, seems to have spent 115,000 guilders to arm the Free Corps. How much Harris distributed on the Orange side is not clear, but it was at least £70,000 or over 800,000 guilders.[20]

The Princess of Orange, as the crisis grew, seizing the initiative from her flabby husband, started on a dramatic journey, with two companions, from Nimwegen to the Hague, there to rally and inspire the

[19] On British captures and demands, Manger, *Recherches*, 17; Van Goens, *Brieven,* III, 209, 230, 234. Frederick II's letter to the Princess of Orange is printed by H. T. Colenbrander, *De Patriottentijd*, Bijlage v. On secession of Zeeland, Colenbrander, *op.cit.*, Bijlage VII; Geyl, 133; A. Cobban, *Ambassadors and Secret Agents: the Diplomacy of the First Earl of Malmesbury at the Hague* (London, 1954), 82-83. On the Orangist desire for the British to intervene, while keeping their activity as invisible as possible, see Van Goens, 212, 239, 241, and the memorandum of the Princess of Orange published by Colenbrander, Bijlage XIII.

[20] Cobban, *op.cit.*, 133-35, 177.

bewildered followers of the Prince. She declared that no one would dare to stop her; she was in fact stopped by the Free Corps. She was obliged to go back to Nimwegen, her mission unaccomplished. This affair caused a great sensation. A handful of armed burghers had interfered with a great lady's freedom of movement. The Princess' brother was now King of Prussia, and he declared that his sister must receive satisfaction for the indignity she had suffered. The Patriots offering only to send delegates to a conference, and otherwise refusing to humble themselves, the King despatched 20,000 Prussian troops into the Netherlands. Harris' diplomacy, the opportune involvement of Austrian and Russian forces in a Turkish war, and the known fact that France was disabled from intervention by mounting troubles at home, all persuaded the Prussian King to spare so sizable a portion of his army. The Prussians were commanded by the Duke of Brunswick, the same who was to command them in the invasion of France five years later. In 1787, as in 1792, he issued a "Brunswick Manifesto." This one was milder than the one against revolutionary Paris; it only announced that no one allowing the Prussians to pass would be harmed. The Prussians in short order occupied Utrecht and Amsterdam. Few shots were fired; the Free Corps dissolved; the citizen-soldiers disappeared before the regular Prussian forces. Patriots everywhere changed or concealed their opinions, or fled from the country. The House of Orange was restored to its former position. "I could not keep my eyes from watering," remarked Sir James Harris, at the gratitude of the Prince and "of those who compose the uppermost class of the people."[21]

It was a great diplomatic triumph for Great Britain to hold the United Provinces outside the orbit of France. The balance of power was "maintained," according to Cobban; actually, it would seem that, with the weakening of France, the phenomenal increase of British and Prussian power since the Seven Years' War had been carried further. Sir James Harris became Baron Malmesbury (later Earl), it being ascertained that his income of £4,000 a year was enough to support the honor; and he was permitted, by a singular favor of the Prince whom he had rescued, to write *je maintiendrai*, the motto of the House of Orange, against an orange background on his crest. Fox, Pitt, Burke, were enthusiastic. It all reminded him of an old romance, said Burke: "a chivalrous king, hearing that a princess had been affronted, takes his lance, assembles his knights and determines to do her justice." One

---

[21] *Ibid.*, 188. Cobban, Vijlbrief, and Geyl agree that it was mainly Harris who restored the Prince, though their feelings toward the fact are very different.

sees already his "delightful vision" of Marie Antoinette in the French Revolution, and the ten thousand swords flashing from their scabbards in her defense. Nor was Burke much inclined to be troubled by scruples: "It was not necessary for us to trouble ourselves with definitions of the legality of the government of this or that country, or the strict construction of the constitution; but it was enough if we saw an opportunity of restoring that party to power, which was most likely to prove a valuable friend of Great Britain." The King of Prussia, for his part in this mixture of knight errantry and *Realpolitik*, carried off five tons of gold, or half a million guilders, as a "free gift" from the rejoicing city of Amsterdam. It must be admitted that the French charged much more in 1795 for saving the democrats.[22]

Sir James Harris continued to be very active during the first months of the restored government. It was with his advice that various offices were filled with reliable men; and, since Dutch bankers would not lend to the Orange regime, he distributed more money, in the form of British loans to the federal and local bodies, than he had previously done to bring the restoration about. The Princess of Orange demanded a good many arrests, so that a "rod of terror," as Harris said, should threaten "the heads of factious leaders."[23] The press was put under severe restraint, and an oath was required of regents, councillors, gildsmen, clergymen, and militia, in which they swore to acknowledge the sovereignty of the Estates and the hereditary stadtholdership of the

[22] *Ibid.*, 200-05. Cobban's book is a detailed and almost purely diplomatic history in which he gives little attention to internal Dutch affairs; but he concludes, or at least states at the close of the book, that the Dutch Patriot movement was "part of an international current of democracy which had already manifested itself in England, America, and Geneva. . . . It exhibited for the first time the strength of a revolutionary democracy possessed of organization, leadership and an ideology." He speaks also of "the uncompromising nature of the new ideology." Dutch writers on whom I have depended all judge the Orangists to have been far more uncompromising than the democrats. They would agree also, I think, with my own view that the Patriot movement was characterized by its lack of a developed "ideology"; it did not formulate its demands in terms of any universal ethical affirmations or any theory of world history. It will be obvious to the reader that I consider the Patriot movement to have been part of "an international current of democracy," but I would think the American Revolution to have had a far more effective "organization, leadership and ideology." Professor Cobban, in apparently turning against *all* revolution, seems like others to wish to spare the Americans from this "disgraceful imputation," as J. Q. Adams put it. On the other hand, even Thomas Jefferson, then in Paris, thought the Dutch democrats too extreme. See my article "The Dubious Democrat: Thomas Jefferson in Bourbon France," in *Political Science Quarterly*, LXXII (Sept. 1957), 388-404. John Adams, in London, while admiring the Patriots and regretting their failure, thought that it had been their weakness "to be too inattentive to the sense of the common people of their own country" and too willing to rely on France. *Works*, VIII, 462.

[23] Blok, *History*, V, 253; Harris, *Diaries and Correspondence* (London, 1845), II, 357.

Prince of Orange. The beginning of legal investigations frightened thousands of Patriots, with their families, into exile.[24] Van der Kemp emigrated to the United States, where he lived until 1829. Van der Capellen had died. Thousands, including Ondaatje, took refuge in France, where the King granted them a small subsidy and allowed them to congregate at St. Omer. Other thousands crossed into the Austrian Netherlands, where they soon became involved in the Belgian revolution. Most of these émigrés returned only in 1795, in the wake of the French republican army.

The Orange regime had made enemies of the most vital elements of its population. It represented the Prince's own followers, the more hardshelled people of the Reformed Church, and the amorphous populace who would still shout *Oranje boven,* "up Orange," in the streets. The chief federal executive from 1787 to 1795, the Zeelander Van de Spiegel, was the man who had offered Zeeland to the British. Able enough, he saw the need for modernization in the ancient fabric of the republic; but he could accomplish nothing, since the Prince and his favorites really wanted no more to happen. The republic drifted. It went to war with France in 1793, with something less than enthusiasm on the part of its people.[25] Secretly, in every town, there were men who had been Patriots, who had drilled in the Free Corps and stood by to let the Prussian regiments pass in 1787, men now in communication with émigrés beyond the frontier, and who believed, from their own bitter experience, that there could be no democratic revolution in the Dutch provinces except in alliance with the French army.

The Orange regime was guaranteed in 1788 by Great Britain and Prussia. "The once so mighty Republic of the United Netherlands had, thanks to the Orange victory, put itself under foreign care."[26] The Dutch Republic first lost its independence, not to the "Jacobins" in 1795, but to the already well developed forces of the European counterrevolution in 1787.

[24] Blok, v, 254. The traditional figure of 40,000 Patriot émigrés, given by Blok and others, is thought by later writers to be exaggerated.

[25] In February 1793, says Geyl, "stand bij ons Willem V met zijn aanhang van oligarchen en predikanten los van die natie"—William V stood apart from the nation with his following of oligarchs and preachers. It is doubtful that Geyl would accept Cobban's conclusion that Sir James Harris, by putting back the Orange party, made possible the Orange restoration in 1814. After all, even the Bourbons were restored then, in Spain and Naples as in France. The strength of the modern House of Orange derives from the very different policies of William V's *son.*

[26] Vijlbrief, 168.

The Belgian Revolution

"Governed by their own laws, secure in their property and their personal liberty, paying only moderate taxes which they lay upon themselves, the Belgians enjoy the finest gifts of a free constitution."[27] So it seemed to an English traveller in the Austrian Netherlands. Nor was he mistaken, though there was much in the laws, the property, and the liberty that came in time to provoke discontent. Satisfaction with their constitution was as characteristic of the Belgian provinces as of England. Not even English Whigs or American colonials dwelt so fervidly upon rights and liberties set forth in documents of long ago. Each province had a kind of historic charter. That of Brabant, the most important, was called the Joyous Entry, from the guarantees issued by the Duke of Brabant in 1355. The tax burden was also gratifyingly low, perhaps a tenth of that of neighboring Holland and England. It may even have been the lowest in the world of European civilization, except for the disorganized Poles and the fortunate Americans.[28] In short, although Belgium belonged to the Austrian monarchy, it was hardly affected by that fact before 1780.

Belgium was a museum of late-medieval corporate liberties. To begin with, it was a bundle of provinces. There were ten of them known as the Austrian Netherlands, here called Belgium, which comprised the territory of modern Belgium and Luxemburg, excluding, however, the bishopric of Liége, which, running from the Dutch to the French frontiers, cut the Austrian provinces in two. The only government common to the ten provinces was supplied by the Austrian Emperor. Practically all his officials, under the level of his viceroy, were native Belgians.

Since the sixteenth century the country had been immunized against change. The struggle against Calvinism had left the people solidly and

---

[27] T. Juste, *Histoire des Etats-généraux des Pays Bas, 1465-1790,* 2 vols. (Brussels, 1864), II, 122. For the most part, however, the present section depends on the admirable study by Suzanne Tassier, *Les démocrates belges de 1789: étude sur le Vonckisme et la Révolution brabançonne* (Brussels, 1930), in *Mémoires de l'Académie royale de Belgique, Classe des lettres,* 2nd series, vol. XXVIII: and on P. von Mitrofanov, *Joseph II: seine politische und Kulturelle Tätigkeit, aus dem russischen ins deutsch übersetzt* (Vienna, 1910), where events in Belgium are seen in comparison with those in other parts of the Hapsburg empire. See also J. Gilissen, *Le régime représentatif avant 1790 en Belgique* (Brussels, 1952). For local case histories see for example V. Fris, *Histoire de Gand* (Ghent, 1930) (favorable to Joseph II and to Vonck), and J. Lefevre, "Le gouvernement du comté de Hainaut au XVIIIe siècle," in *Anciens pays et assemblées d'états,* V (Louvain, 1953), 23-47 (more favorable to the old order). The literature is very large.

[28] See estimates in the Table in Chapter VI above.

devotedly Catholic. Half the land belonged to great abbeys and other ecclesiastical bodies. The clergy, high and low, were sober men with little of the frivolity or indifference that had crept into the churches of France or England. The nobility were old-fashioned; some were well to do, but they lived without ostentation, and they invested their savings in land and mortgages, considering commercial enterprises too undignified or too risky. The peasantry, as in France, were legally free, but subject to the dues and payments of the manorial system. The load borne by the peasants was the lighter, however, in that the upper classes had acquired so few habits of modern extravagance, and because the Austrian government raised little money and few troops in its Belgian possessions. Business and financial development had been arrested. The Dutch, in winning their independence, had obtained the closing of the Scheldt river to seagoing ships. This closure of the Scheldt, written into many international treaties, was in the eighteenth century also strongly insisted on by Great Britain. The intent, and the result, was to destroy the port of Antwerp. The population of Antwerp dropped from 100,000 to 50,000 between the sixteenth century and the eighteenth, while Amsterdam and London more than quadrupled in size. Town life and burgher interests in Belgium, like the habits and outlook of clergy and nobles, remained those of a bygone day.

Belgium was in short an intermediate country, in a state of suspended animation between old and new. The Dutch Patriots who flocked across its frontier in 1787 found it backward, superstitious, priest-ridden, and oligarchic.[29] To the French it was the desert of culture. Seen from farther east, as from the imperial capital at Vienna, it was a far more lively place, the wealthiest of Hapsburg possessions, and distinguished among all parts of the Hapsburg empire (along with Milan) by its free rural population and its great number of busy towns.

Towns, nobles, clergy all had their historic liberties and their privileges. All were represented in the several assemblies of Provincial Estates—except that in Flanders, urbanized since the Middle Ages, the nobility were excluded. There could be, in Belgium, no sharp antagonism between an unprivileged Third Estate and two higher privileged orders. All three orders had an interest in preserving their liberties. On the other hand, the corporate liberties, or rights of the "orders," were by no means equally favorable to all persons within the respective orders or estates.

[29] See P. Geyl, "Noord-Nederlandse patriottenbeweging en Brabantse Revolutie," in *Nieuw Vlaams Tijdschrift*, No. 6, 1953, 3-20.

The Estates of Brabant, for example, met at the Hotel de Ville in Brussels. Though they voted as three houses, they met in a single room. Clergy and nobles sat in upholstered armchairs, while the Third Estate perched on benches, almost out of sight in the embrasures of the windows. Certain great abbots sat *ex officio* as the First Estate; neither bishops nor parish priests had anything to do with the assembly. As for the nobles, only those with four quarters of nobility and 4,000 florins a year could take part. In the Third Estate only the three *chefs-villes* of Brabant were represented—Brussels, Louvain, and Antwerp. What the Third Estate represented was actually the *corporations des métiers*, or gilds of these three towns. The gilds were trade associations of small employers, who resisted economic modernization. Each gild, in each town, characteristically required that apprenticeship be performed in the town itself; that no gild member employ more than a certain number of workmen; that no "foreigner," or non-townsman, engage in the trade within the town or the surrounding country; and that no new masterships or gild memberships be created. The gild memberships, thus fixed in number, had become mainly hereditary. Sons, nephews, or sons-in-law followed their elders in a known routine. The gilds stood firmly against economic expansion, new markets, or new methods, at a time when a quarter of the population of Antwerp, Ghent and Bruges was on poor relief.[30]

The power of the gilds was enormously magnified through the procedures used at the Brabant assembly. Unanimity of the three orders was necessary to the approval of any measure. The Third Estate thus had a veto. It voted only after obtaining the views of its constituents, the gilds of the *chefs-villes*. Hence any gild, in any of the three towns, could prevent action. Despite the modesty of the seating arrangements, and the custom of humbly voting last, the Third Estate of Brabant, that is the *doyens des métiers*, were persons of consequence whose desires were heeded, and opinions sought, by prelates and noblemen. "It is characteristic," according to one authority, "that in August 1787," at the beginning of the Belgian revolution, "not the Duke of Arenberg or the Count of Mérode was sent to Vienna as spokesman for the Estates, but Monsieur Petit."[31]

The other provinces had arrangements much as in Brabant. No Estates General of all provinces met from 1634 to 1790.

[30] On the central problem of the gilds see, in addition to Tassier and Mitrofanov, R. Ledoux, *La suppression du régime corporatif dans les Pays Bas autrichiens* (Brussels, 1912), in *Mémoires de l'Académie royale de Belgique*, 2nd series, vol. x.

[31] Mitrofanov, *Joseph II*, 626.

The politically active or privileged elements, under the Joyous Entry and other such provincial constitutions, were in short the great land-owning abbeys, certain of the nobles, and the gildmasters of certain towns. The agricultural population had no voice, but was well off and without sense of grievance. The urban poor were silent. The unrepresented towns did not care. The secular clergy were content. The most eminent lawyers handled the business of the great landed convents and nobles, with whom they were closely allied. There were lawyers with more modest clients, and also, among those excluded from political life, a few men of modern economic interests, even under the unfavorable conditions obtaining in Belgium: bankers who wished a wider field for profitable investment; organizers of manufactures, eager to break the gild regulations, hire an enlarged work force, or set up domestic industries in rural districts; merchants willing to expand beyond the town market, open the Scheldt, and even acquire an island in the West Indies. Such men, however, were fewer and less powerful than in neighboring countries. The wealthiest banker in Belgium, for example, the viscount Edouard de Walckiers, had an income of 140,000 francs a year, not much when compared to the revenues of the great Amsterdam houses, or the French banker Laborde, or the £100,000 a year (2,400,000 francs) of William Beckford of London.

It remains true that the dominant sentiment in Belgium was satisfaction with things as they were. Revolution came from outside. Placid Belgium, the Boeotia of Europe, was excited by the energetic emperor, Joseph II, by the sight of American independence, and, finally, by the revolution in France.

Native stirrings created a susceptibility to these outside forces. Belgians contributed no books to the European Enlightenment, but they read them. Political journalism began in 1772 with the *Esprit des journaux français et étrangers*. There were half-a-dozen such periodicals by 1785. Forbidden to discuss domestic political questions, they enabled their readers to take part vicariously in the politics of other countries. Debates in the House of Commons were printed in Belgian papers as soon as it became legal to print them in London, in the early 1770's. The Belgian press followed the American Revolution with interest, and published the texts of the American state constitutions.[32] It gave long accounts of the Dutch Patriot agitation. Even the conservative journals contributed to the habit of discussion. The abbé Feller praised

[32] Mlle. Tassier lays great emphasis on the effects of the American Revolution: *Démocrates belges*, 5, 84, 87, etc.

Blackstone and Burke, criticized Gibbon and Adam Smith, and refused to publish the constitution of Massachusetts, but he set people to thinking about them. And he reported, though with disgust, the *vraie fureur* created by the presentation of the *Mariage de Figaro* at Frankfurt on the Main, where people came from fifteen leagues around to relish its equalitarian sentiments.

It was nevertheless the Emperor Joseph II who threw Belgium into commotion. Joseph II, and his brother and successor Leopold II, carried on the program of reform from above, or enlightened despotism, that we have already seen to be characteristic of the Hapsburg monarchy at the time, and which had already brought it, and was to bring it again, into serious conflict with the estates of Bohemia and Hungary. Belgium so far had been only sporadically affected, but when Joseph became sole ruler in 1780, on his mother's death, he launched on a program of forcible modernization in all parts of the empire, Belgium included. In Belgium, as the most advanced of his dominions, he expected to find sympathetic support. He thought that in Belgium, with its large burgher class, his antinoble policies would be welcomed. He was doomed to disappointment. The most profound of his reforms, the abolition of serfdom, had no application to Belgium, where there were no serfs. It thus created no sympathy for the emperor among the peasantry, as it did elsewhere. On the other hand, the restrictions he placed on municipal independence caused him no trouble in his eastern lands, where towns were weak, but the same curbing of town autonomy drove the privileged towns of Belgium to revolt. He tried to free the port of Antwerp, and sent a loaded cargo vessel down the Scheldt, only to have it fired on and driven back by the Dutch; but this action favored only those Belgians who were thinking of the world market, and had no appeal for the economic interests that had political influence in the estates. Towns, nobles, and clergy combined against Joseph II, and no Belgian except a few who worked for the government spoke in his favor. Later, to be sure, by 1790, those Belgians who had become "democrats" looked on the Hapsburg monarchy with more sympathy.[33]

Joseph began by abolishing torture, decreeing toleration for Protestants, forbidding burial in churches, censoring sermons to prevent political opposition, and launching an investigation of the University of Louvain, where it was found that the curriculum had not changed since 1617. To reduce idleness, and increase productivity, he suppressed a few monastic establishments that he regarded as superfluous, pro-

[33] Mitrofanov, *Joseph II,* 587, 659-63.

hibited group pilgrimages, and ordered all kermesses or popular festivals throughout the country to be celebrated on the same day. He tried to relax the trade monopolies of the gilds, and ruled that masters might employ as many workmen as they pleased. Each of these measures antagonized someone.

Belgians began to fear for their constitutional liberties, the more so since in the thought of the day the "constitutional" was ill defined. There was no sense of two levels of law, no distinction between the constitutional and the merely statutory, such as was coming to be felt in America. As in England the Test Act, and even the game laws, could be defended as essential parts of the constitution, so in Belgium the admission of non-Catholics to public office (few as they were), or the forcing of reform on the University of Louvain, were regarded as unconstitutional measures, breaches of the social contract, violations of the Joyous Entry. The abbé Feller quoted Montesquieu to prove it.

In any case the determined Joseph II, to make the country more amenable to his rational government, did in 1787 embark on constitutional change, in the sense of change in the foundation and distribution of public power. He reorganized, unilaterally by his own will, the whole administrative and judicial system. Courts dependent on manorial lordships, estate assemblies, and town councils were abolished. Judicial and administrative power, blended in the old courts, were now separated, as recommended by philosophers of the Enlightenment. A new General Council was set up for executive functions, with intendencies throughout the country. Law courts were uniformly organized into higher courts and courts of first instance. The reform, like Maupeou's reforms of 1770 in France, anticipated the progressive developments of the century to come. But the old courts were basic instruments of government for the older governing class. And they involved not only the concept of the constitution but the concept of property, which also was not as strictly defined as it was to be later. Property included property in office, or inherited private rights in the exercise of public authority.

"Our right to judge is our property, Lord Emperor," pleaded the nobles of Alost. "We do not hold it by grace, but have received it from our fathers [hence it was constitutional] and bought it with blood and gold. It should not be taken from us against our will." Church bodies and town corporations, because they also owned manors, could have said the same. The numerous lawyers bred by the old system of courts (there were 260 at Mons alone) also protested. "Many of us," declared the Brussels lawyers, "have sacrificed all our means to obtain a post costing 700 florins; from our youth we have labored to acquire the needed knowledge, and we hope thereby to support our wives and children, since our rights rest on the sacred and inviolable Joyous Entry."[34]

The issue was clear. It was between social change and constitutional liberty. Reform would come at the cost of arbitrary government overriding the articulate will and historic institutions of the country. Or liberty would be preserved at the cost of perpetuating archaic systems of privilege, property, special rights, class structure, and ecclesiastical participation in the state. The Belgian Revolution was in its origin conservative. It was a revolution against the innovations of a modernizing government—in a sense, a revolution *against* the Enlightenment. It was not in this respect untypical of the time. The American Revolution had also been conservative in a way, a defense of historic liberties against a modernizing government in Great Britain, which was by no means unenlightened, at least in its colonial policy. The difference lay in the content of conservatism, and the meaning of liberty, as between the American colonies and the Belgian provinces. Nor was the Belgian Revolution essentially different in its origins from the French, as is often asserted. The French Revolution really began in this same year, 1787, with the resistance of nobles and prelates to the modernizing program of Calonne. In all cases, American, French, and Belgian, upper-class people took the lead in the first marshalling of discontent, and in all these cases a democratic movement soon emerged. The same was true to a degree in the Dutch Patriot movement, and in the parliamentary reform movements in Ireland and England, though no one had to resist forcible enlightenment at the hands of William V or George III.[35]

At the end of 1788 the Estates of Brabant and of Hainaut refused the grant of subsidies to the Emperor. Joseph II thereupon declared himself absolved from the Joyous Entry. Revolutionary manifestations occurred in the early months of 1789. A brewer of Brussels painted the

[34] *Ibid.*, 574-75.

[35] Professor Geyl, in the article cited in note 29 above, draws a sharp distinction between the Dutch Patriot movement, sharing in the general Franco-Anglo-American Enlightenment, and the conservatism of the Belgian Revolution, since in Belgium it was the government that was "enlightened." But the matter was complicated, because of ultimate ambiguities in liberty and equality themselves.

door of his house with the colors of Brabant: red, yellow, and black. It was the first tricolor.[36]

Resistance to the Austrians concentrated about two men, H. Van der Noot and J. F. Vonck. Both were lawyers of the Brussels bar, but Van der Noot was wealthy and related to the nobility; Vonck was the son of a farmer in easy circumstances. Van der Noot preferred dramatic action, and looked to the large stage of international affairs. Vonck, who was always in poor health, preferred to work behind the scenes. In 1788 Van der Noot, after publishing a ringing pamphlet, escaped the Austrian authorities by leaving the country. Vonck at the same time, after an illness, returned to his home in Brussels. Two very different lines of political action were thus initiated.

Van der Noot, setting up at Breda across the Dutch frontier, began overtures with the restored Orange government and with Great Britain and Prussia. He counted on the intervention of one or all of these powers to support the Belgians against the Emperor. We have the record of his secret conversations with the Dutch Van de Spiegel. He told Van de Spiegel that he represented "important men" in the Austrian Netherlands, that their aim was to set up an independent republic like that of the Dutch, and that they would favor having the second son of the Prince of Orange as a stadtholder, to which the difference of religion need be no bar. We know, too, that Van de Spiegel, the Princess of Orange, and the Amsterdam merchants were all cool to this idea. The Princess wanted no such rickety establishment for her Calvinist son, and Amsterdam wanted no union or affiliation with Belgium, no opening of the Scheldt, and no Antwerp or Ostend merchants turning up in the Indian Ocean. The Dutch wanted Belgium to remain as it had been—and the French to keep out. British interests were the same. Van der Noot's program was in fact hopeless, though he continued to pursue it.[37]

---

[36] Tassier, *Démocrates belges*, 89. The French tricolor appeared in July 1789; the Italian tricolor—red, green, and white—in May 1795; the Dutch tricolor—red, white, and blue in horizontal stripes—in September 1795; a Swiss tricolor—red, black, and yellow—in 1798. After vicissitudes, these are the national colors of these countries today, except that Switzerland in 1840 adopted the white cross on a red field. The present Irish, Yugoslav, Rumanian, Syrian, South African, Mexican, and other Latin American tricolors betray the same inspiration. I do not know whether the Irish tricolor has any connection with the rebellion of 1798. Certain Germans wishing a Rhineland Republic in 1797 raised a standard of red, blue, and green; but I know of no anticipation in this period of the later German republican colors, the present German tricolor, red, black, and gold.

[37] Van de Spiegel's notes and other documents in H. T. Colenbrander, *Gedenkstukken der algemeene Geschiedenis van Nederland van 1795 tot 1840*, I (The Hague, 1905), 137-49.

Vonck meanwhile, from February 1789, was holding secret meetings in his house in Brussels, at first among his friends. He knew of Van der Noot's plan, since the two were working in the same cause, but he had no faith in it, in view of what had happened in the Dutch Netherlands, and of the roles of Britain and Prussia in suppressing the Dutch Patriots, of whom there were at one time thought to be 17,000 in Antwerp alone. Vonck's group therefore counted on action by the Belgians themselves. Their plan, since the Austrians were still in power, was to have a certain number of young men cross the frontier, form military units, arm, and drill; and meanwhile to create a clandestine organization in the Belgian villages and towns, so that return of the armed companies would coincide with an uprising throughout the country, and the Austrians thereby be driven out. Vonck thus created the society *Pro Aris et Focis*—for Hearth and Altar—a name which had already been used by some of the Dutch Free Corps. It was a secret society, using false names, invisible ink, cyphers, double talk, and a system by which each member knew the identity only of the member who had enrolled him. The Belgian Revolution was the only one of the period brought about by conspiratorial methods. These methods, however, revealed a serious weakness. When the uprising came, even the members of Vonck's own society did not know of his part in it. Most of them thought that the main leader of the Belgian Revolution was Van der Noot, operating in patriotic limelight across the border.

It should be added that people of all groups and classes at first joined in *Pro Aris et Focis*. Van der Noot's own brother rejected his plan, and favored Vonck's. The great Abbot of Tongerloo, other abbots, and the bankers of Brussels financed the sojourn and the arming of patriots across the frontier. One of Vonck's most persistent followers, even after Vonck became a democratic leader in 1790, was the Duke of Arenberg, who had 732,000 florins a year. But most of Vonck's partisans were middle-class townspeople outside the gilds.

On June 18, 1789, Joseph II, who could see that Van der Noot was at Breda, and surmise that secret internal preparations were being made, suppressed the Estates of Brabant and annulled the Joyous Entry. It was the very moment when the French were afraid that Louis XVI would dissolve the Estates General. The very day before, on June 17, the French Third Estate had proclaimed the National Assembly, in which segregation of the three orders was abolished. News of this event had a great repercussion in Belgium. On August 18 revolution broke out in Liége.[38] This too immediately affected the Austrian Netherlands. The Orange regime did not favor the rally of armed Belgian subversives within its borders. The Liége revolutionaries enthusiastically welcomed them. By October there were over 2,000 arming and drilling in the territories of Liége. They were mostly very young men of the burgher class. Vonck found a professional army officer, the Flemish Colonel Van der Mersch, to command them. The colonel said that with 3,000 such men, a third in uniform, supported by a general rising, he stood a good chance of driving out the Austrians without foreign aid.

And so it happened. The Austrian authorities remained to the end, if anything, too unperturbed. The agents of the enlightened Joseph II could hardly be charged with counterrevolutionary hysteria. Trautmannsdorf, reporting the assembly of 2,800 men in Liége, expressed no concern; from such burgher youths nothing was to be feared. It was only of the aristocracy that eighteenth-century governments were really afraid. The Austrians, by remitting taxes in 1789, and propagating the idea that discontent was instigated by fanatical priests in favor of oligarchic estates, managed to keep many of the peasantry loyal.

Nevertheless, the Austrian regime collapsed abruptly at the end of 1789. The armed companies streamed in, riots and demonstrations broke out in the towns; there were few Austrian troops present, many being engaged in the war with Turkey. Each province separately declared its independence, Flanders appropriating a few words from the American Declaration of 1776.

Now, with independence, two distinct parties began to form. One favored keeping everything in Belgium as it had been. It had fought only for independence. Van der Noot became its leader. He had never believed in stirring up the lower classes anyway; he would have favored a respectable diplomatic intervention by foreign powers. Those of the other party "were called Vonckists by their enemies, democrats by themselves."[39] They wanted internal changes, now that change seemed to be possible.

[38] Neither space nor the requirements of clarity allow development here of the complex and interesting phenomena of the Liége revolution. See P. Harsin, *La Révolution liégeoise de 1789* (Brussels, 1953). The philosophical views of its prince-bishop allowed Liége to become an important center, after 1750, for the publication of books and periodicals of the Enlightenment. See G. de Froicourt, *François-Charles comte de Velbrück, prince-évêque de Liége, franc-maçon* (Liége, 1936), and U. Capitaine, *Recherches historiques et bibliographiques sur les journaux et les écrits périodiques liégeois* (Liége, 1850).

[39] Suzanne Tassier, "Les Belges et la Révolution française, 1789-1793," in *Revue de l'Université de Bruxelles*, xxxix (1934), 453. For Belgian use of the word democrat see Chapter 1 above.

In the brief turmoil of ejecting the Austrians the insurrectionary committees prepared by Vonck came to life. Their members—at Brussels, Ghent, Bruges, Mons, Namur, and elsewhere—were often men who had hitherto had no role and no interest in politics—"merchants, small landowners, lawyers, who desired to take part in public life, to interest themselves directly in public affairs."[40] Their methods, according to one conservative report, were very different from those of the sixteenth-century revolution against Philip II. Then, it had been magistracies and estate-assemblies that acted. Now "individuals" (significant word) "in each province sit with provincial bodies, in which persons of all classes are placed. . . . The people renew their magistrates, and assume an active authority to oversee all operations."[41] At Menin, where no mayor had been really elected since 1578, one was elected on December 12, 1789. Town revolutionary committees began to exchange delegates, to form provincial congresses, and to think of a National Assembly. A really revolutionary way of talking began to be heard. The Belgians, according to one pamphlet, were now "precisely as at the moment of issuing from the hands of the Creator."[42] The state of nature was in effect; the nation was sovereign, and it should summon a national convention to bring a new state into being. Old provincial constitutions should disappear.

Such ideas came from France, or indeed from America, or, rather, from the application by Belgians, in their own struggle and to solve their own problems, of observations that they had made on developments in America or France. The French Revolution, however, had also the contrary effect. Those with an interest in the old order were alarmed. The French, on the preceding August 4, had repudiated all forms of provincial, ecclesiastical, class, gild, and corporate privilege. In November they nationalized the property of the Church. It was not for this that Van der Noot and other higher-ups in the Belgian Revolution had rebelled against Joseph II. They turned to conservative arguments. When democrats urged equal representation for all persons as citizens, the Abbot of Tongerloo gave the classic reply: virtual representation, and the constitution. "The abbots as a group represent the secular and regular clergy, and indeed they represent the whole rural country as well, being the largest landowners; and, finally, usage has always been this way, and should remain so, since it is constitutional and the Constitution cannot be changed."[43]

[40] Tassier, *Démocrates belges*, 198.   [41] *Ibid.*, 199.
[42] *Ibid.*, 208, quoting a pamphlet by Doutrepont, *Qu'allons-nous devenir?*
[43] *Ibid.*, 190.

The Estates of Brabant, suppressed in June, reconvened in December. The abbots, the noblemen, and the bigwigs of the *chefs-villes*, to forestall the democratic agitation, announced themselves as the true and only sovereign in Brabant. They invited the estates of other provinces to send delegates to a conference. The conference met and pronounced itself to be the Estates General of the [Belgian] Netherlands, defunct since 1634. It adopted an Act of Union which created the United States of Belgium. The Act was closely modeled on the American Articles of Confederation, which in places it textually followed. It set up a Congress as the federal government (Congress and Estates General both existing for a while), whose powers were carefully limited to foreign policy and defense. As in America before 1789, the member states remained sovereign. Van der Noot became chief minister to the new Congress.[44]

It is worth noting that the framework of the American Articles of Confederation, which according to one view was more "democratic" than the United States federal constitution of 1787, was perfectly suited to the perpetuation of oligarchy in Belgium. The framework, in both countries, was designed to guard the position of men whose importance lay in local assemblies; it was also conservative, reflecting resistance to new ideas. In Belgium, however, as generally in Europe, the emphasis on local assemblies and on customary sentiments expressed the privileges of lord, burgher, and cleric. In America, to recur to the ambivalence of the American Revolution, the customary and the ancient were already radical by European standards; and in any case the American states, before adopting the Articles of Confederation, had undergone internal revolution, some more than others.

The Belgian democrats objected to the assumption of sovereignty by the Estates of Brabant, and to a union which was only a confederation of such estates. Such a regime, they said, was in fact more aristocratic than what had existed before. The "intermediate powers" were now sovereign; the doctrines of Montesquieu were violated. Who would now watch out, as the Emperor had done, for the interests of persons who had no voice in the estates—the bankers, the greater merchants, the investors of capital, the emerging industrialists, and even the common people?[45]

---

[44] On Belgian use of United States constitutional models see T. K. Gorman, *America and Belgium: a Study of the Influence of the United States upon the Belgian Revolution of 1789-1790* (London, 1925), in which a great many quotations are gathered to establish the fact of "influence," but without critical observation.

[45] Tassier, *Démocrates belges*, 215-17.

The American state constitutions were also brought into the argument by the democrats, to justify reorganization of representative and electoral machinery within the particular provinces. The Estates party, as it came to be called, replied that the American Revolution had been primarily only a war of independence. Few Belgians denied the appropriateness of American precedent. They differed only on the nature of the American Revolution.

The democrats could do little except write pamphlets and organize political clubs. There was no lower-class upheaval, in town or country. From lists of persons later imprisoned for "Vonckism" we can form an impression of who the democrats were. One list gives the names of seven lawyers, a notary, two doctors, a surgeon, an apothecary, an architect, three merchants, three who called themselves only *rentiers*, three wig-makers, three coffee-shop proprietors, two printers, and three priests.[46] The banker Walckiers was an important member of the party, and so was the wealthy Duke of Arenberg. As a group the democrats were not anti-Catholic, nor even anticlerical; there were priests in good standing among them, though the weight of the clergy was thrown against them. Men who followed Vonck in their youth founded the Belgian Catholic liberal party in their middle age.[47]

Vonck, always cautious, drew up a detailed plan for broadening the representation in the Brabant estates. He intended to allay the fears aroused by the more radical among his associates. As Pitt in his reform bill of 1785 tried to anticipate the opposition of Burke, so Vonck tried to make room for the privileged interests in the existing Brabant assembly. His plan, like Pitt's, was compromising and complicated, and hence not easy to appreciate or to explain. It became, however, the official program of the Brabant democrats.[48]

Vonck objected to the claim of full sovereignty made by the estates, but he did not expound the alternative doctrine of the sovereignty of

[46] *Ibid.*, 381-83.

[47] Tassier insists that the democrats were not anti-Catholic, except for a handful of Josephists like the Doutrepont mentioned in note 42 above. This is confirmed from a different direction by H. Haag, *Origines du catholicisme libéral en Belgique (1789-1839)*, (Louvain, 1950), 82. Haag holds that such anticlericalism as developed in Belgium, beginning in 1790, was the direct consequence of the incredible vindictiveness and terrorism of certain churchmen in the estates party. Haag maintains that the views of the abbé Feller, important in Belgium as a founder of traditionalist philosophy, were not derived from St. Augustine or Bossuet, as has been said, but from Bellarmine and Edmund Burke. Feller was one of the many former Jesuits active after the dissolution of the order in 1774.

[48] Tassier, *Démocrates belges*, 233-44, for a long analysis of Vonck's *Considérations impartiales sur la position actuelle de Brabant*, published on January 29, 1790.

the people. He demanded no National Assembly. Far from repudiating the estates, he proposed that there be four of them instead of three. He would have the abbots continue to sit in their own right, but would add elected deputies of parish and chapter clergy to the First Estate. He would have deputies of the Second Estate elected by all nobles. He would divide the Third Estate into two chambers: one for the three *chefs-villes*, but with more citizens in these towns taking part in election of delegates; and a new chamber for the small towns and for country people who were neither nobles nor clerics. He would have these four chambers deliberate and vote apart, and possess all legislative power, the executive to be given to a council to which each estate elected a member. He argued for this plan, not by appealing to natural right, but by insisting that it was historically entirely compatible with the Joyous Entry.

The Estates party would have none of it. The abbots and the *doyens des métiers* had the most to lose by such an absorption of new deputies into the chambers, and they stood firm against any concession. The abbé Feller, their great spokesman and journalist, found the democratic principles too rationalistic and abstract.

Moderation was expressed also in an opposite quarter by Leopold II, who succeeded Joseph as Emperor in February 1790. Leopold was one of the most reasonable men ever to occupy a European throne. A few years before, as Grand Duke of Tuscany, after study of the American state constitutions, he had devised a constitution for that duchy. He accepted the role of ruler as defined by the enlightened philosophy. In January he wrote to his sister, Marie Christine, the ousted regent of the Austrian Netherlands, in the very words of a "philosopher": "The sovereign, even a hereditary one, is only a delegate employed by the people. In each country there should be a fundamental law to serve as a treaty between the subjects and the monarch and limit the rights and authority of the latter. The sovereign who does not respect this contract thereby loses the position that has been given him only on this condition."[49] Their late brother Joseph, he gave his sister to understand, had in fact violated the liberties of the Belgians, who therefore had reason for their rebellion. In March he offered a basis of reconciliation to the Belgian estates. Explicitly repudiating Joseph's policies, he offered autonomy to Belgium under the revived Estates General, to which he would grant full powers in legislation, taxation, and ap-

[49] *Ibid.*, 315. This often quoted letter was first published in A. Wolff, *Leopold II und Marie Christine: ihr Briefwechsel* (Vienna, 1867), 85-86.

pointment to office. Some Belgian writers express astonishment that the Estates of Brabant never even replied to Leopold's offer of compromise.[50] We need be less surprised, in view of the attitude of the American Congress to similar British proposals in 1778. The Belgian estates were committed to independence.

It was to be an independence, however, from both crown and people. Neither a moderate democratization nor a modern constitutional monarchy was desired, especially by the Estates of Brabant—for those of Flanders, Hainaut, Tournai, and Malines showed more disposition to reconsider "ancient laws." In the circumstances, the democrats were more inclined than the Estates party to listen to Leopold and to put faith in the known liberalism of his ideas. The democratic wing of the Belgian revolutionaries could therefore be suspected of royalism and reaction. On the other hand, the Estates party charged them with sympathy for the French Revolution. The Belgian democrats, in this view, were mere doctrinaires determined to force a foreign ideology upon their country. They were accused of desiring a National Assembly in place of the Three Orders, and of intending to destroy the Catholic and Christian church. These charges were in part fabricated for political purposes, against the known public statements of Vonck and his chief followers, and in part they reflected the genuine fears already aroused by the neighboring revolution in France, the belief that moderates were the dupes of extremists, and the feeling that an inch of concession would become the ten thousand miles of total revolution.

In March 1790 the Estates party won out, after various scuffles and disorderly episodes. Van der Mersch was imprisoned at Antwerp. Vonck, Walckiers, and hundreds of others fled to France. The democrats were hounded, arrested, silenced, or driven into exile. A true terror broke out, conducted mainly by regular clergy, who were faithful to their great abbots. Vonckists and Royalists were damned to the third generation, said one monk in a sermon. Anyone meeting a Vonckist, said another, should simply kill him on sight. A Brussels watchmaker was struck a dozen times with a sword for a few words in criticism of the Estates. There were innumerable such cases. Forms of justice need not be observed, said Feller in his journal. "They are respectable, no doubt . . . but when they lead the country to ruin . . . they are detestable."[51] For the first time in this Belgian revolution there was a genuine mass upheaval, reminiscent of the Great Fear among the

[50] Tassier, *Démocrates belges*, 313-14.   [51] *Ibid.*, 387.

French peasantry the year before. It was, however, of opposite political tendency, being religious and deeply conservative. Every day throughout June 1790 thousands of the country people, led by their priests, poured into Brussels from the villages of Brabant. Some 20,000 arrived from a dozen villages on June 8 alone; 12,000 on June 21. They carried with them symbols or apparatus for the intimidation of democrats. One band brought a hangman's scaffold; another, a noose; in a third, women carried cutlasses; and the crucifix was much in view.[52] Nothing but religious excitement could have aroused so many people. The outraged prelates of Brabant thus made exhibition of their strength. The democratic movement—in the sense of a desire for broader participation in public life, or modernization and liberalizing of legal and constitutional structures—did not, in Belgium or in various other countries, arise by demand of the populace, least of all at the wish of virtuous and simple agrarians.

The democrats in refuge in France established contact with agents of Leopold II.[53] They had every reason to expect consideration from him. The Austrian government, if only out of dislike for the obstructionist estates, and memories of resistance to its own reforming program, was actually inclined to look on the democrats with favor. In December 1790 the Austrian authority in the Belgian provinces was in fact restored, against the selfish, quarrelsome, and self-defeating rule of the momentarily victorious estates. For the democrats the return of the Austrian troops was "almost a deliverance"[54]—in contrast to the effects of the Prussian army on the Dutch Patriots. The Belgian democrats were allowed by the Austrians to return home, and even to form political clubs.

The irony and tragedy of the great Revolution now became very apparent. The Belgian democrats returned to Belgium more radical

[52] *Ibid.*, 390-93. Mlle. Tassier remarks that at the moment when all France was on the move in the Fête de la Fédération to found the new commonwealth, Belgians trudged the roads in a way recalling phenomena of the Crusades.

[53] Vonck in France in April 1790 refused an offer of 2,000,000 florins by the Austrians for his assistance toward an Austrian restoration. The offer was made through the Belgian-born Brussels banker, Proli. This Proli later went to Paris, joined the Jacobin club, and was executed at the wish of Robespierre as a member of the "foreign conspiracy" in which Robespierre believed. The historian Albert Mathiez, like Robespierre, regarded Proli as an Austrian spy, and cited Proli's case as a piece of evidence for the reality of a conspiracy in the sense meant by Robespierre. It seems reasonable to agree with Mlle. Tassier that Proli was more likely a progressive Belgian, favorable both to the democrats and to the reforming Hapsburgs, and mediating between them in good faith in 1790, out of opposition to the old regime. The incident suggests how a comparative view, which Mathiez never attained, throws light on the French Revolution itself. *Démocrates belges*, 363, n. 3.

[54] *Ibid.*, 412.

than they had left it. Most of them were positively anticlerical, convinced that there could be no desirable change except by getting the church out of politics. More were convinced that compromising and halfway measures were a waste of time. There was more willingness to admire and imitate France, and even to look to revolutionary France for moral support or political intervention. There was a sense of a Europe-wide or "world" revolution of which Belgian affairs were but a part. The grounds for these sentiments lay in Belgium, not in France.

On the other hand, the very Austrians who could see the point of view of the democrats were afraid of them—because of the French Revolution. Marie Christine observed to her brother, Leopold, that the Belgian democrats were "the most enlightened men in the country."[55] But she thought he should not trust them. Immediately after the Austrian restoration there arrived in Brussels, in January 1791, as temporary governor-general, the Austrian diplomat Mercy-Argenteau, better known to general history as the counsellor to Marie Antoinette during all her years at Versailles. Mercy-Argenteau favored the Belgian democrats, as a means of weakening the Estates party. He even received suggestions for reform from their spokesmen. He reported to Vienna that their number was growing in important circles. But he was afraid of them. It was clear to him that their views were in the long run incompatible with Hapsburg rule. And he feared the French Revolution.

"The Estates," wrote Mercy, "no doubt are not very deserving; but there is a danger in leaning too easily and too precipitately toward the opposite party, considering the example of the misfortunes of France, and the French emissaries who are here, and of whom I am apprehensive."[56] In short, by 1791, even the enlightened monarchy of Maria Theresa, Joseph II, and Leopold II, and even Leopold II as a man, unique in a world peopled by Louis XVI, George III, and William V in the lengths he might go to conciliate democratic reformers, were thrown by fear of the French Revolution into a position of supporting constituted bodies, privileged classes and entrenched aristocracies.

The restored Austrian regime did not last long. In April 1792 France and Austria went to war, and in the following November the French republican army poured into the Austrian Netherlands. When General Dumouriez won the battle of Jemappes, there were Belgians who welcomed him, but this touches on a later part of the story.

A View of Switzerland

There was no monarchy in Switzerland, not even the shadow monarchy of the House of Orange. There was no nobility, not even the subdued nobility of the Dutch provinces or the well-behaved nobility of Belgium. There was no foreign rule to generate movements of independence. That the Swiss cantons nevertheless suffered from the same problems as were common elsewhere only reveals more clearly the basic issues. As Peter Ochs observed, in an amusing description of all the kinds of people in his own town of Basel who resisted change, the most respected and influential voices, without king, nobility, or Catholic Church, were "aristocratic."

There was no Swiss state. There was only the *Eidgenossenschaft*, the oath-fellowship of thirteen sovereign cantons, perpetually leagued together for external defense. Except for a few cantons that were mountainous, rural, and Catholic, these "oath-fellows" were essentially certain German-speaking and Protestant towns, notably Bern, Zurich, and Basel. French-speaking Vaud, Valais, Neuchatel, and Geneva were not cantons, and Geneva did not even belong to the league. Town oligarchies, in Switzerland as elsewhere, ruled over townspeople and countryside. More will be said when the time comes to consider the Helvetic Republic of 1798. It is enough here to observe, as a sign of the complexity of lordships and jurisdictions, that Switzerland until 1798 had a hundred different tariff zones.

The little democratic revolution at Geneva in the 1760's has been recounted in Chapter v. The party of the Burghers and Citizens, who may have composed a quarter of the population, had clashed with the governing Small Council and Council of Two Hundred. The Burghers, calling themselves *Représentants*, had asserted the right of the town meeting or General Council to elect, at its own free choice, the men to sit in the Small Council or executive government. Partisans of the Small Council were called *Négatifs*, from the right which they claimed to negative, or veto, the remonstrances of Burghers or actions of the General Council. A dilemma had ensued under the "constitution" of 1738, which was "guaranteed" by France, Zurich, and Bern. To obtain the necessary changes or clarifications in the constitution, the *Négatifs* had appealed to the guarantor powers, and the *Représentants* had asserted, more from the logic of their situation than from the logic of Rousseau, the doctrine of the sovereignty of the people. By the "people" they meant those who already enjoyed Burgher rights, assembled in the General Council. There had been a compromise in 1768, a compromise which the young democrat Delolme refused to accept, but which allowed the government to be carried on.

In 1782 this compromise broke down.[57] The intervening years had not been quiet. Burghers continued to meet in their "circles," the neighborhood discussion groups which had become the instruments of political action. For the first time also the Natives entered significantly into politics, demanding the political rights from which they were excluded, but having mainly in mind an occupational and economic equality from which the laws debarred them. Since it was the Burgher *Représentants*, as much as the conservative *Négatifs*, who wished to keep Natives out of profitable or prestige-conveying lines of work, the Natives were divided in their political tactics, some favoring alliance with *Représentants* against *Négatifs*, others the reverse. Most Natives inclined to the Burgher or *Représentant* party.

The Burgher party became somewhat more liberalized in the seventies. Their ideas evolved from burgherdom to citizenship. It may be recalled that in 1770 the Burghers suppressed a Native protest with menacing determination. Whether from the passage of time, the spread of "enlightenment," the ideas made so public by the American Revolution, the growing strength of the Natives, or the need of allies against the obstinate *Négatifs*, the Burghers adopted a broader position. After another Native uprising in 1781, the General Council voted to admit Natives of the third generation in Geneva to Burgher rights. About 460 Natives would thus become Burghers, thereby considerably enlarging the General Council, which hitherto had rarely mustered as many as 1,200 voters. If naturalization after three generations seems little enough, it nevertheless fundamentally altered the old constitution of Geneva.

The Small Council refused to recognize this wholesale conversion of Natives into Burghers. Thus the question of authority, or sovereignty, as between the Small and General Councils, was again raised, as in 1766. The Small Council and the *Négatifs* again appealed to the guarantors, France, Zurich, and Bern. And again the arguments raised in this miniscule affair took to high and general levels. One might suppose all civilization and all humanity to be involved. The Geneva troublemakers, said a Bern official, were "sectaries of J. J. Rousseau and other false philosophers of the day." There was a premonition of the Holy Alliance and the Protocol of Troppau when one of the Geneva Small

[57] For the following paragraphs see E. Chapuisat, *La prise d'armes de 1782 à Genève* (Geneva, 1932).

Council, Micheli du Crest, writing to the French foreign office, and expatiating on "the atrocious and unprovoked horrors of sedition," urged collective intervention "in the cause of all legitimate governments and of all sovereigns." On the other hand, a Geneva democrat, a painter then in Paris named Bourrit, was able to get personally to Vergennes and use language like that of Vergennes' own protégés, the Americans. Bourrit, like the Americans, brought in various purely historical arguments, but also became more abstract: the sovereign at Geneva was the General Council, the Small Council was only the government—"if the government is abusive, and instead of being the guardian of the laws becomes their violator, the sovereign has the right to change it."[58]

France, Zurich, and Bern intervened with troops. Vergennes, willing enough to sponsor democratic revolution in America or in Holland to undermine the British empire, saw no such advantage in Geneva at his very doors. French and Swiss soldiers besieged the city for three weeks. Patrols circulated inside; various Small Councillors were held as hostages; St. Peter's church, Calvin's own church, became a storehouse for gunpowder, and the banker, Etienne Clavière, a Burgher leader, mounted guard with a thousand or so others. Brissot was in the city, forming his ideas on revolution, and so was the future conservative Mallet du Pan, making observations of contrary tendency on the same subject. A proposal for reconciliation, urging the *Négatifs* to give up their *politique aristocratique,* was signed by 1,020 Burghers. Nothing came of it, and the troops forced their way into the city.

The guarantor powers, consulting with the *Négatifs,* drew up an Edict of Pacification. This was submitted to the General Council for its approval. Only half the authorized voters appeared, and of these 113 voted against it. One syndic, several patricians, and most of the Reformed clergy were in this number; that is, they supported the Burghers against restoration of the old system by foreign arms. The new statute, accepted by the General Council, 411 to 113, was soon denounced as the Black Code.

The Pacification, or *code noir,* undid the actions not only of 1782 but of 1768. The General Council lost the right of deliberation. Syndics were to be declared elected if they obtained one-quarter of the votes cast in the General Council. The "circles" were abolished and replaced by public cafés, and militia exercises were forbidden. Three hundred of the 460 Natives recently admitted to Burgher rights now lost them. Fifteen persons were banished for ten years. Others went into a tech-

[58] *Ibid.*, 52-53, 76, 80.

nically voluntary exile. In addition, as if to add insult to injury, and with implications that readers of Chapter v will perceive, the restored patricians insisted against manifest opposition on building a theater. Even Mallet du Pan thought this unwise.

Aristocracy was resurgent at Geneva after 1782, but its enjoyments were to be brief, for there was more trouble in 1789, followed in 1794 by a terrible retribution, when Genevese Burghers put to the guillotine certain fellow townsmen who had brought in the French twelve years before.

Meanwhile Etienne Clavière lived in France (as other Genevese, Dutch, and Belgian refugees were to do), became allied with Brissot, joined his Gallo-American society, collaborated with him on a book on America, and plunged with him into the politics of the French Revolution, becoming French financial minister in 1792. Their friend of that time, Mme. Roland, was given new cause to lament the ordeals of virtue. "Virtue and liberty," she wrote in 1782, "have no more asylum except in a few honest hearts."[59] But the best way to conclude on the affairs of Geneva, as they stood on the eve of the great European struggle, is with the words of another Genevese exile, Francis d'Ivernois. In 1789 he published a book on the recent history of Geneva. From it one should learn, he said, that "whenever there exists in a State a numerous class rejected by the constitution, and which is conscious of this fact and complains of it, either this class must be made associates in the constitution, or the constitution will be in danger of being smothered by the very ardor with which the excluded class tries to embrace it."[60]

Of the rest of Switzerland, or Switzerland proper, since Geneva did not belong to the confederation, there is nothing to report in the way of spectacular events in these years, and it would be necessary in any case, and prohibitively repetitious and lengthy, to follow the story canton by canton. Political ideas were taking shape here as elsewhere. The number and the circulation of periodicals increased, and reading and discussion clubs formed in various towns. Pestalozzi, the famous educational theorist, belonged to such a group of young men in Zurich, and as early as 1766 opposed the use of Zurich troops at Geneva, getting into a scrape for which he spent three days under house arrest. Isaac Iselin at Basel heralded the progress of civilization and Johannes von Müller was moved to add six hundred new facts to his history.

[59] Ibid., 130.
[60] F. d'Ivernois, Tableau historique et politique des dernières révolutions à Genève (London, 1789), I, viii-ix.

The correspondence of Peter Ochs, recently published, allows us to see clearly into this fermentation of ideas.[61] A member of one of the ruling families at Basel, whose great moment was to come in the revolution of 1798, Ochs came of age about 1770. Completely bilingual, writing in his younger days a once-famous history of Basel in German, and conducting all his correspondence in French, and with a sister who married an Alsatian, he had a wide acquaintance in the Swiss cantons, Germany, the Low Countries, and France. At the University of Basel, Iselin was one of his teachers, and another professor there was later tutor to the son of the Prince of Orange. He remained in contact with these men also.

Early in his life he came to share in the generous and humanitarian sentiments of his time. His doctoral dissertation at Basel, dated June 4, 1776, began with an introduction on the dignity and the rights of man, in the course of which he regretted that Negroes in the West Indies should wet the earth with their tears to give Europeans a better breakfast.[62] With Iselin and his other friends he hailed the American Revolution for its promise of a new era.[63] It seems significant that, while we have his letters from 1770, it is not until the American Revolution that we find him taking any political attitudes, that is, thinking in terms of action to bring about expected change.

His political development was slow, and natural for a man in his position. He was no literary sentimentalist, no combative doctrinaire, and no rebel. Being what he was, he entered the governing council at Basel in his twenties, and was presently elected *Oberzunftmeister*, or Uppergildmaster, which amounted to a kind of associate mayor. He knew and said that Basel was a tight little aristocracy, with a sovereign council that chose its own membership from a narrow circle, "democratic" only in that commercial employments did not "derogate." Yet he did not propose to do anything about it. "I adore my wife and idolize my son, now four months old," he wrote to a friend in 1781; "I like my garden, my birds, my rabbits and my chickens far more than things that are so avidly striven for in the great capitals. All I ask

[61] "Recently" for the slow-moving science of history. The Ochs correspondence was published as long ago as 1927-1937, but I know of no work in English that has made any use of it. G. Steiner, ed., *Korrespondenz des Peter Ochs*, 3 vols. (Basel, 1927-1937). On the very great importance of these documents see the review by Guggenbühl in *Zeitschrift für schweitzerische Geschichte* (1936), 339-41. For political institutions at Basel and in Switzerland see Chapter II above.

[62] *Korrespondenz*, I, 93 n. 2. "Hominis dignitas, jura eius, mediaque illa servandi, haec sunt objecta, quibus meditandis pauca incumbunt."

[63] See above, Chapter IX, p. 242.

is to go on with my present existence in peace until my son is grown up, and then die."[64]

In 1785 he received a long letter from a man named Bonstetten, one of a dissatisfied group at Bern. They were trying at Bern, said Bonstetten, to build up a network of correspondents throughout Switzerland to exchange political ideas and factual information. For example, where at Bern in 1680 there had been 500 *regimentsfähigen* families, or familes qualifying to hold office, there were in 1780 only 230; and of 200 men now in the Bern council 57 were childless and 90 had only one son. What were the facts in the other Swiss republics? Bonstetten said that they needed men of the standing of Ochs, "a man of position, rich, well regarded," to give them leadership and to attract coworkers. Remember, he concluded, that we are all Swiss.[65]

Ochs replied with a sympathetic exchange of letters, which, however, soon died (temporarily) "for want of interesting events." He and some others organized a reading club at Basel. It had two rooms, one for reading and one for conversation, open every day from one to eight o'clock, with magazines, newspapers, maps, and pamphlets. In 1787 there were 75 subscribers, and the chief magistrates of the town and all the professors at the University belonged.[66]

Basel adjoined Alsace, where Ochs' sister and brother-in-law lived, and he was excited by the French Revolution, by "representative democracy" (as distinguished from direct democracy and aristocracy), and by the "sublime" proclamation of the rights of man. Here at Basel, he said, our basic statute starts out by talking about the office of burgomaster, and says nothing of any rights of citizens, peasants or men as such. His work in the Basel council began to disgust him. "Would you believe it? The secret council at Bern has begged our secret council to prohibit any newspaper from writing in favor of abolition of the tithe or legal proceedings without cost." As early as October 1789 he saw a chance of war between France and Europe, thought France would win, and revolution spread; but as a prudent Swiss he decided to reduce his French investments.[67]

Ochs' brother-in-law, Jean Dietrich, was elected in 1790 to be the first mayor of Strasbourg under the new regime. A frequent visitor, Ochs was in Strasbourg in June 1790, and witnessed the *fête de la fédération* there, as William Wordsworth did at the same time at

[64] *Korrespondenz*, I, 123-24.   [65] *Ibid.*, 157-61, 167, 173.
[66] *Ibid.*, 195.   [67] *Ibid.*, 212-20, 227, 244.

Calais. He even wrote a poem about it, which, if it fell short of Wordsworth's recollections in the *Prelude,* still expressed his opinions:

> Que les temps ont changé! Qui l'eût jamais pu croire?
> L'égalité civile ennoblit les Français . . .[68]

The next year found him in Paris on the business of Basel, to collect the compensation money due for the loss to Basel citizens that followed abolition of tithes in Alsace. In Paris he saw the sequel to the episode of Varennes, and observed the growth of republicanism, which is to say the discrediting of the French King and Queen. Ordinary people speak of them without ceremony, he reported, "as Mr. and Mrs. Louis XVI."[69]

His feelings mounted as the international crisis became more acute. With the approach of war he was back in Basel. "The revolutions of America, France, and Poland obviously belong in a chain of events that will regenerate the world."[70]

The war came, and a few days later, at his sister's house in Strasbourg, a captain of engineers named Rouget de Lisle composed the Marseillaise. We were having some people in, she explained to her brother, and, as you know, it is always necessary to invent something to do; so we began to make up a song; it is like Gluck, only more lively; I myself arranged the parts for the various instruments, and "my husband, a good tenor, sang the passage that is so stirring and has a certain originality."[71]

Such, in brief, is the story of how a Swiss patrician, between 1776 and 1792, turned from the author of a Latin dissertation on human dignity into a collaborator with the Revolution in France.

Reflections on the Foregoing

We have now surveyed the course of events, roughly between the American and the French Revolutions, in the Dutch Netherlands, Belgium and Switzerland, and in England and Ireland in the preceding chapter. I have tried to hold the story, so far, short of the time when the French Revolution could have had any determining influence, though with difficulty in the case of Belgium. The events traced, in each country, are events that had native causes and reflected internal conditions. What pattern or comparative generalizations do they make it possible to reach?

[68] *Ibid.,* 239, 469. [69] *Ibid.,* 302.
[70] *Ibid.,* 325. [71] *Ibid.,* 353.

In each of the five countries just named there had been, by 1790, a substantial democratic movement, which among the Dutch and Belgians and at Geneva had reached the point of revolution, and which, according to various British writers, had amounted to "near" or "missed" revolution in England. The democratic movement had identified its opponent as "aristocracy." Aristocracy meant the rule of certain constituted bodies, which claimed sovereignty for themselves, were self-perpetuating in a limited number of families, and denied the right of outside persons, or excluded classes, to have any influence on their policies or their personnel. The democratic movement, in one way or another, whether through William Pitt, or the student Ondaatje, or the lawyer Vonck, or the banker Clavière, sought to broaden the basis of participation in political life, and to make the government accountable to some kind of a public. Actual proposals were moderate and even empirical: to reassign borough rights, and give a vote to long leaseholders in England and Ireland; to set up *geconstitueerden* at Utrecht, and a fourth chamber at Brussels; to grant burgher rights to third-generation Natives at Geneva. Historical arguments were as common as those postulating natural right. The most common historical idea—except in Ireland, where it could not be used—was the belief in a trend to hereditary monopolizing, generally since the sixteenth century, of public bodies which had been more fully representative in their medieval origins. If this idea was not wholly true, it lay closer to the pole of truth than to that of downright error.

No one demanded universal suffrage, except the Westminster Committee in England, and it appears that in all these countries the mass of the population, perhaps the bottom three-quarters of society, was politically apathetic, disinclined to change, and attached to their customary superiors. The "people" in the new doctrine did not mean everyone. It meant a political community outside the government and in some sense above it. It is here argued that the theory of the sovereignty of the people, in each country, as in the revolutionary American colonies, had arisen in the needs of an actual political situation, or in answer to the actual arguments of adversaries, more than from any special predilection for rationalistic philosophy. The democrats and the democratically oriented reformers were not "sectaries of J. J. Rousseau," though it is true that Rousseau, in the *Social Contract*, had laid the deepest moral foundation for a democratic theory of the state. The point is that, at this time, and for many reasons, men of various types and in numerous countries converged in their principles. In none of the countries here considered, however, had the idea of the sovereignty of the people led on, as it had in America, to the more truly revolutionary idea of the people as a constituent power, which the French were again to invoke in 1789. There was much talk, in Ireland, England, Holland, and Belgium, of associations, assemblies, congresses, and conventions. What was meant was a kind of public scrutiny or inspection of government, or more freedom to elect a few representatives to existing bodies. No one expected to create a new system of government to supersede that of the past. No one supposed that government must be constructed and authorized by a single act, in a constitutional document written by a constituent convention deemed to speak with the authority of the people itself.

The democratic movement in each of these cases failed. The parliamentary classes in the two British islands prevented any broadening of the representation, and the Anglican interest in England prevented the equalization of political rights for Dissenters. Orange and aristocratic partisans in the United Provinces put down the Dutch democrats; by the same operation, the Dutch Reformed Church prevented the admission of Catholics and of minority Protestants to public affairs. In Belgium the estates party crushed the democrats before being itself overthrown by the Austrian restoration. At Geneva the patricians of the governing councils staged a triumphant counterrevolution. The general conception of an "aristocratic resurgence," which we shall soon apply to events in eastern Europe and France, can reasonably be applied to England, Ireland, Holland, Belgium, and Geneva in the 1780's.

Whether it should also be applied to America is a question. Condorcet and others in France detected a kind of aristocratic resurgence in the American federal constitution of 1787. Strongly disapproving of this constitution, Condorcet wrote to Franklin in July 1788 (and Franklin may have agreed) that "an aristocratic spirit seeks to introduce itself among you."[72] When the famous Pennsylvania constitution of 1776 came to an end in 1790 this belief was reinforced. Various American schools of historians have in effect agreed with Condorcet. My own view is that, while a new upper class was undoubtedly growing up in the United States, it was clearly more dynamic, more oriented to the future, more receptive to change, and less hostile to popular representation than the governing classes in Europe, even, or perhaps one should say especially, those in European republics. What I have

[72] *Works of Benjamin Franklin* (N.Y., 1904), XI, 434-35.

said on the United States constitution, or the political ideas of John Adams, or the use by Belgian conservatives of the American Articles of Confederation, is enough to suggest doubt that what happened in America, with the adoption of the new constitution, reflected any aristocratic resurgence significantly comparable to that of Europe.[73] The Philadelphia convention, in the boldness of its actions and principles, outdistanced not only the European conservatives but even the European democrats, if by the latter one means Henry Flood, Alderman Sawbridge, Ondaatje, Vonck, or the Genevese Burghers, or even the French Constituent Assembly of 1789-1791, which of course could make no provision for an elected executive, and surrounded the popular choice of deputies with many intricate safeguards.

The aristocratic party, except in England, showed a strong tendency to depend on foreign aid. The Geneva patricians three times during the century, and for the last time in 1782, called on the guarantor powers, over democratic protest, to settle internal Genevese problems. In Holland the Orange party depended wholly on England and Prussia. The Dutch in 1787 even had their Flight to Varennes and their Brunswick Manifesto. The Belgian Van der Noot, rather than stir up the Belgian people, worked for intervention by Holland, Prussia, and Britain. The Irish magnates, though often restless under government from Westminster, began to see their ultimate dependency on the British connection. Even in America the old aristocracy of the colonial era, the true conservatives that Americans have forgotten, those who ended up in the ranks of the Loyalist émigrés, depended on the British connection to sustain their position. But although aristocratic interests in America, Ireland, Holland, and Belgium showed this dependence on Britain, it would be unfair to single out Britain as unique in this regard. At Geneva the aristocracy willingly depended on France. Events were to show that some in Poland would rather bring in the Russians than accept a new constitution. It was perfectly rational for the French to believe, as early as July 1789—whether to hope or to fear—that a foreign intervention, at the urging of French nobles and émigrés, might be brought to bear against the Revolution.

On the other hand, even before 1789 or 1792, the leaders of democratization showed an affinity for France. It was to France that American insurgents and Dutch Patriots looked for help, from France that emerging Irish radicals expected encouragement, and in France that democratic refugees found a haven. France before 1789 was full of

[73] See above, 229-32, 271-75, 352.

Dutch, Belgian, Swiss, Irish, and even English political expatriates. It was these men, as much as or more than the French themselves, who were to preach world revolution. No one doubts that the French monarchy patronized foreign revolutionaries more for political advantage than from ideological sympathy. The same is probably true of the French republic, even in 1792, despite all we have been told of world-salvationism in the psychology of the French Revolution.

The democratic movement failed everywhere, before 1789, except in America. Not merely did it not transform the world or introduce a heavenly city, which it hardly intended. Moderate though it was, or seems in restrospect, it failed to obtain any concessions at all. In Ireland the Test Act was repealed for Protestants, and at Geneva a hundred and fifty Natives remained Burghers after 1782. But in general it is true to say, and must be emphasized, that all the efforts of English and Irish parliamentary reformers, and of Dutch, Belgian, and Genevese democrats, had come to absolutely nothing. Indeed, matters were if anything worse, for the fear and the vindictiveness of threatened oligarchies had been aroused.

The democratic movement had failed for various reasons, in some places because the forces of the old order had successfully called upon foreign aid, and in all cases because the democratic interests, though important and enlightened, were a numerical minority in the community as a whole. They had no mass following. The "mass," outside London, Paris, or Amsterdam, really meant the rural population. Country people at lower income levels, in the countries now being considered, were politically unaroused or not much aware of having any serious grievances. So far as the ruling aristocracies drew their incomes from land, or their influence from the good will of their tenantry, they had little to fear from disaffected lawyers or impudent pamphleteers; the one thing that would undermine them was wholesale defection on their own estates. This did not happen until it happened in France in the summer of 1789.

If these events prove anything, it is perhaps that no purely middle-class or "bourgeois" revolution could succeed. Lawyers, bankers, merchants, shopkeepers, students, and professors could not alone unseat the holders of political power. They had done their best: they and their sons had armed and drilled; they had formed armed companies or national guards in Ireland, Holland, Belgium, and Geneva. They had gone down, in Holland and at Geneva, before a regular or foreign army. One reason was the lack of experience of the burgher class in military service and military command. In the latter the aristocracy still had all the advantages. The Dutch Patriots had called on a French army officer to take command against the Prussians—with unfortunate results. The Americans had learned a good deal from French and European professional officers. Another reason for the democratic failure, applying at least to Holland, Belgium, and Geneva, was that these countries had the misfortune to be small, and hence easy objects for intervention. The attempt of conservative Europe to intervene in France in 1792 was to have a very different outcome.

"The French Revolution," Albert Schweitzer once observed, "is a snowstorm falling on trees in blossom."[74] The eminent humanitarian echoed in these words a common idea, evoking the picture of a humane, tolerant, open-minded, moderate, increasingly liberal, and satisfactorily progressing Age of Enlightenment, unfortunately cut short by violent and sanguinary popular revolt. The corollary is that an inflexible conservatism appeared after, and in reaction to, the French Revolution. Readers of the preceding chapters, if they at all agree with the author, will find it hard to see the trees in blossom, and may be prepared to think, as the following chapters will to some extent show, that revolution was itself a reaction against an immovable conservatism already formed.

The two sides were taking shape before 1789. Aristocrats and democrats, known by these names, had already been at each other's throats. Revolutions had been attempted, and counterrevolutionary doctrine was already in the making. Democrats, though moderate in their actual proposals, did speak of the Majesty of the Nation and the Sovereignty of the People. They questioned the legitimacy of the Orders, and of church membership as a qualification for political rights. Such ideas did in fact undermine the constitutions of all European countries as they then existed. Conservatives were not mistaken in making this diagnosis. What they may more reasonably be blamed for is that they provided no means of lawful readjustment, insisted on the immutability of the existing arrangements, and failed to see what they later blamed radicals for failing to see, the wisdom or desirability of evolutionary change.

The artillery soon to be directed against the French Revolution had already been perfected in lesser engagements. The American Revolution was the work of "mechanics and country clowns"—it was a South Carolina Anglican clergyman who said so. America was "in a state

---

[74] *Philosophy of Civilization* (N.Y., 1949), 176.

of dreadful confusion," according to Burke in 1779. It suffered, said the American Galloway, from its own "Wickedness and Folly" under a regime that was "Tyrannical and oppressive." The authors of the Irish Reform Bill were "system mongers." Those of the English reform bill really wanted to destroy the English constitution, said Burke, whose whole conservative philosophy was mapped out in 1784. The Geneva Burghers of 1782 were the victims of "false philosophers of the age." "The cause of all legitimate governments" was at stake. Whether the American revolutionaries had employed "terror" is a question of what one chooses to mean by terror. The French revolutionaries used a kind of terror as early as 1789. But terror—meaning forced oaths, legal proceedings against political offenders, repression of the press and the right of assembly, imprisonment, banishment, exile—had been employed for more conservative purposes, in the little terror at Geneva at the end of 1782, the "rod of terror" that Harris advised for the Dutch in 1787, the very real terror against the Belgian democrats in 1790. The point is not to justify or impugn or recriminate, but only to make clear the division and the struggle, not wholly latent, that already existed at the end of what is called the Age of Enlightenment.

THE LIMITATIONS OF ENLIGHTENED DESPOTISM

Every subject should expect security and protection from his Sovereign, while the Prince is expected to determine and clearly delineate the rights of his subjects, to guide their actions in a way more consistent with the public and private good.—EMPEROR JOSEPH II, 1786

THE LIMITATIONS OF ENLIGHTENED
DESPOTISM

THE forces of aristocracy, which in some countries in the 1780's prevailed over democratic movements, prevailed in others over monarchy itself. This chapter takes up a thread left hanging at the close of Chapter IV. It was shown there that, by the middle 1770's, or just before the American Revolution, the Kings of France and of Sweden, and the Queen of Hungary and Bohemia (to which titles the Hapsburg monarchy owed most of its stature), had asserted royal authority and put the constituted bodies of their several realms under restraint. In France, Chancellor Maupeou abolished the old parlements, in Sweden the Freedom Era came to an end, in Hungary no central diet met after 1764, and in Bohemia none met after 1775. Victory at the moment went to enlightened despotism. Rulers forced through programs of reconstruction by suppressing institutions that had or claimed a representative character. Maupeou and Terray initiated important reforms in tax assessment and judicial organization, while Maria Theresa labored persistently at the alleviation of serfdom.

The following fifteen years made clear the limits beyond which enlightened despotism could not go. However held down, the constituted bodies—estates, diets, parlements, and the like—had strong powers of survival and resurgence. In France, a resistance to government begun by the two higher orders soon developed a more democratic phase. The result was the French Revolution. In Eastern Europe, though demands of a democratic character within the definitions used in this book were by no means wholly absent, the serf-owning aristocracy was the only really important political class, and to this class royal governments had to make concessions. The result was a reaction against the Enlightenment, or a new understanding between throne and nobility, which was in general to last until the beginning of the twentieth century in Eastern Europe.

The present chapter deals mainly with the Hapsburg monarchy under Joseph II and Leopold II, with observations, since not everything can be told, on Prussia, Sweden, and Russia. No attempt is made to discuss enlightened despotism in Spain, Naples, or Denmark. After a chapter on the special case of Poland we shall turn to France, examine the conflict which developed there between a reforming monarchy and a resurgent aristocracy, and trace the beginnings of the French Revolution. Events in these countries will be followed to the eve of the war of 1792.[1]

Joseph II: The Attempted Revolution from Above

What happened at Pressburg in Hungary on April 13, 1784, or at least is reported to have happened, may serve as a parable on the reign of Joseph II. The Emperor had ordered the crown of St. Stephen removed to Vienna. Four officers of the Hungarian Noble Bodyguard arrived to escort the venerable object with appropriate honor and ceremony. When the climactic moment came, all four declared themselves ill, to avoid having to execute so horrifying a command. The keepers of the crown bolted the doors to the strong room and hid the key, so that a locksmith had to be brought to let the Emperor's agents in. A weeping throng surrounded the castle. As the crown was at last borne through the gates, a perfectly clear sky gave out three loud claps of thunder. They were an omen of punishment, people said, for this profanation of the religion and the freedom of Hungary.

The crown of St. Stephen, first worn by that king who had brought the rude Magyars into the Christian and Roman church, was the supreme emblem of Hungarian nationality and independence. It was regarded with profound awe; when it was safe, Hungary was thought to be safe. In its troubled history, it had once been held by the Turks. After 1945 it was for some years in the custody of the United States, to the great annoyance of Hungarian communists, not otherwise given to royalist imagery or historic forms of superstition. Joseph II, on

[1] The two following sections depend mainly on P. von Mitrofanov, *Joseph II: seine politische und kulturelle Tätigkeit, aus dem russischen übersetzt* (Vienna and Leipzig, 1910); F. Valsecchi, *L'assolutismo illuminato in Austria e in Lombardia*, 2 vols. (Bologna, 1931); R. J. Kerner, *Bohemia in the 18th Century: a Study in Political, Economic and Social History with Special Reference to the Reign of Leopold II, 1790-92* (N.Y., 1932); H. Marczali, *Hungary in the 18th Century* (Cambridge, Eng., 1910) (translated from the Hungarian); and on articles by two of my former students, Donald A. Limoli, "Pietro Verri: A Lombard Reformer under Enlightened Absolutism and the French Revolution," *Journal of Central European Affairs* xviii (1958), 254-80, and Peter F. Sugar, "The Influence of the Enlightenment and the French Revolution in 18th Century Hungary," *ibid.*, xvii (1958), 331-55.

taking it to Vienna, demonstrated his obstinacy, showed what he meant by centralization of the empire, and paraded his contempt for the national, constitutional, and religious sentiments that rose up against him. And he provoked the thunders in which his reign came to an end.

The name of Joseph II, "the revolutionary Emperor," has become a byword for colossal failure. He was not inexperienced in affairs, having been coruler with his mother for fifteen years before her death; nor did he labor quite alone, for many devoted public servants, of all the Hapsburg nationalities, worked with him for the modernization of the empire. They were and are called Freemasons and Jansenists, but this is only to say that many believers in the Enlightenment joined Masonic lodges, and that "Jansenists" were Catholics who thought the church too wealthy, too much estranged from the true Christian religion, and too much dominated by Rome. Joseph disliked the French *philosophes* and the philosopher king, Frederick of Prussia, regarding them as smart-aleck *littérateurs*, but he was a philosopher himself in the sense then current, a philosopher in a position of power, the very type of the enlightened and educable prince to whom reformers looked to put through legislation that they wanted. He was also a democrat in a way, "a democrat from head to foot," as his biographer puts it,[2] in the sense that he had no respect for the established aristocracy whatsoever. He even had religious feelings, along somewhat modern lines of social concern. A child's parents give him only his body, he once said; his mind and soul he draws from God alone, and the development of this mind and soul depends on environment. A profound humanitarian, Joseph II believed that his various peoples could be helped by government action. He hated the past, the organized nobility, and the organized church as mere impediments in the way of reforms which without them would be easy.

He had the outlook of the true revolutionary, far more so than most of the democratic radicals so far considered in this book. He thought in terms of society as a whole: there was a right form of society, knowable to science or reason, and which the course of history was to bring about. The state—a just, strong, efficient, and modern state, operated by men who knew what was right—was the instrument to be used for social change. It would reorder society itself, emancipate the small man from dependence on the great, enrich, educate, enlighten, and elevate the people. To try to govern by agreement was a delusion, to seek acceptance of policies in advance was a waste of time, for most people did not know what they really wanted, and those who did

[2] Mitrofanov, 582.

wanted selfish ends. Joseph was a good deal like Robespierre, cold in personal relations yet with a genuine sympathy for what common people had to endure, inflexible in his principles, and distrustful and suspicious, easily ascribing the worst motives to those who opposed him. He saw no need to compromise with those whom he regarded as merely selfish, backward, or wrong-headed. And he saw no need to wait. He had waited long enough, he would say; and his views were indeed the product of experience as well as of temperament and enlightened philosophy. For fifteen years, as coruler, he had watched his mother's tactics of compromise. She had said that she "got to know people" from the Hungarian diet of 1764, and Joseph, when he became sole ruler in 1780, at last free from his mother, had formed a low opinion of the uppermost classes of his empire.

A quick review of his decrees (most of them too short-lived to be called reforms) may begin with the struggle for the mind, which involved a contest with the Catholic Church. Joseph in these actions was typical of the day, when the prestige of Rome was at a low ebb among Catholics, with Jansenism a significant force in France, Italy, and even Spain, and Febronianism favored by archbishops in Germany. Much of Joseph's program was in fact reminiscent of sixteenth-century Protestantism (as Catholic writers, more than Protestants, take pleasure in pointing out), a negative Protestantism, to be sure, without positive religious message, but full of the old objections to the Roman church. Candidates in theology were required to favor the religion of Jesus over "jejune scholastics."[3] Latin gave way to popular languages in the liturgy. The use of music and incense was restricted, and pilgrimages were forbidden. Contemplative religious orders were abolished as merely idle, and some 700 monastic houses (almost two-thirds) were suppressed, over 80,000,000 florins' worth of church property being confiscated. The state took on the responsibility of poor relief and care of the sick. Magic, apostasy, and marriage with non-Christians disappeared as crimes from the penal code. Protestants were freely tolerated, and the rights of Jews, as to place of residence and taxation, were extended. Marriage was recognized as a civil contract, and the validity of contested marriages was put under jurisdiction of civil courts. Husbands were allowed to keep illegitimate children in the home even against the wife's disapproval. And, as if to anticipate the French Revolution in laughable detail, illegitimate children re-

[3] Valsecchi, I, 108. F. Maass, *Der Josephinismus*, in *Fontes rerum austriacarum*, vols. 71 and 72 (Vienna, 1951-1953) is a collection of documents on church affairs.

ceived the right to the legal proceedings which the French called *recherche de la paternité.*

Parish priests were required to put civil above canon law in giving burial to Protestants, atheists, and suicides. They were also instructed to preach good citizenship in their sermons, including the acceptance of military conscription. Regular clergy were forbidden to recognize religious superiors outside the empire. Bishops were obliged to take an oath to the Emperor, and to obtain approval from the civil authorities before issuing pastoral letters to their dioceses. Boundaries of dioceses were redrawn, to correspond with administrative divisions of the civil government. Bishops and parish clergy received salaries payable by the state. As a beginning of democratization of the hierarchy, Joseph appointed a non-noble to be bishop of Olmütz, over the unanimous objection of the cathedral chapter. The canons were afraid, according to one observer, that Joseph would find too many "mere energetic common men" willing to accept bishoprics at only 12,000 florins a year.[4]

Joseph maintained the censorship of the press, but he used it to silence clerical opposition, and to favor all kinds of spokesmen of Jansenism and the Enlightenment. Never since the days of Luther had there been such an inundation of anti-Catholic writings. Clerics were travestied on the stage. Training schools for Catholic clergy were set up under government auspices. The universities were opened to Protestants. Their role, for Joseph, was the preparation of enlightened government officials; their textbooks were controlled, with a view to instilling love of country and usefulness to society.

The pope, dismayed, and fearing a complete schism, made a trip to Vienna. He obtained next to nothing from Joseph, and Prince Kaunitz greeted the Holy Father with no more than a civil handshake. The clergy itself, in the various Hapsburg dominions, with the exception of Belgium, offered little effective resistance. They had long been used to a certain subordination to the dynasty, and it was characteristic, in most Catholic countries before the French Revolution, for Catholic clergy to shy away from any exercise of authority on the part of Rome.

The Emperor also attacked the nobility, from a combination of humanitarian, military, and fiscal motives. In the elegant Vienna of Mozart, he subjected noblemen convicted of crimes to the same humiliating penalties that were inflicted on lesser people. He gave free rein to burghers in his civil service, and he put Jews in the army, and even made a few of them into nobles, as indeed his mother had done.

[4] Mitrofanov, 684 n. 2.

"Feudalism" was more a reality in Eastern than in Western Europe, for the ordinary country person was legally the subject of his lord rather than of the Emperor. "Subjection" or "hereditary subjection," *Untertänigkeit* or *Erbuntertänigkeit*, were the accepted legal terms for the relation of lord and peasant, the more extreme word for serf-dom, *Leibeigenschaft* or "body property," being usually avoided. The agrarian regime bore a resemblance to the system in parts of America. The landowner, in return for granting precarious and often revocable tenures, might receive payments in cash or kind, but he might also, as on American plantations, receive uncompensated and compulsory labor from his "subjects." He adjudicated disputes with them in his own court, which was usually a sitting room in his own house; he exercised police powers over them, and decided which of the young men should be taken from agricultural labor and taught skilled trades and crafts. None of his people might leave except with the lord's per-mission; if they left, they could be legally apprehended as fugitives. Nor could they marry off the premises without the lord's consent. Free neither to move nor to change occupation, they remained a labor force that went with the land itself. The landed property or dominion carried with it a local government over the local inhabitants. Great landowners with many estates, such as the magnates in Hungary or the higher nobility in Bohemia, thus enjoyed little subordinate mon-archies of their own.

Joseph's aim, in effect, in his agrarian program, though radical, was far from utopian; it was to convert the peasantry of his empire to the status of the peasantry in France or Western Germany before the French Revolution. Or, at least, the condition of the most fortunate West European peasant was his model. The peasant was to be a direct subject of the crown, something of a "citizen," an economic enter-priser, a taxpayer, and a potential soldier in his own right. While still having a "lord," he would pay what he owed to this lord not in forced labor but in money; and he would enjoy secure tenure of a piece of land, a tenure which could be inherited, sold, or mortgaged, and which would give ownership of the crop, in such a way as to approach private property in the modern sense. There is no doubt that this was what many peasants in the Hapsburg empire wanted for themselves. When in 1786 an agrarian revolt broke out on the Moravian border against Prince Liechtenstein, the rebels announced that they wished to be the emperor's not the prince's subjects. And such a development filled the landed nobility with alarm. "The peasant as a property-owner," declared one of the estate-assemblies, "will take an even more puffed up attitude toward his lord than he does already."[5]

Joseph II never abolished serfdom in the absolute and abrupt way in which slavery was later abolished in the United States. He proceeded by stages, though they were rapid; and he intended, to the end, that the lords should continue to draw substantial incomes from peasant labor. It is desirable to look closely at his agrarian program, for the better appraisal both of its revolutionary character and of the opposition that it aroused.

His first step was to abolish that personal dependency which reformers denounced as *Leibeigenschaft*. Maria Theresa had already abolished it on lands where she had sufficient control, that is, those that belonged to the crown. Joseph declared it abolished on lands of the church and aristocracy also. By decrees beginning in 1781 peasants gained the legal freedom to depart at will from landed estates, to take up new trades on the estates or elsewhere, and to marry without permission. The peasant was authorized to appeal from his lord's court to the emperor's district chief, though only after protest and notice given orally to the lord. This might be embarrassing to the peasant, who was required in many places to kiss hands and bow to the ground on approaching the lord or the lord's agents. Joseph tried for years to do away with this custom, in which he saw a badge of servility; doubtless to others it seemed the natural etiquette of interclass relations. The decrees, however, stated emphatically that the peasants, while now personally free, still owed, so long as they remained as agricultural workers on the estates, the same obedience and labor services as before; and they provided that recalcitrant workers might be chained, imprisoned on bread and water, or subjected to corporal punishment. Excessive punishment was forbidden; and the law prohibited certain new machines invented to facilitate the administration of floggings.

It became apparent to Joseph and his advisers that the peasant would never become an independent producer, or reliable taxpayer, so long as the lord had control of his time through exaction of labor services. Maria Theresa had attempted to limit these labor services, or robot, to three days a week. Joseph in 1783 made provision for optional conversion of robot to money payments by agreement of lord and peasant in individual cases; but since the lords preferred to keep control of their labor force very few such agreements were made. The problem of

[5] *Ibid.*, 600, 649.

forced labor became part of the problem of the great estates or lati-fundia, and so part of the problem of taxation.

The great noble estates, though not tax-exempt, were seldom ap-praised for tax purposes in correspondence to their real income. We have seen how in England land was valued for tax purposes at its valuation in 1692, and how in France repeated attempts were made to obtain realistic assessments. The problem was universal, and it was one of Joseph's main objectives to draw up a modern cadaster, or official register of true land values. He hoped thus to equalize the tax burden both among social classes and among regions of the empire. It was Joseph's belief, as it was that of Turgot and the French economists, that a direct tax on land, in proportion to income, might replace a complex array of indirect taxes that interfered with economic develop-ment. Such a tax, he observed in 1783, with "no difference between the possessions of men, to whatever estate or order they might belong," with no difference "between the property of noble and peasant, or of state and church," would allow all internal tolls and tariffs to be abolished, "and a free trade among twenty million people to emerge."[6] To enlarge the source of such a land tax, as well as to give incentive for production, Joseph offered crown lands and lands confiscated from the church for sale to private owners, though with some difficulty be-cause of the lack of private capital in his dominions. The new civil code, published in 1786, also favored the multiplication of individual properties, by prescribing equal division of inheritance in place of primogeniture, and restricting entails.

Several years passed in the preparation of the new cadaster. Valua-tions were based on actual income for the previous ten years. Owners had to make declarations of income, and surveyors, appraisers, and agricultural experts went to work. The result was the decree of Feb-ruary 10, 1789, in many ways the climax and turning point of Joseph's reign.

The decree again announced the principle of taxation in proportion to income from land regardless of social order. All landowners, in all provinces, were to pay twelve per cent of annual revenue, except that in Galicia they would for a time pay only eight per cent. Under the new system Bohemia, Austria, Styria, and Carinthia would pay less than in the past; Hungary, Moravia, Silesia, Gorizia, Carniola, and Galicia would pay more. (Belgium and Lombardy were not included.) The same decree, explaining that the state desired the peasant to be a

[6] *Ibid.*, 418.

property-owner, and able to pay his taxes, set forth a solution to the problem of forced labor. "The subject," announced the decree, meaning the peasant who was to have a secure and heritable tenure of land, "shall retain 70 gulden in a hundred of his gross income for his own needs, and only the remaining 30 shall be used for payments due to the nobleman and to the state."[7] Optional conversion of forced labor into money payments having led nowhere, conversion was now required. The law was not, however, inflexible. Money was rare in the villages, and peasants and lords were allowed, if they wished, by agreements in each case, to convert the money payments into payments in kind; but no such agreement could run for over three years (that is, they must not become perpetual); and all such agreements must be approved by the Emperor's district chief. In any case, the peasant, while free from forced labor, still owed payments to his lord as well as to the state. And in any case the lord, whether he received money or produce, would lose the forced labor. The government was to send special lawyers into the villages to counsel the peasants and assist them with legal papers. It may be surmised that their arrival was not anticipated by the gentry with much satisfaction.

The difficulty in Joseph's position was that it expressed no general or public demand, no groups of interested parties with formulated ideas and habits of working together. There was no one to whom he could appeal. His important followers were his own bureaucrats and officials. In the Hapsburg empire—the empire proper, without Belgium and Lombardy—property, position, education, breadth of awareness, and attention to public affairs were in large measure to be found, outside the government, only among the nobility. Significant middle-class people were those who worked for the state. State and nobility were the two big political forces, the church being successfully subdued. Only between the state and the nobility could there be a resounding quarrel. And the state represented only itself, drawing on no strength but its own. There was no large economically rooted middle class, pursuing affairs of importance and enjoying a certain independence. In the Hapsburg empire the extreme case was offered by Hungary, where the aggregate population of all towns was about equal to the number of the nobility—and not over a tenth of townsmen could be thought of as bourgeoisie. Nor was there sustained action toward realizable goals. There were numerous agrarian rebellions, and these might be useful to the government as an embarrassment to the nobles;

[7] *Ibid.*, 617.

but no one could manage or direct them; and they might easily turn against the government itself. The peasants were neither lawyers nor politicians, and understood nothing of needs other than their own. Freed to move, they objected to the labor services that remained. Freed of the labor services, they objected to the money payments that replaced them. Insurrections broke out after the decree of February 1789, especially as it became clear that landlords would resist its enforcement. Peasants refused to work, refused to pay, plundered manor houses, and committed atrocities against the landlords—as in France in the same year, and, at least locally, with even more violence. There was no upper stratum of the Third Estate, as in France, to make common cause for the time being with the rural masses. On the contrary, the peasant violence, by threatening actual anarchy, gave new arguments to the landlords, who could say with some truth, though hardly as the whole truth, that Joseph II had brought the country to ruin.

The only organized centers of opinion or action, outside the government, were the estate-assemblies or diets. These, it will be recalled, were conventions of landlords: Prague was the only city represented in the diet of Bohemia, all Hungarian cities had one vote in the diet of Hungary, thirty-one towns had one vote in the diet of Styria. It was the precise opposite of burgher Holland, where there was one vote for all nobles, and one for each city. The fact that the towns of Bohemia and Hungary were so largely German, even Budapest in the eighteenth century still being a German cultural colony, kept them apart from the surrounding life, separated the classes, and inhibited the growth of effective public opinion.

Joseph, who if not a mere doctrinaire was certainly a revolutionary, simply did not believe that the diets had any just or really legitimate powers. He regarded them merely as vested and special interests, and his propagandists kept repeating that the vaunted Hungarian constitution existed for only 300,000 persons. He saw nothing wrong if the Hungarian and other diets never met. And when the Hungarian county assemblies, in which the political strength of the country lay even more than in the diet, protested against conscription, against the cadaster, against peasant emancipation, and against almost everything else, he tried to suppress these assemblies also.

He could therefore put through his program only by "despotism," that is, by perfecting and enlarging his corps of administrators, inspectors, experts, and officials. They were indeed numerous, and were generally the most enlightened class in the empire; but they were not numerous enough, nor did they enjoy popular acceptance. There was a general repugnance toward men sent out from the capital. "It is inconceivable," said the estates of Lower Austria, "how such important matters [as agrarian reform] could be taken from the gentry [the *Adelsherren*] and turned over to a district chief who does not understand the local situation."

Many of the officials were nobles, if only because there were not enough university graduates or other trained persons from the middle class for the purpose. Nobly born officials often disapproved or sabotaged the imperial orders. In Hungary they resigned in droves. Joseph tried exchange of officials throughout the empire, sending Germans to Hungary, or Hungarians to Bohemia, or the Italian Martini to Belgium. He also created a political police, to watch over opposition and make confidential reports on the work of officials. Indeed, police work of this kind, in its modern form, seems to have begun with Joseph's attempted revolution. The word "police," at this time, it may be said, still retaining connotations of "polish," referred to the promotion of civil order in the sense of civilization itself.

Joseph also decided that, outside Belgium and Lombardy, there should be only one language for official business, and that this should be German. Educated Czechs already used German, and the Magyars used not Magyar but Latin as their political language, so that the decision to employ German was less of an outrage than later nationalist writers have sometimes made it seem; but as a sign of unwanted centralization, with connotations of German superiority, it aroused a good deal of opposition, and in fact the Czech and Magyar renaissances of the following generation were part of the reaction against Joseph II.

Lombardy was affected by Joseph's reign only in certain ways. There was no nobility with seigneurial powers, and no serfdom, so that the most fundamental difficulties did not arise. The Italians took their Catholicism more lightly than the Belgians, with ecclesiastics less potent and Jansenists more numerous than in Brabant; so that the Emperor's church policies caused no excessive consternation. Nevertheless, the reign of Joseph followed the same pattern in Lombardy as elsewhere. Attempts at reform in taxation, fiscal and economic matters, and legal and judicial organization ran up against the usual resistance, in this case that of urban magistracies and patriciates. It has been observed in Chapter IV, for example, that although Beccaria had written in Milan a famous book against torture, and the city was full of liberal thinkers, and although Maria Theresa had ended judicial torture in her German-Bohemian states, torture could not be ended in Milan because the Milanese magistrates believed it necessary to public security.[8] Joseph, here as elsewhere, ended up by crushing the local constituted bodies. He began to replace them with new courts and a new and more modern administrative system, manned by his own appointees and taking instructions from Vienna. His revolution reached its high point, in Lombardy, with the suppression, in 1786, of the Council of Sixty and of the Senate, the chief indigenous bodies of the city and the duchy respectively.

The reign of Joseph II thus presented for the whole empire the same dilemma as in Belgium: reform with despotism, or constitutional liberty with firm resistance to innovation. On the one hand there was the crown, with a program of centralization, looking toward a kind of equal though entirely passive citizenship for all persons as individuals. On the other hand were the historic and constituted bodies, committed to a society of stratified orders, to local autonomy, regional liberties, states rights, or estates rights in which local and class privileges were inseparable. The dilemma, abstractly considered, was not peculiar to the Hapsburg empire. Something like it had occurred in America in 1774, when the British government, in the interests of equalization within the empire, had annulled the charter of Massachusetts. Something like it occurred in France in 1788, when Brienne suppressed the Parlement of Paris. The dilemma as between despotism and purely historic liberty was broken in France and America by revolution. Neither horn was accepted. The subjects of the Hapsburg empire were tossed from one horn to the other.

Leopold II: The Aristocratic Counterattack

Joseph II died in February 1790, before his forty-ninth birthday. During his last illness the empire was in an uproar. Belgium had asserted its independence, and there were revolutionary manifestations in Hungary, where some of the leaders solicited foreign intervention, in this case Prussian, in support of independence, as Van der Noot was doing in Belgium. By the time of Joseph's death there was also general excitement over the French Revolution, from which various classes drew contradictory inspiration. To some, the French Revolution,

[8] Above, p. 106.

as seen in 1790, meant above all the assembly of the Estates General and the ending of royal despotism after almost two hundred years. This view could fire the enthusiasm of men interested in the Hungarian and Bohemian diets, for whom other aspects of the French Revolution were excesses. Burghers and peasants saw French events in a different light. The former, few as they were, began to talk of the *droits de l'homme* in the various languages of the empire. The peasants were in enough touch with the world to hear of French peasant rebellions and of the abolition of feudalism. The news from France, however, only inflamed a situation already agitated by internal causes. It was their emancipation by Joseph II, not an imaginary future emancipation by French example, that the peasants of the Hapsburg empire fought to preserve. And it was the control over their peasants, and other political liberties, of which Joseph II had deprived them, that the upper classes wished to regain.

Leopold, on succeeding Joseph, did not differ much from him in the substance of his ideas. His private opinion of nobility and clergy, and his hopes for a modernized Hapsburg empire, were much the same. Where Joseph, however, was willing to rely on himself and his own subordinates, and had only contempt for opposition, Leopold preferred to enlist support as widely as possible, if only, as Valsecchi has said, to divide up the responsibility. Leopold was something of a constitutionalist. I have already quoted the letter he wrote to Marie Christine at his accession, called forth by the revolution in Belgium, but expressing his actual principles, and applying to the disturbed condition of the whole empire as he found it. Here he stated, somewhat *en philosophe*, his idea of the social contract: that the sovereign drew authority from his people or peoples, that he had only such rightful powers as they had agreed to assign him, and that if he exceeded these powers they were absolved from obedience. Such ideas might seem subversive to the advisers of kings, but they were by no means novel; neither Locke nor Montesquieu had exactly invented them, for they came out of the Middle Ages and out of traditions of elective monarchy which still had vitality in eastern Europe. They were the common stock of political argument from the Transylvanian Alps to the Pennsylvanian Alleghenies.

Leopold, before becoming emperor, had been Grand Duke of Tuscany for twenty-five years, and had there carried out a remarkable series of reforms, in the spirit of the Enlightenment, in taxes, tariffs, land valuations, the gild regime, town government, and church affairs.

He had even worked out a project for a Tuscan constitution, to which a certain interest attaches in the context of the present book.

During the American war Leopold received a visit from the Tuscan-born Philip Mazzei, who hoped to borrow money from him for the State of Virginia. They naturally discussed American issues, and the newspapers at Florence, as elsewhere, gave attention to the American rebellion and the American constitutions. Leopold worked on his constitutional project from 1779 to 1782, during which it is clear, from the use of certain phrases, that he had the constitution of Virginia on his desk. The idea of proclaiming a constitution was probably suggested to him by events in America, but he drew its content from the European Enlightenment as a whole, and from his immediate practical needs in the politics of the grand duchy. What he needed was support against the nobility and the church, and he provided, therefore, for a representative assembly to be elected by taxpayers as taxpayers, not by members of the existing status groups. He hoped thereby to awaken the propertied middle class to political life as his own allies, and believed that his government, and in principle any government, would be the stronger if it rested explicitly on public approval and a measure of public participation. It was not that he expected his own authority to be reduced; on the contrary he expected it to be greater, for the assembly was to be consultative only, to learn what the ruler intended, and supply him with information: the first servant of the state, as enlightened princes now called themselves, would lead an interested people against "feudalism" and "clerocracy." Leopold's project never went into effect, because his own Italian advisers advised against it, insisting, probably rightly in 1782, that the people were not as interested as Leopold thought, and that if anyone was to clash with feudalism and clerocracy they much preferred that the Grand Duke do it himself.[9]

At any rate, when Leopold II in 1790 became Archduke of Austria and King of Hungary and Bohemia he probably thought that Virginia had a better constitution than any of his own numerous domains. On the other hand, he did not believe it possible, as Joseph did, to govern in outright defiance of all constituted bodies in the empire. He began to pacify his irate subjects by promising them their old constitutional

[9] C. Francovich, "La rivoluzione americane e il progetto di costituzione de granduca Pietro Leopoldo," in *Atti del XXXII Congresso di storia del Risorgimento italiano* (Rome, 1954), 201-07; F. Valsecchi, *Le riforme dell' assolutismo illuminato negli stati italiani, 1748-1789* (Milan, 1955), 217-22. Valsecchi discusses the constitutional project without reference to American influence.

liberties. He offered reconciliation to the estates of Belgium. He invited the Milanese to inform him of their desires. And on May 1, 1790, during his journey from Florence to Vienna, he summoned the estates of Bohemia, Moravia, Silesia, Upper Austria, Lower Austria, Styria, Carinthia, Carniola, Gorizia, and the Tyrol, each to meet in its usual provincial capital, and to bring in each case, according to the ancient custom, its lists of gravamina, complaints, grievances, and proposals, as the French Estates General had brought their *cahiers de doléances* to Versailles a year before. He prepared himself to hear from the diets of Hungary and of Transylvania, to whose meeting Joseph had been forced to consent shortly before his death. He made peace with Turkey, and reached enough of an agreement with Prussia to restrain the Hungarians.

The year 1790 may therefore be thought of as a time of active parliamentary life throughout much of the Western world. Not only was the French National Assembly busily at work, and of course the Parliament of Great Britain (as we have seen in discussing the Test Act), but the Congress of the United Belgian States was enjoying its brief year of life, the First Congress of the United States of America was assembled, and the great Four Years' Diet was sitting in Poland. And in every part of the miscellaneous Hapsburg empire indignant deputies were convening to uphold their rights.

What rights did these deputies wish to uphold? This question is fundamental to an understanding of the European counterrevolution of the 1790's. It is also readily answerable, for the *cahiers de doléances* of the Hapsburg empire, though very unlike those of France in 1789, were equally explicit.

All the diets made broad statements of constitutional principle. A constitution, declared the Estates of Bohemia, was "a treaty or agreement between the sovereign and the nation which . . . must bind both parties equally." There must be an "indestructible constitution," with government by "consent" and security for "the persons and property of inhabitants of the kingdom."[10] The Bohemian diet drew on Montesquieu's doctrine of intermediate powers: "There can be no simple abstract idea of the State as consisting only of the monarch and a single class of subjects. . . . Between the two there must be unrestricted intermediate orders, each of whose individual members governs a portion of the people. In the kingdom of Bohemia these are the estate-owners, who, through their influence over their dependents, form a vigorous

[10] Kerner, *Bohemia*, 130-32.

instrument of the Ruler's executive power."[11] In short, each seigneur should govern his own peasants. Above the local level, the estates interpreted the separation of powers to mean that the diet possessed legislative powers; the ruler, executive.

Hungary, which had retained far more of its autonomy than Bohemia, was even more constitutionally minded. The Hungarians were fond of comparing themselves to England in the matter of parliamentary liberties; a hundred copies of Delolme's *Constitution of England* were sold in one day on October 14, 1791. The Hungarians insisted that their diet or parliament was the legislature, the King the executive. They claimed, however, more than Delolme would have ever conceded, namely, the right to make a new contract with each King at the time of his coronation. Since Joseph II had refused to be properly crowned as King of Hungary, and had even removed the crown physically from the kingdom, the Hungarians took the position that they owed him no allegiance. Coronation, announced the county assembly of Bihar, was no empty or superstitious ceremony, but the sign "that the Nation confers power on the King it crowns," and that "he can become King only by our consent and by the force of the laws." Or as the county of Pest affirmed, in the language of the day: "By the social contract which creates the state, sovereignty lies in the hands of the people; Mother Nature has written this maxim in all hearts, and no right minded Ruler could bring it into doubt."[12]

Even the Tyrol said it should crown its ruler in return for a confirmation of liberties, and little Upper Austria insisted on the distinctiveness of its own constitution and privileges.

Leopold was not personally inclined to doubt the social contract in principle. He retorted, to justify absolutism in the empire, and echoing his late brother, that none of the diets really represented its "nation." In Bohemia, with almost 3,000,000 people (excluding Moravia), there were only 174 noble family names, most of them not even Czech, but a medley of O'Kelleys, Desfours, Schwarzenbergs, Trautmannsdorfs, Vrbnas, and Haugwitzes, deposited in that country by the Hapsburgs after the revolt of 1618. Only these nobles, with a few clergy, sat in the diet, the peasants and cities (except Prague) having no representation of their own. The Magyar nobility was more numerous, running from great magnates to small county gentry. If, as said, there were 300,000 of them, in a country of 7,000,000 (without Transyl-

[11] Mitrofanov, 628.
[12] *Ibid.*, 300-01.

vania), they constituted over 4 per cent of the population. In this case they were over twice as numerous proportionately as the French *noblesse*, and more numerous than the more genteel classes in England.[13] They were still, as Leopold said, hardly identical with the nation. Nor were the Magyars as a whole identical with Hungary. One of the worst features of the peasant revolts of 1789 was the ethnic hatreds they revealed. When the Vlach peasants rebelled in Transylvania they spared Rumanian or German landlords but turned ferociously against those who were Magyars.

In Belgium, when the estates revolted against the Emperor, a recognizably democratic party soon took form, which wished an enlargement of representation in the estates as well as mere liberation of existing estates from the central power. We have seen the rise of these Belgian democrats, and their annihilation by the estates party. It has been explained, also, how Leopold and his advisers in Belgium, though sympathetic in a way to the democrats, were unwilling to give them any support, partly from an alarm caused by the French Revolution. Something of the same development was evident, though less marked, in the other Hapsburg lands.

At Milan, for example, Leopold restored the Senate and the Council of Sixty which Joseph had abolished. These were exclusive bodies of oligarchic patricians. Reformists at Milan, men like P. Verri, Melzi d'Eril, and F. Visconti, men who for years had favored the Austrian absolutism as the means of carrying through reforms, and who had turned against it only in 1786 when Joseph destroyed Milan's ancient political bodies, now favored the restoration of the Senate and Council which they had long criticized as obstructions to progress. These liberals had turned from absolutists to constitutionalists after 1786. They did not stand fast, however, merely on the existing constitution. They wished the magistracies of the city and duchy to be somewhat broadened and opened up. Verri, when Leopold solicited Milanese opinion in 1790, asked for a fixed constitution, with inviolable laws and security of property, but he also went further by asking for some sort of elected representative body. He and his friends called for more

[13] Kerner, *Bohemia*, 70-71; Marczali, *Hungary*, 104, 164. The highest estimate for the French nobility is 400,000 in a population of 25,000,000. Patrick Colquhoun, *A Treatise on Indigence* (London, 1806), in his careful tabulation of social strata, put 314,000 people in the classes down through "gentlemen and ladies," higher civil servants, the law and "eminent clergymen," but excluding all merchants, out of a total estimated English population of 9,344,000. It may be that relatively more had a role in political life in Hungary than in England.

freedom of discussion for the Council within itself, with full participation by all sixty of its statutory members, not merely by the inner coterie. The dominant patricians refused all such demands. Leopold took their side, choosing to work with men who had actual power rather than those who had mere ideas. The Lombard liberals, disillusioned with the Austrian absolutism in 1786, and with their own aristocracy in the years that followed, looked with increased sympathy on the French Revolution, and collaborated with Bonaparte on his arrival in 1796.

In the empire proper the towns had long since been reduced to political nullities, and little was to be feared from the urban middle class. The estates, being so largely agrarian, objected that individual burgher non-nobles had sometimes risen to high office under Joseph. The Bohemian diet asked for an end to this practice, "since a whole series of occupations is open to burghers, whereas nobles can look forward only to a few civil and military employments, which in justice should therefore be reserved to them."[14] When it seemed that Leopold, to please the Hungarian diet, might restrict public office to nobles, he drew sporadic protests from lesser Magyars, some of whom reasoned suspiciously like the Abbé Sieyès: "Nature itself has made men equal. It is surely nothing to reproach us with, if we think ourselves a necessary estate in the country. We are workers who supply all necessities; craftsmen who furnish comforts; merchants and manufacturers who bring foreign products into the land; teachers and writers who form hearts and minds; in a word, we are the estate that teaches, protects, and supports—*der lehrt, wehrt und ernährt.*"[15]

Even the peasants made efforts to obtain political recognition. Indeed it was only from the peasants that the estates had much to fear. In Bohemia, early in 1792, by some concerted action that seems not well understood, peasants in many districts took it into their heads to send uninvited delegates to the diet, and a good many actually started for Prague. The police and army, alerted throughout the country, turned back or arrested various rustics on the roads. Self-styled deputies from two districts actually reached the city, where of course they could accomplish nothing.

In Transylvania, the eastern part of the kingdom of Hungary, the

---

[14] E. Denis, *La Bohème depuis la Montagne Blanche*, 619.

[15] Mitrofanov, 660. Compare the sarcastic Latin of an *Oratio pro Leopoldo II* at the time of the diet of 1790: "Populus in hac sanctione sunt praelati, barones, magnates et nobiles; exiguus hic hominum numerus superbia . . . inflata sese super humanitatem extollit." *Ibid.*, n. 2.

same basic problem presented itself with national complications. The Transylvanians did not attend the Hungarian diet; their estates met at Klausenburg, or Cluj. The Transylvanian constitution put heavy emphasis on Protestant liberties and on the rights of the three Transylvanian "nations"—the Magyars, the Székelys, who were like Magyars, and the Germans, who were called Saxons. The mass of the population, however, and hence of the agricultural workers, was of a kind of Rumanian then called Vlach. With the help of two bishops they submitted a petition called the *Supplex Libellus Valachorum*, requesting equality with the three dominant Transylvanian nations, and hence representation in the diet. Leopold referred the petition to the diet itself, where it caused a sensation, of which the outcome could be predicted. The diet concluded that, though a few Vlachs were nobles, they were generally not a landowning class and so had no basis on which to claim political rights, and that they were in any case too crude and uneducated to be given a share in public business. No more was heard of the Vlach petition.[16]

It was Hungary, of all Hapsburg lands except Belgium, that came closest to revolution in 1789 and 1790. In their counties and in the two houses of their parliament the Hungarians were used to a good deal of political action. County assemblies formed committees of correspondence, and extorted the summoning of the estates from the dying Joseph, with much exclamation over the French Revolution, and much talk of the Belgian Revolution as an uprising of fellow Hapsburg subjects; nor was the "convention of Philadelphia" overlooked in the search for analogies. The meeting of the diet at Pest instead of Pressburg was itself a revolutionary departure. Spectators, including women, were admitted to the galleries, and people wore cockades to demonstrate their zeal.

It had long been the custom, at the accession of each King, to issue an agreement between the King and the diet, called a Diploma, usually adapted from the Diplomas of preceding reigns. Now, however, the radical group in the diet maintained that an entirely new social contract was necessary before Leopold could reign. They held that, since Joseph had never been crowned, no monarchy really existed

<hr/>

[16] See N. Iorga, *Études roumanes: Idées et formes littéraires françaises dans le Sud-est de l'Europe* (Paris, 1924), 57; E. Pascu, "Mémoires et protestations des Roumains de Transylvanie et de Hongrie de 1791 à 1892," in *Revue de Transylvanie* (1939), 330-36; H. Marczali, *Magyarország Története III Károlytól a bécsi Congressusig* (History of Hungary from Charles III to the Congress of Vienna) (Budapest, 1898), 541 ff., for knowledge of whose contents I am indebted to Mr. Peter F. Sugar.

in Hungary at all, and that Hungary was at the moment in a state of natural liberty, free to contrive an entirely new Diploma in which new and different institutions of government should be set up. The Hungarians thus acted out both their own constitutional principles and the little stage play of European political theorists, by which man in a state of nature sat down to bargain with his future ruler.

Meanwhile, offstage, quite apart from parliamentary life, the peasant insurrection raged, the worst in Hungary since 1514. Though the first disturbances were among the Rumanian peasants to the east, they soon spread to the Magyar-speaking peasants of the central plain. Class barriers were greater than language barriers, and class sympathies stronger than national sympathies, among the lower classes as among the upper. The Magyar peasant looked across an unbridgeable gulf to the Magyar noble who spoke the same language, particularly detesting the numerous lesser nobles, landless or nearly landless, who lived from the work of two or three serfs or from the income of some county office. Only in the sense ascribed to Joseph II were these peasants "democratic": they disliked the nobility, they had no faith or interest in diets or parliaments, and they willingly accepted government absolutism as favorable to themselves. In fact, the lawyers stationed in the villages by Joseph II to befriend the rural population now helped to give expression to the unrest. A Decretum of the Peasants, of unknown authorship, was distributed through several counties of central Hungary in May 1790. Since it well reveals the violent tenor of life in this land of servile labor, and has not, I think, been hitherto published in English—the whole agrarian radicalism of Eastern Europe that coincided in time with the French Revolution having probably been underestimated further west—it is worth extended quotation.

The Decretum began by complaining that peasants were yoked by the landlords like oxen, "six days out of the week." (Six days of robot was contrary to the laws of Maria Theresa.) The lords, it was said, "want to consider our blood like that of dogs and pigs so as to mistreat, beat and kill us as they please. They say they have bought us out of their pockets, like pigs, and can therefore kill us as pigs. They want to force the king to yield them this power over us. . . .

"Are we pigs? Do we not have human blood, too? . . . Are the armies that faithfully serve the king not composed of our sons? . . . Do we not deserve for all this that each of us should own a small piece of the country's soil?

"Let us advance . . . raise up our sticks, pitchforks and axes against the cruel, parasitic, time stealing, country ruining, king robbing lords."

There followed seven numbered demands, of which the first was that no comma be changed in Joseph's edicts—"holy, useful and just as if God had dictated them." Male servants should abandon their lords within one week; otherwise the lord's household would be murdered. Should a village stand by its lord, even the peasant children would be killed. County officers should go away; those who stayed would be hung up by the legs and have their flesh torn with pincers. Taxes should be paid to the King alone. "We elect as king the man against whom they have rebelled because of Joseph's justice . . . the brother of our dear Joseph, Peter Leopold II." A wooden column should be built in each village in honor of Joseph, until a stone one could be provided.

"Why should we have a diet? We need none, since we have a king. If there is nevertheless to be one we had better be informed; otherwise we will arrange for a diet the like of which was never seen."[17]

The spirit shown in this document and in others, more the spirit of a Mau Mau rebellion than of the French peasant revolts of 1789, naturally spread terror in Hungary. Where in France, in August 1789, the Assembly pacified the peasants, and avoided appeal to the army, by enacting the August decrees for the "abolition of feudalism," no such concessions, or any concessions, came from the diet at Budapest in 1790. Given the composition of the diet, concession to dangerously enraged serfs was scarcely possible. At war with its own people, the diet was in a weak position against the king. An army of peasant soldiers would be poor defenders of the famous Hungarian constitution. Class struggle made impossible any successful revolution in Hungary.

The internal or purely parliamentary politics of the diet, though significant, was therefore somewhat unrealistic. Since the nobles were numerous and divided, the small gentry being opposed to the magnates, and since the towns sent deputies who could speak, though restricted in voting, and since Hungarians were by no means unacquainted with ideas of the European Enlightenment, two parties or groupings formed in the preparation of the new Diploma to be presented to Leopold before his coronation. One group wanted things as

---

[17] *Ibid.*, with thanks again to Mr. Sugar for translation of the Decretum. On the Hungarian diet of 1790-1791 there is a two-volume work by Marczali which I have not been able to use: *Az 1790-91-diki Országgyülés* (Budapest, 1907).

they always had been. Another, accused of susceptibility to French ideas, wanted diets in the future to meet in a single house only, the King to have only a suspensive veto for three diets, a civic oath by all persons including clergy to uphold the constitution, a national army, and a national guard. These ideas were in fact inspired by the example of France, as were some of the arguments. It was to have "one country, one law, one public good" that an upper chamber of higher nobles and prelates was to be abolished. The contrary argument was ancient long before the French Revolution: that "without a nobility we shall all be brothers and Quakers."[18]

Then on August 15, 1790, Budapest learned that Leopold was moving eleven regiments of Austrian soldiers into Hungary. His aim was to impress the diet and to quell the peasants. It was one of the steps (followed by the sending of troops to Belgium the next December) by which he restored his authority in his shattered empire. On the news of the troop movement, the two factions in the diet came to a speedy compromise. They submitted a Diploma to Leopold, which he refused to accept. He offered, and they accepted, the Diploma which Maria Theresa had negotiated in 1740, favorable to the Hungarian political classes and abrogating most of Joseph's edicts, but with a few modifications, as will be seen, in favor of the peasants.

The peasant problem, the problem of serfdom, of the relation between the lord and his labor in the remotest villages, or, conversely, the relation of government with its subjects, was the fundamental issue underlying constitutional and political argument throughout the empire. The diets advanced an array of reasons for the necessity of forced labor and personal subjection. Their view of the qualities of European white men five or six generations ago will remind Americans of views heard nearer home in other connections. The picture they drew was probably not wholly mistaken, given the unfortunate history of the East European peasantry for three centuries before 1790; but they did not propose anything that would improve it.

The agricultural worker was said to be so lacking in self-respect, honor, civilized sentiments, foresight, industry, self-control, responsibility, and general motivation that only the fear of corporal punishment kept him in the fields. "The vulgar spirit of the Bohemian peasant," according to the diet of Bohemia, "was not affected by any injured feeling of honor," so that it was useless to put him under arrest.[19] Jail, as provided in Joseph's penal code, was illusory as a means

18 From a seminar paper prepared by Mr. Sugar. 19 Kerner, 292.

of correcting laziness because the health officials had closed the land-lords' jails, according to the Bohemian estates, or because jail was more comfortable than the peasant's home, according to those of Galicia.[20] In fact, abolition of *Leibeigenschaft* was bad even for the peasants, declared the Galician diet, since peasants would starve without a friendly master's aid in time of famine. The people, said the Hungarians, were beginning to lose the feelings of "gratitude, obedience, loyalty and respectfulness which they had so gladly shown so long as the old laws lasted." The lower classes did not know how to use freedom, and if left alone would sit idly in taverns. On the other hand, one need not feel too sorry for them, since they were accustomed to hard work. They were so desperately poor and so ignorant, lacking animals, tools, and knowledge, that they could never carry on cultivation by themselves. They were too childish to respond to monetary incentives. "The harvest," said the Galicians, "will depend on the caprice of the peasants, who cannot be made to work even for wages. . . . They would only lounge and drink all the more, and not pay a Kreutzer to the landlord or the state."[21] We hope Your Majesty does not suppose that we wish to oppress anyone, pleaded the assembly of the Hungarian county of Pest; "we only wish to curb a licentiousness that is harmful to the common people themselves and may have unfortunate consequences for the general welfare." Scripture allows the *subjectio servorum*, said the county of Szabolcs. Of course all men are equal *ante societatem*, but in society there must be ranks. We realize that all human beings desire to be free (this from the county of Hont), but Providence has made men kings, nobles, and servants; and toward our servants we shall always show Christian mercy. The people are still so far from a desirable state of civilization (*a desiderata civilisatione*, in the Hungarian Latin of another county) that "they would fall into sad extremes if they were freed from the wholesome effects of corporal pains."[22] Direct physical punishment by estate managers is necessary, announced the Diet of Moravia, "since it is certain that all classes of men and the brutal masses of peasants in particular cannot always be brought to obedience by good treatment, since it is also known that the extreme insubordination of the rural populations is provoked by the numerous formalities nowadays required [such as

---

[20] *Ibid.*, and Mitrofanov, 629-37.

[21] *Ibid.*, 635-36, 645; Denis, *Bohême*, 619. The Bohemian Estates warmly favored the *nexus subditelae* (Mitrofanov, 631 n. 2), rather than the "cash nexus" contemplated by Joseph and deplored by Carlyle and other nineteenth-century antiliberals.

[22] Mitrofanov, 636.

Joseph's provision for corporal punishment only with knowledge of the district chief], and since in a word a few blows inflicted on the spot have more effect than severer penalties that may be too delayed."[23] The whole peasant trouble, said the Moravian count Poteani, was stirred up by agitators and outsiders. It was outrageous for revolutionary scribblers to refer to compulsory labor as slavery.

At one time, in the Bohemian diet, the remarks on the vulgar and slovenly Bohemian character became so extreme that a few members, mainly nobles who were Czechs themselves, took offense that "part of the nation" should be so insulted. Most of the diet was puzzled to hear peasants called part of the nation. The episode was significant, for the truth is that in Bohemia and Hungary, as in Galicia and the part of Poland that was still independent, the "nation" did mean the political nation of nobles and gentry. It should be added that men who worked for the imperial government, from Joseph and Leopold down through the central administration, consistently denied that the peasants were as bad as they were said to be by their own lords.

Leopold II, in the two years of his reign, managed at least to hold the Hapsburg empire together. Most of Joseph's reforms he was obliged to repeal. He yielded on all fronts to the aristocratic demand for constitutional liberties. Only in detail could he maintain parts of the reforms in which he really believed. On the peasant question the most that he could obtain was a compromise. The estates accepted Joseph's abolition of *Leibeigenschaft* in 1781, and the peasant remained free in law to change his place of residence or his occupation. But Joseph's decree of February 1789 was rescinded. Peasants who stayed on the land, as most of them did until the industrial era, remained subject to forced labor and corporal punishment until the revolution of 1848. The compromise greatly favored the landlords. Enlightened despotism in the Austrian empire was over. Aristocracy, estates rights, states rights, traditional constitutions, and constituted bodies had prevailed.

This outcome has often been ascribed to fear of the French Revolution, and presented as one phase of a European reaction to that event. In this view the violence of the French Revolution is seen as a cause, or even a justification, for a conservative resurgence throughout Europe. It seems more likely that, while the revolution in France heightened feeling on all sides, causes native to the Hapsburg empire are enough to explain the failure of Joseph II. Had Joseph lived, he

[23] Denis, 619; Kerner, 292.

could have done only as Leopold did. Effects of the French Revolution became more evident a little later, after the war began and the French monarchy was overthrown. Meanwhile the course of revolution in France was affected by the state of the Hapsburg empire. The disaffection of peasant soldiers did not strengthen the Hapsburg armies in the War of the First Coalition, and the eleven regiments that were kept in Hungary were unavailable for use against France. The warlike Magyars, like the peaceful Dutch, lacked enthusiasm for the monarchist crusade of 1792; not until 1797 did Hungarian volunteer forces appear in the field against the French Republic.

It is said also, in what may be called the school of the history of ideas, that Joseph was a pure rationalist engaged in a vain attempt to change the realities of the world. His reign, says Professor Valsecchi, was a war of reason against history, and it was the *vendetta della storia,* the revenge of history, that destroyed his work. To me it seems that something tougher than history was against him.[24]

Three Charters of the North

The problem in this book is not to give equal attention to the separate histories of all countries, but to indicate trends on the eve of the Wars of the French Revolution, and in particular, in the present chapter, to show the point at which disputes between crown and nobility had then arrived. It is to set forth also the limitations of enlightened despotism, or disadvantages or unacceptable choices inherent in that form of polity: namely, either that the monarchy prevailed over nobility and other kinds of privilege, at the cost of arbitrary power, as in the case of Joseph II; or that the monarchy, in order to govern at all, and to assure itself of necessary support, granted concessions, as in the case of Leopold II, to the very feudal or aristocratic interests that enlightened despotism made it a principle to oppose.

[24] If we are wary of the philosophical conservatism in Valsecchi's view, *Assolutismo,* I, 138, which sees Joseph in terms of *il regno della ragione* and the *vendetta della storia,* we can derive even less satisfaction from recent Hungarian Marxist studies, which blame the Hapsburgs for "arresting our bourgeois national evolution," find their "so-called enlightened absolutism" designed to preserve feudalism, and assert as a dogmatic principle that "absolute monarchy is the highest stage of feudal society." See *Études des délégués Hongrois au Xe Congrès international des sciences historiques à Rome* (Budapest, 1955), 18, 19, 73. For these writers the Hapsburgs were colonialist exploiters, and it was the broad masses, not the aristocracy, that represented the desire for national independence. There is more evidence for Mitrofanov's repeated statement that the peasants in all parts of the empire remained *Kaisertreu.* Maria Theresa, Joseph, and Leopold represented the highest stage of "feudalism" in that feudalism was precisely what they did not want—but could not wholly get rid of.

Little has been said of Spain in the present pages. It is not that Spain was unaffected by currents of the time. On the contrary, a good many Spaniards were alive to some of the main ideas of the European Enlightenment; but what mainly concerned them was to reverse the long deterioration in Spain itself, to revive Spanish commerce, to improve mining technology, to make administration more efficient, and stress the practical arts and the ideal of social utility as against the older religious outlook of the country. In Charles III Spain possessed one of the most celebrated and successful of the "enlightened despots." Compared to France or the Hapsburg empire, however, it was a non-political kind of "despotism"; there was less conflict between the monarchy and constituted or corporate bodies representing the nobility or other privileged interests. Nor does any acute class consciousness between bourgeoisie and aristocracy seem to have developed. Even so, according to a recent study, the effect of the French Revolution, in Spain as elsewhere, was to throw doubt on enlightened despotism as a means of social progress.[25]

The limitations of enlightened despotism, the lengths beyond which it could not go in the reconciling of social classes, may be seen in Sweden, Prussia, and Russia. They become particularly evident in connection with three important documents contemporaneous with the French Revolution: the Charter of the Nobility in Russia in 1785, the Swedish Act of Union and Security of 1789, and the Prussian General Code of 1791. Since apparently none of these is available in English, though all were of lasting significance in their respective countries, they are printed as an appendix at the end of this book, together, for contrast, with the preamble to the revolutionary French constitution of 1791.

It has been told in preceding pages how the young Gustavus III, in 1772, put an end to the Freedom Era in Sweden, supplanting a half-century of noble domination with an enlightened absolutism which was more favorable to the non-noble classes, and which won the praises even of the Genevese democrat turned constitutionalist, J. L. Delolme.[26] Gustavus proved, however, to be a fantastic monarch. Much enamored

[25] R. Herr, *The Eighteenth-Century Revolution in Spain* (Princeton, 1958).
[26] See above, pp. 99-103 and 146; for the present paragraphs R. Svanström and C. F. Palmstierna, *Short History of Sweden* (Oxford, 1934), 264-94; R. N. Bain, *Gustavus III and His Contemporaries*, 2 vols. (London, 1894); B. J. Hovde, *The Scandinavian Countries, 1720-1865: the Rise of the Middle Classes*, 2 vols. (Boston, 1943), I, 191-94, 207-19; *Sveriges historia till våra dagar, Vol. X. Den Gustavianska Tiden 1772-1809*, by Ludwig Stavenow (Stockholm, 1925), 207-39, for knowledge of whose contents I am indebted to Professor Arne Odd Johnsen of Oslo.

of France, both of the court life and the men of letters whom he had seen there in his youth, he spent large sums to adorn his nothern Versailles, wrote poems and dramas, sponsored the arts, and indulged in an array of extravagant pleasures, which included an unnatural predilection for the numerous page boys in his entourage. He also entertained military ambitions, laying plans to conquer Norway from Denmark, and avenge Sweden on Russia. Members of the nobility continued to resist him, looking back with regret on their era of freedom, and now aroused by the spectacle of America. Sixty-four Swedish officers had served in America in the French forces, of whom the most famous was Axel de Fersen, Marie Antoinette's admirer. In Finland, which belonged to the Swedish crown, and where the nobility were Swedish, there were noblemen who dreamed of a war of independence in which one of them would be the George Washington. At the diet of 1786 the King asked for a modern army, to be paid for from taxes, in place of the levies of peasants supplied locally by the lords. Led by the nobility, all four estates in the diet—nobles, clergy, townsmen, and peasants—expressed opposition to this project. The King, nevertheless, when Russia became involved in a war with Turkey, seized the opportunity to launch an attack on St. Petersburg.

Some of the nobles in both Sweden and Finland, disapproving of this adventure, and regarding Gustavus III as their main adversary, made collusive arrangements with the Russians. To Gustavus this was of course treason in wartime. It revealed the old habit of disunion, by which parties within Sweden had long brought in rival foreign powers against each other; and it threatened Sweden with the fate of Poland, from which Gustavus claimed to have saved it in 1772. In fact a group of Swedish officers and noblemen appealed to the tsarina to make peace, and signed an agreement with each other in 1788 at Anjala near the border, very much like one of the "confederations" of Polish nobles, and in particular the confederation of Targovica of 1792, which led to the second partition of Poland.

The Swedish diet met again in February 1789. Like the French Estates General of that year, it fell into a schism between the nobility and the other orders. The difference is that Gustavus III did what some have wished Louis XVI had done. He took the side of the commons against the nobles—and confirmed the nobles in their inveterate hostility to himself. Ordering the nobles out of the hall, he carried on the proceedings without them—"a strange sight," said an observer, "a king with nothing but commoners around him . . . but not an unpleasant one." He put nineteen noblemen under arrest, including Axel de Fersen's father. In a speech to the three non-noble orders he called for unity against foreigners and equality of rights among citizens, and he then read his Act of Union and Security, which the three "unredeemed" orders enthusiastically accepted. A week later the nobility met to consider the act and flatly rejected it; the King, taking the chair in person, declared it passed.[27]

The Act of Union, while restating the constitution of 1772, actually put greater powers in the hands of the King, while also assuring more civil equality for the population in general. "All subjects enjoy the same rights," it declared, six months before the French Declaration of the Rights of Man and Citizen; and all were to be judged in the same courts. There must, however, be both noble and non-noble judges in these courts. "All orders of the state have the same right to possess or acquire land." Offices "shall be accessible to all subjects of whatever rank or condition," except that the very highest offices and the court dignities were reserved for nobles. The diet had the right to consent to taxation, but in other matters to deliberate only on proposals which the King put before it. All future kings of Sweden were to be required to accept the act.

The Act of Union was as successful an example as we may find of enlightened despotism providing civil equality and even a measure of public participation in government. It gave general satisfaction, so much so that Swedish burghers and peasants, though interested, watched the subsequent revolutionary events in Europe with a feeling of detachment. The act carried with it, however, two troublesome corollaries: it left the King free to pursue projects dangerous to the country, and it left the nobility a dissatisfied and potentially revolutionary class.

Gustavus extricated himself from the Russian war by a lucky victory at sea; developed a vague aspiration to become King of Poland, putting himself and his court into Polish costume; and, as the last of his fantastic projects, offered to lead the European powers in a crusade against the French Revolution. With his high ideas of kingship, he had even less use for popular than for aristocratic rebellion. Kept at a distance by his brother monarchs, who could not agree on a policy toward France, and who in any case thought Gustavus' volunteering to lead their forces eccentric, he became involved in plans

[27] Svanström and Palmstierna, 283; for the Act of Union see Appendix III, item 3, below; the King's speech was printed in the British *Annual Register* for 1789 (London, 1792), 334-36.

to rescue the French King and Queen. To this end he worked with Axel de Fersen, whose father he had arrested two years before. He had a notion that after landing with 16,000 Swedes and 8,000 Russians in Normandy he could cut through to Paris, while French troops presumably loyal to their King and Queen marched on Paris from the east, after which the French King, restored to independence, would convene the old provincial parlements or estates, pronounce the National Assembly illegal, and undo its work. Nothing came of this grand design. He therefore concocted another, and on June 16, 1791, arrived with fanfare at Aachen in the Rhineland, intending to use that city as a dramatic meeting place with Louis XVI on the latter's escape from France. This plan failed, too, as is well known, because the coach in which Louis XVI and Marie Antoinette were riding, driven by Axel de Fersen, was stopped on June 21 at Varennes.[28]

Meanwhile, a kind of revolutionary sentiment spread among the irritated nobility of Sweden, many of whom, like nobles in Hungary, understood revolution to mean the downfall of kings, and admired the French Revolution as the nemesis of tyrants. A handful of them resorted to direct action. Gustavus III was assassinated at the opera in Stockholm on March 16, 1792. It was only a month before the war between France and Austria. All those involved in the death of the monarchist crusader were noblemen. There is an illuminating postlude with the same ironic message. When another king of Sweden died in 1810, it was again popularly suspected (though falsely) that he had been done to death by a conspiracy of nobles. Count Axel de Fersen, celebrated in French royalist annals as the paladin of monarchy, was murdered in the streets of Stockholm, in 1810, by a mob which believed him to be guilty of poisoning the king of Sweden.

Mr. Liston, the British Minister at Stockholm, reported at the time of Gustavus' death that members of the conspiracy could not agree on what they wanted. The "elder part," he said, "desired the ancient form of the Swedish government [before 1772], or to imitate that of England; while the younger men were eager to adopt the greatest part of the modern ideas of France."[29] In fact the government remained unchanged in 1792, since the dead King's supporters were not dislodged. An enlightened absolutism remained in effect. It assured advantages to the non-noble classes; but its weakness was that the no-

---

[28] For details of Gustavus' "crusade" against the French Revolution see Bain, *op.cit.*, II, 103-52.

[29] Great Britain, Historical Manuscripts Commission, *The Manuscripts of J. B. Fortescue Preserved at Dropmore*, 10 vols. (London, 1892-1927), v, 518.

bility remained very unmanageable, and the King himself not even personally safe.

More concessions were made to aristocratic principles in Russia and in Prussia. These were both very different countries from Sweden. In Sweden all four estates had long enjoyed rights of one kind or another, and the diet in which they met had a lively tradition. In both Russia and Prussia (most of Prussia then lay east of the Elbe) the country people were mostly serfs, the towns were small, sparse, few, and feeble, and the important class was the serf-owning landlords. Nothing like a European assembly of estates had ever developed in Russia, and those of the component regions of the Prussian monarchy had mostly fallen into decay.

Of the Russian empire in the eighteenth century it may be said that no one had any lawful rights on whose continuing enjoyment he could rely. This was as true of the upper classes as of the lower. Indeed, European commentators noticed a lack of class structure as they understood it. There were big men and little men, there were rich and poor, and those higher or lower on the ladder of government service, and some who made a boast of their ancestry. There was not, however, the respect for birth and station that were common in Europe. High rank gave no assurance of independence, nor of that "honor" said by Montesquieu to be necessary to free monarchy, nor even any security from physical punishment or public humiliation. The Empress Anna, on one occasion, annoyed at Prince Golytsin, made him squat in the corner pretending to be a hen, clucking and cackling on a pile of straw as if laying an egg. "A gentleman is nothing here," reported the German Schlözer in 1781. "Birth here gives but little claim to preference or consideration," said an Englishman; "both are regulated by the degree of rank acquired by service."[30] Service meant the state service which had become an obligation for all classes.

With the Empress Catherine II there began to be significant changes. The horrors of Pugachev's rebellion, the worst servile uprising in generations, made her realize her dependency on the landlords for the effective government of the empire, and her expansionist foreign policy made it necessary for her to have a reliable officer corps. She had reason also to know, more than a king of Sweden, the actual

[30] A. Leroy-Beaulieu, *The Empire of the Tsars and the Russians*, 3 vols. (London and New York, 1893), I, 391; Bruckner, *Katharina die Zweite* (Berlin, 1883), 473; W. Tooke, *View of the Russian Empire* (London, 1799), 308. See also A. Goodwin, ed., *The European Nobility in the 18th Century* (London, 1953), 172-89 for an account of the Russian nobility by Max Beloff.

dangers of assassination if noblemen became too disaffected. On the other hand the nobility, or what corresponded to nobility in Russia, were the only people who could effectively make their wishes heard. Catherine's short-lived husband, Peter III, had freed them from punishment by the knout in 1762, and at the Legislative Commission which she assembled in 1767 there were nobles who asked for recognition as an "order," with corporate privileges and corporate guarantees. As the nobility became more Westernized, and more familiar with the meaning of noble status in Europe, they became more aware of their own disadvantages.

Catherine's needs, and noble wishes, came together in the Charter of Nobility which she issued in 1785. What this amounted to was an attempt, in an enormous agrarian empire that rested on unfree labor and on military force, to map out an area of personal status, liberty, and security for those persons without whom the empire could not carry on. In effect, if not by design, the charter introduced nobility on the Western model into Russia. It is an instructive contrast between two rulers often lumped together as enlightened despots, that at the very time when Joseph II tried to turn the serfs of his empire into something like West European peasants, Catherine II, called the "Great," largely to hold down the serfs, moved to convert her landlords into something like Western aristocrats.[31]

The Charter of 1785 began by defining noble estate or status, which it said was a superiority of rank, or of good birth, originating in service to the state, and transmissible to descendants. The word used most commonly in the charter was *blagorodnyi*, "high born" or "honorable." It was to people thus born that the charter gave guarantees. They could not lose their status, honor, property or life without judicial proceedings, and could be judged only by judges of equal birth with themselves. They were exempted from corporal punishment. Highborn persons in lower military ranks were to be liable only to such punishments as were prescribed for the higher. They received permission to leave state service at will, to take service with foreign governments, and to travel outside the country. They were given the right to sign their names (like European nobles) with territorial titles. They were reconfirmed in their right to "buy villages" (that is serfs), and to engage in wholesale or overseas trade in the agricultural or industrial products of their workers. Nobles, as defined in the charter, were also exempted from personal taxes. In general, by Article 17: "We guaran-

[31] For the charter, see Appendix III below.

tee independence and liberty to the Russian nobility for all time by inheritance in future generations."

The charter, besides promising such individual and family guarantees, set up the nobility as an organized and corporate estate. The nobles in each province were to meet in an assembly, elect a marshal, have the right of collective petition, exercise police powers, and name local officials, while enjoying, as an assembly, immunity from molestation or arrest. According to one writer, Catherine hoped to create bodies like the Provincial Estates of France. These rights the Russian nobility continued to enjoy throughout the nineteenth century.

Catherine also issued a charter of the cities, organizing them on paper like European towns of the old regime, with various levels of inhabitants enjoying various levels of burgher rights. Townsmen of merchant status, for example, were freed from forced government service, and those of the first two merchant categories, or higher, were exempted from corporal punishment. The towns, however, were of very little importance in the empire. Growth of a Russian burgher class was held down by the importance of foreign merchants on the one hand, and, on the other, by the business activity of many landed nobles using servile labor.

Under Catherine, in short, whose reputation for enlightenment was due mainly to Western intellectuals, the tsardom reached a great compromise with those whom it recognized as nobles; indeed, in a sense, it created an aristocracy, the better to govern, or rather to dominate, the mass of the people. For some to have a sphere of rights due to special birth or rank was doubtless better than for no one to have any assured rights at all. For some to have a certain independence in the face of power was better than autocracy unmixed. Catherine doubtless believed, like many Europeans (she was herself of German birth), that a stratified society in general, and a hereditary and respected noble class in particular, were signs of an advanced state of civilization. Governor Bernard argued as much in Massachusetts. But she systematized the institutions of hereditary nobility, and of peasant subjection, at the very time when these were being questioned in Europe. While the Austrian monarchs, and even the Prussian, emancipated the serfs on crown estates, she not only did not do so but gave away state domains, peasants and all, to her lovers and favorites. It is estimated that she thus simply handed over almost a million "souls" to nobles.[32] Serfdom reached its low point in her reign.

[32] "Almost a million human beings were robbed of all personal rights by this princely

The Kingdom of Prussia, a showpiece of enlightened despotism, was in the eighteenth century a country of very marked aristocratic resurgence. This took two forms: an actual come-back of the old landed nobility after 1740, and the development of the newer civil service into a self-conscious governing group with an aristocratic code of values. In Prussia, as in the Russia of Catherine, and in the Hapsburg empire of Leopold, the monarchy made concessions to the groups that were indispensable to its rule.[33]

The limitations of enlightened despotism are well seen in the famous Prussian General Code, first promulgated in 1791. Its purpose was to provide a territorially uniform, orderly, known, and predictable body of laws and procedures for all the heterogeneous parts of the monarchy. The code was celebrated in its time as one of the great legal accomplishments for the age, and it gave Prussians a proud sense of living in a *Rechtstaat*, or under a government of laws where arbitrary power had no place. Many Prussians, indeed, after 1789, were inclined to take an indulgent view of the French Revolution, believing, erroneously, that the French were trying only to obtain what the more fortunate Prussians already enjoyed. Even Napoleon regarded the Prussian code as a precedent when he superintended the codification of French law in 1804. But where the Code Napoleon came after a great revolution, and codified the equality of rights, the Code of Frederick the Great—under whom work on it began, though it was completed under his successor—was a codification of the aristocratic society, the *Ständestaat*. It may be taken to represent the farthest point that enlightened absolutism could reach in a society of legally differentiated orders.

The Prussian code began with certain general statements, which lend themselves to comparison with the almost simultaneous French Declaration of Rights.[34] Neither liberty, nor equality, nor the rights of man were absent from the Prussian code; but they were quite otherwise defined than in the French declaration.

On natural liberty the Prussian code observed: "The laws and ordi-

generosity of the Semiramis of the North," V. Gitermann, *Geschichte Russlands*, 2 vols. (Zurich, 1945), II, 244.

[33] Hans Rosenberg, *Bureaucracy, Aristocracy and Autocracy: The Prussian Experience, 1660-1816* (Cambridge, Mass., 1958), 57-108, 175-201. My treatment of Prussia at this point draws heavily on Professor Rosenberg. See also A. Goodwin on the Prussian nobility in *European Nobility in the 18th Century*, 83-101.

[34] *Allgemeines Gesetzbuch für die preussischen Staaten*, 4 vols. (Berlin, 1791). The clauses quoted above appeared in the *Landrecht* of 1794 unchanged with one exception: the clause on restriction of natural liberty was omitted. See Appendix III below.

nances of the state should no further restrict the natural liberty and rights of citizens than the public welfare demands." In the abstract, this was not very different from the French declaration. The code acknowledged the rights of man, but with a special angle: "The rights of man arise from his birth and from his estate. . . . The particular rights of a state-member rest upon the personal relationships in which each one stands toward others or toward the state." As for equality, the code called for an equality of obedience: "The laws bind all members of the state without difference of estate, rank or family." By equality it also meant an equality among social equals: "Persons to whom, by their birth, destination in life or principal occupation, equal rights are ascribed in civil society, make up an estate within the state, *einen Stand des Staats*. Members of each estate have, as such, certain rights and duties." The theory of the state was corporatist: "Civil society consists of many small societies and estates, connected to each other by nature or law or by both together." Rights accrued to the individual according to the estate to which he belonged. There were many such estates, and hundreds of pages of the code were devoted to the particular rights and duties of each. There were 20 pages on rights and duties of *Herrschaft und Gesinde*, that is, of manorial lordship and certain forms of compulsory labor. There were 50 pages on the Peasant Estate, 100 on the Burgher Estate, only 10 on the Noble Estate (whose rights were specified elsewhere), 20 on civil servants, 150 on the clergy, 20 on institutions of learning.

The Prussian code thus fell well short of any general conception of citizenship. The Prussian monarchy remained very much a monarchy of the old regime, that is, a conglomeration of separate kinds of people held together by nothing more than higher authority. The ideal was rigidly hierarchic. Everyone had some rights, but some people had much better rights than others. The code systematized the segregation of classes that had become a main policy of the kingdom. Land and property were classified as people were; nobles, burghers, and peasants could not acquire land out of their class, lest the operations of a common market bring a burgher admixture into the martial and agrarian virtues of Junker squires. The landed nobility and the government service were the two favored classes. They tended to merge, or to feel akin in their values and attitudes, in what Professor Rosenberg calls an "aristobureaucracy," which maintained itself into the twentieth century.

Always with a view toward showing what the international revolutionary disturbance at the end of the eighteenth century was about, I have argued, in preceding chapters, that before the revolution of 1789 in France, or before the war of 1792 by which the revolution was intensified and extended, the position of governing or politically privileged classes was if anything growing stronger. The distinctive thing about these classes—since all societies have upper classes and governing groups—was the high degree to which they were hereditary, self-perpetuating, or self-recruiting, their claim to hold their positions in their own right, and their insistence on maintaining an independence, as Charles Fox said in the Commons in England, against the pressure of either King or people. These "aristocrats," to use the term created by the revolutionary movement itself, were by no means in retreat, and the turmoil of democratic revolution did not merely carry forward a long evolutionary process which might more peacefully have accomplished the same end. The great generalization of Alexis de Tocqueville, that history exhibits a centuries-long movement toward a greater equality of conditions, seems true to me only if it includes the thought, as a subordinate generalization, that men have at times fought for this increase of equality against contrary tendencies and against very positive opposition. At the risk of excessive schematism, but in the attempt to draw a picture of Western Civilization as a whole, evidence has been assembled to persuade the reader that everywhere, except in the United States, the problem of taking wider classes of people into the community was either not recognized as a problem, or was plainly denied to be a problem, or was unsolved. Aristocracies had defeated democratic movements in England, Ireland, Holland, Belgium, and Geneva. They had won concessions from monarchs in the Hapsburg countries, Prussia and Russia; and on failing to win similar concessions in Sweden, they endangered the viability of the monarchy itself. We turn now to the two countries which along with America were then the most famous for revolution—Poland and France. These two were obviously very unlike, yet they have a resemblance under the schematism that has been set up. Both the Polish and the French revolutions began with a kind of aristocratic resurgence, the former against anarchy, the latter against royal absolutism. And in both the revolution reached a life-and-death crisis in the war of 1792.

THE LESSONS OF POLAND

What is the subject of any country? It makes no difference, slave black or white, he is a man, in no way unlike us. In Europe and in any part of the world, he is our equal, a citizen of the earth.—HUGO KOLLONTAY, 1790

Yet we must be fair. Considering where the people of Poland began, they have made relatively as great a leap toward liberty as we have.—CAMILLE DESMOULINS, 1791

THE LESSONS OF POLAND

IT HAS been the fate of Poland, more than of most countries, that outsiders have been mainly concerned to see in it a spectacular object lesson, hurrying on from interest in the Poles themselves to find evidence for general truths of wider application. Very much this same treatment will be accorded to Poland in this chapter, which is a compressed account of the Four Years' Diet of 1788-1792 and its background; but it may be said, as an apology to the Poles, that in this book the affairs of all other countries are presented in the same way, so as to fit them into a story of political disturbance in the Western World as a whole. Poland will first be exhibited as a land of aristocracy triumphant. The question will then be asked, as it was asked of the American Revolution in Chapter VII, whether the Polish Revolution of 1791 was a revolution at all, and if so in what sense; and what observers in other countries—such as Burke in England, the revolutionaries in France, and the rulers of Prussia and Russia—thought that they learned from it.

Jean-Jacques Rousseau drew lessons from Poland in 1771. With the country dissolving in civil war, subverted by Russia, and sinking into the First Partition, the author of the *Social Contract*, at the request of certain Polish patriots, offered his diagnosis of their situation. The conservatism of his advice has often been pointed out. "Don't shake the machine too abruptly," he said; don't multiply enemies within the state by sudden changes; don't in your attempts at reform lose the liberties that you have.[1] His diagnosis nevertheless went to the root of the matter. The trouble with Poland, he thought, was that it had no *consistance*, no staying power to resist pressure and infiltration from outside. What it needed was character, a character of its own, resting on the collective consciousness or will of its people—"national institutions which form the genius, the character, the tastes, and the customs of the people, which make them what they are and not something

[1] *Considérations sur le gouvernement de la Pologne*, in *Oeuvres* (Paris, 1827), x, 146, 15.

else, and inspire that warm love of country founded on habits impossible to uproot."[2] He deplored the appalling class divisions in Poland, by which burghers were "nothing," and peasants "less than nothing," and he favored a gradual emancipation and a humanizing of the serfs. The inequalities of wealth between rich nobles and poor nobles seemed to him altogether too great. In practice, he addressed himself only to the nobles, the one political class in the country, but to them he tried to impart a fundamental message: that if only they would form a general will and acquire certain civic and moral virtues, including respect for each other as equals and a willingness to support each other and their state as the vehicle of their freedom, Poland might yet be saved.

John Adams also drew a lesson. In London in 1787, writing his *Defense of the Constitutions of the United States*, and surveying all known republics, ancient, medieval, and modern, he came to the "regal republic" of Poland, and he found in it abundant confirmation of his principal doctrines. He was horrified to learn that in Poland a "gentleman" was fined only fifteen livres for killing a peasant. Poland, with its feeble monarchy, proved to Adams that the welfare of the people required a strong king, "meaning by the word king a first magistrate possessed exclusively of the executive power." A government without three independent branches, he insisted, would degenerate either into absolute monarchy or into aristocracy, as in Poland, and in an aristocracy the "nobility will annihilate the people, and attended with their horses, hounds and vassals, will run down the king as they would hunt a deer."[3]

A country ruined by having no spiritual solidarity or common basis of loyalty—thus Rousseau. A country ruined by one-class rule and by having no executive government—thus Adams. Most historians have agreed with them.

The Gentry Republic

Poland in 1788, like the Dutch Republic, lived under a constitution "guaranteed" by outside powers. In both cases the guarantee was designed to preserve the historic liberties and the existing upper classes of the country. The Polish constitution, guaranteed by Russia in 1773 after the First Partition, was essentially the old Polish constitution as it had developed over the past two centuries. Except in age, in aristo-

---

[2] *Ibid.*, 23.   [3] *Works* (1851), IV, 371.

cratic complexion, and in dependence on foreign support, the Polish and Dutch arrangements were diametrical opposites, for, in the United Netherlands even the patricians were burghers, while in Poland they were exclusively agrarian landlords, the Dutch being the most commercial people of Western Civilization, the Poles nearly the least so.

The Republic of Poland, whose titular head was an elected king, comprised two parts: the "kingdom of Poland," or Poland proper, and the grand duchy of Lithuania to the east.[4] The two parts, in the 1780's, had somewhat over 8,000,000 people, or about the population of England. Population density was only a third of that of England or France. About 725,000 persons were of families somewhat misleadingly translated into French and English as "noble." About 500,000 persons were of the town classes, not counting the 900,000 Jews, who were mostly scattered in very small businesses in the smallest towns and in the open country. Though the tendency of recent Polish historians is to emphasize the Polish nationality of the burgher class, it is agreed that a significant number of them spoke German and felt as transplanted Germans, while a certain number were Greeks or Armenians, and since the Jews spoke Yiddish, lived apart, or were concentrated in ghettoes, the classes corresponding to the townspeople of Western Europe were prevented by language and religion from developing any feeling of unity. Warsaw was rapidly growing, leaping in size from 30,000 to 120,000 people between 1764 and 1791, but most other places were small, and all the people in the fifty largest towns taken together—of whom few could be called "bourgeoisie"—were only a little over half as numerous as the nobles.

Three-quarters of the population were peasants, most of them serfs, as in the Hapsburg empire, Prussia, and Russia. As in these countries, and indeed more so, the mass of the country population were subjects of their lords, not of the King. "The nobility," according to a Polish lawbook of 1742, "has the right of life and death over its subjects attached to the soil (*glebae adscriptos*), not otherwise than as slaves were

[4] For conditions in Poland before the Four Years' Diet see R. H. Lord, *The Second Partition of Poland* (Cambridge, Mass., 1915); J. Fabre, *Stanislas-Auguste Poniatowski et l'Europe des lumières* (Paris, 1952); R. N. Bain, *The Last King of Poland and His Contemporaries* (London, 1909); the special number of *Przeglad historyczny* (Historical Review), XLII, 1951, devoted to Poland in this period, containing articles with French summaries by C. Bobinska, A. Korta, J. Kott, W. Kula, B. Lesnodorski, J. Michalski, and E. Rostworowski; B. Lesnodorski, "Les facteurs intellectuels de la formation de la société polonaise moderne au Siècle des lumières," in *La Pologne au Xe Congrès international des sciences historiques à Rome* (Warsaw, 1955); *Polish Encyclopedia* (Geneva, 1921), II, 104-21.

considered to be among the Romans."[5] Though such information is hard to come by, it may be assumed that there was in Poland very little of the intermarriage and family relationship between townspeople and peasantry that were so common in France, since in Poland the countryman, as a serf, was not free to move, and might even speak a different language. The sharp separation between town and country, the inability of burghers and agricultural people to enter into each other's interests and points of view, characteristic also of Germany in lesser degree, was one of the fundamental differences between Eastern Europe on the one hand, and Western Europe and North America on the other—always with the reminder that race differences and slavery gave parts of America a resemblance to Eastern Europe.

Persons counting as nobles were exceedingly numerous in Poland, making up over eight per cent of the population. They were more numerous even than in Hungary, where, as seen in the last chapter, the nobility was larger proportionately than the *noblesse* of France or the gentry and aristocracy of England. Since one person in twelve was noble, and the nobles outnumbered the burghers, and in all societies the mass of the people remains somewhat anonymous, it has been possible for some writers to compare the lesser gentry to a yeomanry, and to see a kind of agrarian democracy in the old Poland. The trouble in this view is that the 725,000 nobles were themselves very mixed.

The biggest and richest were the twenty-odd families of magnates, such as the Potockis, the Czartoryskis, the Radziwills, and the Branickis. Their main strength lay in the eastern and southeastern part of the country, in White Russia and the western Ukraine, which remained under Polish control even after the First Partition. Here the landlords, Polish in origin or in culture, descendents of men who had conquered the land from Russians, Tartars, or Turks, held vast latifundia worked by the White Russian or Ukrainian peasantry. Felix Potocki, for example, possessed estates of over 6,500 square miles, larger than Connecticut, or half as large as the Dutch Republic. He kept a court of 400 persons, and had an annual income of 3,000,000 Polish florins. This was a third as large as the income of the Polish crown. A few such magnates together could raise as much money, and as many armed men, as the King himself. They lived like princes, built palaces, gave lavish entertainments, sponsored the arts, spoke French, went on grand tours, and felt it natural for men in their position to maintain their

[5] Quoted from Zalaszowski, *Jus regni Poloniae* (1742), i, 39, by P. Mitrofanov, *Joseph II* (Vienna, 1910), 592.

own foreign policy, being often seen at the courts of St. Petersburg, Berlin, or other great capitals.

Half the nobles, however, were landless or nearly so. Some, possessing a few acres and a horse, made a shabby living by doing the farm labor themselves. Travelers saw them going into the fields wearing their swords, which they hung on trees as they went about their plowing or their digging. Others, having no property, income, skills, or settled occupation, might be called a proletariat except for a sense of class superiority that they maintained, by which they set a high value on birth, physical courage, political liberty, and riding horseback (they were the "equestrian order"), and a low value on work, routine, and the orderly payment of debts. Some Polish noblemen were admirable products of European civilization; one thinks of Adam Czartoryski in the next generation, or the poet and patriot Niemcewicz, who lived for years in New Jersey after the failure of Kosciusko's rebellion. The bulk of the Polish nobility, however, were rude, slovenly, uneducated, and provincial, equally unaware of what French philosophers or a Russian tsarina might be thinking; out of touch with the world, their horizons bounded by the narrow limits of their own way of life; unaccustomed to dealing on equal terms with people unlike themselves; naïvely unpolitical, but inclined to political oratory, and more than willing to join the following of some chieftain. Poor nobles lived as retainers to the great. The great nobleman, the princely magnate, counted his importance by the number of his dependents, the thousands of subjects or unfree peasants who labored on his estates, and the swarms of freemen or nobles, who might also number thousands, that flocked in to do him honor and eat dinner in his country house, and might be rallied as a political force in times of public disturbance.

"Your *aristoi*," Adams wrote to Jefferson in their old age, "are the most difficult animals to manage of anything in the whole theory and practice of government. They will not suffer themselves to be governed."[6] Adams was speaking in general; but his remark puts the political history of Poland for two hundred years before 1788 in a nutshell.

At the close of the Middle Ages Poland had had flourishing towns, and a peasantry as free and as well-off as in most parts of Western Europe. The landed nobility had extorted increasing privileges from the King, who found insufficient strength in the burgher class to resist the neo-feudal demands; and the nobles gradually deprived the

[6] *Works* (1851), x, 51.

King of his powers, and other classes of their rights. The peasantry, as elsewhere in Eastern Europe, fell into bondage. Burghers were thrust aside; when the central diet was definitively constituted in 1505 no city except Cracow received a clear right of representation, and such occasional participation as a few towns enjoyed was finally ended by a law of 1768, with exceptions for Danzig and Thorn. Ceasing to exist as an estate of the realm, the burghers lost their rights of municipal self-government also, and were helpless before the legislative predilections of an agrarian gentry, as when in 1565 the Diet forbade native merchants to engage in foreign trade, and in 1643 it limited their profits to seven per cent, or three per cent in the case of Jews. The Polish towns became very dilapidated.

The landowners, great and small, met in about fifty local assemblies, one for each palatinate or province in the country; and these local assemblies, after 1500, gathered to themselves the power to authorize and to collect taxes, and to maintain armed forces. The country became a loose federation of half a hundred little noble republics. Each sent deputies to the lower house of a central or national diet, where they were bound by imperative mandates of their constituents. The upper house consisted of prelates and great officers of the crown. The nobles elected the King, convening for this purpose in a grand special assemblage, a kind of enormous town meeting which every gentleman in Poland had the right to attend, and where as many as a hundred thousand might actually appear. It was the magnates who financed and directed these turbulent encampments, which always imposed on the King whom they elected certain articles of agreement, called the *pacta conventa*, by which the liberties of Poland were secured. The aristocracy thus prevented the accumulation of powers in the crown from one generation to the next; each generation remained "free," uncommitted by the past, in an odd variation on the doctrine of Jefferson or Thomas Paine.

The gentry and magnates were as reluctant to see power vested in their national diet as in a king. They developed, therefore, a procedure for nullification, the famous Liberum Veto, which came into habitual use in 1652. By this procedure any deputy in the central diet, acting as the representative of his home assembly (and in practice carrying out the will of some magnate) could arise in the diet and by pronouncing the formula, *sic nolo, sic veto*, not merely block the legislation in question, but force the dissolution of the diet itself. Forty-eight of fifty-five diets held between 1652 and 1764 were thus arbitrarily dissolved by minority or indeed individual interests. There was a general atrophy of institutions of government.

The Polish scholar, Konopczynski, in his study of the Liberum Veto, has made some observations so enlightening for constitutional theory, and for the history of self-government, that even in a condensed account it seems well to make room for them. The free veto meant the principle of unanimity, or the denial of majority rule in deliberative bodies. Acceptance of majority rule, Konopczynski reminds us (and it is easy to forget it) is in fact a difficult, artificial, and acquired habit of mind. It depends on several prerequisites: first, that votes be counted, not evaluated in importance according to the identity of the voter; that is, all votes must be considered equal. In the order of business discussion must be distinctly followed by voting, lest nothing emerge but a vague sense of the meeting, or apparent unanimity in which responsibilities are indefinite and differences of opinion are temporarily covered up, only to break out later. There must be a party of some kind, personal, political, religious, or economic, willing to work for years to carry out a decision, and to resist its reversal. It is well to have a settled and fixed population, for if dissidents can simply go away, or retire so far into the depths of the country as to be forgotten, they never learn to submit to majority wishes, nor does the majority learn to govern. A strong executive is useful, for there can be no majority rule unless minorities are obliged to accept decisions once made. Lastly, persons who in their own right are the masters of men, sovereigns on estates with subjects of their own, submit with reluctance to a majority even of their own equals; majority rule has always seemed more reasonable to middle classes than to seigneurs.[7]

Few of these conditions obtained in Poland. The Polish nobleman bowed to no one. Liberty reigned, the *aurea libertas* of Polish annals. So did equality and fraternity, in a way, for in law all nobles were equals and supposed to address one another as "brother." The Poles looked down on the slavish monarchies that surrounded them. They were forever on guard against "despotism," and they watched with zeal over their "contracts," the *pacta conventa*. They boasted like Englishmen of the virtues of their ancestors and the wisdom of their constitution. They liked to compare their Republic to the best times of Greece and Rome. A deputy exercising the Liberum Veto became in this view a bold tribune of the people; and Polish liberty, if it rested on slaves, was all the more Athenian in its character.

[7] L. Konopczynski, *Le Liberum veto: étude sur le développement du principe majoritaire* (Paris, 1930), 19-23.

Actually there was less ground for gratification. The result of Golden Liberty "was the omnipotence of a single caste carried to a point unparalleled in any other European country."[8] It was usual enough in the eighteenth century for the landed aristocrats to enjoy superior privileges. Elsewhere in Eastern Europe they ruled over serfs under monarchical auspices. In England and for a time in Sweden they even governed. In Poland, having monopolized all organs of state, they could neither govern nor suffer themselves to be governed. Central authority became a shadow. The Polish army in the mid-eighteenth century consisted of 24,000 men, almost all cavalry. Few taxes were raised. The revenues of the Republic in 1750 are said to have been one thirteenth those of Russia and one seventy-fifth those of France. In the 1780's after reforms, they amounted to about 12,000,000 French *livres*, compared to 140,000,000 for Russia and 430,000,000 for France.

As in Sweden during the Freedom Era, so in Poland the great noblemen readily called on foreign aid in their rivalries with each other. Some magnates favored Russia, others Turkey, Sweden, or France. Foreign powers paid money to obtain votes in the diet, and important Poles considered such income as their normal due. The diet became an international meddling place, and many a Liberum Veto was initiated by a foreign bribe, but the meetings at which the nobles elected a king were the most notorious for this kind of intervention. As Russia entered into European politics with Peter the Great, it became the most influential of the powers in Poland. In 1764 the diet elected a Polish nobleman, Stanislas Poniatowski, as king, carefully checking him, as in all such elections, with all sorts of guarantees of the national liberties. King Stanislas, a former lover of Catherine of Russia, was still her protégé and became King of Poland by her will. He was a philosopher-king and a patriot, who understood the cause of his country's troubles, and favored many projects of reform; but he was well aware, from having lived there, of the massive might of Imperial Russia, and he understood the difficulty of getting the magnates to make any changes in a system of which they were the main beneficiaries. All three partitions of Poland occurred in his reign. The First Partition, effected in 1772, of which no more will be said here, was a natural consequence of the weakness of Poland confronted by aggressiveness of Prussia and Russia. The Second and Third Partitions were to be less simple.

The shock of the First Partition speeded up the development of a

[8] Lord, *Second Partition*, 15.

new kind of political consciousness that had come into evidence since the middle of the eighteenth century. It is hard to form an accurate impression of the social changes or emerging interests that motivated the new ideas. Polish historians in recent years have devoted a good deal of thought and research to this period. Their work seems to me, by the usual Western standards, to be the best that has been done in any of the countries where a Marxist frame of history is officially prescribed.

In Marxism, not much can happen in history without a "bourgeoisie," and the new writers therefore point to a bourgeois development. They note, for example, how Warsaw quadrupled in size in the thirty years after 1764. This does not necessarily prove much in the way of economic progress in the eighteenth century, when Palermo was larger than Lyons, and Dublin twice as big as Manchester; still, the number of Polish burghers, of a certain level of wealth, was undoubtedly increasing. The new school emphasizes, however, that it was usually the landed nobles who functioned as "bourgeois." In Poland it was the nobles who controlled the means of production. Using their rights of lordship and their unfree labor, they undertook to enter more profitably into a market economy, either by intensifying their agriculture, or by exploiting the mineral and forest wealth on their estates. There was no strong separate productive or manufacturing interest, distinct from the nobles; and since the nobles, even the economically enterprising ones, used their incomes mainly for consumption, to obtain the amenities of civilized living from the West, or to keep up their political followings, capital accumulation was very slow. Nevertheless, some nobles came more often into association with merchants, bankers, and other burghers, and were even prepared for legal changes in which burghers would have the right to buy and own land, since the value and flexibility of landed assets would thus be heightened. Town capitalists, on the other hand (such as existed in Poland), that is, burghers desiring to develop new industries, behaved somewhat like nobles in their reliance on servile labor. The new Polish school finds also that serf rebellions were more common than bourgeois historiography has allowed for. The same argument exists in American historiography, on the alleged degree of contentment or rebelliousness of Negro slaves before 1861, and, all things considered, it seems likely enough that sporadic serf uprisings were common, or more common than one would gather from the works of many historians. There was not, however, in Poland, even in 1794, any such mass upheaval as in Russia under

Pugachev in 1773, or in France during the revolution of 1789, or in Hungary or even in Bohemia at the same time. That burghers offered no leadership to peasants, that burghers and peasants felt no common ties, that burghers in eighteenth-century Poland were not vehemently antiaristocratic, that some nobles were beginning to operate as capitalist entrepreneurs, that capitalism in Poland developed in conjunction with a kind of feudalism and carried over attitudes toward labor inherited from the days of serfdom, and that all this was decisive for the history of Poland and Eastern Europe, and of capitalism and socialism, into the twentieth century—seem to be propositions that historians under no obligations to Marxism can share with the new Polish school.

Poland, too, had its intellectual Enlightenment, which as in all countries in varying degree was both native and imported. The papal dissolution of the Society of Jesus was followed, as in other Catholic countries, notably France, by important educational reforms. The Educational Commission set up in Poland in 1773 has been called the first national ministry of education. It introduced new programs into the schools vacated by the Jesuits, and the aim in these programs, made more urgent by the lesson of the First Partition, was to offer a new training in citizenship and the arts of state, in place of the older literary and rhetorical emphasis. The University of Cracow was modernized by Hugo Kollontay, who observed that "we want no colonies of Plato's republic," and sought to give a practical training in public responsibilities.[9] The Jesuits, in their system of teaching, had provided for a kind of Oxford Union, or mock parliament, in which young men learned how to conduct themselves in the diet, and, in particular, how to execute a Liberum Veto with éclat. Reformers now saw the Liberum Veto as a main source of Poland's ills, and in the new schools, as in the Collegium Nobilium of the Piarist fathers at Warsaw, where many leaders of the revolutionary generation received their schooling, the Liberum Veto was dropped from the academic exercises of the youth.[10]

By the 1780's the works of Beccaria and Filangieri, of Adam Smith, Locke, and Blackstone, of Voltaire, Diderot, Rousseau, Montesquieu, Mably, and Condillac were all known in Polish translation. The organization of Freemasonry also provided international contacts, and various of King Stanislas' reforming advisers, like the Swiss Glayre

---

[9] Lesnodorski, in *Pologne au X⁶ Congrès*, 187.

[10] B. Lesnodorski, *Dzielo sejmu czteroletniego* (The Work of the Four Years' Diet) (Wroclaw, 1951), 87. I am indebted to Mr. André Michalski for examining this and other works in Polish for me.

and the Italian Piattoli, were Masons. These foreign associations, and the reading of foreign books, give evidence of a fermentation of political and intellectual interests, but the idea that the Polish revolution was caused by Masons and *philosophes*, though it has been alleged, is hard to sustain. Experience was to show that no foreign Masons were to support the Polish revolution, and the influence of Rousseau operated in contrary directions. For example, the patriot Wielhorski, the man who had induced Rousseau to write his tract on Poland, had two sons, one of whom supported the constitution of 1791, while the other fought against it, both loudly declaring that they were carrying on their father's and Rousseau's true ideas.[11] Montesquieu's doctrine of the balance of powers was appealed to both by the old-fashioned party that sensed despotism in any strengthening of the King, and by the reforming party that desired a more independent executive. Elsewhere in Europe, Montesquieu was generally the favorite of the aristocratic upholders of the constituted bodies—of the Hungarian diet, the French parlements, or the English House of Commons. It seems that in Poland Montesquieu was an oracle for the monarchists also, for the party that is, that sought to achieve reforms by counterbalancing the aristocracy in the diet.[12]

The first Polish periodical appeared in 1763, and by 1789 there were about a dozen of them, mostly in Polish, but some in German for German-speaking burghers, and some in French for the Warsaw diplomatic community and for more cosmopolitan Poles. The first public theater was established at Warsaw in 1765, so that the stage ceased to be the exclusively private pleasure of aristocratic houses. Efforts were made to modernize the Polish language, and increase its use in place of Latin, German, and French; thus a book of 1782 set forth a vocabulary of Polish terms for the iron industry. The twenty years following 1772 saw the appearance of 109 books devoted to agriculture, in which such far-reaching questions as the free market in land, and emancipation of rural labor, were sometimes raised. By the 1780's, books and pamphlets on political questions were fairly common. A few reforms, of incidental kind, were enacted before 1788: the lord lost the right of capital punishment over his serf, and judicial torture and the crime of witchcraft were abolished. There had come to be,

---

[11] On Masonry and the influence of Rousseau, see Fabre, *Stanislas-Auguste*, 501, 656-57.

[12] On the uses made of Montesquieu in Poland see Lesnodorski, *Dzielo*, 112-13, and W. Smolenski, *Monteskiusz w Polsce w 18 w* (Warsaw, 1927), for knowledge of whose contents I am indebted to Mr. Michalski.

in place of the old speechifying of rustic assemblies, a public opinion of more modern kind on modern questions.

The two leading spokesmen of this Polish enlightenment were Stanislas Staszic and Hugo Kollontay. Staszic, a burgher, in a book of 1785 that was widely read, called for a hereditary instead of an elective monarchy, abolition of the Liberum Veto, higher taxes, a larger army, industrial development, and emancipation of the serfs. Kollontay, born into the lesser nobility and trained for the church, and already known as the reformer of the University of Cracow, was to be the chief luminary of the "bourgeois" or Western-type revolution in Poland, active both in the Four Years' Diet and in the ensuing rebellion under Kosciusko. In 1788, just before the opening of the Four Years' Diet, he began to publish his influential *Anonymous Letters*, in which he demanded much the same radical changes as Staszic. On the basic requirements of a reviving Poland the most active-minded nobles and burghers were agreed, and together they formed the patriot party; but for reasons that should now be clear, most of the reformers were in fact nobles.

The Polish Revolution: The Constitution of 1791

Neither Russia nor Prussia desired a strong or independent Poland on its borders, and Catherine II in particular, enjoying a paramount influence throughout the whole country after the First Partition, wished for matters in Poland to remain just as they were. Since she now expected to dominate Poland through the Polish government itself, she did force the diet, in 1773, to create a few new executive organs, notably a Permanent Commission of thirty-six members, who subdivided into special branches which functioned as ministries. She also kept Russian troops in occupation of the country. Otherwise she was an eloquent partisan of the "Polish liberties" under the old constitution. It was this constitution, with its elective monarchy, its Liberum Veto, and its fifty regional assemblies, modified only by the addition of the Permanent Commission, that she guaranteed in 1773. European monarchs, as Rousseau told the Poles, were fond of liberty for their neighbors because they believed that liberty made men weak. Nor can this cynical opinion be called mistaken, so far as liberty meant the *aurea libertas* of Poland, or the Swedish liberties of the Freedom Era, or the *ware vrijheid* of the Dutch, or the liberties of the ancient Holy Roman Empire or of new American states under the Articles of Confederation.

The reform party therefore had two adversaries to contend with: on the one hand, a strong group among the Polish magnates, and, on the other, Russia.[13] Among magnates partial to the old ways, the most important were the Branicki and Felix Potocki, whose holdings in the Ukraine have been described. They saw in the Russian influence a protection for liberty and for serfdom. Prominent in the reform party was King Stanislas himself, restless in the satellite position to which Catherine had consigned him, surrounding himself with Polish and West European liberals, wishing well to all his people, even the Jews— for he had met Amsterdam Jews in his youth, and seems to have been the only Polish reformer to take an interest in the Jews of Poland, and in the problem which they presented. Eagerly receptive to all kinds of new ideas, Stanislas in 1788 hired Jefferson's friend, Philip Mazzei, as his agent in Paris, to report on events there, and to plant the picture of a new and reviving Poland in the press of France and Holland. The reforming group was led also by certain of the magnates, notably Ignace Potocki, the Radziwills, and the Czartoryskis; and it shaded off, as an incipient national party, into the ranks of the middling gentry and of those burghers who were emerging from the timidity of second-class citizenship, and beginning to have opinions on political subjects.

The patriots awaited the momentary embarrassment of Russia to begin action on their program. The opportunity came in 1788, when Russia became involved in the Turkish war. A diet, to be called the Four Years' Diet, met at Warsaw in October 1788. It soon "confederated" itself, that is, took an action which freed it from the Liberum Veto in matters of taxation and the army. In the Diet three parties soon appeared. One called itself Republican; these were the conservative magnates, with their hordes of *glota*, the barefoot gentry who were their retainers. Nostalgic for the old-time freedom, quick to sniff out despotism in the plans of their opponents, they were also pro-Russian. In the middle was the party of the King, humane and benevolent, brought by Mazzei and others to share the ideas of the American Revolution, yet deterred and frustrated by the belief, which was realistic

[13] On the Polish Revolution, 1788-1792, see the works cited in notes 4 and 10 above; C. Dany, *Les idées politiques et l'esprit publique en Pologne à la fin du 18ᵉ siècle: La constitution du 3 mai 1791* (Paris, 1901); J. Klotz, *L'oeuvre legislative de la Diète de Quatre Ans* (Paris, 1913). The chief account by participants available in a Western language is that published anonymously in 1793, in two volumes in German translation, by Kollontay (Kołłątaj) and others: *Vom Entstehung und Untergang der polnischen Konstitution vom 3 may 1791.* I shall deal later with the more fully revolutionary effort of Kosciusko's rebellion of 1794.

enough, that any effective reform in Poland would awaken the displeasure of Russia. Bolder than the King's party were the Patriots, a mixed group which ranged from those who wanted only a few constitutional changes, such as a stronger executive, through those who felt a need for economic legislation to stimulate production, on to true radicals like Kollontay, who hoped, in addition, for emancipation of the serfs. The Patriots accepted the friendly approaches of Prussia, which, for its own purposes, to offset the Russian influence, and in the hope of obtaining Danzig and Thorn in exchange, decided in 1788 to support the party of reform. The Patriots allowed themselves to make the most inflammatory anti-Russian speeches. They succeeded in getting rid of the Permanent Commission, which they detested as a Russian device, and even in inducing Catherine to withdraw the Russian soldiers. With Russian pressure thus relieved, the way seemed clear for an integral reconstruction. For a long time nothing much happened except more harangues in the Diet. *Oratoribus periit Graecia,* the King wrote to Mazzei, for he was keenly aware of the passage of time, and was afraid that after all the insult and provocation to Russia, when the Turkish war ended, as it soon would, the Russian hold would be clamped more firmly upon the country.

Outside the Diet not much happened, at least in Poland itself. There was no unusual violence, no popular upheaval bringing pressure on the Diet from outside. The Polish revolution remained, as it were, within parliamentary channels—for which in some quarters it was later much praised. It may be that in this Polish revolution the greatest event was the revolution in France. Mazzei, in Paris, denounced the obstructionism of French aristocracy in his bulletins to Warsaw.[14] News of the fall of the Bastille created a sensation. Conscious of a revolution in their own midst, learning excitedly of the one in Paris, and remembering the one in America at the opposite extremity of Western Civilization, where Kosciusko and Pulaski and a dozen others had fought, the Poles formed an impression of revolution on a worldwide scale. The abbé Switkowski, a former Jesuit, and now editor of the chief Polish language journal in Warsaw, published the American and French Declarations of Rights. "In 1789," he wrote in February 1790, "the world was shaken by convulsions and a new era began for the

---

[14] On Mazzei's service to Poland see Fabre, *Stanislas-Auguste*, 507-22 and *passim;* R. Ciampini, ed., *Lettere di Filippo Mazzei alla corte di Polonia* (Bologna, 1937). There seems to be no special study of any influence of the American Revolution in Poland, but M. Haiman, *Poland and the American Revolutionary War* (Chicago, 1932), gives details on over a dozen Poles in America during the Revolution.

human race in Europe. . . . There has been nothing like it since the crusades. . . . As men then fought for the Holy Land it is now for Holy Liberty that they fight. The desire to be free has become a madness at Paris, and has spread East, West and South." Switkowski favored this "madness"; he even approved the French Civil Constitution of the Clergy.[15]

The great event in Poland in 1789 occurred in November. Over a year had now passed since the diet met, and nothing positive had been done, when on November 24, urged on by Kollontay, spokesmen for 141 towns signed an Act of Union at Warsaw. It seems very likely that the level of their expectations had been raised by news of events in France. The act, submitted as a petition to the King, modestly requested a few burgher rights, including representation in the diet itself.

In the diet the general feeling was one of shock. Some members were so incensed that they threatened to leave the assembly if burghers were admitted. All members were gentry and noble, and even the patriots among them had hardly imagined that anyone else should take part in saving the country. There was something subversive about 141 towns banding together. The effects of the French Revolution cut both ways. However moderate the real intent of a Polish reformer might be, if he spoke with favor of the French Revolution, or of the Americans, or alluded to the revolutionary character of the age, or saw in it a sign of the direction in which Poland should be moving, he aroused alarm and consternation, and called up visions, even in 1790, the mildest year of the French Revolution, of aristocrats humiliated by lawyers and country gentlemen insulted by peasants gotten out of hand. Another year passed in the Polish diet with much talk and no action. In the end what happened was a good deal of a compromise.

Late in 1790 the diet adopted the first of three measures for which it is remembered. It excluded landless nobles from attendance at the regional assemblies. This move was a blow against the magnates, and constituted a victory for the reform party, or for the middling nobles who sought to "democratize" Poland by curbing the great lords with their troops of personal followers. This accomplished, the reformers again took up the plea of the towns. There was still much opposition; there were many who thought it outrageous, after disfranchising almost half the nobles, to consider the grant of political powers to the burgher class. At the same time there was a sense of crisis. The designs of

---

[15] J. Grossbart, "La presse polonaise et la Révolution française," in *Annales historiques de la Révolution française*, vol. xiv, 1937, 139. Lesnodorski, *Dzielo*, 84.

Prussia on Danzig and Thorn were known, and Russia, concluding its Turkish war, could be expected soon to make its will felt in Poland. The high point in the debate on the towns was a speech by Niemcewicz. It expressed one of the revolutionary ideas of this revolutionary era, soon to be demonstrated also in France: that liberty, and the extension of rights, far from making a country weak, as the old doctrine held, actually might contribute to its power and its capacity for survival.

"The nobility by itself," said Niemcewicz, "is incapable of defending the country against the ambitious designs of its enemies. Only by a joining of all estates can the Republic increase its strength and its powers of resistance. No one knows to whom Washington owes his birth, and no one knows who Franklin's ancestors were. Yet it is to these two famous men that America owes its liberty and independence." We *need* the burghers, declared the noble Niemcewicz, and it is in our interest for them to be prosperous and productive. Let us offer liberty and property rights, "and we shall see swarms of immigrants from foreign regions come and settle under our government."[16]

A few days later, on April 18, 1791, the diet enacted the Statute of the Cities, the second of its principal acts. So great, however, was the conflict in these debates, so acute was the mounting danger from neighboring powers felt to be, and so much time had been lost since October 1788, that the reform party despaired of obtaining a new constitution by deliberation and agreement. Prince Radziwill, Ignace Potocki, Hugo Kollontay, and others held a series of secret meetings with King Stanislas, who produced a paper that he called "Thoughts of an Elderly Citizen," and which his patriot coworkers seized upon as a very acceptable draft constitution. By prearrangement, at a meeting of the diet from which a good many of the conservatives were absent, the King made a speech on the national emergency and the need for instant action, and he produced his draft, which a tumultuous diet forthwith adopted "by acclamation." Thus arose the famous Constitution of the Third of May. It explicitly incorporated the Statute of Cities, and the two together may be regarded as the Polish constitution of 1791.[17]

The monarchy was made hereditary in the house of Saxony. The

16 Klotz, 357-58; Dany, 189-90.

17 The text of the Constitution of May 3 is printed in French by Klotz, and was printed in French at the time in the Paris *Moniteur* of May 24, 1791. For the text of the equally important Statute of Cities, persons not knowing Polish must apparently resort to the old K. H. L. Pölitz, *Die europäischen Verfassungen seit dem Jahre 1789* (Leipzig, 1832-33), III, 4-8. For the constitution see also Appendix III, item 4, below.

executive was made stronger and more independent, its weakness in the past being called the main source of Poland's troubles. Separate articles, in the manner of the United States constitution of 1787, but inspired more directly by Montesquieu and the theory of the British constitution, provided for executive, legislative, and judicial branches of government. The Liberum Veto was declared abolished, and decision by plurality vote was required. Roman Catholicism was announced to be the national religion, with toleration promised to others. Landed nobles were confirmed in historic rights. Nothing was done for the peasants, except for a specious clause assuring government protection for voluntary bilateral agreements between master and serf. The opening phrase, that Stanislas was King by grace of God and "the nation," was more likely to annoy his fellow monarchs than to strengthen Poland.

It is the new relationship between burghers and nobles that is of most interest. There was nothing like the new principle of national citizenship currently laid down in France. Indeed, one of the concessions made by the Patriots to the conservatives, during the debates, was to avoid the very words "citizen" and "nation" in the drafting of the new law.[18] Rights for burghers were to be burgher rights, and to depend on affiliation with a particular town, but modern principles of the state were admitted in one way, in that all burghers were to enjoy the same rights. A burgher moving from one recognized town to another was to possess the same rights in the new town as in the old. No town could refuse the burgher right to any qualified person who applied for it. Even this much, as readers of this book will perceive, would appear "revolutionary" in Nuremberg or Geneva. The towns lost some of the old privileges and autonomies of medieval type. Lvov, for example, lost the old staple right which had required all goods passing through the city to be stopped and resold for the benefit of Lvov merchants.

It was only to Royal Cities that the Statute of April 18 applied, cities,

[18] Lesnodorski, *Dzielo*, 156. Lesnodorski contrasts the petition of the towns and the projects drafted by Kollontay and Ignace Potocky with the final enactments of the diet. He believes that the diet made the burgher rights purposely complicated in order to befuddle the issue and grant less in reality than in appearance; and he quotes a remark of Ignace Potocky to the King, that it was necessary to "flatter" peasants and burghers, but that it would later be possible "gradually to remove all that which is excessive." See p. 155. He attributes, however, the disinclination to grant rights to burghers, or more executive power to the King, not so much to the magnates as to the agrarian republicanism, with corresponding patriotic and literary traditions, of the gentry as a whole. Here again I am indebted to Mr. Michalski.

that is, which held or might receive charters from the King. Populated centers having "the form of a city," if on royal lands, would receive charters on request. Populated centers on lands belonging to nobles, if inhabited by freemen or by peasants that the lord was willing to free, might be set up as cities by the lord if he so wished, and upon petition by the lord to the King they might receive a royal charter.

Every resident of such a town, if a freeman (not a serf), and a Christian (not a Jew), was to have himself enrolled as a burgher in the Burgher Book. Nobles might enroll as burghers if they wished; those owning property or doing business in a town were required to enroll, and to come under burgher law, without prejudice to their noble status. Towns were to enjoy local self-government, and all property-owning burghers were to elect, and be eligible to, the town offices. Burghers were allowed to buy and enjoy full property rights in "noble" land, that is, rural estates. They received access to public office, to higher appointments in the church, and to commissions in the army, except the cavalry. To them was granted the historic right of the nobles, *neminem captivabimus nisi prius victus*; that is, the King would not imprison them unless they were first convicted in a court of law.

A compromise was reached on burgher representation in the diet. Twenty-one towns were to send representatives, but since the opinion prevailed that only nobles sent by the provincial diets could be "deputies," the town representatives were called "plenipotentiaries," as if the spokesmen of a somewhat alien power. These town delegates were to sit on the tax and police commissions of the diet. They could not be refused the right to speak, but could cast a vote only on commercial matters or other matters affecting the cities. The idea persisted that burghers were unsuited to affairs of state, and a law subsequent to May 3 prescribed that cabinet ministers must be men of inherited noble rank.

It was made easy, however, for burghers to be promoted to the nobility. This provision, among all constitutions of the period, was peculiar to the constitution of Poland, and it reveals, on the one hand, how remote from its authors' minds was the idea of abolishing legal status, and, on the other, how the Polish nobility was less jealously exclusive, less preoccupied with pedigree, more conscious of being simply a general upper class, even in a vague sense more "democratic," than most of the aristocracies in the West. By the statute, any burgher who bought an "entire village," on which he paid at least 200 guilders

in taxes, could become a noble. Burghers serving two years as town delegates in the diet, and those reaching the rank of captain in the army,
were also to be nobles. In addition, each diet was to ennoble thirty
burghers who had obtained distinction in the army, the government
service, as factory owners, or as merchants selling native products. In
short, burghers of notable achievement, or those especially useful to
the country, were to be absorbed, or drained off, year by year, into
the noble class.

A Game of Ideological Football

News of the Polish Revolution was at first received with satisfaction
throughout the Western World. Persons of the most contrary opinions
found something in it to approve, but precisely in the universality of
these praises there lay a danger, for by 1791 the world of Atlantic
Civilization, if the term be permitted, had become aware of deep
ideological cleavages, and it aroused the suspicion of each party to
hear Poland so loudly eulogized by the other. As always, observers
used Poland to draw a lesson or read a lecture. Poland was caught in
the cross-fire of argument over the French Revolution. It was kicked
about in a game of ideological football.

"A great and important Revolution in favor of the rights of man
. . . happily begun without violence or tumult . . . a most wonderful
revolution. . . ." So said the *Gazette of the United States*, published
at Philadelphia. It put to shame, according to these Americans, the
constitution given to Canada at the same time by the British. Toasts
"to the King of Poland" were drunk at Philadelphia and at Richmond.
Poets warmed to the subject:

> Waked by the vernal breeze, see Poland, France
> With youth renew'd and vig'rous health advance.

Thomas Paine considered applying for Polish citizenship, and Joel
Barlow, also in Europe and caught up in the international revolutionary
spirit, wrote a long and enthusiastic letter to the Polish King.[19]

In Holland, the *Leiden Gazette* thought that "if there are any
miracles in this century, one has happened in Poland." The London
Critical Review, surveying the new Polish, French, and United States
federal constitutions together, found that the Polish had "caught its
spirit" from the American. Peter Ochs, at Basel, saw in the Polish

[19] M. Haiman, *The Fall of Poland in Contemporary American Opinion* (Chicago,
1935), 38-62.

revolution, as in the French and American, a sign of world renewal.[20]

In France the revolutionaries, who had now been remaking France for two years, at first hailed the Polish revolution with delight. The sections of the revolutionary Paris municipality sent their congratulations. Lyons did likewise, and little Marenne and Neuf-Brisach and Valognes and many others. The first reports of the Warsaw correspondent of the *Moniteur* were enthusiastic.[21] In France, in May 1791 (a month before Varennes), there was a growing fear of a conspiracy of kings, including Louis XVI, against the Revolution. The journalists of Paris therefore brandished the virtuous King of Poland in the face of his royal brothers. The monarchs of Europe, declared Prudhomme in his *Révolutions de Paris*, had better make haste to issue a constitution to their peoples, like the King of Poland, before their peoples rebelled against them as in France.[22] Camille Desmoulins took a less elated but still menacing tone. In 1789 he had founded a newspaper called the *Révolutions de France et de Brabant*, which in April 1791 he significantly reentitled the *Revolutions of France and other Kingdoms which by demanding a National Assembly . . . will deserve a place in the annals of Liberty*. He observed scornfully that the new Polish constitution confirmed the nobles in their old privileges, and that in the admission of burghers to the army an exception was made for the cavalry, "the horse being so noble an animal that it can be constitutionally mounted only by a gentleman." "Still," he concluded, "we must be fair. Considering where the people of Poland began, they have made as great a leap toward liberty as we have. Doubtless they will come closer to the Declaration of Rights, for *il n'y a que le premier pas qui coûte*."[23]

Such praises from the revolutionary direction, such intimations that events in Poland were a mere first step, had many disturbing repercussions. They were embarrassing to King Stanislas and the Polish reformers. They proved, so to speak, the worst that the Russian tsarina and the unreconstructed Polish magnates could say about Jacobinism in Poland. And they induced other admirers of the Polish Revolution (as, indeed, of the American) to dismiss any such association with France with a shudder, and to argue that in reality, and strictly speaking, there had been no revolution in Poland at all, or at least to dwell

---

[20] *Gazette de Leyde*, numbers 37, 39 and 40 of 1791; *Critical Review*, Sept.-Dec. 1791, 443; on Ochs, above, 364.

[21] Fabre, *Stanislas-Auguste*, 526-30; *Moniteur*, May 7, 1791.

[22] *Révolutions de Paris*, May 14-21, 1791, VIII, 274.

[23] *Révolutions de France . . .* , number 79 (April, 1791), 33-37.

with approval on its great moderation. The purpose in this line of argument was to discredit the French Revolution.

The editor of a German-language paper at Warsaw, the *Warschauer Wochenschrift*, found the new Polish arrangements far more to his taste than the French. "In both countries the burgher estate feels more fortunate, but how different the way in which it has become so! There, the burgher drives the noble out of the temple. Here, the noble offers the burgher his hand. There, discord, women and democrats. Here, friends, men, substance."[24] Mallet du Pan and others of conservative disposition throughout Europe amplified essentially this same simple message. Most notable among them was Edmund Burke. In the words of a modern French scholar, Burke assumed a "philosophical protectorate over the Polish revolution."[25] He had lately published his *Reflections* on the Revolution in France. He now took the occasion to show what he meant by a revolution that was good and constructive.

There is, or was, in the archives at Warsaw a series of letters from Burke to King Stanislas, in which he expressed his enthusiasm.[26] For the English, he expressed it in his *Appeal from the New to the Old Whigs*.

"Anarchy and servitude at once removed . . . ten millions of men in a way of being freed gradually. . . . Everything kept in its place and order; but in that place and order everything bettered. . . . Unheard of conjunction of wisdom and fortune. . . . Not one drop of blood spilled. . . . No studied insults on religion, morals, or manners. . . . True and genuine rights and interests of men. . . . Regular progress . . . towards the stable excellence of a British Constitution."[27]

Burke, of course, like everyone else, was using Poland as a stick with which to beat his own enemies, particularly the French Revolution and those New Whigs who felt a certain sympathy toward it. Poland proved that the French Revolution was entirely unnecessary. Why did these New Whigs, he asked, these people like Fox and Sheridan and Mackintosh, persist in their partiality to the French Revolution, and show such embarrassed reservation in their praises of the Polish, unless it was that they wished to undermine the constitution in England? And he reviewed the history of the era and of his own opinions, to refute the charge that he had contradicted himself: he had favored the American Revolution because it made no demand for new liberties,

---

[24] Grossbart, as in note 15 above, 249.   [25] Fabre, 527.
[26] For these letters of Burke's see Fabre, 679, notes 118-20.
[27] Burke, *Writings* (1901), IV, 195-97.

but was purely defensive, the only issue being novel Parliamentary taxation; and it was perfectly consistent for him, as a warm friend of true liberty, to oppose the instruction of members and the so-called reform of Parliament, to prevent the introduction of French principles into the Canada Act, to view with alarm the sprouting of English political clubs, and to see no merit in the French Revolution (and he might have added the Dutch), while calling attention to events in Poland as a model of orderly liberation.

In France, the revolutionaries soon perceived that the success of the Polish Revolution, or its alleged success (which was to be brief), was being used against them. It was being exploited to represent the French as wildly visionary and wantonly violent. Prudhomme, of the *Révolutions de Paris*, changed his tune in one week. Our enemies harp on Poland to discredit us. "The monarchs, our neighbors, to escape the great revolution that menaces them in their own countries, are going to provoke little ones themselves. They will reach understandings with their subjects. To prevent imitation of us, they will take care to exaggerate our losses and to minimize our gains, and will glory like Stanislas in their moderation."[28] The truth is, he said, that the Polish revolution is a fraud. There has really been none. The serfs remain where they were, and the burghers have been thrown crumbs from the noble table. The same view was taken by a then well-known revolutionary militant, Mehée de la Touche, who early in 1792 published his *Histoire de la prétendue révolution de Pologne*. He poured contempt on Poland and the Poles. He observed that neither serfs nor Jews had obtained any rights. "I suppose that no one," he said, "can seriously argue that the ennoblement of a few bourgeois is a good thing for the bourgeoisie."[29] It became the settled opinion, in France, to scoff at the Polish Revolution as a mere agitation among aristocrats. Meanwhile, however, the praises at first received from revolutionaries and radicals in the West—from the Paris sections, the London clubs, Joel Barlow, Condorcet, Sieyès and others—had put King Stanislas into a difficult situation. He felt obliged to dissociate himself from charges of Jacobinism. By parading his own moderation he hoped to ward off intervention by Russia or Prussia, and to win the support of gentry and nobles for the new order.

"Our law of May 3, and everything that has come out of it since," said King Stanislas in April 1792, as Europe was going to war, "are

[28] *Révolutions de Paris*, May 21-28, 1791, VIII, 311-16.
[29] Pp. 2, 143; see also *Moniteur*, January 7, 1792.

almost the opposite of the French Revolution and keep us very far from democracy, and hence all the more from the Jacobins." He insisted, to gain confidence in his leadership, that he had himself suppressed peasant rebellions by force, and dissolved the artisan associations that might have grown into political clubs. "The Polish bourgeoisie," he averred, "far from affecting a tone of equality with the nobles, has always evinced the greatest respect for its superiors, whom it rightly regards as its benefactors."[30]

By the first part of the year 1792, in short, there was general agreement that nothing had happened in Poland that was at all like the French Revolution. Western Conservatives and revolutionaries, and the Polish King himself and some other makers of the Third of May, each took this position, each for his own reasons.

Yet there had been, it seems to me, as it seems to Professor Lesnodorski and other modern Polish writers, a significant and even a dangerous revolution in Poland, or would be if the new constitution could be maintained.[31] This revolution ignited a center of conflagration in Eastern Europe secondary only to the one in France. The comparison and the contrast to the French Revolution were after all in large measure irrelevant. By the French standard, in either action or principle, the Polish Revolution was a tame affair. It was not so tame for Poland, or for Eastern Europe. In Poland, the constitution of May 3 threatened to end the oligarchy of the magnates. The middling landed nobles who were the chief gainers, reinforced by less numerous burghers, were not wholly negligible in numbers; if there were 400,000 of them in a population of 8,000,000 they constituted over a twentieth of the population, probably not very different from the proportion that voted for Parliament in Great Britain.

Eastern Europe, except for Poland, at this time meant the Russian, Austrian, and Prussian monarchies. In none of them, with exceptions for Hungary, was there any elected parliamentary body with powers like those now contemplated for the Polish diet. All of them were lands of peasant serfdom, and while the Polish constitution did nothing to emancipate the peasants, it was in part the work of men, like Kollontay, whose thoughts moved in this direction. In none of the three monarchies did towns enjoy such self-government as was envisaged for Poland. Even in the West, even in England, there were

[30] Fabre, 531.
[31] Lesnodorski on p. 211, Jablonski on p. 256 of *La Pologne au Xe Congrès international*; but they see the uprising of 1794 as far more truly revolutionary.

few towns where each property-owner could actually cast a vote for councilman or mayor. In neither Russia, Prussia, nor the Hapsburg empire were burghers as free to acquire rural land as under the new Polish laws. Nor could they so readily rise into the gentry. It was easy for French democrats to laugh at the Statute of Cities, or for conservatives of all Western nationalities to praise its realistic correspondence to the facts of Polish life. It was nevertheless disturbing for Eastern Europe. There is evidence, indeed, that East Europeans saw it as such, and agreed with Niemcewicz that it might threaten neighboring powers by attracting immigrants into Poland. The Austrian minister at Warsaw, on April 27, 1791, was of this opinion, "Would it not be prudent," he inquired of Vienna on reporting the terms of the new Statute, "to take the necessary measures to prevent emigration of our Galician burghers?"[32] The monarchs and the hierarchs of Eastern Europe were by no means mistaken in detecting in the Polish constitution a disconcerting odor of Jacobinism. Leopold II of Austria, characteristically enough, was the only one who said anything in its favor, and he soon died.[33]

Neither its touted moderation, nor the hearty approval of Edmund Burke, was enough to save the Polish constitution from extinction. Moderation was not at bottom the true issue. Nor was it the bloodshed and the "excesses" of the French Revolution that caused the most resentment. Modern principles of the state, or ideas with a democratic tinge, even when moderately stated, as by Dutch Patriots, Belgian democrats, Genevese Représentants, English and Irish parliamentary reformers, or William Pitt himself, had for ten years met with nothing but repression or failure. The same happened in Poland. Disgruntled magnates, led by Felix Potocki and the Branicki, formed the Confederation of Targowica. Raising up their followers they declared war on the new regime. They accepted Russian intervention to crush it. "I shall fight Jacobinism, and beat it in Poland," the Empress Catherine wrote to Grimm in 1792.[34] This she did, with aid from the King of

[32] Dany, *Idées politiques*, 195-96.

[33] On reaction of the East European courts see the French summary of the Polish work of S. Smolka, "L'Europe et la constitution du 3 mai 1791," in *Bulletin international de l'Académie des sciences de Cracovie*, 1891.

[34] *La Pologne au Xe Congrès international*, 216. John Adams remarked, in a note added to his *Defense* at some time not before 1797, that a constitution may fail because of "circumstances having nothing to do with its intrinsic excellence," and that if the United States were in the geographical position of Poland, given the controversies that existed in America, it was "at least an open question" whether troubles as bad as those of Poland might not have developed under the constitution of the United States. *Works* (1851), IV, 374 n.

Prussia. The Polish constitution of 1791 survived only a year, and Poland itself was cut up by the Second Partition. But we encroach here on the story of the international counterrevolution, which I shall develop at length in a later place.

There was another country too big to be bullied, then the most populous state in the world of Western Civilization, still at the height of its cultural leadership, in the forefront of science, engineering, and the military arts, busy and wealthy, full of peasants who were not serfs, of aristocrats who were not cowboys, and bulging with bourgeois, the most brilliant and the most dangerous of all the peoples of Europe, as it seemed to Tocqueville. It is time, after the involved narrative of preceding chapters, to turn to the French Revolution.

THE FRENCH REVOLUTION: THE
ARISTOCRATIC RESURGENCE

The Monarchy might become an aristocracy of magistrates, as contrary to the rights and interests of the nation as to those of the sovereign power.—LOUIS XVI to the Parlement of Paris, 1788

No, Sire, no aristocracy in France, but no despotism either.—THE PARLEMENT OF PARIS in reply

THE FRENCH REVOLUTION: THE
ARISTOCRATIC RESURGENCE

THAT the French Revolution had points of resemblance to movements of the time in other countries is the central theme of this book. Like them, it arose out of circumstances characteristic of Western Civilization, and it was to merge with them, especially with the war that began in 1792, into a great struggle that no political borders could contain. From the beginning, however, there was much that was unique about the revolution in France.

The very size of France was enough to make its Revolution a special case. Fifty French cities in 1789 were larger than the Boston of the Tea Party. Paris, except for London, was by far the greatest city of Europe, having, with over 600,000 people, three times the population of Amsterdam or Vienna. Twenty-six million Frenchmen outnumbered the British and the Spanish by more than two to one. Only small and divided German and Italian states lay along France's eastern border. The French outnumbered the subjects of the Russian Empire until after the partitions of Poland; and if they were not much more numerous than those of the Hapsburg dominions, they greatly excelled them in wealth, in national unity, and in complexity of social structure. The actual revenues of the Bourbon monarchy, whose inadequacy brought on the Revolution of 1789, nevertheless approached 500,000,000 livres a year, and were larger than those of Great Britain, twice as large as those of the Hapsburg monarchy, over three times those of Russia, Prussia, Spain, or the Dutch Republic, and twenty-five times those of the United States federal government in the 1790's. France in 1794 was to put almost a million men into uniform, a feat accomplished nowhere else until much later.

This huge country was no monolith. It was extremely diversified, and different conditions obtained from one province to another. A few generalizations may yet be made. The nobility, at the highest estimate, numbered 400,000 persons of all ages and both sexes, so that, though numerous, it made up less than two per cent of the population, in contrast to the four to eight per cent in Hungary and Poland. There were not over 100,000 priests, monks, and nuns, a surprisingly low figure for a Catholic country, for the proportion of clergy in Protestant England seems to have been much greater. Clergy and nobility, as is well known, were legally the two higher "orders." No one knows the number of bourgeois, the word itself being hard to define; but the aggregate population of the fifty largest towns was about 2,200,000. Where in Poland all the people in the fifty largest towns were less numerous than the nobles, they were over five times as numerous as the nobles in France. Only a fraction of townsmen could be called "bourgeois," but on the other hand, in France, a good many "bourgeois" lived in small villages or in the country. The interpenetration of town and country was in fact one of the distinctive features of French society. Lawyers, government employees, innkeepers, a few doctors, retired soldiers, people drawing income from property, lived among the agricultural population. Often there were family ties between townsmen and countrymen. The latter might have matters of business that took them into town. The peasants lived within a kind of manorial system, but there was little that recalled personal serfdom. Peasants could be landowners, as landed property was defined in the manorial context; and although most peasants owned either none or not enough, there were a good many that owned enough land, and raised enough of a crop, to be an embryonic rural bourgeoisie. There were wide variations from region to region, but on a rough average for the whole country it is thought that peasants owned over thirty per cent of the land, the nobles considerably less, the bourgeoisie about twenty per cent, the clergy ten or less, and the crown the remainder. The mighty barriers of Central and Eastern Europe between town and country, or class and class, were worn down in France to fences that could be seen across and even climbed. It was possible for ideas to circulate throughout rural France with remarkable speed, and enough common ground existed for town and country to react alike, and together, to an economic or political or psychological stimulus. Causes of class conflict existed, but when France is compared with the rest of Europe it is the extent of community that seems most important.

Large and complex, France enjoyed a qualitative preeminence also. It was the most active center of the European Enlightenment. Its language was the most international of all modern tongues. The French thought it natural to be imitated by others; they had been imitated in the age of the Gothic cathedrals, and again in the age of Louis XIV, and in the eighteenth century the upper classes of courts and salons, and the intellectuals of academies and reading clubs, commonly looked to France as a country from which much might be learned. The French Revolution occurred in one of the most advanced centers of civilization. The same country which had had irresistible attractions for the upper classes offered after 1789 attractions equally irresistible to the lower. This fact made the French Revolution more shocking and unintelligible to beneficiaries of the old order everywhere. It distinguishes it also from the Russian and other twentieth-century revolutions, whose resemblance to the French, of which much has been made, would be the greater if Marx's revolution had first come about, as he and Lenin expected, in an advanced capitalist country such as England or Germany.

The French Revolution went beyond all others of the period in its scope. It remained primarily political, like other movements of the time, on the supposition that all spheres of life were to be transformed by reorganization of the state, along with introduction of new laws or abolition of old ones. But in its effects on society and social and moral attitudes it went far beyond the merely political, more so than the American Revolution, and much more so than anything contemplated by the Polish, Dutch, Belgian, Genevese, English, or Irish reformers or revolutionaries described in the preceding pages. The French Revolution changed the very nature and definition of property, and to some extent its distribution; it transformed, or attempted to transform, the church, the army, the educational system, institutions of public relief, the legal system, the market economy, and the relationship of employers and employees. It introduced new crucial values, new status strivings, new levels of expectation. It changed the essence of the community and of the individual's sense of his membership in it and his relationship to fellow citizens and fellow men. It even changed the feeling for history, or the idea of what could or ought to happen in history and in the world. Leopold von Ranke once remarked that the growth of historical studies in the nineteenth century was a form of reaction against the Napoleonic empire. As much might be said for the French Revolution and the European Revolution of which it was the largest part. A whole system of civilization seemed to have fallen, and a new one to be struggling to be born; and men of all shades of opinion, whether to further such a change òr to oppose it, took a new view of the possibilities, the hopes, the delusions, and the dangers in the evolution of the human race itself.

The Problem of the French Revolution

For so vast an upheaval vast explanations have usually been found. It has been the habit of historians and political commentators to set the Revolution in a long context of centuries, finding for it distant origins and underlying causes. Thus for Hegel the Revolution represented the emancipation of Mind, the point in history at which Mind, becoming fully conscious, set about determining the conditions of its further existence in the world. For Hegel, for liberals and for democrats, the Revolution was one of a very few great events, such as the introduction of Christianity and the Protestant Reformation, by which the slow growth of freedom had been attained. For Tocqueville it was a climax in the age-long movement toward equality of conditions and growth of central power and public authority. For Marx it signalized the victory of the bourgeois over the feudal order. For Carlyle and for Michelet it was brought on by centuries of misery and oppression of the common people. Others, contrariwise, both Marxists and non-Marxists, have seen it as the outcome of the growing prosperity, wealth, education, ambition, and self-confidence of the French middle classes. Talleyrand attributed it in the last analysis to human vanity, of which he thought the French had more than their share. For Burke the actions of the French in 1789 were "an unforced choice, a fond election of evil," having no more compelling cause than human perversity itself, a vast enough cause, to be sure. For Pope Pius VI, a contemporary, the Revolution was another outbreak, which he compared to Jansenism and Calvinism, in the long history of menaces to true religious faith. Other Catholics, including Pius VII, have been less negative toward it. Various modern writers, usually seizing upon some of the insights of Tocqueville, or agreeing with Taine that the Revolution arose from a fanatical commitment to abstract ideas, have seen in it an anticipation of the totalitarian state.

Recently in France there has been much interest in demographic studies, and the Revolution has been attributed to the rapid increase of population in the eighteenth century, which raised the pressure of people on the land, under existing conditions of agriculture and alternative employments, and produced a population with a very high proportion in the younger, bolder, and more restless age-groups. The population of France did increase from eighteen or nineteen to twenty-five or twenty-six millions between 1700 and 1789, and growth in England, Italy, and other countries was in the same ratio. Professor Godechot of Toulouse, who favors this explanation, half humorously attributes the Revolution of the Western World to the discovery of America, finding a certain elegance in relating these two "capital steps in the history of mankind."[1] His argument is as follows: Population increased because improvements in nutrition, through the growing use of foods originating mainly in America, such as sugar, potatoes and Indian corn (the latter used to fatten poultry and livestock) allowed greater numbers to survive, especially among the poor; but though they survived they did not live well, many remaining underemployed, while meanwhile new discoveries of gold in Brazil, and improvements in silver mining in Spanish America, by increasing the European money supply drove up the price level at a time when wages lagged. The long trend of rising prices, with low wages, contributed to the prosperity of the bourgeoisie and the more substantial farmers, and the bourgeoisie was further benefited by the growth of foreign and colonial trade; but the swelling numbers of landless or nearly landless peasants, of unskilled and unemployed workers, and of paupers and vagrants, built up the mass discontent of which the revolutionary leaders were to make successful use.

Of all these explanations it may be said that they explain too little and too much. Some characterize the course of modern history as a whole. Others make it understandable that there should have been a great disturbance or convulsion at the end of the eighteenth century. They do not explain the form which this disturbance took. They explain everything except the Revolution itself. The Revolution was not simply a chaotic upheaval, but a purposeful political movement accentuating certain recognizable if not always very definite concepts—"feudalism," "aristocracy," "constitution," "citizen," "sovereignty of the people," "nation," "law," "liberty," "equality," "nature," and "natural rights."

These words have the value at least of suggesting what the men of the French Revolution thought they were doing. We come, therefore, to the role of "ideas" in the Revolution, and to "psychological" explanations of its origin and course. The importance of ideas as a

---

[1] J. Godechot, *La Grande Nation: l'expansion révolutionnaire de la France dans le monde*, 2 vols. (Paris, 1956), I, 32-37. For more detailed analysis of effects of price and wage movements see C. Labrousse, *La crise de l'économie française à la fin de l'ancien régime* (Paris, 1944).

cause has long been stressed on all sides of the question. From a point of view favorable to the Revolution, from the profundities of Hegel to the quick assumptions of those engaged in the struggle itself, it has been supposed that men carried out a revolution because they had lived through the Enlightenment, or desired to realize liberty because they had formulated the idea of it in their minds. The argument that ideas cause revolutionary troubles has always, however, been especially congenial to persons less favorable to revolution, or even to change, always with the corollary that ideas, or the ideas in question, are impractical in character, unrelated to actual problems, utopian, visionary, or millennial (sometimes they are compared to a religion), and at any rate are the notions of mere intellectuals (*philosophes* before 1789) without experience of real human nature or real affairs. The effect is to reduce revolution to nonsense, or to the realm of the impossible, though it is of course the very possibility of revolution, or fear that it may be possible, that motivates this line of argument. It is an old and yet ever-living theory. In 1783 Mr. George Ponsonby dismissed the proposal for Irish parliamentary reform as "system mongering," and Burke used the same argument against parliamentary reform in England before applying it to the Revolution in France; and in 1957, in the learned *Political Science Quarterly*, an American historian called Robespierre's idea of the good society a "syllogistic paradise."

If we know anything of human psychology, however, we know that men's behavior is not fully explained by their ideas, in the sense of their concepts, and that we must look not only to the manifest but to the latent content of their minds. What really lay behind the magic words—"liberty," "equality," "nation," "sovereignty," and the others? Bourgeois interests, according to one widely diffused school of thought. Nationalism, according to another. Incipient totalitarianism and fateful trust in the omnipotent state, according to a third. Vanity, according to Talleyrand. A desire for better government appointments on the part of frustrated lesser officials (*ôtez-vous de là que je m'y mette*) according to Metternich—to which Professor Alfred Cobban in one mood seems to subscribe. Fanaticism, according to J. F. La Harpe. Error and confusion, according to F. L. C. Montjoie, who in 1797 published a discussion of twenty-one terms, including *liberté, égalité, volonté générale*, and *pouvoir constituant*, the misunderstanding of which he thought had unfortunately brought about the French Revolution. Nothing at all lay behind these expressions, according to still another observer—not a sophisticated twentieth-century logical positivist, but an angry counterrevolutionary of 1792—who wrote in an early semantic treatise: "*Aristocrat*: arrangement of syllables which produces strange effects on the animal called *democrat*. . . . What has this revolution produced? What do the words *aristocrat, liberty, equality* have to offer except arrangements of syllables?"[2]

Many "psychological" interpretations of the French Revolution have in fact sounded somewhat like counterrevolutionary polemics. When Gustave Le Bon, a founder of social psychology, wrote a book on the French Revolution, the result was hardly distinguishable from the work of Taine. To expose the irrationality of the revolutionaries, the disparity between word and deed, the conjunction of idealism with ruthlessness, or of sentimentality with self-interest, to dwell on supposed contradictions (such as "forcing men to be free"), to convert one thing into another, and to reduce a desire to transform the community into compulsions of an unbalanced mind, as if revolutionaries were only unadjusted individuals, or victims of some public mania or craze, have generally appealed both to persons with a certain interest in psychology, and to those who for political reasons dislike the French Revolution, or revolutions in general. The common feature, in these interpretations, is to deny or minimize the need or reason for the behavior or the opinions that are being examined.

Yet a serious psychology need not lead to this pitfall. A study made by three social psychologists in the 1950's is relevant to the present connection. It is a study of the origin of political ideas, and of their relation to inner conditions of personality. The opinions of fifty selected adult male Americans on the subject of Soviet Russia were used as the medium for this investigation. The men chosen were of various psychological types, and their opinions on Russia were very diverse. The authors concluded that opinion is the inseparable result of three factors: "reality demands, social demands and inner psychological demands."[3]

This finding of social psychology may be constructively applied to the problem of the French Revolution. An extraordinary number of

---

[2] See A. Cobban, *The Myth of the French Revolution: An Inaugural Lecture* (London, 1955); J. F. La Harpe, *Du fanatisme dans la langue révolutionnaire* (Paris, 1797); F. L. C. Montjoie, *Histoire de la Révolution française* (Paris, 1797); *Nouveau dictionnaire pour servir à l'intelligence des termes mis en vogue par la Révolution* (Paris, 1792); F. Brunot, *Histoire de la langue française des origines à 1900*, 12 vols. (Paris, 1905-1953), IX, 652 and *passim*.

[3] M. Brewster Smith, J. S. Bruner, and R. M. White, *Opinions and Personality* (New York, 1956), 275.

people at that time developed very pronounced opinions on liberty, equality, the rights of the people, national sovereignty, the constitution, the royal veto, the aristocracy, the "aristocratic conspiracy," the "foreign conspiracy," and much else. They showed strange mixtures of suspiciousness, aggressiveness, naïveté, and simple faith. It might be shown, though with difficulty, how these attitudes reflected "inner psychological demands," such as frustrations, anxieties, hostilities, and daydreams derived from childhood or other private experience. It might be shown how they reflected "social demands," for many people who shouted "aristocrat" or cried *vive la nation* did so because of social pressure, because so many others were doing the same, or because not to show enthusiasm might be dangerous. It could also be shown how these ideas met "reality demands." Burke notwithstanding, it seems likely that they grew out of actual circumstances, and had a direct relevancy to problems which really existed. The key words of the Revolution were not always misunderstood by the revolutionaries, nor were they mere arrangements of syllables. Robespierre did not really work for a paradise, nor expect the new France to be syllogistic. The ideas of the Revolution, even when most exaggerated or fantastic, had an actual base.

The real problem of the French Revolution is to explain why it was so radical at the very beginning. In a way the first leaders, those of June and July 1789, were moderate enough. Intending no violence, and with no expectation of mass upheaval, they would have preferred to work harmoniously with Louis XVI at the task of national reorganization, and most of them would have been satisfied to obtain, in 1789, about what Louis XVIII was to concede in 1814. The rush of events was soon to make them realize how moderate they really were, for much was to happen that the original leaders could not accept. Nevertheless, it can be misleading to think of a "moderate" revolution of 1789 which took more extreme forms in 1792 and 1793. The contrary could as well be maintained: that it was the alleged moderates of 1789 who in a few rapid strokes destroyed the existing order, leaving what Taine disapprovingly called a spontaneous anarchy, and the half-million little men of the Jacobin clubs of 1793, who in an enormous wave of citizen self-help, having ousted their former rulers or been deserted by them, and with no new institutions yet accepted and effectively functioning, undertook to consolidate the revolutionary program, maintain a government, and carry on an international war in the face of military invasion.

Edmund Burke, in his *Reflections* written in 1790, was right enough in perceiving the radicalism of the Revolution at its outset. By "radicalism" I mean a deep estrangement from the existing order, an insistence upon values incompatible with those embodied in actual institutions, a refusal to entertain projects of compromise, a mood of impatience, suspicion, and exasperation, an embittered class consciousness reaching the point of hatred, a determination to destroy and to create, and a belief that both destruction and creation would be relatively easy. In such a mood the men of 1789 took steps which never could be retracted. The Oath of the Tennis Court, the decrees of August, the Declaration of the Rights of Man and Citizen, the repudiation of legal class, the relegation of the King to the position of a first magistrate, the expropriation of the church, all accomplished or at least proclaimed before the end of 1789, were a series of such irrevocable commitments. They left no room for maneuver, for tactical retreat, for gaining time, for gradualism, for conciliation, or for convenient silence on general principles. They publicized and they maximized an absolute difference of principle between the old regime and the new. What followed flowed as a consequence from this initial work. It has been said, notably by Aulard, that the rest of the Revolution was mainly "defensive," and this is offered in justification of the unpleasantness that followed; but if defensive, it was defense of the advanced position taken in 1789, and one that was tenable only with difficulty because of the opposition that it aroused.

Nor was this radicalism of 1789 to be found only in the assembly which sat from May to October at Versailles and thereafter at Paris. The real revolution erupted throughout the country as a whole, in the agrarian rebellions of the summer, and in the municipal revolutions of Paris and the hundreds of towns, great and small, throughout the length and breadth of the provinces, where new men turned local oligarchs out of office. These events were so uniform and so nearly simultaneous as to raise the suspicion, then and since, of conspiratorial methods. Actually, it is hard to find anything more conspiratorial than the committees of correspondence of the American Revolution. Though such judgments can only be impressionistic, there seems to have been a more nearly universal rising in France in 1789 than in America in 1775.

So much being said for the uniqueness of the French Revolution, the pattern used in foregoing chapters will be applied to it in the following pages. Reforms favored by the government, along the lines of enlightened despotism, were opposed by the upper classes, which played a political role in certain constituted bodies, notably the parlements and the Provincial Estates. These classes were in fact enjoying an "aristocratic resurgence," for the French aristocracy was by no means decadent, and many of its members desired more active positions in public life. The constituted bodies defended what they called the historic constitution of the kingdom, and favored a form of constitutional monarchy, in which, however, their own powers and privileges would be preserved or extended, and a society of ranks and orders would be maintained. They obtained the convening of the Estates General, with representation by "order," but the bulk of the country refused to embody itself according to these older forms. Demand arose for representation of persons, not of status, and for an entirely new constitution for France. The idea of the people as a constituent power, able to make or unmake all political institutions, and to issue grants of authority, was applied in France, as nowhere else except in America up to this time. The sovereignty claimed for the people meant that no one else, neither hereditary magistrate, nor manorial seigneur, nor even the King, could hold public authority by virtue of his own right or status. There should be no irremovable persons in government, with delicate reservations for the King himself. There should be no self-recruiting public powers. The law should know no classes or orders. All persons should be citizens, with equality of rights. Constitutionally at least, this was the essence of the Revolution of 1789.

Ministers and Parlements, 1774-1788

If the Revolution seemed to begin in 1789 with astonishing violence, it was because it had not really begun in 1789 at all. In a way it had begun a quarter of a century before, with the propaganda campaign of the *philosophes*, and especially with the quarrels between the royal government and the parlements, whose climax in the 1760's has been described in Chapter IV.

The French parlements, as has been explained, were corporate bodies, or benches of judicial magistrates, each acting as a supreme court of law for its part of the country, and asserting the power to "verify" laws or taxes proposed by the crown, which in effect meant to consent to them before enforcing them in the courts. These magistrates, who numbered about eleven hundred in all the parlements combined, were mostly nobles, often of several generations of noble descent; and they owned their seats as a form of property, acquired them usually by inheritance, and occupied them irremovably and for life. They were by no means councils of grave old men, for since most of them owed their position to family the average age was surprisingly low, as in the House of Commons. In 1789 over half the members of the Parlement of Paris were under thirty-five. Some were very wealthy; Le Peletier de Saint-Fargeau (who in truth became a Jacobin, and friend of Robespierre) had 500,000 livres a year; and First President d'Aligre was rumored to have an annual income of 700,000 and a nest-egg of five million in the Bank of England.[4]

In what I have called the quasi-revolution of the 1760's the parlements had had a grand conflict with the King's ministers. Protesting against modernization of property assessments, they had banded together in an *union des classes*, or a super-parlement claiming to be representative of the whole kingdom. On the one hand, a royalist pamphleteer denounced the parlements as a "monstrous hereditary aristocracy." On the other hand, the parlements, as early as the 1760's, put a good deal of incipient revolutionary language into wide circulation—*citoyen, loi, patrie, constitution, nation, droit de la nation*, and *cri de la nation*. It seems likely that the parlements had more positive influence than the *philosophes*, especially among lawyers and other makers of public opinion, to whom they spoke out as weighty and reputable bodies in Paris and a dozen provincial capitals. Louis XV had tried to silence them in 1766, in the *séance de la flagellation*, then in 1771 had simply abolished them by a monarchical *coup d'état*. Louis XVI, however, at his accession in 1774, restored the old parlements in their historic form.

Twenty-two years after the *séance de la flagellation*, Louis XVI was at odds with his parlements as much as his predecessor had been, and was even, in his turn, declaring that if they had their way they would become "an aristocracy of magistrates," harmful to "the rights and interests of the nation." This accusation the Parlement of Paris indignantly rejected. The danger to France, it warned on May 4, 1788, came not from aristocracy but from despotism. "The right of freely verifying the laws does not make the parlements an aristocracy of magistrates. If it had happened that your parlement had refused to accept useful laws, we should have to pity humanity but still not make the

[4] On age, see J. Egret, "L'aristocratie parlementaire française à la fin de l'ancien régime," in *Revue historique*, ccviii (1952), 12-13; on wealth, H. Carré, *La fin des parlements* (Paris, 1912), 2ff.

king a despot, destroy the constitution, or establish servitude. . . . But is it true that your parlement need reproach itself with such refusals?"[5] The parlement thus invited an examination of its record.

The record shows that the parlement took a strong stand for important liberal principles, that it helped to school the country on the evils of unchecked government power, that it long enjoyed the support of public opinion, that non-nobles were slow in turning against it, but finally did so abruptly and with devastating effect, since the parlement associated its liberalism with palpable class interest.

The young Louis XVI in 1774 wished above all else to be a good king, no "despot," and to act as differently as possible from his discredited grandfather. Hence he restored the parlements. He also appointed the reformer Turgot as his chief minister. These two steps soon proved to be incompatible. Turgot was a tenth-generation noble, but he was also a physiocrat and an experienced government servant, who had in mind a general reconstruction of the French government and economy. He wished, for example, to temper the royal absolutism by associating the administration with the country, through provincial assemblies in which property-ownership, not legal class, should be the basis of representation. He also desired the toleration of Protestants, and their admission to all offices and occupations. On these larger matters of church and state he kept discreetly silent. His troubles arose over points of detail, designed mainly to loosen up the French economic system so as to increase national income and so raise government revenues. In particular, he proposed certain incidental tax reforms, internal freedom of the grain trade, abolition of craft gilds, and conversion of the *corvée royale*, the labor services of peasants on the royal highways, into a money tax to be paid by landowners of all classes alike. He drafted Six Edicts, which the Parlement of Paris refused to accept.

Of all these proposals, that concerning the *corvée royale* should have been the most innocuous. The *corvée* was performed only a few days in the year, and only by peasants who lived near the royal highways. It was by no means vital to the social structure of the country, and was in fact only fifty years old. The Parlement of Paris nevertheless not only refused to countenance its abolition, but drew up a sweeping remonstrance, which it took care to publish. Issued in 1776, four months before the American Declaration of Independence, it was a

[5] *Remontrances du Parlement de Paris . . . presentées au roi le 4 mai 1788*, pp. 2, 10, 12.

[450]

kind of declaration of independence of the French noble order. Indeed, in the same year, as if to show that anyone could use such language, the Estates of Brittany also insisted on their "imprescriptible and inalienable rights."

"The first rule of justice," according to the Parlement of Paris in this declaration of 1776, "is to preserve for everyone what is due him, a fundamental rule of natural right and of civil government, and one which consists not only in upholding rights of property but in safeguarding rights attached to the person and born of prerogatives of birth and estate." It was very dangerous, "under an appearance of humanity," to establish among men "an equality of duties," to destroy social distinctions, "to overturn civil society, whose harmony rests only on that gradation of powers, authorities, preeminences and distinctions which holds each man in his place and guarantees all stations against confusion.

"This order . . . takes its source in divine institutions; infinite and immutable wisdom in the plan of the Universe has made an unequal dispensation of powers and genius. . . . It is this law of the Universe which, despite efforts of the human mind, maintains itself in every empire and supports the order by which it subsists.

"What dangers then there are in a project produced by an inadmissible system of equality, whose first effect would be to confound all orders in the state by imposing on them the uniform burden of a land tax!

"The French monarchy, by its constitution, is composed of several distinct and separate estates. This distinction of conditions and persons originated with the Nation; it was born with our customs and way of life."[6]

Such appeals to an historic constitution should remind the reader of the protests in the Hapsburg empire against the reforms of Joseph II. The appeals to harmony, order, place, and the divine government of the world, reinforced by warnings against efforts of the human mind, may remind him also of Edmund Burke. I have already, in discussing Burke, pointed to the extraordinary lack of proportion that he could show. Small matters sent him into soaring outbursts on the nature of human society and of man's position under God. It may be doubted whether this was either very good religion or very good

[6] *Remontrances du Parlement de Paris contre les edits . . . presentées en mars, 1776* (Amsterdam, 1776). Reprinted in J. Flammermont, *Remontrances du Parlement de Paris*, 3 vols. (Paris, 1898), III, 278-79, 287.

conservatism. The same may be said of the Parlement of Paris. It equated a week of peasant labor on the roads with the very essence of the French monarchy, the constitution, the prerogatives of birth, the Three Orders, and divine justice.

The parlement likewise defended the craft gilds and trade associations against Turgot's efforts to suppress them. Some of its arguments sound strangely modern, or rather express that resistance to modernity still found in twentieth-century France: to abolish these protective associations "would put the small businessman, the most likely to be crushed by competition, between two equally extreme and ruinous alternatives, either to abandon at a loss a business he can no longer carry on, or to run the risk of bankruptcy if he remains in it."[7] Of more immediate importance was the fact that the parlement, in defending the gilds, did so by defending the whole hierarchic and corporate structure of French society. The cause of the gilds became the cause of the Three Orders; the rights of the commoner became the rights of the noble. When the government proposed to open a military school at Auxerre for noble and non-noble youths alike, the parlement objected to this also. Since noble and non-noble had in fact for centuries attended the same civilian schools, the argument had to be carefully qualified; and what the parlement professed to fear was that for young men of the commercial class to receive a specifically military training, designed for the nobility, would confound the three orders. "Each estate has its own occupations, ideas, duties, genius and manner of life, which should not be adulterated or confused by education."[8]

Neither in the royal *corvée*, nor in the gilds, nor in the school at Auxerre did members of the parlement have any material, direct, or personal interest. Upkeep of the principal roads from tax funds would not perceptibly increase their taxes, nor did the gilds directly concern them, nor was there any novelty in army officers of bourgeois birth. What concerned them was the principle of the thing, or the drift of events that they perceived in every specific proposal. They had developed a defensive, even an obsessive, frame of mind on the matter of rank and order. It was too early, in 1776, for the American Revolution to have had any influence in France, but the whole literature of the *philosophes* and *économistes*, the attempts made by the royal government itself for a generation, and the actual abolition of the parlements in 1771, had made them hypersensitive on every concrete

[7] *Ibid.*, 371.   [8] *Ibid.*, 392.

issue. They were aware that Turgot's real ideas went far beyond the proposals that he submitted. They were not mistaken if they thought that the essence of French law and society might come into question. Thus pressed, they assumed an offensive or counteroffensive, in which they acted as spokesmen for the nobility as a whole, for nobility as an institution necessary to society itself.

Indeed, if everything was abolished together in 1789 it was because everything had been defended together at least as early as 1776. If the special rights of class, province, town, and gild went up in a common conflagration in the night of August 4, it was because the defenders of these rights had long been throwing them into a common pile. If revolutionaries had a "system," so did their opponents. If small things in 1789 could make a man cry "aristocrat," small things in the past had made the parlements cry "prerogatives of birth and estate." The years after 1776 saw a hardening of this kind of rigidity.

Turgot was dismissed in 1776. The party favoring intervention in the American troubles, led by Vergennes, was against him, since for financial reasons he opposed embroilment with England. Courtiers and tax farmers regarded him as a menace, but it was the Parlement of Paris that mainly put an end to him and to his program. He left office convinced of the pernicious influence of special *corps* within the state, organized corporate "bodies" having interests different from those of the "nation." We have already noted his letter of 1778 to Richard Price on the new American constitutions, and the ensuing constitutional discussion in France in the 1780's, in which followers of Turgot expressed their repugnance to balances and counterchecks, and their preference for a single assembly acting with the sovereign authority of the nation considered as a homogeneous whole.

Turgot was followed by Necker, who tried to finance the American war mainly by loans, as Pitt was to finance the French war of 1793. Too discreet to risk new taxes, Necker attempted to increase the yield of those already existing, and hence undertook, like many of his predecessors, and like ministers of other Continental monarchies, to get new tax rolls in which the appraisal of land for taxation should be brought more nearly up to true values. The Parlement of Paris strenuously objected. It even declared, in 1778, that existing valuations must stand so long as taxes were not authorized by taxpayers in some kind of parliamentary body.[9] It may be again observed that in England, under parliamentary rule, taxable land values had not changed

---

[9] *Ibid.*, 395-413.

since 1692, and that though Parliament might occasionally raise the rate of the land tax, most British revenue came from indirect taxes paid by the general population.

Necker accomplished very little, and was followed by Calonne.[10] Up to now no one had ever had a clear idea of French government finances. Accounting methods were sporadic; numerous unrelated estimates of expense had been made, but not combined in a budget, nor projected in terms of a year or any set period of time. It was Calonne who really discovered the deficit. He concluded that it was annual and recurring, and that it had existed all through the century, but had been greatly increased by the American war. It had apparently risen from about 37,000,000 livres a year in 1776 to about 110,000,000 a year in 1786. The debt had risen to over four billions.

Calonne, alarmed, drew up a comprehensive set of measures. His ideas were essentially those of Turgot, but he meant to introduce them in less piecemeal and guarded fashion. He was the first and last minister before 1789 to propose a general plan of structural reorganization. He was the first also to appeal to public opinion.

He was convinced, as most historians have been, that France was a wealthy enough country to support the expenditures of its government. Half the expenditures went for debt service, a quarter for the armed forces, about nineteen per cent for civilian objectives; and the upkeep of Versailles and the whole royal establishment absorbed only six per cent. Distribution of public expenditure in England was much the same. The trouble with the French budget was on the side of income. And if revenue was chronically insufficient, it was in part because wealthy people paid so little in taxes. Nobles were exempt from the *taille* on principle, and many bourgeois by special arrangement. Nobles and bourgeois alike evaded the *vingtième* by false declarations of income. A mass of provincial liberties, special immunities, privileges, deals, bargains, commutations, and *abonnements* spared taxpayers of many kinds from the full impact of the fisc. Calonne thought that by abolition of such exemptions and evasions the financial crises could be surmounted.

Briefly, his plan was threefold: he would obtain the cooperation and understanding of the country through new provincial assemblies, to be elected by taxpayers without regard to the three orders. He

[10] On Calonne see A. Goodwin, "Calonne, the Assembly of Notables and the Origins of the *Révolte Nobiliaire*," *English Historical Review* (1946), 202-34, 329-77; P. Jolly, *Calonne* (Paris, 1949); G. Lefebvre, *Coming of the French Revolution* (Eng. trans., Princeton, 1947), 21-37.

would replace the *vingtième* with a new tax on landed income payable by all landowners equally, whether clergy, noble, or commoner, and he would equalize the tax burden as between provinces by abolishing the exemptions that some of them enjoyed. And he would stimulate production by getting rid of the royal *corvée*, internal tariffs, excises on certain manufactures, and restrictions on the grain trade.

In France, more than in Eastern Europe, and more than in England, land ownership was widely spread among all classes. Some nobles, some bourgeois, and even some peasants were substantial proprietors. A plan for all landowners to be taxed alike, without privilege of social position, and to be represented simply as landowners in elected public bodies, without reference to legal status or corporate grouping, struck at the foundation of the society of estates. And since Calonne intended to have anyone owning land worth 600 livres a year (about £25) take part in his elected assemblies, he undercut the social structure at a point pretty far down in the pyramid.

Calonne won the King's support for his program, but knew that the parlements would never accept it. He considered calling the Estates General, which had not met since 1615, but decided that such a course would be too uncertain and too slow, and would in any case favor the organized nobility and clergy. He decided therefore to lay his plan before a selected group of important persons, an Assembly of Notables, an ancient device last used in 1626. He hoped that endorsement of his plan by a body of such commanding prestige would oblige the parlements to accept it also. The Notables met in February 1787. Designated by the King, they were mainly prelates and great noblemen, with a few members appointed to represent the Third Estate, and they included over forty of the very *parlementaires* that Calonne was trying to outflank.

The meetings of the Notables were highly acrimonious. Calonne informed them of the deficit. They were incredulous, as well they might be, for no one supposed the grandest monarchy in Europe to be so deplorably embarrassed—it may be remembered that Dutch bankers, no mean judges, had for several years been shifting investments from England into France. Calonne insisted on the urgent need of more revenue. The Assembly replied that economy would serve the purpose better. Calonne denounced "privilege." The Assembly countered with allegations of "despotism." Persuaded finally of the reality of the crisis, the Notables announced their acceptance in principle of equal liability to taxation. They refused, however, to endorse the tax proposed by Calonne, or to agree to elected assemblies in which the difference between noble and commoner should have no place. Such assemblies, they warned, would become "democratic or despotic." They declared that they had no powers to bind anyone to any program. Their aim was to throw the whole matter back into the hands of the parlements. Some, including Lafayette, even talked of the Estates General.

I have observed on an earlier page that the failure of the Bourbon monarchy was in part a failure of public relations, that it had shrouded its most justifiable policies in an administrative secrecy, and exhibited its most objectionable features to the world. Calonne now broke the tradition of government secrecy. He appealed to the public, inundating the country with free copies of an *Avertissement* in which his case was stated. He told the country that its fiscal system was unjust. He said that it favored the rich against the poor. He openly denounced privilege, and it was in fact Calonne, speaking in the King's name, who more than anyone gave this word its revolutionary significance. He also broke the tradition of absolutism, or of absolutist methods of reform, by offering to consult with the country, or at least with the taxpayers, through the experiment of elected assemblies. He was not trusted. The government could not so easily live down its reputation for being arbitrary, devious, and extravagant. The court at Versailles was widely detested, by nobles and non-nobles alike. Its worst features were dramatized by the Queen, Marie Antoinette, who was regarded as frivolous, petty, unthinking, capricious, intriguing, and outrageously wasteful. The affair of the Diamond Necklace in 1785 seemed to prove the worst that could be believed. The best churchmen, the soundest provincial nobility, the parlements, and the enlightened bourgeoisie all suspected any minister or program that emanated from the court.

Calonne was driven from office, and was replaced by the Archbishop of Toulouse, Loménie de Brienne, who attempted to carry Calonne's program in a modified form through the parlements. Brienne battled the magistrates for a year, using all the weapons at the King's disposal, *exil, lettres de cachet, lits de justice.* The parlements became the upholders of political liberty. They denounced arbitrary taxation and arbitrary arrest; they laid down as fundamental to the laws of France the principle of consent to taxation, the liberties of the provinces, and the *inamovibilité des magistrats*, that is their own inalienable right to office. The Frenchman, they said, loves his King, "but what he pays to the King he really owes only to the State." The King is only a national treasurer, and "what is not used for the common good belongs to the citizens." This was a "principle founded on the rights of man and confirmed by reason." "Man is born free." "The nature of man is to unite with his equals (*ses semblables*) and to live in society subject to some general conventions, that is, laws." To Thomas Jefferson, then in France, these utterances of the Parlement of Paris all seemed reassuringly Anglo-Saxon. France, he thought in 1787, would soon have a "revolution" like that of England against the Stuarts, but without the bloodshed.[11]

It is one of the puzzles of the Revolution that class animosity, or antagonism between noble and non-noble, should have been so little in evidence in 1787 and much of 1788. The Parlement of Paris, despite all that could be known of it from its own published remonstrances, enjoyed a wide popularity with both Third Estate and nobility at this time. There were of course exceptions: Condorcet, Dupont, Morellet (the school of Turgot) suspected the Parlement of Paris as Voltaire had suspected it twenty years before. That it nevertheless enjoyed wide support can be explained only on the ground that most politically conscious persons at the moment were concerned mainly with absolutism, and would admire any group of men that stood up against arbitrary and non-responsible government.

The parlement in 1787 proved a little more flexible than in the past. It accepted, for example, the abolition of the *corvée* which it had refused to Turgot. It declined, however, to "verify" any new taxes. New taxes, it now openly maintained, could be authorized only by a meeting of the Estates General, the national gathering of the three orders, whose complete dormancy for over a century had seldom been regretted except by a few nobles. Meanwhile the fiscal crisis grew worse, so that it appeared that the government could not carry on. Louis XVI (it was now that he called the parlements an "aristocracy of magistrates") came to the same conclusion as Louis XV. In May 1788 he in effect abrogated the parlements by reducing them to mere judicial organizations.

The May Edicts deprived the parlements of their political power, their right to verify taxes and legislation. This power was vested in a new body, a Plenary Court, which was to sit in Paris and serve for the whole country. The provincial parlements thus sustained a great

---

[11] Flammermont, *Remontrances*, III, 671, 714-15; my article, "The Dubious Democrat: Thomas Jefferson in Bourbon France," in *Political Science Quarterly* (1957), 388-404.

reduction of stature, losing a political power which, though regional, had made them equals to the Parlement of Paris. They felt victimized by centralization. All parlements, those of Paris and the provinces alike, at the same time had their jurisdiction confined to legal cases involving more than 20,000 francs. Smaller cases were assigned to lesser, more decentralized and more accessible courts. The parlements thus lost out in income, in volume of business, and in general importance in the world of lawyers.

The outcry against these May Edicts was universal. Pamphlets poured from the presses in all parts of the country. Opinion was more freely expressed in them than in regular periodicals that were more subject to censorship, so that the pamphlets offer the best, though an imperfect, indication of public opinion. A recent attempt at statistical analysis shows over five hundred published in the four months following May 8, 1788.[12] By far the greatest number appeared in provincial towns, now roused to a high degree of political agitation. It seems that roughly half may have come from the Third Estate, half from the nobility. The most common theme of these writings was the May Edicts. And in this outburst of pamphlets, widely representative of classes and regions, only a pitiful tenth of them supported the government. Nine-tenths attacked the royal policy, which is to say that both nobles and non-nobles rallied to the parlements against the crown. The parlements were idealized as defenders of liberty. The new Plenary Court was denounced as a drumhead body, a group of royal appointees set up to give obsequious approval to government measures. The country rejected the Plenary Court as in any way representing it, and accused the government of crushing the bodies that had ventured upon opposition.

The Aristocratic Revolt

If revolution means the concerted defiance of government, the French Revolution began in the summer of 1788. It then took the form of a great stirring of the constituted or corporate bodies against the king. A German historian, Martin Göhring, has called this phenomenon of 1788 the *Triumph der ständischen Idee*, a triumph of the moment only, followed in 1789 by the "breakthrough to the modern state."[13] The French call these events of 1788 the *révolte nobiliaire*.

[12] R. W. Greenlaw, "Pamphlet Literature in France during the Period of the Aristocratic Revolt," in *Journal of Modern History* (1957), 349-54.

[13] These are chapter headings in M. Göhring, *Weg und Sieg der modernen Staatsidee in Frankreich* (Tübingen, 1947).

The nobility seized the initiative, while the Third Estate, unused to politics, lacking channels of joint action, and still feeling the timidity of a middle class, was willing enough, for the time being, to let the authorities be defied by persons of greater consideration. Even of America it had been said that there could be no revolution without leading families. France now saw a demonstration of Montesquieu's principle, or of the eighteenth-century truism, that nobility served as a check upon despotism, or, in broader terms, that an absolutist regime could best be resisted if there were some kind of grandees outside the machinery of the state itself.

The French aristocracy had been strengthening its position since the death of Louis XIV. We saw, as long ago as Chapter III, the wavering between segregation and assimilation in the relations of nobility to bourgeoisie. There had been a good deal of assimilation in France, more so than anywhere east of the Rhine. Hence in France some nobles and some bourgeois saw a good deal of each other socially, especially in Paris. Hence, also, there were nobles who were not yet aristocrats—*anoblis*, nobles for life only, nobles of *noblesse inachevée*—so that the nobility was by no means a solid class. On the whole, however, aristocratic self-segregation had prevailed, along with a mounting aristocratic class-consciousness. Parlements had adopted regulations to assure the social purity of their membership. After 1783 every one of the 135 French bishops was a nobleman. Of the seventy-five ministers in office from 1718 to 1789 only three were not nobly born; of these, Dubois was a cardinal, Sartine a nonentity, and Necker a foreigner. Half these ministers were of six or more generations of noble blood. Noble also, in the time of Louis XVI, were all the intendants, who might have been called provincial governors were that term not reserved for an honorary office even more aristocratic. Failure had followed the attempts of royal officials to use noble status as a kind of legion of honor for meritorious persons in business and the professions. The attempt to confer noble status on bourgeois army officers had also been blocked by spokesmen for true or hereditary nobility.[14]

The army ordinance of 1781 has remained famous as a symbol of this aristocratic resurgence. It prescribed that officer candidates, in the future (with a significant exception for men rising directly from the ranks) must have no less than four generations of noble descent. The young man on joining a regiment had to submit to his colonel a certificate obtained from the royal genealogist, and to obtain this

[14] See Chapter III above.

certificate he had to assemble a huge dossier of papers, including the marriage contracts of his grandfather and great-grandfather, old deeds, wills, extracts from tax rolls and much else. This absurd perversion of bureaucracy occurred in a war office that was in many respects already highly modernized, and in an army where a fifth of the officers, including a number of generals, were not nobly born.[15]

It must be remembered that in France at the time, as in some other countries since, positions in the army, the church, and the government were of the greater significance, since the private professions were undeveloped, and important salaried employments outside the government were very rare.

Since the death of Louis XIV, and never more effectively than under Louis XVI, the parlements had enlarged their political role, and had upheld, in public and private, noble ideas of good government and society. The successes of the Assembly of Notables against Calonne marked another bid by the nobility for a positive voice in the determination of policy. The way in which Calonne's provincial assemblies worked out showed the same trend. He had intended them to be classless, in the sense then relevant; but Brienne had yielded to noble objections, and the assemblies which actually met in 1787 represented the three orders, and each had to have a member of the clergy or the nobility as its presiding official.

These short-lived provincial assemblies, an experiment that led nowhere, at least advanced the political education of a great many people. In the assembly of Orléanais the clergy and Third Estate, finding that the Duke of Luxembourg paid no taxes at all, engaged in protracted arguments with the nobility. The plebeian Abbé Sieyès

---

[15] Estimates of the number of non-noble officers, as repeated by recent writers, seem to go back to L. Hartmann, *Les officiers de l'armée royale et la Révolution* (Paris, 1910). Hartmann probably exaggerated the number of non-noble officers in the 1780's, since he assumed that among officers receiving commissions before the ordinance of 1781 the proportion of non-nobles remained the same as during wartime conditions of the Seven Years' War. If, however, we disregard the thousands of honorary officers, and those of the royal bodyguard (whose officers were all noble); if we consider only the 9,578 officers assigned to troops in 1789 (infantry, cavalry, artillery, and engineers); if we include as officers the 1,100 *officiers de fortune*, commissioned from the ranks and used mainly for routine duties at the company level; if we assume that all *officiers de fortune* were of non-noble birth; and if we reduce by as much as one-half Hartmann's estimate of the number of non-noble officers other than *officiers de fortune*; then it still seems likely that about 2,000 of the 9,578 officers assigned to troops in 1789 were not of noble birth. That a few officers of non-noble origin were still being promoted to the rank of general in the 1780's is apparent from the chapter on general officers in L. Tuetey, *Les officiers sous l'ancien régime: nobles et roturiers* (Paris, 1908). Tuetey concluded that it was harder for a *roturier* to get into the officer corps at the bottom than to be promoted once he was in it.

learned a good deal as a member of this body. The assembly of Auvergne, of which Lafayette was a member, set itself firmly against new taxation, ignored the King's explicit charge of tax evasion by wealthy landlords, urged respect for provincial liberties, and asked for the revival of the old Estates of Auvergne, which had not met since 1651. The ancient Estates, more than the new provincial assembly, would give a prominent role to the organized nobles and the upper clergy.[16]

Before 1787, only in Brittany and Languedoc were the Provincial Estates of importance. Elsewhere they had died out by the middle of the seventeenth century. In 1787 demands were heard for revival of Provincial Estates in various parts of the country. It was a long-delayed reaction against Richelieu and Louis XIV, a demand to make France a constitutional monarchy, not on the English model, but on the model of a France that had long since passed away. It would be a France in which the King ruled over a confederation of provinces, each guarding its own liberties and exemptions in taxes and administration, and each carrying on its own affairs through its own churchmen, its own nobles and gentry, and its own opulent dignitaries of the King's good towns.

In Provence, for example, no estates had met since 1639. The province, by its liberties, enjoyed certain advantages in taxation. It was one of those outlying parts of France where the law distinguished "noble" from "common" land, somewhat as in Eastern Europe, with the all-important difference that the distinction had become fictitious, since it was estimated in Provence that six times as many commoners as nobles owned land of this noble type. Noble land was free of certain onerous taxes. Alarmed by Calonne's attack on tax exemptions in 1787, and aroused by the humbling in 1788 of the Parlement of Aix, certain leaders brought about the revival of the Estates of Provence. By the precedents of 1639 only fief-owning nobles sat for the nobility, and only mayors and other oligarchs sat for the twenty-six privileged towns. In 1787 there were a great many nobles who owned no fiefs, and a great many bourgeois who did not feel themselves properly represented by the mayors. A lively political struggle developed at this local or provincial level, significant in illustrating the complexity of the issues. It was no simple dispute between noble and bourgeois, but

---

[16] An account of the Orléanais assembly may be found in P. Bastid, *Sieyès et sa pensée* (Paris, 1939), 42-45; of that of Auvergne in L. R. Gottschalk, *Lafayette between the American and the French Revolution* (Chicago, 1950), 331-63.

one more accurately described as a clash between privileged and non-privileged persons, the former comprising fief-owning nobles, *parlementaires*, mayors, owners of noble land, and others who benefited from the old provincial constitution; the latter consisting of nobles who owned no fiefs, numerous bourgeois, and others who had no advantage to gain by the maintenance or revival of historic liberties of Provence. From this lively scene Mirabeau was elected in 1789 to the Estates General.[17]

North of Provence, in Dauphiny, much the same happened, with significant differences. The Parlement of Grenoble, to defend itself against the May Edicts, took the lead in organizing the nobility of the province, along with various lawyers and notables of the bourgeois class, in a revival of the Provincial Estates. These met at Vizille, where they showed themselves more open to new ideas than those of Provence, in that they organized with double representation for the Third Estate, and vote by head, not by order. The Vizille assembly was thus something like a modern parliamentary body, and it set a precedent that was to be of great importance at the national level in 1789. Nevertheless, the insurgents in Dauphiny had in mind certain of their own privileges also, hoping to preserve tax advantages for noble land that resembled those of Provence, or at least not to lose them without compensation. The leading representative of Dauphiny in the Estates General of 1789 was to be J. J. Mounier, of whom more will be said.[18]

Brittany was an old irritant to the monarchy, and now became a hotbed of class conflict and incipient revolution. Its parlement was the most exclusively noble in all France. In its estates, which were very active, some 3,000 seigneurs and gentry enjoyed the personal right to sit in the noble chamber, and hundreds came to every meeting. In the inaccessible interior of the peninsula, these gentry retained more of an ascendancy over the peasants than was now found in most parts of France. At Rennes, much of the population lived by service to the parlementary and noble families who congregated there on public business. On the other hand, in the port towns, such as Saint-Malo and Nantes, an important commercial bourgeoisie had grown up, less wedded to the historic liberties and established authorities of the province.

[17] J. Egret, "La pré-Révolution en Provence, 1787-89," *Annales historiques de la Révolution française* (1954), 97-126.

[18] J. Egret, *La Révolution des Notables: Mounier et les Monarchiens, 1789* (Paris, 1950), 7-50; and see the same author's "La Révolution aristocratique en Franche-Comté et son echec, 1788-89," in *Revue d'histoire moderne et contemporaine*, 1 (1954), pp. 245-71.

After the May Edicts, the Breton parlement and estates rushed anew to the defense of provincial liberties against the central power. They warmly upheld the old Breton constitution, by which they enjoyed a good deal of autonomy, and the lowest per capita tax burden of all France, less than half that of neighboring Normandy and Touraine. The nobles, as elsewhere, sought the support of the bourgeoisie against the crown, but were less successful in obtaining it. Provincial liberties were by no means of equal advantage to all persons within the province; as in Hungary, they favored the existing upper class. The merchants of Nantes, and other bourgeois of modern views, while not opposed to provincial liberties as such, complained that the Provincial Estates levied the taxes inequitably as between individuals, and that they were not really represented by the comfortable municipal mandarins that sat *ex officio* for the Third Estate at Rennes. Inspired by the movement in Dauphiny, they demanded a reorganization of the Provincial Estates on the model of the Vizille assembly. The nobles of Brittany refused what those of Dauphiny had conceded. Class struggle broke out; there was a pitched battle at Rennes between university students and young gentlemen reinforced by their footmen, porters, and assorted retainers. Both sides developed an organization of correspondence committees and exchanges of delegations. The Breton deputies sent to Versailles in 1789 were to transfer these methods to the national stage, and contribute to the formation of the famous Jacobin club of Paris.[19]

The church also, or its governing hierarchy, who were all nobles, lost no time in protesting against the May Edicts, the humiliation of the parlements, and the royal program of taxation. The Assembly of the Clergy met in June 1788. It passed resolutions against the May Edicts. It rejected the principle of taxability of its properties, which amounted to between five and ten per cent of all the landed property in the country. As a tax-exempt body, the French Church had long been in the habit of making a "free gift" to the royal government. The two grants of 1780 and 1782, intended to help pay for the American war, had amounted to 46,000,000 livres, and another 18,000,000 had been granted in 1785. The Assembly of 1788 granted only 1,800,000. It was the lowest free gift in many generations. The prelates intended, like their noble cousins, to use the financial crisis of the monarchy to preserve their own liberties, and for the advantage of the church and

---

[19] J. Egret, "Les origines de la Révolution en Bretagne," *Revue historique*, CCXIII (1955), 189-215; H. Freville, *L'intendance de Bretagne*, 3 vols. (Rennes, 1953).

the country as they understood it. The truth is that the church itself was in an incipiently revolutionary condition, with a good many priests and lesser clergy dissatisfied with the way in which the prelates managed its affairs and handled its wealth. But in 1788 the great bishops and abbots spoke for the church. What they wanted was a constitutional monarchy in the manner of Montesquieu, in which despotism was prevented by the influence of intermediate powers, one of which was the church.[20]

"Despotism" again yielded, as so often in the past. The combined outburst of parlements, provincial estates, and the church, the outcry of the aristocracy for the most part supported by the bourgeoisie in a massive wave of national indignation, were too much for the benign Louis XVI to withstand. In September 1788 he withdrew the May Edicts. As in 1774, he again reinstated the Parlement of Paris and the provincial parlements with their former powers. By this action he also convinced the country that he was in earnest in what he had promised in the preceding July, the summoning of the national Estates General, which was set for the following May.

Victory in September thus went against the royal absolutism. It lay with a movement of constitutional resistance that was primarily noble in its inspiration, or at least represented the interests of those who stood to gain by existing privileges of class and province. The question was whether, with despotism overthrown, aristocracy would succeed it.

Leaders of opinion, noble and bourgeois, now agreed that France should have constitutional government, taxation by consent, and payment of taxes by persons of all classes alike. They agreed that there should be freedom from arbitrary arrest, and a "legitimate" freedom of press and opinion. They agreed that the country should take part in the operations of government. They did not agree on how this was to be done. Were existing constituted bodies—clergy, nobles, Third Estate; parlements, provinces with corporate liberties—to be the units of political participation? Was France really made up, or "constituted," of these? Or should such bodies, and France itself, be "reconstituted"? Should the old elements be transmuted into a "nation," a community

[20] For the amounts of *dons gratuits* see M. Marion, *Dictionnaire des institutions de la France au 17e et au 18e siècles* (Paris, 1923), 105. For its political views see the remonstrances printed without date or place by the Assembly of the Clergy: *Remontrances du clergé présentées au roi le dimanche 15 juin 1788*, upholding the parlements; *Remontrances du clergé . . . sur ses droits, franchises et immunités*, on tax exemption of church property. The Assembly also protested against the grant of civil rights to Protestants by the royal government in 1787: *Remontrances du clergé de France assemblé en 1788, au roi, sur l'édit . . . concernant les non-Catholiques* (Paris, 1788).

made up of individual persons, or at least of proprietors and taxpayers without legalized special status?

The Parlement of Paris, no sooner restored, gave its answer to these questions, an answer that should have surprised no one familiar with its record, but which aroused the ire of a bourgeoisie now heated to a high degree of political consciousness. The coming Estates General, the parlement announced as its considered legal opinion, should be organized in 1789 as at their last meeting, in 1614-1615. That is, they should be a convocation of the Three Orders. They should remain so for all future time.

A second Assembly of Notables, dominated like the first by princes and great noblemen, published similar opinions in December 1788. The problem before the country, declared one of its most eminent spokesmen, was "to distinguish the three constitutional orders of the State, whose essence is to act separately in their deliberations in the Estates General." But even in this august body there was a dissenting view, hinted at by the Provost of the Merchants of Paris, who was no plebeian. The true problem, he said, was "for all orders to be united and merged in the Order of Citizen, the primitive Order of nature, reason and duty."[21]

The issue was joined at the end of 1788. The Third Estate knew what it wanted, as will be seen in the next chapter. But opposition to it was also forming, and before the year 1788 was out there were hints of a program that was to characterize the counterrevolution for the next dozen years. The princes of the blood published a statement at the close of the second Assembly of Notables. If the Third Estate, they warned, demanded too much in the coming Estates General, the upper two orders might repudiate the Estates, secede from them, and deny their legality. The higher orders would turn instead to the parlements as the only bodies able to define the law. They would urge the people to refuse taxes. They would disseminate the idea that no action of these illegal Estates General could be accepted as the national will.[22]

This princely pronouncement infuriated the Third Estate. "Are we Russian slaves or Polish serfs?" one of them demanded. We know that France was very different from Poland.

---

[21] *Discours prononcés à la cloture de l'Assemblée des Notables* (n.p.n.d. [1788]), 9, 15.
[22] See H. Carré, *La fin des parlements, 1788-90* (Paris 1912), 63-64.

THE FRENCH REVOLUTION: THE

EXPLOSION OF 1789

You will see that these are materials for a superb edifice.—THOMAS JEFFERSON to Thomas Paine, Paris, July 1789

We shall return in three months.—THE COUNT OF ARTOIS to Count Esterhazy, Valenciennes, July 1789

THE FRENCH REVOLUTION: THE
EXPLOSION OF 1789

THE FIGURE of Philip Mazzei has been seen from time to time in these pages. A cosmopolitan Italian, he had settled in 1773 in Virginia, where he was almost immediately caught up in the movement against England. He had then returned to Europe to solicit loans for the new state, talked at Florence with the future Emperor Leopold about the American constitutions, gone to Paris, written a book to correct French misunderstandings of the United States, and while remaining in Paris had become a kind of news agent for King Stanislas of Poland. In Paris, late in 1788, he belonged to a group that included Jefferson, Lafayette, Condorcet, Morellet, Dupont de Nemours, and the Duke of La Rochefoucauld. They often met at one another's houses, and naturally had a good deal to say about the American Revolution as a precedent to the crisis in France.

In this group, at this moment, at the height of what historians call the Aristocratic Revolt, it was the American Jefferson who was the most conservative in his ideas of what should be done. In his eyes, despotism was the main issue. In all the careful and detailed reports he sent home on events in France, he had not yet even used the word "privilege" or "privileged classes." He thought the coming Estates General should go slowly: "if they do not aim at too much they may begin a good constitution," he wrote to Madison in November.[1] He was having discussions with Lafayette about a French declaration of rights, but such ideas were now by no means unusual in Paris. The Americanized Mazzei was less cautious than Jefferson, but far more so than Dupont or Condorcet. The Americanized Lafayette was al-

---

[1] *Papers of Thomas Jefferson*, XIV (Princeton, 1958), 188; my article, "The Dubious Democrat: Thomas Jefferson in Bourbon France," *Political Science Quarterly*, LXXII (1957), 388-404.

ready being called an "aristocrat," still in a friendly way, by Condorcet, Mirabeau, and the Abbé Sieyès.

The devil himself is now posing as an American, said Condorcet to Mazzei; "the devil of aristocracy," disguised as a wise and prudent citizen of the New World, was tempting the French with his plausible arguments. Actually, as always, the devil was false. You wise Americans, Condorcet told Mazzei, never had any respect for old abuses such as ours. "You had no ambitious, hypocritical and immensely wealthy clergy calling itself an order in the state," no nobility as a second order, no insidious tax exempt interests, no self-perpetuating tribunals executing an absurd jurisprudence and holding a veto over the lawmaking power, no vicious system of tax collection "tied to the pretensions of your orders and your bodies of magistrates."

You moderate Americans, said Condorcet, would not have tolerated such conditions any more than we will. Mazzei agreed in principle, but sagely observed that it was not possible to destroy everything at once.

"Who ever talked of destroying everything at once?" retorted Condorcet. What the French wanted, he said, was to avoid giving a new lease of life, a new formal sanction, to the old institutions. "And this is what the aristocratic spirit that is dominant today will bring about." If the aristocratic spirit prevailed, he thought, even gradual abolition of the old evils would never be possible.[2]

In this chapter, instead of attempting the hopeless task of a full and rounded account of the French Revolution, for which there is no room and probably no need, I shall select a few points for more detailed treatment: how the year 1789 opened with a fully developed revolutionary psychology, what the Revolution essentially consisted in, and why the French Revolution, though inspired by much the same principles as the American, adopted different constitutional forms and took on a magnitude unknown to the upheavals of Western Civilization since the time of the Protestant Reformation.

The Formation of a Revolutionary Psychology

Great revolutions are not made by professional revolutionists, nor are they manifestations of abnormal psychology in any ordinary meaning of the word. Later on, when the revolution is under way, both professionals and abnormal types (which need not be the same) may

[2] R. Ciampini, *Lettere di Filippo Mazzei alla corte di Polonia* (Bologna, 1937), 17, 53-56.

seize positions of power. But the revolution occurs, in the first place, when men who are ordinarily unexcited by politics, generally moderate, and engaged in their own private affairs, are drawn into revolution as a course to which no acceptable alternative seems to exist. If their behavior becomes abnormal, it is because such behavior represents the reaction of normal minds to extraordinary conditions. It would be hard to explain otherwise how whole peoples turn revolutionary.

Rousseau is rightly considered the father of the Revolution, at least in the sense of those who like to single out ancestors among a multitude of actual forebears. He had expressed the main idea: that individual human beings, as free and equal citizens, make up the community and the law by the unforced action of their own moral will. He had also been deeply alienated from society, which he thought hardly worth preserving, believed himself to be virtuous and others bad and dishonest, thought himself surrounded by enemies, felt himself to be misunderstood, disliked, conspired against, and betrayed. His sentiments make a certain sense when seen against the social environment in which he lived; yet it is undoubtedly true that, by later standards of mental health, Rousseau would have been a candidate for psychiatric treatment. He was entirely non-political. In France there was no chance for him to take any political action, but even at Geneva, when explicitly asked, he had refused to join the group that made the little Geneva revolution of 1768. We have seen also the combination of insight and moderation in his recommendations for Poland.

Maximilien Robespierre developed many of the traits of Rousseau, and some of these are disagreeable to well-balanced people under favorable conditions, but it is doubtful that Robespierre had any need for psychiatric attention. Thirty-one years old in 1789, a reasonably successful self-made man in the American phrase, Robespierre, unlike Rousseau, was a lawyer coping adequately with the problems of life at Arras in northern France. The province of Artois was one of the few in which Provincial Estates had continued to meet. Robespierre believed that the Estates did not represent the inhabitants. This belief was shared by many others, including parish priests who did not sit in the First Estate, or elect those who did, and *nobles non-entrants* who did not sit in or vote for the Second. He believed (and it was true) that the Third Estate was represented *ex officio* by officeholders who bought or inherited their posts and were in some cases of noble status. The Estates of Artois, like those elsewhere, took advantage of the royal embarrassment to advance their own claims. Robespierre suspected an aristocratic maneuver. He began his revolutionary career in January 1789 with a pamphlet, *A la nation artésienne*, in which he called the Provincial Estates "a league of a few citizens" against the people. In March, during the elections for the Estates General, he gave legal assistance to the shoemakers' gild, thus already identifying himself with the common people. When the town dignitaries, some of them noble, tried to control the elections of the Third Estate in Arras, he published a second pamphlet with the ominous title, *Les ennemis de la patrie démasqués*. Elected to the electoral assembly of the province, where the clergy and nobility offered to give up certain privileges, to the applause of the Third Estate, Robespierre refused to take part in the vote of thanks. No thanks were due, he said, for the surrender of abuses which had always been indefensible. In June, at the Estates General at Versailles, he quite unfairly denounced the clergy as "subversive." In August, when the assembly was discussing consent to taxation, Robespierre rose to insist (nor was he mistaken according to the modern theory of the democratic state) that the country did not, strictly speaking, "consent" to taxation; it authorized and raised the taxes by its own agents and its own name.[3]

Robespierre had developed the class hatred, the intolerance, the self-righteousness, and the quarrelsome habit of seeing great principles in passing incidents that may be said to characterize a revolutionary psychology.

There were endless other evidences of the same state of mind. There was Brissot's feeling that no theory could be more "atrocious" than existing reality. There was Mirabeau's execration of "the eternal race of aristocrats." There was repudiation of ordinary social bonds: "since you degrade the Third Estate by your scorn, it owes you nothing."[4] There was utopianism, as in Dupont's faith in a "perfect society," a *beau idéal*, even better than that of the Americans. There was the habit of seeing questions of policy as plain clashes between truth and error: the function of lawmaking bodies is to legislate "the truth," according to Condorcet. And always there was the sense of outrage, of burning injustice, of true merit humiliated by a false system of values. "What a society," cried Sieyès, "in which work is said to *derogate*; where it is honorable to consume, but humiliating to produce, where the laborious

---

[3] *Oeuvres de Maximilien Robespierre* (Paris, 1950), VI, 6-9, 19, 30-31, 66-67.
[4] *Le dernier mot du Tiers Etat à la noblesse de France* (n.p. n.d., January, 1789), 6. For the references here to Brissot, Mirabeau and Dupont, see above pp. 261, 270, 279.

occupations are called vile, as if anything were vile except vice, or as if the classes that work were the most vicious!"[5]

Nevertheless, if the French people—or a good many of them—were in a radical mood at the beginning of 1789, they had been brought to it by their own hitherto accepted superiors. The King himself, and Calonne, had hurled the words "abuse," "privilege," "aristocracy." The parlements had flung back the epithet "despotism." Each had undermined confidence in the good faith of the other. Both had raised up great expectations. The King had spoken of the need for equalization of taxes, and for elected assemblies based on equal representation of landowners. The parlements had publicized the need for a constitution, for public participation in government, and for security of individual rights. Both had given the impression that something was radically wrong with the country, that great evils existed, and that these must and soon could be corrected.

This belief was in harmony with the whole philosophy of the century, and had been powerfully reinforced by the American Revolution. In the drama of the continents the cause of liberty and equality appeared as a world-wide movement, and it seemed that a new era had already dawned.

Repeatedly, however, expectations had been disappointed, and hopes had been raised only to be let down. The first Assembly of Notables had come to nothing. The new provincial assemblies had ended up too often in bickering between the orders. The country had come to the defense of the Parlement of Paris against the May Edicts, and during this controversy the King's promise of the Estates General, as demanded by the Parlement, had aroused a sense of imminent national renewal. There was therefore a sense of betrayal, or a feeling that a veil had been torn aside, when the Parlement of Paris, on its reinstatement, made it a first order of business to declare that the coming Estates must meet as in 1614, and hence presumably in three houses, with one vote for each order.

This action of the Paris Parlement opened the breach of a sharp class antagonism between Third Estate and nobility. It was an action by no means necessitated by a tenderness for constitutional law, since even in 1614 there had been no fixed form of assembly for the Estates General, and more pertinent modern precedents could be found, in Dauphiny and Languedoc, for the joint session of the three orders.

[5] Condorcet, *Lettre à M. le comte de Montmorency* (Paris, 1789), 14; E. Sieyès, *Quest-ce que le Tiers Etat?* (3rd ed., 1789), 83-84.

The ruling of the Parlement seemed purely political, and leaders of the Third, who in supporting the Parlement had supposed that they shared in a national protest against ministerial despotism, now concluded that they had only played the Parlement's game. We begin now to hear sarcastic references to the *all noble Parlement*, and to find phrases where aristocracy and despotism are coupled together as a common evil, as that "aristocracy is despotism at retail." Nor did the Parlement hold the good will of the Third Estate when, immediately after declaring for a "legitimate" freedom of the press, it lacerated and burned one of Sieyès' pamphlets at the steps of the Palais de Justice on December 17, 1788, and condemned one of Mirabeau's tracts in the following February.[6]

The French bourgeoisie, the leaders of the Third Estate—lawyers, government officers, merchants, emerging industrialists, doctors, writers, printers and publishers, owners of what might be called government bonds, "bourgeois" living on landed rents—had no economic grievances at all commensurate with the anger that they now felt. It was the lower classes that had the economic troubles. The upper stratum of the Third Estate had prosperity; it wanted status, or a better status than the existing status-system afforded it. Its members believed, as did the minority of liberal nobles, that the old "orders" no longer described the real character of the French people. It seemed absurd for men otherwise so much alike to be segregated only by law. If the Revolution was not the work of vanity, as Talleyrand held, it was the work of a deeply wounded self-respect. For generations the French bourgeois had accepted the social system. He had accepted the scale of values which made his own position inferior. In relations between noble and bourgeois there had been class consciousness, but not much

[6] *Arrêt de la cour du Parlement, rendu les chambres assemblées, les pairs y séant, qui condamne un imprimé ayant pour titre Délibération à prendre par le Tiers Etat dans toutes les municipalités du Royaume de France à être lacéré et brulé par l'exécuteur de la Haute Justice* (December 17, 1788). It seems likely that this refers to the *Délibérations à prendre* . . . drafted by Sieyès in conjunction with the group about the Duke of Orléans and published with *Instructions données par S.A.S. Monseigneur le duc d'Orléans à ses représentants dans les bailliages* (n.p., 1789). See also P. Bastid, *Sieyès et sa pensée* (Paris, 1939), 50-51. This *arrêt*, together with the *arrêt* of December 5, gives an excellent statement of the conservatism or aristocratic reformism of the Parlement as of the end of 1788, as Sieyès does of the radicalism of the Third Estate. The Parlement expresses dismay that, at a time when the upper orders have agreed to a surrender of tax privileges, this *Délibération* . . . should be found in the ordinary mails in great numbers, circulated by a concerted movement, and breathing *un esprit de système qui cherche à préparer sourdement une révolution dans les principes du gouvernement*. The Parlement condemned Mirabeau's *Histoire secrète de la cour de Berlin* in February 1789, on the eve of the elections to the Estates General.

class conflict. Embarrassment, resentment, frustration, envy, humiliation, hostility, if felt, had somehow been suppressed as useless or unworthy or part of life's ordinary course. Now, at the end of 1788, these things seem to have come to the surface. The class issue was politicized; it seemed possible to do something about it. Inequalities were condemned by the government itself, by the Americans, by the course of history, and the enlightenment of the age. What had been accepted and lived with now met with hot rejection.

But the situation was not visibly improving at the end of 1788. If the Estates General were to assemble in 1789 with a sharp emphasis on the orders, and if France should be governed in the future through such Estates, there would be an accentuation (a "new sanction" in Condorcet's phrase) of legal differences that had been easier to put out of mind so long as no Estates General ever met at all. Shoals of pamphlets protested against the ruling of the Parlement of Paris. The King called another Assembly of Notables to adjudicate the matter. Another disappointment, or even insult: the Assembly agreed with the Parlement, and even threatened to boycott the coming Estates if the difference of orders were not observed. The government had long shown an inclination to side with the Third, and Necker (recalled to office in September) now announced that the Third Estate should have double representation; that is, it should send to Versailles as many deputies as the two other orders combined. This was encouraging to the Third, but also disappointing, and in the circumstances seriously inadequate and evasive. Necker and the King, alarmed and confused by the rising spirit of protest, and warned against concession by various persons at the court, remained noncommittal on procedures to be used after the Estates assembled. If the Estates were to sit, deliberate, and vote as three separate chambers, it would obviously make no difference how many deputies any one chamber might contain. A few tens of thousands of noble families would have an equal voice with the rest of twenty-six million people. Two plus two would make five, as Sieyès said.

The King's government again contributed to the revolutionary education of the country by the procedures that it instituted for the choice of deputies to the Estates General. For one thing, the government called for actual elections. Elections themselves were a new and exciting experience for the world of the day, for even where Provincial Estates had been active in France, as in Brittany and Languedoc and Artois, the deputies of all three orders sat in them either by personal right, or *ex officio*, or by appointment; the same was true of the Belgian and Dutch estate-assemblies, nor was actual election of members the most characteristic feature of the British or Irish House of Commons. The royal electoral ordinance of January 1789 prescribed that all deputies to the Estates General should be elected: nobles by nobles, clergy by clergy, Third Estate by Third Estate.

The elections took place in March and April. There was no individual voting in the privacy of a polling booth. Elections occurred in open meetings, somewhat as in America at the time, or in the English counties and open boroughs, or in the General Council at Geneva. Each meeting, in addition to choosing its deputies, and in accordance with the royal ordinance and the now revived ancient usage, drew up a statement for the deputies to take with them, a *cahier des doléances* or memorandum of grievances in which all kinds of ideas on local and national affairs might be expressed. The electoral meetings thus became deliberative assemblies, in which speeches were made, and people had the chance to express and compare their ideas and discover how many others there were who agreed with them. Each meeting was a little school of political education, and there were forty thousand such meetings.

The royal government authorized a nearly universal manhood suffrage, and more people actually participated in the election of 1789 than in any election in France for many decades to come. Louis XVI, by his electoral ordinance, aroused the whole country down to the remotest village to a high pitch of political expectation. He invited all his subjects to reflect upon their troubles and formally state their complaints. The sense of a new era took on a more definite and practical tone; everywhere there was a feeling that changes of great magnitude were actually going to be made. But in this heightened state of political consciousness the legal difference in order was at the same time reinforced.

It was not easy, in the absence of any established machinery, for so large a country to choose a few hundred delegates to go to Versailles, and to choose them in such a way that they would have any real representative authority when they got there. Electoral assemblies were therefore arranged at various levels. At the top were about two hundred principal district assemblies, the *bailliages*, at which the men who were to go to the Estates General were actually chosen. Below the principal districts were various subdistricts and subassemblies. In the incidence of these subdistricts the difference between the legal orders was very great.

For example, in any one of a hundred towns a nobleman, a priest, and a lawyer might live as neighbors and acquaintances in the same street. For the election, each went his separate way to a different assembly. The nobleman proceeded directly to the principal district assembly, where he met with other noblemen of the whole district, all noblemen (with the usual disputes over cases of marginal status) having the right to appear personally in the noble assembly at this level. The priest likewise went directly to the principal district assembly, where he met with the bishop or bishops of the district (if any), with all the other parish priests in person, and with a few delegates sent by monastic houses and cathedral clergy. The lawyer, however, simply went to a meeting with other lawyers in his own town. For the Third Estate, in the towns, the lowest assemblies were meetings of the gilds and other occupational associations, to which another meeting was added for *non-corporés* who belonged to no such gild or association. Each of these various bodies—like the shoemakers at Arras whom Robespierre befriended—deliberated, drafted a *cahier,* and sent deputies to an assembly of the town as a whole, which in turn deliberated, drafted a *cahier* and sent deputies to the principal district assembly (there might even be another intermediate step), where they met with other deputies from other towns of the district, and with the deputies sent by the peasants. The peasants, meanwhile, met in their villages, where all men twenty-five years old and listed on the tax rolls were admitted to the assembly, and where they too deliberated, drafted a *cahier,* and sent deputies to meet with those of the towns at the principal district assembly. Here, where townsmen and especially lawyers gained an easy ascendancy over deputies of the peasants, if only by greater fluency in public speaking and knowledge of public affairs, another *cahier* was drafted for the whole Third Estate of the district, and deputies were chosen to represent the Third Estate at Versailles. Many of these electoral assemblies, their business done, appointed permanent committees of correspondence to remain in touch with the deputies. Electoral organization in some places developed into revolutionary organization. In Paris and other cities, in the summer of 1789, it was the electors who took over the city government in the municipal revolutions.

The complexities in the electoral process are worth noting for several reasons. They illustrate the corporatist legal framework which the principle of uniform national citizenship was so soon to demolish. They show how the whole country could be suddenly aroused to political action without previous habit or experience. And they explain why the Estates General, when they met in May, exhibited the characteristics that they did. The noble suffrage, at the district level, had favored the numerous country nobility who had the longest lineage and the least modern ideas. The three hundred noble deputies at the Estates General were usually bound, as Lafayette was, by mandates from their constituents which forbade any merger of the three orders. For the clergy, on the other hand, the electoral system favored the parish priests, who were close to the people, at the expense of monastic and cathedral clergy, who were likely to be more aristocratic, or withdrawn from the world, or both. The three hundred clerical deputies at Versailles were predominantly *curés*, with a sprinkling of liberal bishops (since it was liberals among the bishops that the *curés* at the district level most willingly elected), so that the clergy, in the Estates General, was to a large degree in a mood for very extensive renovation in both church and state. For the Third Estate, the sifting through successive assemblies had favored the most active, articulate, persistent, and politically interested kinds of men. Well over half the 648 deputies of the Third at the Estates General were lawyers. As many as 278 held some kind of government office, 166 were lawyers in private practice from prominent barristers in Paris to small country notaries, 85 were merchants or business men, 67 lived by the income or management of their own property, usually land, and 31 were of various professions, mainly doctors.[7]

It is in fact hard to identify a single peasant or workingman among these 648 deputies of the Third. Their absence is of course not remarkable, at a time when the lower income groups were barely literate, if at all, and would scarcely even be worthy of comment, were there not whole schools of modern historians who make an issue of the bourgeois and undemocratic character of the leadership in the revo-

---

[7] For these figures and their significance see A. Cobban, *The Myth of the French Revolution: an Inaugural Lecture* (London, 1955), with the reply to it by G. Lefebvre, *Annales historiques de la Révolution française* (Oct.-Dec., 1956), 337-45. For the elections to the Estates General see B. Hyslop, *Guide to the General Cahiers of 1789* (N.Y., 1936), pp. 3-31; G. Lefebvre, *Coming of the French Revolution* (Eng. trans., Princeton, 1947), pp. 62-75, and the more recent J. Cadart, *Le régime électoral des Etats-Généraux de 1789* (Paris, 1952), a law school work with a doubtful thesis, in which the author, by stressing the nearly universal suffrage and almost ignoring the difference of orders, argues that Louis XVI's "royal democracy" was more democratic than the constitution of 1791.

lution of 1789. It cannot be demonstrated, because it probably is not true, that more general popular participation would have favored a more equal, free, liberal, progressive, productive, open, tolerant, or dynamic form of society. The lowest classes were the most faithfully attached to customary superiors. The year 1789 in France, among its other surprises, was to produce a peasant rebellion, but it was nevertheless the smaller kinds of tenants and agricultural laborers, along with the hordes of domestic servants and other dependents, who most willingly accepted the preeminence of the nobility. It was not the conservatives that feared mass support. The Parlements of Paris and of Grenoble both urged a fully universal male suffrage, wider than the King granted, and there were many proposals that peasant deputies should be themselves peasants. The purpose was to weaken the upper stratum of the Third Estate. Had the Third, at Versailles in May and June 1789, had a great admixture of peasants and artisans it would have in all probability been more docile. "In France, in Holland and elsewhere," said Sieyès in January, probably thinking of the brawls at Rennes and the Orange party in Holland, "we have terrible examples of the coalition between the last class of society and the privileged orders. Let us tell the truth: in every country in the world the R——— belongs to the Aristocracy." By R——— (which he wrote C———, for *canaille*) he meant the rabble; it was already necessary not to say such things too bluntly.[8]

The Overturn: May to August 1789

The Estates General met at Versailles on May 4, 1789.[9] It was a tremendous event, the climax of the earnest labors of forty thousand lesser assemblies. Again there was disappointment. The ancient etiquette was absurdly incongruous and politically explosive. Nothing could have more flagrantly asserted the differing dignity of the orders. In the ceremonial opening procession the six hundred deputies of the Third Estate marched first, meekly clad for the day in black "bourgeois" costume, and followed by the noble order alive with color, then by the dark mass of priests who preceded the magnificent bishops, with the King and the royal family at the end. The opening session fell very flat. The country had looked forward to it for months, as to a salvation in time of trial; but none of the speakers rose to the

[8] *Tiers Etat*, 41n.
[9] The present section mainly follows Lefebvre, *Coming of the French Revolution* (Eng. trans., Princeton, 1947).

occasion, and Necker's address was lengthy, technical, and monotonous. Neither Louis XVI nor Necker had made any decisions; they had no proposals for which they sought backing or which they were prepared to enforce. They left matters in the hands of the deputies, expressing the hope that everyone would prove reasonable and cooperative. This was a good deal to ask of men who for the most part had never seen each other before, who had no organization or accepted basis of leadership, and among whom each one had only the vaguest ideas of what his colleagues from other parts of France might be thinking or how far they were prepared to go.

It is not easy to do justice to all parties in the deadlock that followed. The great immediate issue, and what the Third Estate desired, was that all three orders should merge and sit as a single house, in which decisions would be made by a majority of the twelve hundred members, considered as individuals, so that the nobility and the clergy would cease to exist as separate chambers and could on occasion be outvoted. Such a merger, however, was obviously intended only as a step toward further changes. The nobility firmly resisted. The Third Estate, supported by a few noblemen and a good many priests, was obviously in a revolutionary frame of mind. The King was indeed irresolute, but he had an impossible choice: whether he sided with a now revolutionary Third Estate, or with an equally aroused nobility, he would by choosing one make an enemy of the other; and it would take power as well as good will to mediate between them. The noble order was indeed obstinate, but any nobleman might be excused if after reading Sieyès on the *Tiers Etat*, or Mirabeau on the Order of the Cincinnati, he thought that concessions would endanger the fundamentals of his way of life. And it was Sieyès and Mirabeau who were now emerging as leaders of the Third, if only because in a group of men who did not yet know one another the authorship of a famous pamphlet was enough to make a man known.

For six weeks the Three Estates engaged in parliamentary maneuvers. The Third refused to consider itself as an estate at all. It urged the others to join with it, as a few of the clergy did, whereupon the Third, again calling on the others to unite, proclaimed itself the National Assembly, the only true representative of the French people. It even had the audacity to "authorize" existing taxes, implying that such authorization might be withdrawn, and taxpayers invited to withhold payment if the government proved obdurate. To this revolutionary arrogation of power the King replied by locking the deputies out. They met in the Tennis Court and took their famous oath: that wherever they might meet the National Assembly would be in being, and that they would not dissolve before writing a constitution.

The King now at last offered a program on which he asked for agreement. There would be equality of taxation, assurance of individual liberties, freedom of the press, numerous reforms of detail, and consent to legislation and taxation in periodic future meetings of the Estates General. But the estates should remain as estates. There should be constitutional monarchy, but "the ancient distinction of the three orders" was to be "conserved in its entirety as essential to the constitution of the realm." Provincial Estates were to be introduced in all parts of the country. In each of them, half the members would be Third Estate elected by Third Estate; three tenths, nobles elected by nobles; two tenths clergy elected by clergy, with a certain number of those elected required to be bishops.[10]

The King's program of June 1789 was less than he had supported in Calonne's time two years before. It was about what the parlements and the provincial estates had wanted in 1788. The King's rallying to such a program represented the high point of the aristocratic resurgence, and the same ideas of a France governed through parlements and estates were to remain for ten years one of the orthodoxies of the counterrevolution. What had happened was that the King of France, forced to choose, had chosen to side with the nobles, probably neither quite willingly nor quite knowingly, perhaps with an obscure feeling that, if force must be used, it would be easier and more fitting to force the Third Estate than to force the nobility. In any case, monarchy and aristocracy were now allied in a way quite new in French history, in an alliance which in time was to prove fatal to them both. Even the most moderate of deputies of the Third, in June 1789, men like Malouet, a high official in the naval administration, refused to accept the royal peace offering, and insisted on pursuing the plan for a new constitution according to the oath in the Tennis Court.

The King now began to assemble troops around Versailles and Paris. The only reasonable supposition was that he intended to disperse the recalcitrant assembly and perhaps start over with new estates more carefully selected. A few soldiers could easily have put the leaders under arrest and sent the others fleeing for home or into

---

[10] The King's speech of June 23 may be found in *Archives parlementaires*. The King favored joint meeting of the three orders "for the present session of the estates only."

exile. This was prevented by the violent mass upheaval which now took place.

Until July 1789 the revolution had been mainly an orderly process, an affair largely of lawyers and writers, taking place in assemblies convened by the King himself. It now became a popular movement, and the popular revolution, by infecting the army, disarming the government, and disabling the nobility in the ultimate strongholds of their own landed estates, made it possible for the National Assembly to remain in existence, while at the same time forcing it in some ways to go beyond what its boldest members had intended.

It is here that economic and demographic conditions must be brought into the explanation of what occurred. Peasants had long objected to high taxes, to tithes, to payments due to the owners of manors. Those who owned land wished to get rid of encumbrances upon what they considered to be their own property. The landless demanded the chance to work land on terms that would enable them to live. Prices of agricultural products had been declining for more than a decade, so that the burden of rents, dues, tithes, and taxes was heavier on the peasants; and by the phenomenon known to French historians as the "feudal reaction," the owners of manorial rights—who might be nobles, church bodies, bourgeois, or even well-to-do peasants—were attempting to maintain or enlarge their incomes by a more exact collection of dues that had sometimes fallen into disuse. Conditions in the mid-century had been more favorable to the bulk of the agricultural population, so that unrest in the 1780's was due not merely to poverty but to a sense of pauperization. In addition, all western Europe in 1789 was in the grip of an economic depression; trade was bad, so that there was much unemployment, not only in the towns but also in the country, where many peasants gained part of their living by industrial occupations. The harvest of 1788 had been disastrously bad, so that bread was scarce. In the limited diet of the lower classes bread was a principal item, and by the purely short-run fluctuation, due to shortage, its price was momentarily higher than in almost a hundred years. Unemployment, poverty, restlessness, desperation, all were made abnormally explosive by the political situation. Poor as well as rich had been stirred by the summoning of the Estates General, by the town and village assemblies of March and April, by the news of the meeting of the Estates in May and June. If the lower classes had no interest in a constitution, and cared little for the disputes between nobility and bourgeoisie, they did expect the

Estates General to do something to relieve their own misery. Here again there was an air of universal expectancy. It was easy to believe that good King Louis was surrounded by evil advisers.

The whole Third Estate began to feel itself plotted against and betrayed. The idea of an aristocratic conspiracy, as Professor Lefebvre has said, is a necessary key to the understanding of the whole Revolution, not only in the days of the Terror but in 1789. There was not yet in any literal sense any conspiracy of aristocrats in the summer of 1789, but there was much in the recent past that gave a certain credibility to the idea: the action of the parlement in the preceding September, the threats of the Notables in December, the vacillation and hesitancy of a government that had at times clearly favored the Third Estate, the speeches and pamphlets of noblemen, the delaying action of the nobility in the Estates General, the King's locking out the Third Estate on June 20, his ambiguous proposals, and now his unaccustomed summoning of regiments of the regular army to Paris. On July 11, by dismissing Necker, the King gave further evidence that he planned to use force to disband the Assembly. It was known that Joseph II had dissolved the Estates of Brabant three weeks before.

In Paris people of all kinds, from bankers to shopkeepers and young café orators like Camille Desmoulins, combined in the agitation that led to the fall of the Bastille. There were a few cases of popular lynch-law, and heads were cut from corpses and impaled on pikes, but since governments themselves commonly exposed the heads of defunct malefactors to public view, it is not wholly germane to harp on atrocities of this kind. The bourgeoisie of Paris, acting through the "electors" elected in the preceding March, took over the government of the city, and organized a national guard to preserve life and property. The king proved unwilling or unable to use his army to put down this disturbance. He came to Paris, recognized the Parisian revolution, and accepted the existence of the National Assembly at Versailles.

Agrarian insurrection raged throughout the country. Peasants refused taxes, tithes, and manorial payments. They invaded chateaux and burned the legal papers on which their obligations rested. What they intended was no less than a social revolution, in that they meant by their own action to destroy the manorial or "feudal" system and the forms of property and income that this system represented. In places they were seized for a while by the panic called the Great Fear, believing that their fields and villages were about to be assaulted by brigands in the pay of aristocrats.

Although Louis XVI, under these pressures, recognized the National Assembly and seemed to accept the Revolution, his brother, the Count of Artois, along with the Prince of Condé and others, left the country during the latter part of July. Thus began the emigration. It was known that these émigrés would seek foreign aid, and it was already rumored that the British were about to land in support of the aristocrats, and that the King of Sardinia had the same intention. These rumors were wholly groundless, but they were by no means wholly absurd in a world where revolutions in Holland, Geneva, and Poland had been suppressed by foreign intervention. Such thoughts inflamed the idea of an aristocratic conspiracy, and the belief in such a conspiracy already produced anticipations of what would one day be the Terror. Barnave, commenting on the street murders, had already let fall the dreadful query, *Ce sang était-il donc si pur?* There was talk of committees of investigation and of special courts to try crimes against the state. The great lawyer Target, the small lawyer Robespierre, the Protestant lawyer Barnave, the nobleman Gouy d'Arsy, all agreed that drastic measures were justified in what amounted to civil war; and a month before the Declaration of Rights, it was said that civil liberties could be suspended in time of dire public emergency.

The Assembly had no means of pacifying the peasants. It could not ask the King to restore order by use of the army, which, if it could be used successfully against the peasants, might be turned against the Assembly itself. The peasant intransigence was embarrassing, because men of various classes were owners of manorial property. On the whole, however, the peasants in destroying the manorial system were destroying the economic foundations of the nobility. Peasant and bourgeois were at war with the same enemy, and this is what made possible the French Revolution.

The Assembly decreed what it could not prevent. It "abolished feudalism" on the famous night of the 4th of August. This extraordinary session was in part a parliamentary stratagem, contrived by a radical minority group, and in part the work of men overstimulated by the rush of events of the past few weeks, baffled by peasant rebellion, and worn out by years of debate on the complexities and eccentricities of intermeshing masses of special laws and privileges of all kinds, in which the peculiar rights and advantages of persons, orders, estates, gilds, corporate bodies, provinces, certain property owners, and certain taxpayers were incomprehensibly intermixed.

What was abolished, in this famous abolition of feudalism, was "feudalism" in its eighteenth-century meaning: the seigneurial relationship between landlord and tenant, the manorial forms of income and property, the differences between nobles and commoners in taxation and in the penalties inflicted by law for the same offenses, the immunities and liberties of provinces, and the confusion between public authority and private position represented in varying ways by the gilds, the seigneurial courts, and the institution of property in office.

All peasant obligations thought to have arisen from domination or lordship were abolished outright. These included the vestiges of serfdom, such labor services as remained, hunting rights or game laws favorable to the seigneurs, and the seigneurial or manorial courts. Obligations thought to represent a historic form of property were abolished with compensation. These included most of the payments in money or kind that the peasant proprietors had actually made. In practice it proved impossible to distinguish between the two kinds of "feudal dues," and in any case, as the Revolution continued, all compensation for such dues was abolished in 1792 and 1793. On equality of taxation, in August 1789, there was no longer any disagreement whatever. Provincial privileges were defended, for the sense of regionalism was still strong, but Brittany, in many ways the most privileged province, took the lead in the surrender of all provincial liberties. This was because, as a result of the political troubles in Brittany, the delegation from that province was composed of advanced revolutionaries of the Third Estate, and no delegation of the Breton nobles had come to the Estates General at all. On the gilds, which the Parlement of Paris had defended against Turgot, the Assembly decreed that they should be thoroughly reformed if not suppressed. In putting an end to property in office, the Assembly took on a huge addition to the public debt, for the value of the eleven hundred abolished seats in the parlements, not to mention other proprietary offices, was later set at half a billion *livres*. Since so much has already been said of the parlements, it may be remarked here that somewhat over 400 of the *parlementaires* eventually received compensation, which they generally converted from paper money into land; that about 140 received no compensation because condemned to death in later years of the Revolution; and that about 400 refused compensation because, having emigrated, they worked instead for reinstatement in their old positions through a victory of the counterrevolution.[11]

[11] H. Carré, *La fin des parlements* (Paris, 1912), 260.

The same session of August 4 decreed the abolition of tithes, pluralism in church appointments, and the annates paid to the court of Rome. A revolution was thereby initiated in the financial substructure of the church, and was carried much further in the following November, when all property of the church was confiscated, on the ground that it was not really private property anyway, and that, if it was sold off to new owners, the proceeds could be used to pay the royal, or now public, debt. Naturally some churchmen who had accepted merger of the orders in June, and so contributed to the Revolution, were repelled by these high-handed developments, but the loss of property and income was never the basic issue in the conflict of church and state during the Revolution, and even in 1791 there were still ninety priests in the Assembly considered to be on the Left. The "irreligion" of the first two years of the Revolution was more apparent to its political enemies, French and foreign, than to the French Catholic clergy as a whole.

The resolutions of the night of the 4th were worked out in detail in a series of August decrees of the ensuing weeks. The King showed great hesitancy in accepting these August decrees, but meanwhile, in a sense, they wiped clean the slate on which the outlines of a new France might be drawn. The way seemed open for the great work of regeneration so fervently expected. That there would be a new constitution was now certain. The Assembly prefixed it, on August 26, 1789, after a month of discussion, with a Declaration of the Rights of Man and Citizen.

Most of the arguments since levied against this famous document were heard in the Assembly that enacted it: that the concept of natural rights was dubious anyway, that men should be reminded also of their duties, that a ringing declaration would arouse expectations that could not be fulfilled, that the constitution, when it came, would seem drab and disappointing in comparison with the promises of this initial announcement. The Assembly overruled all such objections. Doubtless many were carried away by political excitement, but there were practical considerations also. The Declaration, far from being the work merely of a debating society, was a political act of the first magnitude. Its purpose was to raise a highly visible standard, to hold and rally a country aroused by the uprisings of preceding weeks, to keep alive the sense of struggle toward a goal, pending the long and disputatious process of constitutional and institutional change. The Declaration was no law book, but rather, in Lefebvre's phrase, a direction of intention, advertising to the country and to the world the shape that the new laws were to have. It was primarily an ethical affirmation, denying the moral foundation of the old order, vindicating the forcible overthrow of authority that had already occurred, and justifying in advance what was yet to come. If it was the death certificate of the Old Regime, in the words of Lefebvre and Aulard, it was also a birth certificate for the new.

It is probable that the idea of listing rights, in a numbered series, in a document distinct from the constitution itself, was suggested to the French by what they knew, which was a good deal, of the American bills of rights.[12] There was in fact a remarkable parallelism between the French Declaration and the Virginia Declaration of 1776. This parallelism can be readily explained by the presence of Jefferson in Paris and the activity of his friend Lafayette in the preparation of the French document; but this explanation is hardly necessary, since the wording of the first three articles, the principal articles of the French Declaration, was devised not by Lafayette but by Mounier, who, though familiar with American bills of rights, was not in much contact with Jefferson. The content of the French declaration was indigenous to France, and resemblances to American declarations are evidence of the community of ideas, and of basic problems as felt and identified on the two sides of the Atlantic. The French declaration, in comparison to the American ones, was more condensed, systematic, and abstract as a statement of public law. It gave a sharper definition to the conception of citizenship, individual liberty, and rightful public authority.

It is hard to comment on the Declaration without quoting it *in extenso* and verbatim. "Men are born and remain free and equal in rights," according to the first article, whose intent, of course, was to repudiate all legal and hereditary differences of rank or order. There may be "social distinctions," if based on "common utility." The natural rights, for whose preservation the state is to exist, are said to be "liberty, property, security and resistance to oppression." The liberty of each man is bounded by the rights of others; its limits can be de-

---

[12] See for example O. Vossler, "Studien zur Erklärung der Menschenrechte," in *Historische Zeitschrift*, vol. 142 (1930), 516-45, which will lead back to the older studies by Jellinek and Marcaggi. The textual comparison of the French and Virginia declarations, presented in Appendix IV below, should help to clarify this ancient subject of scholarly polemics. Professor Gilbert Chinard has analyzed a French publication of 1791 giving textual comparison of the French and American declarations and thus anticipating the whole historical discussion; see his "Notes on the American origins of the *Déclaration des droits de l'homme et du citoyen*" in *Proceedings of the American Philosophical Society*, vol. 98, No. 6 (December 23, 1954). See also Crane Brinton in the *Encyclopedia of the Social Sciences*, art., "Declaration of the Rights of Man."

termined only by law. There must be liberty to consent to laws and taxes, to communicate thought and opinion, to have equal access to all public office according only to "virtues and talents," to be free from arbitrary arrest, unduly severe punishment, or molestation for religious belief.

Half the Declaration is concerned with the nature of law and authority. "The principle of all sovereignty rests essentially in the nation. No body, and no individual, may exercise authority which does not emanate from the nation expressly." No man, or set of men, in other words, may hold public power by virtue of status, rank, family, inheritance or group membership, or by divine right, special training, special expertness, elite status, or other leadership principle of any kind. Royal absolutism, dynastic right, parlements, seigneurial jurisdiction, church courts possessed no coercive authority of their own. Men may be compelled only by law; law must express the general will; arbitrary use of power is a crime; but true law must be obeyed "instantly." The law must be the same for all. Armed forces must exist, but they exist for the benefit of the public, not of those who command them. Public expenditures must be publicly authorized. Public officers are accountable to the public for their conduct in office. Public need may require the condemnation of private property, but only by legal process, and only with fair compensation.

The Declaration, in short, simultaneously derived both liberty and authority from the same principles, while relating both to legal equality. Defending the individual against the state, it set up powers for the state as well. The rights it declared were not those of "man" only, and still less those of man in a state of nature, but of man as "citizen," a member of an organized civil community, in which each citizen was considered to share in the sovereignty and in the formation of that law which alone had any rightful power of coercion. It is in this respect, for example, that the Declaration of 1789 differs from the Declaration of the Rights of Man published by the United Nations in 1948. A "citizen" possesses power as well as rights.

The Declaration of 1789, by laying down the principles of the modern democratic state, remains the chief single document of the Revolution of the Western World. Printed, often on a single page, in hundreds of thousands of copies, it was publicly posted in all parts of France. Translated into a dozen languages, it was soon read and known in other countries, though in most of them, to be sure, it would be audacious if not actually dangerous in 1789 to post it in public.

The Constitution: Mounier and Sieyès

The Assembly now proceeded in August and September to make its main decisions on the constitution. These had already been prefigured in the discussion of the American constitutions, related in Chapter IX, in which Turgot, Mably, and Condorcet had played leading parts. The main disagreement was between those who favored a two-house legislature with a strong independent executive and those who preferred, like the late Turgot, a single assembly in which the national sovereignty should be concentrated.

The two chief constitutional thinkers were J. J. Mounier and the Abbé Sieyès. Mounier had always been one of the least known of the Revolutionary leaders outside of France. His writings and speeches show that he was fully familiar with the United States, which he thought had the best government in history up to that time; and he alluded often to recent events in Britain, Holland, Sweden, and Poland. In favoring a balance of powers in government, and in a certain realism of mind, Mounier was a kind of French John Adams, with much of Jefferson in him also. The Abbé Sieyès, more abstractly dogmatic, has always been well known as the great theorist of the Revolution of 1789. It was he, in his *Tiers Etat*, who translated the ideas of the *Contrat social* into the language of 1789. To judge by his writings, Sieyès had no more than a slight interest in America. Yet it was Sieyès, more clearly than anyone else, who expressed in France what I have called the essential revolutionary idea of the American Revolution: the idea of the people as a constituent power, working through a special convention conceived as outside and prior to government, and creating, by its sovereign action, the organs of state to which it grants a delegated authority.[18]

Mounier, with his balanced government, and Sieyès, with his constituent power, each stood for ideas that had their parallel in America. A comparison of the two, showing how Sieyès prevailed over Mounier, should not only explain much in France but illuminate the relationship between the French and American revolutions, which remains one of the principal problems of the period.

Mounier was the son of a cloth merchant of Grenoble, where he was befriended in his younger days by the grandfather of Stendhal. He became a lawyer, and in 1782 had been able to purchase a minor

[18] See J. Egret, *La Révolution des Notables: Mounier et les Monarchiens, 1789* (Paris, 1950); P. Bastid, *Sieyès*; P. Duclos, *La notion de constitution dans l'oeuvre de l'Assemblée constituante de 1789* (Paris, 1932).

judicial office, and so had acquired a "personal" or non-hereditary noble status which still kept him in the Third Estate. He was a moving spirit in the revolution of 1788 in Dauphiny which led to the Vizille assembly. More than anyone else, he had brought the nobles and bourgeois of Dauphiny together, with double representation for the Third and vote by head in the revived provincial estates, and so had taken the first step in what his fellow Dauphinois, Barnave, called the "democratic revolution." Elected to the Estates General, Mounier hoped for the same voluntary merger of the orders that he had seen happen in Dauphiny. This failing, he joined with the most aggressive spirits in the Third, and became a main author of the Oath of the Tennis Court. After the three orders were fused in the National Assembly, Mounier was elected to the first committee on the constitution. Skeptical of abstract declarations of rights, convinced that if there were to be such a declaration it should not be published until the constitution was completed, Mounier nevertheless went along with the majority and composed a draft of his own. In fact, the first three articles of the Declaration officially adopted on August 26, the most famous affirmations in the whole document, were in Mounier's language and represented his conceptions.[14]

Sieyès also originated in the lesser bourgeoisie, his father having held positions in the financial and postal administrations of the royal government. He had been trained for the church, because it offered careers to men like himself, and had in fact had considerable experience in ecclesiastical administration. Spending several years in Brittany, he had sat with the clergy in its Provincial Estates, where he had formed a low opinion of the hordes of nobility in that body. Transferred to Chartres, he had been an aide to the bishop there, and in this capacity had sat in the Orléanais provincial assembly of 1787. Here the Abbé Sieyès, his bishop (the liberal Lubersac), the eminent scientist, Lavoisier, and the Count de Rochambeau who had commanded in America, all vainly urged the nobility to give up some of their privileges. Where Mounier in Dauphiny found a basis of agreement for

[14] On Mounier and the Declaration, see Egret, *Mounier*, 114-17, and *Archives parlementaires* (première serie, 209 vols., Paris, 1867-1913), VIII, 289 and 463. Mounier submitted his draft to the Assembly on July 27. On August 20, late at night, after a fatiguing discussion on the phrasing of the first three articles, Mounier proposed the language which the Assembly thereupon adopted, and which closely echoed his own draft of July 27. It is rarely pointed out, especially by the more unfriendly and conservative critics of the Declaration, that its opening articles were devised by a man of relatively conservative disposition, who was well aware of the inadequacy, in Burke's phrase, of something written on a piece of paper about the rights of man.

nobles and bourgeois, Sieyès in Brittany and the Orléanais had had the opposite experience. It was from his own participation in real affairs that he acquired some of the cold and contemptuous hatred of the nobility that made him famous. In the last days of 1788 he penned his *Qu'est ce que le Tiers Etat?* which soon went through several editions, and of which the drift was that the nobility was utterly useless, and that the Third Estate could better form a complete nation without it. Sieyès, made famous by his pamphlets, became one of only three clerics elected by the Third Estate to the Estates General. His very rigidity made him a leader of the Third at Versailles in the face of the noble resistance. Where Mounier hoped for voluntary integration of the three orders, Sieyès preferred that the upper two be peremptorily summoned. It was Sieyès, against Mounier's more cautious judgment, who persuaded the Third to adopt the term National Assembly, on the ground that the nation was assembled whether the privileged orders were present or not. Sieyès, like Mounier, was elected by the Assembly to its constitutional committee in July.

Mounier and Sieyès, though they came to stand for opposite views, actually agreed on a good deal. Both detested the society of orders and estates. "Aristocracy is the worst form of government," said Mounier; "it degrades the public character."[15] Sieyès could have said no more in so few words. Both were alarmed by popular disturbances; both went along with the August decrees because they felt obliged to; both were concerned for property, law, and order; both wanted a fixed and firm constitution which would be durable, and under which no organ of government would exceed the limits assigned to it. Both saw the need of obtaining in government a true and authoritative representation of the people, one that should not only truly reflect the national will, but have power to commit its constituents and have its policies properly enforced. Both, as men of the eighteenth century, like Adams or Jefferson, saw as one of the dangers in government a tendency for elected personages to become self-perpetuating or even hereditary, to serve their own interests, to cease to be truly representative, and yet become very difficult to control or to remove. It was in means and procedures, more than in ends, that Sieyès and Mounier differed. To explain why Sieyès prevailed in every case is to explain a good deal of the Revolution.

[15] *Considérations sur les gouvernements et principalement sur celui qui convient à la France* (August, 1789), 14.

To begin with, there was an important question of principle. Did the National Assembly have to *negotiate* a constitution with the King? Were the Assembly and the King independent legal authorities whose agreement was necessary for every clause? Could the Assembly put into the constitution only what the King would willingly approve? No American constitutional convention had ever faced these questions.

Mounier was inclined to avoid such questions as a little too theoretical, to take a common sense view, arguing that the King already existed as a reality, that the country deeply respected the royal authority, that the Assembly enjoyed prestige because the King had convoked it, and that the King in any case would be responsible for enforcing the new constitution, so that it was only reasonable to seek his genuine agreement on its terms. France, said Mounier, was not a *tabula rasa*, nor in a state of nature, nor just "emerged from the forest"; nor in his opinion was the Assembly a true *convention nationale*. It is significant that this term, which was to take on its full meaning in 1792, was already in use in August 1789, to signify a body outside of all government, sprung directly from the people, and authorized to create institutions, as it were, *de novo*. The Americans, according to Mounier, may have been in such a juridical condition in 1776, because they had repudiated their King; but the same was not true of France, where the King still existed, and where in fact no one dreamed of doing without him.[16]

Sieyès took a sour satisfaction in preferring principles to common sense. He was also less inclined than Mounier to overlook the King's recent partisanship for the nobility. Moreover, the King was refusing his approval to the Declaration of Rights and to the August decrees, which, if not wholly desirable to Sieyès, were necessary to keep harmony between the Assembly and the country. To Sieyès it was clear that the Assembly should not have to seek the King's permission on constitutional matters, that the Assembly alone possessed the full *pouvoir constituant*, that the King must be under the constitution and not a coauthor of it, and that Louis XVI, like everyone else, should have only such lawful powers as the constitution might confer upon him. If Louis XVI was antagonized, it made no difference to Sieyès.

The Assembly would have preferred, like Mounier, to avoid an open clash with the King on such topics, but it was drawn on increasingly to agree with Sieyès, because it really had no alternative. Mounier's own position was contradictory: he could not both get rid

16 *Ibid.*, 37-38.

of aristocracy and let the King share in making the constitution. Given Louis XVI as he was, and given a revolution against royal absolutism and the society of estates, it was impossible to escape the principles so loftily handed down by the chilly wisdom of the Abbé Sieyès.

On the content of the constitution, as distinguished from its origin, Mounier at first had a majority in the constitutional committee, and it was his ideas that were laid before the Assembly at the end of August. He and his followers were dubbed Monarchicals or Anglomaniacs by their opponents. Actually, it was at least as much to American as to British examples that they pointed.

Mounier's committee proposed a threefold organization of government: The King, even supposing that for the constitution itself his consent was not necessary, was to have, as the national executive, once the constitution was in operation, a power of veto over legislation. The upper house, for which they used the American term "senate," was to be composed of men of property and standing; the committee did not specify the qualifications or mode of selection, but made it clear that the new senate would not be hereditary, nor composed only of nobles, so that, in its view, there was no danger of "aristocracy." For the lower house, often called a house of representatives in the debates, there was to be a very wide popular suffrage, but with property qualifications for the members. Mounier and his friends repeatedly cited the new United States federal constitution and the state constitutions, including the new one about to be adopted in Pennsylvania (in place of the famous democratic constitution of 1776), to justify the executive veto, bicameralism, and property qualifications for house and senate. "One must have a bold philosophy, indeed," he plaintively remarked, "to be more free of prejudice than the Americans."[17] He insisted that his views were shared by Jefferson, still in Paris as American Minister; nor is there any reason to doubt it. Like everyone else, he selected his arguments, not noting, for example, that there were no property qualification in the new United States federal constitution, and that the qualifications he had in mind were considerably higher than in most American states. In any case, it was the executive veto and the upper house that were in dispute.

The Assembly debated these proposals for ten days. Feeling ran very high, and was confused by popular agitation from the militants of Paris, who were now enraged by the very words Veto and Aristocracy. Mounier and his friends were even threatened with physical

[17] *Ibid.*, 15.

violence. There was no privacy in the chamber; the galleries hooted and applauded as they chose. Nevertheless the debate took a fairly high level, and in all the hubbub it represented a conflict of actual arguments.

As one analyzes these arguments, it becomes clear that what all agreed on was the need of keeping government within lawful limits. All opposed royal absolutism. All admitted that elected assemblies might "err." All feared that a body of men originally elected might become oligarchic and self-perpetuating. How was this to be prevented? How were deputies to be kept responsive to those who deputized them, and made to stay within the powers assigned to them by the nation? How could the constitution be made to stick? All agreed that insurrection and revolutionary defiance, though justifiable in rare circumstances, were not appropriate constitutional methods to prevent the abuse of power.

Mounier and his friends talked much like John Adams. All men love power and domination, said Lally-Tollendal, and a *pouvoir unique,* as in an unchecked single assembly, "will end up by devouring all."[18] There must be two houses, and a strong independent executive. The King, said Mounier, Mirabeau, Malouet, and others, represents the people as much as the deputies do. There is more to be feared from aristocracy than from monarchy: "never has the throne lost authority except to give place to the degrading yoke of aristocracy . . . to defend the independence of the crown is to defend the liberty of the people."[19] The King must have a veto. He may represent the true will and interest of the country more than the deputies do; and even the new President of the United States has an "absolute veto" unless two thirds of both houses are against him.

Arguments in favor of the royal veto often took on a popular or democratic cast, which the prejudices of the time and the clichés of historians have obscured, but which is not really surprising in view of the long association of royalism and antiaristocratism in France. The Abbé Maury, for example, a leading conservative, favored an "absolute veto," and cited the case of Holland, where, he observed, the assemblies, unchecked by any veto, had turned into a *noblesse* and a *monstrueuse aristocratie.* Others thought of the veto as a form of *appel au peuple.* There was a good deal of opinion in favor of execu-

[18] *Archives parlementaires,* VIII, 515.

[19] *Ibid.,* 559. This speech of Mounier's was separately printed as *Motifs présentés au nom du Comité de constitution sur divers articles du Plan du Corps législatif, et principalement sur la nécessité de la sanction royale.*

tive dissolution of the assembly—a doctrine, as is well known, never favored in French parliamentary circles. If the King insisted on vetoing an action of the assembly, said Mirabeau, he should immediately dissolve it and call for new elections. He should have, in the public interest, this power to confront the deputies with their constituents. Mounier, La Rochefoucauld, Lameth, and Rabaut Saint-Etienne also favored this "absolute veto" with immediate dissolution and immediate new elections. Others, preferring only a "suspensive veto," thought of it as an "appeal to the people" at the ensuing periodic election, where voters would choose between the policies of the King and those of the deputies. Very few seem to have thought that a king should simply block an assembly without more ado.

On the other side, against the veto and the upper house, there were obscure deputies who got up and said that nothing could rightly interfere with the rights of man and the sovereignty of the nation. Someone said there should be no veto because there was none in the constitution of Virginia. Most arguments were more concrete. Deputies of all shades of opinion, and both nobles and non-nobles, objected that an upper house would lead back to the "orders" and to monstrous aristocracy. Condorcet now repeated what he had said in criticism of the American constitutions: that the way to control government was to have a single assembly subject to frequent election and to clear declarations of popular rights. John Stevens' rebuttal of John Adams, in the French version mentioned in Chapter IX, with its notes by Condorcet, Dupont, Mazzei, and others, was praised and rejected by various speakers. At least two deputies, the Marquis de Sillery and Dr. Salle from Lorraine, pointed to a fundamental problem, and one that sharply distinguished the French and American revolutions. In France, they said, there was so much that required change that years must pass in basic reconstruction; there was no means of clearly separating ordinary from fundamental laws, or of mapping out a constitutional from a merely legislative sphere; it would long be uncertain whether a piece of legislation was constitutional or not; and meanwhile there must be no royal veto or upper house. They offered as an example the decrees of August 4, which the King had not yet accepted.

Sieyès delivered a great speech against Mounier's proposals. As always, he set up high principles and strict deductions.[20] There must be equality of voting power, he said; one man, one vote, counting men as individuals; anything else would be a throwback to the "distinction

[20] *Archives parlementaires*, VIII, 592-601.

of orders." Hence there could be only one house of legislation; if a senate of fifty men could stop an assembly of five hundred, what was this but that inequality of orders repudiated in the preceding June? The King was one man. He was also hereditary and irremovable. His advice would always be sought, and his influence respected. But his *will*, or vote, could count only as one. Hence he could have no veto over the majority in the Assembly. The authority of the National Assembly must be unquestioned. Its will must be accepted as the will of the nation. Hence, not only must it be free from interference from a second chamber, or from a royal veto; it must be free from that appeal to the people with which the veto was associated. No possibility must exist for the King or anyone else to appeal over the Assembly's head. There would be thousands of subordinate assemblies in the new France (and everyone had in mind the actual electoral assemblies of the preceding spring); if there were ever any doubt as to which of these assemblies the will of the nation really lay in, the country would fall into anarchy and dissolution. The National Assembly must bind its constituents, not be bound by them. Most men were busy with their own affairs; they were in fact "work machines." Since they had to obey the laws they had the right to consent to them; but this meant only that they might choose representatives without dictating what these representatives should be obliged to do. There could be no "democracy" in France (that is "direct democracy"), with thousands of little assemblies each pursuing its own program or forcing its will on the national government.[21] There should be *gouvernement représentatif*, in which representatives were put into or taken out of power by the voters, but, while in power, governed according to their own judgment under orders from no one. As to those who urged a second chamber merely to prevent hasty and ill-considered action, Sieyès had

---

[21] At the beginning of 1789, on the eve of elections to the Estates General, Sieyès had been of a contrary opinion on the referral of important decisions to subordinate assemblies. He then said that the coming National Assembly (a term he already used) should confine itself to a few basic constitutional changes, and should consult with provincial, district, and parish assemblies before legislating on other matters. (See *Instructions données par S. A. S. Monseigneur le duc d'Orléans à ses representants dans les bailliages* [n.p., 1789], *passim*.) For Sieyès' change of mind, and later distrust of such habitual referenda, various historians have found it an adequate explanation to call him a bourgeois, alarmed by the violence, the popular tumult, and the threats to property of the summer of 1789. Sieyès was indeed a bourgeois, with 13,000 francs a year from various church benefices in 1789. Robespierre went through a comparable evolution, from appeals to the *assemblées primaires* when he was out of the government, to attempts to control them when he was in the government, in 1793 and 1794; he, too, has been explained as a bourgeois. But there is, after all, a problem of government itself.

a favorite proposal to make to them: the single National Assembly could subdivide into small groups for leisurely deliberation, then combine again for voting, by numerical majority, to express its authoritative decision.

Sieyès' logic was hard and even repellent, but it is not easy to dismiss it as mistaken. It was perfectly true that the Assembly, if it was to hold to the advanced position taken in the Declaration of Rights and the August decrees, would be threatened from two directions: both from the side of the King and of those who surrounded him in the use of a veto, and from the side of a people already aroused to habits of direct action by the experience of revolution. The coming years were to be characterized by a kind of absolutism in the national representative body, tempered by the King's pursuit of his own designs, and by appeals of malcontents, both radical and conservative, to various regional and local assemblies against the government in Paris. This is only to say that during the Revolution France was deeply divided, with no authority widely enough accepted to make civil peace.

The vote in the Assembly proved to be a disaster for Mounier. The bicameral principle was defeated almost ten to one, with 849 votes for a single house, 89 for two houses, and 122 abstaining.[22] Where Mounier had insisted on the absolute veto, the Assembly adopted a suspensive veto by 673 to 325. The King himself made it known, through Necker, that he did not want Mounier's absolute veto, believing it politically too dangerous ever to use in practice. The suspensive veto was soon defined to mean that a measure passed against the King's veto by two successive biennial legislatures, in addition to

[22] On this elementary yet highly significant point there still seems to be confusion after more than a century and a half of intensive work on the French Revolution. One often obtains the impression that partisans of aristocracy voted for an upper chamber, with the implication that bicameralism was an aristocratic and unicameralism a more democratic belief. The *Moniteur* (issue of September 8-12, 1789) gives only 499 as the number of those voting for a single house; it is followed by the *Archives parlementaires* and by Buchez and Roux. The *Moniteur* is not a true source, however, for dates before November 24, 1789, and it seems likely that this figure is a typographical error, since the *Journal des débats* for September 10, 1789, gives the figure 849, which is adopted by Egret, *Révolution de Notables*, p. 152, as also by Mathiez. All sources that give figures at all give only 89 as the number voting for two houses. Some authorities (Egret, Lanzac de Laborie, Lacretelle) accuse the Right of following a *politique du pire*, that is, of voting for a single house in order to produce an unworkable constitution. Lacretelle says that he remembers many having said, *tout ne va pas encore assez mal* (*Histoire de l'Assemblée constituante*, Paris, 1821, I, 202); and Lanzac de Laborie attributes to Maury the cynical remark that *si vous établissiez deux chambres votre constitution pourrait se maintenir*. I do not know on what contemporary evidence such allegations may rest. I follow Egret in his conclusion on why Right and Left combined to swamp Mounier by favoring a single house.

the one in which the measure originated, would become law without his approval. The King thus received a power to delay, for as long as six years, a program repeatedly endorsed by the legislature and presumably by the electorate. This was surely a dangerous kind of *appel au peuple*. In any government such institutionalized confrontation or stalemate would have been impolitic; in time of revolution and war it might be fatal, and in 1792 it was to prove ruinous to the constitution and to the King, "Monsieur Veto," himself.

It is clear that the materials did not exist in France for a constitution on the American model, with "balanced government" in the manner of John Adams. In fact, it seems that Adams himself would have voted against Mounier in 1789. Stoutly defending his principles, Adams nevertheless thought that temporarily a single house might be best for France, because a senate would "be formed, most probably, of princes of the blood, cardinals, archbishops, dukes and marquises; and all these together would have obstructed the progress of the reformation in religion and government, and procured an abortion to the regeneration of France."[23] This was precisely the view of the Left, as it was already called, in the French Assembly. Patriots feared that even an elected upper house would be dominated by the nobility, or turn in some way into a special "body" or "order" like the old parlements or estates. But even the French Right in 1789 would not vote for an upper house. What the truly conservative aristocrat desired, the little nobleman from the country, was the old-fashioned "order" in which he had been born, to which he owed his status, and which had been dissolved in the Estates General against his will. He did not want an English House of Lords or an elective senate on the American model, for such a body would be filled by wealthy and prominent nobles or bourgeois, and the ordinary nobleman or gentleman of the provinces, if he went into politics, would have to enter a lower house by soliciting votes from the common people.

There was wisdom in the arguments of Mounier and Mirabeau for a strong executive independent of the elected assembly. But the strong governor created in 1780 by the constitution of Massachusetts was an elected officer of limited term, as was the strong President created at the Philadelphia convention for the United States. In an appeal to the people he could be voted out. The French King, as Sieyès observed, was hereditary and irremovable. He was also a carryover from former

[23] *Discourses on Davila* (1790) in *Works* (1851), VI, 274.

times, not really in sympathy with the new. The King could not be wholly trusted even by moderate partisans of the new order. Yet his very existence made it impossible for the French to create a new executive office as the Americans had done. Never during the Revolution, if indeed after it, were the French quite to solve the problem of the relation of the executive to the national representation.

Mounier and his followers immediately resigned from the constitutional committee. There followed the October Days, when rioters invaded Versailles and obliged the King and the Assembly to remove to Paris. Disgusted by such violence, believing that the Assembly was now at the mercy of city mobs, and being actually in some danger of his own life, Mounier returned to Dauphiny. Here he found opinion divided, some favoring the National Assembly, the August decrees, the Declaration, the steps taken toward a new constitution—and some opposed. The former gathered in a popular club to uphold the Assembly—a future Jacobin club of the provinces. The latter Mounier tried to rally in the Provincial Estates, which he himself had helped to bring into being at Vizille the year before. The Provincial Estates became the organized center for opposition to the National Assembly, even threatening civil war. The National Assembly thereupon prohibited the meeting of all Provincial Estates and all "assemblies by Orders" throughout France. Thus another line was drawn between Revolution and Counterrevolution, and another step taken toward concentration of sovereignty in the Assembly at Paris. Mounier then went abroad. Two years later, from his place of exile, in a book explaining why the French had failed to "become free," he was denouncing the new France as impossibly "democratic," and urging royal dictatorship as the only solution for France's troubles.[24]

It is important, most especially perhaps for American readers, to explain how J. J. Mounier, the merchant's son, the enemy of noble privilege, the hero of the Tennis Court, the coauthor of the great Declaration, the moderate revolutionary of 1789 whose ideas were in so many ways close to those of Americans, passed as early as the end of 1789 into the Counterrevolution. For I believe that Mounier was tragically mistaken. His position was untenable. The existence of monarchy and aristocracy in France, as they really were, made his system unworkable and unacceptable. It was not even desired by the King and nobility. If the French were to carry out the principles that they

---

[24] *Recherches sur les causes qui ont empêché les Français de devenir libres, et sur les moyens qui leur restent pour acquérir la liberté* (2 vols., Geneva, 1792), II, 203.

shared with Americans and with men elsewhere in Europe, as described in preceding chapters—principles set forth notably in the Declaration—they would have to do so by concentrating sovereign power, the power to destroy and to create, in a single assembly somewhat as outlined by the Abbé Sieyès—and which wielded, in principle, that awful "supreme, sovereign, absolute and uncontrollable power" ascribed in 1776 by the General Court of Massachusetts to the people. They would have to take account of the wishes of peasants and workers; the Revolution could not succeed if "bourgeois" alone. It could not, as Mounier preferred, be only a revolution of respectable men. Lawyers, businessmen, lesser officeholders, writers, and humanitarians could not, by themselves, defeat the interests of monarchy and aristocracy which were now allied. Moderate revolution was eminently desirable, but it was not one of the possible choices. Moderation in Belgium, Holland, Geneva, Milan, England, Ireland, and Poland had accomplished nothing.

After the October Days of 1789, which led to the transfer of its sittings to Paris, the Assembly remained at work for two years, applying in all directions, and not merely to government, the revolutionary principle of the people as constituent power. The old France which had fallen to pieces was put back together according to a new pattern. National sovereignty, equality of rights, and universality of free citizenship were the most prominent features of the new design. The formerly sovereign King became an officer under the constitution. Nobility and all its titles were abolished. The old constituted bodies, as they have been called in preceding pages, the thirteen parlements and the various Provincial Estates, disappeared. All other "bodies," corporate groups, and special interests faced a similar liquidation. Trade and professional gilds, employers' associations and workingmen's unions were proscribed as contrary to individual liberty and equality. The right of free access to any private occupation or any public office for all qualified persons was proclaimed, with the understanding that qualifications should depend only on the nature of the task to be performed. The church was reorganized, and its bishops and parish clergy were made elective. Protestants and Jews received the same rights as Catholics; or rather, religious affiliation was made irrelevant to citizenship, or to membership in the civil community called the nation. Property, like government, was freed from the lingering idea of lordship; this was the essential meaning of the abolition of feudalism. In the redefinition of property, there could be no property in public office or manorial forms of income; these were abolished with compensation. The Assembly assumed the old royal debt as a public or national obligation, which no government of the Revolution ever expressly repudiated. To pay it off, the property of the church was confiscated, on the ground that it had always been held in trust for the public anyway. The state took on the responsibility for the costs of religious worship, as for social services and education. Taxes, law courts, army, schools, scientific and literary academies were all revolutionized.

The abolition of the provinces and of regional liberties made the same rights and obligations prevail uniformly throughout the country. The basis of representation and the liability to taxes became geographically homogeneous. Various local administrations and officials were made locally elective. The constitution gave the vote to over half the adult male population; or to more than two-thirds of those over the required age of twenty-five. Voters, as such, voted only for electors, who in turn chose the national deputies and the lesser elected officials; but those who might qualify as electors were very numerous, certainly more numerous than those who could read a newspaper or compose a written message, probably being half the men of twenty-five or older. When "equality" was talked of in the eighteenth century, universal suffrage was one of the last things it called to mind; but even if democracy be anachronistically identified with the number of persons entitled to vote, the government set up in France by the constitution of 1791 was incomparably more democratic than any other in the Western World at the time, with the sole exception of certain states in the American Union.[25] Under revolutionary conditions, however, in which people of all classes had been politically aroused, the exclusion of a considerable segment from the vote led to disturbance, especially with the beginning of war and the raising of a popular army in 1792. The Constituent Assembly, on finishing its work in 1791, did not submit the new constitution to any form of popular ratification, such as had occurred for the federal and some of the state constitutions in America. Here again, not without reason, the Assembly was afraid of lesser assemblies throughout the country, many of which might not agree with it, and some of which, even those influenced by "aristocrats," would claim to represent the people more than the National Assembly itself. As Sieyès said, the authority of the National Assembly

[25] See Appendix v.

must be upheld, and no authentic national will could be known except as expressed by it.

After the fall of the Bastille, Camille Desmoulins began to publish a political paper in which he liked to emphasize the international character of the Revolution. He called it the *Révolutions de France et de Brabant*, and in December 1789 he added *etc.* to "Brabant." He put in news items from all kinds of places: there were "fermentations" at Rome, "murmurs" in Hungary, troubles in Denmark, Spain, and Poland, and at Geneva, Liége, and London. In March 1790 he took note of the French émigrés, among whom such incongruous person-ages as Mounier and the Count of Artois were now included, and of the agitation of the émigrés for intervention in France by foreign powers. Against intervention he made the counterthreat of interna-tional subversion. "I would not advise their Sardinian, Bohemian, Spanish, Neapolitan, and Prussian Majesties to get mixed up in our affairs. Four or five million armed men would fight for liberty and *pro aris et focis* against mercenaries at four sous a day." And he said that the American Revolution proved that citizen soldiers could stand against regular armies. And that foreign troops would be subverted by "our cockades and our decrees."

The new French constitution went into effect in September 1791. "The Revolution is over," said Robespierre, in a phrase often quoted. What he said was that the Revolution was over if the constitution was firmly established, if all concerned would live under it peaceably, if it had no dangerous enemies either inside France or beyond its borders. These conditions did not obtain. The Revolution was therefore by no means over. Only a challenge had been issued to the old order; the real struggle was yet to come.

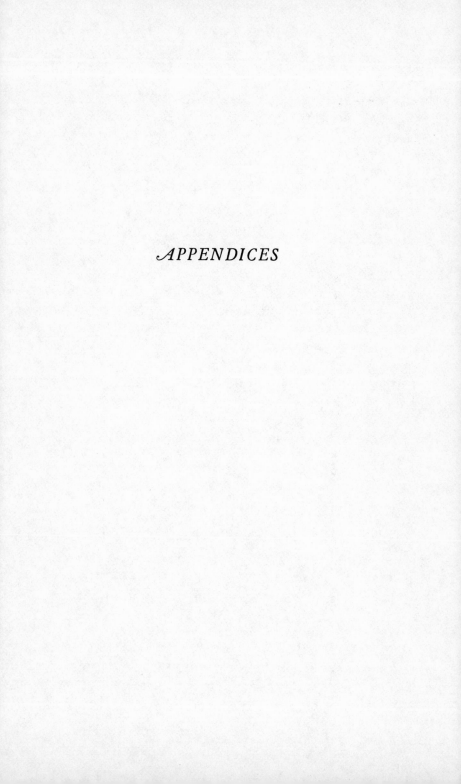

APPENDICES

APPENDICES

✭ APPENDIX I ✭

References for the Quotations at Heads of Chapters

I. G. K. van Hogendorp, *Brieven en Gedenkschriften* (The Hague, 1876), III, 60-61.

II. Montesquieu, *Esprit des lois*, in *Oeuvres* (Paris, 1826), I, 146-52.

III. Burke, *Writings* (Boston, 1901), IV, 175; Paine, *Rights of Man*, Everyman ed., 59.

IV. B. Lacombe, *Résistance janséniste et parlementaire au temps de Louis XV* (Paris, 1948), 108; R. L. de V. d'Argenson, *Considérations sur le gouvernement de la France* (Amsterdam, 1765), 183.

V. *Encyclopédie ou Dictionnaire raisonné* (Paris, 1751-1765), art. "Genève"; *Encyclopedia britannica* (Edinburgh, 1797), art. "Geneva."

VI. Blackstone, *Commentaries on the Laws of England* (Sharswood ed., Philadelphia, 1868), I, 160.

VII. J. Sparks, *Life of Gouverneur Morris* (Boston, 1832), I, 158; M. C. Tyler, *Literary History of the American Revolution* (New York, 1897), II, 124-25; *Writings of George Washington* (Boston, 1835), VII, 159-61.

VIII. C. Rossiter, *Seedtime of the Republic* (New York, 1953), 408-09; J. W. Fortescue, *Correspondence of King George III* (1927-28), III, 248, 282.

IX. M. J. Chénier, *Oeuvres* (Paris, 1826), I, 218; V. Alfieri, *Rime* (Florence, 1933), 308; *Berliner Monatschrift*, April 1783, 368-91; A. Loosjes, *Gedenkzuil, ter gelegenheid der vrij-verklaring van Noord-Amerika* (Amsterdam, 1782), 31; A. Radishchev, *Izbrannye filosofskie sochineniia* (Moscow, 1949), 435.

X. *Correspondence between the Rt. Hon. William Pitt and Charles Duke of Rutland, Lord Lieutenant of Ireland* (London, 1890), 52; Burke, *Writings* (Boston, 1901), VII, 101.

XI. Adams, *Works* (Boston, 1851), VIII, 455.

XII. F. Valsecchi, *L'assolutismo illuminato in Austria e in Lombardia* (Bologna, 1931), I, 128-29.

XIII. Académie polonaise des sciences, *La Pologne au X⁰ congrès international des sciences historiques à Rome* (Warsaw, 1955), 201; C. Desmoulins, *Révolutions de France et de Brabant*, No. 79 (April 1791), 36-37.

XIV. Lavisse, *Histoire de France* (Paris, 1910), IX, 344; *Remontrances du Parlement de Paris . . . presentées au roi le 4 mai 1788* (Paris, 1788), 6.

XV. Julian P. Boyd, ed., *The Papers of Thomas Jefferson*, xv (1958), 269; H. Carré, *La noblesse de France et l'opinion publique au 18⁰ siècle* (Paris, 1920), 365.

★ APPENDIX II ★

Translations of Metrical Passages

P. 238

This vast continent that the seas surround
Will soon change Europe and the world.
There arise for us, in the fields of America,
New interests and a new system of politics.

M. J. Chénier, Charles IX, 1789

The raging storm,
Which is bringing salvation and liberty to us.

V. Alfieri, America Free, 1783

O land to the singer dearer than Fatherland!

Anon., The Freedom of America, 1783

My friends! Each of you sees
The well-being of this state in American liberty.

A. Loosjes, The Independence of
North America, 1782

To you my inflamed soul aspires,
To you, renowned land. . . .
Your example has revealed the goal.

A. Radishchev, Ode to Freedom, 1782
(with acknowledgments to R. H. Mc-
Neal and C. E. Black for the transla-
tion)

P. 255

Venerable Congress, of a people free and good
You have cemented the glory and union;
You have delivered America and its waters
From the furious Leopards, the tyrant of two worlds:
Clear-headed scrutinizers of our vain prejudices,
You have descended to the depth of our hearts;
You plunge into them a torrent of light,
Which brings clarity to this sad hemisphere,
Strikes its tyrants, and from their shameful yoke
Invites us to break the detestable bonds.

Where without distinction of birth or rank,
The most honest man, the most worthy of respect,
The most useful in short, is always the greatest.

P. 257

Be free! (say it in high victory note,
Enraptured song!) free, free now, America!

Thine example calls out loud to the Nations:
"Free is, who free will be, and is worthy to be!" . . .

O land to the singer dearer than Fatherland!
The first shoots of thy freedom grow quickly
  To the tree. . . .

Where sweet equality dwells, and the spawn of nobles,
The plague of Europe, does not defile the manners of
    simplicity,
Without desert, in spite of better men.

O take, beloved, take the stranger up,
The weary stranger; let me at your breast
    Allay the long consuming sorrows,
    The bitter pangs of secret grief.

Why do I tarry? Still clank the iron chains,
Reminding me, poor me, that I am a German.
    I see you, lovely scenes, disappear,
    Sink back into the depth, and weep.

From Goethe:
  Here or nowhere is America
      and
  America, thou hast it better
  Than our continent, the old one.

P. 258

And man was now again man; many noble beings
Planted eagerly the seed of truth.
    Far on Philadelphia's shores there glowed
    A milder dawn.

P. 364

How the times have changed! Who could ever
    have believed it?
Civil equality is ennobling the French. . . .

⭐ APPENDIX III ⭐

The following are excerpts from basic legal or constitutional documents of ten countries between 1782 and 1791, chosen to illustrate provisions with respect to nobility, hierarchy, corporate society, inheritance of legal status, equality or inequality of rights, and uniformity of citizenship.

I.
Russia: Catherine II's Charter of the Nobility, 1785

1. The noble calling is the result, rising out of the qualities and virtues of men who held high office in the past, and distinguished themselves by their merits, by which they transformed the service itself into a dignity, and won for their descendants the noble appellation.

2. It is not only useful for the empire and the throne, but also just, to preserve and firmly establish the honorable estate of the well-born nobility; and hence the dignity of nobility shall remain inalienable from oldest times to the present, and for all time by inheritance to the descendants of those families that now enjoy it, as follows:

3. The nobleman transmits his noble status to his wife.

4. The nobleman transmits his well-born noble status by inheritance to his children.

8. Without judicial proceedings no well-born person can lose noble status.

9. Without judicial proceedings no well-born person can lose his honor.

10. Without judicial proceedings no well-born person can lose his life.

11. Without judicial proceedings no well-born person can lose his property.

12. The well-born person can be judged only by his peers.

15. Corporal punishment may not be inflicted on any well-born person.

16. Noblemen serving in the lower ranks of our Army shall be liable only to such punishments as our military regulations prescribe for higher officers.

17. We guarantee independence and freedom to the Russian nobility for all time, by inheritance in future generations.

18. We guarantee to noblemen, now in our service, the right either to continue in service or to apply for release from it according to regulations now in effect.

19. We guarantee permission to noblemen to enter the service of other European powers allied with us, and to travel in foreign lands.

20. [Duty of nobles to defend the state.]

21. The well-born person has the right to sign his name [as owner of a landed estate].

22. [Rights of sale, alienation and testament.]

23-25. [Miscellaneous.]

26. Well-born persons are confirmed in the right to purchase villages.

27. Well-born persons are confirmed in the right to sell at wholesale what has been harvested in their villages or produced by handicraft.

28. Well-born persons are permitted to have manufactories and industrial works in their villages.

29. Well-born persons are permitted to set up market towns on their estates and to open annual or other markets in them, as provided by law, with the knowledge of the governor and the administration of the province. . . .

30. Well-born persons are confirmed in the right to possess, build or buy houses in the cities, and to carry on manufacturing enterprises therein.

31. [Nobles may obtain burgher rights.]

32. Well-born persons are permitted to sell products raised on their estates at wholesale overseas or to have them exported through the designated ports. . . .

33. Well-born persons, in accordance with the ukaz of June 28, 1782 are confirmed in the right to possess, not only the surface of the lands belonging to them, but also whatever minerals or plants may be present in the depths beneath the soil or waters, and likewise all metals extracted therefrom, in the full sense and scope of the aforementioned ukaz.

34. Well-born persons are confirmed in the right to possess the forests on their estates, and in the right of free use of these forests. . . .

35. In the villages the house of the lord shall be exempt from military quartering.

36. The well-born person is himself freed from personal taxes.

Translated from the German text in V. Gitermann, *Geschichte Russlands*, 2 vols. (Zurich, 1945), II, 470-72, I am indebted to my colleague, Professor Jerome Blum, for comparing the translation for accuracy of meaning with the original Russian. Further clauses granted the nobles the right of provincial assemblies.

2.

The Prussian General Code, 1791
Introduction: On the Laws in General

1. This general code contains the provisions by which the rights and obligations of inhabitants of the state, so far as they are not determined by particular laws, are to be judged.

6. *Decrees or other measures of higher authority, which have issued in contested cases without judicial cognizance, create neither rights nor obligations.

9. *Particular favors, privileges and exceptions to the law, arising from the action of the sovereign, are valid only so far as the particular rights of a third party are not thereby injured.

26. The laws of the state bind all its members without difference of estate, rank or family.

58. Privileges and grants of liberty, in doubtful cases, must be so interpreted as to do the least damage to third parties.

77. *The welfare of the state in general, and of its inhabitants in particular, is the aim of civil society and the general objective of the laws.

79. *The laws and ordinances of the state should restrict the natural liberty and rights of citizens no further than the general welfare demands.

83. Every inhabitant of the state has a right to demand its protection for his person and property.

84. No one therefore is entitled to obtain his rights by his own powers.

89. The rights of man arise from his birth, from his estate, and from actions and arrangements with which the laws have associated a certain determinate effect.

90. The general rights of man are grounded on the natural liberty to seek and further his own welfare, without injury to the rights of another.

91. The particular rights and duties of members of the state rest upon the personal relationship in which each stands to others and to the state itself.

93. Rights which are not supported by the laws are called imperfect, and give no ground for complaints or pleas in court.

94. Actions forbidden by neither natural nor positive law are called permissible.

Part I: Title I
Of Persons and their Rights in General

1. Man is called a person so far as he enjoys certain rights in civil society.

2. Civil society consists of a number of smaller societies and estates, bound together by Nature or Law, or by both.

6. Persons to whom, by their birth, destination or principal occupation, equal rights are ascribed in civil society, make up together an estate of the state.

7. Members of each estate have, as such, and considered as individuals, certain rights and duties.

9. The rights and duties of various societies in the state are further defined by their relation to each other and to the supreme head of the state.

Part II: Title IX
On the Duties and Rights of the Noble Estate

1. The nobility, as the first estate in the state, most especially bears the obligation, by its distinctive destination, to maintain the defense of the state, both of its honor without and of its constitution within.

21. In regard to the essential rights and attributes of the noble estate there is no difference between old and new nobility.

PRIVILEGES OF THE NOBILITY

34. Persons of the nobility are normally subject to the jurisdiction only of the highest court in the province.

35. The nobleman has an especial right to places of honor in the state for which he has made himself fit.

36. But the sovereign retains the power to be the judge of fitness and make selection from among candidates.

37. Only the nobleman has the right to possess noble property.

38. Which properties are noble is determined by the particular constitutions of the several provinces.

40. Only the nobleman may create entails and family trusts for noble properties.

41. Noble property-owners have the right to exercise, in their own name, the hunting rights appertaining to their property.

42. They may have the jurisdictional powers pertaining to their property exercised in their name.

43. They possess the honorific rights that go with church patronage.

45. They may use the names of their property as personal names, and in official documents or on public occasions, use the possession thereof as a special title.

46. Only the resident nobility normally have the right to appear in the noble assemblies of circles and provinces, and to have a voice on matters under consideration there.

51. Persons of the burgher estate cannot own noble property except by permission of the sovereign.

60. Burgher owners cannot convey ownership of noble property to other persons of burgher estate, except by special concession.

76. Noblemen shall normally engage in no burgher livelihood or occupation.

77. Where a wholesale business is not associated with a gild, a nobleman may enter upon it.

79. No nobleman, normally, except with special permission of the sovereign, may become a member of a closed merchant gild.

80. Particular rights and duties of the nobility, as belonging either to the whole estate, or to individual members, with respect to their person and property, are determined by the special laws and constitutions of the different provinces.

81. Whoever, by concealing or denying his noble estate, slips into a gild or corporation and carries on a burgher trade, will suffer the loss of his noble rights.

82. The same is all the more true when anyone of noble birth chooses a dishonorable way of life, or any way of life by which he sinks into the common people.

Translated from *Allgemeines Gesetzbuch für die preussischen Staaten,* 4 vols. (Berlin, 1791). The clauses printed above appeared in identical form in the *Allgemeines Landrecht für die preussischen Staaten* of 1794, except that those marked with an asterisk were simply deleted, presumably because in 1794 they too much suggested the principles of the French Revolution.

3.
Sweden: The Act of Union and
Security, 1789

1. The king is hereditary; he has full powers to govern and defend the realm, declare war, conclude treaties of peace and alliance with foreign powers; grant pardons, life and restoration of honor and property; dispose at his good pleasure of all royal employments, which must be held by Swedes; administer justice and provide for execution of the laws. Other affairs of state are conducted in the manner he judges most useful.

2. All subjects enjoy the same rights, under protection of the laws; hence the royal high court to which cases are evoked must be composed of both noble and non-noble members. Great and small persons must be judged by the legal tribunals.

3. All orders of the state have the same right to possess and acquire land. The equestrian order and the nobility, nevertheless, are confirmed in their ancient privilege of allodial possession. Peasants shall also have the right to lease crown lands and are guaranteed in their possession.

4. The high dignities and principal offices of the kingdom, and employments at court, are exclusively reserved for the equestrian order and the nobility. Other offices shall be accessible to all subjects of whatever birth or condition.

5. The Swedish people have the incontestable right to discuss and reach agreements with the king on all things concerning subsidies to the state.

6. In meetings of the diet only matters proposed by the king may be deliberated upon.

7. The privileges of each order are confirmed in all respects not contrary to the present Act of Union and Security.

8. The present Act of Union and Security will be personally signed by all kings of Sweden on their accession to the throne, and no change herein made; and in the event of extinction of the dynasty, the Act will bind the new king to be elected.

9. The form of government of 1772 will be preserved inviolably in all respects not changed by the present Act.

Translated from a French text in L. Léouzon Le Duc, *Gustave III* (Paris, 1861), 367-69.

4.

Poland: The Constitution of May 3, 1791

In the name of God, etc. we, Stanislas-Augustus, by the grace of God and the will of the nation, king of Poland, etc. . . . . decree the present constitution. . . .

1. *Religion of the Government.* The Catholic, Apostolic and Roman religion is and will remain forever the national religion. . . . However . . . we assure a free exercise of all religions and forms of worship throughout the extent of Poland. . . .

2. *Landed nobles.* . . . We guarantee . . . to the body of the nobility . . . all its liberties, immunities and prerogatives, likewise the preeminence pertaining to it in private as in public life, and notably the rights and privileges granted to this estate by Casimir the Great, Louis of Hungary, Ladislas Jagellon etc. . . . We declare the noble estate in Poland equal in dignity to that of all other countries; we establish the most perfect equality among all members of this body, not only in the right of possessing all offices in the republic, and filling all honorable and lucrative functions, but also in the liberty of uniformly enjoying all liberties and prerogatives attributed to the equestrian order. It is our will above all that individual liberty and security, and property in real and personal estate . . . shall be forever respected in each citizen. . . .

3. *Towns and Burghers.* It is our will that the law decreed by the present diet, under the title, *Our royal towns declared free throughout the extent of the republic,* shall have full and entire force . . . and be regarded as forming part of the present constitution.

4. *Coloni [colons,* field workers, serfs] *and other inhabitants of rural districts.* [Humane principles favored; agreements made between owners and serfs must be respected.]

5-11. [Executive, legislative, judicial, military organs of the state.]

Translated from the complete French text in the *Moniteur* (Paris), May 24, 1791.

5.

Hungary: The Coronation Oath of 1790, as prescribed in the Diploma agreed to by Leopold II and the Hungarian Diet

We, Leopold II, by grace of God elected Emperor of the Romans, always august; of Germany, Hungary, Bohemia, Dalmatia, Croatia, Slavonia, etc., Apostolic King; Archduke of Austria, etc.: As king of the aforesaid Kingdom of Hungary and other kingdoms and regions annexed to the same, we swear by the living God, and by His most holy mother the Virgin Mary, and by all the saints, to preserve the churches of God, the lords prelates, the barons, magnates, nobles, free cities and all inhabitants of the realm in their immunities, liberties, rights, laws, privileges and good and approved ancient customs; and to do justice to all. . . .

Translated from *Corpus juris hungarici*, 5 vols. (Budapest, 1901), v, 150.

6.

Belgium: The Declaration of Independence of Brabant, 1789

The three Estates representing the people of the Duchy of Brabant, having decreed on December 26 and 27, and also on December 29 and 30, 1789, the following points. . . :

1. That the sovereignty lately exercised by the former duke shall be henceforth exercised by the three Estates of Brabant.

2. That otherwise the constitution of this province remains intact on all points.

3. And in particular that the Council of Brabant will preserve all its preeminencies, rights and prerogatives. . . .

In consequence, on December 31, 1789 . . . at the Town Hall of Brussels, in the great hall prepared for the occasion (a crucifix and a copy of Holy Scripture having been placed in the room), there assembled the abovementioned three Estates of Brabant, to wit:

Of the First Estate, His Eminence the Cardinal Archbishop of Malines, His Illustrious Greatness the Bishop of Antwerp, etc., etc. . . .

Of the Second Estate, the Prince of Grimbergue, the Marquis of Wemmel, etc., etc. . . .

And of the Third Estate, from the chief-town of Louvain M. Henri Tielens, acting burgomaster . . . from the town of Brussels . . . from the town of Antwerp. . . .

The ceremony opened with prayer. . . .

And the three estates then took an oath . . . [to uphold] the rights, privileges, statutes, usages, properties and exemptions of the churches . . . [and swearing] faith and homage to the three Estates representing the people of Brabant . . . and . . . to support the constitution in all points on the basis of the Joyous Entry, and of the above resolutions.

Translated from F. X. Feller, *Recueil des représentations . . . des Pays-bas autrichiens,* 17 vols. (n.p. 1787-1790), xv, 123-28.

7.

Geneva: The Edict of Pacification, 1782

Title I. On the various Orders in the Republic, and on its Sovereignty

1. All the various Orders which compose the government of Geneva—to wit, the four Syndics, the Small Council or Council of Twenty-five, the Council of Sixty, the Council of Two Hundred or Great Council, and the General Council—will preserve each its particular rights and attributes, in such a way that none of the above named Orders shall encroach in any way on the rights and attributes of the others.

2. The Syndics may be chosen only from among the Council of Twenty-five; members of the Council of Twenty-five may be chosen only from among the Council of Two Hundred; those of the Council of Sixty, only from among the Council of Two Hundred; those of the Council of Two Hundred from among the Citizens and Burghers; and only the Citizens and Burghers of a full twenty-five years of age shall have the right of entrance to the General Council, along with the Syndics and the members of the Small and Great Councils.

3. The sovereignty of the republic belongs to no one of the Orders taken separately, but the General Council alone shall be called the Sovereign Council.

Translated from *Edit de pacification de 1782 imprimé par ordre du Gouvernement* (Geneva, 1782).

8.

Great Britain: The Canada Act, 1791

. . . May it therefore please Your Most Excellent Majesty that it may be enacted; and be it enacted by the King's Most Excellent Majesty, by and with the Advice and Consent of the Lords Spiritual and Temporal, and of the Commons, in this present Parliament assembled, and by the Authority of the same. . . .

5. That every member of each of the said Legislative Councils [of Upper and Lower Canada] shall hold his seat therein for the term of his Life. . . .

6. That whenever His Majesty . . . shall think proper to confer . . . under the Great Seal of either of the said Provinces, any Hereditary Title of Honor, Rank or Dignity of such Province . . . it shall and may be lawful . . . to annex thereto . . . an Hereditary Right of being summoned to the Legislative Council of such Province . . . and that every person on whom such Right shall be so conferred, or to whom such right shall severally so descend, shall thereupon be entitled to demand of the Governor . . . his Writ of Summons to such Legislative Council. . . .

Great Britain: *Statutes at Large*, 31 George III 31. The provision for a hereditary and titled upper house never went into effect in Canada; its significance is its reflection of views in the British Parliament.

9.

The United States

(1) *The Federal Constitution*, 1787

Article I, Section 9. No title of nobility shall be granted by the United States: and no person holding any office of profit or trust under them, shall, without the consent of Congress, accept any present, emolument, office or title of any kind whatever from any king, prince or foreign state.

Article IV, Section 2. The citizens of each state shall be entitled to all privileges and immunities of citizens in the several states. . . . No person held to service or labor in one state, under the laws thereof, escaping into another, shall . . . be discharged from such service or labor, but shall be delivered up on claim of the party to whom such service or labor may be due.

(2) *The Pennsylvania Constitution*, 1790

Article I, 5-6. The senators shall be chosen for four years by the citizens . . . apportioned among the districts according to the number of taxable inhabitants in each. . . .

Article IX. That the general, great and essential principles of liberty and free government may be recognized and unalterably established, we declare:

1. That all men are born equally free and independent. . . .

24. That the legislature shall not grant any title of nobility or hereditary distinction, nor create any office the appointment of which shall be for a longer term than during good behavior.

F. N. Thorpe, *Federal and State Constitutions*, 7 vols. (Washington, 1909), v, 3093, 3099, 3101.

10.

France: The Constitution of 1791
Preamble

The National Assembly, wishing to establish the French constitution on the principles that it has recognized and declared, irrevocably abolishes the institutions that have done injury to liberty and to the equality of rights.

Nobility no longer exists, nor peerage, nor hereditary distinction of orders, nor feudal regime, nor patrimonial courts, nor titles, denominations or prerogatives deriving therefrom, nor any order of chivalry, nor any of the corporations or decorations for which proofs of nobility used to be required or which presupposed distinctions of birth, nor any other superiority than that of public officers in the exercise of their functions.

Property in office, and its inheritance, no longer exist.

No privilege or exception to the common law for all Frenchmen any longer exists for any part of the nation or for any individual.

Gilds and corporations for professions, arts and crafts no longer exist.

The law no longer takes cognizance of religious vows or any other engagement contrary to natural rights or to the Constitution.

Title I: Fundamental Provisions
Guaranteed by the Constitution

The Constitution guarantees as natural and civil rights:

1. That all citizens are admissible to all positions and employments without other distinction than that of virtues and talents.

2. That all taxes shall be apportioned among all citizens equally in proportion to ability to pay.

3. That the same offenses shall be punished with the same penalties without distinction of persons.

The constitution likewise guarantees as natural and civil rights [liberty of movement, speech, publication, religion, assembly, petition, property, relief of the poor, work for the unemployed and observance of patriotic holidays].

A code of civil law common to the whole kingdom will be drawn up.

Translated from M. Bouchary, ed., *La Déclaration des droits de l'homme et du citoyen et la constitution de 1791* (Paris, 1947), 17-18. For the whole constitution in English see J. H. Stewart, *Documentary survey of the French Revolution* (New York, 1951), 231-62.

★ APPENDIX IV ★

Below are printed, in such a way as to show the resemblances, most of the Virginia Declaration of Rights drafted by George Mason and adopted by the Virginia assembly on June 12, 1776, and most of the Declaration of the Rights of Man and Citizen adopted by the French National Assembly on August 26, 1789:

Virginia, 1776	France, 1789
1. That all men are by nature equally free and independent, and have certain inherent rights, of which, when they enter into a state of society, they cannot by any compact, deprive or divest their posterity; namely, the enjoyment of life and liberty, with the means of acquiring and possessing property, and pursuing and obtaining happiness and safety.	1. Men are born and remain free and equal in rights. . . . 2. . . . These rights are liberty, property, security and resistance to oppression.
2. That all power is vested in, and consequently derived from, the people; that magistrates are their trustees and servants, and at all times amenable to them.	3. The principle of all sovereignty rests essentially in the nation. 15. Society has the right to hold accountable every public agent of administration.
3. That government is, or ought to be, instituted for the common benefit, protection and security of the people, nation or community. . . .	2. The aim of all political association is to preserve the natural and imprescriptible rights of man.
3. . . . when a government shall be found inadequate or contrary to these purposes, a majority of the community hath an indubitable, unalienable and indefensible right to reform, alter or abolish it.	2. . . . resistance to oppression.
4. That no man, or set of men, are entitled to exclusive or separate emoluments or privileges from the community but in consideration of public services, which not being descendible, neither ought the offices of magistrate, legislator or judge to be hereditary.	3. . . . No body, and no individual, may exercise authority which does not emanate from the nation expressly.

[518]

Virginia, 1776	France, 1789
5. That the legislative, executive and judicial powers should be separate and distinct.	16. Any society in which . . . the separation of powers is not determined has no constitution.
6. That . . . all men having sufficient evidence of permanent common interest with, and attachment to the community have the right of suffrage, and cannot be taxed, or deprived of their property for public uses, without their own consent, or that of their representatives. . . .	6. . . . All citizens have the right to take part, in person or by their representatives, in the formation [of the law]. . . .
	14. All citizens have the right, by themselves or through their representatives, to have demonstrated to them the necessity of public taxes, to consent to them freely. . . .
8. That in all capital or criminal prosecutions a man hath a right to demand the cause and nature of his accusation, to be confronted with the accusers and witnesses, to call for evidence in his favor, and to a speedy trial by an impartial jury of twelve men of his vicinage, without whose unanimous consent he cannot be found guilty; nor can he be compelled to give evidence against himself; that no man be deprived of his liberty, except by the law of the land or the judgment of his peers.	7. No man may be indicted, arrested or detained except in cases determined by law and according to the forms which it has prescribed.
9. That excessive bail ought not to be required . . . nor cruel and inhuman punishments inflicted.	8. Only strictly necessary punishments may be established by law. . . .
	9. Every man being presumed innocent until judged guilty, if it is deemed indispensable to keep him under arrest, all rigor not necessary to secure his person should be severely repressed by law.
10. That general warrants, whereby an officer or messenger may be commanded to search suspected places without evidence of a fact committed, or to seize any person or persons not named . . . ought not to be granted.	7. . . . Those who instigate, expedite, execute or cause to be executed arbitrary orders should be punished. . . .

Virginia, 1776	France, 1789
12. That the freedom of the press is one of the great bulwarks of liberty. . . .	11. Free communication of thought and opinion is one of the most precious of the rights of man. Every citizen may therefore speak, write and print freely, on his own responsibility for abuse of this liberty in cases determined by law.
13. That a well-regulated militia, composed of the body of the people, trained to arms, is the proper, natural and safe defense of a free State; that standing armies in time of peace should be avoided as dangerous to liberty; and that in all cases the militia should be under strict subordination to, and governed by, the civil power.	12. Preservation of the rights of man and the citizen requires the existence of public forces. These forces are therefore instituted for the advantage of all, not for the private benefit of those to whom they are entrusted.
15. That no free government . . . can be preserved . . . but by a firm adherence to justice, moderation, temperance, frugality and virtue, and by a frequent recurrence to fundamental principles.	PREAMBLE. . . . that this declaration, by being constantly present to all members of the social body, may keep them at all times aware of their rights and duties; that the acts of both the legislative and executive powers [may be] liable at every moment to comparison with the aim of all political institutions. . . .
16. That religion, or the duty which we owe to our Creator, and the manner of discharging it, can be directed only by reason and conviction, not by force or violence; and therefore all men are equally entitled to the free exercise of religion. . . .	10. No one may be disturbed for his opinions, even in religion, provided that their manifestation does not trouble public order as established by law.
. . . it is the duty of all to practice Christian forbearance, love and charity towards each other.	PREAMBLE. . . . in the presence and under the auspices of the Supreme Being.

The Virginia declaration differs from the French in its emphasis on freedom and frequency of elections and on jury trial, in its concrete warnings against excessive bail, general warrants, suspending of laws and standing armies, and its more explicit reference to Christian and moral virtues. The French declaration differs from that of Virginia in its clearer formulation of citizenship, its definition of law as the expression of the general will, its definition of liberty as the right to do what does not harm another, its more explicit provision that the law must be the same for all and public office open to all alike on the basis of abilities, its greater reserve in relating freedom of thought and religion to law and order, its provision that property may be taken for public use only with due compensation, its less explicit reference to moral virtues and its adoption of a deistic rather than a Christian tone.

The resemblance remains remarkable. Resemblance in the sequence in which ideas are presented is a stronger indication of filiation than resemblance in content.

✦ APPENDIX V ✦

"Democratic" and "Bourgeois" Characteristics in the French Constitution of 1791

It seems desirable to perform, for the French constitution of 1791, an operation resembling, in a lesser way, the one recently performed by Robert E. Brown for the Massachusetts constitution of 1780 and the United States federal constitution, that is, to assemble evidence that the French constitution of 1791 was somewhat more "democratic," and somewhat less "bourgeois," than has been commonly said in the past half century.

Conservatives in 1791, such as Burke and Mounier, regarded the constitution as "democratic," meaning that it applied the elective principle very extensively, based representation on numbers, and did away with inheritance of public position. As late as Taine it was customary for conservatives to stress, though with disapproval, the breadth of popular participation in politics under the constitution of 1791 (*Origines de la France contemporaine,* 1882, II, 263-70). With Madelin, on the conservative side, we get an emphasis on narrowly bourgeois provisions which belied the Declaration of Rights (*Rev. fr.,* 1912, pp. 108-09). Burke, defending "a permanent landed interest," had already, in 1791, identified the French experiment in political democracy with a kind of bourgeois rule, or government, as he said, by "tradesmen, bankers and voluntary clubs of bold, presuming young persons: advocates, attorneys, notaries, managers of newspapers, and those cabals of literary men called academies" (*Works,* 1839, IV, 13).

On the democratic side, in 1789-1791, Robespierre, Desmoulins, Grégoire, Marat, and others objected to the limitations placed by the constitution on suffrage and electoral powers. By the time that Michelet and Louis Blanc treated the subject, shortly after the Revolution of 1848, the question was already an old one, with Michelet emphasizing the democratic character of the constitution, offering figures, and denying that the constitution was "essentially bourgeois, as has so often been repeated," and Louis Blanc maintaining that it "was essentially bourgeois, whatever M. Michelet may say." "It is not a question of figures," added Blanc, "but of justice" (Michelet, *Rev. fr.* ed. 1868, II, 381; Blanc, *Rev. fr.,* ed. 1854, VI, 99). A half century later, Jean Jaurès, a social democrat and a Marxist, but a humane and perceptive historian, reached a rounded judgment on the work of the Constituent Assembly, which he found to be halfway between the democracy of universal suffrage and the *bourgeoisie censitaire* of 1815-1848. He concluded that only the "sub-proletariat" had been unfranchised in 1791 (*Hist. socialiste,* I, 378-98).

Many of the French academic school have shown a less judicial tone than the socialist Jaurès. For Aulard, "the bourgeoisie formed itself into a politically privileged class" (*Hist. pol. de la Rev. fr.*, Paris, 1905, p. 70), for Sagnac "the bourgeoisie monopolized power" (in Lavisse, *Hist. de Fr. contemp.*, Paris, 1920, I, p. 165), for Mathiez an "aristocracy of wealth replaced that of birth" (*Rev. fran.*, Paris, 1922, I, 115), for Villat the electoral regime was "a system of bourgeois selfishness" (*Rev. et empire*, Paris, 1936, I, 72-73), and for Godechot "only the rich could vote" (*Institutions de la France sous la Rev. et l'Empire*, Paris, 1951, p. 73). These views have passed into many histories of the French Revolution written in English. They all reflect Louis Blanc's impatience with figures.

The Constituent Assembly, by an actual count based on local returns, determined on May 27, 1791 that there were then 4,298,360 "active citizens" in France, that is, adult males, at least twenty-five years of age, domiciled locally for one year, not in domestic service, and paying an annual direct tax equal in amount to the wages of three days' unskilled labor. Only these active citizens received the vote. The population of France at this time was probably between 25,000,000 and 26,000,000 (not 27,190,023 as stated by the Assembly, which made no pretense to knowing or having counted the total population); and as for age distribution, both Moheau and Lavoisier estimated that 44 per cent were under 21 years old, and 59 per cent under 31. (Levasseur, *Population française*, 1889, I, 276.) We may assume that half the males were under 25, and half 25 or older. The highest possible figure for total men of 25 and over is thus 6,500,000; and if there were 4,298,360 active citizens, Mathiez was exaggerating in saying that "3,000,000 poor were excluded from the rights of citizenship" (Mathiez, I, 114). Counting all men of 21 and over, it is apparently true that about 3,000,000 were excluded from the vote, since there would be about 7,280,000 men over 21; but these "passive citizens," without the vote, included young men under 25 of all social classes, men living with parents and hence paying no tax, those not yet domiciled locally for a year, and domestic servants, as well as persons too poor to be liable for the required tax. It must be remarked also that the tax reforms of the Constituent Assembly, by replacing many indirect taxes of the Old Regime with a direct tax on real and personal property, carried the liability to direct taxation far down in the social scale. Assuming the accuracy of the figure of 4,298,360 for active citizens (which may be debatable, but is not in fact contested), I would judge that a quarter of adult males may have been excluded from the vote by reason of poverty. Young people, transients, and newcomers in particular areas, of various economic levels but all without the vote, would, however, be a force of political importance, especially in revolutionary times. In practice in 1791 the distinction between active and passive citizens was often locally uncertain. In principle, it is hard to see how the Assembly excluded more than a quarter of the population on economic grounds.

Active citizens had the right to vote only for "electors," who in turn, in electoral assemblies, chose the national deputies, the bishops and various local officials. It was these electors who exercised true political citizenship, and the heart of the question is how many persons were qualified to be chosen as electors. To be an elector, one had to be an active citizen paying a tax equal to ten days' wages of common labor. Various writers state that only about 50,000 persons in all France could qualify as electors; see Gottschalk, *Era of the Fr. Rev.* (1929), p. 172; Gershoy, *Fr. Rev.* (1947), p. 147; J. M. Thompson, *Fr. Rev.* (American edition, 1945), p. 136; Göhring, *Grosse Revolution* (1951), II, 52; Kläy, *Zensuswahlrecht und Gleichheitsprinzip ... 1791* (1956), p. 85. I have also fallen into this error in my *History of the Modern World* (1956), 347. The enormity of the misrepresentation may be seen by the fact that the number qualifying as electors, though not really known, is estimated at 3,000,000; see Sagnac, p. 165 and Godechot, p. 74.

The error has arisen from a confusion of the number qualified to serve as electors with the number actually chosen and functioning as electors in 1791, which was in the neighborhood of 50,000—naturally so, since the constitution provided that there should be one elector for each hundred (or local fraction thereof) of the active citizens, who, as stated, were found to number 4,298,360 in 1791. It was of course not always the same 50,000 persons who functioned as electors, or at least such was not the intent or provision of the constitution. Electors were chosen in 1790; new electors were chosen in 1791; and the constitution provided for a new choice of electors by active citizens in March 1793 and every two years thereafter. Three-quarters of the active citizens, and some three-sevenths of all men over 21, were in short qualified to serve as electors. The extent of participation is illustrated by a curious incident of June 15, 1791, when the constitutional committee recommended to the Assembly, for the forthcoming election of national deputies, the use of a kind of mechanical tabulating device to count the vote in electoral assemblies. One of the reasons offered was to prevent the deception of "electors who cannot read and write." This is very different from the picture of a France ruled by 50,000 of the "rich"; in this respect, at least, Taine's picture of a bustling popular political activity in 1791 seems far more realistic.

It has been usual even for historians with all the figures at hand to reach conclusions somewhat at variance with them. Thus Sagnac and Godechot both tell us that 3,000,000 qualified as electors, but that the wealthy bourgeoisie controlled the state; that there were only 967 electors in Paris (meaning that 967 were chosen in the election of 1791), which of course signifies that there were about 100,000 active citizens, which in a city of 600,000 would in turn signify that only a minority of adult males were "passive";

and they intimate that had the system been less "bourgeois" the electors would have been more numerous, whereas actually absenteeism was chronic in the electoral assemblies, and sometimes there were only 200 present and voting in the electoral assembly of Paris, because most of the electors could not afford to spend several days away from their normal occupations. It is true that such absenteeism in the assemblies threw decisions into the hands of the most assiduous, who might be the more economically independent, but included also those who made a business of politics.

The majority in the Constituent Assembly did conclude, in August 1791, with the rise of radical republicanism after Louis XVI's flight to Varennes, that it had gone too far in a democratic direction, and did make changes whose purpose was to confine the significant vote, that is, the vote of the electors, more definitely to the middle class. It left the qualifications for active citizens untouched. For electors, however, who before August 1791 had qualified by the payment of a direct tax equal to the value of ten days' wages (and it was by this system that the election of 1791, including choice of national deputies for the forthcoming Legislative Body, had already taken place), the Constituent Assembly, in August 1791, prescribed more restrictive qualifications. These resemble those of the British Reform Bill of 1832, in that they based the electoral right on amounts of property or rental varying from place to place. To qualify as an elector, by the provisions of August 1791, it was necessary (1) in cities of more than 6,000 inhabitants to own real property assessed on the tax rolls at an annual income value equivalent to 200 days' unskilled labor, or to lease a dwelling worth an annual income value (or rental) of 150 days' labor, (2) in cities with less than 6,000 inhabitants, the same, with 150 in place of 200, and 100 in place of 150, (3) in rural districts to own real property of an annual value of 150 days' labor, or to lease, or to work on shares (*métayage*), real property of an annual value of 400 days' labor. I have seen no estimates of how many persons lost their right to be chosen as electors by these changes. At the same time, where before August 1791 it had been necessary to pay a direct tax of 54 livres (the *marc d'argent*) to qualify as a national deputy, after August 1791 any active citizen might so qualify. The changes are significant only of the intent of the Constituent Assembly toward its end, since the constitution did not last long enough for them to take effect.

There has been no attempt, to my knowledge, to make a comparison of the property qualifications under the French constitution of 1791 with those obtaining at the same time in Great Britain and America, though these were often mentioned in a general way during the debates in the French Assembly. Were such comparisons realistically made, it would be difficult to say, for example, that the Constituent Assembly, in prescribing a marc d'argent for national deputies, wished to "reserve the seats for a landed aristocracy, as in England." (Godechot, *Institutions*, 74.) In England, a member of the

House of Commons representing a county was required by law to own land of an annual income value of £600, or 15,000 French livres. Since the French tax of 1791 was intended to represent about one sixth of annual income from property, a tax of a marc d'argent, 54 livres, would represent an income of about 300 livres from property. The difference between 15,000 and 300 reflects a difference between conflicting theories of society.

Comparison is made difficult, but by no means impossible, by the setting of the French qualifications in terms of days' labor, as well as the differences between livres, dollars, and shillings. As for the relevancy of the comparison, it must be emphasized that the great difference in the three countries lay in the distribution of land ownership, small properties being very common and indeed almost universal in Massachusetts, less common but not uncommon in France, and increasingly rare in England.

The accompanying table converts all property qualifications into dollars. The first United States dollars were authorized and defined in 1792, and the error will not be too great if we assume that a dollar of 1792 equaled five Massachusetts shillings of 1780, four English shillings, and five French livres. The money value of a day's unskilled labor in France, for determination of electoral qualifications, was set locally according to local conditions, but, by a ruling of the Constituent Assembly, it could nowhere be set for this purpose at less than half a livre or more than one livre per day. A tax of "three days' wages" thus meant a tax of between 1½ and 3 livres. In 1791 the Assembly replaced various old taxes with a direct tax of 300,000,000 livres on real and personal property, or rather on the income from such property—land, farm equipment, business property, mechanics' tools, etc. The average mean incidence of this tax was thus about 12 livres per capita, or, assuming as many as 6,000,000 taxpayers, about 50 livres per taxpayer; and, while this gives no indication whatever of the distribution of property, it suggests that the livre of taxes required for active citizenship, or the 5 to 10 livres required for electors, were not actually very high. Indeed, even the marc d'argent, or the 54 livre tax required to qualify as a national deputy, and which aroused such controversy, was not far in amount from the probable mean average tax; according to one estimate expressed in the Assembly on August 12, 1791, about 60,000 to 80,000 persons paid a direct tax of at least a marc d'argent. One is led to conclude, if the total of men over 25 was about 6,500,000, that almost seventy of them in a hundred had the vote, about fifty in a hundred could serve as electors, and one in a hundred could qualify as a national deputy, before August 1791.

It is certain that the Constituent Assembly wished to reduce and screen the direct impact of the mass of the population upon government; but only from a modern Marxist point of view can its work be meaningfully described as predominantly bourgeois; nor did Jaurès himself so describe it. Whatever the high hopes of early democrats, political democracy seems to

PROPERTY QUALIFICATIONS FOR VOTING AND ELIGIBILITY, 1791
(in dollars of 1792)

	Voter	*Elector*	*Deputy*
France			
To August 1791	Direct tax of 30 to 60 cents a year	Direct tax of $1 to $2 a year	Direct tax of $11 a year
August 1791	Same as above	Rural districts: Real property worth $15 to $30 a year; or lease or *métayage* worth $40 to $80 a year Towns under 6,000: Real property worth $15 to $30 a year; or lease worth $10 to $20 a year Towns over 6,000: Real property worth $20 to $40 a year; or lease worth $15 to $30.	Same as for voter
England	Counties: Real property worth $10 a year; freehold only, copyhold excluded Towns (if represented as boroughs): Various		Counties: Real property worth $3,000 a year Towns (if represented as boroughs): Real property worth $1,500 a year
Massachusetts	Real property worth $12 a year, or any property worth $240 capital value		Lower house: Real property worth $400 capital value, or any property worth $800
Pennsylvania (constitutions of 1776 and 1790)	Taxpayers and their grown sons		Taxpayers and their grown sons
U.S. Federal Constitution	As determined by states		No property qualifications

work best when little more is asked of the voter than to pause briefly at a convenient polling place and mark his choice among candidates on a ballot prepared beforehand. This requires a complex system of decentralized polling places, and organized political parties which draw up lists of candidates for the voter. Neither existed in any country in 1791. It was necessary for voters to meet in assemblies where the names of candidates could be proposed and their merits discussed. The electoral arrangements made by the Constituent Assembly must be explained by mechanical and administrative needs as well as by political objectives.